Y0-CVH-504

University Casebook Series

ACCOUNTING AND THE LAW, Third Edition (1964), with Problem Pamphlet
   The late James L. Dohr, Director, Institute of Accounting, Columbia University,
   Ellis L. Phillips, Jr., Professor of Law, Columbia University.
   George C. Thompson, Professor, Columbia University Graduate School of Business, and
   William C. Warren, Professor of Law, Columbia University.

ACCOUNTING, LAW AND (1949)
   Donald Schapiro, Instructor in Law, Yale University, and
   Ralph Wienshienk, Visiting Lecturer in Law, Yale University.

ACCOUNTING, MATERIALS ON, (1959), with 1968 Supplement
   Robert Amory, Jr., Esq.,
   W. Covington Hardee, Esq., Third Edition by
   David R. Herwitz, Professor of Law, Harvard University, and
   Donald T. Trautman, Professor of Law, Harvard University.

ADMINISTRATIVE LAW, Fifth Edition (1970), with Problems Supplement
   Walter Gellhorn, Professor of Law, Columbia University, and
   Clark Byse, Professor of Law, Harvard University.

ADMIRALTY (1969)
   Jo Desha Lucas, Professor of Law, University of Chicago.

ADMIRALTY (1954)
   The late Stanley Morrison, Professor of Law, Stanford University, and
   The late George W. Stumberg, Professor of Law, University of Texas.

ADVOCACY, INTRODUCTION TO (1970) with Supplementary Cases Pamphlet
   Board of Student Advisers, Harvard Law School.

ANTITRUST LAW (1967), with 1969 Supplement
   Harlan M. Blake, Professor of Law, Columbia University.
   Robert Pitofsky, Professor of Law, New York University.

ARBITRATION (1968)
   Shelden D. Elliott, Professor of Law, New York University.

BANKRUPTCY ACT (Annotated) 1967 Edition
   The late James Angell MacLachlan, Professor of Law Emeritus, Harvard University.

BIOGRAPHY OF A LEGAL DISPUTE, THE: An Introduction to American Civil Procedure (1968)
   Marc A. Franklin, Professor of Law, Stanford University.

UNIVERSITY CASEBOOK SERIES — Continued

BUSINESS ORGANIZATION: EMPLOYMENT—AGENCY—PARTNERSHIP—ATTORNEYS, Third Edition (1965)
Alfred F. Conard, Professor of Law, University of Michigan, and
Robert L. Knauss, Dean of the School of Law, Vanderbilt University.

BUSINESS ORGANIZATION: CORPORATIONS (1948)
A. A. Berle, Jr., Professor of Law, Columbia University, and
William C. Warren, Professor of Law, Columbia University.

BUSINESS PLANNING (1966) with 1971 Problem Supplement
David R. Herwitz, Professor of Law, Harvard University.

CIVIL PROCEDURE, see Procedure

COMMERCIAL AND CONSUMER TRANSACTIONS (1972)
William E. Hogan, Professor of Law, Cornell University.
William D. Warren, Professor of Law, University of California, Los Angeles.

COMMERCIAL AND INVESTMENT PAPER, Third Edition (1964) with Statutory Materials
Roscoe T. Steffen, Professor of Law, University of California, Hastings College of the Law.

COMMERCIAL LAW, CASES & MATERIALS ON, Second Edition (1968) with Statutory Supplement
E. Allan Farnsworth, Professor of Law, Columbia University.
John Honnold, Professor of Law, University of Pennsylvania.

COMMERCIAL PAPER (1968), with Statutory Supplement
E. Allan Farnsworth, Professor of Law, Columbia University.

COMMERCIAL PAPER AND BANK DEPOSITS AND COLLECTIONS (1967) with Statutory Supplement
William D. Hawkland, Professor of Law, University of Illinois.

COMMERCIAL TRANSACTIONS—Text, Cases and Problems, Fourth Edition (1968)
Robert Braucher, Professor of Law, Harvard University, and
Arthur E. Sutherland, Jr., Professor of Law, Harvard University.

COMPARATIVE LAW, Third Edition (1970)
Rudolf B. Schlesinger, Professor of Law, Cornell University.

CONFLICT OF LAWS, Sixth Edition (1971)
Willis L. M. Reese, Professor of Law, Columbia University, and
Maurice Rosenberg, Professor of Law, Columbia University.

CONSTITUTIONAL LAW, Third Edition (1963) with 1971 Supplement
Edward L. Barrett, Jr., Professor of Law, University of California, Davis.
Paul W. Bruton, Professor of Law, University of Pennsylvania, and
John O. Honnold, Professor of Law, University of Pennsylvania.

CONSTITUTIONAL LAW, Eighth Edition (1970) with 1971 Supplement
Gerald Gunther, Professor of Law, Stanford University.
Noel T. Dowling, late Professor of Law, Columbia University.

CONSTITUTIONAL LAW, INDIVIDUAL RIGHTS IN (1970) with 1971 Supplement
Gerald Gunther, Professor of Law, Stanford University.
Noel T. Dowling, late Professor of Law, Columbia University.

UNIVERSITY CASEBOOK SERIES — Continued

CONTRACTS, (1965) (Successor Volume to Patterson, Goble & Jones, Cases on Contracts) with Statutory Supplement

    Harry W. Jones, Professor of Law, Columbia University.
    E. Allan Farnsworth, Professor of Law, Columbia University.
    William F. Young, Professor of Law, Columbia University.

CONTRACTS (1971) with Statutory and Administrative Law Supplement

    Ian R. Macneil, Professor of Law, Cornell University.

CONTRACT LAW AND ITS APPLICATION (1971)

    Addison Mueller, Professor of Law, University of California, Los Angeles.
    Arthur I. Rosett, Professor of Law, University of California, Los Angeles.

CONTRACT LAW, STUDIES IN (1970)

    Edward J. Murphy, Professor of Law, University of Notre Dame.
    Richard E. Speidel, Professor of Law, University of Virginia.

CONTRACTS AND CONTRACT REMEDIES, Fourth Edition (1957)

    Harold Shepherd, Professor of Law Emeritus, Stanford University, and
    Harry H. Wellington, Professor of Law, Yale University.

CONTRACTS AND CONTRACT REMEDIES, Second Edition (1969)

    John P. Dawson, Professor of Law, Harvard University, and
    Wm. Burnett Harvey, Dean of the Law School, Indiana University.

CONVEYANCES, Second Edition (1941)

    Marion R. Kirkwood, Professor of Law Emeritus, Stanford University.

COPYRIGHT, Unfair Competition, and Other Topics Bearing on the Protection of Literary, Musical, and Artistic Works (1960)

    Benjamin Kaplan, Professor of Law, Harvard University, and
    Ralph S. Brown, Jr., Professor of Law, Yale University.

CORPORATE REORGANIZATION, with Statutory Supplement (1950)

    The late E. Merrick Dodd, Professor of Law, Harvard University, and
    DeForest Billyou, Professor of Law, New York University.

CORPORATIONS, Fourth Edition—Unabridged, 1969

    William L. Cary, Professor of Law, Columbia University.

CORPORATIONS, Fourth Edition—Abridged (1970)

    William L. Cary, Professor of Law, Columbia University.

CORRECTIONAL PROCESS (1971) (Pamphlet)

    Reprinted from Miller, Dawson, Dix and Parnas's Criminal Justice Administration & Related Processes

CREDITORS' RIGHTS, Fifth Edition (1957)

    The late John Hanna, Professor of Law Emeritus, Columbia University, and
    The late James Angell MacLachlan, Professor of Law Emeritus, Harvard University.

UNIVERSITY CASEBOOK SERIES — Continued

CREDITORS' RIGHTS AND CORPORATE REORGANIZATION, Fifth Edition (1957)

    The late John Hanna, Professor of Law Emeritus, Columbia University, and The late James Angell MacLachlan, Professor of Law Emeritus, Harvard University.

CREDITORS' RIGHTS AND SECURED TRANSACTIONS, 1967

    William E. Hogan, Professor of Law, Cornell University.
    William D. Warren, Professor of Law, University of California Los Angeles.

CRIMINAL JUSTICE, THE ADMINISTRATION OF, CASES AND MATERIALS ON, Second Edition (1969)

    Francis C. Sullivan, Professor of Law, Louisiana State University.
    Paul Hardin III, Professor of Law, Duke University.
    John Huston, Professor of Law, University of Washington.
    Frank R. Lacy, Professor of Law, University of Oregon.
    Daniel E. Murray, Professor of Law, University of Miami.
    George W. Pugh, Professor of Law, Louisiana State University.

CRIMINAL JUSTICE, Third Edition, 1968, two volumes: I. Criminal Law, II. Criminal Law Administration, with 1971 Supplement

    Fred E. Inbau, Professor of Law, Northwestern University.
    James R. Thompson, Professor of Law, Northwestern University, and Claude R. Sowle, President, Ohio University.

CRIMINAL JUSTICE ADMINISTRATION AND RELATED PROCESSES (1971)

    Frank W. Miller, Professor of Law, Washington University.
    Robert O. Dawson, Professor of Law, University of Texas.
    George E. Dix, Professor of Law, Arizona State University.
    Raymond I. Parnas, Professor of Law, University of California, Davis.

CRIMINAL LAW (1969)

    Lloyd L. Weinreb, Professor of Law, Harvard University.

CRIMINAL LAW AND ITS ADMINISTRATION (1940), with 1956 Supplement

    The late Jerome Michael, Professor of Law, Columbia University, and Herbert Wechsler, Professor of Law, Columbia University.

CRIMINAL LAW AND PROCEDURE, Fourth Edition (1972)

    Rollin M. Perkins, Professor of Law, University of California, Hastings College of the Law.

CRIMINAL PROCESS (1969)

    Lloyd L. Weinreb, Professor of Law, Harvard University.

DAMAGES, Second Edition (1952)

    The late Charles T. McCormick, Professor of Law, University of Texas, and William F. Fritz, Professor of Law, University of Texas.

DECEDENTS' ESTATES (1971)

    Max Rheinstein, Professor of Law Emeritus, University of Chicago.
    Mary Ann Glendon, Professor of Law, Boston College Law School.

DECEDENTS' ESTATES AND TRUSTS, Fourth Edition (1971)

    John Ritchie III, Dean and Professor of Law, Northwestern University, Neill H. Alford, Jr., Professor of Law, University of Virginia, and Richard W. Effland, Professor of Law, Arizona State University.

UNIVERSITY CASEBOOK SERIES — Continued

DECEDENTS' ESTATES AND TRUSTS (1968)
   Howard R. Williams, Professor of Law, Stanford University.

DOMESTIC RELATIONS (1970), with Statutory Supplement
   Monrad G. Paulsen, Dean of the Law School, University of Virginia.
   Walter Wadlington, Professor of Law, University of Virginia.
   Julius Goebel, Jr., Professor of Law Emeritus, Columbia University.

DOMESTIC RELATIONS: STATUTORY MATERIALS
   Monrad G. Paulsen, Dean of the Law School, University of Virginia.
   Walter Wadlington, Professor of Law, University of Virginia.

DOMESTIC RELATIONS—Civil and Canon Law (1963)
   Philip A. Ryan, Professor of Law, Georgetown University, and
   Dom David Granfield, Associate Professor, Catholic University of America.

DYNAMICS OF AMERICAN LAW, THE: Courts, the Legal Process and Freedom of Expression (1968)
   Marc A. Franklin, Professor of Law, Stanford University.

ENVIRONMENTAL PROTECTION, SELECTED LEGAL AND ECONOMIC ASPECTS OF (1971)
   Charles J. Meyers, Professor of Law, Stanford University.
   A. Dan Tarlock, Professor of Law, Indiana University.

EQUITY, Fifth Edition (1967)
   The late Zechariah Chafee, Jr., Professor of Law, Harvard University, and
   Edward D. Re, Professor of Law, St. John's University.

EQUITY, RESTITUTION AND DAMAGES (1969)
   Robert Childres, Professor of Law, Northwestern University.

ETHICS, see Legal Profession

EVIDENCE (1968) with 1969 Supplement
   David W. Louisell, Professor of Law, University of California, Berkeley,
   John Kaplan, Professor of Law, Stanford University,
   Jon R. Waltz, Professor of Law, Northwestern University.

EVIDENCE, Fifth Edition (1965) with 1970 Supplement
   John M. Maguire, Professor of Law Emeritus, Harvard University.
   Jack B. Weinstein, Professor of Law, Columbia University.
   James H. Chadbourn, Professor of Law, Harvard University.
   John H. Mansfield, Professor of Law, Harvard University.

EVIDENCE (1968)
   Francis C. Sullivan, Professor of Law, Louisiana State University,
   Paul Hardin, III, Professor of Law, Duke University.

FEDERAL COURTS, FIFTH EDITION (1970) with 1971 Supplement
   The late Charles T. McCormick, Professor of Law, University of Texas,
   James H. Chadbourn, Professor of Law, Harvard University, and
   Charles Alan Wright, Professor of Law, University of Texas.

FEDERAL COURTS AND THE FEDERAL SYSTEM (1953)
   The late Henry M. Hart, Jr., Professor of Law, Harvard University and
   Herbert Wechsler, Professor of Law, Columbia University.

FEDERAL RULES OF CIVIL PROCEDURE, 1971 Edition

UNIVERSITY CASEBOOK SERIES — Continued

FEDERAL TAXATION, see Taxation

FREE ENTERPRISE AND ECONOMIC ORGANIZATION, Fourth Edition (1972)
Louis B. Schwartz, Professor of Law, University of Pennsylvania.

FUTURE INTERESTS AND ESTATE PLANNING (1961) with 1962 Supplement
W. Barton Leach, Professor of Law, Harvard University, and
James K. Logan, Dean of the Law School, University of Kansas.

FUTURE INTERESTS (1958)
The late Philip Mechem, Professor of Law Emeritus, University of Pennsylvania.

FUTURE INTERESTS (1970)
Howard R. Williams, Professor of Law, Stanford University.

HOUSING (THE ILL-HOUSED) (1971)
Peter W. Martin, Professor of Law, University of Minnesota.

INSURANCE (1971)
William F. Young, Professor of Law, Columbia University.

INTERNATIONAL LAW, See also Transnational Legal Problems and United Nations Law

INTERNATIONAL TRADE AND INVESTMENT, REGULATION OF (1970)
Carl H. Fulda, Professor of Law, University of Texas,
Warren F. Schwartz, Professor of Law, University of Virginia.

INTERNATIONAL TRANSACTIONS AND RELATIONS (1960)
Milton Katz, Professor of Law, Harvard University, and
Kingman Brewster, Jr., President, Yale University.

INTRODUCTION TO THE STUDY OF LAW (1970)
E. Wayne Thode, Professor of Law, University of Utah.
J. Leon Lebowitz, Professor of Law, University of Texas.
Lester J. Mazor, Professor of Law, University of Utah.

INTRODUCTION TO LAW, see also Legal Method, also On Law in Courts, also Dynamics of American Law

JUDICIAL CODE: Rules of Procedure in the Federal Courts with Excerpts from the Criminal Code, 1971 Edition
The late Henry M. Hart, Jr., Professor of Law, Harvard University, and
Herbert Wechsler, Professor of Law, Columbia University.

JURISPRUDENCE (Temporary Edition Hard Bound) (1949)
Lon L. Fuller, Professor of Law, Harvard University.

JUVENILE COURTS (1967)
Hon. Orman W. Ketcham, Juvenile Court of the District of Columbia.
Monrad G. Paulsen, Dean of the Law School, University of Virginia.

UNIVERSITY CASEBOOK SERIES — Continued

JUVENILE JUSTICE PROCESS (1971) (Pamphlet)

Reprinted from Miller, Dawson, Dix & Parnas's Criminal Justice Administration & Related Processes

LABOR LAW, Seventh Edition 1969 with Statutory Supplement

Archibald Cox, Professor of Law, Harvard University, and
Derek C. Bok, President, Harvard University.

LABOR LAW (1968) with Statutory Supplement

Clyde W. Summers, Professor of Law, Yale University.
Harry H. Wellington, Professor of Law, Yale University.

LABOR RELATIONS (1949)

The late Harry Shulman, Dean of the Law School, Yale University, and
Neil Chamberlain, Professor of Economics, Columbia University.

LAND FINANCING (1970)

Norman Penney, Professor of Law, Cornell University.
Richard F. Broude, Professor of Law, Georgetown University.

LAW, LANGUAGE AND ETHICS (1972)

William R. Bishin, Professor of Law, University of Southern California.
Christopher D. Stone, Professor of Law, University of Southern California.

LEGAL DRAFTING (1951)

Robert N. Cook, Professor of Law, University of Cincinnati.

LEGAL METHOD, Second Edition (1952)

Noel T. Dowling, late Professor of Law, Columbia University,
The late Edwin W. Patterson, Professor of Law, Columbia University, and
Richard R. B. Powell, Professor of Law, University of California, Hastings College of the Law.
Second Edition by Harry W. Jones, Professor of Law, Columbia University.

LEGAL METHODS (1969)

Robert N. Covington, Professor of Law, Vanderbilt University,
E. Blythe Stason, Professor of Law, Vanderbilt University,
John W. Wade, Professor of Law, Vanderbilt University,
Elliott E. Cheatham, Professor of Law, Vanderbilt University,
Theodore A. Smedley, Professor of Law, Vanderbilt University.

LEGAL PROFESSION (1970)

Samuel D. Thurman, Dean of the College of Law, University of Utah.
Ellis L. Phillips, Jr., Professor of Law, Columbia University.
Elliott E. Cheatham, Professor of Law, Vanderbilt University.

LEGISLATION, Second Edition (1959)

Horace E. Read, Vice President, Dalhousie University.
John W. MacDonald, Professor of Law, Cornell Law School, and
Jefferson B. Fordham, Professor of Law, University of Pennsylvania.

LOCAL GOVERNMENT LAW (1949)

Jefferson B. Fordham, Professor of Law, University of Pennsylvania.

MENTAL HEALTH PROCESS (1971) (Pamphlet)

Reprinted from Miller, Dawson, Dix & Parnas's Criminal Justice Administration & Related Processes

UNIVERSITY CASEBOOK SERIES — Continued

MODERN REAL ESTATE TRANSACTIONS, Second Edition (1958)
  Allison Dunham, Professor of Law, University of Chicago.

MUNICIPAL CORPORATIONS, see Local Government Law

NEGOTIABLE INSTRUMENTS, see Commercial Paper

NEW YORK PRACTICE, Second Edition (1968)
  Herbert Peterfreund, Professor of Law, New York University,
  Joseph M. McLaughlin, Dean of the Law School, Fordham University.

OIL AND GAS, Second Edition (1964)
  Howard R. Williams, Professor of Law, Stanford University,
  Richard C. Maxwell, Professor of Law, University of California, Los Angeles, and
  Charles J. Meyers, Professor of Law, Stanford University.

ON LAW IN COURTS (1965)
  Paul J. Mishkin, Professor of Law, University of Pennsylvania.
  Clarence Morris, Professor of Law, University of Pennsylvania.

OWNERSHIP AND DEVELOPMENT OF LAND (1965)
  Jan Krasnowiecki, Professor of Law, University of Pennsylvania.

PARTNERSHIP PLANNING (1970) (Pamphlet)
  William L. Cary, Professor of Law, Columbia University.

PATENT, TRADEMARK AND COPYRIGHT LAW (1959)
  E. Ernest Goldstein, Professor of Law, University of Texas.

PLEADING & PROCEDURE: STATE AND FEDERAL, Second Edition (1968)
  David W. Louisell, Professor of Law, University of California, Berkeley, and
  Geoffrey C. Hazard, Jr., Professor of Law, Yale University.

POLICE FUNCTION (1971) (Pamphlet)
  Reprinted from Miller, Dawson, Dix & Parnas's Criminal Justice Administration and Related Processes

PROCEDURE—Biography of a Legal Dispute (1968)
  Marc A. Franklin, Professor of Law, Stanford University.

PROCEDURE—CIVIL PROCEDURE (1961)
  James H. Chadbourn, Professor of Law, Harvard University, and
  A. Leo Levin, Professor of Law, University of Pennsylvania.

PROCEDURE—CIVIL PROCEDURE, Temporary Second Edition (1968)
  Richard H. Field, Professor of Law, Harvard University, and
  Benjamin Kaplan, Professor of Law, Harvard University.

PROCEDURE—CIVIL PROCEDURE, Second Edition (1970)
  Maurice Rosenberg, Professor of Law, Columbia University,
  Jack B. Weinstein, Professor of Law, Columbia University.
  Hans Smit, Professor of Law, Columbia University.

UNIVERSITY CASEBOOK SERIES — Continued

PROCEDURE—FEDERAL RULES OF CIVIL PROCEDURE, 1971 Edition

PROCEDURE PORTFOLIO (1962)
>James H. Chadbourn, Professor of Law, Harvard University, and
A. Leo Levin, Professor of Law, University of Pennsylvania.

PRODUCTS AND THE CONSUMER: Defective and Dangerous Products (1970)
>W. Page Keeton, Dean of the School of Law, University of Texas,
Marshall S. Shapo, Professor of Law, University of Virginia.

PROPERTY, Second Edition (1966)
>John E. Cribbet, Dean of the Law School, University of Illinois,
William F. Fritz, Professor of Law, University of Texas, and
Corwin W. Johnson, Professor of Law, University of Texas.

PROPERTY—PERSONAL (1953)
>The late S. Kenneth Skolfield, Professor of Law Emeritus, Boston University.

PROPERTY—PERSONAL, Third Edition (1954)
>Everett Fraser, Dean of the Law School Emeritus, University of Minnesota
—Third Edition by
Charles W. Taintor II, late Professor of Law, University of Pittsburgh.

PROPERTY—REAL—INTRODUCTION, Third Edition (1954)
>Everett Fraser, Dean of the Law School Emeritus, University of Minnesota.

PROPERTY—REAL PROPERTY AND CONVEYANCING (1954)
>Edward E. Bade, late Professor of Law, University of Minnesota.

PROPERTY, REAL, PROBLEMS IN (Pamphlet) (1969)
>Edward H. Rabin, Professor of Law, University of California, Davis.

PUBLIC UTILITY LAW, see Free Enterprise, also Regulated Industries

RECEIVERSHIP AND CORPORATE REORGANIZATION, see Creditors' Rights

REGULATED INDUSTRIES (1967) with Statutory Supplement
>William K. Jones, Professor of Law, Columbia University.

RESTITUTION, Second Edition (1966)
>John W. Wade, Professor of Law, Vanderbilt University.

SALES AND SECURITY, Fourth Edition (1962), with Statutory Supplement
>George G. Bogert, James Parker Hall Professor of Law Emeritus, University of Chicago.
The late William E. Britton, Professor of Law, University of California, Hastings College of the Law, and
William D. Hawkland, Professor of Law, University of Illinois.

SALES AND SALES FINANCING, Third Edition (1968) with Statutory Supplement
>John Honnold, Professor of Law, University of Pennsylvania.

UNIVERSITY CASEBOOK SERIES — Continued

SECURITY, Third Edition (1959)
    The late John Hanna, Professor of Law Emeritus, Columbia University.

SECURITIES REGULATION, Second Edition (1968) with 1971 Supplement
    Richard W. Jennings, Professor of Law, University of California, Berkeley.
    Harold Marsh, Jr., Professor of Law, University of California, Los Angeles.

SOCIAL WELFARE AND THE INDIVIDUAL (1971)
    Robert J. Levy, Professor of Law, University of Minnesota.
    Thomas P. Lewis, Professor of Law, University of Minnesota.
    Peter W. Martin, Professor of Law, University of Minnesota.

TAXATION, FEDERAL, Sixth Edition (1966) with 1970 Supplement
    Erwin N. Griswold, Solicitor General of the United States.

TAXATION, FEDERAL ESTATE AND GIFT, 1961 Edition with 1965 Supplement
    William C. Warren, Professor of Law, Columbia University, and
    Stanley S. Surrey, Professor of Law, Harvard University.

TAXATION, FEDERAL INCOME, 1960 Edition integrated with 1961 Supplement and a 1964 Supplement
    Stanley S. Surrey, Professor of Law, Harvard University, and
    William C. Warren, Professor of Law, Columbia University.

TORT LAW AND ALTERNATIVES: INJURIES AND REMEDIES (1971)
    Marc A. Franklin, Professor of Law, Stanford University.

TORTS, Second Edition (1952)
    The late Harry Shulman, Dean of the Law School, Yale University, and
    Fleming James, Jr., Professor of Law, Yale University.

TORTS, Fifth Edition (1971)
    William L. Prosser, Professor of Law, University of California, Hastings College of the Law.
    John W. Wade, Professor of Law, Vanderbilt University.

TRADE REGULATION, Fourth Edition (1967) with 1970 Supplement
    Milton Handler, Professor of Law, Columbia University.

TRADE REGULATION, see Free Enterprise

TRANSNATIONAL LEGAL PROBLEMS (1968) with Documentary Supplement
    Henry J. Steiner, Professor of Law, Harvard University,
    Detlev F. Vagts, Professor of Law, Harvard University.

TRIAL ADVOCACY (1968)
    A. Leo Levin, Professor of Law, University of Pennsylvania,
    Harold Cramer, Esq., Member of the Philadelphia Bar. (Maurice Rosenberg, Professor of Law, Columbia University, as consultant).

TRUSTS, Fourth Edition (1967)
    George G. Bogert, James Parker Hall Professor of Law Emeritus, University of Chicago.
    Dallin H. Oaks, President, Brigham Young University.

UNIVERSITY CASEBOOK SERIES — Continued

TRUSTS AND SUCCESSION, Second Edition (1968)
George E. Palmer, Professor of Law, University of Michigan.

UNITED NATIONS IN ACTION (1968)
Louis B. Sohn, Professor of Law, Harvard University.

UNITED NATIONS LAW, Second Edition (1967) with Documentary Supplement (1968)
Louis B. Sohn, Professor of Law, Harvard University.

WATER RESOURCE MANAGEMENT (1971)
Charles J. Meyers, Professor of Law, Stanford University.
A. Dan Tarlock, Professor of Law, Indiana University.

WILLS AND ADMINISTRATION, 5th Edition (1961)
The late Philip Mechem, Professor of Law, University of Pennsylvania, and
The late Thomas E. Atkinson, Professor of Law, New York University.

WORLD LAW, see United Nations Law

University Casebook Series

EDITORIAL BOARD

LON L. FULLER
DIRECTING EDITOR
Professor of Law, Harvard University

EDWARD L. BARRETT, Jr.
Dean of the Law School, University of California, Davis

JEFFERSON B. FORDHAM
Professor of Law, University of Pennsylvania

HARRY W. JONES
Professor of Law, Columbia University

PAGE KEETON
Dean of the Law School, University of Texas

BAYLESS A. MANNING
Professor of Law, Stanford University

LOUIS H. POLLAK
Professor of Law, Yale University

WILLIAM L. PROSSER
Professor of Law, University of California, Hastings College of the Law

JOHN RITCHIE, III
Dean of the Law School, Northwestern University

SAMUEL D. THURMAN
Dean of the Law School, University of Utah

WILLIAM C. WARREN
Professor of Law, Columbia University

CASES AND MATERIALS

ON

THE LEGAL PROFESSION

By

SAMUEL D. THURMAN
Dean of the College of Law, University of Utah

ELLIS L. PHILLIPS, JR.
Professor of Law, Columbia University

ELLIOTT E. CHEATHAM
Professor of Law, Vanderbilt University

Successor Volume
to
Cheatham: Cases and Materials on The Legal Profession,
2nd Edition

Mineola, N. Y.
THE FOUNDATION PRESS, INC.
1970

COPYRIGHT © 1970
By
THE FOUNDATION PRESS, INC.

Library of Congress Catalog Card Number: 73–123245

Thurman et al., Cs. Legal Prof. UCB
1st Reprint—1972

PREFACE

This book is based upon a fresh consideration of the legal profession and its responsibilities and standards.

The period of rapid social change of which we are all a part brings new opportunities and responses by the profession. Our extraordinarily productive economy has made essential new methods of rendering legal service to business. New claims are being asserted by the disadvantaged, and better methods of making legal services available have been made possible by the Congress and the Supreme Court of the United States. The population explosion and the shrinkage of space by swift methods of transportation may call for different methods of political and social organization. The legal profession is giving more sustained attention to its responsibilities, as illustrated by the new Code of Professional Responsibility, the American Bar Association project on Minimum Standards for Criminal Justice, and the ferment in the law schools. There continue the lasting and troubling problems of the lawyer arising out of his partisan position in the adversary system of law administration within the competitive economic system.

Accompanying these developments and increasingly insistent are problems of authoritative control over the profession generated by our fragmented system of government. One set of problems arises out of our federal system: the nation with its "Law of the Land" effective throughout the country; the fifty states each with its own laws and courts and legal profession; the multitude of federal courts (not to mention other tribunals)—district courts, courts of appeal, supreme court—with their several rules and bars. Another set of problems is the product of the tripartite system of government of the nation and the state. Every one has its own legislative, executive, and judicial departments with accompanying questions as to the reach of its powers over the bar and even over the bench.

It is a thrilling time to observe, to think over, and to offer or, far better, to work for developments in the profession. Along with this book there is available a Teacher's Discussion cast in the form of a round table discussion of the book by some of its users with the editors. A continuing dialogue through suggestions and criticisms of the book by other users, whether teachers or students, will be most welcome.

SAMUEL D. THURMAN
ELLIS L. PHILLIPS, JR.
ELLIOTT E. CHEATHAM

April, 1970

SUMMARY OF CONTENTS

	Page
Preface	xi
Table of Contents	xiii
Table of Cases	xix

PART ONE. THE FOUNDATIONS

Chapter
I.	AN OVERVIEW	1
II.	MAKING LEGAL SERVICES AVAILABLE	55
III.	STANDARDS, SUPPORTS AND SANCTIONS	142
IV.	FOREGROUND AND COMPARISON	196

PART TWO. THE LAWYER AT WORK

V.	THE LAWYER IN HIS OFFICE	220
VI.	NEGOTIATION AND COMPROMISE	250
VII.	THE ADVOCATE	272
VIII.	THE LAWYER AND THE LEGISLATURE	334
IX.	THE GOVERNMENT LAWYER	355
X.	PUBLIC RESPONSIBILITY	376

PART THREE. THE CLIENT AND THE LAWYER

XI.	THE ESTABLISHMENT OF THE RELATIONSHIP	411
XII.	SOME CONSEQUENCES OF THE RELATIONSHIP	435

PART FOUR. PERSONNEL OF THE PROFESSION

XIII.	THE LAWYER: EDUCATION, ADMISSION, DISCIPLINE	469
XIV.	THE JUDGE	502

Epilogue	533
Code of Professional Responsibility	535
Index to Code of Professional Responsibility	591
Index	603

TABLE OF CONTENTS

	Page
Preface	xi
Summary of Contents	xiii
Table of Cases	xix

PART ONE. THE FOUNDATIONS

CHAPTER I. AN OVERVIEW ... 1
Section
1. A Look Ahead ... 1
2. The Roles of the Lawyer ... 5
3. The Qualities of the Lawyer ... 32
4. The Setting of the Lawyer's Work ... 35
5. The Interlocking Objectives of the Lawyer ... 37
6. The Need for the Lawyer ... 39
   A. Defense Counsel ... 39
   B. Civil Cases ... 51

CHAPTER II. MAKING LEGAL SERVICES AVAILABLE ... 55
Section
1. The Traditional Methods ... 57
2. The Middle Groups ... 66
   A. Lawyer Referral ... 66
   B. Group Legal Services ... 69
3. The Poor ... 80
4. The Hated ... 89
5. Personal Injury and Death Claims ... 98
   A. The Public Concern ... 98
   B. Solicitation of Personal Injury Claims ... 101
   C. Contingent Fees ... 111
   D. Proposals for Change ... 113
6. Publicity and Solicitation ... 117
7. Lay Experts: Rivals or Collaborators ... 128

CHAPTER III. STANDARDS, SUPPORTS AND SANCTIONS ... 142
Section
1. The Standards ... 142
2. Supports and Sanctions ... 147
   A. The Court ... 148
   B. The Organized Profession ... 155
   C. The Public ... 170
   D. The Individual ... 181
3. The Authoritative Sources of the Standards and Supports ... 189

TABLE OF CONTENTS

	Page
CHAPTER IV. FOREGROUND AND COMPARISON	196

Section
1. The English System 196
2. The American Scene 201
3. A Glance at Other Systems 213

PART TWO. THE LAWYER AT WORK

CHAPTER V. THE LAWYER IN HIS OFFICE 220
Section
1. The Nature of His Work 221
2. Advice on the Borderline—or Beyond 244

CHAPTER VI. NEGOTIATION AND COMPROMISE 250
Section
1. The Importance of Negotiation and Settlement 253
2. Skills and Techniques 258

CHAPTER VII. THE ADVOCATE 272
Section
1. The Nature of a Trial 272
2. The Zeal of the Advocate 280
3. Candor 297
4. Witnesses 317
5. Alternatives to the Adversary System 329

CHAPTER VIII. THE LAWYER AND THE LEGISLATURE 334
Section
1. The Lobbyist 336
    A. The Professional Standard 339
    B. The Legal Standard 345
2. The Legislative Investigating Committee 351

CHAPTER IX. THE GOVERNMENT LAWYER 355
Section
1. The Prosecutor 362
    A. The Decision to Prosecute and Plea Bargaining 362
    B. The Prosecution 366
    C. The Prosecutor and Private Practice 370
2. Other Government Lawyer Roles 371

CHAPTER X. PUBLIC RESPONSIBILITY 376
Section
1. Political Leadership 378
2. Leadership in Public Affairs 386
3. Law Administration 403
4. The Extension of Professional Knowledge 409

xvi

TABLE OF CONTENTS

PART THREE. THE CLIENT AND THE LAWYER

Page

CHAPTER XI. THE ESTABLISHMENT OF THE RELATIONSHIP 411

Section
1. A Case Offered 411
2. Loyalty 414
3. Commencement, Protection and Termination 428

CHAPTER XII. SOME CONSEQUENCES OF THE RELATIONSHIP 435

Section
1. Control Over the Case 435
2. Financial Relations 439
   A. Gifts and Contracts 439
   B. Fees 443
3. Confidential Communications 454
4. Competence and Care 456
5. Injuries to Third Parties 464

PART FOUR. PERSONNEL OF THE PROFESSION

CHAPTER XIII. THE LAWYER: EDUCATION, ADMISSION, DISCIPLINE 469

Section
1. Legal Education 469
2. Admission and Discipline 487

CHAPTER XIV. THE JUDGE 502

Section
1. The Qualities of the Judge 502
2. The Function of the Judge 507
   A. The Trial Judge 507
   B. The Appellate Judge 512
   C. Extrajudicial Functions 513
3. Selection and Tenure of Judges 516
4. Court Organization and Administration 526

Epilogue 533

Code of Professional Responsibility 535

Index to Code of Professional Responsibility 591

Index 603

TABLE OF CASES

The principal cases are in Italic Type. Cases quoted or cited are in Roman Type. References are to Pages.

A. and B., Attorneys-at-Law, In re, 373
Abrams v. United States, 453
Adams v. Stevens & Cagger, 446
Ades, In re, 94, 97, 127
Ahto v. Weaver, 374
Alltmont v. United States, 320
Anastaplo, In re, 500
Ander, In re, 284
Anders v. California, 44
Anderson v. Canaday, 246, 465
Andrewes v. Haas, 437, 446
Appell v. Reiner, 191
Association of the Bar of the City of New York, New York County Lawyers' Association and Bronx County Bar Association, The, 105
Atchison, Topeka & Santa Fe Ry. Co. v. Andrews, 108
Attorney, Matter of an, 496

Barrett v. Ball, 430
Barton v. The State Bar of California, 120, 155
Benson, In re Estate of, 319
Bernard Bercu, In re, 135
Berger v. United States, 366
Betts v. Brady, 40, 41, 45, 53
Biakanja v. Irving, 467, 468
Bingham v. Sheldon, 430
Blackman v. Hale, 460
Blankenbaker v. State, 466
Blumenberg v. Neubecker, 451, 457
Bond & Mortgage Guarantee Co., In re, 425
Bonnifield v. Thorp, 435
Bowles v. United States, 322
Brady v. Maryland, 369
Brotherhood of Railroad Trainmen v. Virginia ex rel. Virginia State Bar, 74, 77, 78, 120, 271
Brown v. Board of Education, 391, 407
B. R. T. v. Virginia, 121
Buckley Case, 467
Buckley v. Gray, 466
Bullen v. Wisconsin, 245

Bullowa, In re, 249
Buttle v. Saunders, 188

Cammarano v. United States, 346
Cammer v. United States, 153
Carlisle v. Barnes, 437
Carpenter v. The State Bar, 268
Cherry Creek Nat. Bank v. Fidelity & Casualty Co., 318
Chicago, B. & Q. Ry. v. Babcock, 480
Chopak, In re, 286
City of. See under name of city.
New York, Matter of City of, 433
Clark v. United States, 322
Clifford v. Hughes, 325
Cohen, In re, 166
Cohen v. Hurley, 501
Commissioner of Internal Revenue v. Tellier, 51
Commissioners v. Younger, 436
Commonwealth v. Hunt, 292
Commonwealth v. Sacco, 368
Comunale v. Traders & General Ins. Co., 432
Connelly, In re, 120
Cowles v. Rochester Folding Box Co., 325
Crocker Point Association v. Gouraud, 459
Croswell v. The People in New York, 94

Davis v. Wakelee, 305
Degen v. Steinbrink, 459
Desist v. United States, 44
De Vito v. United Air Lines, 292
Dillon v. United States, 50, 365
Doe, In re, 286
Douglas v. California, 44
Downer v. Dunaway, 93
Duane Jones Co. v. Burke, 59
Durant, Matter of, 152
Duttenhoffer, Estate of, 439

Eastman v. Blackledge, 446
Edler v. Frazier, 430
Escobedo v. Illinois, 43
Estes v. State of Texas, 176, 178, 278

TABLE OF CASES

Fairfield County Bar v. Taylor, 152
Farmer, In re, 172
Farmers Insurance Exchange v. Henderson, 426
Fasano v. City of New York, 437
Fenaille v. Coudert, 459
Fishgold v. Sullivan Drydock & Repair Corp., 369
Flamm v. Nobel, 318
Florida Bar, In the Matter of the, 64
Freedman v. Oppenheim, 459
French v. Robert S. Abbott Publishing Co., 448
Frost v. Bachman, 442, 477

Gair v. Peck, 111, 449
Gardner v. State of California, 50
Garland, Ex parte, 153
Garrett v. Moore-McCormack Co., 271
Garrison v. Louisiana, 287, 466
Gault, In re, 47, 329
Gebhardt v. United Railways Company of St. Louis, 321, 456
Gelman, Matter of, 263
Giboney v. Empire Storage Co., 160
Gideon v. Wainwright, 39, 43, 45, 49, 53, 54, 76, 344, 460, 461
Giles v. Maryland, 370
Glasser v. United States, 43, 414
Goldsmith v. U. S. Board of Tax Appeals, 195
Grand Rapids Bar Ass'n v. Denkema, 131
Green v. Metropolitan Street Ry. Co., 325
Greenberg, In re, 306
Gregoire v. Biddle, 465
Grievance Committee of the Bar of Hartford County v. Rottner, 415
Griffin v. California, 500
Griffin v. Illinois, 50, 169
Grubbs v. State of Oklahoma, 439
Gunnels v. Atlanta Bar Ass'n, 82, 95

H., Matter of, 151
Hackin v. Arizona, 78
Hackin v. Lockwood, 488
Hallinan, In re, 497
Hallinan v. Committee of Bar Examiners, 489
Hanson v. Kline, 430
Hardaway v. State, 297
Hardenbrook, Matter of, 322
Harkin v. Brundage, 305

Hartford-Empire Co. v. Hazel-Atlas Glass Co., 302
Hatch, In re, 493
Hazel-Atlas Glass Co. v. Hartford-Empire Co., 302
Hearn v. Commissioner, 119
Heimsoth, Matter of, 305
Heinrich, Re, 108
Heller v. Connecticut, 45
Herbits v. Constitution Indemnity Co., 431
Herman v. Dulles, 195
Herron v. Southern Pacific Co., 510
Herron v. State Farm Mutual Ins. Co., 431
Hickman v. Taylor, 240, 319, 320, 321, 456
Hildebrand v. State Bar, 76
Hill v. Hall, 430
Holt v. Commonwealth of Virginia, 466
Huffman's Estate, 447
Hughes v. Wilson Sullivan Co., 319
Hyer v. Flaig, 468

Illinois State Bar Ass'n v. United Mine Workers of America, District 12, p. 70
Integrated Bar, 159
International Ass'n of Machinists v. Street, 159, 160
Investment Corp. of Florida v. Buchman, 468
Isserman, In re, 286

Jacksonville Bar Ass'n v. Wilson, 66
Johnson v. Avery, 45, 138, 141
Johnson v. New Jersey, 44
Johnson v. Ravitch, 438
Johnson v. United States, 510
Johnson v. Zerbst, 42
Jones, In re, 120

Keller v. Wisconsin ex rel. State Bar of Wisconsin, 134
Kent v. Fishblate, 446
Kent v. United States, 47
Kingsland v. Dorsey, 301
Kitz v. Buckmaster, 430
Kline v. Charles, 430
Knight v. Wedderburn, 94
Konigsberg Case, 499
Konigsberg v. State Bar of California, 75, 407, 498, 501
Kopleton, In re, 107
Krause v. Hartford Acc. & Indem. Co., 431
Krooks, Matter of, 432, 446

TABLE OF CASES

Lamb v. Schmitt, 466
Langley, In re, 363
Langlois v. Langlois, 269
Laskey Bros. v. Warner Bros. Pictures, 421
Lathrop v. Donohue, 157, 158, 158, 403
Lawrence v. Tschirgi, 428
Law Students Civil Rights Research Council, Inc. v. Wadmond, 489
Lefton v. City of Hattiesburg, Mississippi, 178
Levy, Matter of, 433
Liles v. Terry, 442
Linder's Estate, In re, 446
L. R., an Attorney at Law, Matter of, 132
Lucas v. Hamm, 466, 468
Lunce v. Overlade, 461

MacLeod v. Vest Transportation Co., 438
Madera v. Board of Education of the City of New York, 329
Mahoning County Bar Ass'n v. Ruffalo, 109
Malloy v. Hogan, 500
Marco v. Dulles, 455
Martin v. Camp, 437, 446
Maternally Yours, Inc. v. Your Maternity Shop, Inc., 191
Martinez v. Del Valle, 293
Maulsby v. Reifsnider, 465
McCarthy v. Spring Valley Coal Co., 292
McCarthy v. United States, 365
McDonald v. Hewlett, 443
McGlone v. Lacey, 443
McGregor v. State Bar, 497
McIntosh v. Flynn, 326
Meinhard v. Salmon, 171
Mempa v. Rhay, 45
Metzger, In re, 282
Michel v. Louisiana, 49
Milone v. English, 422
Miranda v. Arizona, 44, 47
Mitchell v. United States, 49
Mogel, In re, 414
Mooney v. Holohan, 369
Moran v. James, 458
Moura v. State Bar, 490
Murphy v. Washington American League Baseball Club, Inc., 422

NAACP v. Button, 72, 75-78, 120-122, 127
Nash v. United States, 245

National City Bank v. Republic of China, 170
Neece v. Joseph, 325
New York Cent. R. R. Co. v. Johnson, 290
New York Times Co. v. Sullivan, 287
Nye Case, 153

O'Connell v. Superior Court, 433
O'Keefe, In re, 325, 327
Oscanyan v. Arms Co., 436

Palko v. Connecticut, 42
Paschal, Matter of, 433
Patterson v. Colorado, 174
People v. Alexander, 141
People v. Beggs, 264
People v. Clark, 248
People v. Green, 465
People v. Kor, 456
People v. Kresel, 246
People v. Marcus, 248
People v. Wilkes, 369
People ex rel. Chicago Bar Ass'n v. Bereznick, 120
People ex rel. Conn. v. Randolph, 50
People ex rel. Courtney v. Association of Real Estate Tax-Payers of Illinois, 70
People ex rel. Ill. State Bar Ass'n v. People's Stock Yards State Bank, 69
People ex rel. Karlin v. Culkin, 147, 149, 150
People ex rel. Perkins v. Moss, 248
Pepper, Doris H., 186
Percy, Matter of, 152
Perssion's Estate, 443
Potts, Matter of, 448
Powell Case, 174
Powell v. Alabama, 41, 43, 48, 53, 95
Pueblo of Santa Rosa v. Fall, 430

Quercia v. United States, 510

Radiant Burners, Inc. v. American Gas Ass'n, 456
Railway Employe's Dept. v. Hanson, 158-160
Randall v. Brigham, 152
Ratner v. Lehigh Valley R. R. Co., 439
Resner v. State Bar of California, 501
Rex v. Benchers of Gray's Inn, 196
Rex v. Lincoln's Inn, 196
Rhoades, Incorporated v. United Air Lines, Inc., 437

xxi

TABLE OF CASES

Rivette, In re, 439
Robinson, In re, 107
Robinson, Matter of, 325
Rodkinson v. Haecker, 446
Rondel v. Worsley, 412
Roth v. United States, 42
Rothman, In re, 131
Rouss, In re, 495
Rouss, Matter of, 152, 285
Ruffalo, In re, 501
Ruffalo, John Jr., In the Matter of, 108, 110, 111
Rulnick v. Shulman, 122

Sacher, In re, 267, 284
Sacher v. Association of the Bar of the City of New York, 286
Sawyer, In re, 287, 466
Schapiro, Matter of, 325, 327
Schware v. Board of Bar Examiners, 75, 488, 490
Schwarz, In re, 120
Scopes v. Tennessee, 95
Shedden v. Shedden, 94
Shellhammer v. Lehigh Valley R. Co., 306
Sheppard v. Maxwell, 278, 290
Silverman v. State Bar of Texas, 463
Simis v. McElroy, 459
Skidmore v. Baltimore & O. R. Co., 290
Sheppard Case, 174
Sheppard v. Maxwell, 175
Snyder, Matter of, 437
Spanos v. Skouras Theatres Corp., 189
Sparrow, Re, 149
Spaulding Case, 271
Spaulding v. Zimmerman, 269
Sperry v. Florida ex rel. Florida Bar, 134
Spevack v. Klein, 500, 501
Spilker v. Hankin, 443
Spivak v. Sachs, 191
Staedler v. Staedler, 311
State v. Borst, 45
State v. Kavanaugh, 177
State v. Langley, 363
State v. Rush, 50
State v. Smith, 94
State v. Van Duyne, 176, 177
State Bar of Arizona v. Arizona Land Title and Trust Co., 129
State ex rel. State Bar of Wisconsin v. Keller, 132

State ex rel. The Florida Bar v. Nichols, 120
State Street Trust Co. v. Ernst, 468
Stern, Matter of, 154
Summers, In re, 490
Superior Oil Co. v. State of Mississippi, 245

Tannehill v. State, 297
T. C. & Theatre Corp. v. Warner Bros. Pictures, 417, 456
Tenney v. Berger, 433
Third Great Western Turnpike Road Co. v. Loomis, 281
Thorp v. Goewey, 430
Tierney v. Flower, 301
Tot v. United States, 161
Touchett v. E Z Painter Corp., 446
Tracy v. Willys Corp., 424
Trimboli v. Kinkel, 458
Trist v. Child, 347
Tuckiar v. The King, 434
Turco v. Trimboli, 458

Ultramares Corp. v. Touche, 468
Unification of New Hampshire Bar, In re, 158
United Mine Workers of America v. Illinois State Bar Ass'n, 76, 78, 79
United States v. Bartone, 456
United States v. Chicago, Milwaukee, St. Paul & Pacific R. Co., 304
United States v. Dennis, 97, 284
United States v. Empey, 66
United States v. Ford, 322
United States v. Francioso, 492
United States v. Harriss, 345
United States v. Hartford-Empire Co., 302
United States v. Johnson, 273
United States v. MacIntosh, 183
United States v. Marzano, 510
United States v. Sacher, 285
United States v. Standard Oil Co. of New Jersey, 375, 421
United States v. Wade, 44
United States v. Wurzbach, 245
United States ex rel. Berlandi v. Reimer, 497
United States ex rel. Darcy v. Handy, 461
United States ex rel. Goldsby v. Harpole, 93
United States ex rel. Seals v. Wiman, 93

xxii

TABLE OF CASES

Van Duyne Case, 174
Viereck v. United States, 368

Wall, Ex parte, 152, 286
Walsh v. O'Neil, 432
Waugh v. Dibbens, 464
W. E. Bassett Co. v. H. C. Cook Co., 420
Webster v. Kelly, 439
Weil v. Weil, 317
Wessinger v. Sturkie, 453
Willner v. Committee on Character and Fitness, 490, 500

Winberry v. Salisbury, 149
Wisconsin v. Keller, 134
Witherspoon v. Illinois, 407
Woerz v. Rademacher, 458
Woodard v. State Bar, 490
Woods v. City Nat. Bank & Trust Co., 424
Woodward v. Jewell, 458

Yarnall v. Yorkshire Worsted Mills, 437

the whole difference between moral firmness and the mere knowledge of rules which even the rascal can acquire. The students' development will be deeply affected by the unexpressed attitudes of their fellow students and of the instructors in their day to day work, as Justice Holmes emphasized when he said that "education, other than self-education, lies mainly in the shaping of man's interests and aims" and urged that it is the business of a law school "to teach law in the grand manner," * So the third purpose of the book, the development of a sense of responsibility, can be advanced along with the first two since the heightening of a sense of responsibility may come from a realization of the importance and opportunities of the profession, and of the accompanying obligations on those who enjoy its privileges.

Study and teaching in this field offer special difficulties to students and teachers alike. In the ordinary law school courses the subject is covered by cases, which are usually explicit as to the narrow issues involved and are at times clear on the considerations of policy underlying the decisions. There are no court cases, however, on many of the topics included in this book. Even as to matters covered by court decisions, the ordinary case method of treatment is not satisfactory. In the usual law course the precise limits of the law are considered or sought for; but in this subject the cases mark only the outermost bounds beyond which even the crassest rarely stray, and they seldom indicate the narrower limits which public considerations and professional or personal standards prescribe for the lawyer. Moreover, the usual case method of instruction, with its critical dialogue between instructor and student, may be corroding and destructive. As stated of the great teacher, "When we compare Xenophon and Plato, we cannot but feel that the negative effect of Socratic reasoning must have been argumentatively stronger than the positive; so that on minds intellectually active and penetrating, but without moral earnestness, the former may easily have been the sole effect."** And, as the same author points out, the quasi-legal treatment of morality involved in the development of casuistry in the late Middle Ages, "aiming as it did at a precise determination of the limits between the prohibited and the allowable, with doubtful points closely scrutinised and illustrated by fictitious cases, would have a tendency to weaken the moral sensibilities of ordinary minds." * * *

The book is divided into four Parts. Part One, The Foundations, includes a survey of the roles of the lawyer in society, a study of the methods of making his services available, an analysis of the relevant standards of lawyers, a brief glimpse at the history of the

---

* The Use of Law Schools, collected Legal Papers (1921) p. 35.

** Henry Sidgwick, Outline of the History of Ethics, Chapter II, p. 29 (1931 Ed.)

*** Id., Chapter III, p. 153.

profession, and a comparison with some other systems. The six chapters of Part Two, The Lawyer at Work, describe in more detail the varied roles. Part Three, The Client and the Lawyer, emphasizes the lawyer's affirmative loyalties and a few of the other significant consequences of the relationship. The Fourth Part, Personnel of the Profession, looks at the education of lawyers, their admission to practice and their discipline and concludes with a chapter on the judge.

Examining the individual chapters we find an introductory overview in Chapter I of the lawyer's roles, the necessary qualities in properly discharging them and the setting of his work. In addition there is an essay on his interlocking objectives and a study of the constitutional right to counsel.

No more significant recent changes directly affecting the legal profession are to be found than those considered in Chapter II, Making Legal Services Available. Chapter I, Section 6, introduces the topic of the right to counsel and Chapter II extends the inquiry. Included is a survey of the traditional methods of supplying legal services with an accompanying study of the professional restrictions on solicitation and publicity. Special problems affecting four segments of society are dealt with in separate subsections, the middle classes, the poor, the personal injury claimants, and the hated. Another subsection considers the growing significance of non-lawyer involvement in legal matters, described as lay collaboration or "unauthorized practice of the law." Central to the chapter is a study of recent United States Supreme Court decisions concerning group legal services, decisions which constitute a major threat or promise to the legal profession.

Chapter III is devoted to a study of professional standards, the set of values by which the profession strives to live. The several competing loyalties of the lawyer are explored and the general study points forward to the specific problems of succeeding chapters wherein the standards are applied to the varying roles of the lawyer. The major portion of Chapter III looks at the supports and sanctions behind the standards, these being the court, the organized profession, the public and the individual himself. A final section explores briefly the impact of our complex governmental structure, primarily the federal system and the principle of separation of powers, upon the standards of the profession and their sanctions.

Chapter IV, Foreground and Comparison, describes briefly the English background of our profession, sketches the development of the profession on this side of the Atlantic, and concludes with a brief glance at several foreign legal systems. The point is made that the forces which have shaped the profession in the past will continue to do so in the future.

Chapter V, The Lawyer in His Office, begins the detailed treatment of the many roles of the lawyer outlined in Chapter I. It deals with the lawyer's role as counselor in general as well as in more specific fields such as business, taxation, labor relations and the family; with his roles as legislator, as draftsman, and as an administrator of the law. Interwoven are questions dealing with the qualities called for in discharging these functions, qualities such as creativity and sensitivity to the feelings and needs of the persons with whom the lawyer deals, as well as questions as to what may be done in the law school years to develop these qualities. The chapter concludes with a number of troublesome problems on the borderline of professional violation.

Negotiation and compromise take up a major portion of the time of most lawyers in a wide variety of settings. Chapter VI emphasizes the lawyer's role in settlement of pre-existing disputes as well as in the negotiation of future arrangements. The skills and techniques of negotiation are examined along with the ethical responsibilities of the lawyer-negotiator to clients, third persons and society generally.

An analysis of the adversary system of trial is found in Chapter VII, The Advocate. The trial lawyer's sometimes conflicting obligations to client, court, and the public are highlighted by problems in various settings.

The lawyer is frequently a legislative lobbyist and Chapter VIII examines his responsibilities in this area. Unlike the advocate in court the lawyer as lobbyist has lay competitors. Questions as to the existence of professional norms arise as well as questions concerning the various legal standards for control of lobbying. The chapter also includes material on the lawyer as the representative of a client before a legislative investigating committee. A comparison of such investigations and court proceedings is made.

Government Lawyer is the title of Chapter IX with primary focus on the role of the public prosecutor. His discretion to prosecute and the process of plea bargaining are examined along with many of the instances of the prosecutor's special responsibilities, responsibilities differing from those of the attorney for private interests. The chapter concludes with a look at other government lawyers, asking questions as to the extent of and the reasons for their special obligations.

A key chapter deals with the public responsibility of the lawyer (Chapter X). Here there is rising need for lawyer leadership and for student participation. Attention is directed to the lawyer as a holder of public office and as a citizen participant in public affairs. Also included are topics dealing with the obvious areas of lawyer expertise, the administration of justice, the improvement of the substantive law, and the extension of professional knowledge.

Chapter XI is devoted primarily to the lawyer's affirmative duty of loyalty to his client, a duty observed in a variety of settings where conflicts of interest may arise. Brief attention is paid to the freedom of the lawyer in accepting a case and to the factors involved in commencing and terminating the relationship of lawyer and client.

Given a professional relationship, Chapter XII deals with several of its significant consequences. Control over litigation or its subject matter, the fixing of compensation with special attention to contingent fees, the privilege that extends to communications between attorney and client, and the duties of competence and care with the emergence of legal specialists are all considered.

Chapter XIII raises questions concerning the education of lawyers and ends with a consideration of admission to the bar and discipline of attorneys.

The final chapter, XIV, is devoted to the qualities and functions of members of the judiciary. It examines the varying methods of selection and retirement and concludes with the subject of judicial administration and its improvement.

SECTION 2. THE ROLES OF THE LAWYER

Introduction. The most obvious and broadly descriptive role of the lawyer is implicit in the derivation of his name—"law-yer"— one who deals in or is concerned with law. No meaningful study of the lawyer's function can be made without some understanding of the process with which he deals, the law.

Other courses in law school reveal this process at work in a wide variety of settings though the cases may concentrate on rules of law rather than on the process which gives them life. These courses describe law as an instrument of government for the preservation of order, for the regulation and advancement of society, and for the protection of the individual against other individuals and against government itself. An important characteristic is the pervasiveness of law in this country where political problems take legal form and where the economy is constantly in need of legal advice. Law making goes on overtly through legislation and regulation and quietly through court decision. Other law school courses deal with the law's dispute-settling function, its facilitation of future-conduct arrangements, its resolution of public discontent, and its striving for consistency and predictability through the rule of precedent and the use of analogy. They reveal its sense of justice, its striving for stability, and its recognition of the need for change. A major emphasis of legal education is on the role of law in solving the problems of individuals and their society. This book is designed to add to that learning some knowledge of the lawyer's role in the resolution of those problems.

Defining a lawyer as one who deals with and is concerned with law unfolds broad horizons but also proves too much. Such a definition comprehends all members of society, each of which is subject to law and must concern himself therewith. Daily all are compelled to interpret never-ending streams of legislative enactments, local, state and national, usually without the advice of an attorney. Most have no hesitancy in advising friends and others in the process. The same enactments became law in large part through the efforts of non-lawyers, official and non-official, and to a similar extent the executive branch of government is manned by laymen who interpret and execute the law. Even in the process of judicial administration, where the lawyer's claim to exclusivity is strongest, non-lawyers play significant roles as informants, police officials, witnesses, clerks, jurors, etc. Although this book will suggest that the potential of a lawyer in modern society is greater than that of any other professional, later chapters will also examine limits to the lawyer's exclusive function in dealing with law for we shall see that law is not always the sole province of lawyers. Much is left to other specialists, to paraprofessionals, and to laymen, despite the complaints of unauthorized practice committees of the bar.

An analysis of the many roles of the lawyer compels a scrutiny of his function more searching than that suggested by the definition of a lawyer as one who deals with law. High on any list of functions must be the individualization of the law through its application in case or controversy and its utilization in planning with the reduction of such plans to legal form. For the most part these tasks are performed by members of the legal profession who give meaning to the law, both where the directions are explicit and, more important, in areas where leeway is left. As an expert in application of general rules to the needs of specific situations the lawyer may be called upon to use these skills as office counselor, adviser and draftsman (Chapter V), as negotiator (Chapter VI), and as advocate of a client's position (Chapter VII). Each of these partisan roles, it must be observed, is discharged in the setting of the adversary system, a system that assumes an ability to further the cause of clients and at the same time remain faithful to one's responsibility as an officer of the court.

This itemization is obviously not exhaustive and to it must be added the duties of lawyers found in special types of employment outside of private practice. Many of their functions would fit within those just enumerated but they are likely to play distinctive roles as well. Over 40,000 American lawyers are employees of governmental agencies, including 10,000 judges (Chapter XIV), and approximately 30,000 are employees of private concerns. Any complete treatment of the roles of lawyers must at least indicate the duties inherent in such special types of employment.

Finally, beyond the client-representing roles of members of the legal profession there is increasing importance of another lawyer activity, whatever the nature of his other functions. This role is that of public leadership in its broadest sense. (Chapter X). Here we find the lawyer, acting either individually or as a member of a law or lay group, seeking to advance the interests of society on a broad front. A major emphasis of later chapters is on this topic.

LAW AND THE LAWYER

ROSCOE POUND, THE LAWYER FROM ANTIQUITY TO MODERN TIMES *

Pages 24–28 (1953).

It will be worthwhile to remind ourselves why it is that law, lawyers, and a profession of lawyers have come to be developed in all civilized societies and have maintained themselves so persistently that in Soviet Russia it has been found necessary more and more to restore them as an institution. The task of law is to adjust relations and order conduct so as to give the most effect to the whole scheme of expectations of man in civilized society with a minimum of friction and waste. Unless this task is performed, a politically organized society tends to be disrupted or to be dissolved. Controversies must be decided and the general security requires that they be decided according to law, that is, by applying an authoritative technique to authoritative norms or patterns of decision provided for like cases. This can be done well only by judges experienced in the technique and trained in the norms of decision after argument by lawyers who know the technique and have had experience in applying it. Nor are the questions of fact upon which tribunals must pass as a rule so simple or so easy to solve that the untrained man may pass upon them with assurance without assistance of argument by trained advocates. Usually what seems a plain proposition of fact and, when determined, is put as a simple result, follows from a complicated series of disputed facts, frequently disputed in good faith at almost every step in the series. The average controversy is likely to have two sides, each believed in, in good faith by honest

---

* This book was written as a part of the Survey of the Legal Profession under the auspices of the American Bar Association (see Chapter III, page 165 note (5) infra). Roscoe Pound, born in 1870, was one of the most distinguished scholars and members of the American legal profession during the past century. His professional career began as a botanist before he turned to the law, later serving as Commissioner of the Supreme Court of Nebraska, as President of the Association of American Law Schools, as a member of several law faculties, and as Dean of the Harvard Law School for twenty years.

men. In order to decide such controversies satisfactorily the case of each party must be presented thoroughly and skilfully, so that things are put in their proper setting and the tribunal may review the whole case intelligently and come to a conclusion with assurance that nothing has been overlooked, nothing misapprehended, and nothing wrongly valued. The litigant cannot do this adequately for himself. It can only be done by well trained specialists.

Furthermore proper presentation of a case by a skilled advocate saves the time of the courts and so public time and expense. It helps the court by sifting out the relevant facts in advance, putting them in logical order, working out their possible legal consequences, and narrowing the questions which the court must decide to the really crucial points. Good advocacy reduces the work which falls upon judges to decision upon the vital points in carefully selected, appraised, and presented materials. Experience has shown abundantly the waste involved in inexpert presentation of cases by laymen or by inexperienced or inept practitioners.

Along with training and experience, in order to be a help to the courts and an aid to the administration of justice, advocacy demands the professional spirit. In order to further justice, in order to insure that the machinery of justice is not perverted, those who operate the machinery must not merely know how to operate it, they must have a deep sense of things that are done and things that are not done. They need the guiding restraint of the professional spirit to prevent misuse of the machinery, to prevent waste of public time in useless wrangling, to promote proper forensic treatment of witnesses so that witnesses will not be unwilling to come forward to testify. They need it to inspire confidence on the part of courts in being able to rely upon what counsel represent to them instead of having to waste time in looking up everything because unable to assume the face of things as presented by the advocates.

No less important in the busy and complicated world of today is the function of the agent for litigation (attorney, solicitor, proctor). Simply from an economic standpoint there is a very great saving of public time and public money in having cases prepared thoroughly and intelligently in advance of trial. The trial brief, prepared carefully beforehand for the advocate, insures that the crucial points will be distinguished from irrelevant details, that time will not be wasted during the trial on matters which a careful preliminary investigation would have settled, and that the energies of judge and advocate will be directed to the real issues in the controversy.

As to the function of advising upon the law, the sound lawyer is a needed guide for those engaged in enterprises and entering upon undertakings, and those settling trusts or making wills or administering estates or trusts, as well as those seeking reparation of injuries or relief from wrongs in a complex economic order calling for increasing legislation and administrative regulation. The adviser has a function of prevention of or forestalling controversy, preventing needless resort to the courts, and keeping enterprises and undertakings to the straight paths prescribed by law. Every man his own lawyer is even more wasteful than every man his own advocate.

NOTE

Compare Barry and Berman, *The Soviet Legal Profession*, 82 Harv. L.Rev. 1 (1968):

"Over a hundred thousand jurists—advocates, advisers to state institutions, procurators, judges, legal scholars, and others—form a cohesive profession which plays an important part in Soviet society. Although the jurists are in no sense opponents of the Soviet political system, by virtue of their profession they are committed to legal values of freedom and justice, which are sometimes in opposition to the political values of the Soviet government and the Communist Party leadership."

The authors state that there were only 15,000 Soviet jurists in 1928.

REGINALD HEBER SMITH,[*] MEMORANDUM CONCERNING COMPLAINTS AGAINST LAWYERS, THE SURVEY OF THE LEGAL PROFESSION

Page 21 (1949).

The men whose works I have cited all feel that there is a more fundamental reason for complaints against lawyers. As Professor Radin explains it succinctly, I quote him:

"The real reason for the dislike of lawyers is a different one, which shows itself in so many ways that there can be little real doubt about it. People resent the existence of lawyers as a profession in a way they do not resent the existence of any other specialized profession. They do not see why there should be any lawyers at all. . . . they are, in fact, completely unnecessary.

That is the real complaint of the lay public against lawyers."

The end of law is justice, and each man feels that he knows what is justice as well as any other man. He would like to be able to go into court and tell his story to the judge in his own words.

Men realize that they must have doctors for their health, engineers to build bridges, priests and ministers for their spiritual guidance.

---

[*] A leader of the American bar, a pioneer in the field of legal aid, and Director of The Survey of the Legal Profession. His articles on law office management in Volume 26 of the American Bar Journal have been brought together by the Association as a monograph.

But why should they have to pay someone to tell them what the justice of their cause is? That is bad enough, but what is infuriating is to be told in technical jargon they can hardly understand.

This perfectly natural feeling has been intensified in the United States by the democratic impulse. In the Jacksonian era the principle that one man was as good as another tended to become perverted into the conception that one man could do anything as well as another.

Anyone could administer justice. Anyone could be a lawyer if he had a moral character. Several states so provided in their constitutions.

It has taken the bar a long time to recover from the ground it then lost. The weakness of bar associations traces back to that era.

Mr. Root points out that the layman's trouble begins when he has a dispute with another layman whose idea of justice is exactly opposite.

The law must force them to adjudicate their quarrel in court instead of by assault and battery. History has proved that to let a judge decide according to his own notions leads to arbitrary and capricious judgments. Hence he is required to do justice according to law.

NOTE

Erwin N. Griswold, Solicitor General of the United States, and former Dean of the Harvard Law School, delivered the Hamlyn Lectures in England in 1964 describing some of the background of our legal system and the lawyer's roles therein. Griswold, Law and Lawyers in the United States (1964).

A MULTIFACETED ROLE

ELLIOTT E. CHEATHAM, A LAWYER WHEN NEEDED*

Pages 4–7 (1963).

The American lawyer is a paradox within paradoxes. The larger social system within which he works rests on seeming inconsistencies. The economy, yielding so abundantly that its surpluses are embarrassing, is predominantly competitive and purposefully directed to profit rather than to abundance. The needs of society, even the basic ones for food, clothing, and shelter, are met through the strivings of individuals undirected and uncoordinated by government, with the producer compensated by those who seek his product.

At the heart of law itself there are antitheses that a great judge has called The Paradoxes of Legal Science. Stability and progress,

---

* Part of the Carpentier Lectures. Copyright 1963 Columbia University Press. Reprinted by permission.

precedent and equity, justice that is universal yet individual, the one and the many, liberty, equality, and order, such as these are "fundamental opposites [that] clash and are reconciled." *

In its method of administration our law is paradoxical. A trial, which the state employs in settling unresolved controversies, is not a cooperative effort by state agencies to determine the facts and apply the law. The judge, the only impartial participant, is passive —listening, moderating, and passing on what is submitted to him. The lawyers are the active agents who investigate, present, and urge their views of the facts and the law.

The position of the lawyer, too, is paradoxical. Though engaged in the public function of the administration of law, and its most influential participant, he is privately retained by one side, and he aids, guides, and defends that side alone. While called an officer of the court, he is a partisan representative relying on private retainers for his livelihood. This is the adversary system of law administration. Through it, so we believe, "the interested striving of two contending parties is, in the long run, an infinitely better agency for the ascertainment of truth than any species of paternalistic inquiry." **

Under this system something more is required than wise and just laws. Men expert in the law are needed to individualize the law, to apply it, to employ it, and even to develop it in concrete cases. In court, where the law is graphically applied, the work of lawyers makes this need manifest. In our country especially the need for lawyers in court cases is great. In no other nation does the representative of the public, the judge, have so limited a role in court, and the partisan representatives, the lawyers for the parties, so dominant a part.

In office matters the need for lawyers, though less obvious, is equally real. Guidance is needed on legal rights and obligations so that the directives of the law may be observed and its potentialities utilized. In this field of work, too, the need for lawyers is greater in this country than elsewhere. Our malleable economic and social relations and the limited role of governmental functionaries result in delegation to individuals of a large share in determining their mutual relations under law. The individuals to whom these powers are delegated often seek new forms and methods rather than standardized types to fit their desires. In advising and in shaping and defining these relations to suit the infinite variety of human circumstances there is need for a designer and builder of legal relations. He is the lawyer who can draw on and individualize the existing resources of the law to give dependable form to the plans of the par-

---

* Cardozo, The Paradoxes of Legal Science 5 (1928).

** Millar, *The Formative Principles of Civil Procedure*. 18 Ill.L.Rev. 1, 16 (1923).

ties, and who may with imagination and judgment develop new institutions of the law to meet changing needs.

For larger reasons beyond the needs of the immediate parties it is important that lawyers be available to those who need them. Our polity is a legal polity, with many political issues taking legal form. At its beginning the American Revolution was justified because of the violations of the right of the subject and citizen under the law, and the preliminary skirmishes that helped to shape and sharpen the issues were fought in courts of law. Today the protection of the citizen against government and of the alien as well are given reality by lawyers attacking the acts of government. The vague but powerful words "due process of law" and "equal protection of the laws" are defined and made concrete by lawyers and courts. Governmental controls over the economy, whether big business or big labor, are exercised through law, and these controls, too, get their meaning and vitality through the work of lawyers.

Beyond the representation of clients these are other responsibilities that the American lawyer has always carried. From the earliest days of this nation he has aided in forming and guiding public opinion and thus in shaping the institutions of government. In largest measure he has manned the higher levels of the institutions he has shaped. Outside government, among a people who have achieved so much through private initiative, the lawyer still develops and guides innumerable institutions that in the fullest sense are public, though not political. These institutions, private in their administration but public and charitable in their purpose, have provided much of the leadership for the nation in education, the arts, and works of benevolence.

The lawyer's part in these other responsibilities bears directly on our subject. The lawyer reshapes other political and social institutions so that they may better attain their social ends. Naturally it falls to him to reexamine his own institution, the profession of law, so that it, too, will perform its social purpose of providing Equal Justice Under Law.

REPORT OF THE JOINT CONFERENCE ON PROFESSIONAL RESPONSIBILITY *

* In 1952 a Joint Conference on Professional Responsibility was established by the American Bar Association and the Association of American Law Schools with the declared objective of bringing home to the law student, the lawyer and the public an understanding of the nature of the lawyer's professional responsibilities. At various places throughout this book will be found relevant excerpts from the Report of the Joint Conference on Professional Responsibility, an eloquent statement which was approved by the House of Delegates of the American Bar Association at the Midyear Meeting, February 23–24, 1959, and by the Association of American Law Schools at its Annual Meeting, December 28–30, 1958.

44 A.B.A.J. 1159 (1958); 1958 A.A.L.S. Proc. 187 (1958).

A true sense of professional responsibility must derive from an understanding of the reasons that lie back of specific restraints, such as those embodied in the Canons. The grounds for the lawyer's peculiar obligations are to be found in the nature of his calling. The lawyer who seeks a clear understanding of his duties will be led to reflect on the special services his profession renders to society and the services it might render if its full capacities were realized. When the lawyer fully understands the nature of his office, he will then discern what restraints are necessary to keep that office wholesome and effective.

Under the conditions of modern practice it is peculiarly necessary that the lawyer should understand, not merely the established standards of professional conduct, but the reasons underlying these standards. Today the lawyer plays a changing and increasingly varied role. In many developing fields the precise contribution of the legal profession is as yet undefined. In these areas the lawyer who determines what his own contribution shall be is at the same time helping to shape the future role of the profession itself. In the duties that the lawyer must now undertake, the inherited traditions of the Bar often yield but an indirect guidance. Principles of conduct applicable to appearance in open court do not, for example, resolve the issues confronting the lawyer who must assume the delicate task of mediating among opposing interests. Where the lawyer's work is of sufficient public concern to become newsworthy, his audience is today often vastly expanded, while at the same time the issues in controversy are less readily understood than formerly. While performance under public scrutiny may at times reinforce the sense of professional obligation, it may also create grave temptations to unprofessional conduct.

For all these reasons the lawyer stands today in special need of a clear understanding of his obligations and of the vital connection between those obligations and the role his profession plays in society.

. . .

In modern society the legal profession may be said to perform three major services. The most obvious of these relates to the lawyer's role as advocate and counselor. The second has to do with the lawyer as one who designs a framework that will give form and direction to collaborative effort. His third service runs not to particular clients, but to the public as a whole.

NOTE

Does the reader find the analysis and statement of the role of the lawyer given in this section to be accurate and helpful? He may believe more useful the analysis by Chief Justice Vanderbilt which in a few words is: "These five—counseling, advocacy, improving his profession, the courts and the law, leadership in molding public opinion and the unselfish holding of public office—are the essential functions of the great lawyer. Education in these five functions of the lawyer is partly the province of the college, partly the duty of the law school, but in large measure it is the responsibility of the individual lawyer not only while in law school but throughout his working years. This is practicing law in the grand manner—the only way it is worth practicing." Vanderbilt, *The Five Functions of the Lawyer*, 40 A.B.A.J. 31, 32 (1954). Arthur T. Vanderbilt was President of the American Bar Association, Dean of the New York University School of Law, and Chief Justice of the Supreme Court of New Jersey. The most notable result of his work was the reorganization of the judicial system of his state through a new constitution in the drafting and adoption of which he had a major part.

STANLEY F. REED,[*] THE BAR'S PART IN THE MAINTENANCE OF AMERICAN DEMOCRATIC IDEALS [**]

24 A.B.A.J. 622 (1938).

Within the members of our profession is found every type of individual. There are those men of action who will undertake to organize, manage or liquidate every conceivable kind of business or social enterprise. To them, their clients entrust many phases of their affairs quite far away from the humdrum routine of the law. They are advocates with the heart of advocates, bold, persuasive, intense. Opposition even defeat, feeds the fires of their purpose. They are crusaders for a cause or for a client. After one conference, many fuse right and their clients' interest into a single lance with which they will joust with all the world. No hour is unsuitable, no work too difficult for these shock troops of the law. Singly or in groups they attack the problems and find in action itself a reasonable outlet for their energies. These are the lawyers who spin the engines of life. They speed up the documents so that the issues may come out on time. They delve, continuously, for facts and more facts. Facts derived from witnesses, circumstances and background. They check the lives of jurors, draw from the knowledge of experts in every field, and weigh the predilections of judges. Their qualities are those of action.

Others of us are men of reflection. We judge the future by the past. From the experiences of others we determine what course to follow. If rocks and shoals have been encountered in an effort to reach an objective, we counsel our clients as to the dangers of the voyage and seek ways to avoid the difficulties. Precedents count

---

[*] Associate Justice of the Supreme Court of the United States. As Solicitor General of the United States Mr. Reed had earlier argued before the Supreme Court many of the important cases arising out of New Deal legislation.

[**] Copyright 1938 by the American Bar Association. Reprinted by permission.

much in the lives of such lawyers. They ransack the reports to find decisions on all fours with their cases. Apart from the complications of active affairs, these men search for the truth. They revel in the history and philosophy of the law. As teachers or judges they contribute greatly to the understanding of jurisprudence. They are sought as analysts, as originators of theories to conform present facts to former rulings.

There is another group of lawyers whom we will call men of vision. They see the law not as a perfect sphere, complete and finished, but as an aggregation of material ready for the builder. Whatever may be the need of the times may be constructed from the supplies on hand. To these men of vision, the past and present merely offer suggestions as to the way to attain the more perfect justice which is always beyond. These lawyers deal not with the present or the past but with the future. They reason not from precedents but toward objectives. Not what the law is but what it should be. Their interests lie in the continuity of legal process, the discovery of the trend. They study to see how opinions are expanded to meet the changing needs of society,—how acts and statutes may be drafted to cover weaknesses or to meet new conditions.

RICHARD W. NAHSTOLL, REGULATING PROFESSIONAL QUALIFICATION in LAW IN A CHANGING AMERICA *

Pages 125, 127 (1968).

It is surely appropriate that standards of qualification relate to the functions to be performed by the person whose qualifications are to be tested. In short, if a test assumes to measure whether one is qualified to play the role of a lawyer, the role should be understood. The requirements for legal education and the content of bar examinations assume that there is a definable lawyer's role and that the personal equipment required to play it has measurable attributes. This equipment includes acquaintance with legal doctrine, particularly the legal doctrine involved in what are assumed to be the general, usual or common aspects of the "practice of law." The "practice of law" is conceived as centering or at least beginning with the function of appearing in court and directing participation in the litigation procedure. In one respect this is appropriate, for whatever

---

* This publication was prepared for background reading at the 1968 Assembly of the American Bar Association and The American Assembly of Columbia University. Over 100 persons prominent in the legal profession and in the worlds of education, the clergy, communications, business, and government met to consider the "goals for the legal profession in the years ahead in the light of the social changes of the present and recent past." Mr. Nahstoll served as President of the Oregon State Bar and was the winner of the American Bar Association's Ross Essay Contest in 1964.

Copyright 1968 by The American Assembly, Columbia University. Reprinted by Permission of Prentice-Hall, Inc., N. J.

else may be included in the "practice of law," the right to participate in litigation is within the exclusive monopoly conferred by the license to practice law. As a result the bar examination procedure centers on, or at least begins with legal doctrine related to litigation.

Beyond this point, however, there is confusion and difficulty. Participation in litigation does not exhaust the work of a lawyer, nor does the lawyer in performing non-litigation tasks enjoy a professional monopoly. "The work of a lawyer" includes those things which a lawyer does, in common with others, largely because his talents and training are presumed to place these functions within his calling. In common with bankers, realtors, insurance consultants, securities counsellors, and others, the lawyer ventures investment advice and invests the assets of clients. In common with physicians, ministers and social workers, the lawyer gives personal and family advice. In common with accountants, bankers, market analysts, economists and technical persons of all sorts, the lawyer gives business and corporate advice, non-legal in nature. In common with others, the lawyer functions in various ways and situations as a "peacemaker"—negotiating, arbitrating, seasoning his client's demands with a sprig of objectivity or structuring a situation to allow people, essentially desirous of working their way out of a situation which they find distasteful, to "save face" and re-establish communication.

What is the legal doctrine that the lawyer should know to perform *these* tasks? And what examination can be devised that would determine whether he knows enough of it? The process of bar examination assumes, with more confidence than their real difficulty would seem to permit, that there are answers to these questions.

If these questions are difficult, more difficult still is the question whether mastery of doctrine is itself the aspect of the lawyer's technical proficiency that is most important to measure. Fundamental to the broad spectrum of the lawyer's work is the art of communication—communication both sending and receiving, communication in the relatively informal setting of *ex parte* interviewing of clients, witnesses or associates, communication in the relative formality of the courtroom, communication in the negotiation process, communication (perhaps to an unidentified audience) through the written word, whether the document be a letter to be understood on receipt of tomorrow's mail, or a lease or contract to be understood ten (10) years hence. Nor, as we have more recently been made aware, can the subleties of "non-verbal communication" be ignored.

Compounding the problem for the lawyer performing his broader function is the fact that, generally, he is dealing with people at their psychological and emotional ebb. Their potential for avarice is at full flower and, consciously or unconsciously, their personal stake in the matter at hand influences their participation in the affair and their handling of relevant information. Ideally, the lawyer's handling of these nuances would exact of him a high level of sophistication in several of the behavioral disciplines.

Nor is the lawyer's concern with the humanities of significance only in his one-to-one relationships with other persons. If lawyers are to make meaningful contributions to the solution of the social ills of which the recent riots and unrest are symptomatic, it will be to the extent they are able to appreciate, and hopefully to utilize, the relationship of the law to sociology, anthropology, mass psychology, political science, and perhaps other social sciences.

The failure of the legal fraternity to respect these complexities of its work has contributed to what many now appreciate to be the inadequacies of our admissions system. In default of appreciating the need for and developing procedures for testing whether an applicant is qualified to do a lawyer's work, admissions authorities have quite unimaginatively copied the testing procedures of law schools. They undertake to test essentially, and only, those things which law schools have chosen to recognize and acknowledge as within the scope of legal education. At the same time, by process of anticipation, the law schools in varying degrees organize legal education according to what will appear on the bar examinations. The *Rule in Shelley's Case* is examined on by the bar because it is taught in law school, because it is on the bar examination, because it is what the students have been instructed in. . . .

QUINTON JOHNSTONE & DAN HOPSON, JR., LAWYERS AND THEIR WORK*

Page 33 (1967).

. . . the legal profession is so varied and stratified that lawyers of one kind generally have quite limited familiarity with or understanding of the work or problems of most other kinds of lawyers. This is so not only of different sorts of specialists but is particularly true of lawyers in different prestige strata. . . . Thus, for example, the professional vision and values of big firm partners tend to be quite different from those of neighborhood practitioners, even in the same city. Similar disparities tend to exist between local government prosecutors and lawyers on the staff of the United States Solicitor General, and between teachers in marginal kinds of night law schools and those in national law schools.

NOTE

Lawyers and Their Work divides the lawyer's "work tasks" into a variety of categories—negotiation, drafting, litigation, investigation, research, lobbying, brokering, public relations, filing, adjudication, financing, property

---

* Copyright 1967 by the Bobbs-Merrill Co. Reprinted by permission.

management, referrals, supervision of others, emotional support for clients, and all manners of advice to clients. (pages 77–130) Closely related to such an analysis is the question of the extent to which legal services are coming to be performed increasingly by laymen.

It is not too early in this book to begin to inquire into this latter question. What is the practice of law? It is a major concern of bar associations and will be dealt with at various points herein. See Cohen, *Pluralism in the American Legal Profession*, 19 Ala.L.Rev. 247 (1967). See Chapter II, Section 7, page 128 infra.

ADJUDICATION AND LEGISLATION

LON L. FULLER, WHAT THE LAW SCHOOLS CAN CONTRIBUTE TO THE MAKING OF LAWYERS

1 Jour.Leg.Ed. 189, 192–3, 194–5, 196–7 (1948).

. . . The lawyer is a participant, and usually the most active and responsible participant, in two basic social processes: adjudication and legislation. Both terms are here used in a somewhat broader sense than is customary.

The adjudicative process has to do with the case-arguing and dispute-deciding aspect of the lawyer's work. As I use the term, it refers to all forensic methods of deciding disputes, including informal arbitration and the work of administrative tribunals as well as the traditional processes of our courts. Adjudication presents the lawyer in his role as advocate, or judge, or office counselor advising a client of the likely decision of a cause. All of these activities center about a single process, that by which controversies are argued and decided.

The legislative process, on the other hand, presents the lawyer in his rule-creating, structure-giving role. It presents him as a planner, negotiator, and draftsman. As I use the term "legislation" it refers not merely to the planning and drafting of statutes, but includes the negotiation and drafting of contracts and other private documents. Thus, the drafting of a will is, in this sense, legislation, since it establishes a legal framework within which the estate of the testator is administered after his death. . . .

Adjudication has to do with forensic facts. If we are dealing with appellate decisions, the facts reported have been filtered through the rules of evidence and purged of their natural ambiguities by presumptions and rules about the burden of proof. . . .

Legislation, on the other hand, deals not with forensic facts, but with what may be called managerial facts. It is not the task of the lawyer acting as planner, negotiator, and draftsman to reduce the facts to a neat pattern, but to see them as a whole, in all their disorder, in all their ambiguity. He must gear his decision to a range of factual probability, and must devise a plan that will anticipate, and absorb without disruption, future changes in the facts.

Other differences between the processes of legislation and adjudication may be brought out by such a simple inquiry as: What is a contract? For the lawyer concerned with the adjudicative process a contract is a legally enforceable agreement, and its meaning is that which a court will give to it in the event of litigation. For the lawyer bringing a contract into existence it may be primarily a framework for cooperative effort, which performs its function without regard to its enforceability or the interpretations a judge would give to it. Often in phrasing the terms of an agreement the lawyer has to balance the desiderata against each other: (1) that of placing his client in a position to win any lawsuit that may grow out of the contract, and (2) that of creating an instrument of collaboration that will function effectively and not produce lawsuits. If he cannot have both these things, he may properly favor the second at some cost to the first, since his role as practical legislator for the situation may be more important than his role as advocate in a hypothetical future adjudication. . . .

[T]he concept of the legislative process seems to me to furnish a standard that will simplify our problem of what to teach. As I have defined that process it covers a multitude of apparently disrelated activities—all the way from drafting a will in the quiet recesses of a five-name firm on State Street in Boston to negotiating a labor contract under the threat of strike on the Galveston water front. And what a disparate set of skills and aptitudes this process demands of those who participate in it! The negotiator must have tact and insight into others' motives, a sense of timing, a capacity for what may be called visceral decisions. The draftsman must have the capacity for painstaking logical analysis and clear, orderly English—and a horror of visceral decisions. Unless some common core can be found in these skills and activities we must despair of educating a lawyer in less than ten years.

But I believe there is such a common core, which I would define as the accommodation of opposed interests and the reduction of the pattern of that accommodation to clear verbal expression. I think we may even say that the man drafting a will is learning negotiation. He is considering how the interests of the widow can be accommodated to those of the children, and how the testator's desire to be generous toward his alma mater can be reconciled with his obligations toward his family. Such a draftsman is not like a man playing solitaire, but more like a player who plays in turn each of the hands in a bridge game. So that even the task of drafting a will may convey an insight useful in negotiating a contract. By the same token, negotiating and drafting a contract compels a man to perceive the demands contained in the task of drafting a statute and securing its passage. . . .

NOTE

The lawyer as policy maker: "It should need no emphasis that the lawyer is today, even when not himself a 'maker' of policy, the one indispensable adviser of every responsible policy-maker of our society—whether we speak of the head of a government department or agency, of the executive of a corporation or labor union, of the secretary of a trade or other private association, or even of the humble independent enterpriser or professional man. As such an adviser the lawyer, when informing his policy-maker of what he can or cannot *legally* do, is, as policy-makers often complain, in an unassailably strategic position to influence, if not create, policy . . .

"For better or worse our decision-makers and our lawyers are bound together in a relation of dependence or of identity. . . . The lawyer, it must be recalled, is a member of a learned profession—of a skill group which has the temerity to make a profession of tendering advice to others. To no one else can clients and members of the public reasonably be expected to look for that enlargement and correction of perspective, that critical and inclusive view of reality, that is based on the disciplined exercise of skills which the layman is not given the opportunity to acquire." Lasswell and McDougal, *Legal Education and Public Policy: Professional Training in the Public Interest,* 52 Yale L.J. 203, 208–211 (1943).

BENJAMIN N. CARDOZO, MEMORIAL ADDRESS ON JOHN G. MILBURN

Year Book, 1931, Ass'n of the Bar of the City of New York,
Pages 439–440.

The loss to the courts in these latter years was the gain of the office chambers, where the professional adviser took the place of the advocate. I know there is a tendency to deplore the disappearance of the advocate as the dominant figure in the lawyer's life, and to contrast the part he has played in the development of law with the part played by the adviser, and this to the latter's disadvantage. Deplore the change I do, for selfishness, if nothing else, would lead me to lament it. There would be a new joy in the day's work if the leaders were before us daily to stimulate and enlighten when interest droops and flags, as I may tell you, in strictest confidence, it has a tendency to do if the argument of counsel has neither a beginning nor a midde nor, what counts for even more, an end. These personal tribulations must not lead me, however, to overlook the truth that in the literature of the law there has been a tendency to underestimate the importance of the role that is played by the office adviser, not merely in keeping his client out of jail or in avoiding civil liability, but even in shaping and directing the institutions of the law itself. He is much more than a traffic officer, warning of obstructions and keeping travellers to the travelled path. He is a creative agent just as truly as the advocate or the judge. In our complex economic life, new problems call from day to day for new methods and devices. The lawyer in his office formulates a trust receipt, or stock certificates with novel incidents, or bonds, municipal or corporate, with privileges or safeguards till then unknown to the business world. At times legislation is necessary to make the innovation lawful. More often, the new device establishes itself in practice, is taken up by business men generally as one of the accepted moulds of conduct. When that happens, the function of the court becomes in a sense supervisory and secondary. The innovation must still be tested for possible infringements of the behests of public policy and justice. Even so, except in rare cases—cases where the infringement is serious and manifest—the form that has thus worked itself into the methods of business life will be accepted almost automatically as postulates of the legal order. The courts do no more than set the imprimatur of regularity upon methods that have had an origin in the creative activity of an adviser, working independently of courts in the quiet of an office. In this creative activity Mr. Milburn played his full part in the years that I have styled the years of his second epoch. What he did then may console us to some extent for what he ceased to do during that epoch by methods more contentious.

DILLON ANDERSON, A LAW FIRM—AND WHAT IT EXPECTS FROM YOU in LISTEN TO LEADERS IN LAW *

Page 67 (1963).

. . .

There is more to be said about pertinacity; there is its relationship to resourcefulness, another quality which, in my judgment, is one of the greatest assets which a lawyer can bring to a firm—or to the profession in any connection. And resourcefulness surely grows with experience. While a part of this rare quality is doubtless born in some more than in others, and while an imaginative approach becomes easier to some than it does to others, I believe resourcefulness is a trait which can be cultivated and that the plow is pertinacity.

The client wants and will pay handsomely for these qualities in your service. One of the highest compliments I heard paid to my late partner, Jesse Andrews, was that he had the knack of "telling his clients what they could do instead of what they couldn't do." Granted, the client may sometimes have to be told that what he wants to do is illegal. But aside from things which are illegal, the client is entitled to your expert help in doing what he wants to do.

* Copyright 1963 by Tupper and Love, Inc. Reprinted by permission.

He should be able to find, with his lawyer's dedicated help, the best legal avenue to accomplishing his valid business objectives.

The above point was perhaps never better illustrated than it was in the early days of World War II in Washington. Statutes altogether inappropriate and inadequate for the scale and speed of procurement required were still on the books. The capital was alive with bureaucrats who could cite chapter and verse on why many needed things could not be done. Judge Robert Patterson, then Under Secretary of War, brought into the service a group of civilian lawyers whose task was to deal with the pressing needs of mobilizing our resources for waging war. Their task was to find ways, within the law, of doing things *that had to be done*. Their experience in representing civilian clients provided the resourcefulness required, and, indeed, their service in the vital procurement program became an unsung, but significant, chapter in the early months following Pearl Harbor.

. . .

PUBLIC LEADERSHIP

JAMES WILLARD HURST, THE GROWTH OF AMERICAN LAW *

Pages 352–356 (1950).

Another function of the bar throughout our history proved to be the supply of a considerable percentage of the directing personnel needed in large public and private affairs. This was not an unnatural aspect of a profession which was so directly and regularly called on to exercise wide-ranging skill in adjustment of human relations.

. . .

From 1790 to 1930, about 66 per cent of United States Senators were lawyers, and about 50 per cent of the members of the House; the percentages appear to have been about the same over the whole time span. Lawyers numbered between one half and two thirds of state governors. . . .

Lawyers played an important part in public affairs outside of public office and off the platform. From the first days of the republic lobbying was an important item in the practice of the more influential and financially successful lawyers. Law-trained men figured in the inner circles of party politics from the days of Jefferson and Hamilton to those of Taney and Webster, Jeremiah S. Black and Thaddeus Stevens, John P. Altgeld and Elihu Root, John W. Davis and Charles Evans Hughes, Benjamin Cohen and John Foster Dulles.

* With the permission of Little, Brown & Co., publisher.

Probably as important as these more obvious public activities was the cumulative weight of lawyers' unofficial, unpaid, nonpartisan service. Intellectual pride and regard for the public welfare entered, in imponderable mixture, into the amazing, singlehanded battle which David Dudley Field waged for codification of the laws from the 1840's to 1887. In the post Civil War generation an aristocrat at the bar, William Allen Butler, concerned himself with housing, hospital, and charity problems that came with the growth of great cities. . . .

Despite such public and private display of civic consciousness among some of the profession, certain twentieth-century observers saw a material decline in the bar's general participation in public affairs. . . . In 1934 Mr. Justice Stone expressed his sober appraisal that:

> . . . candor would compel even those of us who have the most abiding faith in our profession, and the firmest belief in its capacity for future usefulness, to admit that in our own time the Bar has not maintained its traditional position of public influence and leadership.

The unanimity of such testimony from responsible observers was impressive. On the other hand, though there was a plausible case for the proposition that the bar had lost much in public influence, the case rested largely on opinion. So far as anyone sought to produce tangible evidence, it tended to be directed mainly at an attempt to show that there were fewer lawyers in public office. However, it was hard to establish even this last point by quantitative evidence; available data were incomplete. . . .

Toward mid-twentieth century, however, it appeared that events might be maneuvering lawyers back toward a greater position of constructive public influence. . . . In 1937 the Supreme Court finally affirmed Congress's control of the national economy. In a large measure this only shifted the battleground, but at least it shifted the fight toward more constructive efforts to reach working accommodations between private and public direction of affairs. The lawyer had won his public leadership in the past largely because his profession helped make him a more objective and resourceful mediator of forces. Perhaps he was returning to this basis of leadership. Writing in 1949, the leader and historian of a famous New York law firm seemed in effect to say this. Mr. Robert T. Swaine saw a critical challenge presented to the bar:

> Today the American lawyer deals with the problems of his business clients on a much broader basis, considers substance as more important than form and attempts to relate legal problems to their political, economic and social implications. . . .
> The clients of today also generally recognize the interrelation of legal questions with political, economic and social questions.

. . . Big Business, Big Labor and Big Government are all here to stay. But in the gigantic concentrated power of their aggregate collectivism there is real danger that they may be leading us along the road to state collectivism. If we believe that such an end would be a tragedy, and that individual freedom of opportunity in a system of private enterprise should be maintained, it behooves all of us who render "specialized service to business and finance" to seek such solutions of the legal problems of our clients as are compatible with the changing social concepts and as will avoid the abuses of economic power to which our profession too often contributed in past decades.

ELLIOTT E. CHEATHAM, THE LAWYER'S ROLE AND SURROUNDINGS

25 Rocky Mountain L.Rev. 405, 406–407 (1953).

The System of Law Administration. A second responsibility of the lawyer [in addition to *The Individualization of Law*] concerns the system of law administration. The development and operation of an adequate system of administration rests principally with lawyers. They know whether or not the existing system is working well. They should know what changes can be wisely made. Three elements of an adequate system may be noted. One is the machinery of law administration, that is, the instrumentalities and officials directly charged with the administration of law. A second element is the structure of the legal profession, a structure which will make the services of competent lawyers available in fact to those who need them. A third element is the spirit of the legal profession, its ideals and its standards in everyday work. Machinery and structure are important. They make possible or facilitate measures which otherwise would be difficult or impossible. More important than machinery is the spirit of those who operate it. This spirit can make even poor machinery work passably well; or it can ruin even the best machinery. So it is with the legal profession.

Political and Public Leadership. There is a third function which lawyers largely exercise. It is political and public leadership.

The rules of law must be developed and modified for new situations. Part of this development comes about as a by-product of the individualization of law mentioned above. In the application of the law to concrete cases, the lawyer is aiding also in the development of the rules of law. It is the very nature of the common law thus to grow through cases. The poet has written of the common law broadening down from precedent to precedent, and any volume of court reports will serve as illustration.

With conditions changing swiftly, the development of the law cannot be left to the courts. Law-making must go on through the legislature. Here, again, the dominance of lawyers is a commonplace. The dominance exists in the legislative and the executive branches of the nation, of the states, and of the municipalities. It is so as a matter of course in the representation of interests before legislative committees where so much of our legislation is hammered out.

There are other areas of our public life no less important, though not involving political office. They include the schools, the charities, the churches, the cultural institutions. These myriad activities, by their freedom from political or governmental direction, make possible public services beyond the government and reduce the threat of excessive centralization of power. Here lawyers who do not desire political office or would be unacceptable to the electorate contribute much to public life.

Other areas of our community life include the activities of the large groups which dominate so much of the economy of the nation, such as the industrial and financial corporations, the labor unions, and the growing co-operatives. Here, the corporation lawyer has come to recognize to an increasing degree his responsibility as a guiding force.

Outside of these organized activities there is the vague but fundamental matter of the formation and crystallization and expression of public opinion. From the earliest days of our nation, lawyers have had a predominant part. Hamilton and Jay, along with Madison, in *The Federalist Papers* are familiar illustrations.

NOTES

(1) "The chief characteristic of the professional activity of American lawyers is its rich variety. This variety may be illustrated by the careers of the Justices of the United States Supreme Court prior to their appointment to that tribunal. Supreme Court Justices are, to be sure, unusual among American lawyers in the distinction of their abilities and achievements. Moreover, characteristically they have been more than usually active in public affairs and government before assuming the bench. Even so, the diversity of their professional experience is representative of the American legal profession.

The experience of the justices who composed the Supreme Court in 1965 includes being a lawyer in private law practice (all of them), in large law firms (Justices Harlan and Stewart) and small ones (Justices Clark, Brennan and Goldberg); a public prosecutor (Chief Justice Warren and Justice Black); Attorney General of the United States (Justice Clark); a United States Senator (Justice Black); an officer of local government (Justice Stewart served as city councilman), state government (the Chief Justice was Governor of California), and federal government (Justice Goldberg was Secretary of Labor, Justice Douglas was Chairman of the Securities and Exchange Commission, Justice White was Deputy Attorney General); a law teacher (Justice Douglas); and a judge (Justice Brennan was a trial judge, intermediate appellate judge and justice of a state Supreme Court).

And all nine justices had served in two or more of these capacities at one time or another in their careers. In addition, throughout their professional lives they have been public citizens—active on committees, on boards of directors of charitable and educational institutions, in law reform organizations and on special public commissions." American Bar Foundation, The Legal Profession in the United States,* 1, 2 (1965) (a monograph).

(2) "If one goes back to the days of the making of the Constitution in 1787, he finds that great document largely the fruit of the thought and the patriotism of the lawyers of that day. From that time down to this, all our forward steps in the remodeling of our institutions or in devising new ones have first been the thoughts of . . . lawyers, and they have been promulgated largely through the advocacy and explanations of lawyers. . . . It may well be that great contributions to the institutional and constitutional development of our country have been initiated in the minds of philosophers, but certainly the practical adaptation of them and the adoption of them into the practices of the country have been brought about by using the body of the Bar as the agency for popular advocacy and exposition. . . ." Newton D. Baker, *The Lawyer's Function in Modern Society,* 19 ABAJ 261–262 (1933).

WILLIAM T. GOSSETT, IN THE KEEPING OF LAWYERS **
10 Wm. and Mary L.Rev. 427, 432–434 (1968).

Let me refer you to a related area, though less novel in its content. A distinguished Pennsylvania judge, Curtis Bok, once said:

"In the whole history of law and order, the longest step forward was taken by primitive man, when, as if by common consent, the tribe sat down in a circle and allowed one man to speak at a time. An accused who is shouted down has no rights whatever."

The legal profession long ago developed a term to describe the ancient custom of allowing one person to speak at a time, of allowing the accused to speak without being shouted down. As you know, we call it "due process of law". Due process represents procedural decency and fairness; it came down to us from the Magna Carta, through the common law; and it is embedded in the Constitution of this nation.

In the language of the Supreme Court: "[Due process] is the primary and indispensable foundation of individual freedom. It is the basic and essential term in the social compact which defines the rights of the individual and delimits the powers which the State may exercise." (In re Gault, 387 U.S. 1, 20 (1967).) Without the decency of treatment that is the foundation of due process, there is no free-

---

* Copyright 1965 by the American Bar Foundation. Reprinted by permission.

** The Sherwell Lecture delivered at the Marshall-Wythe School of Law, College of Wm. & Mary, by Mr. Gossett, President of the American Bar Association. Copyright 1969 by the College of William and Mary. Reprinted by permission.

dom, doctrinal or practical, for the individual. Consequently, if lawyers are crusaders at all, as they must be, they are first and foremost crusaders for due process. And if lawyers are public teachers, as they are and must be, they have a continuing responsibility to enlighten the public on the necessity and utility of decency in the law's attitude toward the individual.

. . .

There are many areas of life today that cry out for a sharpened sense of due process on the part of all of us. Equal access to the law is one. A person without legal advice because he cannot afford it is, because of that fact alone, deprived of due process. Unpopular people and those serving unpopular causes can be and often are, because of that fact alone, deprived of due process. An accused who is detained in ignorance of his rights or denied a prompt hearing or the right to counsel, because of that fact alone, can be deprived of due process.

. . .

This matter of due process should be the concern of all Americans, but it is overwhelmingly the concern of lawyers. And the lawyer's continuing responsibility for diligent action in the affected areas goes beyond his professional functions and, indeed, beyond his sworn duty as an officer of the court. It reaches to the very core of his life and of his convictions. Even if every other individual and every institution in our society should forget or subvert process as the cornerstone of our civilization, the lawyer—alone, if necessary; defiant, if challenged; resolute, if discouraged—should never yield on the right of any man, good or bad, rich or poor, revered or hated, to the benefits of due process; should never relax his efforts to enlighten the public about it; and should never silence his demands for it.

DECISION MAKER

ASSOCIATION OF AMERICAN LAW SCHOOLS, SELECTED READINGS ON THE LEGAL PROFESSION, ETHICS IN DECISION MAKING *

Pages 177–179 (1962).

. . . What binds these functions together is that in each category the lawyer must make decisions. Issues for decision flood in upon him day after day in quantities and varieties which are beyond the comprehension of the general public. It is not enough that on each of these occasions the lawyer must make up his mind; in all too many cases he must keep it made up. That is to say, once he has made an election among various possible choices, much of the time he is out on a limb. . . .

---

* Benjamin F. Boyer, Albert J. Harno, Robert E. Mathews, John S. Bradway, Editors. Copyright 1962 by West Publishing Co. Reprinted by permission.

Therefore it is professionally desirable that the decision be "right". What do we mean by "right"? We may test it for instance: in terms of whether it is a correct statement of the law; or as to whether it conduces to the economic benefit of the client; or whether the client himself is satisfied; or on some other basis. In this part of the book our concern is that the decision should be *ethically* "right". We recognize that the process of decision making involves bringing to mind certain factors and applying to them certain tests so that a conclusion is reached. One of those factors is the moral quality of the decision. If a lawyer makes decisions either without including the moral factor, or by improperly emphasizing it, the consequences may be catastrophic both for the individual and, in due course, for the profession itself.

The law student will probably find it difficult at first to acquire the habit of prompt and orderly decision making. In his role as student there may be quite a bit of time for him to deliberate, to weigh factors, to listen to arguments on both sides of a proposition. In law practice there will be, all too many emergencies when his ability to formulate a problem and to give it a reasonable (even a "right") answer must be almost automatic, instinctive, something which springs instantly from his subconscious mind. Of course, there will be other situations in which a longer period of evaluation is afforded him; but he will be well advised to concentrate on improving his reflexes so that when he must say or do something on the spur of the moment, what he says or does is as nearly "right" as he can possibly make it. . . . . . .

The mental process of counselling in which there are ethical factors takes place ordinarily in a very simple pattern. There are two persons present, the attorney and the client. The latter raises the factual situation. The lawyer formulates the question and answers it. But the task of answering is far more extensive than an automatic response. The lawyer analyzes the question and separates the various factors including the ethical implications. If he fails to recognize that there are moral questions implicit the consequences for himself as well as for his client may be far reaching.

The mental process of negotiating has a more complex pattern. There are basically three persons involved, the client with the problem, the lawyer who is to try to solve the problem out of court, and the adversary. Sometimes there are two lawyers. The task of the lawyer is to persuade, convince, induce a solution which is satisfactory to his client but which at the same time is acceptable to the adversary. There are other occasions still in this area of negotiating where the lawyer appears not on behalf of a client, but as moderator between two adversaries. These latter may or may not be represented by counsel. Where the lawyer is moderator his decisions approximate those which are required of the judge. But in conciliation meetings there is less formality, an absence of rules of evidence, a relaxation of courtroom protocol which is appropriate to litigation. The lawyer-moderator occupies a most responsible and difficult position.

The most dramatic decision-making technique recognized by the legal profession is litigation, a process by which a series of decisions by litigants and their lawyers culminate in a formal decision in the form of a final judgment. Even the judge's decision instead of deciding the legal issues raised by the trial may only create new ones which must be resolved by a superior decision-making agency, an appellate court.

The court's decision, whether in the form of rulings of law made during the proceedings, or the final judgment itself, is recorded, and affords opportunity for study and evaluation. The advocate's decision when articulated during the trial is a part of the record and is preserved for study. But no less important are the decisions of the advocate either made silently, or made outside the courtroom. In fact, the most important decision of all may be the attorney's evaluation of the merits of his client's case made after the first interview, particularly if he should influence his client to drop his case without pursuing it further. The silent or unpublished decisions have ethical overtones that are too often ignored, since the published decisions are easier to find, classify and evaluate. . . .

NOTE

"But there is something that the lawyer must have that the student does not necessarily have. What is that one element without which the lawyer fails? It is dangerous to be categorical in such matters and yet I feel reasonably confident that I am right when I tell you no lawyer succeeds without it and that I have never known a lawyer to be a complete failure who possessed it.

I believe gentlemen that this one indispensable element may be defined briefly as the power to make decisions. . . .

. . . Having studied his facts and his law, having posed his legal problem before him and having solved it, he must then drop the role of student and become the man of action by deciding what to do and by doing it.

It is amazing how many men fail at this crucial point. . . .

The important thing is that you must acquire this power of decision when you are young. I believe that it is largely a matter of habit. . . . Do not try to dodge it or evade it. Meet it head-on the first time. The next time will be easier and so the next and next. . . .

Sooner or later, wherever you are, you will have to face the test. How you face it, will, I believe, be the turning point in your careers." Comley, *The Power of Decision*, 26 Conn.Bar J. 82 (March 1952).

THE NON-LAWYER

J. J. CAVANAUGH, THE LAWYER IN SOCIETY *
Pages 73–79 (1963).

There is a fairly recent graduate of the Harvard Law School who has made quite a success for himself. He is not corporate counsel, or the new partner in a firm. He is not a district attorney, or clerk to a Supreme Court justice. He is a chicken rancher in the Near East. The story is that he went east to run some errands for an oil company, saw the local need for eggs, went into partnership with a local man to supply them, eventually found chickens more profitable, and now raises and sells them. He had no background in this field on which to draw. He started from scratch, with no knowledge and little capital, but soon had cornered an opportunity. His case is not as unusual as it sounds.

This phenomenon seems peculiar to the legal profession. There are, to be sure, engineers (Herbert Hoover) and doctors (W. Somerset Maugham) who drift to other fields. Every profession has its mavericks; but none seems to approach the legal profession in the percentage who drift away. . . .

. . .

There are more non-lawyers than non-doctors or non-engineers simply because the elements that make up the lawyer are more easily adaptable to sundry pursuits. Indeed, it might be accurate to define the legal profession as that profession which teaches adaptability. There is much evidence that for centuries law has been regarded as *the* liberal education, *completing* the liberalizing begun by the traditional basic subjects. Most advanced education is a *specialization*, departing, strictly speaking, from the purpose of education. . . .

. . .

The result of dealing always with facts and with such heterogeneous facts is to give the lawyer a respect for all practical things and a certain methodology for dealing with them. This in turn opens doors of opportunity for the lawyer rather than closes any; and he finds himself as easily pulled beyond his profession as left in it. This diffusion of opportunity and capacity is thus a prime reason for the lawyer being so often confronted by his alter-ego, the non-lawyer.

. . .

Perhaps the greatest world figure in literature outside of Shakespeare is Goethe. While there is a fascinating and never-ending debate over who Shakespeare really was, the most plausible argument,

---

* Copyright 1963 by Philosophical Library Inc. Reprinted by permission.

if he was not Shakespeare from Stratford, is that he was the Earl of Oxford, known to have a legal education. In fact, most of the arguments questioning the Stratford man's identity as the author of the plays are based on the fact that Shakespeare's plays are filled with references to legal technicalities. But whatever the uncertainties about Shakespeare, Goethe is well-known. He received a legal education at Strassburg and practiced law at Frankfort for several years before becoming a civil servant at Weimar. Although universal genius is attributed to him, it is interesting to note that the two most productive periods in his life followed closely his association with two more volatile personalities, Herder and Schiller, who stirred the diffused glow of his universality to a creative flame. In exactly the same way the average lawyer is stirred to a specific effort by events outside himself.

Another classic example of the same thing is Johnson's influence on Boswell. Without the utterly preposterous but mesmerizing Dr. Samuel Johnson to act as a goad, the world might never have heard of the obscure barrister, James Boswell. As it turns out, it is Johnson who receives *his* immortality at the hands of Boswell, in one of the world's great biographies. . . .
. . .

The non-lawyer appears in practically every human endeavor, not infrequently occupying foremost rank. For it takes simply a spark of purpose beyond the legalities to amalgamate all the lawyer's humble virtues into a formidable humanity. One of England's greatest actors, David Garrick, was a lawyer. One of the greatest theologians of the Reformation, John Calvin, studied for the law; but when he was twenty-eight his *Institutes of the Christian Religion* became a classic in Christian theology. One of the leaders of the French Revolution, the classic of all revolutions, was Danton, a successful Paris lawyer, who, ironically but typically, was ultimately executed by the other leaders of the revolution for being too moderate and for recognizing that a government overthrown must be supplanted by another.

There is a famous non-lawyer of recent history who comes close to being, like Lincoln, a transfigured lawyer, a lawyer who has simply grown beyond the usual confines rather than grown away from them, who has enlarged the scope of the lawyer's functions rather than changed them, who has kept the virtues of the lawyer and only deepened them. He loved his country and its people; he respected civil authority even while opposing it; his weapons were non-violence and passive resistance; his aims were moderate and realistic; he was willing to negotiate and to advance step by step; he was humble in manner and took as his symbols the simple handcrafts of his people. And true to the negative leadership the lawyer exercises, he became a martyr to his country's liberty. He was an Indian lawyer named Gandhi.

SECTION 3. THE QUALITIES OF THE LAWYER

Introduction. The preceding section highlights the varied nature of the lawyer's roles and suggests that different qualities may be called for in discharging them. Not every lawyer is suited to all roles and each student should consider thoughtfully his own qualities and preferences and seek intelligently to find the kind of work and the setting best suited to him. The reader may find in the following items passages which strike home and which lead him to make use of a strength he perceives or to make good a flaw he observes. An important question to be asked is whether a particular quality is inborn or whether it is capable of development.

WILEY RUTLEDGE, SURVEY OF THE CONFERENCE PROBLEMS—LAW AND LAWYERS IN THE MODERN WORLD

15 Univ. Cincinnati L.Rev. 228, 235 (1941).

I thought all a lawyer had to do was sit and wait for the client to come in and then think up flowery speeches to orate at the trial. Hundreds of lawyers have been made by that, only, in many instances, to their disillusionment when they come to find that the law is not all oratory and flowery language. It is no longer that even in small part. It is hard, close, confining work, and that fact should be brought home to men who begin to think about studying law, and before they make the choice, that is before they begin pre-legal education.

So, also, should some other disqualifications. I have a lawyer friend in a midwestern city who has been a misfit all his life, because he did not know that the law is not the place for a highly sensitive person of definitely individualistic, artistic temperament. He should have been a sculptor, a painter or a musician. But the conflict inherent in the profession has kept his artist's soul in turmoil and him in unhappiness all of his days. There are psychological aptitudes which can be measured, though only a beginning has been made in this, and that information should be brought to boys and girls before they become set in a desire or an ambition which will make misfits of them. I place upon our high schools and universities the charge of failing to perform that duty for them adequately as they are coming through.

PAUL D. CRAVATH, as quoted in SWAINE, THE CRAVATH FIRM

Vol. II, page 266 (1948).

The qualities required for success as a lawyer of affairs, "assuming the fundamental qualities of good health, ordinary honesty, a sound education and normal intelligence" were, he said, "Character, industry and intellectual thoroughness, qualities that do not go to make for charm but go far to make up that indefinable something that we call efficiency. . . . Brilliant intellectual powers are not essential. Too much imagination, too much wit, too great cleverness, too facile fluency, if not leavened by a sound sense of proportion are quite as likely to impede success as to promote it. The best clients are apt to be afraid of those qualities. They want as their counsel a man who is primarily honest, safe, sound and steady. Another quality important for success is loyalty. By that I do not mean common honesty or technical loyalty but that degree of loyalty which becomes devotion. I would also add a sound sense of proportion, the ability to distinguish the essentials from the nonessentials, to concentrate on the things that count and not waste effort and thought on things that are simply interesting." *

CHARLES M. HOUGH, REVIEW OF ALLEN, THE LAW AS A VOCATION

33 Harv.L.Rev. 739, 741–742 (1920).

The most original work in the book, and most valuable for one seriously contemplating strictly professional activities, is the study of those mental qualifications and character traits which may be discovered even in the young, and emphatically make for success at the bar (pp. 23–24). It is of course true that what the writer calls the "necessary fundamental qualities,"—integrity, persistence, judgment, self-confidence, and concentration, will probably insure success in any walk of life. It is the secondary qualities, such as tact, decision mingled with caution, and the like, that turn the scale toward the bar; and of these secondary qualities a long observation of lawyers successful and worthy of success would lead one to put in the foremost place what the writer calls the "gift of sympathy to take the part of

---

* "This was doubtless shrewd insight for a stable society, if not altogether fair to some of his partners. In a world where disaster may be the price of misjudging the forces of social change, will business men be led by their instinct of self-preservation to choose lawyers of imagination, or even of brilliance, suspect as such qualities commonly are? It remains to be seen. Surely business and the business bar will need counsel of imagination and brilliance, resting on a broad understanding of society and its development, as well as a sound sense of proportion, if it is to retain even its present qualified position of leadership in our community." Eugene V. Rostow, *Book Review*, 58 Yale L.J. 650, 655 (1949).

Thurman et al., Cs. Legal Prof. UCB—3

a client properly". Almost any one can learn in the old phrase "to strive mightily" in court; but there is a vast difference between the man who strives by main force and the one who strives sympathetically. The young man who feels (and he soon learns to know the feeling) that he cannot like every client he would like to have, may find delightful and even lucrative professional occupation; but he will rarely if ever rise to the higher planes of advocacy.

LEARNED HAND, THE SPIRIT OF LIBERTY *

Page 222, from the 1949 Harvard Law School Yearbook, p. 9 (1952).

[In writing of the qualities of Charles Evans Hughes, Judge Learned Hand said:] They were a relentless self-discipline in mastering the details of his subject, a reserve against premature commitment while the matter remained in solution, broad horizons to include all the relevant factors, and at the end a solid assurance in the outcome. However, such gifts would not have brought to him the public trust and confidence which followed him in all his undertakings, had it not been for the high purpose apparent in all his incessant public services.

JOSEPH BEAR, SURVEY OF THE LEGAL PROFESSION— WORKMEN'S COMPENSATION AND THE LAWYER

51 Col.L.Rev. 965, 975 (1951).

The conclusion reached from the interviews [with workmen's compensation claimants who had been represented by lawyers] is that a client's satisfaction or dissatisfaction is based primarily on the conduct of his lawyer, and not on the amount of the award, the content of the statute, or the caliber of the administrators. In view of this conclusion it is not surprising that a negative theme in the interview histories is dissatisfaction of the client with his lawyer, because of failure to keep the client informed as to the progress of his case, or laxity in establishing a working relationship with him. . . . A satisfied client—and these were in the majority—resulted when the attorney was able and willing to answer questions and showed a genuine interest in the case.

* With the permission of the publisher, Alfred A. Knopf, Inc.

SECTION 4. THE SETTING OF THE LAWYER'S WORK

ELLIOTT E. CHEATHAM, THE LAWYER'S ROLE AND SURROUNDINGS
25 Rocky Mountain L.Rev. 405, 407–410 (1953).

The setting of the lawyer's work will profoundly affect him. One aspect is the larger setting, the community of which he is a part. Two characteristics of this larger setting will be mentioned: a competitive economy, and the extension of knowledge with the development of new skilled groups.

A Competitive Economy. The lawyer in his work partakes of the characteristics of the larger society of which he is a part. In its economic aspects American society is still predominantly capitalistic and competitive in its nature. The community has a variety of needs, including such basic ones as food, clothing, shelter and security. The needs of the community are met through the individual strivings of its members, undirected and uncoördinated for the most part by government, with the producer compensated by the persons who need his products.

The legal profession shares in this aspect of American society. In meeting the needs for the individualization of justice, the lawyer is retained by the persons who need his services and he is compensated by them.

In stressing the individualistic character of American society, there is no desire to ignore modifying trends. Two of these trends directly affect the work of the lawyer. The first is the increasing activity of government in economic affairs; the second is the formation and increasing influence of large groups in industry and in labor. The result is big government, big business, and big labor—with whatever they may portend. But American life is still permeated with the ideas of innovation, of progress, of individual striving. In short, we are a liberal, democratic, competitive society, which has been moving in the direction of increased state activity. The lawyer is primarily the representative of individual clients, retained and compensated by them.

The Extension of Knowledge and the Development of New Skilled Groups. The second characteristic in our society which deserves mention here is the enormous extension of knowledge and the development of new specialized groups to apply this knowledge to human affairs. Until the latter part of the nineteenth century, the lawyer was almost the only expert in the adjustment of human relations. At times, of course, he was aided or supplanted by the minister or the priest, especially in family matters. The lawyer naturally regarded himself as the all-competent man. "Choate." as a biographer wrote of Rufus Choate, "at various times, was psychologist, sociologist, neurologist, alienist, and father confessor, as well as attorney."

In recent years new fields of knowledge bearing on human relations and their adjustment have developed, and the social sciences are rapidly refining their conclusions. New professions or specialized groups have arisen to help in adjusting these relations, and they are steadily improving their methods. . . .

These new groups may be thought of as rivals, or as colleagues, or as aids to the lawyer in the work of advising and guiding the client. At the very least, they must be taken account of by the modern lawyer.

[Besides the characteristics of the larger community of which he is a part, there is] the specific professional setting of the lawyer [which] has the most obvious bearing on his work. Three elements will be mentioned: a partisan position, the adversary system, and the organized profession.

A Partisan Position. Typically, the lawyer is retained by one side only in a situation. He is privately retained, so he is the representative of a private interest. He is aiding, guiding, defending one side, and not both sides. Therefore, he is a partisan representative. Partisanship must be enlightened and restrained if it is to avoid improper injury to both litigants. Particularly is this true in work in the office as counselor. In office work the lawyer is not under the supervision of a judge or under the instant challenge of an adversary, and the freedom from immediate scrutiny calls for corresponding wisdom and restraint.

The Adversary System. The most distinctive element in the lawyer's work is the method used for the determination of controversies not otherwise resolved. A trial is not a dispassionate and coöperative effort by all the parties to arrive at justice. It is the adversary system, the competitive system in the administration of law. In a court there is a judge, who is to pass on the questions, and there are lawyers on each side. Under the American system, the judge is relatively passive, listening, moderating, and passing on what is offered to him. But neither the judge nor any other representative of the public is active in developing the facts. The lawyers are the ones who develop and present the case. They do so, each for his own side and not for both sides. If one lawyer is poor or lazy, his side suffers accordingly. If the other lawyer is unscrupulous, his side may benefit unduly.

For the layman, it is never easy to understand, much less to sympathize with, the adversary system for the administration of justice. It does involve a seeming paradox—the deliberate reliance on partisan representation to bring out the truth and to achieve justice. It troubles the sensitive man entering the profession. He understands why the soldier should fight his nation's enemy, or why the physician should fight disease, the common enemy of mankind. But what is the justification of the lawyer, "an officer of the court," fighting for what is not just?

Though the adversary system is the last resort in the settlement of controversies, it would break down if it were used for every disagreement. So compromise, adjustment, or reconciliation is the usual method. Reconciliation of competing interests is important between individuals when a single dispute is involved. It is even more important when a continuing relation is envisaged, with business men who will keep on dealing with each other. It is most important of all when it concerns the larger groups in our society.

The adversary system in law administration bears a striking resemblance to the competitive economic system. In each we assume that the individual through partisanship or through self-interest will strive mightily for his side, and that kind of striving we must have. But neither system would be tolerable without restraints and modifications, and at times without outright departures from the system itself. Since the legal profession is entrusted with the system of law administration, a part of its task is to develop in its members appropriate restraints without impairing the values of partisan striving. An accompanying task is to aid in the modification of the adversary system or departure from it in areas to which the system is unsuited.

SECTION 5. THE INTERLOCKING OBJECTIVES OF THE LAWYER

As one about to enter practice you, the reader, have had frequent occasions to put to yourself the question of what you hope to achieve by becoming a lawyer. Consider whether the following analysis is an aid to you. Which portions would you add to or modify?

Three sets of objectives can be set out.

1. Individual objectives or ambitions.
2. Professional objectives or functions.
3. Social objectives or roles.

This is not to suggest that these objectives can or do exist independently of each other. One grouping will derive much of its meaning from the other, and there are large areas of overlap as well as many conflicts which must be reconciled. Insight into the legal profession, however, can be gained by considering these three interlocking objectives of today's lawyer and today's law student.

1. Individual Objectives.

A law student expects to make a decent living for himself and his family through admission to the legal profession. He desires to engage in work that is personally satisfying, intellectually and otherwise, work that makes it possible to be true to himself and to his own standards. In addition to self-respect, public respect will be sought and many will admit to a hope for a measure of public acclaim or even fame. Others will think of independence, wealth, power and influence through a life in the law.

Further reflection will no doubt bring expressions of fairly uniform desires to assist in the solution of human problems, to render effective service to clients, to function successfully within the profession, and to improve and serve society. Here the student looks forward to the second and third of his objectives, objectives that are at the same time individual goals of most lawyers. The combination of these goals may well describe the individual lawyer's overall objective —a well rounded complete life, "A Man For All Seasons," in the language characterizing Sir Thomas More.

2. Professional Objectives.

Included in the individual objectives of almost all lawyers is the desire to be an effective member of his profession, to further the legitimate aims of his clients as ably as possible, and at the same time to play his role as a key figure in the administration of justice.

The generalities of the law require individualization for specific clients and specific controversies. The lawyer must become an expert in the process of applying the general to the specific and much of what follows herein concerns this task and its accompanying duties and conflicts. Later chapters detail the professional role of the lawyer in avoiding and settling disputes for his client, planning future courses of action for him, serving as his advocate before court, commission, board, and legislative body, and acting as an advisor in an unlimited range of activities. The improvement of the profession and its image are also properly a part of his professional objectives.

3. Social Objectives.

This broadest of all lawyer objectives stresses the contribution that society expects of the legal profession and of its members. Society has a vital interest in the individual and professional objectives of lawyers but here the emphasis is on leadership on many fronts. Lawyers are expected to play significant social roles. Clearly this is so with reference to improving the administration of justice and improving the substantive law. It is no less true in other areas of public life. Lawyers furnish much of the leadership of the nation at every level. It is so in political life whether elective or appointive, in the formation of public opinion, in the guidance of the economy, and in organizations which are public though not political in nature, such as charities, churches, universities and cultural institutions. Chapter X of this book will focus on these social roles, roles which are colored by all other lawyer objectives.

SECTION 6. THE NEED FOR THE LAWYER

Introduction. Society joins with the legal profession in seeking to achieve Equal Justice Under Law, a goal that can be fully achieved only if lawyers are available at the proper times. At certain of these times the Supreme Court of the United States has said that there is a constitutional right to counsel or a constitutional prohibition against state interference with non-governmental methods of providing counsel. At other times there are statutory rights. In many more instances although there are neither constitutional nor statutory rights, there may exist moral claims to legal services, claims that are coming to be increasingly recognized. The cases and notes that follow highlight the recent developments in these fields. More detailed treatment is left to other courses in the curriculum and to Chapter II of this book dealing with the methods of making legal services available.

A. DEFENSE COUNSEL

GIDEON v. WAINWRIGHT

Supreme Court of the United States, 1963.
372 U.S. 335, 83 S.Ct. 792, 9 L.Ed.2d 799.

MR. JUSTICE BLACK delivered the opinion of the Court.

Petitioner was charged in a Florida state court with having broken and entered a poolroom with intent to commit a misdemeanor. This offense is a felony under Florida law. Appearing in court without funds and without a lawyer, petitioner asked the court to appoint counsel for him, whereupon the following colloquy took place:

"The Court: Mr. Gideon, I am sorry, but I cannot appoint Counsel to represent you in this case. Under the laws of the State of Florida, the only time the Court can appoint Counsel to represent a Defendant is when that person is charged with a capital offense. I am sorry, but I will have to deny your request to appoint Counsel to defend you in this case.

"The Defendant: The United States Supreme Court says I am entitled to be represented by Counsel."

Put to trial before a jury, Gideon conducted his defense about as well as could be expected from a layman . . . . The jury returned a verdict of guilty, and petitioner was sentenced to serve five years in the state prison. Later, petitioner filed in the Florida Supreme Court this habeas corpus petition attacking his conviction and sentence on the ground that the trial court's refusal to appoint counsel for him denied him rights "guaranteed by the Constitution and the Bill of

Rights by the United States Government." Treating the petition for habeas corpus as properly before it, the State Supreme Court, "upon consideration thereof" but without an opinion, denied all relief. Since 1942, when Betts v. Brady, 316 U.S. 455, 62 S.Ct. 1252, 86 L.Ed. 1595, was decided by a divided Court, the problem of a defendant's federal constitutional right to counsel in a state court has been a continuing source of controversy and litigation in both state and federal courts. To give this problem another review here, we granted certiorari. 370 U.S. 908, 82 S.Ct. 1259, 8 L.Ed.2d 403. Since Gideon was proceeding *in forma pauperis,* we appointed counsel to represent him and requested both sides to discuss in their briefs and oral arguments the following: "Should this Court's holding in Betts v. Brady, 316 U.S. 455, 62 S.Ct. 1252, 86 L.Ed. 1595, be reconsidered?" . . . . . .

The Sixth Amendment provides, "In all criminal prosecutions, the accused shall enjoy the right . . . to have the Assistance of Counsel for his defence." We have construed this to mean that in federal courts counsel must be provided for defendants unable to employ counsel unless the right is competently and intelligently waived. . . . . . .

We accept Betts v. Brady's assumption, based as it was on our prior cases, that a provision of the Bill of Rights which is "fundamental and essential to a fair trial" is made obligatory upon the States by the Fourteenth Amendment. We think the Court in Betts was wrong, however, in concluding that the Sixth Amendment's guarantee of counsel is not one of these fundamental rights. . . .

. . . The fact is that in deciding as it did—that "appointment of counsel is not a fundamental right, essential to a fair trial"—the Court in Betts v. Brady made an abrupt break with its own well-considered precedents. In returning to these old precedents, sounder we believe than the new, we but restore constitutional principles established to achieve a fair system of justice. Not only these precedents but also reason and reflection require us to recognize that in our adversary system of criminal justice, any person haled into court, who is too poor to hire a lawyer, cannot be assured a fair trial unless counsel is provided for him. This seems to us to be an obvious truth. Governments, both state and federal, quite properly spend vast sums of money to establish machinery to try defendants accused of crime. Lawyers to prosecute are everywhere deemed essential to protect the public's interest in an orderly society. Similarly, there are few defendants charged with crime, few indeed, who fail to hire the best lawyers they can get to prepare and present their defenses. That government hires lawyers to prosecute and defendants who have the money hire lawyers to defend are the strongest indications of the widespread belief that lawyers in criminal courts are necessities, not luxuries. The right of one charged with crime to counsel may not be deemed fundamental and essential to fair trials in some countries, but it is in ours. From the very beginning, our state and national constitutions and laws have laid great emphasis on procedural and substantial safeguards designed to assure fair trials before impartial tribunals in which every defendant stands equal before the law. This noble ideal cannot be realized if the poor man charged with crime has to face his accusers without a lawyer to assist him. A defendant's need for a lawyer is nowhere better stated than in the moving words of Mr. Justice Sutherland in Powell v. Alabama:

> "The right to be heard would be, in many cases, of little avail if it did not comprehend the right to be heard by counsel. Even the intelligent and educated layman has small and sometimes no skill in the science of law. If charged with crime, he is incapable, generally, of determining for himself whether the indictment is good or bad. He is unfamiliar with the rules of evidence. Left without the aid of counsel he may be put on trial without a proper charge, and convicted upon incompetent evidence, or evidence irrelevant to the issue or otherwise inadmissible. He lacks both the skill and knowledge adequately to prepare his defense, even though he have a perfect one. He requires the guiding hand of counsel at every step in the proceedings against him. Without it, though he be not guilty, he faces the danger of conviction because he does not know how to establish his innocence." 287 U.S., at 68–69, 53 S.Ct., at 64, 77 L.Ed. 158.

The Court in Betts v. Brady departed from the sound wisdom upon which the Court's holding in Powell v. Alabama rested. Florida, supported by two other States, has asked that Betts v. Brady be left intact. Twenty-two States, as friends of the Court, argue that Betts was "an anachronism when handed down" and that it should now be overruled. We agree.

The judgment is reversed and the cause is remanded to the Supreme Court of Florida for further action not inconsistent with this opinion.

Reversed.

MR. JUSTICE DOUGLAS.

My Brother Harlan is of the view that a guarantee of the Bill of Rights that is made applicable to the States by reason of the Fourteenth Amendment is a lesser version of that same guarantee as applied to the Federal Government. Mr. Justice Jackson shared that view. But that view has not prevailed and rights protected against state invasion by the Due Process Clause of the Fourteenth Amendment are not watered-down versions of what the Bill of Rights guarantees.

MR. JUSTICE CLARK, concurring in the result.

. . .

I must conclude . . . that the Constitution makes no distinction between capital and noncapital cases. The Fourteenth Amendment requires due process of law for the deprival of "liberty" just as for deprival of "life", and there cannot constitutionally be a difference in the quality of the process based merely upon a supposed difference in the sanction involved. . . .

MR. JUSTICE HARLAN, concurring.

. . .

In agreeing with the Court that the right to counsel in a case such as this should now be expressly recognized as a fundamental right embraced in the Fourteenth Amendment, I wish to make a further observation. When we hold a right or immunity, valid against the Federal Government, to be "implicit in the concept of ordered liberty" and thus valid against the States, I do not read our past decisions to suggest that by so holding, we automatically carry over an entire body of federal law and apply it in full sweep to the States. Any such concept would disregard the frequently wide disparity between the legitimate interests of the States and of the Federal Government, the divergent problems that they face, and the significantly different consequences of their actions. Cf. Roth v. United States, 354 U.S. 476, 496–508, 77 S.Ct. 1304, 1315–1321, 1 L.Ed.2d 1498 (separate opinion of this writer). In what is done today I do not understand the Court to depart from the principles laid down in Palko v. Connecticut, 302 U.S. 319, 58 S.Ct. 149, 82 L.Ed. 288, or to embrace the concept that the Fourteenth Amendment "incorporates" the Sixth Amendment as such.

On these premises I join in the judgment of the Court.

NOTES: THE CONSTITUTIONAL RIGHT TO COUNSEL

(1) Gideon was later retried and, aided by appointed trial counsel, was acquitted. For a fascinating and well documented account of the Gideon case see Lewis, Gideon's Trumpet (1964).

(2) The Sixth Amendment to the United States Constitution provides that "In all criminal prosecutions, the accused shall enjoy the right . . . to have the Assistance of Counsel for his defence." This guarantee of the right to counsel to defendants in the federal courts has been rigorously applied. In Johnson v. Zerbst, 304 U.S. 458, 467, 468, 58 S.Ct. 1019, 1024 (1938), a man accused of passing counterfeit money had been tried without counsel, found guilty, and sentenced to imprisonment. On proceedings for habeas corpus, it was held that if the accused "did not competently and intelligently waive his right to counsel", the prisoner was entitled to be set free. The court put the effect of lack of counsel in the strong terms of lack of jurisdiction, saying: ". . . compliance with this constitutional mandate is an essential jurisdictional prerequisite to a federal court's authority to deprive an accused of his life or liberty. . . . If this requirement of the Sixth Amendment is not complied with, the court no longer has

jurisdiction to proceed." See Note, *The Representation of Indigent Criminal Defendants in the Federal District Courts,* 76 Harv.L.Rev. 579 (1963). This right to counsel is not satisfied where defendant's counsel also represented other parties with conflicting interests. Glasser v. United States, 315 U.S. 60 (1942). Page 414 infra, Chapter XI, Section 2.

The Criminal Justice Act of 1964. To implement the Sixth Amendment Congress enacted The Criminal Justice Act of 1964. Pub.L. 88–455, approved August 20, 1964, 78 Stat. 552, 18 U.S.C.A. § 3006A. Under this Act each U. S. District Court is to establish a plan whereby a defendant charged with a felony or a misdemeanor, other than a petty offense, financially unable to obtain counsel can do so, with specified compensation from the United States for legal and other services rendered. The Act applies from preliminary hearing through appeal. There was some disappointment that Congress refused to adopt a public defender program as many states have done. See Shafroth, *The New Criminal Justice Act,* 50 A.B.A.J. 1049 (1964); Oaks, *Improving the Criminal Justice Act,* 55 A.B.A.J. 217 (1969). See page 85 infra, Chapter II, Section 3.

(3) *The Fourteenth Amendment.* Powell v. Alabama, 287 U.S. 45 (1932), referred to in *Gideon v. Wainwright,* was an earlier landmark case in the field of constitutionally protected right to counsel in state courts. Several negroes had been speedily tried and convicted of the rape of white girls with only token representation by appointed counsel. The United States Supreme Court held that due process had been denied in that there had been no reasonable opportunity to secure counsel and no effective appointment by the court. Justice Sutherland, stressing the basic character of the right, emphasized that this was a capital case where the defendants were incapable of making an adequate defense without counsel.

Some of the pre-*Gideon* secondary reference materials on the right to counsel in state courts are: Beaney, The Right To Counsel In American Courts (1955); Fellman, *The Federal Right to Counsel in State Courts,* 31 Neb.L.Rev. 15 (1951); Kamisar, *Betts v. Brady Twenty Years Later: The Right to Counsel and Due Process Values,* 61 Mich.L.Rev. 219 (1962). In 45 Minnesota Law Review 693–896 (1961) is found a series of excellent articles on the right to counsel in a variety of settings.

Gideon v. Wainwright left questions concerning the stage at which counsel must constitutionally be provided.

Counsel Prior to Trial.

Escobedo v. Illinois, 378 U.S. 478 (1964), involved a suspect for murder who was taken into custody and questioned after his request to consult retained counsel had been denied. The Court pointed to a constitutional need for counsel at that earlier stage and put teeth in this pronouncement by excluding from evidence incriminating statements made by the defendant during such questioning. The Court concluded that "the accused has been denied 'the Assistance of Counsel' in violation of the Sixth Amendment to the Constitution as 'made obligatory upon the States by the Fourteenth Amendment,'" citing *Gideon.* (378 U.S. 478, 491).

This decision met with a storm of criticism from law enforcement officers whose long-time practice had been that of early interrogation of suspects in order to obtain confessions, with no right to counsel extended.

For a discussion of the problems of "efficient" law enforcement under *Escobedo,* and European solutions to such problems, see Morrissey, *Escobedo's European Ancestors,* 52 A.B.A.J. 723 (1966).) The need for major changes in police practices and for less reliance upon confessions and the third degree by police and prosecutors was further emphasized in Miranda v. Arizona, 384 U.S. 436 (1966), with no distinction drawn between capital and non-capital felonies. The Court summarized the rules for police interrogation in these words:

". . . the prosecution may not use statements, whether exculpatory or inculpatory, stemming from custodial interrogation of the defendant unless it demonstrates the use of procedural safeguards effective to secure the privilege against self-incrimination. By custodial interrogation, we mean questioning initiated by law enforcement officers after a person has been taken into custody or otherwise deprived of his freedom of action in any significant way. As for the procedural safeguards to be employed, unless other fully effective means are devised to inform accused persons of their right of silence and to assure a continuous opportunity to exercise it, the following measures are required. Prior to any questioning, the person must be warned that he has a right to remain silent, that any statement he does make may be used as evidence against him, and that he has a right to the presence of an attorney, either retained or appointed. The defendant may waive effectuation of these rights, provided the waiver is made voluntarily, knowingly and intelligently. If, however, he indicates in any manner and at any stage of the process that he wishes to consult with an attorney before speaking there can be no questioning. Likewise, if the individual is alone and indicates in any manner that he does not wish to be interrogated, the police may not question him. The mere fact that he may have answered some questions or volunteered some statements on his own does not deprive him of the right to refrain from answering any further inquiries until he has consulted with an attorney and thereafter consents to be questioned." (pp. 444–445)

See also United States v. Wade, 388 U.S. 218 (1967) (right to counsel at post-indictment lineup.)

Johnson v. New Jersey, 384 U.S. 719 (1966) held that the requirements of *Escobedo* and *Miranda* apply only to trials begun after the date on which each decision was announced and were not to be retroactive. The *Gideon* rule, with reference to counsel at trial, has been applied retroactively. 384 U.S. 719, 727. For a discussion of the factors involved in deciding whether to give retrospective effect to a decision see Desist v. United States, 394 U.S. 244 (1969).

Counsel After the Trial. Douglas v. California, 372 U.S. 353 (1963), established an indigent's constitutional right to counsel on appeal from a non-capital felony conviction. Where counsel on appeal was appointed but withdrew, contending there was no merit to the appeal and leaving defendant without counsel, the Supreme Court held that the attorney's conclusion as to the merits of the appeal was insufficient, and the defendant's constitutional rights had been violated. Anders v. California, 386 U.S. 738 (1967). The Court stated that appointed counsel had a duty to defendant to act as advocate, not as *amicus curiae,* and laid down strict guidelines to be followed by an attorney who wishes to abandon what he considers a frivolous appeal. In Mempa v. Rhay, 389 U.S. 128 (1967), the requirements of *Gideon* were extended to post-trial hearings where revocation of probation would result in substantial confinement.

As a consequence of recent Supreme Court decisions, petitioning for habeas corpus has become a major preoccupation at many penal institutions. See Spector, *A Prison Librarian Looks at Writ Writing,* 56 Calif.L.Rev. 365 (1968). In Johnson v. Avery, 393 U.S. 483, (1969) the court held that state prison regulations which barred inmates from assisting other prisoners in the preparation of such writs were invalid as in conflict with the right of habeas corpus where the state did not afford legal assistance. Justice Douglas, concurring, emphasized the present day need for and use of "para-professionals." See pages 138–139 infra. See Note, *Prison "No Assistance" Regulations and the Jailhouse Lawyer,* 1968 Duke L.J. 343.

(4) *Misdemeanors.* A troublesome question for the administration of criminal justice in this country concerns the extent to which counsel must be provided to indigents accused of misdemeanors. The same problem as to the stage at which any constitutional right attaches is also present. American Bar Foundation Field Study and Report, Defense of the Poor in Criminal Cases in American State Courts 123 (1965), estimates roughly that 5,000,000 persons each year are charged with misdemeanors in the state courts of this country compared with 300,000 accused of felonies. Possibly as many as 700,000, the same Report estimates, serve jail sentences for misdemeanors while 140,000 go to prison for felonies. Although completely accurate statistics as to the number of indigents included in these figures are not available, it is probably a safe guess that it would be a very high percentage. (Equal Justice For The Accused 38 (1959), a joint study by a Special Committee of the Association of the Bar of the City of New York and The National Legal Aid and Defender Association, estimates that at least 60 per cent of those charged with crime in the United States cannot afford to retain counsel.) What are the implications from these figures if counsel, now not generally available, must be supplied? *Gideon v. Wainwright* on its facts is limited to felonies but the language of its opinion is broad. Subsequent to *Gideon* the United States Supreme Court on several occasions declined to review cases involving this question. In Heller v. Connecticut, 389 U.S. 902 (1967), certiorari was denied with Justices Fortas and Douglas dissenting, contending that it was time for the court to decide whether the "constitutional guarantee of counsel applies to the present case and to other relatively 'minor' offenses or misdemeanors carrying significant penalties for their violation."

The lower federal courts as well as the state courts since *Gideon* have been in conflict with reference to this question, reminiscent of the *"Betts v. Brady era."* State v. Borst, 278 Minn. 388, 154 N.W.2d 888 (1967), surveyed the cases and had this to say:

. . .

"Until we have a definitive decision by the Supreme Court of the United States as to whether Gideon requires appointment of counsel for an indigent charged with a misdemeanor as defined by our laws, as a Sixth-Amendment right, we choose not to guess at what it may eventually hold by basing our decision on the Federal Constitution or even on our state Constitution. In the exercise of our supervisory power to insure the fair administration of justice, we decide that counsel should be provided in any case whether it be a misdemeanor or not, which may lead to incarceration in a penal institution. In other words, if the court is to impose a jail sentence, counsel should be furnished. We leave for future determination the question of whether counsel must be furnished where only a fine is to be imposed.

. . .

"The arguments most frequently advanced in support of denial of appointed counsel in misdemeanor cases are that it will cost too much and that there are so many of these cases that there are insufficient attorneys to represent all misdemeanants.

"We are persuaded that the possible loss of liberty by an innocent person charged with a misdemeanor, who does not know how to defend himself, is too sacred a right to be sacrificed on the altar of expediency. Any society that can afford a professional prosecutor to prosecute this type of crime must assume the burden of providing adequate defense, to the end that innocent people will not be convicted without having facilities available to properly present a defense.

"As to the latter contention, it may be that our public defender system, which now operates throughout most of the state, may have to be extended to handle this type of case.

"In any event, neither of these arguments is sufficiently persuasive to deny an accused person, who may wind up in jail because he doesn't know how to defend himself, the proper tools with which to present what defense he may have.

"It is clear that there is no magic in the designation of a crime as a misdemeanor, gross misdemeanor, or felony. We must look to the consequences of conviction of crime rather than the classification. The impact on an accused who suffers loss of liberty by incarceration in a penal institution is the same no matter how the crime of which he was convicted was classified.

"The rule we adopt follows substantially the recommendations of a report by the President's Commission on Law Enforcement and Administration of Justice, The Challenge of Crime in a Free Society. The commission recommends the following:

" 'The objective to be met as quickly as possible is to provide counsel to every criminal defendant who faces a significant penalty, if he cannot afford to provide counsel himself. This should apply to cases classified as misdeameanors as well as to those classified as felonies. Counsel should be provided early in the proceedings and certainly no later than the first judicial appearance. The services of counsel should be available after conviction through appeal, and in collateral attack proceedings when the issues are not frivolous. The immediate minimum, until it becomes possible to provide the foregoing, is that all criminal defendants who are in danger of substantial loss of liberty shall be provided with counsel.' "

For a comprehensive Comment on the impact of *Gideon* in the misdemeanor field see Sprecher, *Continuing Echoes of Gideon's Trumpet—The Indigent Defendant and the Misdemeanor; A New Crisis Involving the Assistance of Counsel in A Criminal Trial,* 10 So.Tex.L.J. 222 (1968).

Sobering questions are raised with reference to the right to an attorney when the nation's cities erupt in broad-scale riots. The sheer number of arrests in civil disorders may test the constitutional requirements to their limits. Can enough lawyers be found when riot arrests run into the thousands? Can the warnings required by *Miranda* be given by the police or by troops engaged in emergency police work? Is a replacement of civil law with martial law the only solution in such instances? In the case of campus revolts and anti-war demonstrations leading to arrests *In re Gault* (infra p. 48) has magnified the demands upon the state still further.

For a discussion of the response of the bar to the riot arrests which followed the death of Dr. Martin Luther King see Comment, *The Response of the Washington, D. C. Community and Its Criminal Justice System to the April 1968 Riot*, 37 G.W.L.Rev. 862, 938–949 (1969). (It is estimated that over 400 attorneys, assisted by many law students, volunteered their services. Many of these were government attorneys and the Comment discusses the conflict of interest claims in such cases.)

(5) *The Juvenile's Right to Counsel.* Juvenile courts in the United States have traditionally differed from other courts in that they combine correctional as well as judicial functions. They have not only ruled on alleged offenses but have provided services designed to protect and rehabilitate the child and avoid the harshness of the common law adversary theory. Proceedings have been informal with emphasis upon the juvenile's background in disposing of his case and with heavy reliance on the social sciences for diagnosis and treatment. There has been little or no opportunity for representation of the juvenile by legal counsel or for other procedural safeguards extended to adults accused of crime. See President's Commission on Law Enforcement and Administration of Justice, Task Force Report: Juvenile Delinquency and Youth Crime (Washington: U. S. Government Printing Office, 1967).

In recent years much concern has been expressed over the juvenile court's informal procedures. See President's Commission on Law Enforcement and Administration of Justice, The Challenge of Crime in a Free Society (Washington: U. S. Government Office, 1967), 85–87; Paulsen, *Fairness to the Juvenile Offender*, 41 Minn.L.Rev. 547 (1957); *Juvenile Delinquents: The Police, State Courts, and Individualized Justice*, 79 Harv.L.Rev. 775 (1966). In 1966 the U. S. Supreme Court had this to say:

"While there can be no doubt of the original laudable purpose of juvenile courts, studies and critiques in recent years raise serious questions as to whether actual performance measures well enough against theoretical purpose to make tolerable the immunity of the process from the reach of constitutional guaranties applicable to adults. There is much evidence that some juvenile courts . . . lack the personnel, facilities and techniques to perform adequately as representatives of the State in a *parens patriae* capacity, at least with respect to children charged with law violations. There is evidence, in fact, that there may be grounds for concern that the child receives the worst of both worlds: that he gets neither the protections accorded to adults nor the solicitous care and regenerative treatment postulated for children." Kent v. United States, 383 U.S. 541, 555 (1966).

In re Gault, 387 U.S. 1 (1967), became another landmark decision in the constitutional definition of the right to counsel. Gault was a 15-year old boy who had been charged by the State of Arizona with making lewd telephone calls. After hearings before a juvenile court judge he had been committed to the state industrial school as a juvenile delinquent until he reached majority. An 18-year old could have received a maximum fine of $5 to $50 or imprisonment in jail for not more than two months. The Supreme Court found a deprivation of the procedural safeguards of the Fourteenth Amendment and concluded that children alleged to be delinquent were entitled to adequate notice of charges, the right to confront and cross-examine witnesses and be advised of the privilege against self-incrimination as well as the right to representation by a lawyer retained or appointed. In connection with the latter right the court stated:

". . . The probation officer cannot act as counsel for the child. His role in the adjudicatory hearing, by statute and in fact, is as arresting officer and witness against the child. Nor can the judge represent the child. There is no material difference in this respect between adult and juvenile proceedings of the sort here involved. In adult proceedings, this contention has been foreclosed by decisions of this Court. A proceeding where the issue is whether the child will be found to be 'delinquent' and subjected to the loss of his liberty for years is comparable in seriousness to a felony prosecution. The juvenile needs the assistance of counsel to cope with problems of law, to make skilled inquiry into the facts, to insist upon regularity of the proceedings, and to ascertain whether he has a defense and to prepare and submit it. The child 'requires the guiding hand of counsel at every step in the proceedings against him. (Powell v. Alabama, 287 U.S. 45, 69 (1932)).'" (p. 36)

In re Gault will undoubtedly have a far-reaching impact on the American juvenile court system. See Symposium on the implications from *In re Gault*, 43 Ind.L.Jour. 523–677 (1968); Skoler, *Counsel in Juvenile Court Proceedings—A Total Criminal Justice Perspective*, 8 Jour.Fam.Law 243 (1968); Gossett, *Gault and Juvenile Crime*, 55 A.B.A.J. 503 (1969).

See Furlong, *The Juvenile Court and the Lawyer*, 3 Jour.Fam.Law 1 (1963) for a good description of the pre-*Gault* situation in this country together with a description of a seminar and internship program at Willamette University College of Law devoted to juvenile law and funded by a Ford Foundation grant.

(6) *Competence of Counsel.* Claims that constitutional rights to counsel have been violated due to alleged incompetence of court-appointed counsel have been asserted with some frequency. Such claims have often been rejected under the time-honored rule that the neglect of the attorney is to be imputed to his client. This rule has been applied most frequently in civil cases where counsel has been retained. In a criminal action, where there is less reason to deny a convicted defendant the right to inquire into an attorney's handling of his case, courts are still concerned about the consequences of post-conviction inquiries into the effectiveness of counsel. Should a distinction be drawn between appointed and retained counsel in criminal cases? For general discussions see Comment, *Incompetency of Counsel as a Ground for Attacking Criminal Convictions in California and Federal Courts*, 4 U.C.L.A. L.Rev. 400 (1957); Note, *The Right to Effective Counsel in Crimi-*

nal Cases, 18 Van.L.Rev. 1920 (1965); Comment, *Federal Habeas Corpus—A Hindsight View of Trial Attorney Effectiveness,* 27 La.L.Rev. 784 (1967); Mazor, *Power and Responsibility in the Attorney-Client Relation,* 20 Stan. L.Rev. 1120 (1968). As yet no Supreme Court case has upheld such a claim arising out of a state court proceeding although Michel v. Louisiana 350 U.S. 91 (1955), lends support to the view that a sufficient showing of incompetency might violate the Fourteenth Amendment due process requirement of a fair trial. In Mitchell v. United States, 259 F.2d 787 (D.C.Cir.), cert. denied 358 U.S. 850 (1958), a number of lower federal court decisions involving a similar problem under the Sixth Amendment are reviewed. See Chapter XII, Section 4, page 456 infra.

(7) *Reimbursement of Defense Counsel.* Counsel for indigent defendants are provided under several different systems throughout the United States. In some jurisdictions there are public defender systems and in others defender systems that are privately financed or voluntarily staffed. Frequently there are mixed systems. In many jurisdictions counsel are court appointed as the need arises. See Chapter II, Section 3, infra.

In August, 1962, almost one year prior to *Gideon,* the House of Delegates of the American Bar Association adopted a resolution authorizing the Association's president to appoint a special committee and associate state committees "to study present practices and to initiate, coordinate and accelerate efforts to insure adequacy of the defense provided indigent persons accused of crime in the United States." 48 A.B.A.J. 988 (1962). Defense Of The Poor (1965), a project of the American Bar Foundation with Mr. Lee Silverstein as Director, was the three-volume product of this detailed study by the special committee and its 50 associate state committees. This report contains many statistical tables and details the various systems of providing counsel, together with their financing, that obtain throughout the country. It discusses the major problems such as the stage at which counsel is or should be provided, counsel for misdemeanors, post-conviction counsel, methods of determining eligibility for free counsel, etc.

In the case of court appointed counsel reimbursement is provided for in a variety of ways: See Strong, *Reimbursement of Expenses of Appointed Counsel,* 26 La.L.Rev. 695 (1965):

> "The basic problem is who is to pay the cost of defending the indigent. Certainly the indigent cannot pay it. Unless assistance is made available by such organizations as charitable foundations or the United Fund, there are only two sources of funds, the prosecuting jurisdiction and the appointed counsel. In a majority of jurisdictions in the United States, the burden has fallen on the court-appointed attorneys. But it should be added that part of the burden may sometimes have fallen on the indigent defendants, in the form of an inadequate effort by impecunious counsel.
>
> . . .
>
> "At present the position in the federal courts under the Criminal Justice Act of 1964 is that counsel may be reimbursed for all reasonable expenses, and funds in a limited amount are available for expert witnesses and investigative services. . . .
>
> "At the present time nine of the fifty states and the District of Columbia provide specifically for reimbursement of the expenses of ap-

pointed counsel. In many of the other states, appointed counsel are paid by increasing the compensation allowed by statute in an amount sufficient to cover reasonable expenses without making an allowance for them specifically. In the thirteen jurisdictions that afford complete reimbursement, the only requirement seems to be a showing that the expenses were reasonably necessary.

"In many of the states which have only limited reimbursement, or none at all, there have been recommendations from the bar that adequate funds be made available. Even in the states which allow reimbursement, it is often true that securing the return of expense money is difficult and time-consuming. This complaint is particularly prevalent in New Jersey, where lawyers have found that the cost in time of filling out the required forms to secure reimbursement is often more than the actual expenses themselves."

In Dillon v. United States, 230 F.Supp. 487 (D.C.Ore.1964), the Federal district court held that court appointment of counsel to represent an indigent defendant without compensation was a "taking" of property within the meaning of the Fifth Amendment and ordered compensation to be paid. On appeal the ninth circuit reversed, concluding this was a matter for legislative, not judicial, treatment. (346 F.2d 633 (9th Cir. 1965), cert. denied 382 U.S. 978 (1966).) The Appendix to the opinion cites cases to the effect that representation of indigent defendants is an obligation of attorneys upon admission to the bar. Is a similar argument valid with reference to doctors and needy patients?

Assigned attorneys in People ex rel. Conn. v. Randolph, 35 Ill.2d 24, 219 N.E.2d 337 (1966), fared better where they were required to assume a new residence and forego their law practices in lengthy criminal proceedings. The court concluded that its power to appoint counsel included inherent power to prevent intolerable hardship on counsel and held that a statute limiting reimbursement to $500 for each defendant could not constitutionally apply. Payment of expenses and compensation totalling $31,000 was directed by a writ of mandamus to the state treasurer and auditor of public accounts. See also State v. Rush, 46 N.J. 399, 217 A.2d 441 (1966).

See Ervin, *Uncompensated Counsel: They Do Not Meet the Constitutional Mandate*, 49 A.B.A.J. 435 (1963); Note, *Criminal Justice Act of 1964: A Discussion of the Reasons Why Assigned Counsel Must Be Compensated*, 60 Nw.U.L.Rev. 212 (1965).

(8) *Assistance Other than Counsel.* In addition to a right to counsel the United States Supreme Court has dealt with other necessary assistance in the defense of a criminal action, which must be supplied to indigents by the state. These include a free trial transcript where an indigent has been convicted and desires to take advantage of a right of appeal under state law. Griffin v. Illinois, 351 U.S. 12 (1956). This right was extended to an indigent prisoner whose habeas corpus petition was denied by a lower state court and who requested a free transcript of that proceeding in preparing and presenting a new original petition for habeas corpus to the state supreme court. Gardner v. State of California, 393 U.S. 367 (1969). Various other kinds of assistance in addition to counsel may also be necessary—expert witnesses, investigatory services, etc. See Note, *Right to Aid in Addition to Counsel for Indigent Criminal Defendants*, 47 Minn.L.Rev. 1054 (1963).

(9) *Non-indigent defendants.* It has been suggested that all those accused of crime, whether indigent or not, should have all costs of defense, including attorney's fees, paid for by the state inasmuch as the prosecution is similarly financed. If this becomes a right, constitutionally protected or otherwise, should it be limited to defendants who are acquitted and denied to those convicted? Is Commissioner of Internal Revenue v. Tellier, 383 U.S. 687 (1966), a way station? In that case the United States Supreme Court upheld an income tax deduction to a convicted defendant in a business-related criminal case for fees paid to the taxpayer-defendant's lawyer. The earlier long-standing practice of the Internal Revenue Service permitting such deductions only in the case of acquitted defendants was overturned.

B. CIVIL CASES

An accused in a criminal case has a need for a lawyer that is rapidly becoming a legally protected right. The same statement cannot yet be made with reference to most civil actions although here, as well, the need in fact for lawyers is becoming increasingly clear. The last third of the 20th Century begins with the recognition of unprecedented demands for legal services in a wide range of human activities. The satisfactory meeting of these needs will challenge the legal profession. See Elliott E. Cheatham, A Lawyer When Needed (1963).

A few of the reasons for the dramatic increase in the need for lawyers are set forth in the excerpts that follow.

THE MIDDLE CLASSES

COMMENT, PROVIDING LEGAL SERVICES FOR THE MIDDLE CLASS IN CIVIL MATTERS: THE PROBLEM, THE DUTY AND A SOLUTION

26 U.Pitt.L.Rev. 811, 811–12 (1965).

As a society increases in size, sophistication and technology, the body of laws which is required to control that society also increases in size, scope and complexity. With this growth, the law directly affects more and more facets of individual behavior, creating an expanding need for legal services on the part of the individual members of the society. Presently, the availability of legal services too often is limited to those who can afford to pay its full cost and to those who can afford to pay little or nothing. As legal guidance in social and commercial behavior increasingly becomes necessary, there will come a concurrent demand from the layman that such guidance be made available to him. This demand will not come from those who are able to employ the best of legal talent, nor from those who can obtain legal assistance at little or no cost. It will come from the large "forgotten middle income class," who can neither afford to pay proportionately large fees nor qualify for ultra-low-cost services. The legal profession must recognize this inevitable demand and consider methods whereby it can be satisfied. If the profession fails to provide such methods, the laity will.

NOTES

(1) For a good discussion of some of the steps that might be taken to assist people of moderate means to meet legal expenses see Christensen, *Aids in Meeting Legal Expenses*, 37 Ford.L.Rev. 383 (1969). Some of the suggested aids are: Recovery of attorney's fees as a cost of litigation, legal service financing programs, legal expense insurance proposals, income tax deductions for legal expenses, and direct subsidies. See also Smith, *Legal Services for Persons of Moderate Means*, 1949 Wis.L.Rev. 416; Pedrick, *The Profession and its Reach*, 1 Ind.Legal Forum 132 (1967).

(2) Civil commitment of the mentally ill is an area where the lawyer's role and the rights of the prospective patient have not always been clearly defined. For a study of the need of counsel in this field and an analysis of the laws of the various states with respect thereto see Cohen, *The Function of the Attorney and the Commitment of the Mentally Ill*, 44 Texas L.Rev. 424 (1966).

THE POOR

PATRICIA M. WALD, REPORT TO THE NATIONAL CONFERENCE ON LAW AND POVERTY *

Pages 2–6 (1965).

The lives of the poor suffer from the unwelcome intrusion of outside forces, often utilizing the trappings of the law. Urban renewal disrupts the neighborhood, creditors garnishee wages or repossess furniture, welfare agencies withhold money, and landlords evict into the streets. . . .

. . .

The National Conference on Law and Poverty has been summoned to demonstrate to leaders of the legal profession from all sectors of the country how critical their aid can be in finding ways to reverse self-perpetuating poverty in America. Without the active

---

* In June of 1965 a National Conference on Law and Poverty was convened in Washington D. C. under the co-sponsorship of Nicholas deB. Katzenbach, Attorney General of the United States and Sargent Shriver, Director of the Office of Economic Opportunity. The Conference considered today's need for legal services among the country's 35 million impoverished citizens, defined as individuals with family incomes of less than $3,000 per year. This Report made to the Conference portrayed vividly the extent of this need for lawyers' services and, at the same time, the lack of awareness of the need on the part of the poor.

support of the Bar, the poor will not emerge from the tentacles of slum housing, job discrimination, welfare inequities, unjust criminal procedures, and commercial exploitation.

Lawyers must educate the poor to avoid the pitfalls of unfair leases and installment contracts, to assert their basic legal rights against landlords, sellers, even the police, to seek legal help when they need it, to trust the courts, to utilize the full potential of the law for self-help. The business man does not seek a license, a franchise, a government contract, a subsidy, without his lawyer at his side. Is the need of the poor for shelter, possession of household furniture, sustenance, or custody of his children less important?

Lawyers have many roles to fill in the struggle to overcome poverty. The Bar must accept responsibility for guiding the poor through the daily maze of legal technicalities authored by prior generations of lawyers. It must spearhead efforts to make basic rights more comprehensible and more adaptable to the realities of urban life and to the inequalities of economic status. Lawyers can perform watchdog functions to see that any legislative program designed for the poor is being administered on their behalf. This includes welfare programs, consumer credit reforms, housing programs, social security, workmen's compensation, and the poverty program itself. They can develop and lobby for new legislation to assist the poor in their upward fight.

. . .

Poor people are prone to legal trouble. They are often defendants, rarely plaintiffs. They are bewildered and bemused by legalities they face daily as parents, consumers, tenants, recipients of public assistance, accused offenders. If poverty itelf is at the root of most of their legal troubles, their escape may lie, at least in part, in establishing legal rights that the landlord, the social agency, the neighborhood merchant, and the police will honor.

NOTES

(1) In Powell v. Alabama, 287 U.S. 45, 69 (1932), Justice Sutherland had this to say about retained counsel: "If in any case, civil or criminal, a state or federal court were arbitrarily to refuse to hear a party by counsel, employed and appearing for him, it reasonably may not be doubted that such a refusal would be a denial of a hearing, and, therefore, of due process in the constitutional sense." Turning to *Gideon*, where the Fourteenth Amendment's guarantee of due process, if "life and liberty" are at stake, requires the appointment of counsel for indigents in criminal cases, is it a logical next step to find a constitutional mandate for the appointment of counsel in some civil cases where "property" of an indigent is threatened? See Note, *The Indigent's Right to Counsel in Civil Cases*, 76 Yale L.Jour. 545 (1967), where this argument is advanced. The writer suggests the likelihood of a gradual extension of constitutionally protected rights to counsel in civil cases similar to the development in the criminal field in between Betts v. Brady, 316 U.S.

455 (1942), and *Gideon* (1963). See also Note, *The Right to Counsel in Civil Litigation,* 66 Colum.L.Rev. 1322 (1966), where the equal protection clause is advanced as a possible guarantor of appointed counsel in civil cases for plaintiffs, as well as defendants, unable to afford legal representation. What problems can you foresee in implementing such concepts? See Carlin, Howard and Messinger, Civil Justice and the Poor (1967).

(2) The Committee on Civil Rights of the Association of the Bar of the City of New York has recommended "that a statute or court rule require that all process served in civil cases seeking money damages prominently in bold face type advise the defendant from the very outset of the suit that he has a right to a lawyer and that if he cannot afford one the Clerk of the Court will refer the defendant to an agency which will consider his case." 24 The Record of the Association of the Bar of the City of New York, May 304 (1969).

The problems raised in Chapter II, Making Legal Services Available, are closely related to the topic of this Section, The Need for the Lawyer. Recent decisions, notably those of the United States Supreme Court, and significant legislation such as the Economic Opportunity Act of 1964 and the Criminal Justice Act of 1964 have not only increased dramatically the visibility of unmet legal needs but have at the same time led to unprecedented activity in exploring new methods of meeting these needs.

Chapter II

MAKING LEGAL SERVICES AVAILABLE

Introduction. The old ideal of the legal profession was that of the individual independent lawyer serving directly the individual independent client who chose his own lawyer and paid the fees out of his own funds. For most Americans the ideal is impossible in modern life. Our economy is organized in large groups, big business and big labor, with the individual increasingly dependent on his position in the group. No less important than the economic changes are new social sensitivity to the needs of the poor and disadvantaged as well as of the middle groups and the increased roles of government. These new elements call for a reconsideration of the methods to be employed in providing legal services and of the standards of the bar, as several decisions by the Supreme Court of the United States make mandatory.

In such a reconsideration the guide is as these same decisions make explicit "the public interest." The public interest has several components, involving the clients, the lawyers, and the public in a more general sense. As seen by the prospective clients the methods employed should assure that those who need legal services be able to obtain them within their means and ordinarily do so, and that the services rendered meet the bar's standards of loyalty, competence and zeal. As viewed by lawyers and the public as well the methods should preserve the bar as an independent profession ready to aid its varied clients and ready as well to contribute through support, criticism or opposition to the development of our liberal democratic society. The latter point deserves repeated emphasis for with increasingly large scale organization there is increasing need for protection of individual rights against the large scale organizations and their bureaucracies—big government, big business, big labor. The public interest has the more general meaning of a system of law administration which is carried on with the economy and speed consistent with a fair hearing.

Potential clients are diverse. One form of diversity, based on wealth or lack of it, can be illustrated by a rectangle representing the population of the country and divided into three sections. At one end the section represents business men and the well-to-do. The members of this group recognize the need for legal services, they know where and how to employ lawyers, and they are competent to make and to change the choice. At the other end the segment represents the poor. Individually, they need lawyers almost as much as the well-to-do though for different reasons and collectively they are even more in need of lawyers to press their causes, but they cannot retain them in the usual way. At the very bottom of this segment there is a group of the poor who because of isolation and fear are functionally incompetent in our society and may not obtain the legal services available for them unless the services are brought almost to their door.

In between there is the largest segment, the middle groups in our society, which, with the fortunate leveling up of income, have grown steadily larger as the segment below shrinks. The increase in wealth has brought an increase in the legal problems of acquiring and disposing of property. Yet these growing groups do not obtain in proportionate measure the legal services they need, at least from lawyers. The importance of these two largest groups of our population calls for increased attention to the reasons for the gap between needs and services. One reason on the side of the laymen is poverty, the inability to pay lawyers' fees. Another reason is ignorance of the need for and value of legal services and ignorance of where to find a lawyer and whom to choose. Yet another reason is fear—the unfortunate popular fear of overcharging and overreaching by the lawyer, and fear of the law's processes and delays. Ignorance may be corrected by information, and fear can be replaced by a sense of confidence and security in institutions with which the laymen are familiar and through which legal services are provided.

Lawyers, too, are diverse. The diversity important for the present purpose has little to do with the varieties of practice. It is a diversity which matches the diversity of clients and the stability of the clientele. The lawyers with an established clientele, who make known their availability in an unostentatious way and with clients who know them and return to them, are the organized bar's model of the method of providing legal services. Many lawyers do not correspond to this model, as beginners without clients and older men who desire to make their availability known to clients they wish. Standing in the way are standards and laws going back to the old English prohibitions of barratry, champerty and maintenance.

The chapter deals first with the accepted methods of lawyers in organizing themselves to render services. Then it deals with four kinds of prospective clients for whom special measures may be appropriate—the middle groups, the poor, the personal injury claimants, and the hated. It considers also two sets of professional standards and their bearing on the availability of legal services, the prohibition of publicity and solicitation and the condemnation of the rendition of legal services by laymen.

NOTE

An excellent discussion of the general problems of this chapter is Barlow F. Christensen, Bringing Lawyers and Clients Together (1968). The modest size of this monograph of the American Bar Foundation, prepared in cooperation with the Special Committee on Availability of Legal Services of the American Bar Association, obcures its importance in analyzing the problems, in stating competing values, and in offering proposals.

WARREN EARL BURGER, THE FUTURE OF LEGAL EDUCATION, AMERICAN BAR ASSOCIATION ANNUAL MEETING (1969)

Changes in our society, its growth and increasing mobility and the very structure of large cities have altered life patterns so that the old modes of lawyer-client communication and the role of the lawyer must adjust to meet new needs. In addition the profession must meet new kinds of problems and help devise auxiliary means for the delivery of legal assistance in many situations where it has not been given in the past.

SECTION 1. THE TRADITIONAL METHODS

THE SOLO PRACTITIONER

In the common law the lone, independent practitioner has been taken as the norm. The cases and the opinions of the committees on professional ethics repeatedly refer to the individual responsibility of the lawyer and the direct relationship of the lawyer and the client, which are at their strongest with the independent practitioner. Many American lawyers practice alone, though a large proportion of them share offices with other lawyers and have something like a partnership in office expenses though not in clients or income.

NOTES

(1) Elson, *Book Review*, 30 U.Chi.L.Rev. 784, 790 (1963). "The author chose, for some reason known only to himself, to present the practice of the individual practitioner in negative terms. One can say, as he has, that the solo practitioner handles the dirty work of the bar. On the other hand, one can also say that the solo practitioner carries the primary responsibility of the bar for the administration of justice. The solo practitioner represents almost all persons accused of crime and therefore plays a significant role not only in preserving the rights of the individuals involved, but in developing the law in this field. Similarly, the great bulk of plaintiff's work in the field of personal injury litigation is carried by the solo practitioner. In doing this work, he is in turn playing a vital role in the development of tort law. The same can be said for attorneys who are specializing in the field of family law. Finally, and not without major significance, it is upon the solo practitioner that the burden falls for handling the unpopular cause." See also Gerhart, *Practicing Law: The Case for the Individual Practitioner*, 43 A.B.A.J. 793 (1957).

(2) The 1967 Lawyer Statistical Report, p. 18, compiled by the American Bar Foundation, shows a steady decline of the percentage of individual practitioners from 61% in 1948 to 39% in 1966.

(3) Lawyer's Non-Partnership Arrangements are helpfully discussed and forms for reducing the arrangements to writing are suggested in ABA Comm. on Economics of Law Practice, The Lawyer's Handbook 471–91 (1962).

PARTNERSHIPS

There may be partnerships of lawyers. Partnerships range from the informal two man firm to the large metropolitan office with a score of partners and several times as many associates. Studies have shown that on the average lawyers practicing in partnerships have larger incomes than lawyers practicing alone and the income of each partner goes up with the size of the firm. Certainly, this is not because the formation of a partnership insures a larger income but because most lawyers with wealthy clients find the partnership more effective or even essential in providing the services the clients need.

NOTES

(1) "I wonder if the vast extent and complexity of the law has not made 'solo' practice an anachronism. Also I wonder if 'solo' practice is not so uneconomical that the lawyer's earnings are necessarily low, and if it is not so inefficient as to be the real cause of the rise of competing lay agencies. . . .

"My belief is that a genuine partnership of two men produces twice as good results from the client's point of view. I think the same will be true of four men working as a team, each following his own talents and aptitudes, because law practice calls for men of different types. . . . I am not arguing for large partnerships. Just think of the superiority of even a two-man firm. It takes care of sickness because both are not likely to be sick at the same time. It takes care of vacation. When one is in court, the other can keep the office open and see clients. There can be some division of labor which is the first step towards efficiency." Reginald Heber Smith (1949) *

(2) "It is a striking fact that in over 97 per cent. of the cases which have come before the Discipline Committee since 1919 the solicitor whose conduct was complained of had no partner, and that in that period of fourteen years only five solicitors who were in partnership have been struck off the roll. . . . Quite apart from the fact that partners necessarily operate as a check on each other, there are many valid reasons why a solicitor should have a partner or partners. . . ." *The Single Practitioner and Professional Misconduct*, The Law Journal, London, reprinted in New York Law Journal, vol. 90, p. 2426, Dec. 27, 1933.

(3) Is it ethically or legally wrong for members or employees of a law firm to resign and establish a rival firm with the hope and design of acquiring clients of the old firm? Does the answer turn at all on the nature of the methods used to acquire these clients or on the time at which the methods are used? For a decision involving the employees of a business firm, see

---
* From a letter to an editor.

Duane Jones Co. v. Burke, 306 N.Y. 172 (1954), discussed 54 Col.L.Rev. 994 (1954).

(4) On firm names the American Bar Association Committee, as other committees, has ruled that "where local custom permits, the name of a deceased or former partner may be continued." Opinion No. 318 (1967). In an earlier opinion, A.B.A. No. 267 (1945), the Committee stated:

> "The reason for this is that all of the partners have by their joint and several efforts over a period of years contributed to the good will attached to the firm name. In the case of a firm having widespread connections, this good will is disturbed by a change in firm name every time a name partner dies, and that reflects a loss in some degree of the good will to the building up of which the surviving partners have contributed their time, skill and labor through a period of years. To avoid this loss the firm name is continued and to meet the requirements of the Canon the individuals constituting the firm from time to time are listed."

The legal effects of the death of a partner are helpfully discussed in Note, *Death of a Lawyer,* 56 Colum.L.Rev. 606 (1956).

THE LARGE CITY FIRM

WHITNEY NORTH SEYMOUR, THE PRACTICE OF LAW IN A LARGE CITY, in LISTEN TO LEADERS IN THE LAW *

Pages 234–39 (1963).

The early experiences with a large, or moderately large, firm in a city will vary somewhat; but the following is probably a fair summary of the average. With the size of the firm goes a great proliferation of specialization. Ordinarily there will be one or more partners (sometimes ten) who concentrate on some particular area of law. Among these will be general corporate law (including formation of corporations, corporate mortgages, issuance of securities, SEC registration, etc.), tax law, estate law, litigation, perhaps labor law, and others, depending on the city and the area. . . .

In the firm's hierarchy, usually each partner will have several senior associates and some juniors who work closely with him. Some of these may be general utility men in the field, who are on call to work with a number of partners. But each partner and his preferred colleagues tend to be a rather closely knit group.

Each firm has its own way of launching the new associate. Some shuttle him around the departments for a couple of years with a few months of assignment to each department. This gives broad exposure to the firm's work, but may result in some enforced boredom when he hits a department holding no interest for him. In others, he goes into

---

* Copyright 1963 by Tupper and Love, Inc. Reprinted by permission of Holt, Rinehart and Winston, Inc.

a sort of pool of new talent; out of this he is assigned by someone who acts as an office manager or managing partner to do what is needed. He may do legal research in any of the departments. He may file papers or carry the bag of a litigator who needs a junior in a trial. He may help with a corporate closing where there are an infinite number of papers, or he may sometimes help to proofread the proofs of those papers. In this more hit-or-miss apprenticeship, variety supplies the interest. Gradually, under either system, the young man begins to show a flair for some particular specialty or he feels a call to one. Starting out with a general background, he, like every else, soon tends to be drawn to some particular specialty, and here he turns out to do his best work. Here he can see the best chance of progress and of the greatest satisfaction in his practice. If he really finds himself, he will not want to change. . . .

There is not room here to trace the whole process. The life in a large-city firm is exciting and intensely competitive in a gentlemanly sort of way. It takes great energy and effort. . . .

What rewards are there that take the place of the relatively serene pace at which the profession usually proceeds in smaller communities? First, of course, there is the rather crass notion that lawyers in large firms do well financially. Certainly this brings some able young men to the cities. And it is true that the income of a partner in a large city firm is likely to be several times the income of a partner in a small-town firm; but with taxes, such rewards have largely lost their appeal. The lower cost of living, greater leisure, and easier opportunities for participating in civic affairs in a smaller town, undoubtedly make up for any difference in income.

My impression is that it is the supposed opportunity to deal with legal problems of larger import rather than larger income, which is today the magnet drawing young lawyers to large-city practice. There is much truth in this concept. A large-city office does have a fascinating variety of problems. The corporate matters are likely to involve larger sums and tougher problems. . . . But it is well to remember that there may be quite as many challenging legal problems in a defense to a suit on a three-hundred-dollar note as in a one-hundred-million-dollar debenture issue. I believe the true appeal would probably be in that the large firms have a wider variety of professional challenges, because their clients are more varied, and not because of the amounts involved in any of the matters. Furthermore, where formerly one Wall Street lawyer might aspire to advise Mr. Morgan or Mr. Baker, they are more likely now to talk to office counsel and some career vice president. The notion that they will deal both with big men and big problems is one that may be more true in Texas than elsewhere.

It is fair to say that because of the nature and quality of the clientele of the larger firms, and the agreeable and professional competition between them, the lawyer's work is likely to be superlatively well done. Every possible legal question gets identified and solved. Skilled lawyers look at every alternative. . . .

But even a fast professional pace, and the opportunity to have a constant feast of hard and interesting problems with adequate financial reward, is not enough for most lawyers. . . . Fortunately, the urge to serve both clients and the public interest runs very deep in the profession.

The answer to this is, I believe, that big-city lawyers have the same opportunity to serve the public interest that lawyers anywhere do. Not only the opportunity, but the city lawyers seize it and they discharge it well. . . .

The young lawyer can start at once to gain some of these satisfactions and he can have them the rest of his life. His natural field will be the local bar associations where other lawyers and judges may learn to appreciate him. . . . Through the churches, hospitals, school board, legal-aid societies, chambers of commerce, citizens unions, etc., he can find many demands and outlets for his talents. Cultural activities, too—libraries, art galleries, symphonies, amateur dramatics—all will welcome him. These activities will broaden him, make him a better and more useful lawyer, and, with good luck and the aid of a good wife and alert children, may keep him from becoming too stuffy.

In the end, he will join with his colleagues in smaller communities in remembering two great truths about the profession which deserve repeating. The first comes from Elihu Root's great speech to the Yale Law School in 1904, which goes in part:

"He is a poor-spirited fellow who conceives that he has no duty but to his clients and sets before himself no object but personal success. To be a lawyer working for fees is not to be any the less a citizen whose unbought service is due to his community and his country with his best and constant effort. And the lawyer's profession demands of him something more than the ordinary public service of citizenship. He has a duty to the law. In the cause of peace and order and human rights against all injustice and wrong, he is the advocate of all men, present and to come."

And the second comes from a great friend of the United States and of mine, Lord Evershed, formerly Master of the Rolls and now a Chancery Law Lord, who said, in his 1955 speech at the University of Kansas:

. . . "for the legal profession no standard of scholarship or rectitude can by any means be too high. If it is true to say (as I believe that it is) that the measure of true freedom—freedom of the mind and the spirit as well as of the person—in any country is directly proportional to the respect in which its legal profession is held by the general community, so also is it true that the future liberties of our people, the maintenance of the high standards of stability and values, are in the hands of those of our profession."

NOTES

(1) "[W]hat I am most concerned with is the problem of how lawyers should qualify themselves to best serve the public under known present and probable future conditions. . . . [T]he impact of the broad changes in life in this country and particularly the development of big business, big government and big labor, compelled practicing lawyers to affirmatively make and negatively accept very substantial changes in the ways and means of practice. The question is whether these changes have been in the right direction and have gone far enough and not too far. The answer would seem to be that the Bar has been slow to recognize the existence and the imperativeness of the demand for change and that it is only where the compulsion of the demand has been strongest that it has been adequately met. . .

"The [large] law firm makes available to its clients a number of lawyers, each of whom possesses at least one of the special skills needed by clients. . . . Generally speaking, each client of the firm looks to one particular partner as his lawyer—the lawyer to whom he brings his legal problem for initial discussion unless it happens to be of such a peculiarly specialized nature that this preliminary step would involve a waste of time. Thus, from the large firm there may be obtained by a client precisely the close and confidential counselling which is in the best tradition of the Bar. . . . The instance of the large law firm handling the problems of its clients and particularly those created by big government and big labor, is an outstanding example of an adequate response to the demands of clients for the best possible legal services." Harrison Tweed,* The Changing Practice of Law 8, 11, 13, 15 (1955).

(2) The large corporate office and its demands and impacts on its personnel, including the young lawyers, are excellently examined by a sociologist in Smigel, The Wall Street Lawyer (1964). The corporation lawyer is sympathetically yet critically considered, in part through a description of the creators of some of the Wall Street firms, in Levy, Corporation Lawyer: Saint or Sinner (1961).

See also Eugene V. Rostow, *Review of Robert T. Swaine, The Cravath Firm and Its Predecessors*, 58 Yale L.J. 650 (1949).

(3) ". . . in my own city the best minds of the profession are scarcely lawyers at all. They may be something much better, or much worse; but they are not that. With courts they have no dealings whatever, and would hardly know what to do in one if they came there. Indeed, the

---

* Harrison Tweed was a New York City specialist in Trusts and Estates. His Cardozo Lecture, "The Changing Practice of Law", is an excellent discussion of its subject. He got fun out of giving fresh vision and life to numerous organizations, most notably his local bar association, The Association of the Bar of the City of New York. On the walls of the Association and of the Harvard Law School is his comment on us: "I have a high opinion of lawyers. With all their faults, they stack up well against those in every other occupation or profession. They are better to work with or play with or fight with or drink with than most other varieties of mankind."

situation has become such that I cannot quite see how a system of jurisprudence dependent upon precedent is permanently to get on at all with its best talent steadily drawn away from the precedent makers." Learned Hand, *Have the Bench and Bar Anything to Contribute to the Teaching of Law?*, Proceedings, Ass'n of American Law Schools, 45, 56 (1925).

HOUSE COUNSEL

CHARLES S. MADDOCK, THE CORPORATION LAW DEPARTMENT

30 Harvard Bus.Rev. 119, 136 (1952).

During the past 20 years, more and more industrial corporations have found a need for the day-to-day counsel of attorneys in connection with all aspects of their activities. . . .

The law department is classified as a service department in the corporate organization and is comparable in this respect with personnel, medical, traffic, research, and similar departments.

In general, the law department provides legal counsel and guidance to the officers and directors of the company and to the personnel of all operating and service departments, and has the responsibility of handling or making arrangements for handling all litigation in which the company may become involved. . . .

. . . But great plans, new plants and processes, production and sales volume, all can be stymied entirely or converted from profit to loss if the legal aspects of these steps are not cared for properly. . . .

. . . Corporation law department practice offers a broad field for true professional practice. Whether or not this is so in a particular corporation rests with those responsible for developing policy regarding the law department's relationship to the company. Superior lawyers will not be content to remain with work that is routine or offers no challenge to their ability. The best lawyers will always be found in those companies where the executives and general counsel recognize fully the service that the legal profession can render to American business and take steps to utilize that service to the utmost.

NOTES

(1) Creighton, *Corporation Counsel and Antitrust*, 48 A.B.A.J. 656, 658 (1962). "First, the lawyer must in part be not a lawyer. As a student of the law, which he must always remain, he solves legal problems. Some corporate counsel are prone to do this for their clients. Businessmen, however, have business problems and business objective. Profits, cost reduction, increased sales, keeping the plant at capacity production; these aims may not be the lawyer's direct responsibility but he must understand them. He solves legal problems only because and as that aids the purposes of the business.

"It is true the lawyer's point of view will not coincide with that of the manager. The lawyer will often take a longer range view. Particularly in advising marketing men, for example, counsel may cause a pause for cool analysis and sober judgment. What can corporate lawyers do affirmatively to increase their usefulness? . . . It is fatal, however, for him to view his function as an end in itself as lawyers sometimes seem to do. His function is to render legal service. The emphasis is on 'service'.

"He remains a lawyer, nevertheless, and his clients will respect him as such. All the opportunities for general service in the profession are his. He will have influence in the company as he has stature."

(2) Marden, *The Corporate Lawyer Today*, 20 The Record Ass'n Bar City N. Y. 346, 348–49 (1965). "The reasons for the astounding growth of corporate legal departments are fairly obvious. Legal questions are rampant today in almost every business transaction and large business particularly needs to have well informed counsel close at hand, available on a moment's notice. As John Tennant puts it:

'The two principal advantages [of corporate counsel] are availability and specialized knowledge of the facts. The desire or need for a lawyer available at all times is probably the pervading reason for the establishment of corporate law departments in the first instance and for their continued growth.'

I rather like Leon Hickman's three points at which he feels that the corporate counsel is in a position to be uniquely effective:

'He may practice preventive law; he can be certain of his facts; and he can schedule his work on an acceptable timetable.' . . .

The lawyer who has one client is no less a lawyer than those who have many. He has the same responsibilities, the same obligations and the same rights as the general practitioner."

(3) For a humorous account of a career as counsel for a large corporation see Davis, *Reflections of a Kept Lawyer*, 53 A.B.A.J. 349 (1967).

CORPORATION OF LAWYERS

IN THE MATTER OF THE FLORIDA BAR

Supreme Court of Florida, 1961.
133 So.2d 554.

THORNAL, JUSTICE. The Florida Bar has filed its original petition here requesting approval of certain amendments to the Integration Rule and the Code of Ethics to enable members of the petitioner to qualify under a State Statute known as "The Professional Service Corporation Act," Chapter 61–64, Laws of 1961.

We must decide whether members of The Florida Bar should be permitted to practice law as a corporate entity pursuant to statute above mentioned. . . .

Traditionally, the so-called learned professions have not been permitted to practice as corporate entities. . . . The principal reason for this change in attitude regarding these professional groups appears to arise out of the provisions of the Internal Revenue Code of 1954, U.S.C.A. Title 26, § 1 et seq., which permit an employer to establish a pension fund for the benefit of his employees. Payments by the employer into the fund are income tax deductible. Payments to the employee do not subject him to income tax until he actually receives the pension later in life. Stockholders of corporations can be employees thereof even though they own the corporate entity. Corporate stockholders can thus take advantage of these benefits. . . .

. . . If a means can be devised which preserves to the client and the public generally, all of the traditional obligations and responsibilities of the lawyer and at the same time enables the legal profession to obtain a benefit not otherwise available to it, we can find no objection to the proposal.

As we read Chapter 61–64, supra, implemented by the Rules which we hereafter announce, the highly personal obligation of the lawyer to his client is in no way adversely affected. The individual practitioner, whether a stockholder in a corporation or otherwise, will continue to be expected to abide by all of the Rules and Canons of professional ethics heretofore or hereafter required of him. The corporate entity as a method of doing business will not be permitted to protect the unfaithful or the unethical. As a matter of fact, the corporate entity itself will automatically come within the ambit of our jurisdiction in regard to discipline. In addition to the individual liability and responsibility of the stockholder, the corporate entity will be liable for the misprisions of its members to the extent of the corporate assets. . . . The members will be associated together as stockholders. They will have as their objective the conduct of the affairs of the corporate entity with a division of the profits. There will be continuity of life and centralization of management. There will be liability for corporate debts to the limit of the corporate assets. Finally, there will be a modified form of transferability of interests. There is some limitation on transferability by the requirement which restricts the transfer of stock in a professional service corporation to one who is a member of the profession and subject to the privilege of remaining stockholders to acquire the stock offered for transfer. . . .

Inasmuch as the entire proposal is so completely interwoven into the federal tax structure the members of the Bar are likewise forewarned of the advisability of making certain that any contemplated procedure under the rules and statute meet with the approval of the governing authorities of the United States Treasury Department. . . . We are pioneering in a new field of professional relationships and responsibilities. In the interest of individual clients, the public and the practitioner, care and caution should guide the footsteps of those who venture into this relatively unexplored area.

[The court ordered that The Integration Rule, the Code of Ethics and the Rules Governing the Conduct of Attorneys be amended in the form it prescribed so as to permit lawyers to practice law as a corporation.]

NOTES

(1) The relations of the members of the organization among themselves and to outsiders are governed by state law. But the determination whether the organization is a "corporation" for federal tax purposes is a matter of federal law and as the Regulations state "the label" given by state law is not conclusive. The applicable Income Tax Regulations cited by the court set out six "characteristics of corporations."

(2) The Committee on Professional Ethics of the American Bar Association in Opinion No. 303 (1961), dealing "with the general characteristics which are typically present," expressed the view that the practice of law by lawyers in the corporate form is not improper "provided appropriate safeguards are observed."

(3) In an action by a lawyer member of a professional corporation organized under Colorado law it was held that a Treasury Regulation of 1965 which denied the organization the standing as a corporation for income tax purposes was invalid as inconsistent with the revenue statutes. United States v. Empey, 406 F.2d 157 (1969). See Comment, *Can Professionals Incorporate for Tax Purposes?* 33 Alb.L.Rev. 311 (1969).

SECTION 2. THE MIDDLE GROUPS

A. LAWYER REFERRAL

JACKSONVILLE BAR ASSOCIATION v. WILSON

Supreme Court of Florida, 1958.
102 So.2d 292.

[A lawyer brought an action against The Jacksonville Bar Association for a declaratory decree that the operation of a lawyer reference service by the association with attendant publicity was in violation of Canons 27 and 28 of the American Bar Association adopted by the supreme court of the state. The regulations governing the operation of the service had a prefatory statement:

> The purpose of the Lawyer Reference Service . . . is to provide a method whereby any person who can afford to pay a reasonable fee for legal advice, and who does not have a lawyer, may be referred by The Jacksonville Bar Association to a lawyer willing to give a brief consultation for a fixed fee, and, where necessary, additional legal services for a reasonable fee to be agreed upon between the lawyer and the client.

A typical newspaper advertisement of the Service read:

Lawyer Reference Service

If you do not have a lawyer, contact this official agency of the Jacksonville Bar Association for referral to a lawyer to handle your legal matters for a reasonable fee.

501 Florida National Bank
Dial El. 3-1548

The trial judge granted the decree condemning the service and the Jacksonville Bar Association appealed.]

HOBSON, JUSTICE . . .

The regulations [by the Association] go on to provide that the service shall be operated by a Referrer, who acts as a lawyer functioning under the supervision of a committee of the Bar Association. A prospective client is first interviewed by the Referrer who, if further legal services are required, refers the client to a member of the panel of lawyers who have indicated their willingness to serve. The regulations pertaining to the formation and operation of the panel of lawyers are reproduced verbatim, as follows:

IV. Formation of the Panel . . .

3. In submitting his application for membership on the panel an applicant may, if he chooses to do so, list those branches of legal work in which he considers himself particularly qualified and those which he does not care to handle.

4. By filing an application, each applicant agrees that if he is registered by the committee as a member of the panel:

a. He will personally grant a half-hour consultation for a fee of $5.00, to any client referred to him by the Referrer.

b. Any charge for further service will be limited to a reasonable amount agreed upon with the client and in keeping with the spirit of the Lawyer Reference Service.

c. Any dispute which may arise in connection with the amount of his fee shall be arbitrated by the Committee on Lawyer Reference Service, whose decision in the matter will be accepted by the client and the member of the panel as controlling and final. . . .

The prohibition of advertising by lawyers deserves some examination. All agree that advertising by an individual lawyer, if permitted, will detract from the dignity of the profession, but the matter goes deeper than this. Perhaps the most understandable and acceptable additional reasons we have found are stated by one commentator as follows:

"1. That advertisements, unless kept within narrow limits, like any other form of solicitation, tend to stir up litigation, and such tendency is against the public interest.

"2. That if there were no restrictions on advertisements, the least capable and least honorable lawyers would be apt to publish the most extravagant and alluring material about themselves, and that the harm which would result would, in large measure, fall on the ignorant and on those least able to afford it.

"3. That the temptation would be strong to hold out as inducements for employment, assurances of success or satisfaction to the client, which assurances could not be realized, and that the giving of such assurances would materially increase the temptation to use ill means to secure the end desired by the client.

"In other words, the reasons for the rule, and for the conclusion that it is desirable to prohibit advertising entirely, or to limit it within such narrow bounds that it will not admit of abuse, are based on the possibility and probability that this means of publicity, if permitted, will be abused." Harrison Hewitt in a comment at 15 ABAJ 116 (1929), reproduced in Cheatham, Cases and Materials on the Legal Profession (2d Ed., 1955), p. 525.

Of course, competition is at the root of abuses in advertising. If the individual lawyer were permitted to compete with his fellows in publicity through advertising, we have no doubt that Mr. Hewitt's three points, quoted above, would accurately forecast the result.

But the advertising now before us represents the very antithesis of competition. Here is an organization of lawyers, which all in a given area may join, working cooperatively to lower the barrier between the legal profession and the public. Certainly the public must be attracted, and must be apprised of the availability of the service. We deal every day with cases wherein the client sought legal advice too late, when his affairs had reached the pathological stage and litigation could not be avoided. Counselling, or preventive legal advice before trouble commences, will tend to keep people out of the courts, within the letter and spirit of the Canons of Ethics. And alerting the public to the existence of a service, under bar sponsorship, which will provide such preventive advice at a reasonable fee is not unethical, but must redound to the benefit both of the public and of the bar.

The final declaratory decree appealed from is reversed and the cause remanded with directions to dismiss the suit.

NOTE

"Even though the lawyer referral plan last year brought legal services of one kind or another to approximately 100,000 people, the inadequacy of the plan as it presently exists in most communities is apparent. Reaching 100,000 people on an adult population of over 100,000,000 is a miniscule effect—less than 1 in a 1000. . . . The plan can be effective, but it will become so only through a substantial commitment—of resources, of course, but above all a commitment to change itself—at all levels of the organization. The extent to which the profession is not willing to make such a commitment may well portend, if not determine, the future of the profession." Christen-

B. GROUP LEGAL SERVICES

THREE STATE DECISIONS

PEOPLE EX REL. ILL. STATE BAR ASS'N v. PEOPLE'S STOCK YARDS STATE BANK

Supreme Court of Illinois, 1931. 344 Ill. 462, 176 N.E. 901.

[A proceeding for contempt of court was brought against a bank for engaging in the practice of law. The bank in a community of immigrant industrial workers carried on a real estate and decedents' estates practice for its customers. It actively solicited the work which was done by salaried lawyers in its employ with the fees retained by the bank. Held, the bank was in contempt of court.]

ORR, J. . . . Under the constitution of this State the judicial power is vested solely in the courts. . . . Having inherent and plenary power and original jurisdiction to decide who shall be admitted to practice as attorneys in this State, this court also has all the power and jurisdiction necessary to protect and enforce its rules and decisions in that respect. . . . And so it has been held that the court, which alone has authority to license attorneys, has as a necessary corollary ample implied power to protect this function by punishing unauthorized persons for usurping the privilege of acting as attorneys. . . .

. . . It is no less a usurpation of the function and privilege of an attorney and an affront to the court having sole power to license attorneys, for one not licensed as such to perform the services of an attorney outside of court proceedings. . . .

Respondent, being a corporation, is also prohibited by statute from practicing law in Illinois. . . . The legislature has not attempted to tie the hands of the courts in dealing with contempts of this kind, and any attempt to do so would be an infringement upon the inherent exclusive jurisdiction of the courts. . . .

. . . That it [the bank] used for that purpose the services of licensed attorneys in its employ does not alter the fact that it was thus practicing law. . . .

[The court found the bank was in contempt of court.]

PEOPLE EX REL. COURTNEY v. ASSOCIATION OF REAL ESTATE TAX-PAYERS OF ILLINOIS

Supreme Court of Illinois, 1933.
354 Ill. 102, 187 N.E. 823.

[A proceeding was brought against a non-proft corporation to punish it for contempt of court for practicing law. The corporation was organized for the purpose of giving protection to real estate tax-payers and it attacked in court the system of tax assessment in Chicago. The membership was over 23,000, the average membership fee was $14.50, and the reasonable legal fees and other expenses for the work done by lawyers of the corporation in the attack on the tax assessment system was $200,000. The court held the corporation was in contempt of court.]

FARTHING, J. . . . That relation of trust and confidence essential to the relation of attorney and client did not exist between the members of the respondent association and its attorneys, and whatever relation of trust and confidence existed was between the membership and the association. . . . Much that was said in People v. People's Stock Yards State Bank, supra, is controlling in this case as to the question of the respondent's having practiced law. . . . It is well settled that no corporation can be licensed to practice law. The fact that the respondent was a corporation organized not for profit does not vary the rule. . . .

[The respondent was adjudged guilty of contempt of court.]

ILLINOIS STATE BAR ASS'N v. UNITED MINE WORKERS OF AMERICA, DISTRICT 12

Supreme Court of Illinois, 1966.
35 Ill.2d 112, 219 N.E.2d 503.

[A state bar association filed a complaint against a labor union seeking to restrain it from activities alleged to constitute the unauthorized practice of law. The facts were that shortly after the state's workmen's compensation act was passed nearly fifty years earlier the union began the practice of employing a lawyer on a salary to represent the union members who had claims under the act and who wished his services. The letter of employment of the lawyer states: "You will receive no further instructions or directions and have no interference from the District, nor from any officer, and your obligations and relations will be to and with only the several persons you represent." Under the plan injured members receive a letter from the union advising them to fill out and return accompanying forms describing the accident to "the legal department" of the union. The application for adjustment of claim is prepared by secretaries in the union offices and sent by them directly to the workmen's compensation commission. The salaried lawyer prepares the case from the claim file. The lawyer determines what he thinks the case is worth, presents his views to the employer's attorney and attempts to reach a settlement. If the lawyers reach an agreement the Union lawyer informs the injured man of its terms who then decides whether to accept it. If the settlement is rejected the claim is set down for hearing before the commission. The hearing is ordinarily the first time that the injured man and his lawyer come into personal contact, though the union members understand he is available earlier for advice. The full amount of any settlement or award is paid to the injured person. The trial court granted the injunction against the union and the state supreme court affirmed the decision.]

PER CURIAM. It is clear that under the prior decisions of this court, organizations, including not-for-profit organizations, which hire or retain lawyers to represent their individual members in legal matters are ordinarily engaging in the unauthorized practice of law. . . .

Thought to be of paramount importance to the public is the preservation of the integrity of the lawyer-client relationship involving the highest degree of trust and confidence, and an unswerving dedication of the lawyer's abilities to the interests of his client. Intervention in this relationship of third-party organizations by whom lawyers are directly employed and compensated to handle personal claims of organization members has generally been prohibited. . . .

. . . Even though the terms of the letter of employment indicate no organizational direction will be given, the interests of the employer and the client in a given case may or may not be identical, since as the AFL–CIO *amicus* brief indicates, the interests of the union, collectively, may extend beyond the interest of the injured member.

In our consideration of this case, the policy arguments of the Mine Workers and *amici* are impressive. . . . (See Markus, Group Representation by Attorneys as Misconduct, 14 Cleveland-Marshall Law Review, 1 (1966).) But . . . they are insufficient to override the governing principles in the attorney-client relationship.

NOTES

(1) These three Illinois cases taken together did more, it will be observed, than merely to condemn the kind of group legal services involved. Since the Supreme Court of Illinois held it had the last word on what constitutes the unlawful practice of law, the decisions blocked all efforts by the organized bar or by the legislature to develop group practice unless either the state constitution was amended or else the Supreme Court of the United States stepped in.

(2) The Committee on Unauthorized Practice of the American Bar Association condemned fringe benefits in the form either of legal services rendered by union lawyers to union members or by employers' lawyers to employees. 36 A.B.A.J. 677 (1950). The opinion was criticized by the longtime chairman of the Committee on Professional Ethics of the Association in his book, Drinker, Legal Ethics, which was cited by the Supreme Court of the United States in the cases next ahead.

(3) "Legal Fee Finance Plans" have been proposed under which the clients' notes for the amount of the fees will be discounted by a bank with immediate payment of the fees to the lawyers, a method, as it is said by which hard-pressed clients can buy legal services on the installment plan. The American Bar Association Committee in a carefully guarded opinion expressed the view that the plan is not per se unethical. Opinion 320, 54 A.B.A.J. 476 (1968). As the opinion shows an opposite view has been expressed by some local bar associations.

NATIONAL ASSOCIATION FOR THE ADVANCEMENT OF COLORED PEOPLE v. BUTTON, ATTORNEY GENERAL OF VIRGINIA

Supreme Court of the United States, 1963.
371 U.S. 415, 83 S.Ct. 328, 9 L.Ed.2d 405.

[The National Association for the Advancement of Colored People (NAACP) attacked in the state courts of Virginia state statutes condemning its activities. The Supreme Court of Appeals of Virginia upheld one of the statutes. The Supreme Court of the United States granted certiorari.

The statute in question passed by the legislature in 1956 amended the provisions of the Virginia Code forbidding solicitation of legal business by a "runner" or "capper" to include "an agent for an individual or organization which retains a lawyer in connection with an action to which it is not a party and in which it has no pecuniary right or liability". The basic aims of NAACP are to secure the elimination of all racial barriers which deprive Negro citizens of the privileges and burdens of equal citizenship. In recent years it had concentrated in Virginia upon financing litigation attacking racial segregation in the public schools. The actual control of litigation is with the NAACP's locally retained attorney, though the NAACP continues to be concerned that the outcome of the lawsuit is consistent with its policies.]

MR. JUSTICE BRENNAN delivered the opinion of the Court. . . .

Our concern is with the impact of enforcement of Chapter 33 upon First Amendment freedoms. . . .

We read the decree of the Virginia Supreme Court of Appeals in the instant case as proscribing any arrangement by which prospective litigants are advised to seek the assistance of particular attorneys.

. . . There thus inheres in the statute the gravest danger of smothering all discussion looking to the eventual institution of litigation on behalf of the rights of members of an unpopular minority. . . . We cannot close our eyes to the fact that the militant Negro civil rights movement has engendered the intense resentment and opposition of the politically dominant white community of Virginia; litigation assisted by the NAACP has been bitterly fought. . . .

We hold that Chapter 33 as construed violates the Fourteenth Amendment by unduly inhibiting protected freedoms of expression and association. In so holding, we reject two further contentions of respondents. The first is that the Virginia Supreme Court of Appeals has guaranteed free expression by expressly confirming petitioner's right to continue its advocacy of civil-rights litigation. . . . The second contention is that Virginia has a subordinating interest in the regulation of the legal profession, embodied in Chapter 33, which justifies limiting petitioner's First Amendment rights. Specifically, Virginia contends that the NAACP's activities in furtherance of litigation, being "improper solicitation" under the state statute, fall within the traditional purview of state regulation of professional conduct. . . . The decisions of this Court have consistently held that only a compelling state interest in the regulation of a subject within the State's constitutional power to regulate can justify limiting First Amendment freedoms. . . . A State may not, under the guise of prohibiting professional misconduct ignore constitutional rights.

. . . [R]egulations which reflect hostility to stirring up litigation have been aimed chiefly at those who urge recourse for private gain serving no public interest. . . . For a member of the bar to participate, directly or through intermediaries, in such misuses of the legal process is conduct traditionally condemned as injurious to the public. . . .

Objection to the intervention of a lay intermediary, who may control litigation or otherwise interfere with the rendering of legal services in a confidential relationship, also derives from the element of pecuniary gain. Fearful of dangers thought to arise from that element, the courts of several States have sustained regulations aimed at these activities.* We intimate no view one way or the other as to merits of those decisions with respect to the particular arrangements against which they are directed. . . .

There has been no showing of a serious danger here of professionally reprehensible conflicts of interest which rules against solicitation frequently seek to prevent. This is so partly because no monetary stakes are involved, and so there is no danger that the attorney will desert or subvert the paramount interest of his client to enrich

---

* In a footnote Mr. Justice Brennan cited or referred to several state cases which had condemned such activities.

himself or an outside sponsor. . . . Resort to the courts to seek vindication of constitutional rights is a different matter from the oppressive, malicious, or avaricious use of the legal process for purely private gain. . . .

We conclude that although the petitioner has shown that its activities fall within the First Amendment's protections, the State has failed to advance any substantial regulatory interest, in the form of substantive evils flowing from petitioner's activities, which can justify the broad prohibitions which it has imposed. . . .

Because our disposition is rested on the First Amendment as absorbed in the Fourteenth, we do not reach the considerations of race or racial discrimination which are the predicate of petitioner's challenge to the statute under the Equal Protection Clause. . . .*

Reversed.

BROTHERHOOD OF RAILROAD TRAINMEN v. VIRGINIA EX REL. VIRGINIA STATE BAR

Supreme Court of the United States, 1964.
377 U.S. 1, 84 S.Ct. 1113, 12 L.Ed.2d 89.

Mr. Justice Black delivered the opinion of the Court.

[The Virginia State Bar brought suit against the Brotherhood of Railroad Trainmen, an investigator employed by it, and a lawyer designated "Regional Counsel" to enjoin them from carrying on activities charged to be the solicitation of legal business and the unauthorized practice of law in Virginia. The Virginia courts granted the injunction and the Supreme Court of the United States granted certiorari to consider a constitutional question.] It soon became apparent to the railroad workers, however, that simply having these federal statutes on the books (the Federal Employers' Liability Act and related statutes) was not enough to assure that the workers would receive the full benefit of the compensatory damages Congress intended they should have. Injured workers or their families often fell prey on the one hand to persuasive claims adjusters eager to gain a quick and cheap settlement for their railroad employers, or on the other to lawyers either not competent to try these lawsuits against the able and experienced railroad counsel or too willing to settle a case for a quick dollar.

It was to protect against these obvious hazards to the injured man or his widow that the workers through their Brotherhood set up their Legal Aid Department, since renamed Department of Legal Counsel, the basic activities of which the court below has enjoined. Under their plan the United States was divided into sixteen regions

---

* The concurring and dissenting opinions are omitted.

and the Brotherhood selected, on the advice of local lawyers and federal and state judges, a lawyer or firm in each region with a reputation for honesty and skill in representing plaintiffs in railroad personal injury litigation. When a worker was injured or killed, the secretary of his local lodge would go to him or to his widow or children and recommend that the claim not be settled without first seeing a lawyer, and that in the Brotherhood's judgment the best lawyer to consult was the counsel selected by it for that area.[8] . . .

The Brotherhood admits that it advises injured members and their dependents to obtain legal advice before making settlement of their claims and that it recommends particular attorneys to handle such claims. The result of the plan, the Brotherhood admits, is to channel legal employment to the particular lawyers approved by the Brotherhood as legally and morally competent to handle injury claims for members and their families. It is the injunction against this particular practice which the Brotherhood, on behalf of its members, contends denies them rights guaranteed by the First and Fourteenth Amendments. We agree with this contention. . . .

Virginia undoubtedly has broad powers to regulate the practice of law within its borders;[10] but we have had occasion in the past to recognize that in regulating the practice of law a State cannot ignore the rights of individuals secured by the Constitution.[11] For as we said in NAACP v. Button, supra, 371 U.S., at 429, "a State cannot foreclose the exercise of constitutional rights by mere labels." Here what Virginia has sought to halt is not a commercialization of the legal profession which might threaten the moral and ethical fabric of the administration of justice. It is not "ambulance chasing." The railroad workers, by recommending competent lawyers to each other, obviously are not themselves engaging in the practice of law, nor are they or the lawyers whom they select parties to any soliciting of business. It is interesting to note that in Great Britain unions do not simply recommend lawyers to members in need of advice; they retain counsel, paid by the union, to represent members in personal law-

8. The Brotherhood also provides a staff, now at its own expense, to investigate accidents to help gather evidence for use by the injured worker or his family should a trial be necessary to vindicate their rights. [Footnote by the Court.]

10. The Bar relies on the common law, the Canons of Ethics of the American Bar Association, adopted into the rules of the Supreme Court of Appeals of Virginia, 171 Va. xviii, and several Virginia statutes prohibiting the unauthorized practice of law. The Canons of Ethics to which the Bar refers prohibit respectively stirring up of litigation, control or exploitation by a lay agency of professional services of a lawyer, and aiding the unauthorized practice of law. Canons 28, 35, 47. The statutes respectively set the qualifications for the practice of law in the State and provide for injunctions against "running, capping, soliciting and maintenance." Virginia Code, 1950, §§ 54–42, 54–83.1. [Footnote by the Court.]

11. NAACP v. Button, 371 U.S. 415; Konigsberg v. State Bar, 353 U.S. 252; Schware v. Board of Bar Examiners, 353 U.S. 232. [Footnote by the Court.]

suits,[12] a practice similar to that which we upheld in NAACP v. Button, supra.

A State could not, by invoking the power to regulate the professional conduct of attorneys, infringe in any way the right of individuals and the public to be fairly represented in lawsuits authorized by Congress to effectuate a basic public interest. Laymen cannot be expected to know how to protect their rights when dealing with practiced and carefully counseled adversaries, cf. Gideon v. Wainwright, 372 U.S. 335, and for them to associate together to help one another to preserve and enforce rights granted them under federal laws cannot be condemned as a threat to legal ethics.[13] The State can no more keep these workers from using their cooperative plan to advise one another than it could use more direct means to bar them from resorting to the courts to vindicate their legal rights. The right to petition the courts cannot be so handicapped. . . . "the State has failed to advance any substantial regulatory interest, in the form of substantive evils flowing from petitioner's activities, which can justify the broad prohibitions which it has imposed." 371 U.S., at 444. . . .

We hold that the First and Fourteenth Amendments protect the right of the members through their Brotherhood to maintain and carry out their plan for advising workers who are injured to obtain legal advice and for recommending specific lawyers. . . . And, of course, lawyers accepting employment under this constitutionally protected plan have a like protection which the State cannot abridge.

The judgment and decree are vacated and the case is remanded for proceedings not inconsistent with this opinion.

[The dissenting opinion of MR. JUSTICE CLARK, with whom MR. JUSTICE HARLAN joined, is omitted.]

UNITED MINE WORKERS OF AMERICA v. ILLINOIS STATE BAR ASS'N

Supreme Court of the United States, 1967.
389 U.S. 217, 88 S.Ct. 353, 19 L.Ed.2d 426.

MR. JUSTICE BLACK delivered the opinion of the Court. [The facts are given in the statement of the case in the Supreme Court of Illinois supra p. 70. The Supreme Court of the United States granted certiorari.]

---

12. See Feather, The Essence of Trade Unionism (London, 1963), 42–43. [Footnote by the Court.]

13. Cf. Drinker, Legal Ethics (1953), 167; Hildebrand v. State Bar, 36 Cal. 2d 504, 515, 225 P.2d 508, 514 (Carter, J., dissenting), 36 Cal.2d, at 521, 225 P.2d, at 518 (Traynor, J., dissenting). [Footnote by the Court.]

... The Illinois Supreme Court rejected petitioner's contention that its members had a right, protected by the First and Fourteenth Amendments, to join together and assist one another in the assertion of their legal rights by collectively hiring an attorney to handle their claims. ...

... We start with the premise that the rights to assemble peaceably and to petition for a redress of grievances are among the most precious of the liberties safeguarded by the Bill of Rights. ... We have therefore repeatedly held that laws which actually affect the exercise of these vital rights cannot be sustained merely because they were enacted for the purpose of dealing with some evil within the State's legislative competence, or even because the laws do in fact provide a helpful means of dealing with such an evil. ...

We think that both the Button and Trainmen cases are controlling here. The litigation in question is, of course, not bound up with political matters of acute social moment, as in Button, but the First Amendment does not protect speech and assembly only to the extent it can be characterized as political. "Great secular causes, with small ones, are guarded. . . ."

Nor can the case at bar be distinguished from the Trainmen case in any persuasive way.[5] Here, to be sure, the attorney is actually paid by the Union, not merely the beneficiary of its recommendations. But in both situations the attorney's economic welfare is dependent to a considerable extent on the good will of the union, and if the temptation to sacrifice the client's best interests is stronger in the present situation, it is stronger in a virtually imperceptible degree. In both cases, there was absolutely no indication that the theoretically imaginable divergence between the interests of union and member ever actually arose in the context of a particular lawsuit; indeed in the present case the Illinois Supreme Court itself described the possibility of conflicting interests as, at most "conceivabl[e]."

It has been suggested that the Union could achieve its goal by referring members to a specific lawyer or lawyers and then reimbursing the members out of a common fund for legal fees paid. Although a committee of the American Bar Association, in an informal opinion, may have approved such an arrangement, we think the view of the Illinois Supreme Court is more relevant on this point. In the present case itself the Illinois court stressed that where a union rec-

---

5. It is irrelevant that the litigation in Trainmen involved statutory rights created by Congress, while the litigation in the present case involved state-created rights. Our holding in Trainmen was based not on State interference with a federal program in violation of the Supremacy Clause but rather on petitioner's freedom of speech, petition, and assembly under the First and Fourteenth Amendments, and this freedom is, of course, as extensive with respect to assembly and discussion related to matters of local as to matters of federal concern. [Footnote by the Court.]

ommends attorneys to its members, "any 'financial connection of any kind'" between the union and such attorneys is illegal. It cannot seriously be argued, therefore, that this alternative arrangement would be held proper under the laws of Illinois.

The decree at issue here thus substantially impairs the associational rights of the mine workers and is not needed to protect the State's interest in high standards of legal ethics.' . . .

The judgment and decree are vacated and the case is remanded for proceedings not inconsistent with this opinion.

MR. JUSTICE HARLAN dissenting . . . . Although I agree with the balancing approach employed by the majority, I find the scales tip differently. . . . The State was entitled to conclude that removed from ready contact with his client, insulated from interference by his actual employer, paid a salary independent of the results achieved, faced with a heavy caseload, and very possibly with other activities competing for his time,[13] the attorney will be tempted to place undue emphasis upon quick disposition of each case. . . . In the absence of demonstrated arbitrary or discriminatory regulation, state courts and legislatures should be left to govern their own Bars, free from interference by this Court.[17]

NOTES

(1) These three cases, the Button, Railroad Trainmen and United Mine Workers decisions, have, as their unifying idea, "the public interest." The Court put the burden on the states and the bar to show that the restrictions set by the bar's standards are in the public interest.

(a) What form of groups and of legal services are protected by the constitutional principles enunciated in these cases? Must the protected group be an organization the members of which have a common interest aside from the procurement of legal services, and must the services rendered arise out of activities connected with this common interest? To be specific, would protection be given to a group formed solely to obtain legal service, or

---

13. The attorney employed by the Mine Workers was an Illinois state senator and had a private practice other than the Mine Workers' representation. [Footnote by the Justice.]

17. It has been suggested both in this case and elsewhere, cf. *Hackin v. Arizona, ante*, p. 143 (Douglas, J., dissenting), that prevailing Canons of Ethics and traditional customs in the legal profession will have to be modified to keep pace with the needs of new social developments, such as the Federal Poverty Program. That may well be true, but such considerations furnish no justification for today's heavy-handed action by the Court. The American Bar Association and other bodies throughout the country already have such matters under consideration. See, e. g., 1964 ABA Reports 381–383 (establishment of Special Committee on Ethical Standards); 1966 ABA Reports 589–594 (Report of Special Committee on Availability of Legal Services); 39 Calif. State Bar Journal 639–742 (Report of Committee on Group Legal Services). Moreover, the complexity of these matters makes them especially suitable for experimentation at the local level. And, all else failing, the Congress undoubtedly has the power to implement federal programs by establishing overriding rules governing legal representation in connection therewith. [Footnote by the Justice.]

to a cooperative association formed to obtain for its members a variety of services and goods?

(b) Is the protection confined to this sort of fringe benefit extended by a voluntary association to its members or does it extend to such a benefit provided by an employer for its employees?

(c) Is the protection confined to persons of the middle and lower classes who otherwise may not obtain the services they need? To put the converse of the Mine Workers case, may large self-insured employers band together to employ lawyers to represent them individually in workmen's compensation cases?

(d) In these three cases the Court held that the Constitution casts the burden on the profession and the state to show that the particular standards in question are in the public interest. Is there a similar constitutional burden as to all standards of the profession?

(2) See Voorhees, *Group Legal Services and the Public Interest*, 55 A.B.A.J. 534 (1969), which urges "Group legal services are in the public interest, and the profession should recognize this fact. Other group services, which were resisted by other professions when they were introduced are now accepted, and the dire predictions made about them have proved false."

(3) Opposing views within the bar on group legal services were illustrated by two proposals before the American Bar Association at its 1969 meeting. One proposal was in the form of the report of the Special Committee on Availability of Legal Services under the chairmanship of Mr. F. William McAlpin of St. Louis, published in the 1969 Report of the Association. The Special Committee's report proposed a statement of policy which would give broad approval to the rendition of legal services "to individual members of a group identifiable in terms of some substantial common interest." The report recommended several safeguards which would help to prevent the misuse of group legal services. An opposing proposal called for the condemnation in the Code of Professional Reponsibility of group legal services except "in those instances and to the extent that controlling constitutional interpretation at the time of the rendition of the services requires the allowance of such legal services activities."

The latter was accepted and adopted as a part of the Code. DR 2–103 (D) (5)

(4) An excellent study on legal services, which reaches much beyond its title of insurance, is Stolz, *Insurance for Legal Services: A Preliminary Study of Feasibility*, 35 U.Chi.L.Rev. 417, 476 (1967), commissioned by The American Bar Foundation. The conclusion on its specific subject is: "Legal insurance is a possible way of financing legal service for individuals of modest means. A plan can be constructed that would not be too costly to be sold. For the most part the services that would be purchased through insurance are low cost, preventive law services that the public is not now buying. The primary value of legal insurance would be as a way of encouraging people to use more legal services. For selected groups, legal insurance would be more attractive than group legal services, but, in general, legal insurance cannot achieve the economies of scale possible through group legal services. Legal insurance, accordingly, is far from a complete answer to those concerned about the economic threat of group legal services, nor is it likely to revolutionize the economics of law practice."

(5) The consumer who individually is victimized in a sum too small to justify the costs of litigation is receiving increasing protection through government. For a suggestion of a practicable measure see Wade and Kamenshine, *Restitution for Defrauded Consumers: Making the Remedy Effective Through Suit by Governmental Agency*, 37 Geo.Wash.L.Rev. 1031 (1969).

SECTION 3. THE POOR

Introduction. The needs of the poor for legal services and the barriers in the way are mentioned first in this section. Then several methods of providing the services are indicated. They began with the legal aid societies which were charitable in nature and private in support and in control. They have moved on to a variety of government supported methods, ranging from support to the established legal aid societies in their ordinary work on to government aid to attacks on established but unjust institutions and to methods of aiding the poor to lift themselves out of poverty. The subject is closely related to the *legal* right to have counsel provided in all serious criminal cases. See Chapter I, Section 6, p. 39, supra. The right to counsel" here involved has a broader and more fundamental meaning. It concerns the felt obligation on society and especially on the legal profession to see to it that every person who needs a lawyer shall have a fair opportunity to retain one, whether in a civil or a criminal case, in a litigated or unlitigated matter.

REGINALD HEBER SMITH,* JUSTICE AND THE POOR
Pages 31–34 (1924).

The lawyer is indispensable to the conduct of proceedings before the courts, and yet the fees which he must charge for his services are more than millions of persons can pay. Simple as these propositions are, they are too often forgotten in the discussions concerning the administration of justice. . . . The vast number of persons who are thus debarred from legal advice and the essential services of the lawyer in court, however is not realized. . . . [I]t appears

---

* One spring, Dean Thayer of the Harvard Law School asked a third year man to come to his office. "Smith", the dean said, "next week you will be offered the place of counsel of the Boston Legal Aid Society. It is nothing. You can make it into something." Reginald Heber Smith did more than make the office into something. He wrote Justice and the Poor, a book which gave impetus to the whole legal aid movement. Though he became the managing partner of a large firm and was active in many public causes, he continued a guiding force in legal aid through many lean years ahead. He had fellow leaders worthy of him, both national and local, for legal aid has attracted to it many of the best of the American bar.

that there are in the United States over 35,000,000 men, women, and children whose financial condition renders them unable to pay any appreciable sum for attorney's services. . . .

NOTE

"The law is more than rules of rights and repressions. The law is a dynamic force for social change. . . . It is not only the lack of money that makes a man poor. The shackles that bind to poverty are ignorance of rights, disregard of personal value as a human being, a sense of being abandoned, a conviction of despair as an object manipulated by a system." Bamberger, *The Legal Services Program of the Office of Economic Opportunity*, 41 Notre Dame Law 847, 852 (1966). See Cahn and Cahn, *The War on Poverty: A Civilian Perspective*, 73 Yale L.J. 1317 (1964).

THE LEGAL AID ORGANIZATIONS

EMERY A. BROWNELL, LEGAL AID IN THE UNITED STATES

Pages 3, 8–9, 45 (1951).

Legal Aid, essentially, is the organized effort of the bar and the community to provide the services of lawyers free, or for a token charge, to persons who cannot afford to pay an attorney's fee and whose cases are unremunerative on a contingent fee basis. Such services may involve no more than a professional consultation or they may include assistance in negotiation, the preparation of documents or representation in court. The term "Legal Aid" applies if they are supplied through a facility organized for this special purpose and if they represent something more than the free service which individual attorneys render in the course of private practice. . . .

The predominant forms of Legal Aid organizations . . . are generally classified in six groups as follows: 1. Societies. 2. Departments of Social Agencies. 3. Public Bureaus. 4. Bar Association Offices. 5. Law School Clinics. 6. Public and Voluntary Defender Organizations.

. . . Year after year, these offices have found that approximately three-fourths of the problems which come to them require only consultation service and, in some cases, a referral to some other legal or social service. . . . It demonstrates that it is not only persons of wealth and business corporations who need legal counseling of a preventive sort, but that the well-being of all citizens is promoted by the timely advice of lawyers on the many and frequent questions of law affecting their lives, their property, and their opportunities.

NOTES

(1) Organized private legal aid began in a small way in New York City in the 1870's and about the same time in Chicago. The slow development in

other communities and the dominantly private character of the work is revealed in a 1951 study by the Executive Director of the National Legal Aid Association which showed that 60 per cent of the financial support came from Community Chests, an additional 24 per cent from individual contributions, and only 9½ per cent from public funds.* At that time the societies gave their attention primarily to civil matters and the combined budgets of the local societies was $909,000. By contrast in 1966 the civil offices reporting to the National Legal Aid and Defender Association showed the cost of operations had increased to over $11,500,000, of which over 54 per cent came from the Office of Economic Opportunity.**

(2) In 1949 England initiated a legal aid and advice scheme with four basic elements: (1) all persons needing legal services are able to obtain them regardless of poverty; (2) the services are rendered by lawyers in private practice whom the client chooses and the relation between the client and the lawyer is direct with no intermediary; (3) the plan is administered by the solicitors' organization, The Law Society; (4) the government pays the cost of the services beyond what the client can pay, and the lawyers accept fees somewhat below their usual scale. The English plan at its inception was described by the Secretary of the Law Society. Lund, *The Legal Aid and Advice Scheme,* 4 The Record Ass'n Bar City N. Y. 77 (1949). Its developments are described by Lord Parker in *The Development of Legal Aid in England since 1949,* 48 A.B.A.J. 1029 (1962).

(3) In the Province of Ontario there came into force in 1967, a legal aid plan which is closer in policies and methods to the English plan than to the recent American plan. The plan provides province-wide service wholly financed by the provincial government. . . . "The successful applicant for legal aid is given a legal aid certificate which simply entitles him to help under the Act and makes no mention of a specific lawyer. Legal Aid Clients are urged to hire a lawyer of their own choosing. . . . The drafters of the Legal Aid Act are also very determined that the legislation foster the private practice of law. . . . The official governing body of the legal profession, the Law Society of Upper Canada, is responsible for the administration of the new legal aid plan. . . . [T]he professional services of Ontario lawyers acting under the Act shall be paid 'three-quarters of the fees customarily paid . . . .'" Parker, *Legal Aid—Canadian Style,* 14 Wayne L.Rev. 471, 477, 478, 485 (1968).

(4) The needs for special publicity to bring home to the poor the fact that the legal services are available for them have been repeatedly recognized by the courts and the bar. It was held not improper solicitation for a bar association to make known through the newspapers that a committee would provide free legal services for the poor victims of loan sharks, whether to defend against illegal exactions or to bring actions to recover sums already paid under illegal demands. Gunnels v. Atlanta Bar Ass'n, 191 Ga. 366, 12 S.E.2d 602 (1940). A helpful note reviews the opinions of the American Bar Association committee on the subject. Blakslee, *Legal Aid Offices and Advertising,* 53 A.B.A.J. 1148 (1967).

---

* Brownell, Legal Aid in the United States 232, 237 (1951).

** National Legal Aid and Defender Association, 1967 Summary of Conference Proceedings, at 275.

THE POOR AND COUNSEL IN CRIMINAL CASES

HARRISON TWEED, FOREWORD, EQUAL JUSTICE FOR THE ACCUSED, REPORT

Pages 5–6 (1959) *

Three quite different methods for furnishing legal representation in the criminal courts to those who cannot afford a lawyer have been used. The first is through counsel assigned by the courts, generally without compensation for services and often without reimbursement for expenses. . . . [A] preferable system is that of defender services offered through private legal aid societies or the like. . . . Personally, I have never believed that sufficient funds would be available to make this system an adequate ultimate solution for most communities. . . . A third approach has been the appointment of a so-called public defender—a lawyer selected non-politically for full or part-time work and duly compensated for his services out of tax revenues. . . . The report brings the good tidings that a fourth system has proved successful in the few places where it has been tried. It is the so-called "mixed private-public system." Control is entirely non-political and shared by lawyers and laymen. Substantial fractions of the necessary funds come from both private and public sources.

DELMAR KARLEN, REPORT TO THE MAYOR OF THE CITY OF NEW YORK

Pages 10–11 (1965).

[A 1965 New York statute provided that legal counsel be provided at public expense for the indigent in all criminal cases except minor traffic infractions.*** The statute gave to the counties and cities the option of providing counsel through a public defender, a private legal aid society, a private assigned counsel system, or any combination of them. If private counsel were assigned the compensation was $15 per hour for in-court time and $10 per hour for out-of-court time, with a normal maximum of $300 for each misdemeanor case and $500 for each felony. At that time almost all indigent defendants in New York City for whom there were court-assigned counsel were represented by the Legal Aid Society, to which the City contributed $400,000 out of a Society budget of about $1,300,000. The Society employed full-time attorneys of specialized experience stationed regularly in the courthouse.

---

* The report was made by a Special Committee of The Association of the Bar of the City of New York and The National Legal Aid and Defender Association, of which Mr. Robert von Mehren was the chairman and Mr. Kenneth R. Franey the director.

*** N.Y. County Law §§ 722 to 722–F (Supp.1968–69).

Concern over the financial burdens to the City of New York led to a request by Judge Botein of the Appellate Division to the Institute of Judicial Administration of New York University to conduct a study of the comparative costs of representation by private assigned counsel and by the Legal Aid Society. The report to the mayor of the city by Professor Delmar Karlen, Director of the Institute, November 15, 1965, concluded:]

[I]t is evident that the cost of representing indigent defendants through a system of assigned counsel would be vastly greater than the cost of having them represented by the Legal Aid Society. According to the minimum estimate given above, the cost would be more than four times as great; and according to the maximum estimate, it might be 30 times as great. According to our most moderate estimate and best judgment, the cost would be approximately 10 times as great.

THE POOR AND COUNSEL IN CIVIL MATTERS

In all serious criminal cases, as earlier material makes manifest, there is a constitutional right in the indigent accused to have counsel provided for him. In civil matters, there appears to be no holding that the Constitution requires counsel be provided for those unable to retain them, whether in court cases or in office matters.* Yet the legal right to counsel, in criminal cases is based on something more fundamental than the law itself. It is based on a felt moral obligation by society to one needing a lawyer to see to it that he be able to have one as the surest means of attaining equal justice under law. This same sense of moral obligation, even though it has not taken legal form in civil matters, has led to different kinds of action to make counsel available in fact for the middle classes and for the poor.

One action was taken by the Supreme Court of the United States in a series of decisions culminating in the *United Mine Workers* case, supra 76. It struck down on constitutional grounds standards of the profession which hampered methods of making counsel available to the middle classes.

Another form of action is to provide the services of lawyers to those who need them. Organizations to provide these services to the poor—legal aid societies—are nearly a century old. Though long most inadequately financed they rendered legal services to hundreds of thousands, perhaps millions, of people. Until the 1960's legal aid was provided primarily by these societies which obtained their funds almost wholly from private sources and which rendered services

---

* Justice Douglas has intimated there is such a right. See Douglas, J., dissenting in Hackin v. Arizona, 389 U.S. 143 (1967). Property as well as life, liberty are explicitly protected by the Bill of Rights, and human dignity has come to be recognized as one of the basic values in our society.

essentially charitable in character and in tone. The creation of the Office of Economic Opportunity and its Legal Services Program brought about a revolution. In part the revolution comes from enlarged budgets and personnel. In largest part it comes from a new sense of individual right and social obligation given expression in national law, and from the wider scope of the work envisioned and undertaken on behalf of the poor by their lawyers.

THREE FEDERAL STATUTES OF 1964

In 1964, three federal statutes of importance in the provision of legal services were enacted. The first, the Civil Rights Act of 1964, enlarges the power of the Attorney General of the United States to bring suits to protect the exercise of civil rights. Pub.L. No. 88-352, 78 Stat. 241, 42 U.S.C.A. § 2000 et seq. (1964).

The second, The Criminal Justice Act of 1964, deals with the method of furnishing counsel for the indigent in the federal criminal courts. The Act provides for a decentralized plan, giving to each district court the power, with the approval of the judicial council of its circuit, to establish a plan which is any one of the following: "(1) Representation by private attorneys; (2) Representation by attorneys furnished by a bar association or a legal aid agency; or (3) Representation according to a plan containing a combination of the foregoing." The Act allows compensation not exceeding $15 per hour for time in court and $10 per hour for time out of court, with the ordinary maximum of $500 in a felony case and $300 in a misdemeanor case, and with the possibility of increase in extraordinary cases. The Act provides also for the services of others than counsel Pub.L. No. 88-455, 78 Stat. 552, 18 U.S.C.A. § 3006A (1964).

The third statute, the Economic Opportunity Act of 1964, states its purpose:

> "It is, therefore, the policy of the United States to eliminate the paradox of poverty in the midst of plenty in this Nation by opening to everyone the opportunity for education and training, the opportunity to work, and the opportunity to live in decency and dignity." Pub.L. No. 88-452, 78 Stat. 508, 42 U.S.C.A. § 2701 et seq. (1964).

The statute authorizes support for legal services. The Legal Services Program of the Office of Economic Opportunity has transformed the extent and even more the nature of legal services for the poor. The facts make manifest a revolution brought about by enlarged budgets and even more by a new sense of social obligation. The transformation, as said above, is from legal aid resting on humanitarian and charitable purposes to legal services granted as of right in the administration and development of the law; with legal services a part of the methods by which the poor may lift themselves out of poverty and participate fully in American life.

NOTES

(1) The implementation of the Criminal Justice Act of 1964 was the subject of a comprehensive Report of the Judicial Conference of the United States, reported in 36 F.R.D. 277 (1965). The Judicial Conference of the United States and the Department of Justice have recommended amendments to the system authorized by the Act. One change was an increase in the financial support given to "private defenders" as legal aid societies. Another matter considered was the contribution to their defense of the "marginally eligible" defendants who can pay some, but not all, of the costs of their defense. See Oaks, *Improving the Criminal Justice Act*, 55 A.B.A.J. 217 (1969).

(2) Writing in 1968 the Executive Director of the American Bar Foundation could say: "For some years past, and most clearly since the advent of the federal antipoverty program, it has been urged that a claimant of welfare benefits be treated as an applicant and not as a supplicant. . . . The legal services program of the Office of Economic Opportunity (OEO) has funded legal assistance programs to such an extent that the annual budgets for legal services for the poor have multiplied six times over since 1960 and more than ten times since 1955. . . . In larger perspective social justice for the poor is being rapidly transformed from a claim on private conscience to an institutionalized system of social insurance." Hazard, Social Welfare and Urban Problems, Thos. D. Sherrard, Ed., (1968) 113–116.

(3) The breadth of the activities of the Legal Services Program is shown vividly in "Law in Action", a monthly account of the program. The issue of December, 1968, for example, describes "We Can Help," a plan designed to acquaint the poor with their rights and with the legal services available. Unusual individual cases are mentioned, as one for the protection of a client's livelihood through prevention of suspension of his driver's license. Stress is laid on the protection of groups through test cases or class actions, say, as to widen the scope of food benefit programs and to assure fair hearings before welfare benefits are held up. Most important of all are affirmative measures to help the clients lift themselves out of poverty as through aid in the formation of credit unions and cooperatives.

(4) In November, 1968, the Department of Health, Education and Welfare announced a new legal services program conducted by the Department and directed to the 8,000,000 persons on public welfare. Its program will be coordinated with that of OEO. The governing statement of principles, "Meeting Legal Needs of the Poor", may be obtained from HEW. See Robb, *HEW Legal Services: Beauty or Beast*, 55 A.B.A.J. 346 (1969).

THE COMING OF O.E.O. AND ITS LEGAL SERVICES PROGRAM

HOWARD C. WESTWOOD, A STIR IN THE LAND

50 Judicature 158 (1967).

The Economic Opportunity Act was adopted in 1964, to be administered by the Office of Economic Opportunity. Its program was formulated late that year; it included, most happily, provision for help in the financing of legal aid projects in those communities having the wisdom and initiative to seek them. Then, indeed, did things begin to stir.

The OEO, of course, could not simply hand out funds without inquiry. It had to draw up some general specifications for the projects that it would help finance. In doing so it has performed a great service by emphasizing elements that the pauperized legal aid budgets of the past several years have had grievously to neglect. . . . One such element is that of bringing legal aid service physically closer to the people who need it. . . .

A second element is that of use of the test case and other means for effecting improvement in the law in fields having special impact on the poor, such as in the area of consumer's protection. Lawyers for business enterprise and labor unions have performed distinguished service for their clients in shaping the law for their clients' interest. On occasion legal aid societies also have demonstrated what a great contribution they could make to the suiting of the law to their clients' needs. They have instituted and won notable test cases. . . .

In addition to the elements to which OEO has required attention, two points are emerging about which even OEO has not yet given much thought, but which have long cried for notice and for action.

[The first point the author makes is the incongruity of denying legal aid to the poor man who can barely afford to retain private counsel when the known fact is that the services rendered to marginal clients by marginal lawyers is often incompetent and not infrequently unethical.] . . . Another point is looming. That is the extent of the fundamental right of the layman to a lawyer's service, a right so fundamental as to be of constitutional proportions. The constitutional right to counsel has been recognized in criminal cases. . . . Thus far there seems to have been an assumption that the right is limited to cases involving personal liberty. This is careless. . . .

On these questions legal aid societies have been strangely silent. Until they begin to ask such questions and to demand the answer that the professed principles of our society so plainly dictate, they are, I submit, derelict in the safeguarding of those in the community who are supposed to be in their charge. . . .

All this stir in the land is propelling legal aid forward with jet speed as compared with the snail's pace of only yesterday. It is being brought home to thoughtful people that this legal aid job, is, indeed, an enormous one. . . . Challenged as never before is the old leadership of the bar of legal aid. One may well wonder, and question, whether old leadership is up to meeting the challenge. If not, we need not greatly worry. For coming along in nearly every city is a generation of young lawyers ready and eager. If present leadership falters, stronger hands are reaching to take hold.

All this stir in the land is no passing matter. Legal aid is on the march, its ranks swelling each month. For behind it all there is the appeal of an idea that will never down. It is an idea that has stirred men for more than three hundred years. It can be expressed today no better than it was in earliest times when, at the grand council of officers of Cromwell's army, it was stated in these pregnant terms:

". . . the poorest he that is in England hath a life to live as the richest he."

A PEOPLE'S COUNSEL

[The Administrative Conference of the United States made an interim report in January, 1969, published in the Annual Report of the Conference for 1969. It recommended by divided vote the creation of "People's Counsel." The recommendation follows.]

4. (a) An organization should be authorized by statute to employ a staff to act as "People's Counsel." The People's Counsel should represent the interests of the poor in all Federal administrative rulemaking substantially affecting the poor.

(b) The People's Counsel should be charged with assuring that the views of significant separable minority interests among the poor are represented in such Federal administrative rulemaking. . . .

(d) The People's Counsel should be authorized to participate suitably in its own name to represent the interests of the poor in any Federal agency proceedings in which the poor have a substantial interest.

(e) The People's Counsel should be authorized to provide representation for organizations and groups of the poor who seek judicial review of administrative action substantially affecting their interests. . . .

5. (a) Congress should provide for an appropriate body to perform the functions outlined in Section 4. Deserving of consideration as such body would be a new single-purpose corporation, to be created by Congress, modeled on the Corporation for Public Broadcasting,

Pub.Law 90–129, 81 Stat. 368 (1967), 47 U.S.C.A. § 396, and to be known as the People's Counsel Corporation. . . .

6. All Federal agencies should be required by Executive order to notify the People's Counsel of all proposed rules which would have a substantial impact on the poor. . . .

Without prejudice to creating or empowering any other appropriate body to perform the general functions outlined in paragraphs 4, 5, and 6, any special provision therefor should be so structured as to take maximum advantage of the capabilities in this field of nongovernment organizations, and of other public bodies, including notably the Office of Economic Opportunity.

NOTE

See Bonfield, *Representation for the Poor in Federal Rule Making*, 67 Mich.L.Rev. 511 (1969).

SECTION 4. THE HATED

Introduction. Assume that a man who comes in and asks you to defend him is hated by your community or at least by your clientele. The hatred comes from the nature of the offense charged or the nature of the person or from both. Will you take the case?

The mere mention of a few well known cases will show the abiding nature of the problem: John Adams and his defense of the British soldiers after the Boston Massacre; the Anarchists case in Chicago in the 1880s; the Sacco-Vanzetti case after World War I; the prosecution of the Nazi saboteurs and of one of their accomplices during World War II; the prosecution of the Communist leaders after World War II. The case tendered you is not apt to be such a famous one. It will be one of the kind of which a former student wrote: "perhaps the most abuse I ever received was when as 'an obscure lawyer in a country town' I defended 'a member of a minority group accused of a grave crime' ".

There are strong considerations in favor of acceptance of the case. They include the right of an accused to have counsel; the importance in our pluralistic democracy that radical opinions be freely expressed; the duty of the profession to see to it that needed legal services be provided; the sense of personal obligation to help perform this duty and to aid a person in trouble; at times the benefit derived from the approval by a lawyer's particular's clientele of his participation in such a case.

A consideration against acceptance is the probable visitation on the lawyer of the hatred for his client with a loss of clientele, a consequence that has often occurred. The inexperience of the lawyer in the field in question is a factor, though this may call for association with another lawyer rather than declination of the case. The stage of the lawyer in practice has been mentioned by students in class discussion, with the conclusion proposed by them that the established lawyer is under a greater duty than the beginner. The established lawyer with a position attained and family ambitions to satisfy may reply that it is even more difficult to keep up with or to excel the Joneses than it is to catch up with them.

The organized bar surely has an obligation to see to it that counsel is made available. At a time when public feeling against Communists was particularly strong the House of Delegates of the American Bar Association, pursuant to a report of its Special Committee on Individual Rights as Affected by National Security, adopted the resolution below. Some local bar associations took special measures to help provide counsel in such cases. Later when racial animosities were stirred there was formed a broadly based "Lawyers' Committee for Civil Rights Under Law". And in at least one state especially affected the state bar association adopted a resolution calling for the assistance of counsel for all persons, and the officers have sought to implement the spirit of the resolutions.

Methods may be employed to blunt the effect of the hatred toward the client and the lawyer. They include appointment of the lawyer by the court, joint appointments, the joinder of several lawyers from well known firms in representation, and public statements whether by the lawyers or the bar association on the importance that counsel be provided for the unpopular.

NOTES

(1) In 1953 the House of Delegates of the American Bar Association, pursuant to a report of the Special Committee on Individual Rights as Affected by National Security (78 A.B.A.Rep. 133), adopted the following resolution.

II. *Resolved:*

1. That the American Bar Association *reaffirms the principles* that the right of defendants to the benefit of assistance of counsel and the duty of the bar to provide such aid even to the most unpopular defendants involves public acceptance of the correlative right of a lawyer to represent and defend, in accordance with the standards of the *legal profession,* any client without being penalized by having imputed to him his client's reputation, views or character.

2. That the Association will support any lawyer against criticism or attack in connection with such representation, when, in its judgment, he has behaved in accordance with the standards of the bar.

3. That the Association will *continue* to educate the profession and the public on the rights and duties of a lawyer in representing any client, regardless of the unpopularity of either the client or his cause.

4. That the Association request all state and local associations to cooperate fully in implementing these *declarations of principles.*

(2) Observe the several points of impact of the above declarations of principles made at a time of public concern over alleged Communist subversion: (1) the right of defendants; (2) the duty of the bar; (3) public acceptance; (4) implementation by state and local bar associations. In several cities local bar associations did implement the principles by the voluntary services of lawyers in the defense of the accused. Mr. Peter Holme has described a method used by the Denver Bar Association. Stone, Legal Education and Public Responsibility 51–56 (1959).

(3) Over the years the defense of the unpopular has had the consistent support of some national organizations, as the American Civil Liberties Union and the National Lawyers' Guild. The difficulties in the way of providing effective counsel for Negroes in some Southern states has led to the formation of national organization directed to providing counsel and to activities by students in some law schools.

THE STANDARD OF THE ENGLISH BARRISTER

SIR HARTLEY SHAWCROSS, THE EXPERIENCE OF NATION STATES, GREAT BRITAIN

54 Colum.L.Rev. 734, 741–742 n. 8 (1954).

The tradition [of the duty of a barrister to accept a brief for a hated defendant] was recently re-stated by the General Council of the Bar of England:

"I have recently heard it said that certain members of the Bar in one of Her Majesty's Colonies refused to accept a brief to defend an African, accused of offences of a quasi-political nature against public order. The suggestion is that those barristers made excuses and declined to act, their true reason being they thought that their popularity or reputation might be detrimentally affected by appearing for the defence in such a case. For the prosecution they might appear, but not for the defence.

"If this report were true it would disclose a wholly deplorable departure from the great traditions of our law and one which, if substantiated, both the Attorney General and the Bar Council, of which I happen to be Chairman, would have to deal with in the severest possible way.

"Among laymen on both sides of politics there are some foolish and shortsighted enough to think that a barrister may and should pick and choose the cases in which he is prepared to appear.

"It would be well if those people remembered how the present rule that a barrister must accept a brief on behalf of any client who wishes to retain him to appear before any court in which he holds himself out to practice—was finally established. It arose in 1792 over the prosecution of Tom Paine for publishing the second part of his Rights of Man. The great advocate, Erskine, who accepted the retainer to defend Paine and was deprived of his Office as Attorney General to the Prince of Wales for doing so, said—and said truly—in a famous speech: 'From the moment that any advocate can be permitted to say that he will or will not stand between the Crown and the subject arraigned in the Court where he daily sits to practise, from that moment the liberties of England are at an end.'" Annual Statement at the Bar of England, 1952.

NOTE

The work of Erskine in defending hated reformers is described in Campbell, VIII Lives of the Lord Chancellors. In his own time its effects reached far beyond the particular cases. "Thanks to Erskine's persuasive eloquence, twelve Tory jurymen acquitted Hardy and his fellow prisoners on the special charge, and reminded the government that the method of Robespierre was not wanted over here. . . . This timely check saved England from a reign of terror and perhaps ultimately from a retributive revolution." Trevelyan, History of England, bk. V., ch. 4 (1926, 1952).

AN AMERICAN EXAMPLE

A LAWYER'S DUTY AS TO A RETAINER IN AN UNPOPULAR CASE

34 A.B.A.J. 22 (1948).

A shining, concrete example of what an American lawyer feels called upon to do in behalf of justice and fair play, when he is asked to accept a retainer in a perhaps unpopular cause, is worth more in our profession than abstract canons. On December 2, 1947, Mr. Justice Frankfurter of the Supreme Court of the United States published in the Boston Globe a letter concerning the late Arthur D. Hill, of the Massachusetts Bar (Boston), who died on November 29. The account given as to what Arthur Hill said when he took the retainer in the Sacco-Vanzetti appeal, deserves a place in the annals of our profession, because it fulfills what Sir Norman Birkett and other great advocates have lately said as to the lawyer's duty. Mr. Justice Frankfurter wrote:

". . . Nothing is farther from my mind than to stir the dead embers of a tragic controversy. But I think it is important for the traditions of the law and of this Commonwealth now to make public the circumstances under which Arthur Hill became counsel for Sacco and Vanzetti in the final stages of that affair. . . .

"It was at this stage that I was asked if I would try to enlist Mr. Hill's legal services to undertake a final effort on behalf of the men, hopeless as it seemed by appeal to the federal law. I saw Arthur Hill, told him the situation and, more particularly, that if he undertook this thankless task it would have to be solely as an exercise of the public profession of the law, for it would have to be done without a fee.

"Without hesitation he made an answer that deserves permanence in the history of the legal profession. This is what he said:

" 'If the president of the biggest bank in Boston came to me and said that his wife had been convicted of murder, but he wanted me to see if there was any possible relief in the Supreme Court of the United States and offered me a fee of $50,000 to make such an effort, of course I would take the retainer as would, I suppose, everybody else at the Bar. It would be a perfectly honorable thing to see whether there was anything in the record which laid a basis for an appeal to the federal court.

" 'I do not see how I can decline a similar effort on behalf of Sacco and Vanzetti simply because they are poor devils against whom the feeling of the community is strong and they have no money with which to hire me. I don't particularly enjoy proceedings that will follow, but I don't see how I can possibly refuse to make the effort.' "

NOTES

(1) As a young lawyer, President John Adams defended Captain Thomas Preston, one of the British soldiers who took part in the Boston Massacre in 1770. Later he wrote: "The Part I took in Defense of Captn. Preston and the Soldiers, procured me Anxiety and Obloquy enough. It was, however, one of the most gallant, generous, manly and disinterested Actions of my whole Life, and one of the best Pieces of Service I ever rendered my Country. Judgment of Death against those Soldiers would have been as foul a Stain upon this Country as the Executions of the Quakers or Witches, anciently. As the Evidence was, the verdict of the Jury was exactly right." Legal Papers of John Adams, Wroth and Zobelled, Vol. 3, p. 33 (1965).

(2) In a vivid autobiography of a young lawyer who "travels a road that separates him from his community", mention is made of the influence of his decision on his wife and child, his partner, and on his own economical and political future. "I explained all this to Camille but there was really no need. Along with Jim, she believed that we really had no choice in the matter". Charles Morgan, A Time to Speak, x, 74, 75 (1964).

(3) A hated accused is entitled as of course to full protective measures from his lawyer and also from the judge. When a defendant was tried and convicted under the influence of the presence of a mob, without his lawyer seeking a continuance or a change of venue and without the judge taking such measures on his own initiative, the conviction was upset on habeas corpus. Downer v. Dunaway, 53 F.2d 586 (5th Cir. 1931). When the lawyers for Negro accused were intimidated by local prejudice from challenging the practice of systematic exclusion of Negroes from the grand and the petit juries, the federal court took judicial notice of the intimidation and set the conviction aside. United States ex rel. Goldsby v. Harpole, 263 F.2d 71 (5th Cir. 1959); United States ex rel. Seals v. Wiman, 304 F.2d 53 (5th Cir. 1962).

IN RE ADES

United States District Court, D. Maryland, 1934. 6 F.Supp. 467.

[Respondent was ordered to show cause why he should not be disbarred. One charge against him was that he had volunteered his services to defend several negroes charged with crime, who he believed would otherwise not be adequately represented.]

SOPER, CIRCUIT JUDGE. . . . The Canons of Professional Ethics of the American Bar Association and the decisions of the courts quite generally prohibit the direct solicitation of business for gain by an attorney either through advertisement or personal communication; and also condemn the procuring of business by indirection through touters of any kind. . . .

Notwithstanding these salutary rules, it cannot be laid down as an inflexible maxim that a lawyer may never volunteer his services to a litigant, where the litigant is in need of assistance, or where important issues are involved in the case; and this may be so even though questions of a controversial or political character are at stake. Thus we read in Boswell's Life of Johnson (Hill's Edition), vol. 3, pp. 99, 100, 229, 230, 241, 243, of the habeas corpus proceeding in an English court in the interest of James Somerset, a negro slave who had escaped from his master, 20 Howell's State Trials, 1, 23, Loftt's Reports, 1772, p. 1, where distinguished counsel appeared on the negro's behalf; and of the similar cases in Scotland of Knight v. Wedderburn and Shedden v. Shedden, reported in 20 Howell's State Trials 1, note. In New York, Andrew Hamilton was brought into the libel case of John Peter Zenger in 1734 by the "Sons of Liberty" to assist counsel appointed by the court to defend him. Great American Lawyers, edited by Wm. Draper Lewis, vol. 1, p. 30, 17 Howell's State Trials, 676, 686, 694. Alexander Hamilton gratuitously appeared for the defense in Croswell v. The People in New York in 1804. Great American Lawyers, vol. 1, 373. George Hay and William Wirt in 1800 volunteered to defend James Thompson Callender. Beveridge's "Life of John Marshall," vol. 3, 38, Wharton State Trials, 692. Coming to the state of Maryland, it is recalled that Luther Martin tendered his services in the defense of Aaron Burr, when charged with treason, Beveridge's "Life of John Marshall," vol. 3, p. 428; and that in the Dred Scott Case, in which it was said that the free soil interests were in charge of both sides of the litigation, Reverdy Johnson volunteered his services out of consideration for the court. Ewing on Legal and Historical Status of the Dred Scott Decision, 29, 30; Shouler's History of the United States, vol. 5, 378; Steiner, Life of Reverdy Johnson, 37. Lest it may seem to be a far cry from these historic incidents to the present case, it may be noticed that more recently, in State v. Smith, 84 W.Va. 59, 99 S.E. 332, 333, it was held not to be unprofessional for an attorney to go to the jail and agree to serve five ignorant Russians there confined without specific charge being lodged against them. The court said: "In many, in fact in most instances, it is unethical, and may be a ground of suspension from the practice, but there are many instances in which such would not be the case, and a general statement that one solicited employment without showing that such solicitation was in a dishonorable or a disreputable way is not a sufficient charge to justify suspension or disbarment." In Scopes v. Tennessee, 154 Tenn. 105, 289 S.W. 363, 53 A.L.R. 821, Clarence Darrow, of counsel for the defense, was secured by the American Civil Liberties Union; and in the Scottsboro Case, Powell v. Alabama, 287 U.S. 45, 53 S.Ct. 55, 77 L.Ed. 158, 84 A.L.R. 527, where the Supreme Court set aside the conviction of seven negroes charged with the crime of rape upon two white girls, on the ground that the trial court had not provided counsel for them in the proper manner, Walter H. Pollak, leading counsel for the defense on appeal, was secured by the International Labor Defense. . . . it should be said, lest a wrong conclusion be drawn from this discussion, that repeated attempts on the part of an attorney to volunteer his services, even in needy cases, will be looked upon askance by the legal profession, and will likely lead to a critical examination of the attorney's conduct. . . .

[The court found the evidence failed to sustain the charge that the respondent improperly injected himself into the case, with knowledge of his client's guilt and contrary to the latter's desire. On charges not here relevant, respondent was reprimanded.]

NOTES

(1) It is not improper solicitation for a bar association committee on the enforcement of the usury laws to represent free of charge the victim of a usurious moneylender in defending against illegal exactions and in bringing an action to recover the amounts illegally paid. Gunnels v. Atlanta Bar Ass'n, 191 Ga. 366 (1940).

(2) On the propriety of a group of lawyers who opposed the New Deal and thought its legislation unconstitutional offering gratuitous legal services to indigent persons deprived of their constitutional rights, see American Bar Association Committee Opinion No. 148 (1935), discussed, 36 Colum.L.Rev. 993 (1936).

POLITICAL TRIALS

ELLIOTT E. CHEATHAM, A LAWYER WHEN NEEDED *

Pages 28–31 (1963).

When a solicitous system of law administration gives opportunities for repeated delays, the ordinary crime is troubling enough. Far

---

* With the permission of The Columbia University Press.

more troubling is the political case, which is instituted or which is handled by counsel for one side or the other not so much to secure the conviction or the acquittal of the particular defendant, but to advance some high political end of change and of revolution or counterrevolution. Each one of the elements of the case may have a political motivation: the law on which the prosecution is based, the accused and his conduct, the lawyer for the defense and his tactics, the prosecution and its methods, the judge and his actions, and the public and their attitude. . . . The political trial is disturbing because in all its elements it differs from our ideal of an adversary proceeding. This ideal assumes that the accused and his counsel are seeking acquittal, the prosecution is seeking an adjudication on the narrow legal issue, the judge is impartial, and public feelings are kept out the case.

Political trials keep recurring. In times and places remote from us there were the two most famous trials recorded by history or tradition—the trials of Socrates and of Jesus. In our own times, but in other places, there were the Reichstag fire trial in Nazi Germany, the Communist purge trials, the hippodrome trials of the Castro regime in Cuba, and, of a wholly different tone, the trial of the pacifist agitator Gandhi. Our own history has been studded with such trials. James Otis used court attacks on the writs of assistance, as he employed his pamphlets, to inflame the resistance of the colonies to the mother country. The fugitive slave law cases were effective means of stirring antislavery sentiment. The congressional hearings on Communists have been employed to expose the Party and its members and sympathizers. In our day the sit-in demonstrations and the accompanying arrests, prosecution, and publicity are a form of attack on racial segregation.

Let us consider some of the elements of a political trial and how badly they fit into our traditional values. Begin with the accused. In the ordinary case it is assumed he is seeking acquittal above all other things. In the political trial it may be quite otherwise, as Socrates and Jesus illustrate. Socrates, accused of corrupting the youth and certainly guilty of disturbing inquiry into established ways, sought acquittal only on his own terms. He urged that he was entitled to support at the public expense rather than condemnation, and would not accept freedom through flight. Jesus, as an ancient tradition of sacrifice has it, was fated to die here so that men might live hereafter. He did not seek to escape his fate even from Pilate, "the local commander of the military government of a foreign occupation power." To take a modern illustration, Gandhi, in stating the case in his campaign of civil disobedience, sought the severest punishment and urged upon the judge the reasons for it.

There are other less exalted examples of accused so convinced of the importance and justice of the cause that they insist on the trial being so conducted as to advance the cause regardless of their personal fate. They use the witness stand as a forum for the statement of their views and the trial as a means of exposing the system they attack. They accept conviction content in the knowledge that the blood of the martyrs is the seed of the Church. How can our law deal with and hold within bounds defendants who begin by rejecting the purposes of the administration of law and the whole system of which the law is a part? A partial answer was given in the case of the prosecution of the Communist leaders when one of the accused sought, at the end of a nine-months trial, to substitute himself for his able counsel in addressing the jury. The trial judge denied the permission. The action of the trial judge in denying the request was affirmed by the Court of Appeals for, as Judge Learned Hand wrote: "it is difficult to assign any other motive for his request than that he wished to make a flaming address to the jury which would have reverberations not only inside but outside the court room." [26]

The lawyer for the defense may share the views of his client and may seek to conduct the case for the larger ends they have in common. He may speak over the heads of the judge and the jury to the public in language of the cause he would advance. What an unequaled opportunity when the cause is embodied in the drama of a trial, and when the drama is covered by the press and possibly by radio and television! The lawyer may even spurn lesser grounds of acquittal and, with or without the client's consent, help to secure conviction and execution. What should be done with such a lawyer? Here we are on firmer ground than when dealing with the client himself, for the lawyer is one to whom the profession's admonitions of loyalty and zeal are directed. Certainly the lawyer, guilty of disloyalty to his client because of loyalty to a larger cause, would under our standards deserve the harshest discipline. This is made explicit in the *Ades* case, discussed above, in which Judge Soper stated of the Communist counsel that if he offends, "by subordinating the interest of his client to the interest of the organization employing him, the remedy of proper discipline is in the hands of the court." [27]

NOTE

"Modern means of communication do not restrict participation in or reactions to a trial by those present and, with some delay, by a wider educated public. . . . The dynamics of such an undertaking—the vicarious participation of a virtually unlimited public in the unfolding of a political reality, re-created and severely compressed for trial purposes into categories within easy reach of the public's understanding—fashions a new political weapon." Kircheimer, Political Justice: The Use of Legal Procedure for Political Ends 7 (1961).

26. United States v. Dennis, 183 F.2d 201, 233 (C.A.2d, 1950). [Author's footnote.]

27. In re Ades, 6 F.Supp. 467, 477 (D. C.Md.1934). [Author's footnote.]

SECTION 5. PERSONAL INJURY AND DEATH CLAIMS

A. THE PUBLIC CONCERN

FRANKLIN, CHANIN, AND MARK, ACCIDENTS, MONEY, AND THE LAW: A STUDY OF THE ECONOMICS OF PERSONAL INJURY LITIGATION

61 Colum.L.Rev. 1–5 (1961).*

A. *The Accident Problem.* For its increasing mobility, spreading cities, and booming technology, modern society pays a fearful price in accidental injuries. Each year accidents claim 10,000,000 victims, of whom 100,000 are fatalities. In a nation of 180,000,000 people this means that over 5 per cent of the population annually become accident statistics.

Pale before the human cost, but staggering in its own right, is the economic price of accidents. Evidence for recent years suggests that lost wages and medical expenses alone amount to almost $5,000,000,000 annually. In addition, there are other, more indirect consequences, and the total economic cost of accidents may well exceed $15,000,000,000.

Countermeasures proceed on two principal fronts: reduction of the number of accidents and alleviation of the dislocating effects of those that do happen. Better understanding of human behavior, better designing of human products, and safer habits have helped to check the accident rate and to hold it below the rate of population increase. But as long as man, his machines and his materials are fallible, accidents can be expected, and society must be prepared to grapple with their consequences.

B. *Compensating the Accident Victim.* From earliest times, society has relied primarily upon the cash payment to ease the problems confronting the accident victim. Although everyone recognizes that money is an inadequate substitute for a lost limb or excruciating pain, monetary balm may well have been the only practical way to handle the victim's problems in the past—and that may still be true today. But a more satisfying reason for its use is that with items such as medical expenses and lost income commonly present, much of the loss incurred is susceptible of monetary evaluation.

Society's use of cash payments differs according to the circumstances of the accident. Chiefly, the questions are whether the accident occurred on the job or off, and if the latter, who was at fault?

---

* The monograph is republished in Dollars, Delay and the Automobile Victim: Studies in Reparation for Highway Injuries and Related Court Problems (Walter E. Meyer Research Institute of Law, 1968).

If the victim is hurt on the job, workmen's compensation statutes generally determine the manner and amount of payment. . . .

If the accident is not covered by workmen's compensation, the victim, if he is to have any legal remedy, must seek reparation under the tort law. The common law tort rules are based upon two major premises. First, people should be allowed some freedom of action and should not have to pay for injuries that they cause unless their conduct has fallen below some standard of reasonableness. Second, people should show some care for their own safety, and should not be allowed to recover if their own fault has contributed to the accident. . . .

There has been much criticism of this system, particularly of late, and many have suggested that there be some change. Those who would effect a change, however, do not agree on what is wrong with the present system. Some believe that fault is not a sensible basis for determining the allocation of loss. In our complex society many people are injured in accidents that cannot be ascribed to anyone's legal fault and, the critics contend, these losses should not be left to fall wholly upon the victims, who are usually the ones least able to bear them. Others, while not opposed on theoretical grounds to a reparation system based on individual fault, are concerned with problems that have arisen in its administration. They point, for example, to the long delay often encountered by victims in prosecuting their claims. Many direct their criticisms to the recoveries themselves, contending that they are both inequitable in amount and inadequate in form. Then there are those who are not troubled by the system per se but rather by the role the lawyer plays in it. They maintain, among other things, that lawyers receive too large a share of the recoveries obtained.

Just as the critics do not agree on *why* there should be a change, they also disagree about the type of change needed. A system of benefits somewhat analogous to workmen's compensation has been viewed by many as a panacea for most of our existing problems. It is contended that such a system would guarantee a limited, but equitable, amount of compensation to deserving victims, would provide a remedy for delay, and would prevent excessive lawyers' fees. Others, who are less willing to abandon so deep rooted a system, prefer less drastic remedies: utilization of quasi-judicial personnel to reduce delay, the use of impartial medical experts to ferret out malingerers and to aid juries in resolving disputes between experts, and other innovations intended to modify rather than abolish the common law system.

NOTE

"The present system for compensation of traffic victims continues to draw heavy fire. The serious shortcomings commonly identified in current complaints are inherent in any system founded primarily on negligence law and liability insurance.

"One revealing way of viewing the system is to examine liability insurance as a consumer product. In particular, how much of the premium dollar comes back in net benefits compensating for losses not otherwise compensated? The answer is shocking.

> Disposition of the Liability Insurance Premium Dollar
>
> | | |
> |---|---|
> | General Insurance Overhead | $ .33 |
> | Claims Administration Costs | .23 |
> | Net to Victims: | |
> | Paid as "Compensation" Above Loss | .14 |
> | Paid for Losses also Compensated from Other Sources | .11 |
> | Paid in Compensation of Losses Not Otherwise Compensated | .19 |
> | | $1.00" |

Keeton, *Basic Protection Automobile Insurance—A Reform Tailored to the Need,* 5 Ga.St.B.J. 117 (1968).

THE INDIVIDUALS INVOLVED AND THEIR LAWYERS

The injured party in an automobile accident is, typically, a necessitous person, dependent on his earnings for the support of himself and his family. He does not know where to get a good lawyer. He is a one-shot client who will not return to the lawyer for further services. He cannot himself secure the names of witnesses to the accident or obtain leads to the relevant evidence.

The actual defendant is typically a liability insurance company or else a large industrial company, with a well organized staff of lawyers and claim agents who are on the scene of the accident promptly to seek a settlement or at least to obtain evidence. The defendant is, of course, under no financial pressure to effect a settlement.

There are many lawyers who would like to have tort claims against solvent defendants, varying from the inexperienced, to whom the case is turned over by a friend, to those who are expert in obtaining and handling cases. There is also the lay intruder who, after obtaining from the injured person a written retainer with the lawyer's name in blank, turns the case over to a lawyer who agrees to give him a share of the recovery.

The defendants lawyers are nearly always experienced men with adequate staffs of claim agents and investigators.

At times, the two sets of lawyers are put down as deadly enemies of one another, with the defendants' lawyers seeking to extirpate their adversaries. This is wrong. In a particular case each lawyer does his best for his side, and the claim agents for defendants may seek to use the machinery of professional discipline to hold within bounds the more assertive of their adversaries. Yet looked at in a larger way the two sets of lawyers are complementary with each dependent upon the other for existence. If there were no claimants and claimants' lawyers, there would be no defendants and no defendants' lawyers. The complementary nature of the relation is made obvious in the encyclopedia, "Trials", devoted primarily to personal injury cases. Volume I of the set opens with two forewords, "Plaintiff's Foreword" and "Defense Foreword". The two forewords are alike in urging the continuance of the use of tort law, liability based on fault, jury trials, and the trial bar in this field, and in denouncing those who would do away with them.

B. SOLICITATION OF PERSONAL INJURY CLAIMS

Dear Jim: *

I see by the papers that your Committee is out to make a drive on what it calls "ambulance chasing," and word has reached me via the grapevine that you have decided to make an example of somebody, and that I have been selected as Exhibit A.

I pay you the compliment of believing that you didn't make the selection. You and I have been pretty good friends ever since law school, and I never did you any harm that I know of, and both of us know that there are some mutual debts and favors between us that would make either one of us a plain heel if he went after the other. I think I recognize the fine Italian hand of some other gentlemen on your Committee. Three of them are country lawyers who think that they were entitled to some personal injury cases that came my way instead—one of them with a $27,500 verdict within the last three months. Another one represents a railroad, and the last time he tangled with me the Supreme Court affirmed a $35,000 recovery in a clear liability broken back case that he didn't have the common decency to settle. Two others try some cases for the biggest liability insurance companies in the state, which speaks for itself; and one is a professor at the university law school who is full of eethicks because he never practised a day in his life. It is not hard to see where the shooting is coming from.

I am writing you this letter partly to get it off my chest, and partly to let you know what your Committee is in for if it goes ahead with Exhibit A. You can make any use of it you like, but it isn't going to do any of you any good if it gets into the newspapers—and that is where a copy of it is going if you make it public. I have some friends there who have given me a little help now and then, and don't think they wouldn't love it.

---

* A letter to a member of a Grievance Committee. Printed in Selected Readings on the Legal Profession page 130 (1962) and reprinted by permission of the copyright owner, West Publishing Co., and of the author who, at his own request, remains anonymous.

The charge against me is that I solicit personal injury claims. Granted. I admit it. I'm proud of it. And what the hell is wrong with it?

We will, if you please, leave out a lot of pure baloney that I have no doubt your Committee has been talking. We will forget about perjury and subornation and shanghaied witnesses. You know damn well that I have never done anything like that in my life. And we won't talk about professional incompetence. I have tried cases before every judge in the state, and they will all tell you that I try a clean, fair case, and get everything out there is in it. If you go through with your little disbarment proceeding, I will call every damn one of them as a witness to how I conduct a trial, and make them testify, under subpoena, if necessary. It won't be necessary in very many cases. You know as well as I do that there are plenty of attorneys who are getting away with murder at the trial, and if your committee had the sense that God gave a goose, it would go after them instead of picking on me, and I would be the first to back it up. The criminal law shysters alone would keep you busy for ten years, and for that matter there is one man on your Committee who has no business casting any rocks at anybody, and you know whom I mean. Also, we won't talk about exorbitant fees. I never have collected more than thirty-three and a third, except in some rare cases where I had to do a lot of work and the chances of any recovery at all were very slim. My clients are satisfied, and your Committee hasn't had any complaints from any of them. And finally, for God's sake quit talking about ambulances. I never have chased an ambulance, and I don't know of anyone who ever did. I get some of my information from nurses and internes and desk girls—and why not?—but an ambulance driver isn't worth a damn. Usually he doesn't even know the victim's name.

Leaving out all that poppy cock, what is the matter with solicitation? Every lawyer solicits cases, and you and your Committee know it. He either solicits cases or he starves to death or goes into the real estate business and solicits prospects there. The difference between lawyers is that some of them are not hypocrites and come out and say frankly that they want the business, and the rest do it indirectly. They solicit by joining everything in sight and getting friendly with a lot of people they don't give a damn about in the hope that they will some day conceivably have some legal work, and then inviting them to dinner when they do. I don't want to get personal, but I don't think it was a sudden and powerful attack of religion that made you give up your Sunday golf and take to ushering in the First Presbyterian Church in a wing collar. And I don't think it was only a coincidence that they picked you to draw that trust agreement and handle the suit about the new organ. Maybe you don't call it that, but I say you solicited that business. You wanted it, and you went out and got it.

It's all right with me; I think you had a perfect right to do it, but I claim the same privilege.

A whole lot of lawyers are more direct than that, and some of them are on your Committee. One of them picked up a client at the country club about a month ago by betting him $50 on a golf match, and then offering to cancel the bet when he won, in return for a little legal employment. Another one horned in on a conversation at the bar, asked some questions and handed out some free advice, and wound up by taking over some corporation work that ought to net him a fee of at least $5,000. Another one told the president of a milling concern that his attorney had mishandled a tax matter—P.S. he got the job. And I could go on and fill up the page.

Well Jim, since I heard what was up, I have been collecting affidavits about these little matters on the part of your Committee. If you don't think I've got them ask the boys whom they took those clients away from, and who their friends are—and how well some of that advice panned out. I have evidence now on twenty-three separate cases of solicitation (and I mean direct) by members of your Committee, and by the time you get ready to blow the lid off I will have some more. I haven't got an organization for nothing. The moment you start your little disbarment proceeding, I am going to submit those affidavits to your Committee, and when they refuse to act on them I intend to file them with a petition to the Supreme Court. I don't know what the Court will do about them, but I can tell you what the newspapers will do.

But the horrible thing about me is supposed to be that I solicit personal injury cases. In other words, instead of playing golf with a lot of business men who never move without a lawyer at their elbows, I go out and offer legal assistance to people who are poor and sick and injured, and who are too helpless or haven't the money or the friends or the education or the intelligence to look after their own interests or even to know that they need a lawyer and what he can do for them. I do, and I am damn proud of it. If you could see these clients of mine, Jim, it would break your heart. I am going to have some exhibits of my own in your disbarment proceeding, and some of them are going to come in on crutches and some in wheel chairs, and some are going to be led in because they are blind. They will all testify for me. It will make quite a story for the papers. With pictures.

The Constitution of the United States, and our own state constitution, are supposed to guarantee a man advice of counsel. But the guarantee isn't much good to him unless he can get the counsel. The defendant in a criminal case, if he shows up in court without a lawyer, has some second-rater assigned to defend him; but the plaintiff in a personal injury case never gets into court at all unless he gets the lawyer first. I will defend to the last ditch the proposition that it is the business of the bar to see that he gets counsel, and that when he can't come to the attorney, it is up to the attorney to go to him.

They tell me that I am supposed to wait around until he gets well and somebody tells him I am a good personal injury lawyer, and sends him to see me. And what is supposed to be happening to his case in the meantime? You don't win cases without witnesses; and who is going to get the witnesses for him while he is flat on his back with a broken coccyx or one leg off at the knee? You know as well as I do what even twenty-four hours does to the witnesses of an automobile collision and to their memories even if you ever succeed in locating them. Well, what about three weeks or a month? And what is the defendant doing in the meantime? Whenever the street car company has an accident, it gets statements down on paper the same day from everyone within a hundred yards, and follows up the case for a week. Who gets those witnesses for the man lying there with the fractured skull? And what chance has he got a month later of even finding out their names?

And what about the defendant's claim agent, who arrives as soon as the man is conscious, and talks him into settling the case for ten percent of what it is worth, without "the expense of a lawyer"? One of your Committee sent a . . . around to see a twenty-two year old boy with a leg amputated at the hip and take a release for $100. And he fought me like hell over it when I got it set aside for a $9,000 verdict in court. Another one pulled the old joint tortfeasor release, and sent the driver of a brokendown tin can who was on relief in to settle for $50 and say that was all he had. All that I have to say is that if it is legal or ethical for one lawyer to send an agent in to see a helpless man who is crippled for life and take his claim away from him for the smallest amount he can get by with, it is just as legal and ethical for another lawyer to go to him and say, "Don't sign that; you are entitled to more, and I can get it for you."

But my solicitation is supposed to be "organized," and so I ought to be disbarred. Of course it's organized. It has to be. I need as much of an organization as a liability insurance company, and for a better reason. I have to get to my clients before the claim agents settle with them for as little as they will take; and I have to find their witnesses before the defendants work on them too long. And if I take cases away from other lawyers, at least I offer the client better service than they can, because of that organization. Ask . . . about the case he lost, where I came in afterward and got the new trial on the basis of newly discovered evidence and the $12,000 verdict. I am a specialist in a particular kind of case, and I am organized for the purpose of getting injured human beings compensation for their ruined lives. If there is any better reason to organize, I don't know it.

Well, Jim, your Committee will be pleased to hear that I am coming in with another flock of affidavits, about the claim agents, and that quite a few of them have something to say about some of the Committee, and their clients. If we are going to have a war, it might as well be a good one, and we will drag the whole business out into the open, and try it in the papers. It will be a healthy experience for the bar. I hope your Committee will have the sense to drop this business where it stands—in fact, I haven't much doubt that after this letter gets passed around they will decide that it is all a mistake and I am really purer than the lilies of the field. But if they don't, don't say I didn't warn you. As for the Supreme Court, I'll take my chances. Some of them practised law not so long ago, and what with the last appointments, more than half of them were plaintiff's attorneys.

I don't want this to be personal between you and me. I am a friend of yours, and always will be, and nothing that I turn loose is going to be aimed at you. I am writing this chiefly to let you know where things stand.

Yours, as always,

. . . .

In the Matter of the Petition of THE ASSOCIATION OF THE BAR OF THE CITY OF NEW YORK, NEW YORK COUNTY LAWYERS' ASSOCIATION and BRONX COUNTY BAR ASSOCIATION for an Inquiry by the Court into Certain Abuses and Illegal and Improper Practices Alleged in the Petition.

Supreme Court of New York, Appellate Division, 1928.
222 App.Div. 580, 227 N.Y.S. 1.

DOWLING, P. J. The Association of the Bar of the City of New York, New York County Lawyers' Association and Bronx County Bar Association, the three representative associations of lawyers in the First Department, have presented to this court a joint petition, wherein they set forth that there exists in this department a practice commonly known as "ambulance chasing," that is, the solicitation by lawyers of their employment to prosecute damage cases on the basis of the contingent fees, the amount of which is not fixed with reference to the nature or extent of the prospective services. Such agreements of retainer are frequently signed by injured persons, improvidently or ignorantly, when they are suffering from injuries recently received, which render them incapable of exercising a discriminating judgment.

"Ambulance chasing" is described more in detail as follows: Lawyers engaged in the practice referred to, by themselves or through their agents who are sometimes laymen, promise or give to persons sustaining personal injuries some valuable consideration to induce them to employ such lawyers to prosecute claims for damages for their injuries. Such lawyers, through their agents, in some instances, maintain a well-organized and effective system of solicitation by which they obtain prompt information of accidents resulting in personal injuries, from hospital employees, ambulance drivers, taxicab drivers and others who are so situated as to have early knowledge, and they pay them compensation for such information. Solicitation for such business frequently takes place immediately after an injury has been received, often on the same day, in hospitals, in homes, and at the bedsides of injured persons, while they are in pain or otherwise distressed on account of their injuries.

In some instances the lawyer or his agent agrees to advance the costs of legal proceedings and to assume the payment of hospital expenses and medical bills as an inducement to the employment of the lawyer. The injured persons are solicited to sign printed contracts of retainer, and they frequently do so with only vague comprehension of what the papers contain or of their purpose and effect and without having at the time any knowledge of the character or standing or ability of the person retained except from a person or persons interested, frequently in a pecuniary way, in securing the retainer. It is alleged that "ambulance chasing" pursued in the manner above described has been systematized to such an extent that the lawyers engaged in it control a large number of the so-called personal injury actions upon the calendars of the courts in this department, and these cases constitute a substantial proportion of the cases on the jury calendar of the Supreme Court. It is largely on account of the accumulation of such cases upon the calendars of the Trial Terms of the Supreme and other courts that the present congestion in the courts exists. . . .

The petition further recites that from the practices above described there flow other harmful results, among which are the following: Poor and ignorant claimants are overreached and oppressed by importunate lawyers, insensible to the obligations of their calling, or by solicitors acting in their behalf; claims to a great number and involving a large aggregate amount come into the control of a single lawyer, who in many cases advances filing and jury fees, views the business as a commercial transaction, and settles or litigates the claims on the basis of the pecuniary advantage to himself rather than in the best interest of the client; clients are compelled to pay unconscionable fees, wholly incommensurate with the services performed or the results obtained; lawyers are tempted to, and sometimes do, resort to improper and illegal practices, frequently induced by reason of their financial interest in the result, and they otherwise violate their obligations to the courts and to the profession; and finally, thousands of suits are brought without merit, and without any intention by the attorneys for the claimant to bring them to trial.

It is further averred that the evils inherent in the practice of "ambulance chasing" are by no means confined to the activities of lawyers for the claimants, but they have brought in their wake activities on the part of representatives of defendants in those cases, which are equally improper and unlawful. In many instances, it is a race between solicitors for lawyers, who seek to get retainers from the unfortunate injured persons, and representatives of the prospective defendants, who seek to get releases from the same injured persons for little or nothing, as to which of these would reach the bedside first. In that way the poor unfortunates are overreached, their signatures are obtained to retainers or releases, at a time when, by reason of suffering, ignorance or lack of time to consider, the injured person can exercise no proper judgment in the protection of his or her rights. To the extent that members of the bar are concerned in such practices, on behalf of defendants, either by themselves, or through directing or suggesting the activities of others, their conduct is as reprehensible as that of lawyers for claimants.

The petition recites that there has been widespread public criticism of the practices referred to and that such practices with their attendant evils, tend to undermine public confidence in the administration of justice.

The petitioners, therefore, pray (1) that an investigation be ordered by this court, to be conducted by itself or by such other appropriate procedure as it shall determine, in order that a judicial inquiry may be made into the practices hereinbefore alleged to exist and into any other illegal and improper practices.

(2) That upon the conclusion of such investigation all parties found to have been participating in any such practices be brought into court in some appropriate action or proceeding and dealt with according to law; and that such other remedy or remedies may be granted, and such judicial discipline exercised, as may be found to be effective and proper, to correct the abuses that may be found to exist. . . .

The prayer of the petitioners herein will be granted, and an investigation will be ordered into the abuses complained of. . . .

NOTES

(1) The power of the court to conduct the general inquiry ordered in the principal case was upheld in People ex rel. Karlin v. Culkin, 248 N.Y. 465 (1928), infra p. 150. Is the effectiveness of such an inquiry blunted by the decisions of the Supreme Court of the United States, infra, which extend the protection of the Constitution to a lawyer who refuses to answer questions in disciplinary proceedings on the ground the answer might incriminate him?

(2) The ambulance chaser frequently bases the justification of his conduct in getting and preparing his case on the heinousness of his adversary and the consequent strong measures required for protection of the injured party. The company claim agent replies in kind. See In re Kopleton, 229 App.Div. 111 (1930), and In re Robinson, 151 App.Div. 589 (1912), affirmed

209 N.Y. 354 (1913). The disbarment of a lawyer engaged in solicitation of personal injury cases was denied by a divided court in a case in which the investigation was promoted by an association of railroads. Re Heinrich, 10 Ill.2d 357, cert. den. 355 U.S. 805 (1957); Annot., 67 A.L.R.2d 859 (1959).

(3) The justice who conducted the investigation ordered in the principal case made a report in which he recommended judicial supervision of retainers and of settlements. (1) He urged that a contract of retainer obtained while an injured person is in a hospital or within fifteen days after the occurrence of the accident should be void unless made with the approval of the court. (The question occurs whether the delay in investigation by the claimant's lawyer or his representative during the waiting period would not be harmful to the claimant. Modern disclosure proceedings by which the claimant can obtain much evidence from the defendant might mitigate the harm done by delay in investigation. But most claims are small and do not justify the expense entailed by such proceedings.) (2) As to settlements the justice urged there should be judicial supervision, stating "[i]f the courts are to assume a large measure of control over the relations between injured persons and their attorneys, they should also be required to protect such claimants from imposition by defendants."

(4) A case which describes the organization of solicitation of personal injury claims under the Federal Employers' Liability Act is Atchison, Topeka & Santa Fe Ry. Co. v. Andrews, 338 Ill.App. 552 (1949). A Chicago lawyer organized a family partnership, consisting of his wife and brother to solicit business for him, with agents including numerous railroad employees and with the accidents involved occurring in the southwestern states over two thousand miles away from the place of suit and trial. The court enjoined the solicitation of claims by the lawyer and the partnership and the further prosecution of actions commenced. Does federal law govern the scope of the right and, perhaps, the privileges of the lawyer under the federal law claim?

IN THE MATTER OF JOHN RUFFALO, JR.

United States Court of Appeals, Sixth Circuit, 1966.
370 F.2d 447.

[At the instigation of employees of the Association of American Railroads a proceeding for disbarment was brought in the Supreme Court of Ohio against a Cleveland lawyer who specialized in personal injury and death claims and who had previously been censured for solicitation of practice. The original charges included advancements of living expenses to clients. During the hearing before a Board of Commissioners it appeared that the lawyer had employed surreptitiously a brakeman of the Baltimore and Ohio Railroad Company as an investigator in his off time. The Board then included this conduct as a charge against the lawyer and gave him extended time to meet it. The Board sought to obtain from the lawyer his records as to payments to the brakeman but was unsuccessful, as the lawyer replied: "We worked on that basis [of minimal records] for the particular reason that we didn't want this man to be accused of, which he wasn't doing and which he did not do, but the fact was that I was trying to protect him." The Supreme Court of Ohio ordered Ruffalo suspended indefinitely from practice. (Mahoning County Bar Ass'n v. Ruffalo, 176 Ohio St. 263, 199 N.E.2d 896, 8 A.L.R.3d 1142 (Anno. p. 1155 (1964)). Certiorari was denied by the Supreme Court of the United States. The Supreme Court of Ohio certified its action to the United States Court of Appeals for the Sixth Circuit. The latter court then ordered Ruffalo to show cause why he should not be disbarred from that court, and considered the matter on the basis of the record made in the State of Ohio proceedings.]

O'SULLIVAN, CIRCUIT JUDGE. . . .

The facts as to Charge No. 8 are that Ruffalo during the pendency of their FELA cases, advanced living expenses to three clients. This conduct was found to offend Canons 10 and 42 of the Canons of Professional Ethics. . . . The Supreme Court of Ohio, in agreement with Opinion No. 288 of the Professional Ethics Committee of the American Bar Association . . . expressed its view that, "It is obvious that where the advancement of living expenses is made, as in the instant case, to enable a client and his family to survive, any agreement by the disabled client to repay them would not have the effect of providing the attorney with any reasonable source of repayment other than the proceeds received on trial or settlement of his client's claim. In effect, the attorney has purchased an interest in the subject matter of the litigation that he is conducting."

We need not, and do not, announce a rule for this Circuit that, standing alone, the conduct involved in Charge No. 8 would prompt us to discipline Ruffalo. . . . [W]ith Ruffalo's previous conviction, and the charge making up Charge 13, there is sufficient. . .

The admitted facts of Charge No. 13 are that Ruffalo . . . hired Michael Orlando, an employee of the Baltimore & Ohio Railroad, to act under cover as his agent in investigating cases against various railroads. This under cover work included investigating and obtaining evidence to be used in Ruffalo's cases against Orlando's own employer, the B. and O. . . .

Charge No. 13, . . . was added as a specification of misconduct during the course of the Board of Commissioner's hearing. Mr. Ruffalo objected to this being done, and the Board advised him that he could have time to offer proofs in opposition to the charge. . . . We find no procedural impropriety in this regard. Neither do his counsel raise the question here. They do, however, assert deprivation of due process in that prior to Ruffalo's described use of Orlando, he was never told that such would be looked upon as misconduct. . . . We will not hold that due process requires that our bar associations anticipate every conceivable type of misconduct. . . . Surely our profession is not so morally and ethically naive as to need always advanced definition of what is, and what is not, impermissible behavior.

[The respondent was suspended indefinitely.]

EDWARDS, CIRCUIT JUDGE (dissenting). . . .

The undisputed facts are that out of a very busy practice . . . respondent was shown to have made such loans in two instances [$1,025 to a widow client over a period of four years, and $611 to another such client over a period of three years with an ultimate settlement of her claim for $21,000].

I cannot in good conscience agree that the making of such small loans as to these two admittedly impoverished widows represented purchasing an interest in litigation. If this record showed that making maintenance loans to clients was a general practice employed by respondent so as to become widely known and hence to constitute an economic attraction for potential clients, we would have facts from which such an inference could be drawn. . . .

We recognize, of course, that the American Bar Association's Professional Ethics Committee has published an opinion, No. 288 which may be cited as general support for the view expressed by the Ohio Supreme Court. This view is, however, against the great weight of opinion in the courts in this country. . . .

Respondent's actions in hiring Orlando for the purpose admitted by respondent, in concealing the employment relationship and in being a great deal less than fully cooperative with the Bar Association's investigation of his record in this matter convince the majority that he was aware of the conflict of interest inevitable [for Orlando] in his hiring Orlando to investigate accident cases against Orlando's own employer. These facts also convince me.

This, however, does not end the matter. In order for a lawyer properly to be found guilty of an offense and barred, perhaps forever, from the practice of his profession, he should have advance notice that the act he was charged with was an offence, and prior to his hearing he should have written notice of the charge made against him. Respondent here had neither.

NOTE

The decision of the Court of Appeals was reversed by the Supreme Court of the United States. In the Matter of John Ruffalo, Jr., 390 U.S. 544 (1968). Speaking for the Court Mr. Justice Douglas said: "These are adversary proceedings of a quasi-criminal nature. . . . The charge must be known before the proceedings commence. . . . This absence of fair notice as to the reach of the grievance procedure and the precise nature of the charges deprived petitioner of procedural due process." Mr. Justice Black agreed with the Court's judgment "for reasons stated in the Court's opinion and many others."

The United States District Court had in an earlier decision declined to discipline the respondent. In the Matter of John Ruffalo, Jr., 249 F.Supp. 432 (N.D.Ohio, 1965).

C. CONTINGENT FEES

GAIR v. PECK

Court of Appeals of New York, 1959.
6 N.Y.2d 97, 188 N.Y.S.2d 491, 160 N.E.2d 43.

[A rule specifying the amount of contingent fees in claims and actions for personal injury and wrongful death which had the court's approval in advance was adopted by the Appellate Division, First Department, of New York. The limitation was 50 per cent. of the first $1,000 of the sum recovered; 40 per cent. of the next $2,000; 35 per cent. on the next $22,000; 25 per cent. of any sum over $25,000. A higher percentage could be authorized under extraordinary circumstances, and a fee arrangement of 33⅓ was permitted. The rule ["Rule 4"] further provided that the retention of a larger fee would constitute "the exaction of unreasonable and unconscionable compensation" in violation of the Canons adopted by the New York State Bar Association, unless authorized by a written order of a court. The rule was held invalid as beyond the power of the court by the Appellate Division, Third Department, and an appeal was taken to the Court of Appeals.]

Van Voorhis, Judge. . . .

The record on appeal discloses that in recent years contingent fee agreements have been filed with the Clerk of the First Department at an annual rate of 150,000 or more, of which upwards of 60% have fixed the attorneys' compensation at 50% of the amount of the recovery. . . .

Taking cognizance of this situation, and noting that contingent fees are generally allowed in the United States because of their practical value in enabling a poor man with a meritorious cause of action to obtain competent counsel, the First Department adopted rule 4 with a preamble which concludes:

"When, however, the contingent fee reaches or approaches the 50 per cent level, it ceases to be a measure of due compensation for professional services rendered and makes the lawyer a partner or proprietor in the lawsuit. This is not a permissible professional relationship or a proper professional practice.

"The court considers the schedule adopted to allow ample compensation for the best efforts and services of competent counsel. It recognizes the possibility that extraordinary circumstances may exist in a particular case which would make the resulting compensation inadequate. The court will make special allowance in such cases and grant an application for larger compensation." . . .

Rule 4, *sub judice*, is essential in order to put on record the data necessary to be used as a foundation for taking disciplinary action. . . . The "fee schedule" in rule 4 dispenses with supplying that information where the agreed contingent fee is less than the percentages designated in the rule. If the stipulated fee is greater, the attorney is required to supply the information necessary on which to form a conclusion concerning the value of the professional services which have been rendered. This is merely supplying procedure whereby the lawyer may discharge his traditional burden of justifying his relations with his client where the circumstances prima facie call for explanation. . . .

. . . The scheduling of the graduated scale of percentages in the rule, fair as these percentages are conceded to be for the purposes of the action, concludes nobody. They are simply a procedural means of avoiding the necessity of calling upon every lawyer who files a contingent fee agreement to show what he has done in the case as a basis for determining whether the fee agreement is exorbitant. Plaintiffs have not denied that it is within the power of the Appellate Division to call on all lawyers who have collected contingent fees to do exactly that.

. . . The contention that this is a fee-limiting measure is reduced to an argument that lawyers cannot be disciplined for accepting fees which would be uncollectible in court, if the clients defended on the ground that they are so out of proportion to the value of the work as to be unconscionable.
. . .

The judgment appealed from should be reversed, and declaratory judgment entered in favor of the defendants and against plaintiffs, without costs.*

NOTES

(1) "In my experience, a 50% contingent fee is too high in any, except the most unusual case. . . . On the other hand, an efficient personal injury office cannot operate on less than a ⅓ fee. Not all cases are won, and all a lawyer has to sell is his time and talents, and these become rapidly expendable commodities." Belli, Modern Trials 41 (1954).

(2) The measures taken by the Appellate Division, First Department, for protecting claimants have been increasingly strict, as a result of the inquiry authorized by the case, supra p. 105. The first requirement instituted that claimants' lawyers file statements reporting their contingent fee agreements. Then came the requirement of rather elaborate closing statements showing how funds collected were disposed of. Finally there was the rule

---

* The dissenting opinions of two judges are omitted. Cert. den., 361 U.S. 374 (1960).

considered in the principal case. The several measures are described in MacKinnon, Contingent Fees For Legal Services 160–70 (1964). Rosenberg and Sovern, *Delay and the Dynamics of Personal Injury Litigation*, 59 Colum. L.Rev. 1116, 1118–19 (1959);

(3) *"Self-Restraint of Lawyers.*—When dealing with the fees of members of a profession, the element of self-restraint is an important factor in controlling those instances where the use of standard rates produces excessive charges. This professional self-limitation is a safety factor or governor on the machinery of fee-setting which is overlooked by many observers, who view with understandable alarm the prospect of routine application of rates providing for ⅓ or ½ of the recovery to attorneys, when the recovery is large (about $50,000). Evidence of such self-limitation by individual lawyers is provided by the 1928 Philadelphia study, and by the findings of the Columbia studies. In the latter, analysis of closing statements showed that the actual fee was charged at rates lower than the allowed maximum (all figures in dollars):

Amount Recovered	Rule 4 Rates	Average from Closing Statements
500	250	205
2,000	900	740
14,000	5,150	4,620
33,000	11,000	9,570"

MacKinnon, Contingent Fees for Legal Services 187–88 (1964).

D. PROPOSALS FOR CHANGE

THE VIEW OF PLAINTIFF'S COUNSEL

JACOB D. FUCHSBERG, A LAWYER LOOKS AT PROPOSED CHANGES

51 Judicature 158 (1967).

The most telling thrust in law in this decade has been the broadening of the obligation to entitle every American citizen—regardless of any economic or educational handicaps, whether produced by deep-rooted social problems, or, as with some accident victims, by the acute stress of an injury or death—to a spokesman as available and as skilled as that obtainable by people not so hemmed in by social and economic pressures. . . .

The clear fact is that to base any plan on the premise that lawyers would become less necessary is to plant seeds of injustice. . .

Now, few of the suggestions I am about to make are new, but they are put together with the strong feeling that we can afford them, as we can mass air travel systems, mass housing programs, mass highways, the stratoplane and other things that only limited imaginations have prevented us from reaching toward.

Compulsory Insurance—Liability insurance should be compulsory. . . .

Unlimited Coverage—Coverage should be unlimited. . . .

Comparative Negligence—Comparative negligence should take the place of contributory negligence. . . .

Universal Medical Payments—The compulsory liability policy might have a compulsory medical payments feature, which could be eliminated at the option of the policyholder only by his filing and maintaining proof of equivalent collateral arrangements through other sources. . . . This would, of course, lessen the social impact of such delays as still exist. . . .

Direct Suit v. Carriers—We ought to consider permitting direct suit against carriers. . . .

Insure People, not Cars—This would permit more equitable ratings, the maintenance of better experience records and better incentives for safety and lower cost.

Massive safety campaigns ought to be our first order of business.

We should expand *advance payment and rehabilitation programs.* . . .

We should *abolish guest laws and governmental, charitable and intra-family immunities, and remove death action limits*, where they now still exist.

We should work for an *adequate court system* instead of starved courts. . . .

There should be tough traffic law enforcement, and against the car involved, thus putting family pressure on the careless driver. . . .

If we embrace these, we would be advocating, positively and not negatively, a FULL PROTECTION PLAN.

NOTE

The plaintiff-tort lawyers have their own association, originally called National Association of Claimants Compensation Attorneys (NACCA) and now the American Trial Lawyers Association (ATLA). It publishes the bi-monthly journal, "Trial". Vigorous support for the role of these lawyers and of their association is given in Melvin Belli's book, Blood Money: Ready for the Plaintiff (1956).

METHODS OF INJURY REPARATION

ALFRED F. CONARD, LIVE AND LET LIVE: JUSTICE IN INJURY REPARATION

52 Judicature 105, 106 (1968).

[An] interesting contrast between tort law in the books and tort law in action concerns who pays the bill. Under tort theory, it should be the wrongdoer. But we all know a large part is paid by insurance companies, from funds to which all of us—mostly rightdoers—contribute. The next figure ("Payouts by Insurance Companies and Individuals") is based on the Michigan study showing that 97 per cent of the losses were paid by insurance companies, and just 3 per cent by wrongdoers. The significance of this is that when we talk about the merit of crediting collateral sources, or of paying for pain and suffering, we should not be thinking chiefly about how the *wrongdoer* is affected, but of how the innocent premium-payer is affected.

In most of our discussions about injury reparation, we lawyers naturally focus on the tort action. But there are quite a number of other regimes, all of which contribute significantly to the welfare of the injury victim. Some of the main ones are indicated by the figure entitled, "Comparative Administrative Expense." In addition to tort liability, there are workmen's compensation, private loss insurance (chiefly life and health), public aid, and social security. The columns below the line represent a hundred dollars of reparation from each of these systems. The columns above the line indicate the administrative expense. As you can see, it is about 3 per cent for social security, 5 per cent for public aid, 20 per cent for private loss insurance, 45 per cent for workmen's compensation, and 127 per cent for insured tort liability.

The figure on tort liability is so remarkable that I have prepared another graph ("Costs and Benefits") to show how it is made up. The column at the left illustrates the full social cost of tort reparation, shown as 100 per cent. The public cost of maintaining courts is about one per cent. After we take that off, we have 99 per cent left, which is the liability insurance premium. The next 40 per cent is the cost of running an insurance business—selling insurance, rating the risks, running the company, compensating capital, investigating claims, and adjusting them or defending against them. That leaves 59 per cent as the "payout." But out of that come the collection expenses—mostly lawyers' fees. So about 44 per cent of the total social costs end up as net benefits to injury victims.

STUDIES AND PROPOSALS

The heavy burden of personal injuries and deaths, especially in traffic accidents, has led to many studies. A few are cited in the footnote.* Some of the proposals for change emanating from the studies are sketched below.

1. Speed up the settlement of the claim of the injured person. A group of liability insurance companies are testing a system of prompt but limited payments. Another stimulus would be a penalty for not settling promptly. An analogy is the statutes in some states which call for a percentage increase of the sum awarded against an insurance company when the claim is not settled and goes to trial and judgment. A similar penalty might be related to the offer of settlement. So if the plaintiff offered to accept a stated sum and the judgment was for more than that sum, the judgment would be automatically increased; if the defendant offered to pay a stated sum and the judgment was for less than that sum, the judgment would be correspondingly decreased.

2. Speed up and simplify the court hearings. This change has been advocated and tried through the use of aides to the court.

3. Change the legal basis of liability of the alleged wrongdoer. Now the liability in tort is based on the fault of the defendant, with the claimant barred if he was contributorily negligent. It has been proposed that fault be done away with as a basis of liability as well as contributory negligence as a defense, and there be absolute liability after the model of workmen's compensation laws.

4. Change the measure and method of recovery. If the number of persons entitled to recover is increased, the measure of recovery must be reduced to make bearable the burden of payment on whom-

---

* A Columbia University study of 1932, discussed in a symposium in 32 Colum.L.Rev. 785 (1932), urged a plan similar to Workmen's Compensation. It was an idea whose time had not come. Professor Albert Ehrenzweig, in Full Aid Insurance for the Traffic Victim (1954), sketches a voluntary full aid liability insurance plan. A University of Michigan study by Messrs. Conrad, Morgan, Pratt, Voltz and Bombaugh, Automobile Accident Costs and Payments (1964) presents the results of studies in the economics of injury reparation. Auto Compensation Plans: Public Law Perspective on a Private Law Problem (1965) by Messrs. Blum and Kalven takes a more conservative position. Dollars, Delay and the Automobile Victim, (1968) supported the Walter E. Meyer Research Institute of Law, is a collection of essays by several contributors. "Basic Protection for the Traffic Victim" (1965), a book by Messrs. Keeton and O'Connell, proposes a radical reform. Under it the injured party would be compensated by his own insurance company without regard to fault, instead of by the driver of the other car. In 1970 the State Insurance Department of New York recommended the adoption of such a system, which it said would cut in half the insurance costs for motorists. Governor Rockefeller recommends the adoption of the new system because of his concern over the "spiraling costs of automobile insurance and about the inhumanity of the present system."

ever it is cast. One common proposal is to eliminate the right to recover for pain and suffering. A proposal directed to a related end is that the recovery be used for the rehabilitation of the injured party so far as that is practicable,—a method widely used in workmen's compensation cases. A somewhat similar proposal is that the sum recovered be paid in installments rather than in a lump sum, since most injured persons are without the financial experience to lead them to use a large sum wisely.

5. The source of reparation is now the wrongdoer as tested by tort law. It has been proposed that for the most part the source be the injured party through his own insurance company. Another proposed source is the government, whether state or federal, under a system of social insurance.

6. In 1969 the American Bar Association approved the numerous recommendations of a special committee on automobile accident reparation. The recommendations, designed to simplify procedures and reduce delays in litigation, call for the retention of the right to jury trials but the elimination of the unanimous verdict, and the encouragement of prompt settlements.

SECTION 6. PUBLICITY AND SOLICITATION

Introduction. The methods most lawyers employ in rendering legal services makes some publicity essential for the sake of both clients and lawyers. If prospective clients do not know where a lawyer's office is and do not think he is at least a pretty good lawyer, they cannot or will not retain him to represent them; without some publicity he might as well not be a lawyer at all. The close relationship of publicity with the duty of the profession to make services available is explicitly recognized in the Code of Professional Responsibility.

None the less, limitations have been pronounced on the lawyer's publicity. He is felt to be under stricter rules as to publicity than the layman he represents. Other sections in this chapter deal with several specific kinds of clients. The idea which binds the sections together is that the methods of making legal services available should be determined by the situation and the needs of the clients in question. The same sort of test, "the public interest", as the Supreme Court of the United States put it, is applicable to the more general question dealt with here.

CODE OF PROFESSIONAL RESPONSIBILITY *

EC 2–1

The need of members of the public for legal services is met only if they recognize their legal problems, appreciate the importance of seeking assistance, and are able to obtain the services of acceptable legal counsel. Hence, important functions of the legal profession are to educate laymen to recognize their legal problems, to facilitate the process of intelligent selection of lawyers, and to assist in making legal services fully available.

EC 2–6

Formerly a potential client usually knew the reputations of local lawyers for competency and integrity and therefore could select a practitioner in whom he had confidence. This traditional selection process worked well because it was initiated by the client and the choice was an informed one.

EC 2–7

Changed conditions, however, seriously restrict the effectiveness of the traditional selection process. Generally, the reputations of lawyers are not sufficiently known to enable laymen to make intelligent choices. The law has become increasingly complex and specialized. Few lawyers are willing and competent to deal with every kind of legal matter, and laymen have difficulty in judging the competence of lawyers to render different types of legal services. The selection of legal counsel is particularly difficult for transients, persons moving into new areas, persons of limited education or means, and others who have little or no contact with lawyers.

EC 2–9

The traditional ban against advertising by lawyers, which is subject to certain limited exceptions, is rooted in the public interest. Competitive advertising would encourage extravagant, artful, self-laudatory brashness in seeking business and thus could mislead the layman. Furthermore, it would inevitably produce unrealistic expectations in particular cases and bring about distrust of the law and lawyers. Thus, public confidence in our legal system would be impaired by such advertisements of professional services. The attorney-client relationship is personal and unique and should not be established as the result of pressures and deceptions. History has demonstrated that public confidence in the legal system is best preserved by strict, self-imposed controls over, rather than by unlimited, advertising.

* Copyright 1969 by the American Bar Association. Reprinted with permission.

EC 2-10

Methods of advertising that are subject to the objections stated above should be and are prohibited. However, the Disciplinary Rules recognize the value of giving assistance in the selection process through forms of advertising that furnish identification of a lawyer while avoiding such objections. For example, a lawyer may be identified in the classified section of the telephone directory, in the office building directory, and on his letterhead and professional card. But at all times the permitted notices should be dignified and accurate.

EC 2-14

In some instances a lawyer confines his practice to a particular field of law. In the absence of state controls to insure the existence of special competence, a lawyer should not be permitted to hold himself out as a specialist or as having special training or ability, other than in the historically excepted fields of admiralty, trademark, and patent law.

NOTES

(1) In his federal income tax return, a lawyer deducted, as "ordinary and necessary business expenses" private club dues, cost of entertaining his prospective clients, and expenses for donations and flowers for good will purposes. The amounts listed as "entertainment" ranged from $8,300 to $13,000 a year. The Commissioner and the Tax Court allowed part of these expenses as deductions, the sums varying from $1,200 to $1,700 a year, but disallowed the others, because of indefiniteness of proof. The Court of Appeals affirmed the disallowance. In a concurring opinion, Chambers, C. J. stated: "He contends . . . that the entertainment items were really distasteful to him but that entertain extravagantly he must to make an adequate living professionally in San Francisco. . . . [W]hile the commissioner makes no point of it, there well may be a question in the next similar case . . . as to the legality for such large deductions at all for a lawyer for 'business getting.' I am sure many deduct therefor in a modest way, but I wonder about the cost of an intensive campaign to get legal business. On that, I reserve my dicta." Hearn v. Commissioner, 309 F.2d 431, 433–34 (9th Cir. 1962).

(2) The broad prohibition of solicitation of practice has been criticized largely on the ground that the standards of the profession have been shaped by the laywer with established clients and do not take into account other kinds of lawyers or the needs of clients for information. See Shuchman, *Ethics and Legal Ethics: The Propriety of the Canons as a Group Moral Code*, 37 Geo.Wash.L.Rev. 244 (1968): Note, *A Critical Analysis of Rules Against Solicitation by Lawyers*, 25 U.Chi.L.Rev. 674 (1958); Note, *Advertising, Solicitation and Legal Ethics*, 7 Vand.L.Rev. 676 (1954).

(3) The Code of Professional Responsibility, DR 2–102(F) provides: "Nothing herein contained shall prohibit a lawyer from using or permitting the use, in connection with his name, of an earned degree or title derived therefrom indicating his training in the law."

BARTON v. THE STATE BAR OF CALIFORNIA

Supreme Court of California
209 Cal. 677, 289 P. 818 (1930).

Disciplinary proceedings were filed against a lawyer for newspaper advertising. In his defense the lawyer argued that the Rule of the State Bar which prohibited the solicitation of professional employment by advertisement was an unreasonable regulation because "the law has ceased to be a sacrosanct profession and has become a highly competitive business." In rejecting the defense the court said: "Notwithstanding the declaration of the petitioner, we do not believe that the profession of the law is, or ought to be, merely 'a highly competitive business'. And because it is not, and because it is necessary that the public should not be given the idea that it is so considered by the members of the profession, the rule against the solicitation of business by advertisement is a reasonable regulation."

NOTES

(1) The extent to which self-laudation might go is illustrated in a case where the lawyer referred to himself as "the legal Gibralter of the theatrical profession" People ex rel. Chicago Bar Ass'n v. Bereznick, 292 Ill. 305 (1920), and in another case where as the court stated a solicitation circular "reads like the advance bills of the late P. T. Barnum in heralding the approach of the Greatest Show on Earth," In re Schwarz, 175 App.Div. 335 (1916).

(2) Different results were reached in two cases involving picturesque articles about law offices, in the preparation of which the lawyers had cooperated. In one case involving a personal injury firm the court held there was no violation of the standards of the profession. State ex rel. The Florida Bar v. Nichols, 151 So.2d 257 (Fla.1963). In the other, concerning a small corporate firm, the court condemned the self-laudation. In re Connelly, 18 App.Div.2d 466 (1963).

IN RE JONES

Supreme Court of Missouri (1966).
431 S.W.2d 809.

[In disciplinary proceedings a lawyer was charged with obtaining personal injury cases through the recommendations of a layman to whom by agreement he paid 10 per cent of the recovery for "contingent fee investigation." To the charge he set up the defense of the constitutional right of free speech broadly in three aspects: the layman had the free speech right to recommend him; the clients had the right to retain him; and he had the right to accept the cases. In support of the defense, he relied on the Button and Brotherhood of Railroad Trainmen cases (supra pp. 72, 74). The Court rejected the defense.]

Donnelly, J. In N.A.A.C.P. v. Button, the United States Supreme Court upheld the right of the N.A.A.C.P. to solicit plaintiffs to designate N.A.A.C.P. staff attorneys to represent them in legal proceedings to achieve desegregation. In B. R. T. v. Virginia, the United States Supreme Court upheld the right of the Brotherhood of Railroad Trainmen to advise injured workers to obtain legal advice, to recommend specific attorneys, and upheld the rights of lawyers to accept employment under such circumstances. . . .

We will not expand these rulings beyond the facts in those cases. It is accurate to say that any layman has a right to recommend a lawyer, any injured person has a right to accept such recommendation, and any lawyer has a right to accept employment in a proper set of circumstances. We also recognize some difficulty in reconciling traditional concepts of proper ethical conduct on the part of lawyers with the needs of people in our modern society. However, the facts in this case evidence practices we cannot condone.

THE ENGLISH BACKGROUND

F. B. MACKINNON, CONTINGENT FEES FOR LEGAL SERVICES

Pages 35–36 (1964).

Considering the contingent fee contract as an agreement by a lawyer to render assistance to a litigant in a matter in which he, the lawyer, is not directly concerned, with the expectation of being paid a fee out of the recovery, we find that we must deal with a number of long-standing legal doctrines designed to limit a lawsuit to those immediately affected by it. In Anglo-American law these concepts have taken the following form: the prohibition of assistance to a litigant by one not directly interested in the suit—the doctrine of maintenance; the prohibition of agreements to share in the subject matter of the suit, if successful, in return for assistance in litigation—the doctrine of champerty; the disapproval of the purchase or sale of part or all of an interest which is under litigation—the doctrine of the non-assignability of a cause of action; and the disapproval of those who stir up and stimulate litigation—the doctrine of barratry.

The English History.—Although all four of these doctrines date back at least 700 years, the history of the development and modification of ancient policies against allowing strangers to encourage and assist litigation has left a trail of legal concepts which have direct bearing upon modern contingent fee contracts. Doctrines originally aimed against those who would override the authority of the trial courts of the English kings of the thirteenth and fourteenth centuries have come to be directed against an arrangement by which a lawyer seeks to make his fee depend upon the outcome of the lawsuit.

NOTES

(1) For a consideration of the background, in policy and in history, of the condemnation of solicitation of practice, see Mr. Justice Brennan's opinion in NAACP v. Button, 371 U.S. 415, 438–44 (1963).

(2) The uncritical transfer from feudal England to modern America of the old doctrines of champerty, barratry and maintenance has been sharply criticized. Radin, *Maintenance by Champerty*, 24 Cal.L.Rev. 48 (1935). Certainly, it is hard to fit them neatly into to-day's situation when assignment of contracts is taken for granted and contingent fees are approved. Is this an instance of an unexamined transfer of old terms to new situations and conditions? Or is it an illustration of the continuing vitality of old policies against stirring up litigation?

(3) "The common law of champerty and maintenance has never been adopted in this state or applied in civil actions, and the true and exclusive inquiry and test of these plaintiffs to seek relief from a court of equity is whether the transaction upon which they rely is opposed to public policy." Rulnick v. Shulman, 106 Conn. 66 (1927).

SOME RELEVANT FACTORS

The ideal of the bar has been that the lawyer is passive in getting clients and that the lawyer is already known to clients who will come to him or that his reputation will bring clients. The ideal, which condemns publicity and solicitation by the lawyer, has some supports in policy. There is a public interest against the stirring up of strife and controversy. If there were no restrictions on publicity and solicitation, the least capable and least honorable lawyers would use extravagant measures which would be effective with those most in need of protection against them. Such measures by the lawyers and the hopes of clients would increase the use of evil means to secure the end promised. Despite the Madison Avenue aspects of much of business there is a social value in the qualities of restraint and dignity in the professional man.

There are considerations opposed to the bar's ideal. Legal rights will not be protected and enforced unless counsel are readily available to those in need of them, a fact which is the basis of the recent Supreme Court of the United States decisions in the field. Many lawyers, as the beginners and the less successful, do not have the clients which they believe they would have if only their qualities could be made more widely known. Methods of obtaining clients which are beyond the reach of practicable prohibition, as the use of social, political business and even church relationships and activities, may be less worthy than the more direct methods condemned. Lawyers in politics, a highly important group, are in need of constant publicity if they are to remain in office.

SEEKING A PLACE IN A LAW OFFICE

Of course, a lawyer may seek a place in a law office by personal application. He may seek a place by a blind advertisement in a lawyer's journal, as in the "positions wanted" section of the American Bar Association Journal. He may seek employment with a governmental agency. And he may seek position as house counsel of a corporation. A.B.A.Comm.Ops. 197 and 244.

If he has specialized ability, he may send to lawyers a card informing recipients of this speciality or he may so advertise in a lawyers' journal. Ass'n. Bar City N.Y.Op. 851.

In the United States a lawyer may not purchase the practice of another lawyer, though this is permitted to the solicitor in England. cf. Ass'n Bar City N.Y.Ops. 618, 803.

NOTE

The American Bar Association Journal has a section of classified advertisements. One heading is "Lawyers Wanted", another "Positions Wanted". An illustration under the second heading is:

"Attorney, Tax, Heavy Experience, both corporate and government on federal level, desires opportunity with law firm or corporation. Earning $20,000. Box 8–A 9."

PROFESSIONAL CARD

"Professional Card" means any one of three things: (1) the identifying card which a man carries in his card case as a means of introducing himself; (2) the notice sent by mail announcing the opening of an office or a change in a firm; (3) the simple professional card published in newspapers in some communities. As to the last of them, the view has been expressed that it is no longer permissible. A.B.A.Opinion 182 (1938). As to the second, a joint committee of the two New York City Associations expressed the following view reported as N.Y.Co.Law Assoc.Op. 375 (1946).

I

In the Committees' opinion, it is not improper for an attorney to state in his professional announcement the particular public office from which he is returning to private practice. Such a statement should not go beyond naming the department or agency of the government with which the attorney served and the title of the position which he held therein. The terms of the announcement and its physical setup should be such as to avoid any implication that the attorney is seeking to announce that he is specially qualified to handle matters dealt with by such agency or department or in which he gained experience while holding public office. . . .

II

The Committees are of the opinion that it is improper for such an announcement to state that the attorney intends to specialize in practice before the government department or agency in which he held office.

III

After full reconsideration by the undersigned Committees, they are of the opinion that a distinction should be made between announcements to be sent only to lawyers and announcements to be sent to others. Announcements made to lawyers only, which state the particular branch of law intended to be practiced, are still predominantly informational in character because lawyers are not substantially influenced to employ other lawyers by announcements or impressed by their implications. On the contrary, such announcements have a far greater tendency to impress persons other than lawyers with the obvious implication that the announcer is particularly qualified to handle the type of matter to be specialized in; and hence such announcements constitute improper solicitations of employment when sent to others than lawyers.

Consequently, the undersigned Committees are now of the opinion that an attorney may properly send to lawyers only, both known and unknown to him, an announcement which includes a statement of intention to specialize in a particular branch of the law, whether or not it be a recognized specialty, but that an attorney may not include such a statement in any announcement to be sent to anyone who is not a lawyer unless the specialty be Admiralty, Patents, Copyrights or Trademarks. The exception is made in deference to a long standing and approved custom in the particular fields mentioned.

IV

A professional announcement may be sent by a lawyer to other lawyers, known and unknown to him, and in addition only to non-lawyer individuals and organizations whom he knows personally or with whom his relationships are such as to make it appropriate that they should receive the announcement, i.e., such an announcement may be properly sent to other than lawyers only when "warranted by personal relations." (Canon 27)

No announcement may be published otherwise than in an approved law list or for a limited number of times in a publication published for the use of lawyers primarily.

NOTICES OF SPECIALIZED LEGAL SERVICES
N.Y.C. OPINION NO. 851 (1961)

The New York Law Journal has requested the opinion of this Committee regarding the principles applicable to notices published in the Law Journal advertising the availability of lawyers for specialized legal services to be rendered to other lawyers.

Canon 46 of the Canons of Ethics of this Association and of the New York State Bar Association (and the corresponding Canon of the American Bar Association before a liberalizing amendment in 1956) provides as follows:

"CANON 46. NOTICE OF SPECIALIZED LEGAL SERVICE.

"Where a lawyer is engaged in rendering a specialized legal service directly and only to other lawyers, a brief, dignified notice of that fact, couched in language indicating that it is addressed to lawyers, inserted in legal periodicals and like publications, when it will afford convenient and beneficial information to lawyers desiring to obtain such service, is not improper."

The prior opinions of this and other bar association committees interpreting this Canon appear in many respects to be inconsistent and confusing as applied to the conditions of modern legal practice which call for specialization in an increasing degree. This Committee is now of the opinion that the term "specialized legal services" should not be limited to admiralty, patent, trademark, copyright law or other specialties in which some lawyers practice exclusively. The term should be interpreted with sufficient breadth to permit lawyers to notify other lawyers of their availability for any special legal service that may assist other lawyers in serving their clients . . .

As to the form of the advertisement, brevity and dignity are of the utmost importance and it should be so worded as to indicate that it is addressed to lawyers only. It should not be a display type or contain representations of special ability, diligence or experience, . . .

Its publication should be limited to legal journals published in the locality where the lawyer has his office. Under ordinary circumstances we see no reason for limiting the number of insertions.

To the extent that they may be inconsistent with the foregoing, previous opinions of this Committee are overruled.

NOTE

Compare Code of Professional Responsibility DR 2–105(a) (3).

INFORMING CLIENTS OF CHANGES IN THE LAW

American Bar Association Committee Opinion, No. 210, 27 A.B. A.J. 319 (1941). [Question]: A member of the American Bar Association calls attention to the effect on testamentary dispositions of subsequent changes in general economic conditions, of changes in the attitude or death of named fiduciaries in a will, of the removal of the testator to a different jurisdiction where different laws of descent may prevail, of changes in financial conditions, family relationship and kindred matters, and then inquires whether it is proper for the lawyer who drew the will to call attention of the testator from time to time of the importance of going over his will.

[Answer]: The inquiry presents the question as to whether such action on the part of a lawyer is solicitation of legal employment and so to be condemned.

Many events transpire between the date of making the will and the death of the testator. The legal significance of such occurrences are often of serious consequence, of which the testator may not be aware, and so the importance of calling the attention of the testator thereto is manifest.

It is our opinion that where the lawyer has no reason to believe that he has been supplanted by another lawyer, it is not only his right, but it might even be his duty to advise his client of any change of fact or law which might defeat the client's testamentary purpose as expressed in the will.

Periodic notices might be sent to the client for whom a lawyer has drawn a will, suggesting that it might be wise for the client to re-examine his will to determine whether or not there has been any change in his situation requiring a modification of his will.

PUBLICITY BY CLIENTS

A.B.A. Com.Op. 290 (1956).

We have been asked by a local bar association to reconsider our Opinion 285 and to pass on the ethical propriety of a local firm (*A, B and C*) permitting a municipality or a bond house selling its obligations to publish an advertisement offering its bonds as follows: "These bonds are offered when, as and if issued and received by us and subject to approval of legality by Messrs. *A, B and C.*"

We adhere to Opinion 285.

The value of municipal bonds is peculiarly dependent on the assurance of compliance with all the required legal formalities and it is hence most important for purchasers of them to be confident that the legal steps in their issuance have been in charge of competent lawyers. For the municipality to give such assurance is primarily in its interest and in that of the purchasers. Although some advantage to the law firm may result, this is incidental. . . . The question is always, as we said in Opinion 285, whether under the circumstances the furtherance of the professional employment of the lawyer is the primary purpose of the advertisement, or is merely a necessary incident of a proper and legitimate objective of the client which does not have the effect of unduly advertising him.

NOTE

Does the principle of this opinion apply to proxy contests, to stockholder derivative actions, and to class actions generally? The roles of counsel for the insurgents and for management in proxy contests are discussed in Aranow and Einhorn, Proxy Contests for Corporate Control 14–15, 541 (2d ed. 1968). The lawyer's part in a controversy when there are other persons of similar interests besides his client are considered in Drinker, Legal Ethics, 251 (1953).

PUBLIC CAUSES

Solicitation may be upheld when its purpose is to provide counsel for a hated defendant who otherwise might not have effective counsel. The *Ades* case, supra p. 94, is a good illustration.

It may happen that representation in court cases is used not merely for the advantage of a particular person but for the advancement of a cause or the protection of a group. In the case of *NAACP v. BUTTON*, supra p. 72, the solicitation was for the purpose of protecting the constitutional rights of a disadvantaged group and it was on this stated ground that certiorari was sought. See also Note, "Inciting Litigation", 3 Race Rel. L. Rep. 1257 (1958). Somewhat similar are the situations provided for by statute in which the Attorney General of the United States is authorized to proceed to protect civil rights.

Institutional publicity of several kinds for the bar has been approved by American Bar Association committee opinions. So it has been with lawyer referral services (No. 227 (1941)) a legal check up program (No. 307 (1962)); and a bar sponsored program which dramatized the harm caused by the lack of legal services in drafting a will. (No. 179 (1938)). Publicity for legal aid offices is now accepted as a matter of course.

SECTION 7. LAY EXPERTS: RIVALS OR COLLABORATORS

CODE OF PROFESSIONAL RESPONSIBILITY *
EC 3–1

The prohibition against the practice of law by a layman is grounded in the need of the public for integrity and competence of those who undertake to render legal services. Because of the fiduciary character of the attorney-client relationship and the inherently complex nature of our legal system, the public can better be assured of the requisite responsibility and competence only if the practice of law is confined to those who are subject to the requirements and regulations imposed upon members of the legal profession.

EC 5–1

It is neither necessary nor desirable to attempt the formulation of a single, specific definition of what constitutes the practice of law. Functionally, the practice of law relates to the rendition of services for others that call for the professional judgment of a lawyer. The essence of the professional judgment of the lawyer is his educated ability to relate the general body and philosophy of law to a specific legal problem of a client; and thus, the public interest will be better served if only lawyers are permitted to act in matters involving professional judgment. Where this professional judgment is not involved, non-lawyers, such as court clerks, police officers, abstracters, and many governmental employees, may engage in occupations that require a special knowledge of law in certain areas. But the services of a lawyer are essential in the public interest whenever the exercise of professional legal judgment is required.

NOTES

(1) For an early and ranging discussion of the problems involved under "unauthorized practice of law" see Llewellyn, *The Bar's Troubles and Poultices—and Cures*, 5 Law and Contemp.Prob. 104 (1938). The publications on the subject are numerous. The most extensive one is "Unauthorized Practice News" of the American Bar Association committee which includes many decisions not reported elsewhere. There are source books published by the Committee consisting of compilations of cases and commentaries on the subject, of the applicable statutes, and of the informative opinions issued by the Committee.

(2) "No longer is the petty poacher the major challenger. The challenger is the man who offers or seems to offer something the lawyer does not offer and who gives his services with greater efficiency and economy. The term, 'unauthorized practice of law,' is antiquated and inadequate. The new groups cannot rightly be regarded merely as rivals for work which are to be combatted or whose fields must be rigidly delimited. They must be

* Copyright 1969 by the American Bar Association. Reprinted with permission.

regarded for what they are, collaborators in the common task of advising and guiding clients.* The bar should take measures to examine the whole situation afresh and to see to it that this new expertness is made available to clients who need it in a way which does not involve burdensome and unnecessary fees." Cheatham, *The Lawyer's Role in Modern Society: A Round Table,* 4 J.Pub.Law 1, 48 (1955).

STATE BAR OF ARIZONA v. ARIZONA LAND TITLE AND TRUST CO.

Supreme Court of Arizona, 1961.
90 Ariz. 76, 366 P.2d 1.
Modified, 91 Ariz. 293, 371 P.2d 1020 (1962).

[The State Bar of Arizona and the members of its Committee on Unauthorized Practice filed two complaints for declaratory judgments that the defendants had been engaged in the unlawful practice of law. One complaint was against real estate salesmen. Another complaint, against title companies, charged that they gave legal advice and prepared documents affecting the title to land for their patrons, through lawyers employed by them and by other persons. The trial court approved some of the acts by the defendants and condemned others. The test employed was whether the activities were necessary or proper incidents established by custom or by law to the conduct of lawful business. The plaintiffs appealed.]

LOCKWOOD, JUSTICE. . . . We believe it sufficient to state that those acts, whether performed in court or in the law office, which lawyers customarily have carried on from day to day through the centuries must constitute "the practice of law". See Opinion of the Justices, 1935, 289 Mass. 607, 194 N.E. 313, 318. . . . Many of the Canons of Professional Ethics which attorneys must observe most scrupulously are diametrically opposed to the code by which businessmen must live if they are to survive. Perhaps the most important applicable Canon states that

> "The lawyer owes 'entire devotion to the interest of the client, warm zeal in the maintenance and defense of his rights and the exertion of his utmost learning and ability,' to the end that nothing be taken or be withheld from him, save by the rules of law, legally applied." Excerpt from Canon 15, Canons of Professional Ethics.

---

* "The lawyer cannot properly advise and counsel his clients without the assistance of experts as well as of lawyers who specialize in particular fields. It is suggested that a Canon should be framed stressing the duty of a lawyer in giving counsel and advice to utilize the service of such experts." McCracken, *Report on Observance by the Bar of Stated Professional Standards,* 37 Va.L.Rev. 339, 421 (1951).

The relationship between title company employees and company customers bears none of the characteristics of the attorney-client relationship envisioned in this Canon. . . .

There is further evidence indicating that the relationship between title company employees and company customers may lack the professional posture so necessary when the customers' legal rights are involved. Title company witnesses consistently testified that when dealing with customers, they carefully avoided conversation which would involve a discussion of the customers' objectives, or legal rights and obligations with respect to the property being conveyed. Nevertheless, the title company employee, in "filling in a form", obviously exercises his own discretion as to what form should be used, and what language is to be inserted in the blank spaces. By virtue of his training and professional role, the lawyer is able to question his client freely, advise him of the legal effect of various forms of conveyance or other instruments, and then use such legal documents and language as will best effect the objectives of the client. . . .

. . . If there are adverse interests (and there usually are in a land transaction), the position of the title company attorney is particularly difficult. . . . The title company lawyer is confronted with at least three separate clients: the title company, and each of its customers involved in the transaction. It is difficult to conceive how the title company attorney can maintain the proper professional posture toward each, when at least some of their interests may conflict. . . .

The title companies rely heavily upon the theory that even if some of their acts complained of fall within the definition of the "practice of law", nevertheless by reason of long established custom such conduct has become incidental to their lawful business, and in the absence of specific showing that it is not in the public interest, it should not be considered "unauthorized" practice of law. . . .

We agree with the California court which stated in Agran v. Shapiro, 1954, 127 Cal.App.2d 807, 817, 273 P.2d 619, 625, that "Any rule which holds that a layman who prepares legal papers . . . is not practicing law when such services are incidental to another business . . . completely ignores the public welfare."

The title companies maintain that they may prepare legal instruments in transactions in which they have an "interest" in the subject-matter. With this proposition we agree. We disagree, however, with appellees' view as to what "interest" in the subject-matter of a transaction is sufficient to permit self-representation. . . . We note there may be contractual pecuniary obligations between one or more of the parties, whose rights and obligations to each other are affected by the document or paper, and a third party who has performed services in negotiating the transaction (i.e., a realtor who brings buyer and seller together) which may be appended to a document.

However the mere assertion of these contractual rights in the document itself, naming the third party, does not suffice to make him a "party with an interest" in the transaction, since his interest is not in the subject matter but in fees for his services in bringing it about.

. . .

. . . Everything which we have heretofore stated with reference to appellee title companies applies with equal force and effect to appellee real estate brokers. It must also be noted in this connection that although the legislature may impose additional restrictions which affect the licensing of attorneys, it cannot infringe on the ultimate power of the courts to determine who may practice law. In re Greer, 1938, 52 Ariz. 385, 389–390, 81 P.2d 96, 98. . . .

Judgment of the trial court is affirmed in part, and reversed in part, and the trial court is directed to enter the following declaratory judgment:

It is ordered, adjudged, and decreed that those acts, whether performed in court or in the law office, which lawyers customarily have carried on from day to day through the centuries constitute the practice of law. . . .

NOTES

(1) The year following the decision in the principal case the real estate interests put before the voters by initiative an amendment to the state constitution to the effect that any licensed real estate salesman when acting as broker or agent in the sale, exchange or lease of land should have the right to fill out and also to draft, without charge, all instruments incident to the transaction. The amendment was approved by a large majority. See Marks *The Lawyers and the Realtors: Arizona's Experience*, 49 A.B.A.J. 139 (1963).

(2) "It would be extremely difficult to formulate an accurate definition of the 'practice of law' which might endure, for the reason that under our system of jurisprudence such practice must necessarily change with the ever-changing business and social order." Potter, J., in Grand Rapids Bar Ass'n v. Denkema, 290 Mich. 56 (1939).

IN RE ROTHMAN

12 N.J. 528, 97 A.2d 621 (1953).

[Two young lawyers owned the stock of a corporation engaged in mortgage financing. The corporation advertised extensively during a building boom and had from 45 to 50 mortgage closings a week. ". . . on the sale of a house to a G.I. for $15,000 the mortgage company's fees totalled $483. These fees were made up of 1% G.I. discount, recording fees, the cost of the title policy, three months' taxes, the fire insurance premium, a survey and the closing fee of $150. One of the lawyers represented the mortgage company at the closing and received the fee. Apparently the mortgagors frequently did not retain lawyers to represent them at the closing, but they were free to do so. The Supreme Court of New Jersey, by a vote of four to three, held the lawyers were guilty of violating the Canons of Professional Ethics.]

VANDERBILT, C. J. . . . The controlling authorities in the instant case are the 27th ["Advertising, Direct or Indirect"], 35th ["Intermediaries"], and 47th ["Aiding the Unauthorized Practice of Law"] Canons of Professional Ethics and the unanimous opinion of this court of less than two years ago in In the Matter of L. R., an Attorney at Law, 7 N.J. 390, 81 A.2d 725 (1951). . . . We there held that:

> "The practice which has been referred to as 'a one-package system' is a system whereby commercial services, including a lawyer's fee, are rendered to a person for a single charge"

. . . These canons do not, however, preclude an attorney from engaging in all business. The line of demarcation is clearly indicated in Opinion No. 57 of the Committee on Professional Ethics of the American Bar Association, dated March 19, 1932, which provides in part:

> "It is not necessarily improper for an attorney to engage in a business; but impropriety arises when the business is of such a nature or is conducted in such a manner as to be inconsistent with the lawyer's duties as a member of the Bar. Such an inconsistency arises when the business is one that will readily lend itself as a means for procuring professional employment for him, is such that it can be used as a cloak for indirect solicitation on his behalf, or is of a nature that, if handled by a lawyer, would be regarded as the practice of law."

BRENNAN, J. dissenting. . . . Is Mr. Irving's present situation, . . . so "far removed" from that of innumerable past and present leaders of the bar who have been and are identified in executive capacities, as directors, and as owners, with building and loan associations, insurance companies, savings and loan associations, banks and trust companies, and like socially useful enterprises, with the result and in some cases for the purpose of having their law practices benefit from these connections . . . ?

STATE EX REL. STATE BAR OF WISCONSIN v. KELLER

Supreme Court of Wisconsin, 1962.
16 Wis.2d 377, 114 N.W.2d 796.

[The attorney general of the state acting on relation of the State Bar of Wisconsin brought a quo warranto proceeding against a layman charging that he was usurping the franchise of practicing law.

The complaint alleged that the respondent, a layman, had been an active practitioner for several years before the Wisconsin Public Service Commission on behalf of trucking companies, applying for or opposing the grant of authority to conduct trucking operations. In these proceedings he had examined witnesses and otherwise presented the facts in the cases. The respondent answered that he was familiar with the rules of evidence and with the principles of law applicable to his field of work, as well as with the principles of legal ethics, that in all his work he was acting as a qualified layman, and that the Wisconsin statutes and Administrative Code authorized the appearance of laymen before administrative commission. The respondent answered further that he was a licensed practitioner before the Interstate Commerce Commission as well as the Public Service Commission of Indiana, that his primary representation of his clients involved trucking in interstate commerce, and that a considerable part of his activities before the State administrative agencies was incidental to his interstate work. The relator demurred to the answer. The trial court dismissed the complaint for lack of competence over the subject matter. On appeal it was found the trial court did have competence and the Supreme Court of Wisconsin went on to decide the case on the merits.]

BROWN, JUSTICE. . . . The legislature's creation of the Public Service Commission with its rulemaking powers does not in any way supersede the exclusive power of the judiciary, ultimately residing in the supreme court, to determine what is or is not the practice of law and to restrict such practice to persons licensed by the court to engage in it. . . .

We hold, further, that the alleged lawfulness of respondent to engage in similar activities in other jurisdictions, such as in the State of Indiana or before the Interstate Commerce Commission, is immaterial in the case at bar. Respondent's activities in Wisconsin and his compliance or the lack of it with Wisconsin law are the controlling facts and the law applicable. Foreign bodies can no more authorize persons unlicensed in this state to practice law here than could the Public Service Commission of Wisconsin.

Respondent contends that by his study and experience he has become as well or better qualified than many licensed lawyers in the particular limited field in which he holds himself out to serve his clients, and his activities in that area should not be restrained. These practical qualifications in the instant case may be admitted without affecting the result. Beyond competency in a limited field the lawyer is subject to the discipline and control of the courts. There are obligations to his client and to the public under the supervision of the courts which are lacking in the case of any unlicensed person. We need not and we should not acknowledge a layman's right to practice law in a specialized field because the layman appears to be competent in it. . . .

Respondent has contended that to restrain him from continuing his present practices before the P.S.C. infringes his constitutional right to due process of law and equal protection of the law. We do not find that the United States Constitution assures him of a right to practice law in this state without being duly licensed by this court to do so nor does it protect him if he attempts it. . . .

[T]he respondent should be enjoined from appearing as an advocate for a client in respect to the client's legal rights and to procure an adjudication of legal rights desired by the client. . . .

Order reversed and cause remanded with directions to enter a restraining order not inconsistent with the opinion.

The next stage of the controversy was reported in Keller v. Wisconsin ex rel. State Bar of Wisconsin, 374 U.S. 102, 83 S.Ct. 1686 (1963). The Supreme Court of the United States, without argument, entered the following order:

"Per Curiam.

"The Petition for writ of certiorari is granted, the judgment is vacated and the case is remanded to the Supreme Court of Wisconsin for reconsideration in light of Sperry v. Florida ex rel. Florida Bar, 373 U.S. 379."

(The Sperry case involved a lay practitioner registered to practice before the United States Patent Office, in accordance with regulations issued by the Commissioner of Patents. He maintained an office in Florida where he rendered opinions on patentability, prepared applications for letters patent and papers incidental to them and further represented clients before the Patent Office in Washington. The Supreme Court of Florida had enjoined him from carrying on his activities in Florida. The Supreme Court of the United States reversed the state court decision, holding that the privilege to engage in these activities had validly been granted by federal law and the state could not prohibit the exercise of these privileges even within its borders.)

On remand the Supreme Court of Wisconsin reconsidered the matter and handed down its decision in State ex rel. State Bar of Wisconsin v. Keller, 21 Wis. 100, 123 N.W.2d 905 (1963). In a per curiam opinion the court stated that Keller could appear as a representative of others in hearings of the Interstate Commerce Commission in Wisconsin and that he could give in Wisconsin his opinion to clients on Interstate Commerce Commission matters, but that he could not appear in a representative capacity before the state public service commission. On matters which required the approval of both the federal and the state commissions the court stated:

> "Counsel for Keller contends that there are a number of situations where persons engaged in interstate commerce would require the issuance of permits or other actions both by the Interstate Commerce Commission and the Public Service Commission of Wisconsin, and he argues that this subject matter relationship should make Keller's practice before the Public Service Commission of Wisconsin an incident to his practice before the Interstate Commerce Commission. He also apparently takes the position that where leases and contracts must be approved by the Interstate Commerce Commission, such leases and contracts may be drawn by a practitioner licensed by that commission. We do not consider either contention correct. Although we recognize that he may advise whether a particular lease or contract complies with federal law or regulations, leases and contracts create substantive rights and obligations of parties and to prepare them and advise concerning their significance other than their standing under the interstate commerce laws and regulations would constitute the practice of law outside the scope of his practice before the Interstate Commerce Commission." Id. at 907.*

APPLICATION OF NEW YORK COUNTY LAWYERS' ASS'N. IN RE BERNARD BERCU

Supreme Court, Appellate Division, New York, 1948.
273 App.Div. 524, 78 N.Y.S.2d 209.

[Mr. Bercu, a certified public accountant, gave advice to a New York business firm which kept its books on an accrual basis. The advice concerned the year in which the payment of back city taxes could be used by the firm as a deduction in its federal income tax return. He was not otherwise engaged in accounting work for the firm. For his services he brought suit for a fee of $500. The action was dismissed by the Municipal Court.

Thereupon the New York County Lawyers' Association filed the present suit to punish Bercu for contempt of court and to enjoin him

---

* A petition for certiorari by the lay practitioner was denied. 377 U.S. 964, 84 S.Ct. 1643 (1964). The Court had invited the Solicitor General to file a brief in the case. A memorandum of the Solicitor General and the General Counsel of the Commission agreed with the second Wisconsin decision as to "the authority granted by the Interstate Commerce Commission to practitioners under its present rules of practice." The memorandum also agreed that the rules of practice did not confer "the right to practice before State regulatory agencies, even in regard to matters concerning interstate transportation". As to "the drafting of contracts and leases which require its [the Commission's] approval", the matter was for resolution by the State.

from practicing law. In the later stage of the litigation counsel appeared as amici curiae representing the American Institute of Accountants and several bar associations. The Supreme Court, Special Term, dismissed the proceedings on the merits. An appeal was taken to the Appellate Division.]

PECK, PRESIDING JUSTICE. The case is not an easy one because of the overlapping of law and accounting. An accountant must be familiar to a considerable extent with tax law and must employ his knowledge of the law in his accounting practice. By the same token, a tax lawyer must have an understanding of accounting. It is difficult, therefore, to draw a precise line in the tax area between the field of the accountant and the field of the lawyer. Unless we are to say, however, that because common ground exists between the lawyer and accountant in the tax area no bounds may be recognized between them, some line of demarcation must be observed. . . . The application of legal knowledge in such work, however, is only incidental to the accounting functions. It is not expected or permitted of the accountant, despite his knowledge or use of the law, to give legal advice which is unconnected with accounting work. That is exactly what this respondent did. He was doing no accounting work for the Croft Company within the ordinary or proper conception of an accountant's work. He had nothing to do with the Croft Company's books or its tax return. . . . The question respondent undertook to answer was in nature a question of law, as is made all the more evident when one considers the research respondent undertook in the matter and the legal labyrinth into which any thorough research in the matter would lead. . . .

Fortunately the tax law conforms largely with accepted principles of accounting, as most law conforms with business customs and practices. One need only thumb through the Internal Revenue Code relating to income taxes, however, or listen to the criticism leveled at the tax laws and decisions by some writers on accountancy, to note the many respects in which tax law is at variance with usual accounting principles. And it is certainly contrary to fact to view the advice which respondent gave in this case as following accounting principles. . . .

It is much too narrow a view, and one revealing inadequate perception, to regard the tax law as mainly a matter of accounting. More than most specialties in the law, tax law is drawn from and involved with many branches of law. It bridges and is intimately connected, for example, with corporation law, partnership law, property law, the law of sales, trusts and frequently constitutional law. Quite obviously, one trained only in accounting, regardless of specific tax knowledge, does not have the orientation even in tax law to qualify as a tax lawyer. . . . We must either admit frankly that taxation is a hybrid of law and accounting and, as a matter of practical administration, permit accountants to practice tax law, or, also as a matter of practical administration, while allowing the accountant jurisdiction of incidental questions of law which may arise in connection with auditing books or preparing tax returns, deny him the right as a consultant to give legal advice. We are of the opinion that the latter alternative accords to the accountant all necessary and desirable latitude and that nothing less would accord to the public the protection that is necessary when it seeks legal advice.

Respondent is most persuasive when he challenges the consistency of recognizing an accountant's right to prepare income tax returns while denying him the right to give income tax advice. As respondent says, precisely the same question may at one time arise during the preparation of an income tax return and at another time serve as the subject of a request for advice by a client. The difference is that in the one case the accountant is dealing with a question of law which is only incidental to preparing a tax return and in the other case he is addressing himself to a question of law alone. . . .

It allows the accountant maximum freedom of action within the field which might be called "tax accounting" and is the minimum of control necessary to give the public protection when it seeks advice as to tax law.

The order appealed from should be reversed, respondent adjudged in contempt and fined $50 and an injunction as prayed for issued. . . .

DORE, COHN, and CALLAHAN, JJ., concur.

GLENNON, J., dissents and votes to affirm.

[The decision of the Appellate Division was unanimously affirmed in a memorandum decision of the Court of Appeals of New York, 299 N.Y. 728, 87 N.E.2d 451 (1949).]

NOTES

(1) The tax question on which Mr. Bercu gave advice involved the year in which a deduction could be claimed on the *federal* income tax return. Was the question in the principal case as to the privilege of an accountant to carry on such work governed by federal law or, as the New York courts evidently assumed, by state law?

(2) An excellent discussion of the areas of work which may wisely be occupied jointly or severally by the lawyers and the certified public accountants is given by Dean Erwin N. Griswold in *Lawyers, Accountants and Taxes*, 10 The Record Ass'n Bar City N. Y. 52 (1955).

JOHNSON v. AVERY

Supreme Court of the United States, 1969.
393 U.S. 483, 89 S.Ct. 747, 21 L.Ed.2d 718.

[A man serving a term of life imprisonment filed a crude petition for release from solitary confinement. He had been transferred to "maximum security" because, in violation of prison regulations, he had aided other prisoners to prepare petitions for relief, and refused to desist. Held, the relief should be granted.]

FORTAS, J. . . . It has not been held that there is any general obligation of the courts, state or federal, to appoint counsel for prisoners who indicate, without more, that they wish to seek post-conviction relief. . . . Accordingly, the initial burden of presenting a claim to post-conviction relief usually rests upon the indigent prisoner himself with such help as he can obtain within the prison walls or the prison system. . . . But unless and until the State provides some reasonable alternative to assist inmates in the preparation of petitions for post-conviction relief, it may not validly enforce a regulation such as that here in issue, barring inmates from furnishing such assistance to other prisoners. . . .*

The judgment of the Court of Appeals is reversed and the case is remanded for further proceedings consistent with this opinion.

MR. JUSTICE DOUGLAS concurring. . . .

The increasing complexities of our governmental apparatus both at the local and federal levels have made it difficult for a person to process a claim or even to make a complaint. . . .

We think of claims as grist of the mill for the lawyers. But it is becoming abundantly clear that more and more of the effort in ferreting out the basis of claims and the agencies responsible for them and in preparing the almost endless paperwork for their prosecution is work for laymen. There are not enough lawyers to manage or supervise all of these affairs; and much of the basic work done requires no special legal talent. Yet there is a closed-shop philosophy in the legal profession that cuts down drastically active roles for laymen. . . .

That traditional, closed-shop attitude is utterly out of place in the modern world where claims pile high and much of the work of

---

* In reversing the District Court, the Court of Appeals relied on the power of the State to restrict the practice of law to licensed attorneys as a source of authority for the prison regulation. The power of the State to control the practice of law cannot be exercised so as to abrogate federally protected rights. . . . In any event, the type of activity involved here—preparation of petitions for post-conviction relief—historically and traditionally is one which may benefit from the services of a trained and dedicated lawyer, but it is a function often, perhaps generally, performed by laymen. Title 28 U.S.C.A. § 2242 apparently contemplates that in many situations petitions for federal habeas corpus relief will be prepared by laymen. [Footnote by the court].

tracing and pursuing them requires the patience and wisdom of a layman rather than the legal skills of a member of the bar.

"If poverty lawyers are overworked, some of the work can be delegated to sub-professionals. New York law permits senior law students to practice law under certain supervised conditions. Approval must first be granted by the appellate division. A rung or two lower on the legal profession's ladder are laymen legal technicians, comparable to nurses and lab assistants in the medical profession. Large law firms employ them, and there seems to be no reason why they cannot be used in legal services programs to relieve attorneys for more professional tasks." Samore, Legal Services for the Poor, 32 Albany L.Rev. 509, 515–516 (1968). And see Sparer, Thorkelson and Weiss, The Lay Advocate, 43 U.Det.L.J. 493, 510–514 (1966).

The plight of a man in prison may in these respects be even more acute than the plight of a person on the outside.

MR. JUSTICE WHITE dissented in an opinion in which MR. JUSTICE BLACK concurred.

SOME COMMENTS AND QUESTIONS

The Situation. The lawyer is entrusted with the sole privilege to practice law. Recent developments have brought competitors in the adjustment of human relations. These developments include the expansion and refinement of the social sciences, and the American passion for large-scale methods with consequent economy and speed. The bar has taken three sets of measures to meet the new conditions, affirmative, cooperative and prohibitive. The affirmative set comprises measures to achieve the readier availability of lawyers' services to all classes; the cooperative is illustrated by agreement on the national level on the nature of the work appropriate to each group;[1] the third set is protection of the lawyer's field from encroachment by others, illustrated by cases in this section, that is condemnation of the "unauthorized practice of law".

The Authoritative Sources. The problem of authoritative sources which pervades American law comes from two aspects of our government: (1) the federal aspect with its allocation of powers between the nation and the states; (2) the separation of powers among the three branches of government. The Keller case above dealt with both aspects: the federal government through the Interstate Commerce Commission was held to have power to determine the scope of the privilege of lay practitioners in federal commission matters; the state government through its Supreme Court was held to have the sole power under the state constitution to determine the privilege of the same practitioner to handle matters before the state commission. Are the decisions of the two courts consistent? And in the adjustment of the relations of the bar to other professional and business groups, may judges

---

1. These Statements of Principles are published in the Annual Report of the American Bar Association; e. g. 92 Rep.A.B.A. Appendix, at 37 (1968) and in III Martindale-Hubbell Law Directory, American Bar Association Section 215A–229A (1969).

who are members of the profession fairly and wisely claim and exercise the final power under the constitution to determine the field of each group?

The Fundamental Factors. In determining the relation of the bar to other groups, what are the fundamental factors which a court should consider? Is not the Arizona court above clearly wrong in using history as the test? Is it not wiser to shift the focus of the inquiry from the lawyer and his privilege, to the layman and his needs for legal services and how they can best be met? Is not this shift required by the United States Constitution as illustrated by the three cases above on lay intermediaries? In those cases the Supreme Court of the United States used as the test of constitutionality "the public interest".

The fundamental factors include the variety and needs of prospective clients, the special qualities of the lawyer, and the nature of the rivals and their qualities. The bases of the lawyer's claim to the special privilege include his superior competence, dependability, and breadth of view beyond that of a specialist. They extend as well to the social interest in the preservation of a strong and independent bar, which cannot be maintained if its field is taken over by others. The bar's rivals vary from the university trained and state tested expert, as the certified public accountant, on to the mere aggressive layman, and they include organizations which through lawyers in their employ render services like those of the independent lawyer. Among the reasons supporting the rivals are the readier access of clients to them; the equal or superior value of the rival's kind of expertness; the relation of the legal work as incidental to the laymen's principal work; speed in business transactions; economy and lower charges?

Court Proceedings. The lawyer alone has the privilege, except for the privilege of a litigant to represent himself.

Giving Advice and Drafting Documents. Here, too, the lawyer has greatly superior ability. Yet with the innumerable legal transactions which embody business and even personal relations, there are other factors which often justify lay action. It has been held so at times, but not always, when a legal instrument is prepared or filled in as incident to the business of the party. Compare the bank teller filling in a $100 note for a loan to a workman, with the drafting of a living trust by a trust company. Complexity as contrasted with simplicity have at times been mentioned or rejected as a decisive factor. The certified ability of the layman in his field is surely a factor.

Lawyers and Laymen Jointly. The association of lawyers and laymen might take any one of several forms which are usefully discussed in Opinion No. 297 of the American Bar Association Committee; 47 A.B.A.J. 527 (1961). One professional man may be in the employ of the other on a salary to which there is no objection; though a lawyer so employed continues to be bound by the standards of his profession. Should partnerships of men from two professions be allowed? This could result in superior service to the client but difference in standards and the possible use of the laymen as a cover for the solicitation of practice has so far led the bar to condemn it. Would or should the formation of this kind of partnership be protected by the constitutional "right of association?"

What of dual expertness of the same man, best illustrated by the lawyer-certified public accountant? The bar association opinion last mentioned insists the man must choose and may not practice both professions at the same time. Yet there are two or three thousand of these two-gun men, they have their own national association, and their privilege to carry on both professions has been as vigorously defended as condemned.[2] Is the dual practice socially desirable and constitutionally protected?

Then there is the layman who performs routine services for a lawyer, perhaps while he is studying law. A law clerk may lawfully answer the call of a court calendar to inform the court that his leader is engaged in another court.[3] Should there be a wide development in law of associate professional personnel, para-professionals as medical technicians and trained nurses in the medical profession, so as to free the lawyers for the more demanding part of his work?[4]

The Layman Alone. The opinions in *Johnson v. Avery*, p. 138 supra, illustrate the development of the activities of a layman alone in providing services usually thought of as within the lawyers' domain. What are the basic grounds of the opinions of Justice Fortas and Mr. Justice Douglas, and how far should their reasoning go in protecting laymen whether under the Constitution of the United States or under state law or under the standards of the legal profession? Justice Fortas appears to lay emphasis on "unless and until the State provide some reasonable alternative". Mr. Justice Douglas condemns the "closed shop attitude" of the bar generally and stresses the adequacy of the laymen's services.

---

2. Levy and Sprague, *Accounting and Law: Is Dual Practice in the Public Interest?*, 52 A.B.A.J. 1110 (1966); Mintz, *Accountancy and Law; Should Dual Practice Be Proscribed?*, 53 A.B.A.J. 225 (1967).

3. People v. Alexander, 53 Ill.App.3d 299 (1964).

4. See Johnstone and Hopson, Lawyers and Their Work 544 (1967).

Chapter III

STANDARDS, SUPPORTS AND SANCTIONS

SECTION 1. THE STANDARDS

"THE LAWYER IS HIS CLIENT WITH A LAW DEGREE."
"THE LAWYER IS AN OFFICER OF THE COURT."
"THE BAR IS A PROFESSION."

The characterization of a group under a particular designation may be urged as a guide to the rights and duties of the members of the group in their work. The three statements above are illustrations.

"The lawyer is his client with a law degree. The lawyer should do what the client would do, if the client had the learning and abilities of the lawyer." A student wrote down this statement at the end of a class hour and handed it to an instructor. The next day the instructor put the statement on the board and asked for comments. What comments does the reader have? What relation does the student's statement have to the other two statements at the head of this text note?

The other two statements are often used to characterize the lawyer. Are the statements accurate, and are they useful in guiding the actions of lawyers and judges? One objection to them is that the terms "officer of the court" and "profession" are vague and defy precise definition and should not be employed as the basis of conclusions in specific situations. Certainly, they are not as precise as such legal concepts as contingent remainder or holder in due course. Yet, they are as clear as such legal ideas as unjust enrichment, good faith, fiduciary, reasonableness, and constructive trust, the last of which is, as Judge Cardozo said, "the medium through which the conscience of equity finds expression."

Legal ideas vary in the measure of their definiteness. The fundamental, and therefore more general, ideas guide the development of the definite and specific, so it is no reason to reject an idea because it is fundamental and general.

> "Our discussion will be adequate if it has as much clearness as the subject admits of, for precision is not to be sought for alike in all discussions any more than in all the products of the crafts. . . . It is the mark of an educated man to look for precision in each class of things just so far as the nature of the subject admits; . . ."*

---

* Aristotle, Ethics, Book I, Chap. B.

A good way to begin the consideration of the last two statements at the head of this note is to raise, as to each of them, two sets of questions which run throughout the law. One set involves the operative facts which are relied on as bringing a particular matter within a certain class. If you give an affirmative (or a negative) answer about either of the foregoing statements as to the lawyer and the bar, what facts lead you to place or to refuse to place the lawyer or the bar in the stated class? The second set of questions concerns the consequences drawn from the classification. If you say the lawyer is (or is not) an officer of the court, and if you say the bar is (or is not) a profession, then what consequences of any importance would naturally follow from your action in placing or refusing to place the lawyer or the bar within the class named? The conclusion might be a precise one, as the application of a legal rule, or else a vaguer and more fundamental one relating to ethical attitudes and standards. After answering these specific questions about the quoted statements, the reader may be better able to answer the general questions about their accuracy and usefulness. To this end, the words of Holmes are apt.

"The life of the law has not been logic; it has been experience. The felt necessities of the time, the prevalent moral and political theories, intuitions of public policy, avowed or unconscious, even the prejudices which judges share with their fellow-men, have had a good deal more to do than the syllogism in determining the rules by which men should be governed." *

After considering the questions as to operative facts and conclusions we may be better able to answer the principal questions considered later in this chapter as to the accuracy and usefulness of the characterizations as "officer of the court" and "a profession."

There is a closely related aspect of the statements which a lawyer would naturally raise. He would insist on knowing the specific issue in which one or the other statements is urged or is denied in reaching the result. Let the reader consider the bearing and usefulness of the statements in this chapter, as well as in later cases throughout the book.

FACTORS AND STANDARDS

The profession of law carries on its work under complex conditions and with competing loyalties. The standards of the profession are guides to action which will most effectively further the accomplishments of the bar's responsibilities. Four relevant factors will be mentioned.

* Holmes, The Common Law 1 (1881).

The first is the fact of privilege and trust. The members of the profession, as a group, are given the exclusive privilege to practice and administer the law whether in the office or in the courtroom. The individual lawyer is entrusted by his client with the guidance and management of his affairs that touch the law.

A second set of factors comprises the complexities and difficulties under which the lawyer practices and administers the law. To summarize, the lawyer earns his living as a partisan representative of his clients; he is the most active participant in the public function of the administration of law; he administers the law through an adversary method within the larger competitive economic system; and through it all he shares the obligations all men have of decency and consideration in human relations. The complex setting of the lawyer's work gives rise to different loyalties.

The third set includes our social and political order with its constant changes. Rules of professional conduct, which at one time were appropriate and helpful to the performance of the bar's responsibilities may no longer be so.

Lastly, the standards of lawyers, to be useful, must be affirmative. The lawyer's function is to act, not to refrain from acting. The standards, even when couched in the negative form of restraints, are designed to insure the better performance of his affirmative roles.

The general standards of the profession achieve definiteness through specific rules directed to particular situations, as later chapters illustrate. Conversely, the specific rules should constantly be brought to the test of consistency with the general standards and policies. There is the danger here, as throughout the law, that as standards are transformed into definite rules, they may become rigid and lose sight of the fundamental policies which are the true guides. Changing conditions may call for a modification of an old specific rule when tested by the more fundamental standards in the new context. This twin process of developing the general into the particular and of testing the particular by the general is at the heart of this book.

THE RECONCILIATION OF LOYALTIES

In life and in law there are different affirmative loyalties and they must be wisely reconciled. A familiar illustration is the work of the judge. In any close case there are competing factors, and the judge must determine which set of factors should be given controlling force. In the work of the judge and of the legislator, these factors are ordinarily called policies or values. The same necessity of reconciling affirmative loyalties appears in the work of other men. The statements following concern the work of three different groups, the journalists, the men in public affairs, and the lawyers.

The Journalist. "The American newspaper of today is inescapably an enterprise devoted to four or five different objects at once. It is a private undertaking run for profit and for the support of its staff; that is, it is a business enterprise. It is a semi-public instrumentality for the diffusion of correct information. It is an agency for expressing editorial opinions. It is often the voice of a political party or some other public organization with continuing principles and traditions. That these and other purposes should sometimes clash with one another, and that their conflict should produce defective journalism, are inevitable. Much of the professional code of journalism has been developed to lessen these conflicts; to keep the counting-room from interfering with the editorial page, to prevent the editorial page from interfering with news presentation, and so on." Allan Nevins, The New York Times Book Review Section, December 4, 1938, p. 20.

The man in public affairs. ". . . [I]t is easy for men who have not shouldered any responsibility for public affairs and who have not had to make decisions as representatives or agents of the public to be completely unrealistic in their estimate of the moral problem in Government. The choice between good and evil is inescapable in life—public as well as private. . . . But the simple choice between the public interest and private or personal interest is not the biggest problem to-day. The difficult thing is to choose between or to harmonize various interests, . . ." Ethical Standards in Government, Report of a Subcommittee, Mr. Paul H. Douglas, Chairman, of the Committee on Labor and Public Welfare, United States Senate, 82d Congress, 1st Session, pp. 6–8 (1951).

The lawyer. "In the field of procedure . . . the lawyer is constantly concerned with ethical problems, for that field is the field of professional conduct. Here the question is not what is the law, but what shall I do? Shall I use a capias and arrest the defendant, or a summons and merely give him notice? Shall I annoy my opponent with an attachment? Shall I drag him away from home into a foreign court? Shall I hide my real defense under a general demurrer or a general issue? Shall I ask for a continuance, move for a directed verdict, request certain instructions to the jury, move for a new trial, assign certain errors? All these questions are to be answered by giving moral values to the alternatives of conduct. There are conflicting interests, as in every moral problem. The lawyer must consider his client, but need not wholly forget himself; he must remember that his opponent has a right to fair treatment and that society has a large stake in the successful operation of its judicial agencies. Which elements shall, in the particular case before him, have controlling force? On what basis shall he compromise the inconsistent tendencies? . . .

"If we accept the prevailing theory of utilitarian ethics, which seems peculiarly appropriate in judging the conduct of a public profession, we shall find the true motive of choice to be the greatest aggregate good to the lawyer, his client, the opposing lawyer and his client, the judge, the jury, the witnesses, and the general public. A conscientious consideration of the rights of all these parties to the litigation will result in a true ethical judgment." Edson R. Sunderland, An Inquiry Concerning the Functions of Procedure in Legal Education, 21 Mich.L.Rev. 372, 383–385 (1923).

The presence of several loyalties means that no one can be pressed to its logical extreme and dominate all the others. There must be a reconciliation of all of these loyalties, with each one having its due place and proportion.

Reconciliation is sometimes referred to as compromise. This word unfortunately has come to have a connotation of weakness and flabbiness, even though it has been employed by some great writers in a wholly different sense, as, in John Morley's vigorous essay "On Compromise." What is the guide to reconciliation of these affirmative loyalties? No easy answer can be given. To borrow again from Judge Cardozo, there is no legal calculus to give a precise answer. Wisdom, fairness, and appreciation of the role of the legal profession and the setting of its work—all will contribute to the answer.

THE LOYALTIES OF THE LAWYER

The lawyer owes several loyalties. In his work some of them reinforce one another. Others may come into conflict. The lawyer must reconcile these loyalties in action, giving its due weight to each of them. Let the reader consider whether the statement of loyalties offered below is accurate and helpful. Then let him make his own list. And in the variety of situations presented in the book, let him recur to his list of loyalties and see which ones are involved and which ones should predominate.

1. *Loyalty to the client.* This obvious duty calls for competence and zeal and fairness, unimpaired by competing loyalties to other persons.

2. *Loyalty to the administration of justice.* This calls for respect to the other parties in the administration of justice. (a) To the judge, as a representative of the public and an administrator of the law. (b) To the other side—whether the lawyer, the party or the witnesses—so that the machinery may function well and without obstruction. (c) To his profession, so that he may aid in its development and will avoid conduct which might bring it into disrepute.

3. *To the community.* (a) In his professional work, whether in the forum or in the office, he will aid in the performance of his profession's function of advancing justice through law. (b) He will exercise his powers as a leader, especially in the improvement of the machinery for the administration of justice.

4. *To his associates in practice.* To his partners, his seniors, his juniors, and his helpers.

5. *To himself.* (a) To his own economic interests, so that he may make a fair living through his professional work. This calls for such matters as fair measures to make his abilities known to potential clients, efficient office management, and reasonable fees. (b) To his ethical standards as a man, so he will not violate them in his professional work. The words of Polonius to his son, elevated as they are, will always have force. "This above all—to thine own self be true, and it must follow, as the night the day, Thou canst not then be false to any man."

SECTION 2. SUPPORTS AND SANCTIONS

Introduction. Standards without adherence are shams. Adherence to standards is achieved through supports and sanctions. The supports and sanctions do even more than secure adherence to standards; they affirm, modify or develop them. It is with the standards of the profession as it is with the law itself. The agencies of enforcement are at the same time agencies that shape and reshape the principles they enforce. This section gives a brief view of four kinds of supports and sanctions of professional standards.

The lawyer is bound by the law as he administers the law, so the processes of law enforcement through the courts have an important role. Yet the client is the person on whom falls the burden of the most widely applied court sanctions for the lawyer's failure to follow the law's directives. The dismissal of an action, the reversal of a judgment, the declaration of the invalidity of an instrument may all be the result of the lawyer's failure to observe the law in matters he handles. Illustrations of sanctions of this kind appear throughout this book as, indeed, in every field of law.

The lawyer himself bears the brunt of varied sanctions. They include (1) injunctive proceedings, (2) denial of liens or fees, (3) actions for damages, (4) summary proceedings by clients whose monies he has failed to pay over, (5) contempt proceedings, (6) disciplinary proceedings leading to censure or suspension or disbarment, (7) criminal prosecution. These sanctions appear in application throughout this book and are not dealt with here. The matters raised in this chapter include the general nature of the relation of the lawyer to the court and the authoritative sources of the standards and sanctions of the lawyer.

The supports and sanctions for the standards of the lawyer at work which are considered here are the court, the organized profession, the public, and the individual himself.

A. THE COURT

Introduction. In whom rests the authoritative legal control over the legal profession? The profession itself has great actual power in determining the standards by which its members shall be guided and in helping to enforce them through the pressure of professional opinion, as appears at many places in this book. Yet it seems never to have been contended that the organized profession in the United States has an inherent legal power over its members, as the inns of court have in England by custom over the barristers.

In this country the courts have exercised a large measure of control over the legal profession and matters appertaining to it. The source of the control may be found in statutes assuming to give power to the courts. Even in the absence of statute the power may be found in the principle of separation of the powers of government into three parts, the legislative, the executive and the judicial,—a principle embodied in the state as well as federal constitutions. The language of the constitutions providing for the judicial department varies from state to state, and different conclusions on the extent of the power may turn on differences in language. But the language is rarely explicit on control of the bar. To give content to vague provisions it is necessary to resort to consideration of history, and of the policy on which the constitutional provision rests.

It is well to take note that the principle of separation of powers came into our constitutions through a mistake. The speculation of the French political philosopher, Montesquieu, in his book, "The Spirit of the Laws", as to the English constitution was taken up by the makers of our government and written into all our constitutions. In a foreword to a republication of Montesquieu's book Justice Holmes pointed this out:

> "His England—the England of the threefold division of power into legislative, executive and judicial—was a fiction invented by him, a fiction which misled the makers of our Constitution as it misled Blackstone."

Even before the adoption of the Federal Constitution the authors of The Federalist Papers, No. 47–50 reviewed the constitutions of the states and showed there was "a partial mixture of powers" in all of them. So the constitutional provisions are not to be construed in a letter-bound way but in a way to achieve cooperation in the public interest.

The policy expressed in the principle of separation of powers is, in part, designed to protect against undue concentration of power in one person or in one body. In its affirmative aspect the policy is primarily one of independence—in the present matter, the independence of the judiciary from undue outside influence in the tasks committed to the judges. What does this policy fairly call for in the matter of power of the judiciary over the bar?

The question has arisen in a wide variety of situations. (1) The control over the conduct of individual members of the bar exercised, for example, through contempt or disciplinary proceedings. (2) The consideration and determination of the general standards of conduct of the bar, as, through a general inquiry into their conduct (infra, p. 150, People ex rel. Karlin v. Culkin), or through the promulgation or approval of canons of professional ethics. (3) The determination of who may become or remain members of the bar, as, admission to the bar (infra, p. 487), or disbarment. (4) The form of general organization of the bar, as, the self-governing bar (infra, p. 155). (5) The scope of the bar's exclusive field of activity, as, what is the unauthorized practice of law (supra, p. 128). (6) The inherent power of the courts to determine their own rules of procedure and practice.*

Granted the judiciary has power in the areas mentioned, the question remains as to the degree of its control. Does the control exist free of legislative action? Or is its control shared with the legislature, so that legislative provisions in the field are valid provided they do not unduly hamper the courts in their functions? Or is the power held at the sufferance of the legislature?

Another question concerns the part of the judicial system in which the power is vested. Is it vested in each separate court as to matters before that court, so that, for example, each court could punish for contempt for matters committed before it? Or is it vested wholly in the highest appellate court of the state?

THE CHANGE IN THE TONE OF THE ADMINISTRATION OF JUSTICE IN ENGLAND

W. BLAKE ODGERS IN A CENTURY OF LAW REFORM

Pages 41–42 (1901).*

Of all the mighty changes that have taken place in the nineteenth century, the greatest change has been in the tone of the administra-

---

* Dean Wigmore asserted that the courts have the inherent and exclusive power to determine their own rules of practice and procedure. John H. Wigmore, *All Legislative Rules for Judiciary Procedure are Void Constitutionally*, 23 Ill.L.Rev. 276 (1928); (reprinted in 1940, as *Legislature Has No Power in Procedural Field*, 24 Jour. Am.Jud.Soc. 70).

The New Jersey Constitution of 1947 was explicit in vesting control of practice and procedure in the state Supreme Court. In an opinion by Chief Justice Vanderbilt, the New Jersey Court held that an effort by the legislature to interfere with this power was in violation of the constitution. Winberry v. Salisbury, 5 N.J. 240 (1950). See also Re Sparrow, 338 Mo. 203 (1935).

** By permission of the Macmillan Company, publishers.

tion of both the civil and the criminal law. The manners of our law courts have marvelously improved. Formerly judges browbeat the prisoners, jeered at their efforts to defend themselves, and censured juries who honestly did their duty. Formerly, too, counsel bullied the witnesses and perverted what they said. Now the attitude and temper of Her Majesty's judges towards parties, witnesses, and prisoners alike has wholly changed, and the Bar too behave like gentlemen. Of course if a witness is deliberately trying to conceal the truth, he must be severely cross-examined; but an honest and innocent witness is now always treated with courtesy by counsel on both sides. The moral tone of the Bar is wholly different from what it was when Bentham wrote: they no longer seek to obtain a temporary victory by unfair means: they remember that it is their duty to assist the Court in eliciting the truth. This is due partly to the improved education of the Bar; partly no doubt to the influence of an omnipresent press; but still more to Her Majesty's judges. If counsel for the prosecution presses the case too vehemently against a prisoner; if counsel cross-examining in a civil case pries unnecessarily into the private concerns of the witness; a word, or even a look, from the presiding judge will at once check such indiscretion.

PEOPLE EX REL. KARLIN v. CULKIN

Court of Appeals of New York, 1928.
248 N.Y. 465, 60 A.L.R. 851, 162 N.E. 487.

CARDOZO, CH. J. A petition by three leading bar associations, presented to the Appellate Division for the first judicial department in January, 1928, gave notice to the court that evil practices were rife among members of the bar. "Ambulance chasing" was spreading to a demoralizing extent. . . . The bar as a whole felt the sting of the discredit thus put upon its membership by an unscrupulous minority.

It spoke its mind through its associations, the organs of its common will. The court was asked to inquire into the practices charged in the petition, and any other illegal and improper practices, either through an investigation to be conducted by itself or through some other appropriate procedure. . . .

The court responded promptly. It held (speaking by its presiding justice) that its disciplinary power is not limited to "cases where specific charges are made against a named attorney." It will act of its own motion whenever it has reasonable cause to believe that there has been professional misconduct either by one or by a class. . . .

The order of the Appellate Division designates a justice of the Supreme Court to conduct the investigation at an appointed term with full authority "to summon witnesses and to compel the giving of testimony and the production of books, papers and documentary evidence."

. . .

The investigation proceeded in the form directed by the order. Many witnesses were examined. They were given the privilege at their option of examination in camera. There came a time when the appellant, a member of the bar for twenty-five years, was served with a subpoena. He appeared in court, but refused to be sworn. His practice had involved the trial of many actions for personal injuries. He was called to testify as to his conduct in the procurement of retainers in these cases and in others. There is no denial that the testimony had relation to the ends of the inquiry. His refusal to testify was a challenge to the inquiry as a whole. Upon his persisting in that challenge, the court adjudged him in contempt and committed him to jail until he should submit to be sworn and examined. A petition for his release upon habeas corpus was dismissed. Both orders, the one adjudging the contempt and the one dismissing the writ, were affirmed by the Appellate Division. They are now before this court.

The precise question to be determined is whether there is power in the Appellate Division to direct a general inquiry into the conduct of its own officers, the members of the bar, and in the course of that inquiry to compel one of those officers to testify as to his acts in his professional relations. The grand jury inquires into crimes with a view to punishment or correction through the sanctions of the criminal law. There are, however, many forms of professional misconduct that do not amount to crimes. Even when they do, disbarment is not punishment within the meaning of the criminal law (Matter of Rouss, 221 N.Y. 81, 85, 116 N.E. 782). Inquisition by the court with a view to the discipline of its officers is more than a superfluous duplication of inquisition by the grand jury with a view to the punishment of criminals. The two fields of action are diverse and independent.

. . .

"Membership in the bar is a privilege burdened with conditions" (Matter of Rouss, supra, p. 84). The appellant was received into that ancient fellowship for something more than private gain. He became an officer of the court, and, like the court itself, an instrument or agency to advance the ends of justice. His co-operation with the court was due whenever justice would be imperilled if co-operation was withheld. He might be assigned as counsel for the needy, in causes criminal or civil, serving without pay (Code Crim.Pro. sec. 308; Civ. Prac.Act, secs. 196, 198). He might be directed by summary order to make restitution to a client of moneys or other property wrongfully withheld (Matter of H., an Attorney, 87 N.Y. 521). He might be censured, suspended or disbarred for "any conduct prejudicial to the administration of justice" (Judiciary Law, sec. 88, subd. 2). All this is undisputed. We are now asked to hold that when evil practices are rife to the dishonor of the profession, he may not be compelled by rule or order of the court, whose officer he is, to say what he knows of them, subject to his claim of privilege if the answer will expose him to punishment for crime (Matter of Rouss, supra). Co-operation between court and officer in furtherance of justice is a phrase without reality if the officer may then be silent in the face of a command to speak. . . . [The court reviewed the English and American precedents.]

The argument from history is reinforced by others from analogy and policy. The power of the court in the discipline of its officers is in truth a dual one. It prefers the charges, and determines them (Matter of Percy, 36 N.Y. 651; Randall v. Brigham, 7 Wall. (U.S.) 523, 540; Ex parte Wall, 107 U.S. 265, 2 S.Ct. 569; Fairfield County Bar v. Taylor, 60 Conn. 11, 22 A. 441; Matter of Durant, 80 Conn. 140, 67 A. 497). Preliminary inquiry there must be, at least to some extent, before a decision can be reached whether to prosecute at all (Matter of Percy, supra). Voluntary affidavits or even unsworn statements will often be enough (Matter of Percy, supra; Randall v. Brigham, supra). Occasions may arise where the probe must be more searching if justice is not to fail. The power to inquire imports by fair construction the power to inquire by methods appropriate and adequate, and so by compulsory process if search would otherwise be thwarted. Analogies are at hand to give support to that conclusion. A legislative body may act upon common knowledge or information voluntarily contributed. At times it stands in need of more. There is then power to investigate by subpoena under the sanction of an oath. . . .

We conclude that the refusal was a contempt (Civ.Prac.Act, sec. 406), and that the investigation must proceed. In so holding we place power and responsibility where in reason they should be. No doubt the power can be abused, but that is true of power generally. In discharging a function so responsible and delicate, the courts will refrain, we may be sure, from a surveillance of the profession that would be merely odious or arbitrary. They will act considerately and cautiously, mindful at all times of the dignity of the bar and of the resentment certain to be engendered by any tyrannous intervention. No lack of caution or consideration can be imputed to them here. They did not move of their own prompting, but at the instance of the very bar whose privacy and privilege they are said to have infringed. In the long run the power now conceded will make for the health and honor of the profession and for the protection of the public. If the house is to be cleaned, it is for those who occupy and govern it, rather than for strangers, to do the noisome work.

The orders are affirmed.

NOTE

Would this case be decided differently today because of the privilege of the lawyer not to testify to his own harm? Cf. infra p. 500.

CAMMER v. UNITED STATES

Supreme Court of the United States, 1956.
350 U.S. 399, 76 S.Ct. 456, 100 L.Ed. 474.

[A District of Columbia grand jury returned an indictment charging a person with having filed a false noncommunist affidavit in violation of a federal statute. The indicted person's lawyer mailed identical letters and questionnaires to all members of that grand jury who were employees of the federal government. The questions were directed toward learning whether the government employee jurors might have been influenced by bias or fear to indict persons charged with having had some associations with the Communist Party. The lawyer was ordered by the District Court in which the indictment had been returned to show cause why he should not be adjudged guilty of contempt under 18 U.S.C.A. § 401(2) (1964). The statute provided:

"A court of the United States shall have power to punish by fine or imprisonment, at its discretion, such contempt of its authority, and none other, as—

. . . (2) Misbehavior of any of its officers in their official transactions."

The District Court found the lawyer guilty of contempt, the Court of Appeals affirmed, and the Supreme Court granted certiorari. The lawyer contended that he was not guilty of "misbehavior" and that he was not in this matter engaged in an "official transaction". The Supreme Court left aside these contentions and reversed the Court of Appeals on the ground that the lawyer was not an "officer of the court" within the meaning of the statute.]

MR. JUSTICE BLACK delivered the opinion of the Court. . . .

It has been stated many times that lawyers are "officers of the court." One of the most frequently repeated statements to this effect appears in Ex parte Garland, 4 Wall. 333, 378. The Court pointed out there, however, that an attorney was not an "officer" within the ordinary meaning of that term. . . .

There are strong reasons why attorneys should not be considered "officers" under Sec. 401(2). As we pointed out in the *Nye* case [313 U.S. 33], the 1831 Act was promptly passed by the Congress after the impeachment proceedings against Judge Peck failed by a senatorial vote of 22 to 21. Judge Peck had sent a lawyer to jail and had taken away his right to practice as punishment for an alleged contempt. . . . Those directing the impeachment proceedings, who later brought about the passage of the 1831 Act [from which the statute here in question was derived] expressed deep concern lest lawyers continue to be subjected to summary trials by judges without the safeguards of juries and regular procedure. Congressman James Buchan who made the last argument against Judge Peck stated: . . .

"I hold it to be the imperative duty of an attorney to protect the interests of his client out of court as well as in court. . . . The public have almost as deep an interest in the independence of the bar as of the bench."

We hold that a lawyer is not the kind of "officer" who can be summarily tried for contempt under 18 U.S.C.A. § 401(2). . . . Reversed.

NOTES

(1) Would Judge Cardozo and Justice Black differ in the results they would reach in the two cases next above?

(2) Is the statement that the lawyer is an officer of the court unfortunate because it ignores the nature of much of the lawyer's work? Most of his work is done not as advocate but as counsellor and guide of the client and shaper and draftsman of his client's plans. Even when serving as advocate, the lawyer appears as often before an administrative tribunal as before a court. Would the term proposed by Professor Willard Hurst be a more appropriate one, "an office of the legal order"? Hurst, *The Legal Profession*, 1966 Wis.L.Rev. 967, 976 (1966).

(3) Is the customary statement a useful one, nevertheless, as it is a reminder that a lawyer is something more than a servant of his client and has wider duties to the social order which confers on him his privileged position?

MATTER OF STERN

Supreme Court of New York, Appellate Division, 1910.
137 App.Div. 909, 121 N.Y.S. 948.

CLARKE, J.: Charges of unprofessional conduct having been filed against the respondent, he has interposed a voluminous answer accompanied by supporting affidavits and exhibits. Ordinarily upon charges and an answer a reference is ordered to ascertain and report the facts. We do not think such a course necessary in this matter. The charges are not presented by the Association of the Bar upon a preliminary examination by its grievance committee but by a private prosecutor, a former client of the respondent, who is and has been engaged in a bitter legal contest with the respondent having to do, not with the professional relation of the respondent to him, but arising from the disappointment of the complainant at the provisions of the will of his deceased daughter in which the respondent was named as a legatee. The first charge is frivolous; the second and the third have been the subjects of investigation in court proceedings which resulted favorably to the respondent. They are, upon their face, serious, but they are so because of most important omissions in the narrative of facts intended to support them and are so fully met and disposed of by the answering papers as, in our judgment, to render them unworthy of further consideration. The motive of the attack is obvious, its animus apparent, and should not be permitted to succeed. The duty of this court towards the members of the bar, its officers, is not only to administer discipline to those found to be guilty of unprofessional conduct, but to protect the reputation of those attacked upon frivolous or malicious charges. To dignify these charges by referring them would be to permit the purpose of the attack to be accomplished to a considerable measure. We find nothing to justify the charge of unprofessional conduct and nothing to investigate, and the charges are hence dismissed.

B. THE ORGANIZED PROFESSION

Introduction. The law, along with medicine and theology, is one of the ancient learned professions. Is law still to regard itself as a profession? An answer drawn from history alone is unsatisfying. The answer must be sought in the social facts and in social utility that may justify calling the law a profession.

Dean Pound defined a profession: [1]

"The term [a profession] refers to a group of men pursuing a learned art as a common calling in the spirit of a public service —no less a public service because it may incidentally be a means of livelihood . . . Historically there are three ideas involved in a profession: organization, learning, i. e., pursuit of a learned art, and a spirit of public service. These are essential. A further idea, that of gaining livelihood, is involved in a calling."

A sociologist, while saying there is no absolute difference between professional and other kinds of occupational behavior, insisted on the social importance of a professional attitude and defined professional behavior in terms of four attributes (1) a high degree of systematic knowledge; (2) primary orientation to the community interest; (3) a high degree of self control through codes of ethics; and (4) a set of rewards for work achievement.[2]

The traditional position of the bar as a profession has been challenged on the ground that the practice of law is now a business.

"No amount of preaching can alter the cold, indisputable fact that the law has ceased to be a sacrosanct profession and has become a highly competitive business." [3]

1. Roscoe Pound, The Lawyer from Antiquity to Modern Times 5–6 (1953).

2. Bernard Barber, Some Problems in the Sociology of the Professions, in The Professions in America 18, (Kenneth S. Lynn et al. ed. 1965). In that volume there is a discussion of The Legal Profession by Professor Paul A. Freund. For another general discussion of the subject see Carr-Saunders and Wilson, The Professions (1933, 1964).

3. Argument of counsel in Barton v. The State Bar of California, 209 Cal. 677, 671 (1930).

From this denial of the standing of the law as a profession, the conclusion has been urged that lawyers are free to indulge in practices, such as advertising, permitted to businessmen.[4] A different kind of objection, already mentioned, is that the term "profession" is too general in determining the standards of a lawyer. It is better, so it is urged, to analyze and state the situation of the lawyer and ascertain what loyalties are called for in the light of the situation:

> "A lawyer acts for others. His profession offers peculiar temptations to serve himself at the expense of his clients. Many sins of this sort defy detection or punishment. So too, ill means can be employed to a great extent with like immunity . . . . It seems better to state and emphasize the duty of loyalty rather than to focus attention upon the notion of a profession, from which the same duty may be implied."[5]

A quite different challenge to the old distinction between law and business was made by Justice Brandeis before he went on the bench. He urged, not that law has become a business and therefore lawyers may adopt lower standards, but that business management should be regarded as a profession with the corresponding heightened sense of obligation.[6] The same point was made by Professor Dodd with respect to corporate managers:

> ". . . the legal standard applicable to the directors and other persons by whom our large business corporations are managed will prove extremely difficult of enforcement unless that standard is calculated to appeal to the managers themselves and thus to attain the status of a professional code of ethics rather than that of a legal rule imposed upon an antagonistic group by the community at large."[7]

Justice Brandeis and Professor Dodd evidently assumed that the conception of a profession carries with it a higher individual and group sense of responsibility than is so with many other occupations. For professional men there are room and need, not only for higher standards, but also for sanctions in group attitudes that go beyond the processes of the law.

By contrast, the student's statement quoted on p. 142, (above) pressed the lawyer's obligation to his client to the point of servility. The other two general characterizations as an officer of the court and as a profession are reminders of other duties: first, the duty to aid in the administration of the law; second, adherence to the standards developed by the group in the wise reconciliation and performance of the several loyalties of the lawyer.

---

4. *Id.*

5. Hewitt, Book Review, 35 Yale L.J. 391, 392–393 (1926).

6. Louis D. Brandeis, Business—A Profession 1 (1914).

7. Dodd, *Is Effective Enforcement of the Fiduciary Duties of Corporate Managers Practicable?*, 2 U.Chi.L.Rev. 194, 199 (1935).

LATHROP v. DONOHUE

Supreme Court of Wisconsin, 1960.
10 Wis.2d 230, 102 N.W.2d 404.

[In 1943, the Wisconsin legislature passed a statute providing for the integration of the bar of that state. The Wisconsin Supreme Court held the statute was not binding upon it because the "power to integrate the bar is an incident to the exercise of the judicial power." The State Supreme Court twice rejected petitions for integration; later it ordered integration for a trial period of two years; and still later ordered integration on a permanent basis as the State Bar of Wisconsin. The rules and by-laws of the integrated bar imposed compulsory membership and payment of annual dues upon all lawyers in active practice in the state. They also authorized various activities of the integrated bar indicated below.

The plaintiff, a Wisconsin lawyer, brought an action against the treasurer of the State Bar of Wisconsin to recover $15 paid under protest as annual dues to the State Bar. The grounds of the action were that the integration of the bar violated the rights of the plaintiff under the Constitutions of Wisconsin and the United States, especially his rights of freedom of association and free speech. The plaintiff stated in general terms that the State Bar had used its funds and employees in opposition to the adoption of legislation in Wisconsin which the plaintiff favored. The defendant demurred to the complaint. The trial court sustained the demurrer and dismissed the complaint. On appeal the decision below was sustained by the Supreme Court of Wisconsin.]

CURRIE, J. . . . The rules and by-laws of the State Bar do not compel the plaintiff to associate with anyone. He is free to attend or not attend its meetings or vote in its elections as he chooses. . . . He is as free as he was before to voice his views on any subject in any manner he wishes, even though such views be diametrically opposed to a position taken by the State Bar. . . .

In every instance the legislative measures advocated or opposed have dealt with the administration of justice, court reform, and legal practice. Neither the above-quoted by-laws nor the stated purposes . . . for which the bar was integrated would permit the State Bar to be engaged in legislative activities unrelated to these three subjects. The plaintiff complains that certain proposed legislation, upon which the State Bar has taken a stand, embody changes in substantive law and points to the recently enacted Family Code. . . . We do not deem that the State Bar should be compelled to refrain from taking a stand on a measure which does substantially deal with legal practice and the administration of justice merely because it also makes some changes in substantive law.

We are of the opinion that the public welfare will be promoted by securing and publishing the composite judgment of the members of the bar of the state on measures directly affecting the administration of justice and the practice of law. . . . A voluntary association is free to take a stand on any proposed legislation in any field it deems desirable. This is not true of the State Bar which must confine its activities in legislative matters to those authorized by the rules and by-laws promulgated by this court. . . . This court will exercise its inherent powers to take remedial action should the State Bar engage in an activity not authorized by the rules and by-laws and not in keeping with the stated objectives for which it was created. . . .

When we attempt to balance the competing interests at stake in this action we find no regulation of, or interference with, any of the plaintiff's rights of free speech, assembly, or petition. . . .

The judgment appealed from is affirmed.

NOTE

In Re Unification of New Hampshire Bar, 248 A.2d 709 (N.H.1968), a "unified bar" was established for a trial period of three years.

LATHROP v. DONOHUE

Supreme Court of the United States, 1961.
367 U.S. 820, 81 S.Ct. 1826, 6 L.Ed.2d 1191.

[The Supreme Court of the United States granted certiorari in the Wisconsin case of *Lathrop v. Donohue*, supra p. 157. The Court affirmed the decision by a vote of 7 to 2 with 5 opinions. Speaking through Mr. Justice Brennan, four of the justices (Chief Justice Warren and Justices Brennan, Clark and Stewart) upheld the State Bar against the attack on the ground of freedom of association; but they reserved the question whether the petitioner's right of free speech was infringed if his dues money was used to support the political activities of the State Bar. Three of the justices (Justices Harlan, Frankfurter and Whittaker) would uphold integration throughout. Two of the justices (Justices Black and Douglas) dissented in separate opinions, on the ground the petitioner's constitutional rights were violated.]

MR. JUSTICE BRENNAN announced the judgment of the Court and an opinion in which THE CHIEF JUSTICE, MR. JUSTICE CLARK and MR. JUSTICE STEWART join. . . .

In our view the case presents a claim of impingement upon freedom of association no different from that which we decided in Railway Employe's Dept. v. Hanson, 351 U.S. 225, 76 S.Ct. 714, 100 L.Ed. 1112. We there held that § 2 of the Railway Labor Act, 45 U.S.C.A. § 152, did not on its face abridge protected rights of association in authorizing union-shop agreements between interstate railroads and unions of their employees conditioning the employees' continued employment on payment of union dues, initiation fees and assessments. There too the record indicated that the organizations engaged in some activities similar to the legislative activities of which the appellant complains. See International Association of Machinists v. Street, ante [367 U.S. 740], . . . Given the character of the integrated bar shown on this record, in the light of the limitation of the membership requirement to the compulsory payment of reasonable annual dues, we are unable to find any impingement upon protected rights of association.

However, appellant would have us go farther and decide whether his constitutional rights of free speech are infringed if his dues money is used to support the political activities of the State Bar. . . .

We are persuaded that on this record we have no sound basis for deciding appellant's constitutional claim insofar as it rests on the assertion that his rights of free speech are violated by the use of his money for causes which he opposes. . . . That issue is reserved."

MR. JUSTICE HARLAN with whom MR. JUSTICE FRANKFURTER joins, concurring in the judgment.

. . .

Unless one is ready to fall prey to what are at best but alluring abstractions on rights of free speech and association, I think he will be hard put to it to find any solid basis for the Constitutional qualms which, though unexpressed, so obviously underlie the plurality opinion, or for the views of my two dissenting Brothers, one of whom finds unconstitutional the entire Integrated Bar concept 367 U.S. at pages 877–885, 81 S.Ct. at pages 1856–1860, and the other of whom holds the operations of such a Bar unconstitutional to the extent that they involve taking "the money of protesting lawyers" and using "it to support causes they are against" 367 U.S. at page 871, 81 S.Ct. at page 1852.

For me, there is a short and simple answer to all of this. The Hanson case, 351 U.S. 225, 76 S.Ct. 714, 100 L.Ed. 1112, decided by a unanimous Court, surely lays at rest all doubt that a State may constitutionally condition the right to practice law upon membership in an integrated bar association, a condition fully as justified by state needs as the union shop is by federal needs. Indeed the conclusion reached in *Hanson* with respect to compulsory union membership seems to me *a fortiori* true here, in light of the supervisory powers which the State, through its courts, has traditionally exercised over admission to the practice of law, . . .

Mr. Justice Black, dissenting. . . .

The appellee's contention in this respect rests upon two different arguments. The first of these is that the use of compelled dues by an integrated bar to further legislative ends contrary to the wishes of some of its members can be upheld under the so-called "balancing test," which permits abridgment of First Amendment rights so long as that abridgment furthers some legitimate purpose of the State.

The "balancing" argument here is identical to that which has recently produced a long line of liberty-stifling decisions in the name of "self-preservation." . . .

The second ground upon which the appellee would have us distinguish compelled support of hated views as practiced by an integrated bar from compelled support of such views as practiced by the unions involved in the *Street* case is that lawyers are somehow different from other people. . . .

The mere fact that a lawyer has important responsibilities in society does not require or even permit the State to deprive him of those protections of freedom set out in the Bill of Rights for the precise purpose of insuring the independence of the individual against the Government and those acting for the Government.

I would reverse this case and direct the Supreme Court of Wisconsin to require refund of the dues exacted under protest from the appellant in order to permit the Wisconsin State Bar to advocate measures he is against and to oppose measures he favors.

Mr. Justice Douglas, dissenting. . . .

If the State can compel all lawyers to join a guild, I see no reason why it cannot make the same requirement of doctors, dentists, and nurses. . . .

We established no such precedent in Railway Employes' Dept. v. Hanson, 351 U.S. 225, 76 S.Ct. 714, 100 L.Ed. 1112. We dealt there only with a problem in collective bargaining, viz., is it beyond legislative competence to require all who benefit from the process of collective bargaining and enjoy its fruits to contribute to its costs? . . .

If we had here a law which required lawyers to contribute to a fund out of which clients would be paid in case attorneys turned out to be embezzlers, the present objection might not be relevant. In that case, one risk of the profession would be distributed among all members of the group.

There is here no evil shown. It has the mark of "a lawyer class or caste"—system of "a self-governing and self-disciplining bar" such as England has. The pattern of this legislation is regimentation. . . .

While the legislature has few limits where strictly social legislation is concerned (Giboney v. Empire Storage Co., 336 U.S. 490, 69

S.Ct. 684, 93 L.Ed. 834; Tot v. United States, 319 U.S. 463, 63 S.Ct. 1241, 87 L.Ed. 1519), the First Amendment applies strictures designed to keep our society from becoming moulded into patterns of conformity which satisfy the majority.

NOTES

(1) The bar, as every profession and many specialized groups, has a central organization which has formulated standards for the members and continues to interpret and seeks to enforce them. On what matters may the organized bar wisely establish such standards and seek to enforce them by its own machinery or with the aid of the courts? And what should, or must, be the guides of the bar in the development and enforcement of its standards? In the first three cases on group legal services supra p. 72, the Supreme Court of the United States applied the test of "the public interest" in determining the constitutionality of the standards of the bar there involved. This test should be applied to all standards of the bar, it will be agreed, in determining their validity under state law, and also whether they meet the tests of policy which guides the bar itself in formulating them.

(2) The opinions in the principal case reveal different attitudes on the extent to which the establishment of standards may be wisely undertaken by the organized bar. Mr. Justice Harlan was explicit in approving the "useful and significant" activities of the bar in its sphere of activities. Mr. Justice Douglas was emphatic in condemning the "guild" character of the organization.

As the reader goes through the book he will find that the questions put in the note immediately preceding will recur in many settings. There is the fact that the members of the bar, while representing their clients and aiding in the administration of law, are making their living out of this work and share in the self-interest which affects us all. The self-interest of the bar might distort the stated standards.

Yet it would be erroneous to consider the question of standards by itself. The organized bar in this country has an extraordinary record of achievement in its appropriate fields of concern. This record is sketched by Mr. Whitney North Seymour in the 25th Annual Cardozo Lecture: "The Obligation of the Lawyer to His Profession".* Characteristically, he put his subject in terms not of achievements by the profession but of opportunities and obligations of lawyers to contribute to those achievements. When seen in the larger setting, the shaping and enforcement of standards is a natural part of the organized bar's activities. This part, too, calls for constant attention so the standards will match the public need in these rapidly changing times which bring more law and more work for men of law.

* 23 The Record Ass'n Bar City N. Y. 311 (1968).

THE FUNCTIONS OF PROFESSIONAL ETHICS

ROSTOW, THE LAWYER AND HIS CLIENT
48 A.B.A.J. 25–26 (1962).

No professional group exists, as Durkheim has said, without its own moral discipline, its own ethics.[1] Every man is a citizen, a member of a family, and usually a member also of a variety of social organisms and bodies, private and public, depending on his interests. A lawyer, like members of other specialized professional groups, is subject to the special ethical rules of his guild, which often present problems of conflict and accommodation with the ethical rules applicable to individuals and to families, and to those of citizenship generally. . . .

One of the main functions of codes of professional ethics, Durkheim says at a later point, is to reconcile these contrasts and conflicts between individual and group interests, and those of the community at large. In order for groups within a society to persist, he remarks, "each part must behave in a way that enables the whole to survive". The moral discipline of the professional group, he adds, "is a code of rules that lays down for the individual what he should do so as not to damage collective interests and so as not to disorganize the society of which he forms a part". We might add to Durkheim's exposition the more affirmative thought that the function of professional ethics in the life of the group is not merely to avoid damaging conflicts between the code of the group and that of society, but actively to further, through the work of the group, the fulfillment of goals approved by the society to which the professional group belongs, and which it should serve.

ETHICAL STANDARDS IN GOVERNMENT, REPORT OF A SUBCOMMITTEE (HON. PAUL H. DOUGLAS, CHAIRMAN) OF THE COMMITTEE ON LABOR AND PUBLIC WELFARE
U. S. Sen., 82d Congress, 1st Session, p. 35 (1951).

Codes of professional ethics to guide the behavior of professional groups summarize the sense of obligation which permeates the more thoughtful members of an entire society. When a professional group begins to recognize its character and to be aware of the importance of its public (or socially useful) function, it is ready to think about the specific obligations which rest upon it.

The broad moral code, to which members of society owe allegiance, is not enough. Its principles must also be applied to the pro-

---

1. Emile Durkheim, Professional Ethics and Civil Morals (Lecons de Sociologie Physique des Moeurs et du Droit) pages 14–15 (American edition, 1958). [Author's footnote].

fessional activities in anticipation of the issues and dilemmas which arise, so that professional obligations can be seen clearly and understood, free from the tensions and temptations which beset a busy professional life. Professional codes are a recognition that professional status brings with it the power to exploit its position—to use it for personal rather than professional ends. . . .

When a specific group with a socially useful function begins to wield great power, it stands at a moral crossroads. It must recognize its social or public function and accept its obligation to protect that function against the exploitive tendencies which power brings, or else its exploitive tendencies will tend to become predominant. There are many forms of exploitation, but in a commercial order, commercial forms of exploitation are naturally predominant. Probably the severest pressure on any professional group today is a temptation to commercialize its power. A code is essentially a measure to safeguard the integrity of the professional function. . . .

THE AMERICAN BAR ASSOCIATION

The American Bar Association was organized in 1878. Its constitution provides that its objects shall be: "to uphold and defend the Constitution of the United States and maintain representative government; to advance the science of jurisprudence; to promote the administration of justice and the uniformity of legislation and of judicial decisions throughout the nation; to uphold the honor of the profession of law; to apply its knowledge and experience in the field of the law to the promotion of the public good; to encourage cordial intercourse among the members of the American Bar; and to correlate and promote such activities of the Bar organizations in the nation and in the respective states as are within these objects, in the interest of the legal profession and of the public." Its stated objectives were widened in 1949, "to apply its knowledge and experience in the field of the law to the promotion of the public good."

The Association is an organization of individuals, not a federation of bar associations, and all American lawyers are eligible. In 1970 its members numbered over 140,000, nearly 50 per cent of the lawyers of the country. Law students are now eligible for membership.

The control and administration of the Association are vested in the House of Delegates which is composed of, for the most part, (1) delegates from the states, chosen by the members of the Association in each state; (2) delegates from state and certain local bar associations; (3) delegates chosen by the Assembly; (4) the heads of stated national legal organizations; (5) the Attorney-General and the Solicitor-General of the United States; and (6) the officers of the Association.

The work of the Association is carried forward primarily by standing and special committees and by sections. The subjects range widely over most of the fields of practice as General Practice, Labor Law, Aeronautical Law. They include as well improvements of the law and of law administration (as Civil Rights, Legal Aid and Indigent Defendants, and Judicial Administration). The American Bar Foundation, independently administered, is the research arm of the American Bar Association.

The headquarters of the Association, to which inquiries may be sent, are in the American Bar Center, 1155 East 60th Street, Chicago, Illinois 60637.

NOTES

(1) See Edson R. Sunderland, History of the American Bar Association and Its Work (1953). Chapter X, page 376 infra discusses the public responsibilities of the organized bar.

(2) There are numerous specialized organizations of lawyers. Those organizations which are represented in the House of Delegates of the American Bar Association are listed in the annual report of the Association. Two of these associations, devoted to the improvement of the law, deserve special mention. The American Law Institute is described in Herbert F. Goodrich, *The Story of the American Law Institute,* 1951 Wash.U.L.Q. 283 (1951). The American Judicature Society, which has been notably effective in advancing its purpose "to promote the efficient administration of justice", publishes the Journal, Judicature.

(3) The National Lawyers Guild was organized in 1937. The preamble to its constitution characterized it, as "a professional organization which shall function as an effective social force in the service of the people to the end that human rights shall be regarded as more sacred than property rights". The troubled career of the Guild is set out well in Countryman and Finman, The Lawyer in Modern Society 392–402 (1966).

(4) The National Bar Association, a predominately Negro organization, was founded in 1925 at a time when the American Bar Association did not cordially welcome Negroes to membership. Its stated purposes include advancing the science of jurisprudence, inproving the administration of justice, promoting legislation that will improve the economic conditions of all the citizens of the United States, and protecting the civil and political rights of the citizens and residents of the several States. A volume published in 1963, Who's Who in the National Bar Association deserves quotation at some length. In a Foreword the president, Mr. Robert E. Lillard, described the contributions made by the association "to enhance the stature and promote the efficiency of the Negro practitioner as well as aid the constructive administration of justice." (p. 4) In considering the future of the Association and describing some immediate and detailed programs, Mr. George W. Crockett, Jr. concluded that "the central objective of the National Bar Association should be to work itself out of existence by working, as its Constitution provides, 'for the integration of the American bar.'" (p. 8) And in a discussion of the "Why" of the Association Mr. William S. Thompson in-

cluded a passage from an address in 1959 to the Association by Dr. Martin Luther King:

> "What of the future? Let me answer this by attempting to give the lie to an attitude too often prevalent in society—the feeling that social progress is an automatic phenomenon that can emerge without effort . . . to believe this is to be victimized with an illusion wrapped in superstition. Human progress is neither automatic nor inevitable.
> . . . every step toward the goal of justice requires sacrifice, suffering and struggle; the tireless exertion and passionate concern of dedicated individuals." (p. 14)

(5) In the 1940s, "a broad study of the functioning of lawyers in a free society" was instituted under the name of The Survey of the Legal Profession. The study is described by its director, Reginald Heber Smith, in *Survey of the Legal Profession: Its Scope, Methods and Objectives*, 39 A.B.A.J. 548 (1953). The American Lawyer by Blaustein and Porter (1954) gives in short form the essence of the Survey reports. The reports are listed in an appendix to that book at page 342 as well as in a Note to 39 A.B.A.J. 548, 551 (1953).

STATE AND LOCAL BAR ASSOCIATIONS

The state and local bar associations vary widely in their vigor and activities. A strong state association, which has been notably effective in the continuing education of the bar, is the State Bar of California. A strong local organization with breadth of view in its activities is The Association of the Bar of the City of New York. The most extensive discussion of the history of state and local bar associations is found in Roscoe Pound, The Lawyer from Antiquity to Modern Times (1953).

Most state and local bar associations are voluntary in character. Another form of organization is the all-inclusive bar association, known variously as the integrated bar, the incorporated bar, or the self-governing bar. The first of these bar associations, which include in their membership all the lawyers in active practice in a state, was organized in 1921.

NOTE

An excellent discussion of the government and activities of bar associations is given in Winters, Bar Association Organization and Activities (1954). The book, as the author states in the preface, is "both a handbook for bar association officers and a report to the Survey of the Legal Profession on bar association activities".

The annual report of the American Bar Association gives a directory of the state bar associations with the names and addresses of their officers, as well as a directory of those local bar associations, specialized bar associations and other organizations represented in the House of Delegates of the American Bar Association.

CODE OF PROFESSIONAL RESPONSIBILITY *

The American Bar Association adopted in 1969 a Code of Professional Responsibility. The Code consists of three interrelated parts: Canons, Ethical Considerations, Disciplinary Rules. The nine Canons are "axiomatic" statements of the obligations of lawyers. The Ethical Considerations, as the Preamble states, "are aspirational in character and represent the objectives toward which every member of the profession should strive. . . . The Disciplinary Rules, unlike the Ethical Considerations are mandatory in character and state the minimum level of conduct below which no lawyer can fall without being subject to disciplinary action." In a Prefatory Statement the relationship to the existing Canons was indicated:

> "The present Canons, nevertheless, contain many provisions that are sound in substance, and all of these have been brought forward in the proposed Code."

The Code was drafted by a committee of twelve members with Mr. Edward L. Wright as Chairman and Professor John F. Sutton, Jr., as Reporter.

Frequent references to the Code of Professional Responsibility and to the earlier Canons of Professional Ethics are made in this book. The Code is set forth in full at pages 539, 589 infra.**

NOTES

(1) The Canons of Professional Ethics were adopted by the American Bar Association in 1908. They have been adopted also by many state and local bar associations. In a few states the legislatures enacted the Canons into law, and in other states the courts or integrated bars have promulgated them as professional standards. Their history and a statement of the amendments made are sketched in Drinker, Legal Ethics, pp. 23–26, 309–325. (1953) An excellent appraisal of the background and range of the Canons is given in Hurst, The Growth of American Law, The Law Makers (1950) pp. 329–333.

The typical attitude of courts toward the Canons was illustrated by the Supreme Judicial Court of Massachusetts in a case of suspension of a lawyer for advertising free legal advice:

> "Codes of legal ethics adopted by bar associations of course have no statutory force. . . . They are commonly recognized by bench and bar alike as establishing wholesome standards of professional action." In re Cohen, 261 Mass. 484, 487 (1928).

(2) The Canons of Judicial Ethics were drafted by a committee of three judges and two lawyers headed by the Chief Justice of the United States. The Canons were approved and adopted by the American Bar Association in 1924. They have since been amended in a few aspects. In 1969 the American Bar Association authorized a reappraisal and reformulation of the Canons of Judicial Ethics by a special committee of Bench and Bar leaders to be headed by Chief Justice Roger J. Traynor of the Supreme Court of California with Professor E. Wayne Thode as Reporter.

* Copyright 1969 by the American Bar Association. Reprinted with permission.
** An excellent Symposium on the Code appears in 48 Texas L.Rev. 255–397 (1970).

THE COMMITTEE ON PROFESSIONAL ETHICS

In 1912, a local bar association, the New York County Lawyers' Association, first empowered a Committee on Professional Ethics to advise inquirers on matters of professional conduct. Many state and local associations now have similar committees. In 1922 The Committee on Professional Ethics and Grievances of the American Bar Association was authorized to express its opinion concerning proper professional conduct. The Committee publishes those opinions which it believes to be of general interest to the profession. In a few states the committees on professional ethics have official standing under appointment by the supreme court of the state, and their opinions carry corresponding weight.

Frequent references to the opinions of the American Bar Association Committee and to the opinions of local bar committees are found in this book.

NOTE

The origin of the first committee has been described by its founder. Boston, *Practical Activities in Legal Ethics*, 62 U.Pa.L.Rev. 103 (1913).

For a discussion of the organization and functions of the ethics and grievance committees, and of the availability of the opinions of the ethics committees, see Drinker, Legal Ethics x, 30–32 (1953).

For an outline of the development, work, and publications of these committees in England and in the United States, see Cheatham and Lewis, *Committees on Legal Ethics*, 24 Calif.L.Rev. 28 (1935).

UNIFORMITY OR DIVERSITY OF THE BAR AND ITS STANDARDS

Our society is pluralistic, not monolithic. Its pluralistic character is evidenced by the variety of lawyers no less than of clients. Lawyers differ in temperament, in political and social views, and in the conditions of practice ranging from membership in a Wall Street firm with an established and loyal clientele to the small "independent" lawyer who has catch-as-catch-can clients.

Several recent studies of the legal profession by sociologists or lawyers are directed to different segments of the bar. One is confined to The Wall Street Lawyer.[1] The second concerns lawyers practicing alone in Chicago, especially the less successful part of this group.[2] The third covers a cross section of lawyers in parts of New York City.[3] All of them consider in greater or lesser measure the

---

1. E. Smigel, The Wall Street Lawyer (1964).
2. J. Carlin, Lawyers on Their Own (1962).
3. J. Carlin, Lawyers' Ethics (1966).

quality of integrity in practice. The last of the three has as its focus of inquiry the social conditions of moral integrity in the legal profession, "how the social organization of the profession affects the ethical behavior of lawyers."

Putting aside for the time the individual lawyer's "inner disposition", his "ethical concern", it appears from these studies that a most important element in the social setting of a lawyer is the nature of his clientele: is it stable and continuing or uncertain and intermittent; do clients put pressure on lawyers to do their bidding; is there competition for the work from other occupational groups? Included in the social setting are the public agencies with which the lawyer deals, and his colleagues or "peer" group of the profession and their standards.

The general conclusion as to urban lawyers' ethics are disturbing. The poorer and less stable the clientele, the less ethical is the lawyer, with his insecurity leading at times to dishonesty. The less ethical the public agency with which the lawyer deals, the greater is the chance of corruption. The influence of colleagues is a variable thing, and the unsuccessful lawyer has slight concern with the bar associations made up or guided as they are by the affluent members of the bar. An accompanying conclusion is that the poor get far less of the legal services they need than the well-to-do, that the quality of services is inferior, and that inadequate attention is given to the laws affecting the poor. In short, the lawyers for the lower income groups are less adequate, less ethical, and less prosperous.

The diversity of lawyers and the reported widespread violation of the stated standards of the profession raises the question, should the standards of the profession be uniform for all lawyers alike throughout their work?

This question suggests itself at the places ahead in this course where there are considered the methods of making legal services available to the poor and to the disadvantaged, to the blue and the white collar workers, and to the middle class, supra pp. 66–89.

For the purposes of such an inquiry it may be useful to take note of differences in purposes of the standards and differences in motives for the violations of the standards. Some standards have for their purpose the protection of the client, as the prohibition of representing conflicting interests. Others are directed to the prevention of unfairness to others, as a lawyer's adversaries who would be injured by a distortion of the legal process. Deliberate violations of professional standards are of two general kinds. One kind may be based on a disagreement in basic philosophy, as when a lawyer violates the standard against solicitation of practice by volunteering his services to a disadvantaged person who he believes would not otherwise obtain dependable legal services. Another kind of deviation is based merely on the desire for personal advantage, which in extenuation may be urged to be of the first kind. Perhaps, a third kind of violation is the most common, that is excessive zeal which in the heat of contest obscures the wise limitations on the adversary system, or laziness and lack of zeal which result in lack of preparation and inadequate service.

Differences in fields of practice scarcely give difficulty. There are diverse fields of expertness which are represented by Sections of the American Bar Association with no rejection of the general standards of the bar. Strong differences in political and social views, similarly, give no real difficulty, as there is room for the support of different views within the same organization. An illustration is the American Bar Association which has had at the same time one committee on Education Against Communism and another committee on Individual Rights as Affected by National Security.

In considering a question like this one, it is a safeguard of course, to put ourselves in positions in which the variation of standards would be helpful to our adversaries or competitors as well as those in which they would be helpful to us. With this caution in mind will the reader accept or reject these tentative conclusions?

All lawyers have in common the roles in society pointed out earlier. The standards of the profession, if wisely developed to aid the better performance of these roles, should not vary from lawyer to lawyer or from one field of practice to another.

There is need, however, for perception and judgment and discrimination in the development of standards. There is need, as well, for open-mindedness so that old standards may be rejected and new ones formulated when different or changing conditions make the old standards unsuited as supports to the lawyer's role under the new conditions. So because of our basic views on the need for restraints on government there is a difference in the matter of candor between the prosecuting attorney and the defense attorney in a criminal case. And in the acceptance of a matter tendered that involves illegality or unfairness there is a decisive difference between a case already completed and the case that is being planned. See infra pp. 220ff.

The most important differentiating factor in the development of standards is not the difference between lawyers or their fields of practice but between the kinds of clients, actual or potential. The difference between clients is most important in the methods of making legal services available in fact. The wealthy and sophisticated man cannot be put on the same footing as the poor and ignorant and suspicious. To do so would be to confirm the ironic epigram of Anatole France: "The law, in its majestic equality, forbids the rich as well as the poor to sleep under bridges, to beg in the streets, and to steal bread." *

---

* A. France, John Cornous, A Modern Plutarch 27, quoted in Griffin v. Illinois, 351 U.S. 12, 23 (1956) (Frankfurter, J., concurring).

NOTE

See Cohen, *Pluralism in the American Legal Profession*, 19 Ala.L.Rev. 247 (1967)

C. THE PUBLIC

Introduction. Public opinion is a major force in law making. Every legislator seeks public support for the measures he espouses. The courts are influenced by public opinion in their development of the law.* In law administration public opinion is important, and it may be a disturbing element rather than a support of the standards of the bar. Three aspects of it will here be raised.

(1) *Community Values and Standards.* The lawyer is part of the larger community which he serves, not a member of a monastic order. The values and standards of the community will deeply affect him and may be shared by him. This is especially true in the United States where business lawyers are so closely associated with the day by day activities of their clients. Yet it is the nature of a profession to insist on the qualities called for by its social function even though they are opposed to the general values of the community. The very reason for having a profession is that its members will have standards of competence and judgment and firmness that are different from those of the public. It is a further responsibility of the lawyer, at least in the United States, to help form public opinion, not to be a passive follower. In no respect is this leadership more obviously demanded than in the standards and character of a people. The items from Senator Douglas's committee report on the political leader, from Judge Cardozo on the fiduciary, from Chief Justice Stacy on the lawyer, all show the social importance that a man with a special responsibility, as the lawyer, shall not merge his standards into those of the public.

(2) *The Public Attitude Toward the Bar.* The second aspect is the public attitude toward the bar, "the public image of the lawyer" as a sociologist might put it. In considering material ahead, in this subsection let the reader put to himself, several questions: (a) what is the public attitude; (b) what is the effect of the attitude; (c) what are the reasons for the attitude; (d) what measures should the bar or the individual lawyer take in this matter.

(3) *Public Opinion of a Particular Client or Case.* Difficult and continuing problems raised by public opinion as it bears on a client or case are raised as to two kinds of subjects. One is the past transac-

---

* "The claims of dominant opinion rooted in sentiments of justice and public morality are among the most powerful shaping-forces in lawmaking by courts." Frankfurter, J., in National City Bank v. Republic of China, 348 U.S. 356, 360 (1955).

tion which is before a court. The other is a continuing matter on which future action is sought.

INTERRELATION OF STANDARDS

ETHICAL STANDARDS IN GOVERNMENT, REPORT OF A SUBCOMMITTEE (HON. PAUL H. DOUGLAS, CHAIRMAN) OF THE COMMITTEE ON LABOR AND PUBLIC WELFARE

U. S. Sen., 82d Congress, 1st Session 7, 9 (1951).

The standards of conduct of the legislative, executive, and judicial branches of government are interwoven. The standards of conduct of all these public servants also are interwoven with those of all who actively take part in public affairs, and of all who do business with the government. The morals of official conduct may be distinguished, but certainly not separated, from public morals generally. The moral standards of the country, indeed, provide the ethical environment which in turn conditions the standards of behavior of public officials. . . .

But that is only half of the story. The relationship is not slavish, and there is a two-way action. The conduct of public officials is also a powerful example influencing the general public toward higher or lower standards. . . . The standards of the public will be raised if leaders in public life practice vigorous integrity. They will be lowered if these leaders are lax in their personal or official behavior.

This reciprocal relationship between the ethics of the public and ethics of public representatives was repeatedly emphasized in the testimony presented to the subcommittee. . . . The man who sweareth to his own hurt and changeth not is essential in both the business and political worlds. In maintaining the effectiveness of an organization, the character of men in key positions is recognized to be as important as their intelligence. Americans venerate Washington for his integrity, and Lincoln for his unswerving dedication to the Union. These judgments reflect the enduring values of basic American ideals.

NOTES

(1) The character of a fiduciary's duties has been stated by Chief Judge Cardozo in language applicable to the lawyer: "Many forms of conduct permissible in a workaday world for those acting at arm's length, are forbidden to those bound by fiduciary ties. A trustee is held to something stricter than the morals of the market place. Not honestly alone, but the punctilio of an honor the most sensitive is then the standard of behavior. As to this there has developed a tradition that is unbending and inveterate. . . . Only thus has the level of conduct for fiduciaries been kept at a level higher than that trodden by the crowd. It will not consciously be lowered by any judgment of this court." Meinhard v. Salmon, 249 N.Y. 458, 464 (1928).

(2) In denying an application for admission to the bar Chief Justice Stacy wrote: "An attorney at law is a sworn officer of the court, whose chief concern, as such, is to aid in the administration of justice. In addition, he has an unparalleled opportunity to fix the code of ethics and to determine the moral tone of the business life of his community. Other agencies, of course, contribute their part, but in its final analysis, trade is conducted on sound legal advice. Take, for example, a commercial center of high ideals, another of low standards, and there will invariably be found a difference between the bars of the two localities. The legal profession has never failed to make its impress upon the life of the community." In re Farmer, 191 N.C. 235, 239 (1926).

THE PUBLIC ATTITUDE TOWARD LAWYERS

It is gratifying that surveys of public opinion about lawyers reveal that clients generally have a high opinion of their own lawyers.[1] Yet this opinion of lawyers with whom they have dealt is accompanied by a much lower opinion of lawyers as a group. The lower opinion of lawyers is joined with a misconception of law itself, well described by the executive head of the national legal aid organization:

> "The law is popularly regarded as a negative and restraining force, something darkly mysterious and forbidding—not a positive and constructive social device for regulating human relations in a way which provides a maximum of opportunity and freedom to the greatest number. . . . Few understand the law to be something useful and helpful." [2]

Many think of the lawyer's work as concerned principally with quarrels and litigation rather than with counseling and guidance and the wise and dependable shaping of transactions.

The public attitude has unfortunate consequences. Perhaps, its gravest consequence is the difficulties it raises in the way of the extension of the services of the bar to those who need them. A person in grave need of legal services may be unaware of the need or even unwilling to go to a lawyer because of fear of overreaching. (See supra Chap. II, pp. 80–89.) The public attitude may also encourage clients to ask lawyers to aid them in unsavory matters and make it less easy to hold some members of the bar up to the wise professional standards. The public ignorance of the adversary system of the administration of law may also put difficulties in the way of obtaining counsel for the hated. (See supra Chap. II, pp. 89–97.)

The reasons for public misconception of law and lawyers are varied, and so are the correctives which might be employed. The law's technicalities are derived from efforts to make the law certain and

1. See Drinker, *Laymen on the Competency and Integrity of Lawyers*, 22 Tenn.L.Rev. 371 (1952); Missouri Bar Prentice-Hall Survey 37, 40, 67 (1963).

2. Brownell, *Legal Aid in the United States* 52–55 (1951).

predictable, and periodic reassessment is essential to keep justice from being smothered by certainty. The adversary system of law administration can work admirably with able and decent lawyers on each side, yet it can be exceedingly harsh in cross-examination, in argument and in innuendo. It can degenerate into a brawl unless held in check by the standards of the bench and the bar. Even at its best the system is a troubling one for laymen to appreciate when they observe a lawyer representing an atrocious criminal. The law's delays and the law's expenses have been complained of since Pier's Plowman. Delays can be reduced only by continuing attention to the system of law administration, and expenses may be lessened by attention to clients' needs with more efficiency or through less costly personnel. The financial defaults by lawyers may be remedied by a system of clients' security funds and guarded against by the requirement of periodical office accounting as in England.

In making the public aware of its methods and uses, law is under a handicap when compared with medicine. Physical ills with the consequent need for medical care usually give their signs early through pain or weakness, but the need for legal care may not show itself until a lawsuit. The profession of medicine has important allies. We cannot glance at a magazine or enter a drug store without having pharmaceutical companies tell us of wonder drugs that physicians can prescribe. Newspapers, radio and television do their part. There is news interest in the developments of the biological and physical sciences and their uses in medicine.

Law has no such aids and allies to tell of its services. Newspapers and television portray sensational court cases in which the clever advocate downs his adversary. They ignore the inconspicuous office work that makes up nine tenths of lawyers' services. The contrast between the two professions is a fact to be kept in mind in determining what the bar, individually and as a group, should do in correcting public misconceptions of its work and, no less, in correcting well founded complaints of the bar and law administration.

PUBLIC OPINION OF A CLIENT OR CASE

"Free Press vs. Fair Trial"

Another impact of public opinion is the public attitude toward a particular client or case. The bar's standards on publicity of matters in controversy have been shaped by its conception of the lawyer as a participant in the adjudicative process in which judgment is reached by an impartial tribunal on the basis of past facts brought out in court. The standards are set out in the Code of Professional Responsibility, DR7-107, in Canon 20 of the Canons of Professional Ethics and Canon 35 of the Canons of Judicial Ethics.

The harms to the law's ideal of a fair trial from publicity about a case are essentially two. One is the danger that the jurymen will have reached a conclusion before hearing the evidence because of pre-trial publicity, as illustrated by the *Shappard* case, infra p. 175 ; or worse still, general public opinion will be so inflamed that a fair trial is impossible in the community, as in the *Powell* case supra p. 43.

Contemporaneous publicity creates another danger. It is that the participants—judge, jurymen, lawyers, witnesses—will have their actions distorted by the knowledge that they are performing before the public. This danger, especially strong when a trial is broadcast over radio or television, is stressed in some of the opinions in the Estes case, infra p. 178.

In opposition to the bar's standards there may be invoked the constitutional guaranty of a free press and the policy on which the guaranty rests. The newer news media, radio and television, claim equal rights under the constitution with the old. Another criticism of the bar's standards is occasionally indicated by the use of the phrase, "Star Chamber Proceedings", applied to any effort to limit publicity. The criticism is absurd. No one is seeking to exclude representatives of the press or other news media from a court room, or to prevent publication of the evidence after the trial, or to silence or even to temper criticisms of any of the participants in a trial. The comments by Justice Holmes is pertinent:

> "When a case is finished, courts are subject to the same criticism as other people, but the propriety and necessity of preventing interference with the course of justice by premature statement, argument or intimidation hardly can be denied." [1]

What measures may wisely be taken to prevent the dangers of unfair publicity without impairing the value of a free press? One set of measures is directed solely to the lawyers and the other "officers of the legal process," such as the law enforcement officers. An illustration is the announcement of policy and proposed measures by the Supreme Court of New Jersey in the *Van Duyne* case infra p. 177. Here the conception discussed earlier of lawyers as officers of the court subject to reasonable restrictions imposed by the court in aid of a fair trial is clearly useful. Measures directed at the press are quite a different matter. In England the courts have been stringent in preventing pre-trial publicity of matters which might interfere with the fairness of a trial, yet the English newspapers and their readers appear no less avid for post-trial spicy details than are Americans for pre-trial accounts. The constitutional provision of a free press makes American courts reluctant to claim powers over the press even for the purposes of insuring a free trial. The varied nature and standards of the publicity media make it doubtful that self-regulation would

---

1. Patterson v. Colorado, 205 U.S. 454, 463 (1907).

be attainable. The best hope is to dry up the principal sources of publicity through self-regulation by men of law.

"Future-directed Work". The standards of the bar are to be determined in the light of the processes of which the lawyer is a part and with the standards as aids to those processes. When the processes are concerned with the determination of past facts by impartial men, it is the part of wisdom and fairness to prevent the distortion of those processes by outside publicity.

Some processes in which the lawyer has a part are not concerned with the adjudication of past transaction. They look to the future, they seek change, they are essentially legislative in character, and they are greatly dependent on public opinion. The standards of the bar which condemn publicity about the client and the case may not be suited to this future-directed part of the lawyer's work. Perhaps, the ordinary standards are not entirely suited even to the situation in which the client's reputation and his future business are injured by a pending action and he seeks a lawyer's aid in righting this injury. The lawyer might well and wisely say he will not give his aid in obtaining publicity, since that is beyond his competence and is the task for a public relations man. But should he refuse to do his work as a lawyer in the matter because his client will seek and obtain all the publicity he can for his future-directed case? What standard would you draft, propose and urge for cases of this sort?

SHEPPARD v. MAXWELL

Supreme Court of the United States, 1966.
384 U.S. 333, 86 S.Ct. 1507, 16 L.Ed.2d 600.

[A man accused of murdering his wife was tried and convicted in a state court in the city where the homicide occurred. The conviction was affirmed by the appellate courts of the state, and the Supreme Court of the United States denied certiorari. The present federal habeas corpus petition was filed on the ground the accused had been deprived of a fair trial. The Supreme Court of the United States granted a petition for certiorari after a decision adverse to the petitioner by the United States Court of Appeals.

The evidence on the hearing of the habeas corpus petition showed that there was "massive, pervasive and prejudicial publicity" of the case by the local newspapers and radio and television stations before and during the trial, some of it with the aid of public officials.]

MR. JUSTICE CLARK delivered the opinion of the Court. . . .

We have concluded that Sheppard did not receive a fair trial consistent with the Due Process Clause of the Fourteenth Amendment, . . .

The [trial] court's fundamental error is compounded by the holding that it lacked power to control the publicity about the trial. . . .

As we stressed in *Estes*, the presence of the press at judicial proceedings must be limited when it is apparent that the accused might otherwise be prejudiced or disadvantaged . . . the judge should have adopted stricter rules governing the use of the courtroom by newsmen as Sheppard's counsel requested. . . . Secondly, the court should have insulated the witnesses. . . . Thirdly, the court should have made some effort to control the release of leads, information, and gossip to the press by police officers, witnesses, and the counsel for both sides. . . .

[T]he fact that many of the prejudicial news items can be traced to the prosecution, as well as the defense, aggravates the judge's failure to take any action. . . . Effective control of these sources—concededly within the court's power—might well have prevented the divulgence of inaccurate information, rumors, and accusations that made up much of the inflammatory publicity, at least after Sheppard's indictment.

More specifically, the trial court might well have proscribed extrajudicial statements by any lawyer, party, witness, or court official which divulged prejudicial matters, . . . any belief in guilt or innocence, or like statements concerning the merits of the case. See State v. Van Duyne, 43 N.J. 369, 389, 204 A.2d 841, 852 (1964), in which the court interpreted Canon 20 of the American Bar Association's Canons of Professional Ethics to prohibit such statements. . . . Of course, there is nothing that proscribes the press from reporting events that transpire in the courtroom. But where there is a reasonable likelihood that prejudicial news prior to trial will prevent a fair trial, the judge should continue the case until the threat abates or transfer it to another county not so permeated with publicity. In addition, sequestration of the jury was something the judge should have raised *sua sponte* with counsel. If publicity during the proceedings threatens the fairness of the trial, a new trial should be ordered. But we must remember that reversals are but palliatives; the cure lies in those remedial measures that will prevent the prejudice at its inception. . . .

Since the state trial judge did not fulfill his duty to protect Sheppard from the inherently prejudicial publicity which saturated the community and to control disruptive influences in the courtroom, we must reverse the denial of the habeas petition. The case is remanded to the District Court with instructions to issue the writ and order that Sheppard be released from custody unless the State puts him to its charges again within a reasonable time.

MR. JUSTICE BLACK dissents.

NOTES

(1) In State v. Van Duyne, 43 N.J. 369 (1964), referred to with approval in the principal case, Mr. Justice Francis said: "Control of the matter is largely in the hands of the prosecutor and local police authorities. For example, one district attorney in New York State adopted an office rule prohibiting release of confessions to newspapers prior to trial. 131 N.Y.L.J. 4 (Apr. 22, 1954). In our view Canons 5 and 20 of the Canons of Professional Ethics require a broader and more stringent rule. We interpret these canons, particularly Canon 20, to ban statements to news media by prosecutors, assistant prosecutors and their lawyer staff members, as to alleged confessions or inculpatory admissions by the accused, or to the effect that the case is "open and shut" against the defendant, and the like, or with reference to the defendant's prior criminal record, either of convictions or arrests. Such statements have the capacity to interfere with a fair trial and cannot be countenanced. With respect to prosecutors' detectives and members of local police departments who are not members of the bar, statements of the type described are an improper interference with the due administration of criminal justice and constitute conduct unbecoming a police officer. As such they warrant discipline at the hands of the proper authorities.

"The ban on statements by the prosecutor and his aides applies as well to defense counsel. The right of the State to a fair trial cannot be impeded or diluted by out-of-court assertions by him to news media on the subject of his client's innocence. The courtroom is the place to settle the issue and comments before or during the trial which have the capacity to influence potential or actual jurors to the possible prejudice of the State are impermissible.

"There is nothing in the rules to which attention is now called which interferes with the operation of a free press. Trials of criminal indictments are public proceedings. Nothing is suggested herein which proscribes the reporting of the evidence as it is introduced before the jury by the State and the defendant during the course of the trial."

(2) The American Bar Association created an Advisory Committee on Fair Trial and Free Press. The Committee's proposed standards call for severe restraint by counsel in criminal cases in the release of information about it. The standards were approved by the Association. See Reardon, *The Fair Trial—Free Press Standards*, 54 A.B.A.J. 343 (1968). The substance of the Committee's recommendations as to lawyers in civil and administrative proceedings as well as criminal cases are included in the Code of Professional Responsibility, DR 7–107.

STATE v. KAVANAUGH

Supreme Court of New Jersey (1968).
52 N.J. 7, 243 A.2d 225.

[A Massachusetts lawyer was granted permission to appear in a New Jersey court as counsel pro hac vice for defendants accused of murder. He wrote a sensational letter to the Governor of New Jersey accusing representatives of the State of outrageous conduct in the case and sent copies to 150 persons. The letter reached and was used by the news media. On an order to show cause the permission to appear *pro hac vice* was revoked. The clients accused of murder appealed.]

PER CURIAM. . . . [W]e do not have the slightest doubt that Mr. Bailey intended that letter to reach the press. Nor did anything emerge at the hearing to dissipate the gross ethical impropriety evidenced in the letter itself. On the contrary the hearing demonstrated that the letter also violated a specific order of the trial court. . . . [O]ne of the relevant issues at the hearing was whether Mr. Bailey could give assurance as to future behavior if permitted to stay in the cases. On that score, Mr. Bailey's performance offered no promise. . . .

The final relevant aspect of the matter relates to the impact of Mr. Bailey's removal upon his clients, the intervenors, and their respective counsel. We have no doubt the removal of Mr. Bailey will have an appreciable impact upon all of them in some respect. . . . Since the trial must be postponed, there will be a full opportunity for Mr. Bailey's clients to obtain other counsel. . . . As to the extra dollar hurt to Mr. Bailey's clients, involved in changing counsel, the matter must be left for an accounting between them. . . .

It is not easy for us to oust counsel of a client's choice. But the misbehavior here is so gross that we cannot risk more of it. . . .

Mr. Bailey's clients urge a constitutional right to select an attorney who is not a member of our Bar. So long as the Bar of our State is able, willing and free to provide effective counsel, there is no such right. . . . This is not a situation in which no member of the local Bar will act. See Lefton v. City of Hattiesburg, Mississippi, 333 F.2d 280 (5 Cir. 1964). There is no dearth of competent attorneys in our State ready to meet the constitutional right to counsel. . . .

The order is affirmed.

TELEVISION IN THE COURTROOM

The constitutional status of television in the courtroom is not yet settled. In Estes v. State of Texas, 381 U.S. 532 (1965), a man who had been convicted in a Texas court of a highly publicized crime of swindling urged that he had been deprived of his right to due process of law by the televising and broadcasting of his trial. The conviction was reversed by the Supreme Court of the United States by a vote of five to four with six opinions. There follow passages from three of the opinions.

CHIEF JUSTICE WARREN, speaking for MR. JUSTICE DOUGLAS and MR. JUSTICE GOLDBERG as well, said:

"I believe that it violates the Sixth Amendment for federal courts and the Fourteenth Amendment for state courts to allow criminal trials to be televised to the public at large. I base this conviction on three grounds: (1) that the televising of trials diverts the trial from its proper purpose in that it has an inevitable impact on all the trial participants; (2) that it gives the public the wrong impression about the purpose of the trials, thereby detracting from the dignity of court proceedings and lessening the reliability of trials; and (3) that it singles out certain defendants and subjects them to trials under prejudicial conditions not experienced by others.

". . . I cannot agree with those who say that a televised trial deprives a defendant of a fair trial only if 'actual prejudice' can be shown. The prejudice of television may be so subtle that it escapes the ordinary method of proof, but it would gradually erode our fundamental conception of trial. . . .

"Canon 35 of the American Bar Association's Canons of Judicial Ethics prohibits the televising of court trials. With only two, or possibly three exceptions, the highest court of each State which has considered the question has declared that televised criminal trials are inconsistent with the Anglo-American conception of 'trial'. Similarly, Rule 53 of the Federal Rules of Criminal Procedure prohibits the 'broadcasting' of trials, and the Judicial Conference of the United States has unanimously condemned televised trials.

"The right of the communications media to comment on court proceedings does not bring with it the right to inject themselves into the fabric of the trial process to alter the purpose of that process. . ."

MR. JUSTICE STEWART, with whom MR. JUSTICE BLACK, MR. JUSTICE BRENNAN and MR. JUSTICE WHITE joined, wrote: "I think that the introduction of television into a courtroom is, at least in the present state of the art, an extremely unwise policy. It invites many constitutional risks, and it detracts from the inherent dignity of a courtroom. But I am unable to escalate this personal view into a *per se* constitutional rule. And I am unable to find, on the specific record of this case, that the circumstances attending the limited televising of the petitioner's trial resulted in the denial of any right guaranteed to him by the United States Constitution.

MR. JUSTICE WHITE, with whom MR. JUSTICE BRENNAN joined, added in dissent:

"I agree with Mr. Justice Stewart that a finding of constitutional prejudice on this record entails erecting a flat ban on the use of cameras in the courtroom, and believe that it is premature to promulgate such a broad constitutional principle at the present time. . . . Here, although our experience is inadequate and our judgment correspondingly infirm, the Court discourages further meaningful study of the use of television at criminal trials."

NOTES

(1) The development of Canon 35 of the Canons of Judicial Ethics as set out in the amicus curiae brief of the American Bar Association is given in Mr. Justice Harlan's opinion in the principal case at pp. 596–601. There is a helpful discussion of the general problem in Warden, *Canon 35: Is There Room for Objectivity?*, 4 Washburn L.Jour. 211 (1965).

PUBLICITY FOR CLIENTS: SOME CASES

(1) The A. & P. grocery chain were defendants in a proceeding for alleged violation of the federal anti-trust laws, and the company sought to retain a well-known firm of lawyers to represent it in the case. In the discussion of the matter the company's representatives said that the mere filing of the proceeding had injured it, and that the company to protect its reputation intended to publish a series of newspaper advertisements concerning the particular proceeding as well as the failure of other anti-trust actions against it. The head of the law firm said something like this: "With great regret I have to say we cannot take the case because of your projected advertising campaign. We try our cases in the courts, not in the newspapers." The company's officials asked another firm to take the case, which it did. Was the first firm right and the second firm wrong in its actions?

(2) Would your answer be affected by the fact that the Attorney General of the United States followed the practice of issuing public statements at the time of the institution of major anti-trust proceedings, which outline the nature of the charge and the policy of the government? The Committee on Professional Ethics of the American Bar Association had ruled that such statements are proper, saying in part:

"In the broad aspect the Attorney General is attorney for the body politic. . . . [H]e is reporting to the public. Herein lies a material difference between a report or a press release issued by the Attorney General and one given out by an attorney for a private client. . . .

"While we see no objection to statements reflecting departmental policy, nor to statements of fact relating to past proceedings in the nature of reports, when as here, the statements relate to prospective or pending criminal or civil proceedings, they should omit any assertions of fact likely to create an adverse attitude in the public mind respecting the alleged actions of the defendants to such proceedings." A.B.A. Opinion 199 (1940).

(3) In New Haven, a labor union sought to organize the employees of a manufacturing company and called a strike of the employees to obtain recognition of the union. The union charged that the employer was paying sub-standard wages. The newspapers ignored the strike. At last some Yale students joined the picket lines and they were among the pickets arrested and jailed. This broke the newspaper ban, and in the resultant newspaper articles the nature of the wages paid and of the strike was made known. The strike was won. Was the lawyer for the union, who helped to plan the strategy of the strike, within his privilege as a lawyer? Why or why not? Cf. Waldman, *Sons of Eli Join the Labor Movement*, in Labor Lawyer 164 (1944).

(4) You are the lawyer for a trucking company. There is a bill before a state legislature to increase the taxes on trucks, and the company asks you to aid in opposing the bill before a legislative committee. The company informs you that it and its trade association plan a widespread campaign to show to the public the large amount of taxes already exacted of trucks. Would you refuse to represent the company in the matter?

(5) You are a member of a civic organization which seeks an appropriation from a state or city government in support of legal aid. The president asks you to give your support to the measure before a committee of the state or the city legislative authority. He informs you that he will endeavor to obtain all the newspaper publicity he can on the need for the legislative appropriation. Is it thinkable that you would refuse to give your support because of the newspaper publicity?

D. THE INDIVIDUAL

Introduction. The individual lawyer's own "inner disposition" or resolution may be a powerful, though intangible, support for professional standards. Several questions about it deserve mention. (1) Does individual resolution or inner disposition exist? (2) Is the quality of social importance, whether in private practice or in wider leadership? (3) Whence does a man derive this quality of firmness, and how may he strengthen it—weak as every man must admit he is? (4) In what matters may a lawyer impose his standards on others?

IDEALS AND ACTIONS

DAVID RIESMAN, THE STUDY OF NATIONAL CHARACTER: SOME OBSERVATIONS ON THE AMERICAN CASE

13 Harvard Library Bulletin 5, 24 (1959).

We find it easier to describe the limits on human conduct than the areas of freedom and amorphousness. Studies of national character tend to strike a deterministic note, even when, if they are grounded in history, they show how great and dramatic have been the changes in a nation's ethos within the period of a century or less. It is frequently said that the world is getting more homogeneous and that enclaves, whether national or regional, are bound to disappear, provided we do not all disappear. There is truth in this, of course. But it is also true that the differences among men that will increasingly matter will not arise from geographical location and will hence be more within the realm of the individual. Indeed, the importance of the individual in setting a model for the character of a group has been insufficiently studied by social scientists, though we all know in a general way how identification with great historical figures is one way by which we avoid the parochialism of our particular birth in a particular family. We are only beginning to understand the power of individuals to shape their own character by their selection among models and experiences.

NOTES

(1) "Let the young man take care what he asks in his youth, for in his age he shall have it." Goethe.

"The ideals cherished in the souls of men enter into the character of their actions." Alfred North Whitehead.

(2) "I include in apprenticeship a dedication to the life or the works, or both, of a figure who commands respect and admiration, whether a living figure or a figure understood through history." William J. Brennan, Occasional Pamphlet Number Nine, Harvard Law School (1967).

UNDERSTANDING AND RESOLUTION

REPORT OF THE JOINT CONFERENCE ON PROFESSIONAL RESPONSIBILITY

44 A.B.A.J. 1159, 1218 (1958); 1958 A.A.L.S.Pro. 187, 202 (1958).

To meet the highest demands of professional responsibility the lawyer must not only have a clear understanding of his duties, but must also possess the resolution necessary to carry into effect what his intellect tells him ought to be done.

For understanding is not of itself enough. Understanding may enable the lawyer to see the goal toward which he should strive, but it will not furnish the motive power that will impel him toward it. For this the lawyer requires a sense of attachment to something larger than himself.

For some this will be attainable only through religious faith. For others it may come from a feeling of identification with the legal profession and its great leaders of the past. Still others, looking to the future, may find it in the thought that they are applying their professional skills to help bring about a better life for all men.

These are problems each lawyer must solve in his own way. But in solving them he will remember, with Whitehead, that moral education cannot be complete without the habitual vision of greatness.

NOTE

"I die the King's good servant, but God's first", are the words attributed to Sir Thomas More as he mounted the scaffold to which Henry VIII had sent him. Cf. Hughes, C. J., dissenting in United States v. MacIntosh, 283 U.S. 605, 633, 634 (1931).

"INNER DISPOSITION" AND LAWYERS' ETHICS

JEROME E. CARLIN, LAWYERS' ETHICS: A SURVEY OF THE NEW YORK CITY BAR

Pages 133, 135–136, 148 (1966).*

[Professor Carlin, a sociologist and lawyer, made a study of the New York bar which was directed largely to "the social conditions of moral integrity in the legal profession," "with influences on ethical conduct arising from characteristics of the lawyer's clientele, of the courts and agencies of government with which he deals, and of his colleague group, and with the patterning of these influences by the system of social stratification in the bar." As a part of the study he made a pioneering inquiry into what he called the lawyer's inner disposition and its bearing on the lawyer's actions.**]

The evidence presented thus far indicates that adherence to ethical norms is greatly influenced by circumstances arising from the nature of the lawyer's practice and position in the bar. . . . This chapter considers the way in which lawyers' ethical conduct is affected by basic ethical orientations or disposi-

---

* With the permission of Russell Sage Foundation, publisher.

** To an inquiry from one of the editors the author replied: "I am not aware of any other empirical studies that seek to examine the effect of 'inner disposition' on conformity to ethical standards. Hopefully other researchers will explore further this all-important matter."

tions, and how these are related to situational pressures and the system of stratification in the bar. . . .

Of particular interest is the apparent resistance to pressures shown by lawyers who have the greatest ethical concern. Even when subjected to the combination of high client-related pressures and exposure to lower-level courts and agencies, only 20 per cent of those with high ethical concern are violators, as against 77 per cent of those with low concern. Moreover, high concern lawyers are far less responsive to an increase in situational pressures than their less ethically concerned colleagues. Finally, it should be noted that the least ethically concerned lawyers are likely to violate when exposed to *either* type of situational pressure, moderately concerned lawyers tend to violate only when exposed to *both* types of pressure, and the most concerned lawyers violate very little even when they are exposed to both types of pressure. . . .

Inner disposition and external pressures have a combined, cumulative effect on ethical conduct, and are about equally influential. The lawyer's inner ethical orientation makes a considerable difference in his response to situational pressures, and consequently in his capacity to conform to ethical standards. The stronger his ethical concern, the less likely is he to succumb to pressures to violate ordinary standards and the more likely he is to respond positively to supports for conformity to higher level standards. Adherence to ethical norms, then, is a product of *both* inner disposition, which is more or less evenly distributed in the bar, and situational controls, which are patterned in accordance with the system of stratification in the bar.

OBEDIENCE TO THE UNENFORCEABLE

THE RIGHT HONORABLE LORD MOULTON, LAW AND MANNERS

134 The Atlantic Monthly 1 (July, 1924).[1]

In order to explain this extraordinary title I must ask you to follow me in examining the three great domains of Human Action. First comes the domain of Positive Law, where our actions are prescribed by laws binding upon us which must be obeyed. Next comes the domain of Free Choice, which includes all those actions as to which we claim and enjoy complete freedom. But between these two there is a third large and important domain in which there rules neither Positive Law nor Absolute Freedom. In that domain there is no law which inexorably determines our course of action, and yet we feel that we

[1]. With the permission of the publisher, Macmillan & Co., Ltd.

are not free to choose as we would. The degree of this sense of a lack of complete freedom in this domain varies in every case. It grades from a consciousness of a Duty nearly as strong as Positive Law, to a feeling that the matter is all but a question of personal choice. Some might wish to parcel out this domain into separate countries, calling one, for instance, the domain of Duty, another the domain of Public Spirit, another the domain of Good Form; but I prefer to look at it as all one domain, for it has one and the same characteristic throughout—it is the domain of Obedience to the Unforceable. The obedience is the obedience of a man to that which he cannot be forced to obey. He is the enforcer of the law upon himself. . . .

All these three domains are essential to the properly organized life of the individual, and one must be on one's guard against thinking that any of them can safely be encroached upon. That Law must exist needs no argument. But, on the other hand, the domain of Free Choice should be dear to all. This is where spontaneity, originality, and energy are born. . . . This country forms the other frontier of the domain of Manners and delimits it on the side farthest way from that of Positive Law.

The dangers that threaten the maintenance of this domain of Manners arise from its situation between the region of Absolute Choice and the region of Positive Law. There are countless supporters of the movements to enlarge the sphere of Positive Law. In many countries—especially in the younger nations—there is a tendency to make laws to regulate everything. On the other hand, there is a growing tendency to treat matters that are not regulated by Positive Law as being matters of Absolute Choice. Both these movements are encroachments on the middle land, and to my mind the real greatness of a nation, its true civilization, is measured by the extent of this land of Obedience to the Unenforceable. . . . The true test is the extent to which the individuals composing the nation can be trusted to obey self-imposed law.

In the changes that are taking place in the world around us, one of those which is fraught with grave peril is the discredit into which this idea of the middle land is falling. . . . there is a widespread tendency to regard the fact that they can do a thing as meaning that they may do it. There can be no more fatal error than this. Between "can do" and "may do" ought to exist the whole realm which recognizes the sway of duty, fairness, sympathy, taste, and all the other things that make life beautiful and society possible. . . .
I am too well acquainted with the inadequacy of the formal language of statutes to prefer them to the living action of public and private sense of Duty.

The great principle of Obedience to the Unenforceable is no mere ideal, but in some form or other it is strong in the hearts of all except the most depraved. If you wish to know how strong, remember the account of the Titanic disaster. The men were gentlemen to the edge of death. "Ladies first." Why was that? Law did not require it. Force could not have compelled it in the face of almost certain death. It was merely a piece of good Manners in the sense in which I have used the phrase. The feeling of obedience to the Unenforceable was so strong that at that terrible moment all behaved as, if they could look back, they would wish to have behaved.[2] . . .

Now I can tell you why I chose the title "Law and Manners." It must be evident to you that Manners must include all things which a man should impose upon himself, from duty to good taste. I have borne in mind the great motto of William of Wykeham—*Manners makyth Man*. It is in this sense—loyalty to the rule of Obedience to the Unenforceable, throughout the whole realm of personal action—that we should use the word "Manners" if we would truly say that "Manners makyth Man."

DORIS H. PEPPER

36 T.C. 886 (1961).

[A law firm who were counsel for a small jobbing corporation in New York City, aided the corporation in finding persons who would lend it money. About thirty of the lenders were clients, business and personal friends and acquaintances, and office associates of a member of that firm and they made loans totaling almost $200,000. The head of the corporation was guilty of gross fraud, the corporation went into bankruptcy, and only a part of the loans were repaid by it. The members of the law firm decided it was imperative, if they were to save their law practice, that they prevent those persons who had outstanding loans from losing their money, including persons who had never been clients of the firm. The members of the firm paid over $65,000 to the lenders. In their federal income tax return they listed these payments as an ordinary and necessary business expense. The Commissioner disallowed them and the taxpayers took this appeal.]

TRAIN, J.: . . . We must first determine whether these expenses arose out of petitioners' trade or business. . . . There

---

2. On the Titanic there was one violator of the principle.

"Joseph Bruce Ismay, 74, former owner of the White Star Line and former president of the International Mercantile Marine Co., who survived the Titanic disaster, died yesterday. Mr. Ismay was criticized severely for allowing himself to be rescued from the Titanic, which struck an iceberg in the North Atlantic April 14, 1912, and sank with 1,635 persons on board.

"Mr. Ismay died without making any statement on the Titanic. One of the ship's officers said twenty-two years later: 'Ismay did the worst thing he ever did in his life when he got into that lifeboat.' . . .

"After the inquiry he became a recluse and although a person of great means never again appeared at any public function. . . . Of late years his life had been a solitary one." New York World-Telegram, October 18, 1937, p. 30.

is more to the modern day practice of law than just reading cases, writing briefs, and appearing in trials. There are many things that are not in the purest sense the practice of law, nevertheless they are so integrally connected with it as to be inseparable from it. . . . Hofheimer, a practicing attorney in New York, testified that he and his firm, in many instances, actively sought out financing for clients. . . . Based on the record before us, we are convinced that the transaction which gave rise to petitioners' payments to the creditors . . . arose out of petitioners' "trade or business".

We may assume that the payment to the creditors were necessary, at least in the sense that they were appropriate and helpful. . . .

What is ordinary, though there must always be a strain of constancy within it, is nonetheless a variable affected by time and place and circumstance. . . .

After the swindle was discovered, Morton [a member of the law firm] called Hofheimer [a lawyer who was one of the lenders] not as an investor, but as a friend . . . Hofheimer agreed with Morton that the partnership . . . was obligated to repay the money. On cross-examination, when asked about what he meant by "obligated" Hofheimer testified as follows:

> A. Because he had recommended this investment and as it unfortunately turned out, the borrower was a dishonest person. I told him then and I still feel that it is a risk that an attorney runs when he recommends to anyone that money be invested with a dishonest client.
>
> Q. By that, you mean a moral obligation.
>
> A. I certainly mean a moral obligation, but I think I mean more than that . . . I think that he was legally obligated to pay that money.

Morton also testified that he and Siegel [a member of the law firm] decided it was necessary in order to protect their practice to repay the creditors. . . .

> A. We decided that it was imperative if we were to save our practice, our law practice that we should prevent those people who had outstanding loans . . . from losing their money.

Based on the entire record before us, we conclude that the payments made by petitioners were an ordinary expense of their trade or business. . . .

Respondent's contention that the deduction to petitioners should be disallowed because voluntarily made is without merit. Morton admitted that they were not guarantors, nor were they under any legal obligation to repay the loans . . . . However, there is no requirement that there must be an underlying legal obligation to make an expenditure before it can qualify as an ordinary and necessary business expense. . . .

NOTES

(1) Buttle v. Saunders [1950] 2 All E.R. 193 (Ch.) [Trustees under a trust for land for sale agreed orally to sell the land to Mrs. Simpson for £6,000 and the matter had proceeded so far that one copy of the contract for sale had been signed by Mrs. Simpson and the other copy by one, but only one, of the trustees. Canon Buttle then orally offered £6,500 for the property. The trustees indicated they would go through with the sale to Mrs. Simpson because they felt they were bound by commercial morality to complete the sale to her. An action was filed in the Chancery Division by Canon Buttle and others to restrain the trustees, and the trustees asked for the direction of the court in the matter.]

Wynn-Parry, J. . . . "It is true that persons who are not in the position of trustees are entitled, if they so desire, to accept a lesser price than that which they might obtain on the sale of the property. . . . It redounds to the credit of a man who acts like that in such circumstances. Trustees, however, are not vested with such complete freedom. They have an overriding duty to obtain the best price which they can for their beneficiaries. . . . The only consideration which was present to their minds was that they had gone so far in the negotiations with Mrs. Simpson that they could not properly, from the point of view of commercial morality, resign from these negotiations. That being so, they did not, to any extent, probe Canon Buttle's offer as, in my view, they should have done. . . .

"There being a serious purchaser, I shall give the trustees liberty to sell to Mrs. Simpson for £6,600, that being the highest price offered."

(2) What was the nature of the motives of the lawyers and the trustees in the two cases next above? Would the result in either case have been affected if the court had found that the guide to action was their inner conviction of right conduct as individuals or as lawyers or trustees?

THE INDIVIDUAL'S STANDARDS vs. THE ACCEPTED STANDARDS OF THE BAR

When may a lawyer fairly adhere to his personal standards of conduct, and when should he in fairness act in accordance with the accepted standards of the bar which are lower than his own? Are the answers given below the right ones so far as they go?

When he is acting without harmful effect on a person for whose welfare he is responsible, he is free to apply his personal standards. So it is when a case is tendered to him and he is deciding whether to take it.

When he has accepted a case and is acting as his client's representative, the matter is more difficult. Then the question becomes—will the lawyer give his client the kind of services and protection which the ordinary ethics of the bar would permit and which almost any other lawyer would give (i. e., utilizing the defense of the statute of limitations to defeat a claim), or will he hold his client up to his own standard? May the lawyer impose his ethics on the client without telling the client what he intends to do? Usually this can be done by showing that it would be decent and in his long-time interest to act as the lawyer wishes him to do, and by getting his consent.

SECTION 3. THE AUTHORITATIVE SOURCES OF THE STANDARDS AND SUPPORTS

SPANOS v. SKOURAS THEATRES CORPORATION

United States Court of Appeals, Second Circuit, 1966.
364 F.2d 161, cert. den. 385 U.S. 987 (1966).

[The plaintiff, a lawyer who was admitted to practice in California but not in New York and who was an expert on antitrust laws, was retained by the leader of motion picture theatre companies to aid in a projected federal antitrust suit against the major motion picture producers in the New York City area. The retainer agreement called for the payment of an annual sum and additional fees. The plaintiff spent much time and effort in California on research and in New York in settlement conferences and other phases of the projected suit. He received something over $80,000 in fees and then was discharged by the client. He brought the present action in a United States District Court in New York City for additional compensation. The defendant counterclaimed for the return of the sum already paid, on the ground the plaintiff, an out of state attorney, was entitled to nothing for legal services in connection with a New York action. The District Court awarded the plaintiff additional fees and dismissed the counterclaim. The Court of Appeals, by a divided vote, reversed the judgment for additional fees. On reconsideration in Banc The Court of Appeals, by a vote of seven to two, affirmed the judgment of the District Court.]

On Reconsideration in Banc

FRIENDLY, CIRCUIT JUDGE. . . .

In the first place, we think Judge Wyatt was correct in concluding that a right to recover could be predicated on Rule 3(c) of the District Court for the Southern District of New York providing that "[a] member in good standing of the bar of any state . . . may upon motion be permitted to argue or try a particular cause in whole or in part as counsel or advocate." The contract engaging Spanos to work on the suit for damages under the antitrust laws, 15 U.S.C.A.

§ 15, which defendants proposed to bring in the Southern District can fairly be construed as contemplating court appearances on his part. When the defendants engaged him to that end, they impliedly assumed the obligation of having their New York lawyers in the action make any motion that was necessary to render such appearances lawful. There is not the slightest reason to suppose that if by their lawyers defendants had sought admission *pro hac vice* for the colleague whose services they had been at such pains to secure, the motion would have been denied; . . . We cannot accept the contention that if such leave to appear had been sought and granted, Spanos could recover only for court appearances and not for other legal work in the suit; under 28 U.S.C.A. § 1654, stemming from § 35 of the First Judiciary Act, 1 Stat. 92 (1789), the grant of leave would have given official recognition to his status as an attorney in the district for all purposes of the action and would have insulated him from § 270 of the New York Penal Law with respect to any legal services reasonably incident to the activities the District Court had authorized. Spanos' contract was thus susceptible of being lawfully performed without his being admitted to the New York bar and cannot be considered an illegal bargain. . . .

While this would suffice to dispose of the case, the importance of the problem and the desirability of furnishing guidance to the bar lead us to consider other grounds that have been urged for affirmance. . . . we hold that under the privileges and immunities clause of the Constitution no state can prohibit a citizen with a federal claim or defense from engaging an out-of-state lawyer to collaborate with an in-state lawyer and give legal advice concerning it within the state. . . . We are persuaded, however, that where a right has been conferred on citizens by federal law, the constitutional guarantee against its abridgment must be read to include what is necessary and appropriate for its assertion. In an age of increased specialization and high mobility of the bar, this must comprehend the right to bring to the assistance of an attorney admitted in the resident state a lawyer licensed by "public act" of any other state who is thought best fitted for the task, and to allow him to serve in whatever manner is most effective, subject only to valid rules of courts as to practice before them. Cf. Lefton v. City of Hattiesburg, 333 F.2d 280, 285 (5 Cir. 1964). Indeed, in instances where the federal claim or defense is unpopular, advice and assistance by an out-of-state lawyer may be the only means available for vindication. The broadening of district court rules as to admission suggested in the dissenting opinion is no adequate solution. The federal matter on which the help of a non-resident specialist is sought may be pending in a different state or may not be a suit at all, and specialized legal advice may be needed without the delay or expense incident to admission by a federal court before which the attorney may not have any intention of practicing, even if that were available and would afford sufficient validation. . . .

The Association of the Bar of the City of New York urges us to take an even broader ground that would render the participation of a licensed in-state lawyer irrelevant. A good deal can be said for such a position; for example, in the case just put of the corporation having nationwide operations, it would seem absurd that when the out-of-state trade-mark specialist goes to a local branch, he should be required to obtain the assistance of a resident general practitioner for whose views he would have little regard. Yet there is also a case for the other side. The disparity in requirements for admission to the bar gives a state maintaining high qualification standards some interest in seeing that its residents do not take action even on a federal right solely on the advice of a lawyer from another state; moreover, what is basically a federal claim or defense may depend in part on an "issue or claim which has its source in state law." Maternally Yours, Inc. v. Your Maternity Shop, Inc., 234 F.2d 538, 541 n. 1 (2 Cir. 1956). We thus limit our holding to the situation here presented, where a citizen has invited a duly licensed out-of-state lawyer to work in association with a local lawyer on a federal claim or defense. . . .

The judgment of the District Court in favor of Spanos is affirmed.

HAYS, CIRCUIT JUDGE (concurring in the result).

I subscribe to the position taken in the amicus brief of the Association of the Bar of the City of New York.

LUMBARD, CHIEF JUDGE, with whom J. JOSEPH SMITH, CIRCUIT JUDGE, concurs (dissenting). . . .

. . . Judge Friendly's opinion now supports recovery on the theory that no state can prohibit a citizen with a federal claim from engaging an out-of-state lawyer to collaborate with an in-state lawyer because of the privileges and immunities clause of the Constitution. . . .

Apparently the majority would leave the more than 200,000 out-of-state lawyers from the forty nine other states free to practice federal law in New York without any regulation whatever—none from New York, and none from any federal court, until it was time to appear at trial. . . .

NOTES

(1) In Appell v. Reiner, 43 N.J. 313 (1964), the Supreme Court of New Jersey upheld the claim of a New York lawyer to recover for services rendered in New York and New Jersey to an embarrassed debtor who had creditors in both states. In a somewhat similar situation the Court of Appeals of New York by divided vote denied the claim of an out of state lawyer to recover for services in New York. Spivak v. Sachs, 16 N.Y.2d 163 (1965).

(2) See Flowers, *The Practice of Law by Out-of-State Attorneys*, 20 Vand.L.Rev. 1276 (1967); Note, *Retaining Out-of-State Counsel: The Evolution of a Federal Right*, 67 Col.L.Rev 731 (1967); Note, *Attorneys: Interstate and Federal Practice*, 80 Harv.L.Rev. 1711 (1967). The problem in the international field is discussed in Note, *Foreign Branches of Law Firms: The Development of Lawyers Equipped to Handle International Practice*, 80 Harv.L.Rev. 1284 (1967).

(3) The Committee on Professional Ethics of the American Bar Association has expressed its views on "problems involving the practice of law across state lines. What are the ethical implications of associations of lawyers . . . in different states for the purpose of servicing clients in different states, states in which fewer than all of the partners or associates are admitted?" See Opinion 316: *The Practice of Law Across State Lines*, 53 A.B.A.J. 353 (1967).

(4) "(T)he demands of business and the mobility of our society pose distinct problems in the regulation of the practice of law by the states. In furtherance of the public interest, the legal profession should discourage regulations that unreasonably impose territorial limitations upon the right of a lawyer to handle the legal affairs of his client or upon the opportunity of a client to obtain the services of a lawyer of his choice in all matters including the presentation of a contested matter in a tribunal before which the lawyer is not permanently admitted to practice." Code of Professional Responsibility, EC 3–9.*

OUR GOVERNMENTAL STRUCTURE AND THE PROFESSION OF LAW

The complexities of our system of law which bear on the profession of law have two main sources, the federal system and the principle of separation of powers.

Three aspects of the federal system call for mention. The most obvious is the two sets of laws, one the federal laws and the other the laws of the several states. The Constitution is explicit on the supremacy of federal law within its sphere. Article VI provides:

> "This Constitution, and the Laws of the United States which shall be made in Pursuance thereof; and all Treaties made, or which shall be made, under the Authority of the United States, shall be the supreme Law of the Land; and the Judges in every State shall be bound thereby, any Thing in the Constitution or Laws of any State to the Contrary notwithstanding."

"[T]he Laws of the United States" include the federal common law, for federal courts, as may all common law courts, make common law subject to modification or rejection by the legislature. The Tenth Amendment to the Constitution is complementary to Article VI, explicitly reassuring the States as it does that their laws, too, are supreme within their appropriate sphere:

> "The powers not delegated to the United States by the Constitution, nor prohibited by it to the States are reserved to the States respectively, or to the people."

* Copyright 1969 by the American Bar Association. Reprinted with permission.

The argument might be made that federal law standards for the profession should apply in the enforcement of federal-based rights. The argument gives rise to additional complexities, for the application of federal law is often intertwined with problems of state law. Furthermore, the application of state law may be countered by a defense based on federal law, as the due process clause of the Fourteenth Amendment. Though a case as instituted may be based on one body of law, it may wind up with the decisive element drawn from another body of law.

A second aspect of the federal system is the set of federal courts. These courts have their own standards of admission and of discipline as well as rules of "procedure". It may be that some or even all phases of the lawyers' standards in practice before these courts may be characterized as procedure and so governed by the principles moulded by these courts. While the Rules of Civil Procedure of the United States District Courts were fashioned pursuant to an enabling Act of Congress, the control over the federal courts' bar might be rested on the more fundamental principle of the inherent power of a court to set standards and impose sanctions on those who practice before it. Note that Article III of the Constitution begins, "The judicial power of the United States shall be vested" in indicated courts. The judicial power may well extend over those "officers of the court", the lawyers.

The problems under these two aspects of the federal system may be put in this compact form which combines the aspects of the applicable law and the nature of the tribunal:

1. A federal law cause of action in a federal court.
2. A federal law cause of action in a state court.
3. A state law cause of action in a federal court.
4. A state law cause of action in a state court.

But this simple organization does not encompass the even more troubling aspect of advice and counseling and drafting as to one or the other or both bodies of law, whether or not litigation is contemplated.

The third aspect of the federal system is the interstate aspect. Each of the fifty states may have the power to determine who can practice law within the state and to set standards and sanctions for these practitioners. This checker board system of admission and control for the bar contrasts sharply with our nationwide economic and social systems under which people, goods, funds and ideas move freely across state lines from Maine to Hawaii. It is in contrast, too, with the nationwide reach of federal law, "the supreme Law of the Land." Is the present view that each state may determine the privileges and standards of practice of lawyers within its borders consonant with the needs of our nationwide economic, social and federal law systems?

The separation of powers principle and the problems it creates are common to both the federal and the state governments. The principle derives from the tripartite division of the powers of government among the legislative, executive and judicial branches. It assures that the powers of government are divided among the three branches of government without being concentrated in one, whether it be the King or the President, or the Parliament or the Congress. It helps to assure also that each branch has inherent within it the powers essential to its effective operation, without impairing the cooperation of the several branches to common ends. Two questions under the separation of powers principle have special relevance here. One is, does the legislature as the general law-making body have power to fix standards and sanctions for the profession of law as it may do for other specialized groups in the community, subject of course to constitutional limitations? The other question is, does each branch of government have inherent power to set standards for representatives that appear before it? This latter question can be made more specific by splitting it into three parts. (1) Does the judiciary, whether federal or state, have inherent and exclusive power over those who assume to practice law before the courts or in their offices? (2) Do the several executive or administrative agencies have a similar power over practitioners before them or in the fields of the agencies? (3) Does the legislature have a similar power over advocates and lobbyists who support legislative measures whether before legislative committees or by informal means?

The general questions which this section raises reappear in specific settings at many places in this course. The reader may determine for himself whether the answers in the specific cases are adequate and whether they aid him in reaching a satisfying answer to the general questions.

NOTES

(1) "[T]he United States . . . has perhaps the most complicated legal structure that has ever been devised and made effective in man's effort to govern himself. . . . Only an American who has grown up in the system, and come to think of it as a part of the order of nature, can fail to see how intricate it is." Erwin N. Griswold, Law and Lawyers in the United States 3, 64 (1964).

(2) *Administrative Agency.* "The International Claims Commission of the United States, in the Department of State, found that the appellant, an attorney, had violated certain canons of ethics of the American Bar Association. After a hearing the Commission revoked his right to appear before it. The then Secretary of State, advised by a committee of the District of

Columbia Bar Association that the Commission's findings were correct, affirmed the revocation. On review the District Court entered a summary judgment against appellant. . . . An administrative agency that has general authority to prescribe its rules of procedure may set standards for determining who may practice before it. Goldsmith v. U. S. Board of Tax Appeals, 270 U.S. 117. . . ." Edgerton, J., in Herman v. Dulles, 205 F.2d 715 (D.C. Cir. 1953).

(3) The problem of federal control is discussed briefly in Cheatham, *The Reach of Federal Action over the Profession of Law*, 18 Stan.L.Rev. 1288 (1966).

Chapter IV

FOREGROUND AND COMPARISON

SECTION 1. THE ENGLISH SYSTEM

THE LEGAL PROFESSION IN ENGLAND

THOMAS G. LUND, THE LEGAL PROFESSION IN ENGLAND AND WALES

35 Jour.Am.Jud.Soc. 134 (1952).*

The legal profession in England and Wales is divided into two branches, solicitors and barristers. . . .

From the beginning of the 19th century the four great Inns of Court, namely, Lincoln's Inn, the Inner Temple, the Middle Temple and Gray's Inn, have excluded all attorneys and solicitors and their articled clerks from being members of their societies, which now consist exclusively of barristers. . . .

The bar accordingly developed as the upper branch, an autonomous community eventually independent of both judges and legislature.† . . . No person can be a member of both branches at once, but it is possible to change from one branch to the other and such a course is by no means rare. . . .

Barristers have a monopoly of the right of audience in the superior courts, and it is from their ranks that the higher judicial offices and the law offices of the Crown (those of Attorney-General and Solicitor-General) are filled. Barristers, however, have not a complete monopoly of advocacy as a right of audience is also extended to solicitors in, for example, the county courts and Magistrates' courts. Nor is the work of barristers entirely limited to advocacy: in addition they are consulted from time to time as experts by solicitors—much in the same way as a general medical practitioner may call in to consultation a specialist.

The other fundamental difference between the two branches of the profession is that (with one comparatively unimportant exception where legal aid is granted in certain criminal matters) the bar has by convention no right of direct access to the client; the client can

---

* The author is secretary of the Law Society of England.

† Thus, it has long been recognized that no aspirant to the bar has any legal right to be admitted as student of an Inn (Rex v. Lincoln's Inn, 4 B. & C., 1825), or to be called to the Bar (Rex v. Benchers of Gray's Inn, 1 Doug. 353, 1780) or to be restored if expelled therefrom (Boreman's case (1622) cited in Rex v. Benchers of Gray's Inn). [Author's footnote.]

only approach, consult or instruct a barrister through a solicitor. A barrister must work as an individual and may not practice in partnership whereas a solicitor not only may do so but, as will be seen, generally does. Solicitors indeed do nine-tenths of the work which members of the bar in the United States carry out and it is only specialist advocacy in the Supreme Court which is an English barrister's prerogative. . . .

Apparently no one, not even the Inns of Court themselves, knows the exact number of barristers. Very many people are called to the bar with no intention of practicing, but mainly with the intention of securing some qualification which will advance them in their career. My guess would be that the total number might be somewhere in the region of 2,000. We know that about 1,600 have offered their services for the Legal Aid Scheme, but many of these are no doubt earning their living in some way other than at the bar for the most part, e. g. in journalism. . . . A person wishing to be called to the Bar must join one of the Inns, having first passed a test of general education (of approximately the same standard as that required for entry into a university) and fulfilled certain conditions of fitness and respectability; he must "keep" a certain number of terms (generally twelve), which now involves nothing more than dining in hall on a number of days in each term, 4 terms in a year; and he must pass a qualifying examination of a largely theoretical nature. The examination approximates to those for a university law degree and Bar students frequently keep their terms while at the university. . . . In contradistinction to solicitors, who must be British subjects, barristers may be of any nationality.

The Bar is divided into two ranks; Queen's Counsel who wear silk gowns and are called "Silks" or "Leaders"; and all other barristers who are called "Juniors." Q.C.'s are appointed on the recommendation of the Lord Chancellor and the appointment is generally (but not invariably) a necessary preliminary to elevation to the judiciary. . . . There are probably about 1,000 to 1,200 members of the Bar today who earn their living exclusively from their profession. . . .

The main classification of practicing barristers is into the Chancery and Common Law Bars. . . . The great majority practice in London but a few have chambers in provincial cities. Nearly all common law barristers are also members of a circuit. For the purpose of trials by Her Majesty's judges at Assizes, England and Wales outside London is divided into eight circuits each of which has its own Bar. A barrister can only belong to one circuit and a barrister who is not a member of the circuit cannot hold a brief upon it unless he is paid a special fee in addition to his normal brief fee and unless a member of the circuit is briefed with him.

A barrister's fee is regarded as being an honorarium and he may not sue either the solicitor instructing him or the lay client for it. The solicitor, however, is primarily responsible and The Law Society (the governing body of the solicitors' profession) will exert pressure on the solicitor to ensue its payment. The amount of the fee is a matter for agreement between the barrister and the solicitor, but for certain matters a more or less standard scale has been generally recognized. . . .

While the Bar have at all times been associated with the Inns of Court, attorneys and solicitors were formerly associated with the Inns of Chancery but these Inns, lacking any of the power, authority and prestige of the Inns of Court, became atrophied and slowly decayed. Early in the 18th century there was established the Society of Gentlemen Practicers in the Courts of Law and Equity. . . .

This Society was the forerunner of The Law Society which first came into being in 1823. It was originally established as a joint stock company and was later incorporated by Royal Charter. . . .

. . . In 1951 out of about 22,000 English solicitors engaged in the practice of the law about 16,000 were members. . . . Notwithstanding the voluntary nature of The Law Society, the Society has been entrusted by Parliament with many powers, obligations and duties with respect to the profession. . . .

Parliament has by statute laid down what training is necessary for a solicitor. Apart from barristers and certain "colonial" solicitors of not less than five years' standing, every intending solicitor is required to serve a period under articles of clerkship (or apprenticeship) with a solicitor engaged in the active practice of the law. The term is normally five years but is reduced to three years for university graduates (whether in law or arts). . . .

The management and control of examinations for solicitors has been placed by Parliament in the hands of The Law Society which is empowered to make regulations governing the syllabus, the appointment of examiners and other kindred matters. These regulations, however, must be approved by the Master of the Rolls, the Lord Chancellor and the Lord Chief Justice and the objection of any two of these is fatal. . . .

Parliament has also expressly directed The Law Society to make rules dealing with the money accounts to be kept by solicitors. . . To insure that these rules are observed each practicing solicitor is required to submit annually to The Law Society a certificate signed by a member of one of the recognized accountancy bodies to the effect that the rules have been complied with in the solicitor's practice. Moreover, the Council of The Law Society may at any time, whether upon complaint or otherwise, inspect a solicitor's books of account and bank accounts to ascertain whether he has complied with the rules. . . .

The Law Society also maintains and administers a fund, the "Compensation Fund," from which, at the discretion of the Council, grants are made for the purpose of relieving or mitigating losses sustained by any person in consequence of dishonesty on the part of any solicitor or solicitor's clerk in connection with the solicitor's practice. Every solicitor is required by statute to contribute to this Fund when taking out his annual practicing certificate. . . .

Perhaps, however, the most important of the duties entrusted by Parliament to The Law Society is the administration of the Legal Aid and Advice Act, 1949: . . . This is a scheme whereby those of moderate means can, on payment of a proportion of the costs calculated on their capital and income, receive legal aid and assistance in litigation, the balance, up to 85%, of the lawyer's normal fee payable in each case being met by the state. The administrative details of the service are embodied in a scheme drawn up on the authority of Parliament by The Law Society. The position, therefore, is of a largely state-financed scheme drawn up and operated, subject only to ultimate government consent, by a voluntary organization representative of the profession itself—which is a far cry from nationalization of the legal profession. . . . Apart from London and the larger provincial cities where there are a few firms with up to about ten partners each, it is unusual to find a firm with more than two or three partners and there are, even in London, many solicitors practicing alone. It is, however, probably true that the number of solicitors practicing alone is decreasing and that the growing complexity of the law is tending to result in more specialization so that the size of firms —and the number of partners—is increasing.

THE ENGLISH AND THE AMERICAN SETTING COMPARED

HENRY T. LUMMUS, BOOK REVIEW

46 Harv.L.Rev. 533 (1933).

It is, of course, impossible to transplant to America every detail of English practice and make it live here in a new atmosphere and strange surroundings. Many of the English practices are foreign to our traditions and modes of thought, however much better they may be than ours. They are devised for a body of litigation made small by the expense of English justice; they would have to be applied in America to a mass of litigation swollen by the American theory that the public should pay the entire cost of all litigation that the individual may choose to begin. They are made to be administered by a few judges of great experience and skill; in America, they would have to be administered by many judges, ranging in capacity from those who are equal to the best in England down to those who owe their seats merely to a knack at catching votes. The English practices are administered by judges who are expected to be prompt, efficient, and strong, masters of the trial; in many of our states they would have to be administered by judges who are expected to be merely moderators in a struggle between dominating advocates and are even denied the last word to the jury and sometimes any word at all unless in writing. The English rules, too, are made for a trial bar, small, familiar with practice, and highly disciplined; here, they would have to be used by a bar tremendously large ranging in merit from the peers of the most able English leaders down to the most ignorant pettifoggers that can be stuffed with enough law to get through a bar examination. In England, there is a homogeneous people with pride in strong courts and efficient administration of justice, civil and criminal. In America, the pioneer spirit of which Dean Pound has spoken still survives, among a mixed population, in distrust for the courts, in a liking for the law's delays, in maintaining at enormous public expense the right of jury trial free of cost in every petty dispute, in depressing the judge and elevating the advocate, and in loving the law in proportion as it is weak and impotent against an individual battling for immunity from the civil or criminal consequences of his wrongdoing. Editors may inveigh against it when this spirit runs counter to the wish of the moment; but the pioneer spirit, like Ol' Man River, "keeps rollin' along" and is a force always to be reckoned with. . . .

We must not imagine that the English system of procedure, so much admired on this side of the water, has no critics in the land of its birth. One of the reasons for its success, administered as it is by a body of judges so small as to raise a question as to what so many judges do to keep busy in America, is its cost. The cost keeps the business of the Supreme Court within limits; the overflow that cannot pay the cost goes into the county courts, or is settled without litigation, or suffers a denial of justice. . . .

NOTES

(1) The history of the profession of law in England is outlined in Plucknett, A Concise History of the Common Law, Part II, Ch. 12 and 13 (5th ed. 1956); Holdsworth, History of English Law, Vol. II, Ch. IV and V; Vol. III; Vol. VI, Ch. VIII; Vol. XII, Ch. III (1938).

The institutions and personnel of English law are described in the context of law administration in Jackson, The Machinery of Justice in England (5th ed. 1967). The activities of English lawyers are vividly portrayed in Megarry, Lawyer and Litigant in England (1962).

The standards of the two branches of the English profession are stated in books by the secretaries of the two principal professional bodies, Sir Thomas G. Lund, Secretary of the Law Society of England and Mr. W. W. Boulton, Secretary to the General Council of the Bar. See Lund, A Guide to the Professional Conduct and Etiquette of Solicitors (1960); Boulton, A Guide to Conduct and Etiquette at the Bar of England and Wales (4th ed. 1965). See also Cordery's Law Relating to Solicitors (6th ed. 1968).

A glimpse or a guess of the future is ventured in Lund, The Future Pattern of the Profession, 22 Record Ass'n Bar City N. Y. 22 (1967).

(2) Two recent, unusual books have described and critically appraised the English legal profession. The first, Abel-Smith & Stevens, Lawyers and the Courts (1967), is, as the subtitle indicates, "A Sociological Study of the English Legal System, 1750–1967." It contrasts especially "The Age of Reform: 1825–1875" with both "The Era of Stagnation: 1875–1939" and "The Second World War and After: Prelude to Reform?". The second book, Johnstone & Hopson, Lawyers and Their Work (1967), describes the profession in both England and the United States, and lays stress on how and through whom legal services are to be made available. See especially chapters 11 to 15.

(3) In Search of Justice: [English] Society and the Legal System (1968) by Abel-Smith and Stevens is a descriptive and critical book, the counterpart of which is needed in the United States. "If this book encourages lawyers to question their own assumptions as well as ours", the authors say in the Introduction, "we shall be delighted".

(4) The House of Lords has stated it will no longer accept the principle that its decisions are beyond overruling. See Leach, *Revisionism in the House of Lords: The Bastion of Rigid Stare Decisis Falls*, 80 Harv.L.Rev. 797 (1967).

"[T]he lawyer must, as a member of the society in which he lives, stand back from his daily practice and think about the laws which he helps to administer and enforce; and surveying them, he must originate ideas; he must criticize; he must, by what he says and writes, help to guide society." These words from an address by the chairman of the Law Commission, created by Parliament, may indicate the breadth of view which the Commission will take in its recommendations. Sir Leslie Scarman, *The Role of the Legal Profession in Law Reform*, 21 Record Ass'n Bar City N. Y. 11, 24 (1966).

Legal education in England is being transformed with an increasing role being taken over by the universities. Professional training, which has so long marked the education of both branches of the profession, is being associated with university training. See *Lord Chancellor's Committee on Legal Education: Memorandum from the Society of Public Teachers of Law*, X Jour.Soc.Pub.Tea.Law (N.S.) 157 (1969).

The basic methods in the two oldest universities, the Oxford tutorial and the Cambridge supervision systems, are described in Parry, *The Cambridge Supervision System*, 7 J.Leg.Ed. 1 (1954).

SECTION 2. THE AMERICAN SCENE

Introduction. In a brief sketch of the history of the American legal profession, mention may be made of any one of numerous aspects of its development. It may be laid on the forces which impelled the development; on changes in the subject matter of practice; on corresponding changes in the growth and organization of law offices; on changes in the influence of lawyers in the public life of the nation and in their position in the community. In this section some attention will be given to all these matters.

Stress might be laid on still other aspects, as, on the growth of competitors who would share or take over the work of lawyers; on the growth of bar associations and their activities; on the standards lawyers set for themselves; on legal education and admission to the bar; on changes in the machinery of law administration; on bar leaders who have helped to give direction and impetus to change. In later chapters these aspects are raised.

NOTE

Current national, state, and city data on such matters as the distribution of lawyers and the lawyer-population ratio are collected in American Bar Foundation, The 1967 Lawyer Statistical Report (1968). A triennial volume, the report is based on figures prepared by Martindale-Hubbell Law Directory.

A GLIMPSE OF LAWYERS OF EARLIER ERAS, HAMILTON AND CHOATE

GOEBEL, THE LAW PRACTICE OF ALEXANDER HAMILTON

Book Review, 18 Vand.L.Rev. 1660, 1661–62 (1965).

Hamilton's thoroughness as a lawyer appears throughout the book. When a young man he drafted his own practice manual. He was most careful in preparation. His arguments were directed to basic policies and not to case matching. It had to be so, for there were only English reports when he began his practice. It would have been so, one may hazard, even if there had been an abundance of reports. There were routine cases in his practice to be sure but there were many novel problems of the relations of state with state, and state with nation in the new federal union, as well as the problems of nation with nation. Hamilton's mind was affirmative in character, and was directed to fundamentals at the beginning of his country, which he envisaged as one of the great nations of the world. . . .

Hamilton was master and not subject of the technicalities of practice. His arguments for clients often reflected the larger views of public affairs. In the public mind his place is that of the arch conservative who favored even monarchy. In another view he was the very opposite of the conservative. He was the future-directed man who sought order and strength in the new national government as essentials to the security and development of his country. Who can now doubt that the views on powers of government pressed by Hamilton have prevailed over those of Jefferson?

Yet powers are not ends in themselves; they are instruments to other things. Here Jefferson's ideals have their great place. This generation, no less than the one after 1783, is one of conflict between order and liberty, stability and change. It is Hamiltonian in powers and methods of government, Jeffersonian in its ideals in a society that Jefferson would have abhorred. In our times, too, there is need for lawyers who will lift up their eyes from books and clients and give public guidance. In the Foreword to this book Judge Proskauer cites Hamilton as an examplar of what de Tocqueville urged on American lawyers:

> I cannot believe that a republic could subsist at the present time if the influence of lawyers in public business did not increase in proportion to the power of the people.

CLAUDE M. FUESS, RUFUS CHOATE [*]

Pages 135–138, 140 (1928).

Many acute and discriminating critics who knew Rufus Choate in the full maturity of his powers have agreed that he was the most eminent American lawyer not only of his own time but of any time. . . .

For some years Choate's law office was located at 4 Court Street, an entry famous for the influential men who had quarters there. On the same floor with Choate were Charles Sumner, George S. Hillard, Theophilus Parsons, and John A. Andrew, later War Governor of Massachusetts. On the floor above were Horace Mann, the educational reformer, Edward C. Loring, and Luther Stearns Cushing, the author of Cushing's Manual. Choate and Crowninshield had two rooms,—one for the clerks and one for Choate's inner sanctum. There was none of the elaborate mechanism, the smart looking secretaries and formal atmosphere which one finds on State Street to-day. . . . The place was littered with books, official blanks, legal documents, and other dry looking reading matter, arranged with no particular system. . . . Filing cabinets were then unknown, but he could usually put his hand at once on what he wanted. . . .

In his early days in Boston, Choate was careless in making out his accounts and often set his charges ridiculously low. As a consequence, he accumulated very little property. He himself was indifferent to money, but after 1849, when the new firm was formed, the system was changed. Bell, his partner, now put his fees on a more rational scale, with the result that the average annual receipts of the office from 1849 to 1859, while Choate was engaged in about seventy cases a year, were not far from $18,000. In 1856, his most profitable

---

[*] With the permission of the publisher, G. P. Putnam Sons.

year, he took in more than $22,000. The largest fee accepted by Choate was $2,500,—a sum which he received in only four instances. . . . Choate was versed in every phase of the profession. He was for the defendant in cases of divorce, embezzlement, assault, arson, and murder; he was ready to appear in any court, from that of a Justice of the Peace to that of a Supreme Court Judge; his clients represented an infinite variety of persons, from the lowest to the highest, from rogues to martyrs. He defended a Catholic priest against a charge of criminal assault; he conducted a case for Iasigi, a Greek, against a defendant who had induced the foreigner to sell goods on credit to an insolvent purchaser; and he represented one of the litigants in a quarrel between two branches of a great Christian Church. Studying the cases in which Rufus Choate appeared, we shall be ranging over nearly every aspect of human life, rich with material as interesting as that in the Newgate Calendar, or in a physician's notebook. Choate, at various times, was psychologist, sociologist, neurologist, alienist, and father confessor, as well as attorney.

NOTE

On the history of the legal profession and the development of the organized bar, see Charles Warren, A History of the American Bar (1913); Roscoe Pound, The Lawyer from Antiquity to Modern Times (1953). See also Anton-Herman Chroust, The Rise of the Legal Profession in America (1965), which sketches the development of the profession by colonies and then by fields down to about 1840; The Golden Age of American Law (Haar ed. 1965) which consists of writings by and about lawyers in the period from 1820 to 1860.

THE TYPES OF LAW PRACTICE

JAMES WILLARD HURST, THE GROWTH OF AMERICAN LAW—THE LAW MAKERS *

Pages 295–305 (1950).

So far as the evidence goes, the practice of the law throughout our history closely reflected the main concerns of the society as of any given time. . . . It was not surprising, therefore, that the bulk of law practice consistently dealt with economic affairs—with property, business institutions, and economic conflict. As was natural in the opening of a new country, land and commerce provided the grist of law office activity well past the Civil War. . . .

Marked specialization in fields of practice did not develop until the end of the nineteenth century. But from an early date the inherent diversity of commerce was reflected in the growth of particular types of law business in particular localities. . . .

* With the permission of the publisher, Little, Brown & Co.

Industry and finance gave decided direction to the growth of new types of law business after 1870; and, as we shall later note, this development was paralleled by marked specialization in law practice. The "railroad lawyer" was the first symbol of change. . . . Ambitious men soon found that the centers of power were closer to finance. Able lawyers began to sit on boards of directors. . . . The distribution of the most influential new law business responded to a shift in the center of gravity in the economy. Railroad mergers and railroad finance were the avenue to a whole new field of corporate counseling, and the centers of this work were in a handful of great cities east of the Mississippi.

Important developments in law practice of the late nineteenth and early twentieth centuries clustered about the growth of unprecedented concentration of industrial and financial power. . . . Before the '70's lawyers had relatively little personal injury business, though in the 1840's the first railroad fellow servant case warned of new problems. The spread of mechanized transportation, mining, and industry made the personal injury field a major challenge to legal adjustment. The reality of the problems was attested by the spread of safety laws, employers' liability legislation, and finally workmen's compensation systems. After 1920 the automobile still more drastically revolutionized the personal injury business that passed through law offices.

Population continued to move toward several score of great cities, and this drift provided another focus of change in law jobs. Thus small claims, landlord-tenant disputes, issues arising out of broken homes presented vast totals of potential work for the bar; the work was no less real or important because most of it could not be handled economically as the profession was organized to deal with it. The growth of cities changed the nature of law practice in criminal cases. Through most of the nineteenth century the average practitioner took his quota of cases in defense of persons accused of crime; even lawyers most occupied with large affairs appeared for the defense in criminal cases. But, in the twentieth century the defense of accused persons became more and more the specialty of a small part of the bar, even as the reach of the criminal law greatly expanded. . . .

From 1790 on, law practice included a material amount of dealings with or affecting the government. Such business varied much in type and extent. . . . At first government was primarily the potential source of gifts. This shaped the kind of business that lawyers had before legislatures and executive officers. The high point, as well as the most abused type, of such effort concerned the obtaining of special corporate charters, franchises, and privileges, specially between about 1820–1890. . . .

After 1850, as emphasis turned from government bounty to government regulation, new issues began to bring lawyers before government. . . . Government at all levels in the United States extended the scope of its regulation of business in the twentieth century. In turn this vastly extended the work of lawyers before administrative bodies, as well as before legislatures and courts. . . .

Parallel to the extended reach of government regulation was of course a great expansion in the volume of the government's own law business. . . .

New types of government regulation and services involved individual actions and adjustments, taken under the laws, which ran into figures which would have seemed astronomical to lawyers or administrators of a century earlier. . . .

[In the period since 1790] the most basic change in the nature of lawyers' professional work was the shift in emphasis from advocacy to counseling. Of course lawyers always did office work as well as court work. . . . But before 1870, both in their own eyes and in the common opinion of laymen, lawyers' distinctive business was contest in court; the criterion in handling most matters out of court was how the arrangement would stand up under a later challenge in court; by common consent in the typical community the prizes in reputation, public influence, and wealth were the due of the able advocate. . . .

The years after 1870 showed a more matter-of-fact attitude, a prevailing distaste for litigation as a costly luxury, and an increasing effort to use law and lawyers preventively. . . .

The evidence that we have confirms that the great city business law offices of the early twentieth century set a pattern which simply put in clearest form certain trends which marked the more lucrative and influential practice of the law throughout the country. The first reliable investigations of the economics of the profession were made in the 1930's. These studies tended to confirm the new picture of the lawyer as primarily advisor, counselor, administrator of affairs—in contrast to the image of the frock-coated Daniel Webster, which was the mid-nineteenth-century stereotype of the bar.

NOTES

(1) See Hurst, *Lawyers in American Society, 1750–1966*, 50 Marquette L.Rev. 594 (1967). In this article, Professor Hurst sketches the developments over the years in three roles of the American lawyer: "First the lawyer has been a man earning a living. Second, he has, in the Bar, collectively constituted one of the key institutions of social order in our history. And third, he has been a professional man."

(2) Two European commentators of the American scene, de Tocqueville and Bryce, about half a century apart, had a good deal to say about the legal profession. See Alexis de Tocqueville, Democracy in America, especially Chap. 16, "Causes Which Mitigate the Tyranny of the Majority in the United States—The Temper of the Legal Profession in the United States and How it Serves as a Counterpoise to Democracy"; Lord Bryce, The

American Commonwealth, especially Chap. 98 "The Bar" and Chap. 99 "The Bench".

(3) An unusually interesting anthology of historical and comparative materials with introductory and connecting passages, "based on the radical idea that it is possible to gain education by thoughtful reading", is Honnold, The Life of the Law: Readings on the Growth of Legal Institutions (1964).

THE LAW EXPLOSION

HARRY W. JONES, THE COURTS, THE PUBLIC, AND THE LAW EXPLOSION

Pages 2-3 (1965).

Our courts are now confronted by the mid century law explosion. This, to some extent, is a function of the population explosion—twice as many people, therefore twice as many disputes to be settled, twice as many civil claims to be heard and weighed, twice as many criminal charges to be tried and determined. But that is by no means the whole story of the law explosion; the full truth is that we have a society that is far more complex and vastly more demanding on law and legal institutions. New rights, like those of social security, have been brought into being, and older rights of contract and property made subject to government regulation and legal control. New social interests are pressing for recognition in the courts. Groups long inarticulate have found legal spokesmen and are asserting grievances long unheard. Each of these developments has brought its additional grist to the mills of justice.

Two aspects of the law explosion are of central importance for contemporary judicial administration. In court congestion, the automobile is the villain of the piece, as Maurice Rosenberg makes plain in Chapter Two. Technological advances and dramatic gains in prevailing income standards have put tens of millions of cars on the roads, and one result has been an astronomical increase in accident figures and personal injury suits. This tide of litigation has inundated our trial courts of general jurisdiction. In the great cities, delays run into years, and courtroom adjudication becomes a painful last alternative, to be resorted to only when a tolerable settlement cannot be secured from the insurance company out of court. There is no inherent reason why this must be so. We put up with the situation only because we are used to it and fatalistic about it. How long would the public tolerate comparable delay and inefficiency in the furnishing of any other public service?

Edward Barrett's essay (Chapter Four) provides abundant evidence that the quantitative pressures on the courts are even greater in criminal law administration. There has been a massive increase in crime and other phenomena of social instability. Scholars of society have varying explanations, but all seem to agree that two of the major factors are 1) the waning influence of the family, the church, and other nonlegal agencies of social control, and 2) the vast migrations of population from the small towns and rural areas to the great cities that have taken place in the United States since World War II. Whatever the causes, the consequences for the legal order are manifest. The great mass of criminal cases, divorce proceedings, and adjudications in matters of mental illness, alcoholism, narcotics addiction, and juvenile delinquency are disposed of in any major city on an assembly-line basis, so many cases to the hour. What are the implications for law and social order when untold thousands of people charged with criminal offenses are handled in the lower courts as if they were mere blanks for processing?

Can justice be administered on a mass-production basis? Are there no middle ways between the glacial slowness of the court process in personal injury suits and the frantic speed of the magistrates' courts in misdemeanor cases?

NOTE

"Our changing society now faces challenge to public order and to the realization of American ideals greater than any since the Civil War—the cluster of problems known as the urban crisis.

"Legal institutions provide a network of relationships for co-operation and for reconciling conflict in society, and so are inconspicuous when society is at peace. There inadequacies as well as the importance of their functions become clear in times of trouble. . . .

"The law seeks fair dealing, equity and redress of grievance—these are the benefits of legal order. For many, our institutions have proved inadequate to secure the benefits of equal justice. We must overcome this failure.

"Beyond this, the systematic re-examination and evaluation of the substance or our law, with a view to its continuous improvement, are essential to the legal order and especially important in a period of sweeping social change. It is a professional responsibility of lawyers to create and support the institutions necessary to achieve that end. The lawyer contributes to enhancement of respect for law by assuring that law is truly worthy of respect." *Report of the American Assembly on Law and the Changing Society,* 54 A.B.A.J. 450 (1968).

THE FORCES WHICH WILL CONTINUE TO SHAPE THE PROFESSION

This section is directed primarily to changes in the work, structure and spirit of the American Bar. These changes cannot be seen fully if observed only in isolation for they were not self-generating. Some may have been aided by forces within the profession. Most of the changes have been impelled by forces outside. It is not easy to separate these forces from one another since they overlap and interact. It is possible, however, to look at the development of the profession from the viewpoint of each of several factors in turn—intellectual, economic and social, ethical, political, leadership.

1. *Intellectual.* "Intellectual" means here the efforts of man to understand and to control his environment. Darius, the Persian, could send a message from Susa to Sardis, Sir Winston Churchill wrote, as quickly as the Emperor Charles V, two thousand years later, could send one from Madrid to Brussels, the messengers of both being equally dependent on the speed of the horse. Justice Frankfurter told of a question he would put to his classes in the Harvard Law School, "Who was the most important law reformer of the past two centuries." After the students had proposed such men of law as Mansfield, Marshall, and Bentham, Frankfurter would say, "Watt." James Watt first made practicable the use of molecular power for human purposes through a steam engine, and the use of the released power in industry.* The Industrial Revolution rests on the inventions of Watt and his successors. One of the new revolutions we are witnessing comes from a vastly greater source of power, the use of atomic power released in the fission and fusion of the atom. In two centuries, the source of industrial power has changed from muscular energy to molecular energy released in the burning of fossil fuels to nuclear energy. One of the by-products of new sources of energies is methods of transportation which have brought the site of Washington closer in time to Paris or Peking than it was to Baltimore when our capital was founded. The name of Charles Darwin brings to mind another line of scientific development and its immense impact on man and on his way of looking at himself and his place in the scheme of things. Each reader can make for himself a list of the scientists, the inventors, and the engineers who have made modern society possible and have created a host of opportunities and problems for society.

---

* "There have been two great creative epochs in the history of our civilization: that of ancient Greece and that of today. The one produced critical thought; the other applied it to invent machines. Besides these two contributions to secular society, all others rank as minor. The one stirred into activity that critical intelligence upon which rests our whole apparatus of knowledge; the other made nature our Ally not merely by applying its power to do our work, but also by supplying the means for extending knowledge itself, almost to the infinite." Shotwell, The History of History, Vol. I, p. 246 (1939).

Along with all groups in society the lawyer has shared in the effects of these intellectual creations. It is for him especially to aid in developing the law and his own profession so they may be adequate to the new needs and opportunities. In a more direct sense the lawyer is a debtor of another intellectual group, the social scientists. He may employ economic and social data in drafting legislation and in advising clients, or he may marshal them as an advocate to support a point. He must begin to make terms with the social scientists as collaborators or as rivals.

Economic and Social. Our nation and our profession began with little business in small communities. Little business had only occasional need for legal counsel in the days of little government. Big business and urban sprawl are marks of our day. Economic interests of all sorts make demands on government for favorable treatment ranging from subsidies and tariffs to exemption from taxation or regulation. Big business has its steady stream of legal questions, swelled by the regulations of big government. An engrossing task of many lawyers is that of adviser and guide, with a close identification of much of the bar with these regular clients. This has given rise to the gigantic law firms in the large cities, and it has contributed to the decline of the political position of leaders of the bar. The growth of the large cities has created a need for newer forms of local government. It has made imperative new forms of legal services for a large part of the population. The change of position of the United States has greatly expanded the international activities of business as well as of government, and these have created almost a new dimension in the work of the American lawyer.

Ethical. The sense of justice, or, as Edmond Cahn so well put it, "The Sense of Injustice"—stimulated it may be by religion, has the profoundest effect on the law. As the ethical sense of the nation or the state or the community develops, so does the law. Caveat emptor has given way to protective regulations of many sorts. Racial discrimination has been condemned, and efforts have been made to aid the disadvantaged of all races. Much of this field has become "lawyer's law", with new and more effective forms of legal services for a large part of the population. In the more traditional parts of the lawyer's work much of the change comes from a heightened sense of professional responsibility, as manifested in the continuing efforts to improve law administration at all levels.

Political. Political forces bear on our branches of government at all levels. They bear on the courts as attested by the recent developments of the constitutional rights of the citizens against government, most strikingly illustrated for the lawyer by the right to counsel. Of course, they are felt strongly in the legislature. They impinge on the executive, who is influenced by them and employs them in aid of his program. One illustration is Andrew Jackson with his insistence on the capacity of the common man in every task and the temporary deprofessionalization of lawyers. A political fact of immense importance is our written Constitution with its limitations on government and its influence on the mentality and approach of American lawyers. Even the Declaration of Independence, with its detailed indictment of King George III for his violation of the legal rights of his American subjects, is a magnificent ethical as well as political document. The result of our political system has been that:

> "(A)ll the major issues of American political life would be cast in legal language and, accordingly, would receive their final shape from lawyers rather than from philosophers or political scientists."*

Leadership. It is not necessary to resort to the great man theory of history to observe the effect of leadership. Men with devotion and courage and, if the community is fortunate, with judgment and a sense of timing can do much. They can help to give effective expression to the underlying forces. So it has been with the bar. Each reader will have his own heroes, as well as his own villains who would deflect or block the forces. A few names of leaders in our profession which come at once to mind are John Marshall, David Dudley Field, Evarts and the group with him who formed an effective bar association in New York at the time of the Tweed scandals, Simeon Baldwin the moving figure in the organization of the American Bar Association, Christopher Columbus Langdell and James Bar Ames, Louis D. Brandeis, Charles Evans Hughes, Arthur T. Vanderbilt, Reginald Heber Smith. Whom would the reader add to this list of leaders in his own day and in his own community? The lawyers mentioned were conspicuous leaders. Yet every lawyer is a leader in some measure. His qualities will determine what he does in aiding and guiding his clients, in molding the profession, and so in forming the society of which he and his profession and his clients are parts. He, too, is one of the forces which will continue to shape the profession.

The Past is Prologue.

"One believes that legal history means not only a study of the trends and changes of legal thought in the past, but also, a more subtle task, a study of the trends, and the likelihood of changes of legal thought in the present. So viewed it is the social calculus of the law."**

The perception and forecast of social changes are important for lawyers even in private practice when advising their clients on long term matters. As Professor Willard Hurst has written, "a full-bodied conception of legal history [is] one which treats it not as the history of a self-contained system, but as the story of law in society";

---

* Chroust, The Rise of the Legal Profession in America 54 (1965).

** Joseph H. Beale, Jr., *Social Justice and Business Costs—A Study in the Legal History of To-day*, 49 Harv.L. Rev. 593, 609 (1936).

and again, "so much of effective legal control rests on effective timing."

Each person can point up for himself what has been sketched. Let each person draw six parallel columns, giving them the headings, intellectual, economic and social, and so on, ending with the legal profession. In each of the first five he should put down some dates or names indicating major changes in those areas. For example, under "political" might be put 1787, or 1865, or 1933. Opposite such entries he would enter, in the last column, consequent changes in the work or structure or spirit of our profession.

NOTES

(1) "Of what is past, or passing or to come."

Alfred North Whitehead, Adventures of Ideas Chap. VI (1933). "The recent shortening of the time-span between notable changes in social customs is very obvious, if we examine history. . . . The conclusion to be drawn from this survey is a momentous one. Our sociological theories, our political philosophy, our practical maxims of business, our political economy, and our doctrines of education, are derived from an unbroken tradition of great thinkers and of practical example, from the age of Plato in the fifth century before Christ to the end of the last century. The whole of this tradition is warped by the vicious assumption that each generation will substantially live amid the conditions governing the lives of its fathers and will transmit those conditions to mould with equal force the lives of its children. We are living in the first period of human history for which this assumption is false. . . . The point is that in the past the time-span of important change was considerably longer than that of a single human life. Thus mankind was trained to adapt itself to fixed conditions. Today this time-span is considerably shorter than that of human life, and accordingly our training must prepare individuals to face a novelty of conditions."

Trevelyan, "English Literature and Its Readers", The English Association, Presidential Address, p. 7, 1950. "My friend Sir Lawrence Bragg, the Head of the Cavendish Laboratory in Cambridge, recently gave a lecture in which he said that the advance of science and invention in our times was bringing about a change in the economic and other conditions of man's life which would, ere long, have produced as great a change as that produced by the practice of agriculture some thousands of years ago. Agriculture enabled wealth to accumulate and town life to begin, and thereby made the civilizations of which we know, ancient, medieval, and modern, up to the time of this further change now taking place."

(2) The passage above lays stress on the affirmative and moving factors shaping the profession. There are other and quite different factors which may question, hamper, slow, and block developments even in times of swift social change. Professor Willard Hurst has contrasted drift with direction in his book, Law and Social Process in United States History. Routine and habit, so easy for a profession accustomed to look to precedent for guidance, are more than mere inertia to be pushed aside. They are active defenders of the status quo. Lending strength to them is the fact that changes in law, especially in law administration, mean new burdens of study and learning on

the lawyer with no increment of value to him in his work; by contrast with the physician whose professional abilities are enhanced by advances in medical science and technique. There is the accompanying factor of the naturally conservative temperament, so well illustrated by Lord Halsbury whose name is carried on the principal compilations of English law and statutes and of whom it was said:

> "In each successive generation of his long manhood he readily adapted himself to the most conservative standpoint of the moment and voiced its creed in plain and unvarnished language."*

SECTION 3. A GLANCE AT OTHER SYSTEMS

ROBERT H. JACKSON, THE GENESIS OF AN AMERICAN LEGAL PROFESSION: A REVIEW OF 150 YEARS OF CHANGE

38 A.B.A.J. 547, 616 (1952).

It is not without significance that the most constructive was also the least intellectually isolationist period of our legal history.

A RECONCILIATION OF JUDICIAL SYSTEMS

REPORT [TO THE SECRETARY OF STATE] OF ROBERT H. JACKSON, UNITED STATES REPRESENTATIVE TO THE INTERNATIONAL CONFERENCE ON MILITARY TRIALS

Pages x, vi, 319 (1945).

[The negotiations among the Allied Powers on the establishment of a tribunal to try the leaders of Nazi Germany at the end of World War II furnished a striking example of diversity of views on the operation of legal systems.] Legal systems exhibit disparities in their methods of procedure greater than in the principles of law they serve. Members of the legal profession acquire a rather emotional attachment to forms and customs to which they are accustomed and frequently entertain a passionate conviction that no unfamiliar procedure can be morally right.

. . . a procedure that is acceptable as a fair trial in countries accustomed to the Continental system of law may not be regarded as a fair trial in common law countries. What is even harder for Americans to recognize is that trials which we regard as fair and just may be regarded in Continental countries as not only inadequate to protect society but also as inadequate to protect the accused individual. . . .

---

* See Heuston, Lives of the Lord Chancellors, 1885–1940 at 73 (1964).

A fundamental cleavage, which persisted throughout the negotiations, was caused by the difference between the Soviet practice, under which a judicial inquiry is carried on chiefly by the court and not by the parties, and the Anglo-American theory of a criminal trial, which the Soviet jurist rejects and stigmatizes as the "contest theory". The Soviets rely on the diligence of the tribunal rather than on the zeal and self-interest of adversaries to develop the facts. Another fundamental opposition concerns the function of a judiciary. The Soviet views a court as "one of the organs of government power, a weapon in the hands of the ruling class for the purpose of safeguarding its interests." It is not strange that those trained in that view should find it difficult to accept or to understand the Anglo-American idea of a court as an independent agency responsible only before the law.

. . . I think that in some ways the Continental and Soviet systems are perhaps better than ours.

THE EXCESSES OF CONTENTIOUSNESS IN THE UNITED STATES

EARL WARREN, OBSERVATION: THE ADVOCATE AND THE ADMINISTRATION OF JUSTICE IN AN URBAN SOCIETY

47 Texas L.Rev. 615, 617–619 (1969).

It has been my belief for many years that the most serious problem today in the administration of justice is the manner in which we handle judicial work.

There is some evidence that we have become callous in living day by day with the problems surrounding the administration of our courts. . . . We need constantly to remind ourselves that cases are, for the most part, people waiting for the processes of justice, and in our major cities these people are seeing justice denied by lost witnesses, by forgotten or hazy facts, and by crimes committed by felons who might otherwise be in jail or under supervision. . . .

. . . Dean Pound, perhaps more than any legal scholar in the world, viewed the broad spectrum of the law and its operation on society and pronounced what he saw with a clarity seldom matched.

The man who in 1906 angered many of the leaders in the American Bar Association with his forthright speech on "The Causes of Popular Dissatisfaction With the Administration of Justice" would certainly applaud the efforts of the trial bar to make the administration of justice more effective. . . .

. . . You will all recall the challenge he made to improve the adversary process in that historic speech at St. Paul. Speaking of the judicial process and of the public's view of it, he stated:

> A . . . potent source of irritation lies in our American exaggerations of the common law contentious procedure. The sporting theory of justice, the "instinct of giving the game fair play," as Professor Wigmore has put it, is so rooted in the profession in America that most of us take it as a fundamental legal tenant. . . .
>
> The effect of our exaggerated contentious procedure is not only to irritate parties, witnesses and jurors in particular cases, but to give to the whole community a false notion of the purpose and end of law.

This long quotation presents a direct challenge to our legal system. In a sense, the quotation also illustrates the scope of the challenge. In it, Dean Pound calls on history to destroy any view that there is something sacred about the contentious or gaming theory of judicial administration. He calls on his deep understanding of justice in the civil-law countries to suggest the theory is by no means universal. But, most of all, he expresses his concern about the consequence of the theory in practical application as it gives "the whole community a false notion of the purpose and end of law." . . .

In actuality, the "exaggerated contentious procedure" is at the heart of the malfunctioning of our urban courts.

THE FRENCH AND THE AMERICAN PROCEDURAL SYSTEMS

LE PAULLE, STUDY IN COMPARATIVE CIVIL PROCEDURE

12 Cornell L.Q. 24 (1967).

Taking for granted that common law procedure is known to the reader, we have contrasted it with civil law procedure. But as civil law is more or less an abstraction, we have chosen a concrete example: French procedure as a most representative illustration, since French Law has been taken as a model in many other countries. . . . A great difference between civil and common law procedure is that, in the civil law system, there is always a representative of the State (district attorney) in all civil suits. In a case of breach of contract, for example, the district attorney may argue the case one way or the other, as he believes the law to be. In nine cases out of ten their presence is not necessary, but sometimes it is quite useful to have before the judges an important disinterested exposition of the facts and of the law. . . .

From a comparison of civil and common law procedure, what are the main impressions that may be gathered? . . .

The political conception back of each one is different. The American conception is that in a democracy it is shocking that some individuals may, as a profession, have the fate of some of their countrymen in their hands. So, the idea of a judge deciding the whole case, law and fact, does not agree with the philosophy of the land. Facts must be decided by fellow countrymen, selected by chance; law must be decided by a judge, preferably elected by the people at large.

Now the civil law conception, that claims to be as democratic, reaches quite opposite results and says democracy must be safety against arbitrary human decisions; citizens must be judged by law and not by men; so, those who have to decide the fate of their fellow-citizens must not be picked out by blind chance and brought into the court-room with all the obscure sentiments and instincts of the crowd from which they come. The safeguard of democracy is the coolness of professional judges, their training in inductive process for the discovery of the truth, their lack of sentimental attitude. The Anglo-American philosophy back of its procedure is a sentimental democracy that wants to strengthen the links with the people at large. The Latin philosophy is an intellectual democracy wanting to protect those coming into court from the heart, the nerves, the obscure instincts and passions of the crowd and the mob. Hence in the civil law there is no jury in civil cases, judges are never elected by the people at large, there must be three judges and a representative of the State in each court. . . .

The proceedings in court are much more brief in France; the evidence is all gathered in writing before the trial so the judges in court have only to hear two speeches on arguments of law of which they already know the outline by the "conclusions", and of evidence of which they have had a copy. Hence proceedings in average cases last between ten minutes to one hour. . . .

The element of surprise, eliminated in a civil law trial,[155] is carefully kept as a weapon in the legal fight; the American lawyer hides his evidence from his opponent. . . .

. . . there is no cross-examination in a civil law court; when witnesses must testify, the questions are put by the Chief Justice and the lawyers remain silent, other than to look from time to time to the Chief Justice to put this or that question to the witness; there is no fight with the witness, or with the opponent about interrupting the witness.

At common law, when the two lawyers have taken the positions with their weapons (i. e. evidence), they are left alone in the arena. It would be considered as against the rules of fair game to have a

---

155. Since all evidence introduced by one party must be communicated to the opponent a reasonable time before the trial. [Author's footnote].

third party intervening in favor of one of the champions. In civil law countries, on the contrary, the presence of a district attorney saying freely how he believes the law should be applied, in a suit on a breach of contract, for instance, changes to a considerable extent the attitude of the lawyers.

For these reasons a trial looks more at common law like a fight, at civil law more like an academic discussion and an inductive effort to discover the truth.

Which is the best? It is submitted that such a question has no meaning: there is not one good system of procedure: all are good when they are adapted to the psychology of the people and the spirit of the law to which they apply.

A CONCILIATORY SYSTEM OF SETTLEMENT OF CONTROVERSY: THE ANCIENT CHINESE SYSTEM

WIGMORE, A PANORAMA OF THE WORLD'S LEGAL SYSTEMS

Vol. I, Pages 143 et seq. (1928).

The history and characteristics of the Chinese system of law and justice cannot be appreciated without taking into account the general philosophy of life that underlies it. In the following passage, a modern legal scholar lucidly summarizes that philosophy and points out some of its effects on ideas of law and justice: . . . In general the Chinese look to Moderation, Humanity, Equity, as the governing idea for social relations. The conception of strict logical law, independent of the purpose in hand and the personality of the parties to a dispute, remains an alien notion. The Chinese does not conceive of an absolute right or wrong in law.

"It follows that in general, he seeks a middle road, the golden mean, a compromise which will 'save the face', an adjustment by settlement between the differing contentions. The magistrate, for the Chinese, is a friendly arbitrator, rather than a dominating authority bound to declare the law and to secure its respect." . . .

Another notable consequence of the Confucian philosophy (or Chinese character) is that conciliation and mutual adjustment are looked upon as ideal elements of justice. . . . The German jurist Puchta has concisely stated the antithesis between justice and law:

"The relationships of law are the relations of one man to another, and may be called legal relations. But the various human relationships do not enter, in their full extent, into the sphere of law, because the legal notion of a person rests upon an abstraction and does not embrace the whole being of man. There must, therefore, occur much modification and subtraction before we reach the special relations which alone are involved in the idea of a law. Thus, suppose a man has arisen from a protracted illness, and in order to pay the bill of his physician, to provide for the urgent wants of his family, due to his recent incapacity, and to procure the means of beginning business again, he goes to a well-disposed neighbor, whom he has helped in former times, and obtains a loan at the usual rate. How much of all this must we not leave out in order to ascertain the purely jural relations between the parties! Compare with this the case of the rich man who borrows capital merely to add to his possession by a new speculation, and consider the effort of abstraction which is required in order to assimilate the resulting legal relations. And yet the *legal* relations in these two cases are identical."

To the Anglo-Norman lawyer, accustomed to do homage to strict legal principle as in and for itself the "summum bonum" of law, and to regard legal justice as manifesting itself only in a system of unbending rules, this quotation will indicate better than anything else the great gulf that is fixed between his own system and that which was indigenous to China. By making generalizations into hard-and-fast rules, by strictly eliminating in individual cases a variety of important moral considerations, the Anglo-Normans have succeeded in creating a special type of justice. This tendency of theirs is so strong that English Equity, the one great effort to counteract it, has become in the end identical in these respects with the whole system.

Yet there are peoples to whom this type of justice is utterly alien. The "struggle for rights", which the great German jurist, von Ihering, inculcated as the basis of civic law and order, is alien to Chinese thought. An unyielding insistence upon principle, and a rigid demand for one's due, are almost as reprehensible, as a vulgar physical struggle. Moral force, and the "rule of reason", should control, rather than strict technical rights. Compromise is the highest virtue; intolerance and obstinacy, a mark of defective character. Nothing is so important that it cannot be compromised for human welfare or comfort or dignity. Hence the significance (so misunderstood by the Occidental) of "saving the face", i. e. of obtaining a respectable compromise in a dispute. Hence, also, the universal resort to mediation or arbitration, precedent to going to law, and usually removing that necessity.

NOTE

The brief items in this chapter illustrate at least five systems for the settlement of controversy: (1) the lawyer dominated system (USA); (2) the judge directed system (England); (3) the professionalized system

(France); (4) the avowedly political system (USSR); (5) the conciliatory system, "peace without victory," or better still, "peace without defeat," (Ancient China). In this country, too, there are illustrations of the last four systems: (2) a trial in a federal court before a firm judge; (3) the work of many administrative commissions; (4) the interpretation of our Constitution—however much the political ideals in the USA may differ from those in the USSR: (5) the adjustment of labor-management controversy which to be lasting must be face-saving? Are there other areas in which, to borrow Justice Jackson's phrase, our legal institutions could be "most constructive" through thoughtful consideration and adaptations of other methods?

Part Two

THE LAWYER AT WORK

Chapter V

THE LAWYER IN HIS OFFICE

Introduction. This chapter begins a more detailed treatment of the roles of American lawyers outlined in Chapter I, Section 2. Although these roles are many the lawyer's principal function today as a private practitioner is that of office counselor and adviser. A Daniel Webster at the bar or his television counterpart may be lay images of the lawyer and the case method of instruction, with its heavy emphasis on litigation and on law review concepts of law, undoubtedly contributes to this illusion even among law students. The out-of-court work of attorneys, however, in counseling and planning future courses of conduct and in avoiding litigation by compromise occupies the major portion of the time of most practitioners. Law schools fail to project an accurate picture of this important facet of the lawyer's life.

The lawyer in his office may be one who never sees the inside of a courtroom, never appears before an administrative body, and yet has great influence in ordering the affairs of his fellow men. His may be the task of shaping the form of a great corporation or planning a small business venture. He is frequently the most trusted adviser in his client's personal affairs, the purchase of his home, the settlement of his marital conflicts, the disposition of his estate.

In the pages that follow the lawyer's image as a Counselor-at-Law in a variety of settings will be projected. His advice is sought by government, by business, by labor, and in the solution of every-day family problems, to mention but a few types of legal counseling. The fact that a lawyer must counsel with and advise men and organizations in an almost limitless spectrum of activities requires that he become a semi-expert in as many areas as his clients have problems. This suggests that much of what the lawyer does in his office encompasses human problems and relations beyond the strictly legal. This chapter will explore the lawyer's part in dealing with the clients' problems as a whole and at the same time will point to the necessity of cooperation with others who can assist.

Related and contrasting views of other thoughtful observers of the American legal scene will also be included in these materials dealing with the office lawyer. He is described as a "legislator" who designs and drafts "the framework of collaborative effort." His function as an administrator of the law and as a maker of policy at various levels will be referred to. In each of these roles the creative nature of a lawyer's work becomes evident.

After reading these materials ask yourself whether the multifaceted nature of the lawyer's work has implications for pre-legal education, for law school curricula, and also for continuing legal education following admission to the bar. Are you as a student in a position to suggest at this stage of your training whether you have been poorly advised with reference to your education to date? Thoughtful lawyers, judges and legal educators are doing much soul searching with reference to such questions.

SECTION 1. THE NATURE OF HIS WORK

COUNSELOR-AT-LAW

REPORT OF THE JOINT CONFERENCE ON PROFESSIONAL RESPONSIBILITY

1958 A.A.L.S. Pro. 187, 192; 44 A.B.A.J. 1159, 1161 (1958).

The Lawyer's Role as Counselor.

Vital as is the lawyer's role in adjudication, it should not be thought that it is only as an advocate pleading in open court that he contributes to the administration of the law. The most effective realization of the law's aims often takes place in the attorney's office, where litigation is forestalled by anticipating its outcome, where the lawyer's quiet counsel takes the place of public force. Contrary to popular belief, the compliance with the law thus brought about is not generally lipserving and narrow, for by reminding him of its long-run costs the lawyer often deters his client from a course of conduct technically permissible under existing law, though inconsistent with its underlying spirit and purpose.

Although the lawyer serves the administration of justice indispensably both as advocate and as office counselor, the demands imposed on him by these two roles must be sharply distinguished. The man who has been called into court to answer for his own actions is entitled to a fair hearing. Partisan advocacy plays its essential part in such a hearing, and the lawyer pleading his client's case may properly present it in the most favorable light. A similar resolution of doubts in one direction becomes inappropriate when the lawyer acts as counselor. The reasons that justify and even require partisan advocacy in the trial of a cause do not grant any license to the lawyer to participate as legal adviser in a line of conduct that is immoral, unfair, or of doubtful legality. In saving himself from this unworthy involvement, the lawyer cannot be guided solely by an unreflective inner sense of good faith; he must be at pains to preserve a sufficient detachment from his client's interests so that he remains capable of a sound and objective appraisal of the propriety of what his client proposes to do.

HARROP A. FREEMAN, LEGAL INTERVIEWING AND COUNSELING *

Page 1 (1964).

We Are "Counsellors at Law"

Perhaps the distinction is not so pointed in America where we do not separate lawyers into Solicitors and Barristers. Yet we lawyers need only to look at our Certificates of Admission to the Bar to be reminded that we hold ourselves out as Attorneys *and* Counsellors at Law. Counseling is increasingly becoming recognized as a separate discipline and profession—witness the licensing of psychological and marital counselors in many states. The general image of the "Country Lawyer" has always been that of the wise counselor, knowing the backgrounds of the community people and helping them through the problems that threaten normal living. It is sometimes assumed that as people have become mobile, business has become big and metropolitan law offices have become factories, that the counseling function has departed from the law. Quite on the contrary. While it may be that the production men in large offices grind out S.E.C. statements and corporate reorganizations, the senior partners increasingly perform the function of counselors or policy formers. I recently heard the senior partner of perhaps New York City's largest law firm opine that 90% of his work was counseling in not strictly legal matters.

NOTES

(1) In the Preface to Professor Freeman's book, Erwin N. Griswold makes the following observation:

". . . Thus, the ordinary use of the case system leaves the student largely unaware of the fact that much of the law practiced in law offices is not wholly systematic and never gets into the appellate courts. It gives the student little or no insight into the problems of dealing with people, to the techniques for finding the facts from people, for advising them effectively, and for aiding them effectively in resolving their own problems and in adjusting their relations with other people.

. . .

---

* During 1962–63 the author, under a grant from the Walter E. Meyer Research Institute of Law, conducted a study of counseling by lawyers, doctors and clergymen. He surveyed most professional schools, contacted approximately 10,000 practitioners in the three professions by interview or questionnaire, studied almost 8,000 clients, and analyzed all books and articles in the field of counseling. This book is the result of that study. Copyright 1964 by West Publishing Co. Reprinted by permission.

". . . (A)ppellate court decisions represent, for the most part, the failures in our law. Where there is effective counselling and negotiation, there are no court decisions, and especially no appellate court decisions. Whole areas of the law never get into court. An example may be found in the problems of legal ethics which are considered frequently in every busy law office, but which are resolved by the partners without any court decision. And much business advice consists of caution and forewarning, designed, and usually effectively, to keep the business out of court.

. . .

"Now Professor Freeman has done something about it, and has shown that it is possible to do so. The present book contains no appellate court decisions. Yet it is based, from beginning to end, on cases, on actual cases involving real people, which were handled by real lawyers, and by members of other professions, each of whom was playing his appropriate and useful professional role. These are cases on counselling and negotiation. . . .

". . . In a very real sense, this is almost as much a pioneering book as was Dean Langdell's Cases on Contracts. Just as the concept of that book flowered in the work of others who built upon it, we may hope that the approach taken here may likewise be fruitful, and that this may be the first of a long line of Case-books based on non-appellate-court materials. . . ."

(2) Dr. Andrew S. Watson has described perceptively the emotional barriers implicit in the lawyer's counseling role, *The Lawyer as Counselor,* 5 Jour.Fam.Law 7 (1965). He concludes, page 17: "There are a multitude of ways in which skill in the counseling process may be developed. Most of you have no doubt utilized the tried and true process of experience to promote this capacity. At the same time, experience may have locked you into various attitudes and procedures which ultimately defeat efficiency in the counseling process. While it is true that experience is the best teacher, it is only if the pupil has the capacity to perceive the questions and answers which the teacher puts forth. It is just at this point that personal blindspots such as those mentioned above, get in the way of the learning process.

"The best way to gain skill in counseling, is through the help of a skilled counselor in going over one's own experience in counseling. As you may know, this is routine practice in the field of psychiatry, clinical psychology and social work, and there is no reason why it could not be utilized by lawyers as well. It should be possible for lawyers to seek assistance from skilled counselors who could help them with specific situations from their legal counseling practice, by going over the case material and helping them to see the emotional issues which are present. I have on many occasions, helped lawyers analyze such material and it has usually been possible for them to see parameters of emotional activity and involvement of which they were not previously aware. Merely pointing them out helped clarify the nature of these interactive processes and permitted them to return to their client and explore the problems more fully and productively." See also Watson, *Professionalizing the Lawyer's Role as Counselor: Risk-Taking for Rewards,* 1 Law and the Social Order 17 (1969).

(3) See Mayer, The Lawyers pp. 306–07: (1966)

[T]he highly paid "lawyer is paid for his judgment. He contributes not only that feeling for relevance which is the essence of his profession, but a sense of priorities, which is the next step up from relevance. He knows the applicable law . . . but in addition he knows the problems in public policy which the law raises. And he can make a shrewd judgment of the capacity (i. e., the combination of ability and energy) of his client and of the others in the situation. . . . This does not mean that the advice will always be accepted (or even that it will always be correct . . .) but that he will be able to see in many situations implications that have escaped other people."

(4) It has been suggested that the classroom atmosphere in today's law schools with its case method of instruction teaches contention and argumentation and turns out graduates ill-equipped to listen without interruption or counsel sympathetically. Is this a fair criticism?

(5) In any consideration of the lawyer's counseling role there is the recurring question as to whether the attorney should "make the decision" for the client or whether he should merely outline the advantages and disadvantages of various courses of action. The answer will no doubt depend on the particular relationship involved although the client will often hope for an attorney less timid than the one who merely outlines. The story is told of the frustrated client who claimed to be looking for a one-armed attorney—one who couldn't say: "On the one hand . . . but on the other hand . . .." What is your conception of the proper lengths to which a Counselor-at-Law should go in making the decision for the client? Keep this question in mind in reading the following pages dealing with specific counseling roles. See Code of Professional Responsibility, EC 7–7, EC 7–8, EC 7–9

ROME G. BROWN, SOME APPLICATIONS OF THE RULES OF LEGAL ETHICS

6 Minn.L.Rev. 427, 434–437 (1922).

It is not only the right and privilege, but it is the professional and personal duty of the lawyer, to be judicial in the formulation of his conclusions with reference to his client's business and, above all, to use his utmost endeavor, even to the extent of shrinking or even losing his standing with his client, to keep his client from doing injustice.

The lawyer's function is in the nature of that of a fiduciary or trustee, and he is answerable as such, not only to the particular person standing in direct relation to him of client, but answerable also to all those, whether it be the public or individuals, to whom the client himself owes an accounting. This is particularly true in instances where the client himself occupies a representative position, as when he is the officer or manager for the interests of another or of several others through appointment,—for example, when he is a corporation officer or an executor of an estate or a trustee of property or moneys for either present or prospective beneficiaries. In such cases the lawyer and his conscience, as guardians of a trust, are answerable not merely to the client in person but to the client *as trustee*. The fiduciary capacity of the lawyer, with all its accompanying duties and responsibilities, runs side by side with that of his trustee-client and through and unto the end of every transaction which affects the interests of the ultimate beneficiaries. Much more is this the case when the lawyer in question has been the attorney for the maker of the will or other writing creating the trust and has drawn such writing with the full knowledge of the real intent and purpose of their maker.

Because of these fiduciary capacities and duties, the lawyer must insist, and sometimes even dictate, that the client shall perform fully and honorably all his obligations. His duty persists beyond the point of spirited controversies or even of irreconcilable differences with his client. He must not at the first instance of divergence hold up his hands in despair or sever his professsional relations in defiance. Sometimes a client, ordinarily fair, becomes subject to a selfish or other ulterior motive or influence or even to an honest obsession of error which may prevert his mental processes and seem to stultify his conscience. Then is just the time when the lawyer should stick, and with a persistence, too, that may involve temporarily some sacrifice of his personal or professional pride. But he should persist in his efforts to accomplish in the end his greater duty and responsibility of bringing his client to a right state of mind and to a right view of the facts and of the conclusions upon the points in conflict. The issue may be one involving the jeopardy of large financial interests of the client or it may be one only incidentally and in small degree affecting the client's finances, but at the same time involving the question of great prejudice or injustice to a beneficiary of a trust or other third party. It is the lawyer's duty to keep the client from putting a black mark on his business record and never to yield, nor to permit his client to yield, to the purpose or intent of following a course of persecution or oppression or of any form of fraud or of injustice. In such instances a lawyer should treat his client as a doctor would treat a patient stricken temporarily with bodily or mental weakness. He must not yield his judgment or conscience to the control or dictation of error. Neither must he, by withdrawing, try to avoid responsibility by leaving the client free to injure himself or others. He must never falter in the full performance of his duty as fiduciary or trustee. He should be patient and tactful, but he should never surrender on a square issue of good faith, even though the favor of his client be forever jeopardized.

These phases of applied legal ethics could never be solved by reference to reported cases. They arise from the confidential conflicts between the lawyer and his client. In private practice they are a part only of the esoteric experience of the profession.

NOTE

One of your clients, obviously distraught, comes to your office and asks that a codicil to his will be prepared immediately so as to disinherit a daughter who has just married a man of a different faith. What should you do?

THE CLIENT'S PROBLEM AS A WHOLE

JAMES A. PIKE, BEYOND THE LAW *

Pages 56–59 (1963).

A wise physician said some years ago to a joint conference on medical and theological students, "If I as a whole person am not treating a patient as a whole person, I might as well be practicing veterinary medicine." This applies to the lawyer's profession, too. Referring first to the subject of the physician's sentence, you should not separate yourself as a lawyer from what you are as you. You should not seek to bifurcate your life into the eight-plus hours a day engaged in legal practice and what you are as a person the rest of the time. And to turn to the object of the physician's sentence, when a client comes in as a prospective plaintiff or defendant in litigation, or comes seeking to organize a scheme or to write a will, what has come in is not just a legal problem but a person with a legal problem, or a person who thinks he has a legal problem, or a person who is verbalizing in terms of a legal problem but may be in deeper need. . . .

Legal counseling is simply a form of human interrelationship. In such, communication is never at its best when it is station-to-station. It is better person-to-person. Hence, simply because he is called to be a whole person, every lawyer is called to be a pastor. He is called upon to listen; he is called upon to help clients see the truth, to raise the right question in connection with the whole view of the matter involved.

But this is not a calling to run other people's lives. There is one thing that bothers lawyers when this pastoral claim is laid upon them. They will say in effect, "Who am I to play God for the client?" The answer is, "You certainly should not—nor should any priest, minister or rabbi, for that matter." A good pastor (in the narrower sense of the word) does not tell his counselee what to do; he tries from his overall perspective, and his knowledge of the person, and his grasp of the situation to see what the fundamental nature of his professed problem is, to help the counselee take all factors into account and evaluate them soundly. On the one hand, he seeks to lift burdens that the person may have unnecessarily imposed upon himself, and, on the other, to stimulate the person to a recognition of real obligation. He

---

* These excerpts are taken from the Rosenthal Lectures of Northwestern University Law School. Bishop Pike was a lawyer, author, and clergyman.

seeks to help the person see through his own rationalizations, defense mechanisms, etc. He may suggest possible harm to the counselee or others from a proposed course of action or from a deflection from a course of action. If such a legal counselor senses needs beyond his own depth he will seek to make sound referrals, carrying through, where it is appropriate, as a helpful collaborator with that other professional.

Quite analogous is the role of the lawyer as pastor. He certainly is not expected to tell the client what to do, but he is morally bound to give the best of himself to the client as a person, not simply as the carrier of some legal business.

NOTES

(1) See Cheatham, *Specialized Legal Services,* 16 Vand.L.R. 497, 499–500 (1963):

"The second conclusion is that there is need for something more than a man who knows more and more about less and less of the law. The client is not merely a point or problem of law. He is a human being who seeks advice and help in meeting a problem with personal as well as legal aspects. His problem, even if looked at as an impersonal case at law, often cuts across several fields of law, and its parts are not fragments isolated from one another. So there is need for a lawyer who has the judgment and wisdom to see and to deal with the client's problem and its various specialized elements as an integrated whole."

(2) An increasing number of other professionals have appeared on the American scene in recent years. An important task of the lawyer is that of determining when the clients' best interests can be served by calling upon such persons for assistance. See Chapter II, Section 7, supra. See also Chapter XII, page 435, infra, dealing with the legal specialist.

THE BUSINESS COUNSELOR

The work of the lawyer for large interests, especially for large financial interests, differs from the work of the ordinary lawyer in at least three respects.

The first is that the client's activities are of far greater concern to the community than those of the ordinary small client. It may be thought there is a correspondingly clearer, though not greater, duty on the lawyer to make his client weigh the effect of his actions on others. "Clearer, though not greater, duty",—it was said. The lawyer in ordinary affairs cannot think that their smallness gives a license to help do injustice at retail which would be denied to his more affluent brother at wholesale.

The second is that the client's relations are often with others, —perhaps purchasers of stock or stockholders—who rely on the fairness of the client's statement which the lawyer helps to formulate. Speaking shortly after the hectic 1920's Calvert Magruder said:

> "In a situation of this sort [investment trusts with securities to sell] the lawyer ought to realize that it is not a case of assisting a client to drive a hard bargain with an adverse party dealing at arm's length; rather it is a case of assisting the investment banker to take advantage of the confidence of his clients, from whom the real situation is often concealed by a disingenuous prospectus." *

The third difference is that it is often difficult to know who is the real client to whom loyalty is owed. If the president of a large corporation employs a lawyer for the corporation, to whom is loyalty owed when conflicts of interest threaten—the president and other members of the management group; the stockholders, whether majority or minority; "the corporation", whether parent or subsidiary?

What do the standards of professional responsibility call for under these somewhat unusual conditions?

WHITNEY NORTH SEYMOUR, RELIGION AND THE LAW, in MAN AT WORK IN GOD'S WORLD

Pages 152–153 (1963).

. . . As a result of the growth of business and of government regulation, have we become so accustomed to simply telling our clients what the SEC or the antitrust regulations are that we fail to tell them what they ought to do in the light of their moral responsibilities to the community, to their competitors, to their employees, and to themselves? Whatever may have been the case at the peak of the industrial revolution, I am inclined to think that lawyers have begun to swing in the direction of taking a larger view of their obligation in advice to clients.

I think that the business corporations of this country, perhaps as a result of the series of blows that have been rained upon them in the last twenty-odd years, and the advice of public relations people and the growth of a new generation of executives, have begun to feel themselves that they ought to look at the whole panorama in charting their courses. Many of them recognize a public responsibility going beyond bare legal rights. As a result their lawyers have been encouraged to give a broad kind of advice. That is a good thing. It does seem to me that the city lawyer at his desk, just as a country lawyer, visualizes his client's problem not only as a question of when the Statute of Limitations runs, but, in looking to his community, how

---

* Magruder, *What May Society Expect of Our Profession?* 37 Maryland State Bar Ass'n Transactions 87 (1932).

his moral responsibility will be carried out, and how many nights he is going to spend feeling remorseful if he makes a judgment which is really not fair. . . . We all know that our maximum contribution is made when we can give the broadest kind of advice. That is true of business corporations, but it is more true of individuals.

THE LARGE CITY FIRM

The item appears supra page 59.

HOUSE COUNSEL

The item appears supra page 63.

THE TAX COUNSELOR

NORRIS DARRELL, THE TAX PRACTITIONER'S DUTY TO HIS CLIENT AND HIS GOVERNMENT *

7 The Practical Lawyer 23 (March 1961).

. . .

My subject today encompasses matters of conscience and propriety in relation to the professional tax practitioner's multiple responsibilities—his duty to his client, his duty to his conscience, and his duty to society, including his Government.

. . .

General Advisory Problems

Perhaps the most important everyday ethical problems of the lawyer in tax practice, long antedating the tax return, have to do with general advisory matters. In principle we surely all agree on this: the lawyer's responsibilities include the obligation to make every reasonable effort to equip himself to advise and represent clients wisely, and he must have the stamina and sufficient detachment to tell them the truth.

. . .

You are consulted about a proposed family partnership between husband and wife, valid in form under the laws of the State, but to be operated on the unwritten understanding, which may never be discovered, that the husband will continue to control the property and manage the partnership, that the wife will pay family bills out of her share of the profits, and that the wife will hold her interest subject to his control, even to the point of returning it to him should he need it. What should your attitude be?

---

* Copyright 1961 by the American Law Institute. Reprinted by permission.

Schemes such as this often lead to harsh law and endless litigation, sometimes dragging valid arrangements into the mess. A question of ethics is clearly involved in furthering arrangements which, though superficially appearing to be valid, are factually colorable and artificial. Can we not go further and say that, apart from whether such a scheme would be legally or practically effective, there is an affirmative professional responsibility to discourage abortive tax plans of this sort in the interest of making the tax system work and of relieving the administration and the judiciary of undue burdens?

You are consulted about a corporate reorganization or readjustment, the tax consequences of which may depend upon the existence of a good business purpose, or at least upon the existence of a purpose other than saving taxes. You know that the client is tax conscious and that a tax advantage is an important consideration. Is there any moral objection to your canvassing and seeking to develop with the client all possible nontax reasons that could fairly be given in support of the transaction? And can you properly suggest modifications of the plan to strengthen it from this standpoint?

The same sort of problem arises when clients are concerned over and seek aid in building up a current record that will enable them to put their best tax foot forward with respect to potential liability for accumulated earnings tax, or potential contemplation of death treatment of a gift, or the possible application of section 269 or, indeed, any situation where tax liability may depend upon motive or intent or upon existence of a business as distinct from a personal or purely tax purpose.

Obviously, it is improper to build a house of cards, to manufacture evidence; reasons given must be genuine, and the lawyer must search his conscience and be extremely careful to avoid misleading camouflage. But you would feel free, would you not, to advise on the law, the factual record, and possible amendments to the plan that would strengthen the tax position?

Purposes and motives are often by their nature elusive, and experience shows that clients often need help in thinking out and articulating their own real objectives. But, do you not agree that one must be very careful to avoid feeding motives into a tax-conscious client's mind? In the zeal of the undertaking, it is very easy to cross the dividing line without recognizing it, and we tax practitioners may not always tread carefully enough in these matters.

Tax Return Problems

Lawyers engaged in tax practice are often confronted with problems of another type—problems relating to tax returns. These may arise in a variety of situations, as illustrated by the following.

A client confidentially asks you for legal advice concerning a clearly taxable income item that he inadvertently omitted from his income tax return, filed six months previously, with the preparation and filing of which you had nothing to do.

Should not your advice be to file an amended return, or, if the client were a corporation or other taxpayer subject to annual audit and were not concerned over the running of interest, to put a note in the file to be submitted to the examining agent when he comes in to audit. If the client refuses to heed his advice, does not your responsibility cease?

The attorney-client relationship would appear to prevent you from turning informer, and Treasury Circular No. 230 does not require you to become one. Indeed, this would be true even if the omission had been deliberate and fraudulent, if it be concluded that at the time of the disclosure the fraud was a past and not a prospective or continuing one, disclosed to you in confidence.

. . .

A client engaged in the manufacturing business submits to you for review and approval a federal income tax return reflecting the taxable income of the business, together with a letter from the client's regular auditors stating that in their opinion the return properly reflects taxable income, except that certain expenditures have been taken as current expense deductions which they consider should have been capitalized.

The client concedes that these items are clearly capital in nature but desires to claim them as expense deductions in the hope that, buried in a long list of items, they will not be discovered on audit, or if discovered, will be available to concede in order that the field agent might find an additional tax, which the client believes he would consider a mark to his credit and thereby reduce the likelihood of other unfavorable adjustments. What should you advise?

Is it not clear, there being no doubt as to the law, that you should not advise or encourage action on the basis of what the client may get away with—on the basis of what may slip by on audit, or be available at that time to concede? Indeed, should you not try to discourage the client from reporting on that basis? The practice of deducting items known to be non-deductible is one that I consider quite questionable and that, I regret to say, would be less appealing if the Service through its field agents could convince taxpayers that it does not pay.

. . .

Post Audit Problems

The most common contact lawyers in tax practice have with government officials is in connection with post audit problems, tax settlement negotiations, and litigation. In seeking the most favorable interpretation of the facts and the law applicable to his case, the lawyer can deliberately present the facts and legal precedents in the way calculated to appear most favorable to his client's position, but he must avoid trickery, misrepresentation of fact or law, and concealment of material matters relating to any issue under consideration. Sedulous though he must be in these latter respects, he need not lean over backward to help the Government's case.

. . .

The executors of an estate of a relatively youthful but wealthy former client retain you to defend against an asserted additional estate tax liability based on a claim that certain inter vivos gifts to the decedent's daughter, slightly less than three years before his accidental death, were made in contemplation of death. You had advised the decedent in connection with the gift, and had explained to him the potential income and estate tax savings from the gift. The decedent then had told you privately and confidentially that, while he wanted to save income taxes and provide some income for his daughter, he did not expect to live very long in view of his family history and that he was primarily interested in the potential saving in estate taxes on his estate. The decedent had not discussed with you what you might say should a question later arise. What should you do?

Is it not clear that you cannot tell the whole story because you cannot disclose what you learned from the confidential communication with your deceased client? This being so, would it not be improper to present arguments in support of the nontestamentary motives while remaining silent as to the testamentary motives?

In these circumstances, since you cannot properly make full disclosure of pertinent facts within your knowledge, should you advise the executors to consult other counsel or should you advise them to concede liability? May you not properly explain the situation to the executors and, if in your opinion the gift was in fact clearly made in contemplation of death, recommend that liability be conceded, otherwise that other counsel be consulted?

. . .

Fee Problems

During the year you rendered legal services to an individual client the fees for which will be partly deductible by him (because they pertain to his investment or business affairs or tax advice) and partly not deductible (because they relate to the execution of a will or some other personal matter). How far can you go in loading the fee for the deductible items and lightening the fee for the others?

A lawyer does not work by the clock, and his fees are dependent on many factors, including the time spent, results accomplished, the importance, novelty and difficulty of the matter, custom, and the client's views. He may at times even work without fee. It seems clear that he need not automatically apportion his total charge according to the relative hours spent on all these matters and that he is fully entitled to differentiate on the basis of the above factors, including the factor of tax deductibility.

But, would you not say that, whatever you may charge in respect of the nondeductible items, you should not be influenced by the tax consideration to the extent of charging more for services in respect of the deductible items than can fairly be justified therefor? The Government thus far usually accepts the lawyers' word as to the allocation of his fees; it would be most unfortunate if the time should ever come when his word will not be acceptable.

Your client, suspecting that he might dislike any allocation you might make, requests that you simply bill him for services rendered, without description or itemization of any kind, thinking that this might serve him better. Would you see any objection to your doing this?

Your answer may be influenced by whether this would be a departure from your general custom or your prior custom with the client, or by whether you knew or suspected what he had in mind. But, generally speaking, is not the ethical problem here simply one of avoiding any statement that would mislead the ordinary examining agent and deter him from inquiring into the facts? Or, have you an affirmative duty beyond that? This type of problem may be more acute where a large part of the services was rendered to a controlling corporate stockholder who desires the corporation to be billed.

Problems of Public Responsibility

. . .

A body of public spirited citizens asks you to join with them in signing a petition urging upon Congress a reform in the tax law that you believe to be much needed but that, if adopted, might seriously adversely affect some of your clients. What should you do?

Would you not consider yourself free to join in urging the reform, if you believe in it and it would not conflict with your duty to any client in any matter in which you have been retained? On the other hand, even though there were no such conflict, might you not properly conclude that you would be fully justified in remaining silent, if you believe you would get into difficulties with one or more clients by joining in the appeal; the importance of lending your name to the appeal might not outweigh the damage to your client relationships. I feel sure you will agree, however, that, generally speaking, a lawyer ought to try to participate in those things that he thinks are useful in the public interest; and ordinarily clients do not take offense at this.

Closing Observations

May I conclude with a few general observations. I question the notion that, where his adversary is the Treasury, the lawyer need give less than full devotion to his duty to his client because of a larger duty he owes to the Governor or his fellow citizens. I believe the lawyer surely owes no less devotion to his duty to a taxpayer, who is his client, than he owes to a criminal whom he undertakes to defend. Both are entitled to full legal representation.

Yet, with respect to ordinary, everyday, administrative tax practice, especially where a crystallized controversy headed for the courts is not involved, there may be differences in shading or degree. The questions here are perplexing, and the area is one especially in need of further study and clarification.

It may be suggested, on the one hand, that the obligation of candor and fairness, involving the disclosure of distressing things, should be more strict and rigid when it runs to a court—a judicial umpire whom not even silence should be permitted to mislead—than when it runs to the Treasury which through its representatives of varying attitudes and qualifications is in the equivocal position of investigator, claimant, and administrative judge. On the other hand, it may be thought that this obligation of the lawyer should be at least as, if not more, strict and rigid when he is facing the Treasury, the thought here being that a tax matter is not simply a matter between taxpayer and Treasury but between taxpayer and the Treasury and other taxpayers.

. . .

In most taxpayers, ourselves included, there is a tendency toward a little larceny when it comes to taxation, though none of us would think of stealing a cent from or deliberately hurting our friends. This natural tendency is nurtured whenever tax officials, also human, seem to act in an overzealous and partisan fashion, and it thrives in an atmosphere of distrust of the fairness of the tax law. For these if for no other reasons, may not the tax practitioner be charged with the further duty I mentioned at the outset, namely, a duty to do what he can to help make the tax law more fair, practical, and equitable, and to improve its administration?

. . .

NOTE

Some of the professional responsibilities of lawyers in business and taxation were discussed in a seminar at the 84th Annual Meeting of the American Bar Association at St. Louis, Missouri, August 6, 1961, by Robert Braucher, Norris Darrell, David R. Herwitz and Ross L. Malone. See *Business Planning and Professional Responsibility*, 8 The Practical Lawyer 17 (January 1962) and 39 (February 1962). See also Paul, *The Lawyer as a Tax Adviser*, 25 Rocky Mountain L.Rev. 412 (1953).

THE LABOR UNION COUNSELOR

ROBERT M. SEGAL, LABOR LAW: THE CASE FOR THE UNION LAWYER *

44 A.B.A.J. 1056, 1057 (1958).

. . .

Whereas prior to 1932 the labor lawyer was primarily concerned with injunctions, antitrust and criminal cases, today he performs many valuable new services. Appearances before administrative agencies constitute a substantial part of his practice. He also handles court litigation for unions, arbitration cases, negotiations, approval and administration of collective bargaining agreements, interpretations of union constitutions, and advice to the unions relative to strategy, rights and obligations. He also drafts legislation and interprets the many new labor laws for the unions. He must be familiar with a great mass of specialized background material in the labor relations field.

In addition he does considerable "non-legal" work such as preparing economic and statistical data, drafting speeches for union officials, speaking before labor and other groups, writing articles and other public relations work. To the general public, the labor lawyer is often the public representative of the union, for he appears at lectures, debates, forums, and before legislative and administrative committees. Labor lawyers now have become a vital part of the functioning of labor unions.

With approximately 125,000 collective bargaining agreements in force today setting the "private law of the plant", problems occur frequently involving the interpretation of the terms of the agreement by arbitration. Approximately 30 percent of all labor lawyers regularly do arbitration work and another 40 percent infrequently do such work. At the same time grievance work prior to arbitration is seldom done by attorneys.

The most important work in the labor lawyer's field, collective bargaining, is the "preventive phase" of labor law, designed to stabilize the employment relationship without resort to economic force. It involves the relation of groups of people, both between the group and outsiders and between the group and the individual members of which it is composed. Unlike the problems involved in aggregations of property, this highly personalized field requires a different approach. Although the labor lawyer and the union must know the federal and state law relative to strikes and picketing, as well as the rights and duties of the parties under the labor relations laws, ordinary legal

---

* Copyright 1958 by the American Bar Association. Reprinted by permission.

sanctions are often unavailable, for the highly competitive interests between employers and employees and between groups of employees are scarcely amenable to the ordinary process of adjudication. The labor lawyer must understand the practical problems, relative to seniority, job security, pensions, discharges, wage structures and piece rates, management prerogatives, insurance, grievance and similar clauses, for voluntary adjustments and negotiations are more important than litigation in the emotional and dynamic field of labor relations.

NOTE

See Kennedy, *Union Racketeering: The Responsibility of the Bar,* 44 A.B.A.J. 437 (1958). Mr. Segal's article is written in response to this article by the then Senator from Massachusetts, John F. Kennedy.

THE FAMILY COUNSELOR

FOWLER AND MIRIAM HARPER, LAWYERS AND MARRIAGE COUNSELING

1 Journal of Family Law 73, 79–81 (1961).

. . .

Aside from the professional marriage counsellor, individual marriage counselling is sometimes undertaken by the lawyer and the clergyman. Some of them have had training and have acquired specific skills. Those who have not should be cautious of attempting therapy. The safest course would appear to be to probe into the family difficulties far enough to determine whether the case is hopeless, whether reference to a clinic or a private counsellor is indicated, or whether the situation is so trivial that sympathy and common sense may be sufficient to deal with the difficulty.

So far as the lawyer is concerned, there are some special problems peculiar to his profession. As indicated earlier, frequently the most effective counselling is done when the counsellor sees both parties, sometimes together. As every lawyer knows there is always another side to every case. In a recent field study conducted by a Yale Law School student, attorneys were asked whether, if they accepted as a client a person who wanted a divorce, they would wish to talk to the other spouse. Of 259 responses, 116 said that they would. Indeed a few (9) said they would not take the case unless they could talk to the other spouse.

For a half century the Canon of Ethics of the American Bar Association has referred to the "obligation . . . not to divulge his [client's] secrets or confidences." The question is raised as to how far an attorney can interview his client's spouse about their marital affairs without divulging confidence. Where the client knows, understands, and gives his consent to this procedure, however, and the other spouse understands the capacity in which the attorney conducts the interview and realizes its purpose, there would appear to be no objection.

Again there is the Canon which prohibits a lawyer from representing both parties to a controversy. Indeed, the American Bar Association, the Michigan Committee, and two New York committees have held that a lawyer for one spouse should not even recommend a lawyer for the other.

This is simply recognition of the implications of the adversary system under which lawyers live and have their being. The principle that a lawyer cannot serve two masters is, as a general proposition, accepted by the profession. However, it should be pointed out that this is sometimes a figure of speech. Perhaps he can serve two masters if their interests are not antagonistic. In family difficulties the interests of the parties are frequently antagonistic, but not always so. If a lawyer can avoid an adversary situation, he may be able to serve the interests of both parties. The Canon of Ethics also provides that "whenever the controversy will admit of fair judgment, the client should be advised to avoid or end litigation." If a meeting with the other spouse or with both together would facilitate "fair judgment" or promote reconciliation, it would appear not only permissible but altogether proper for the lawyer to do so. Not infrequently the fundamental difficulty rests in the inconsistent expectations of the spouses and a misconception of each other's expectations in one or more aspects of the marriage relations. By ascertaining these conflicting expectations and misunderstandings through conferences with both parties a lawyer may be able to dissipate much of their hostility and create a favorable atmosphere for reconciliation.

Many lawyers, judges, and social workers regard the adversary procedure, as it is traditionally known in the law, as inappropriate in divorce, custody, and related family matters. It tends to discourage reconciliation and to intensify animosities. To be sure, so long as the usual fault grounds for divorce are retained, it will not be possible to eliminate all adversary situations. However, some of the worst evils are avoided and others mitigated by the philosophy and procedure of the family courts with their staffs of experts. Moreover, the development in recent years of non-fault grounds for divorce, such as the "living apart" statutes, affords some escape from the worst aspects of the adversary system. In any event, if the lawyer can establish a reasonable line between his functions as counsellor and as lawyer, he may be able to perform in both capacities and even if the situation becomes adversary in character, he may serve as both counsellor and attorney for his client, and make the ordeal less unpleasant than it otherwise might become.

NOTES

(1) See Bradway, *A Suggestion: The Family Lawyer*, 45 A.B.A.J. 831 (1959).

(2) If an attorney is consulted by both spouses in an effort to effect a reconciliation but the efforts are fruitless and one party thereafter decides to file an action for divorce, what is the responsibility of the attorney? Can he properly represent either party? See In the Matter of Julius Braun, an Attorney at Law, 49 N.J. 16 (1967).

(3) The importance of well-drafted agreements between separated spouses who frequently look upon the agreement as "some kind of Bible," is emphasized and illustrated in Fisher, *Toward Better Separation Agreements*, 4 Jour.Fam.Law 63 (1964).

THE OFFICE LAWYER AS LEGISLATOR

REPORT OF THE JOINT CONFERENCE ON PROFESSIONAL RESPONSIBILITY

1958 AALS Pro. 187, 192 (1958); 44 A.B.A.J. 1159, 1161 (1958).

The Lawyer as One Who Designs the Framework of Collaborative Effort

In our society the great bulk of human relations are set, not by governmental decree, but by the voluntary action of the affected parties. Men come together to collaborate and to arrange their relations in many ways: by forming corporations, partnerships, labor unions, clubs and churches; by concluding contracts and leases; by entering a hundred other large and small transactions by which their rights and duties toward one another are defined.

Successful voluntary collaboration usually requires for its guidance something equivalent to a formal charter, defining the terms of the collaboration, anticipating and forfending against possible disputes, and generally providing a framework for the parties' future dealings. In our society the natural architect of this framework is the lawyer.

This is obvious where the transactions or relationship proposed must be fitted into existing law, either to insure legal enforcement or in order not to trespass against legal prohibitions. But the lawyer is also apt to be called upon to draft the by-laws of a social club or the terms of an agreement known to be unenforceable because cancelable by either party at any time. In these cases the lawyer functions, not as an expert in the rules of an existing government, but as one who brings into existence a government for the regulation of the parties' own relations. The skill thus exercised is essentially the same as that involved in drafting constitutions and international treaties. The fruits of this skill enter in large measure into the drafting of ordinary legal documents, though this fact is obscured by the mistaken notion that the lawyer's only concern in such cases is with possible future litigation, it being forgotten that an important part of his task is to design a framework of collaboration that will function in such a way that litigation will not arise.

As the examples just given have suggested, in devising charters of collaborative effort the lawyer often acts where all of the affected parties are present as participants. But the lawyer also performs a similar function in situations where this is not so, as, for example, in planning estates and drafting wills. Here the instrument defining the terms of collaboration may affect persons not present and often not born. Yet here, too, the good lawyer does not serve merely as a legal conduit for his client's desires, but as a wise counselor, experienced in the art of devising arrangements that will put in workable order the entangled affairs and interests of human beings.

LON L. FULLER, WHAT THE LAW SCHOOLS CAN CONTRIBUTE TO THE MAKING OF LAWYERS

1 Jour.Leg.Ed. 189 (1948).

(The article appears page 18 supra.)

NOTES

(1) "In carrying out his work as lawmaker, the lawyer is at once the architect and the builder of human relationships. He draws on his legal learning for knowledge of the legal tools and materials he can use and their capacity to bear loads and withstand stresses. At the same time, he draws on his knowledge of human nature and of business practice to gauge the workability of the arrangements he is considering. In addition, he employs his skill in analyzing problems and in using language effectively to make sure that the documents embodying the arrangements he has designed cover all significant contingencies and, at the same time, do not create other risks by ambiguities of plan or language.

"Books and articles have been and are continuing to be written about the judicial process, the legislative process, the administrative process. But I suspect the first book has yet to be written about the process whereby a couple of lawyers bring two militantly hostile parties together in an office, adjudicate their disputes, draw a decree or statute called a contract to govern their conduct for the next ten years, and thereafter administer the law they have written in a way that will sensibly and faithfully carry out the legislative intent." Cavers, *Legal Education and Lawyer-Made Law*, 54 W.Va.L. Rev. 177, 179–181 (1952).

(2) Consider the analogies of the draftsman of a private bill to grant a corporate charter in an earlier era when that was the method of incorporation, with the work of the corporate lawyer today in drafting papers looking to the formation of a corporation, or drafting the corporate charter, or draft-

ing the corporate by-laws. Is the former process any more legislative drafting than the latter? Compare the work of the European lawyer in planning a cartel structure, under which most matters are kept entirely out of court and controversies are handled through arbitration.

THE LAWYER AS AN ADMINISTRATOR OF THE LAW

JUSTICE JACKSON, concurring, in HICKMAN v. TAYLOR
329 U.S. 495, 514, 67 S.Ct. 385 (1947). . . .

It too often is overlooked that the lawyer and the law office are indispensable parts of our administration of justice. Law-abiding people can go nowhere else to learn the ever-changing and constantly multiplying rules by which they must behave and to obtain redress for their wrongs.

REGINALD HEBER SMITH, INAUGURAL STATEMENT
1 Quarterly Report, Conference on Personal Finance Law, 1, 6 (1946).

Justice in this country is administered 10% by judges in court rooms and 90% by lawyers in law offices. In that process we have learned that many of our severest battles are with our own clients; anger and vengeance have to be extirpated from their minds and emotions, and a sense of justice instilled. We have to teach them the limits of law; that, for example, no statute or code can rekindle the flame of love that has been extinguished between a husband and wife. We learn that all opposing parties are not rogues and liars; that there is much on their side—sometimes too much. We learn that opposing counsel are not only able and alert, but also in most cases, with only tragic exceptions, prove to be honorable gentlemen. We learn that misunderstanding, rather than greed or spite, is at the root of many quarrels.

CHARLES HORSKY, THE WASHINGTON LAWYER *
Pages 122-137 (1952).

It is fair to say that he is an essential participant if the governmental process, as we now know it, is to function effectively.

The effect on government which comes from the work of representing clients is perhaps at the same time most significant and least understood in the area where there is little contact with the government itself. That is the function which the lawyer performs in

---

* With the permission of the publisher, Little, Brown & Co.

simply advising his clients, but in which he is in fact operating as an extension of the government's enforcement machinery. . . .

This work of the Washington lawyer in making the mandates of government meaningful is both a part of the lawyer's professional responsibility and a long step toward enforcement. As a Washington tax lawyer has said, "the Government is entitled to the tax lawyer's help in explaining to taxpayers the necessity and reasonableness of many provisions which taxpayers must inevitably dislike." Without this assistance which the lawyer can give—advice to the client on what the government expects him to do and not to do—the government simply could not operate. . . .

But explanations and interpretations are not the whole of the Washington lawyer's contribution to the enforcement of the law. He is consulted by his clients on a proposed course of action, a proposed contract, a proposed form of advertising, a proposed almost everything. He says no, and the proposal is abandoned or modified. To me that is just as significant as an injunction obtained by the government against the same proposal. For every occasion on which the government itself prevents some unlawful course of dealing, either *in limine*, or after it has begun, there must be dozens which have been prevented by the refusal of a lawyer to approve them. I am convinced that my generalization holds: private lawyers, such as the Washington lawyers who specialize in the antitrust field, do more toward enforcing the antitrust laws than ten times as big a government could ever do.

NOTE

In what sense is the lawyer an administrator of the law? Compare the work of the lawyer in advising on tax liability, and the work of the treasury employee who may advise inquirers as to tax liability and may help them to fill out their income tax forms. How many more official administrators would government need were it not for the lawyer's work as private practitioner?

THE DAY BY DAY JOB

The foregoing material in this chapter may give the erroneous impression that the office work of the lawyer is chiefly devoted to the service of large business interests. The fact is, of course, that most lawyers most of the time represent the middle class of the community. Their work consists in making business transactions run smoothly and cheaply through careful draftsmanship, and through wise counsel within a rather narrow range; in a sympathetic and understanding handling of the problems concerned with the family and with trusts and estates; and in timely, careful, and vigorous handling of the disagreements and contests that do arise. This sort of work has always been done by the lawyer, and is not a creation of modern industrial conditions.

Likewise, the material in the chapter may overemphasize the range of the creative work of the lawyer. The desires and plans of most clients can be well carried out through approved and, perhaps, standardized legal conceptions. It is the primary duty of the office lawyer to effectuate these desires and plans in ways which will not be challenged because of their novelty. After fully acquainting himself with the situation, the draftsman will endeavor to foresee the questions that may arise and will either eliminate the basis of these questions or else give the answers in the document itself. There are few clients with the disposition of Sergeant Maynard, who, it is said, deliberately inserted dubious provisions in his own will so that litigation after his death would settle questions that had troubled him in life.

Competence and thoroughness and a clear head in the job to be done are the essentials most of the time; not scintillating brilliance of imagination in the development of novel theories or ingenious devices.

This day by day job may lack glamour. In the aggregate it has immense usefulness. It has, as well, possibilities for grave injury. In drawing a will, say, the incompetent or careless lawyer can leave so many points uncertain as to incite family controversies and poison family relations for generations.

NOTES

(1) *Preventive Law.* Louis M. Brown has been for many years a leading exponent of counseling as a means of preventing legal controversies from arising. He is the author of numerous excellent and informative articles on the subject of Preventive Law. See Brown, Manual of Preventive Law (1950). For a description of a course offered at the University of Southern California Law School see Brown, *Planning by Lawyers—A Law School Course in Client Counseling,* 15 The Practical Lawyer 70 (March 1969).

(2) *Law Office Management.* Although space limitations in this book make impossible any treatment of the many topics included under this heading, the subject is obviously relevant and important for members of the legal profession. A number of helpful sources for guidance and information in the field are available. The American Bar Association, through its Committee on Economics of Law Practice, publishes The Lawyer's Handbook (1962). The Practical Lawyer is a periodical published eight times each year by the Joint Committee on Continuing Legal Education of the American Law Institute and the American Bar Association. Law Office Economics and Management is a quarterly publication of Callaghan & Co., Illinois. For an excellent study of the management of 100 small law firms (four or fewer partners) see Kline D. Strong, An Analysis of Law Firm Management, (1970).

THE OFFICE LAWYER AND THE ADVOCATE

There are two strongly marked characteristics of the work of the lawyer in his office, which can be pointed up by contrast with the advocate.

The first characteristic concerns the time and type of situation to which the two phases of the lawyer's work are directed. The advocate is dealing typically with a past and completed situation, and it is his task to help in determining who shall have the benefits and the burdens of the past. The lawyer in his office looks characteristically to the future, not to the past, for he is concerned with a situation which is still formative. It is his duty to advise on the legality and wisdom of a plan; to aid in shaping it; and then to embody it in documents which are effective and are clear and comprehensive enough to prevent future misunderstanding and controversy.

The second characteristic involves the presence of other persons as safeguards and restraints. Ordinarily the advocate confronts an opposing advocate in a public hearing, and it is the presupposition of the adversary system that each advocate will stress the matters favorable to his side and will put the opposing side to the test. Then there is the impartial judge who, after both sides have been presented, will determine which side has the right. All of this goes on in a public hearing with the safeguards which publicity affords.

At times in the work of the office lawyer, there is an opposing lawyer, as, in large business negotiations. Ordinarily, it is not so, and the situation in its formative stage is essentially unilateral. The office lawyer is working in the privacy of his office, unchecked by the questions and objections of opposing counsel and unrestrained by immediate publicity. Never is there a judge to whom can be shifted the responsibility for decision. In the work in his office, the lawyer's responsibility may well be at its greatest. It may call for more watchfulness and restraint, for the protection of the client, too, than in the more conspicuous work as advocate. And an obligation, real though indefinite, may be owed to the other and unrepresented person who will be asked to become a party to the document or whose fortunes may be governed by it.

NOTE

See E. Wayne Thode, *The Ethical Standard for the Advocate*, 39 Texas L.Rev. 575 (1961), for an excellent comparison of some of the difficult questions confronting the advocate with those of the counselor. Code of Professional Responsibility, EC 7–3, compares the roles of the advocate and the adviser where the bounds of law are uncertain.

SECTION 2. ADVICE ON THE BORDERLINE— OR BEYOND

ADVICE TO DISOBEY THE LAW

NEW YORK COUNTY OPINION 27 (1913)

Question: Is it proper for a lawyer to advise a client, in reply to a query seeking his advice, that in his opinion it would be better for the client to pay a fine prescribed by a certain penal Statute than to obey its directions?

Answer: In the opinion of the Committee, the question should be answered in the negative.

If a lawyer in this state advises a client to do an act forbidden by law and punishable by fine, it would appear that he becomes a principal in a misdemeanor by virtue of section 2, Penal Law (Consolidated Laws of New York). (Cf. Sec. 27.)

It is the lawyer's duty when asked to advise, to instruct the client as to the measure of the penalty prescribed by the law; but he should stop there. For the lawyer, as an officer of the law, owes a peculiar duty to the State and a duty to the profession. He violates his duty to the State when he deliberately becomes party to a crime; and violates his duty to the profession, because deliberate participation in crime by a lawyer tends to bring both the law and the legal profession into contempt.

We are not considering those cases where there is a bona fide intention to test the validity of a law.

NOTES

(1) An attorney for a trucking company whose trucks operate through several states advises the company not to comply with the maximum weight law of the state of Pennsylvania which law is much more restrictive than that of any other state through which the trucks operate. This advice proves to be sound financially inasmuch as the fines paid for overweight violation are less costly than would be the cost of reducing the weights transported in order to comply with Pennsylvania law. Was the attorney acting properly in giving this advice? Would your answer be different depending upon the policies behind the Pennsylvania law? (In Tank Truck Rental, Inc. v. Commissioner, 356 U.S. 30 (1958), the United States Supreme Court held that the payment of such fines by the trucking company was not deductible as a business expense under the federal income tax. To permit such deduction, the court said, would frustrate state policy. Attorney's fees paid in defending against charges of violating such laws would no doubt be deductible today, whether the company was found guilty or acquitted. Tellier v. Commissioner, 383 U.S. 687 (1966). Would the company also be able to deduct the fees of the lawyer who advised the violation?)

(2) On the liability of a lawyer when he advises his client to disobey a court order, a statute, or an administrative order, see Note, *Liability of the Lawyer for Advising Disobedience*, 39 Col.L.Rev. 433 (1939).

(3) See Code of Professional Responsibility EC 7–5.

ADVICE TO USE A DUMMY TO ESCAPE PERSONAL LIABILITY

NEW YORK COUNTY OPINION 30 (1914)

Question: Is it a breach of professional ethics for a lawyer—who knowingly permits—to allow his client, whom he represents, to act as a "dummy" in a transaction, i. e., the making of a loan on bond and mortgage; in other words, when the application for the loan is made, the property to be mortgaged stands in the name of A & B, and, when the loan is closed, the mortgage is given to C—to whom, in the meantime, the property was transferred—and two days after the recording of the mortgage the property is transferred by C to A & B (the former owners), who thereby escape liability, although the loan was in fact made to A & B, and presumably, C, was financially irresponsible?

Answer: As the question does not import that there is any deception or misrepresentation or any imposition upon any one, or that the contract is in any way unlawful, and parties are at liberty to make lawful contracts upon such terms and with such persons and upon such security as may be agreed, the Committee is of the opinion that the question discloses no breach of any lawyer's duty; the lawyer should, however, explain to his client, "the dummy," the liability which he incurs.

NOTES

(1) If the true nature of this transaction, the fact that C is a financially irresponsible dummy who alone had assumed personal liability on the mortgage, were unknown to the mortgagee should the answer be the same?

(2) ". . . The fact that it desired to evade the law, as it is called, is immaterial, because the very meaning of a line in the law is that you intentionally may go as close to it as you can if you do not pass it. Bullen v. Wisconsin, 240 U.S. 625, 630, 631, 36 S.Ct. 473." Holmes, J., in Superior Oil Co. v. State of Mississippi, 280 U.S. 390, 395–396 (1930).

". . . Whenever the law draws a line there will be cases very near each other on opposite sides. The precise course of the line may be uncertain, but no one can come near it without knowing that he does so, if he thinks, and if he does so it is familiar to the criminal law to make him take the risk. Nash v. United States, 229 U.S. 373, 33 S.Ct. 780." Holmes, J., in United States v. Wurzbach, 280 U.S. 396, 399 (1930).

ANDERSON v. CANADAY
37 Okl. 171, 131 P. 697 (1913).

[This is a suit by a judgment debtor, who was compelled by garnishment to pay a judgment, against the lawyer who conceived the plan of collection through garnishment. Plaintiff is a citizen of Oklahoma and an employee of a company doing business both in Oklahoma and Missouri. He was indebted to defendant Holmes for $50. Defendant Anderson, also a resident of Oklahoma, as Holmes' lawyer instituted an action for the $50 in a Missouri court and garnished plaintiff's salary. As the defendant Anderson evidently knew, the exemption of the plaintiff's wages from garnishment under the law of Oklahoma would not be given effect in Missouri, and the claim against him was satisfied out of his wages. Plaintiff charges that defendants combined and confederated together to defeat and defraud him of his rights under the exemption laws of Oklahoma by bringing the action in Missouri. Defendants' demurrer to the petition was overruled and judgment against Anderson was given for the amount of the garnished wages.]

ROSSER, C. It is contended, however, that though the creditor might be liable his attorney is not. An attorney is not ordinarily liable for the acts of his client. The fact that through ignorance he gives his client bad advice, on which he acts to the hurt of another, will not make the attorney liable to that other. But where the attorney is actuated by malicious motives or shares the illegal motives of his client he becomes responsible, the liability of the attorney depends on his state of mind. If he is actuated only by his duty as attorney, he is not liable; but if he shares the illegal purpose and intent of the client he is liable. . . .

The petition in this case alleges that Holmes and Anderson combined and confederated together, in order to defeat and defraud the rights of the plaintiff under the exemption laws of the state of Oklahoma, by bringing an action in the state of Missouri. It stated a cause of action. . . .

The judgment of the trial court should be affirmed.

PEOPLE v. KRESEL
Supreme Court of New York, Appellate Div., 1935.
243 App.Div. 137, 277 N.Y.S. 168.

[This was the prosecution of a lawyer for giving advice which sent his clients to jail. He was convicted of aiding, abetting, counseling and procuring three persons, Marcus, Saul Singer and Pollack, in misapplying the funds of a bank. Marcus, Saul Singer and Pollack were directors of a bank and its several wholly owned subsidiaries. The defendant was the attorney for the group.

When informed by the Superintendent of Banks that the bank was violating the Banking Law by extending too much credit to one borrower, the Singer group devised a plan by which the loans were in large part divided up among the subsidiaries. Defendant was of the opinion that the plan was legal, and on the basis of this advice the directors carried it out. In the prosecution of the directors for violating the Banking Laws, the plan was held illegal and the directors were sent to jail.

It was Marcus or Singer who devised the basic plan of substituting the subsidiaries as debtors. The aid given by the defendant was limited to details.]

HEFFERNAN, J. . . . That brings us to the main inquiry as to appellant's connection with this plan. As I interpret the evidence his sole connection with the transaction was as a lawyer.

The offense of which appellant was convicted involves no moral turpitude and it is undenied that it was based on a transaction which caused injury to no one. . . . He was the adviser of Marcus and Singer, the executives of these institutions. It is not denied that they presented to him the Bolivar plan. Appellant asserts that he believed the proposal to be lawful. On January 11, 1930, he advised Marcus and Singer that before anything was done in the matter the plan should be submitted to the Superintendent of Banks for his approval. It is uncontradicted that appellant's last connection with this transaction was on that date and that his last word was that nothing should be done until the approval of the Banking Department was obtained. Nevertheless, the plan was executed on January 13, 1930, without the knowledge or consent of appellant.

Marcus and Singer of course committed the crime with which they were charged. . . .

In order for one, not an officer or employee of a moneyed corporation, to be an aider and abettor of the crime, he must have an actual criminal intent; he must be guilty of an action involving moral turpitude. . . .

The trial court, however, erroneously charged the jury that the only intent required to be shown as to an aider and abettor was the same intent as is required in the case of a director, namely, an intent to do the prohibited act. The trial court committed serious and prejudicial error in instructing the jury that appellant could be found guilty of the crime charged, even though he were acting in perfect good faith.

There is no evidence that appellant urged or incited any one to commit any offense. The extent of his offending is that he failed to forbid his clients to proceed. He swore that he believed the plan to be within the law. The court of last resort has since held that he was mistaken. When appellant gave his advice the question was unsettled. It is worthy of note that neither the Appellate Division nor the Court of Appeals was unanimous in its construction of the law. A lawyer is not to be held criminally responsible because he honestly gives mistaken advice upon a doubtful question of law. No lawyer is answerable if he is mistaken concerning a question of law on which reasonable doubt may be entertained by well-informed lawyers. . . .

Infallibility is an attribute of neither lawyer nor judge. And yet in this case the trial court said to the jury that appellant was conclusively presumed to know the law and that the law involved herein was plain and unambiguous. It is a silly perversion of the legal fiction that every one is bound to know the law, to insist that, in this field of law, lawyers shall decide all questions in accordance with what the courts may ultimately hold, at the peril that the failure to prophesy correctly the final outcome will make them criminal accessories. . . .

Finally we are convinced that legal guilt was not brought home to Kresel. The evidence is insufficient to warrant his conviction.

CRAPSER, J., concurs; RHODES, J., concurs for reversal and dismissal of the indictment, with a separate memorandum; HILL, P. J., and BLISS, J., vote to reverse the judgment of conviction and for a new trial, with an opinion by HILL, P. J., in which BLISS, J., concurs, with a memorandum.

HILL, P. J. . . . In determining what intent is necessary to establish guilt in his case, our court neither is required nor permitted to reason by analogy from the opinions in cases like People v. Clark (242 N.Y. 313, 151 N.E. 631) and People ex rel. Perkins v. Moss (187 N.Y. 410, 80 N.E. 383), for the Court of Appeals in People v. Marcus (261 N.Y. 268, 185 N.E. 97) has determined the exact question on the very facts here presented. I am unable to agree with Judge Heffernan and the arguments advanced on behalf of defendant that the intent necessary in this case is other than that held sufficient as to Bernard K. Marcus and Saul Singer. As to them, it has been decided that proof of intent to do the act forbidden is sufficient. I do not read the portion of the prevailing opinion in the Marcus case that applies to Herbert Singer as indicating that because he was an attorney it was necessary to establish an intent to do something inherently wrong and criminal as distinguished from an intent to do the act made criminal by statute. . . . A necessary element named in the Penal Law, section 2, was lacking, that, while he counseled, he did not induce the older men to commit the crime, that the advice which he gave was not followed and had no effect upon the determination already formed by them to carry through the essential features of the plan. I agree with the trial judge that the only intent necessary was that

Kresel intended to aid and abet Marcus, Saul Singer and Pollack in doing the act forbidden by section 305 of the Penal Law. . . .

The judgment of conviction should be reversed in the interests of justice, and a new trial ordered.

NOTES

(1) Here the clients went to jail and the lawyer went free. Do you gather from this case that everyone is presumed to know the law except the lawyers? Do we hesitate to apply this presumption to lawyers because they are in the business of advising on the law and the public interest requires that they be not fettered by fear in the performance of this function?

(2) In re Bullowa, 223 App.Div. 593 (1928), a lawyer was charged with having suggested to his client in correspondence between them that the client falsify papers bearing on the value of ships which the government was about to take over. The language used in the letters was capable of several interpretations. The attorney was acquitted, but in its opinion the Court said, ". . . the precise language used by a lawyer to his client is immaterial, if its effect is, not only to advise or counsel, but even to suggest or indicate, a course of action which will enable the client to defraud another, or to set the due processes of law at defiance, or to evade or circumvent them by trickery or fraud."

Chapter VI

NEGOTIATION AND COMPROMISE

Introduction. Lawyers play important roles in the resolution of disputes prior to litigation and frequently serve as representatives when the negotiating process is aimed at planning for the future, the legislative function. In fact, the newly admitted lawyer is surprised to discover that after three years of law study a major portion of his time is devoted to negotiation and compromise, with court action only a remote possibility. That possibility, however, is not insignificant in the bargaining process and the lawyer's accurate estimate of his client's chances in court is perhaps the most important skill he must develop to become an effective negotiator. Hopefully three years of law school have placed the young lawyer on the path to expertise in "prophecying what the courts will do in fact," Holmes' definition of law. Even, however, where the law is fairly predictable in favor of one's client, there are at least two good reasons why a negotiated settlement might be the better part of valor. The facts might not be found by judge or jury as the client asserts them and even victory can be costly to a party due to the fact that attorney's fees are generally not recoverable in this country. Consequently the possibilities of out-of-court settlement must often be explored.

The lawyer functioning as a negotiator finds himself in a wide variety of bargaining relationships which call for disparate skills and techniques and which require a consideration of ethical questions that vary with each relationship. It will be the purpose of this chapter to examine into the several general kinds of bargaining roles in which lawyers find themselves, placing each within one of two broad categories—negotiations to settle pre-existing disputes and negotiations for future arrangements.

It should be observed at the outset that both types of negotiation serve the interests of the client if costly court litigation is avoided even though there might often be the ultimate possibility of victory in a judicial action. The settlement of disputes in court is not only costly in terms of money, time, and emotions but the administration of justice would soon collapse from overload if the great majority of disputes were not settled prior to court action. Society obviously has a major interest in the settlement of most controversies at an early stage. This is true with reference to each of the fields where lawyers function as dispute-settlors. Not quite as obvious but equally apt is the conclusion that a responsible lawyer in negotiating plans for a client's continuing relationship with others serves his client best by creating plans fair to all parties, plans that will avoid later disputes leading to possible litigation. The temptation to "get the better of the deal" may be short-sighted and must be resisted where the parties will have future relations. The reader may consider whether such admonition is less necessary in the settlement of past disputes if a continuing relationship between the parties is not envisioned. In some instances of past dispute-settling, the same parties will face each other again, possibly on a regular basis, and a similar precaution as to short-sighted victories would seem to be in order.

Several frequently encountered bargaining situations will serve to illustrate the two areas of negotiation. In each the question might be asked as to the exclusivity of the lawyer's role for we shall see that non-lawyers, acting either on their own behalf or in a representative capacity, are significant factors in negotiation.

A major area of dispute-settlement through negotiation is seen in personal injury tort claims, especially those resulting from automobile accidents. Here society's interest in out-of-court settlement looms large inasmuch as such claims lead to the great majority of civil jury trials in this country and account for trial delays of several years in most large cities. Settlement prior to trial must terminate almost all of such claims or the judicial system as we know it today would cease to function. Many studies suggest that administrative decision-making should replace court action in this field. Even if this comes to pass it is likely that most controversies of this nature will continue to be settled through negotiation. Lawyers play significant parts in the settlements of these disputes. They are the usual representatives for claimants although many settlements are entered into with the injured parties themselves and some with members of their family. On the defense side most negotiations are carried out with insurance claims adjusters who are generally not attorneys. Is there any reason why lay representatives for claimants have not appeared with greater frequency in the negotiating process prior to trial? Would this constitute the practice of law?

The offices of the Internal Revenue Service are the scenes of many settlements arrived at through negotiation. Here the regulations of the Service permit representation by attorneys or certified public accountants as well as other specified lay individuals. An anomalous rule also permits non-lawyers who pass an examination to represent clients beyond the negotiation stage if the case comes before the Tax Court. Experience has shown, however, that few non-lawyers exercise this right without associating an attorney, the role unquestionably becoming that of an advocate.

A major and continuing area of dispute in our society is that of employer-employee grievances. The alternative to settlement here was all too frequently that of strike, boycott, picketing, and violence, and their responses, the lockout and the court injunction. Seldom was one of these devices, or any combination, a satisfactory solution.

Society's stake in peaceful settlements is high and in this field legislation, federal and state, has been put on the books to force the disputants to the bargaining table. Laws compelling collective bargaining bring into being vast numbers of negotiated agreements pertaining to wages, hours of work, and other working conditions. The agreements themselves generally provide for negotiation of future grievances, with an ultimate resort, not to the courts, but to arbitration. We thus find in labor law a laboratory without parallel for the study of dispute-settlement and contractual compromise through negotiation. Representatives of labor in the bargaining process are generally not lawyers and even where resort is had to arbitration, a process not dissimilar to the judicial, probably no more than half of the representatives of labor are members of the legal profession. Are these representatives practicing law? Employer representatives, both in negotiation and before an arbitrator, are more likely to be company attorneys although this is still far from universally true. One additional and important observation with reference to employer-employee grievances should be made. The disputants in this area, unlike the parties involved in personal injury tort claims or in tax controversies, will have a continuing relation with each other after the settlement of the immediate controversy. This obviously has a bearing on the process of settlement and on the nature of the settlement itself.

Two other fields of negotiation, in each of which the lawyer is the exclusive representative, should be mentioned. One pertains to pretrial settlement conferences after a civil action has been filed, and the other to "plea bargaining" in the criminal field. The usual stated objectives of pretrial are to simplify issues and speed up trials. Many believe, however, that the impetus to compromise afforded by the settlement conference, referred to by some as a "by-product", is actually the major contribution of pre-trial. Here the services of an impartial judge are often available to bring counsel together in a setting less formal than the courtroom. Counsel and their clients are frequently able to view the controversy much more objectively after such discussion and experience has shown that settlements are arrived at and a trial avoided in many cases.

"Plea bargaining," a term objected to by some prosecutors as suggesting unethical conduct, is an important part of the administration of the criminal law. It is clear that if most criminal defendants did not plead guilty there would result an impossible log jam of jury trials and several times the personnel now involved in criminal litigation would be necessary. As a consequence prosecutors make use of several inducements in bargaining with defendant or his attorney for a guilty plea. These inducements include dismissal of some of the charges, acceptance of a plea to a lesser included offense, and a promise of a lighter sentence recommendation. In Chapter IX, Section 1, further reference is made to the discretion of the prosecutor in these negotiations.

Before concluding this survey of the lawyer's negotiating role emphasis should again be laid on the dual nature of the role. The out-of-court settlement of pre-existing disputes is important for society and takes up a major portion of the practice of many attorneys. No less important to society and to the practicing lawyer is the negotiation of contracts and other kinds of arrangements to govern future conduct. Basic questions to be resolved concern the nature of the skills necessary for effective representation in the two areas of negotiation and the ethical restrictions on such representation. Lawyers will in the future continue to be challenged, as they have been in the past, by both questions.

SECTION 1. THE IMPORTANCE OF NEGOTIATION AND SETTLEMENT

In Frank W. Brady, The Settlement of Controversies: The Will and the Way to Prevent Lawsuits,* 45 A.B.A.J. 471 (1959), the following are listed as some of the advantages of out-of-court settlement:

1. Extrajudicial justice moves faster and is far cheaper.

2. It saves much mental anguish and heartache to the lawyer and to his client.

3. It often reconciles the disputing parties.

4. It is generally more satisfactory.

5. In the settlement of a case in your office, *you* are the judge to a great extent.

6. Also, with your client's approval, you have the choice to accept or to reject the final "decision" reached at the conference table.

7. You can handle more work when you settle cases out of court.

8. You attract more clients, as more clients prefer to settle than to litigate. As soon as word gets around that you "specialize" in keeping clients out of court, your success in the profession is assured.

9. Extrajudicial justice generally operates under a mantle of secrecy, unlike judicial justice. It thus keeps your client's name away from unnecessary (sometimes unpleasant) publicity.

10. You and your clients make fewer enemies by settling than by fighting in court.

* Copyright 1959 by the American Bar Association. Reprinted by permission.

11. Judges like you all the more for sparing them hard work; and, without being aware of the fact, you gain their respect and admiration.

PERSONAL INJURY CLAIMS

In Maurice Rosenberg and Michael J. Sovern, Delay and the Dynamics of Personal Injury Litigation, 59 Col.L.Rev. 1115, 1124, (1959), the fate of 193,000 annual personal injury claims in New York City is described as follows:

> In devising improved methods the courts fortunately need not spread their efforts across all the 193,000 personal injury claims made each year. Almost two-thirds of these are settled or abandoned without suit—roughly 77,000 with, and 39,000 without the aid of counsel. Even the remaining group of 77,000 sued cases contains a large proportion that never actually burdens the courts. About 29,000 close without the parties signifying they want a trial by filing a note of issue. Of the 48,000 suits left, roughly 7,000 reach trial, of which only about 2,500 go all the way to verdict. It is these 7,000 or so suits which reach trial that are the heart of the delay problem.

NOTES

(1) In Chicago it is estimated that 85 per cent of all personal injury claims handled by insurers are settled prior to the filing of suit. Only 10 per cent of the suits filed are brought to trial. See Comment, *Settlement of Personal Injury Cases in the Chicago Area*, 47 Nw.L.Rev. 895 n. 5, 902 (1953).

For a study of personal injury claims in New York City and the role and effectiveness of the lawyer in their settlement see Franklin, Chamin, and Mark, *Accidents, Money and the Law: A Study of the Economics of Personal Injury Litigation*, 61 Col.L.Rev. 1 (1961).

See Chapter II, Section 5, supra, for a more detailed treatment of the representation of personal injury claimants and defendants.

(2) A third year law student is employed part time by a firm of attorneys which represents various casualty insurance companies in connection with the adjustment and settlement of claims and the defense of suits against the insured, in accordance with the provisions of the policies. The student has become very effective as an investigator and adjuster and regularly settles many of the claims. Is the firm acting unethically? Is the student practicing law? See A.B.A. Opinion 85 (1932); Johnson, *Unauthorized Practice by Law Students: Some Legal Advice About Legal Advice*, 36 Tex.L.Rev. 346 (1958).

PRETRIAL

ARVO VAN ALSTYNE AND HARVEY M. GROSSMAN, CALIFORNIA PRETRIAL AND SETTLEMENT PROCEDURES *

Pages 169–171 (1963).

Under the 1957 pretrial rules, settlement was considered merely a byproduct of pretrial procedure. . . . The 1963 rules emphasize the settlement objective, however, and have supplemented pretrial conferences with separately conducted, judicially supervised settlement conferences. . . .

. . . (T)oday the settlement of potential litigation commands substantial acceptance among members of the bench and bar, most of whom agree with the view that a reasonable settlement is always better than a risky trial. More fundamentally, promotion of settlements is also widely regarded not only as an appropriate function of the judiciary, but as a duty owed both the public and litigants; the courts are considered to have a responsibility to aid in compromising disputes, so that the rights of litigants will be better served, unnecessary litigation avoided, and public expense eliminated.

Importance of Judicial Supervision

Settlement discussions are frequently standard procedure between experienced counsel. Indeed, the great majority of civil cases filed never go to trial, most of them being disposed of by compromise agreements. . . . The purpose behind the present emphasis on judicial participation in settlement discussions therefore requires some explanation.

There are at least three significant reasons:

First, judicial participation often creates a climate that expedites productive negotiations for settlement. Some attorneys are reluctant to open settlement negotiations for fear their action may be construed as indicating a lack of confidence in the strength of their position. When both counsel share this reluctance, negotiations may never be undertaken or may be deferred too long to be fully effective. Judicial invitation to explore settlement possibilities informally can "break the ice."

Second, the judge contributes the views of an outsider who usually enjoys considerable prestige. Without exerting undue pressure to forego a trial, he may diplomatically explore with counsel the strengths and weaknesses of their respective positions, pointing out possible defects or advantages that may have been overlooked. On

* Copyright 1963 by The Regents of the University of California. Reprinted by permission.

request, or on his own motion, he may also express tentatively his appraisal of the settlement value of the case, or of the range in which settlement discussions may realistically proceed. Counsel whose authority to negotiate is narrowly circumscribed by his client often may find the court's opinion a helpful basis for inducing his client to reevaluate the case and authorize a more realistic compromise. In short, although many cases are settled extrajudicially, even more can be settled with judicial assistance.

Third, a settlement conference presided over by an impartial judge often constitutes a practical substitute for a trial, especially when the parties consider that a matter of principle is at stake and they insist on having their "day in court." After participating in a settlement conference, at which their contentions and those of the opposing parties have been heard and evaluated by the judge, they frequently are satisfied that their case has been properly disposed of with the impartial and objective assistance of the judicial process.

Early Settlement as Pretrial Objective

There are numerous factors which in many cases tend to mitigate against effective settlement negotiations in the early stages of a lawsuit. In personal injury actions, for example, the possibility of later complications from what might appear at first to be a relatively simple injury cautions against serious settlement discussions until the extent of the injuries has become reasonably fixed. Full possession of the facts and development of adequate legal theories of liability or defense as a basis for responsible settlement negotiations often are not possible without extended discovery proceedings. In addition, some attorneys representing insurance companies and defendants understandably feel that time works for them, in view of the burden of proof that a plaintiff must carry and the various pressures which increasingly tend to induce plaintiffs to seek settlement rather than risk the uncertainties of a long-deferred trial. As a consequence, a large number of settlements take place immediately prior to the trial date, or on the date of trial itself—the so-called settlements on the courthouse steps.

One objective of pretrial settlement procedures is to advance substantially the time at which productive settlement negotiations take place. . . .

Settlement in the pretrial stage (ordinarily the pretrial conference is held about four to six weeks before the probable trial date, pursuant to Rule 220) may save the parties final trial preparation and make it unnecessary for witnesses to attend court. It also prevents the trial calendar from collapsing because of unanticipated last-minute settlements, or from being overloaded (with resultant continuances or trailing calendars) because extra cases were set in the realistic but unrealized expectation that a substantial number would be settled before trial. To the extent that pretrial advances the date of effective settlement discussions between counsel the efficiency of the administration of justice is improved.

A DISSENT

For another view on out-of-court settlement, generally referred to by critics as "compromise," see With the Aid of Court, 13 N.Y. County Bar Bull. 203, 205 (1956):

That compromise has achieved "peace in our time" many times is acknowledged by all. But is compromise the best way to settle disputes at the bar? That is the question asked by this essay.

Today under the pressures of crowded court calendars on one hand and a materialism engendered by prosperity and the natural greed of man on the other, we find more and more law suits being settled by compromise—very often not merely "with the aid of the court" but at its insistence. . . .

. . . [T]oo many judges encourage this bypassing of the orderly lawful determination of disputes, citing the number of cases settled rather than the number tried and decided perhaps because that number decided is so few when compared with the total number of disputes brought to court.

This tendency to dispose of all cases by compromise might possibly be condoned in many negligence cases because of the pressure of thousands of cases that otherwise would not be disposed of for scores of years to come, with our present procedures and judicial equipment.

But in the commercial field, in the tax field and the field of decedents estates and criminal prosecutions the case for compromise stands not only on weak legs but implies an abdication of the judicial function that, in the eyes of lawyers and public, makes the courts seem more like market places where justice is done and law and order maintained. The majesty of the law is giving way to a materialistic bartering system that looks only to the immediate case of today with no consideration for the need to establish principles that will guide and control men in their future dealings.

How can the public, particularly those who become entangled in the web of litigation, be expected to respect our judicial process if they find non-judicial methods being employed to determine their rights?

NOTE

For an excellent description and analysis of empirical research into the effect of pretrial procedures upon the disposition of personal injury litigation in New Jersey see Rosenberg, The Pretrial Conference and Effective Justice (1964). See also Holtzoff, *Federal Pretrial Procedure*, 11 Am.Univ.L. Rev. 21 (1962).

SECTION 2. SKILLS AND TECHNIQUES

THEODORE VOORHEES, LAW OFFICE TRAINING: THE ART OF NEGOTIATION
13 Prac. Lawyer 61, 62 (April, 1967).

PREPARATION

Importance

Some lawyers are foolhardy and will attend a settlement conference or other negotiation without advance preparation. They will excuse themselves on the ground that they will go only to listen and not to make commitments, and that they can study the proposition better when they have heard what the other side has to say. This may turn out adversely.

A skilled and well-prepared opponent will come to the meeting with his arguments all lined up, and his thrusts may unseat the lawyer on the other side. The latter may appear an ignoramus if he does not respond in some fashion. He may find himself making concessions. Worst of all, his failure, from the beginning, to be able to put his case in a strong light may prejudice his position through every stage that follows in the course of the negotiation.

Lawyers do not function well *sub silentio*. Even when they are young and inexperienced, they are expected to speak up and defend the interests of their clients on all occasions. An associate's inability to respond forcefully and intelligently at the first and all subsequent meetings will indicate inferiority, and may serve to embarrass him and the law office from which he comes. A strong response requires forethought.

Liaison with Client

A crucial aspect of the attorney's preparation is to make sure that the client approves in advance the position that his counsel is to take, that the client authorizes any specific proposals that may be within contemplation, and that authority is granted for the payment or receipt of the monetary consideration. A negotiation may be too complex or its course too uncertain to permit prior approval of each step to be taken at the meeting. The associate should be counselled to obtain clear instructions on how far he may go in particular directions and when he may rely on his own judgment.

If the client does not want to give him *carte blanche*, he should not be offended. In delicate transactions, the return to touch base and the opportunity to discuss the pros and cons of the pending proposals may turn out to be helpful in the long run.

Specific Types

To turn to specific types of negotiation, preparation for collective bargaining should include study of the full range of the lengths to which the client—the employer or the union, depending on the representation—will be prepared to go, not merely at the first meeting but at all subsequent stages of the negotiation. All the basic underlying facts with respect to the controversy must be reviewed and thoroughly understood. Every argument in support of the client's position must be thought out and polished. Above all, the position of the other side must be visualized, its strengths and weaknesses probed, and the strategy for demolishing its contentions devised.

. . .

Similarly, before going to a real estate settlement or a tax conference, a lawyer should ascertain what problems are to be met, what positions are likely to be taken by the other side, and what course his own client should follow in the negotiations.

As for attendance at a settlement conference in a personal injury case, the attorney should be as well prepared with respect to every aspect of the case as he would be if he were going to court to commence the trial. Thorough knowledge of the strength of his claim or defense, however, is not enough. Counsel should be prepared to plead his case with eloquence, and he should remember that on this occasion his plea is directed to the opposing counsel. If the latter can be shaken, a satisfactory settlement may be attained.

TECHNIQUES

. . .

Candor and sincerity are the most powerful weapons of a good advocate. As soon as the adversary understands that he is dealing with a man of integrity, the discussions can proceed with directness, and the time wasted in beating around the bush may be eliminated.

The negotiator should stake out the ground to be covered and the area in which agreement is to be reached. If the controversy can be narrowed by the statement of the issue, time may be saved by an early attempt to reach agreement as to what the issue really is.

In some instances, it may be well to delineate at the earliest stage certain basic areas in which no agreement is possible. If a client has instructed counsel that under no circumstances will he concede this or that, and his attorney is convinced that such is truly the case, the adversary might as well be so told at the very beginning. If the opposing client has instructed his attorney that agreement in the interdicted areas are *sine qua non*, the parties might well consider whether they should not break off without further waste of time. It should be remembered, however, that an exchange of views often leads to concessions.

Wherever possible, the negotiator should take the initiative, state the position of the client, and present the justification for that position and the arguments that may persuade the other side to accept it.

Obviously, the presentation must be handled delicately. Success will be impeded by an unnecessary antagonizing of the opponent.

There is little point in a negotiation unless there is a mutual interest in reaching agreement. Counsel, therefore, is not giving his case away by indicating his determination to reach agreement if humanly possible. Normally, he should avoid permitting the inference that agreement is so important to his client that major concessions will be made in order to reach it.

Patience should be preserved at all times. On one occasion during a prolonged labor negotiation, Walter Reuther was asked the same question fifteen times. He never gave a sign of irritation and answered the question as carefully and as patiently on the fifteenth time as on the first.

THE GIVE

Few agreements are reached unless each party is prepared to provide consideration. Most negotiations turn on how much the parties are prepared to give.

One of the more important instructions for an inexperienced lawyer should be the handling of the making of concessions. Here, general rules may be found quite dangerous; yet some advice should prove helpful. Inexperience can be costly to the client.

The final price that the client is prepared to pay should not be laid on the table until

Every effort has been made to secure the bargain at a smaller price; or

There is a strong indication that that price will be enough to bring the parties to agreement; or

Even though there is danger that the offer may be rejected, failure to make the offer will lead to a breakoff of negotiations and a loss of any possible agreement.

Concessions should normally be made only when they are balanced by concessions from the other side.

The time may come when a final offer must be made on a take-it-or-leave-it basis. This event calls for a convincing display of candor and conviction.

The associate should be encouraged to develop a sense of timing and a sensitivity as to the proper method of approach. Under ordinary circumstances, it might be foolhardy for a negotiator to start off the discussion by making a major concession. Under others, the temper of the opposition may be such that an immediate exposure of the whole tenor of the client's proposal may be the best way of leading up to an agreement.

SPIRIT OF THE NEGOTIATIONS

Some lawyers negotiate with the other party as though they were at Panmunjon. The adversary has become the enemy, opposing counsel are extended no courtesies, and the discussion is conducted on the level of the Cold War. The interests of the clients could not be more poorly served.

Young lawyers must learn that, at all cost, communication must be maintained during the negotiation of an agreement, and that this may best be accomplished in an atmosphere of friendliness, sincerity, and relaxation. The labor leader or his counsel who presents a visage of eternal belligerency may fool the rank and file into believing that he is representing their best interests. More often than not, he freezes the employer into a counterfoil of intransigent resistance.

Control of temper, patience, and constant courtesy are to be recommended; care and vigilance no less so. The negotiator should keep himself alert so as to divine the meaning and intent of what his adversary is saying to him and to take advantage of all opportunities that may be offered. To get the most for his client he must, at all times, be prepared to give his best.

There is also need for boldness and courage. It is fatal to commence a negotiation with a defeatist attitude or with fear that the client's objective is beyond attainment. A determination to work things out may be enough to carry the day.

CONCLUSION

A lawyer should pride himself on being a good negotiator. In an active practice, there will scarcely be a day when he will not undertake to reach an agreement with another lawyer on some problem, sometimes large and sometimes small.

He does not prove his strength or wisdom when he becomes known as one who always has to have things done his way. A good negotiator finds the method of securing an agreement in such a manner as is within the best interest of his client but compatible, wherever possible, with the desires and convenience of the other fellow as well. In the order of priorities, a lawyer is well-advised to put his own predilections far down the list.

Great satisfaction is derived from the lawyer's role as negotiator, not the least of which is the report to the client of a mission accomplished. Here, as in all other roles that the lawyer plays, the service aspect should be stressed in law office talks to the young lawyers. The profession calls for dedication to the interest of the client and determination to provide superior service. Law office associates need instruction in the employment of their talents and the utilization of professional tools.

NOTES

(1) Many helpful articles on negotiation and settlement are found in the pages of The Practical Lawyer. See McConnell, *Settlement Negotiations—Revisited,* 11 Prac.Lawyer 39 (Feb. 1965); Lorry, *Settlement of a Personal Injury Claim,* 11 Prac.Lawyer 15 (Jan. 1965) (containing a detailed checklist for the evaluation of a personal injury claim); Hermann, *Fair Dealing in Personal Injury Cases,* 10 Clev.-Mar.L.Rev. 449 (1961) (an analysis of the financial disadvantage to attorneys resulting from unnecessary litigation); Armstrong, *How and When to Settle,* 19 Ark.L.Rev. 20 (1965); Sindell and Sindell, Let's Talk Settlement (1963).

See also Stuart, *Some Pointers in Successfully Negotiating With the Internal Revenue Service,* 40 Taxes 59 (1962); Glieberman, *How to Negotiate a Divorce Case,* 45 Chi.Bar Record 139 (1963); Note, *Guilty Plea Bargaining: Compromises by Prosecutors to Secure Guilty Pleas,* 112 Pa.L.Rev. 865 (1964) (Chapter IX, Section 1A, pages 363–366 infra, also deals with this subject.)

There is a wealth of written material on the subject of negotiation in labor relations. See Kuhn, Bargaining in Grievance Settlement (1961). See also Segal, *Labor Law: The Case for the Union Lawyer,* 44 A.B.A.J. 1056 (1958), page 235, supra.

An area of broadened interest in recent years has been that of student-university disputes. What issues have loomed largest here? Are lawyers helpful in settling such controversies? Does the fact of a continuing relationship play an important part in these negotiations? Some have suggested similarities in these disputes to the history of employer-employee disputes. Do you see any?

In Cooper, Living the Law 147–155 (1958), we find an exploration of the disparate bargaining techniques called for in a variety of settings. Professor Cooper divides these into Friendly Negotiations, Negotiations with Public Officials, and Adversary Negotiations.

For a further discussion of some of the ethical problems see King and Sears, *The Ethical Aspects of Compromise, Settlement and Arbitration,* 25 Rocky Mountain L.Rev. 454 (1953).

"One thoughtful lawyer, of whom inquiry was made for The Survey of the Legal Profession, wrote: 'Should there be a special Canon covering negotiations and controversies which do not result in litigation? The present Canons lay too much stress on the lawyer's duty as an advocate.'" McCracken, *Report on Observance by the Bar of Stated Professional Standards,* 37 Va.L.Rev. 399, 423 (1951). Can the same criticism be made of the new Code of Professional Responsibility?

(2) Is it true that the art of negotiation cannot be taught in law school as some contend? If it can, should it be? Few schools have endeavored to do so. For an informative description of a seminar directed towards this end at the Michigan Law School by a law professor and a psychiatrist see White, *The Lawyer as a Negotiator: An Adventure in Understanding and Teaching the Art of Negotiation,* 19 Jour.Leg.Ed. 337 (1967). See also a good description and analysis of a similar course taught at the University of Washington, Peck and Fletcher, *A Course on the Subject of Negotiation,* 21

J.Legal Ed. 196 (1968). An earlier suggestion for such law school training is found in Mathews, *Negotiation: A Pedagogical Challenge*, 6 J.Legal Ed. 93 (1953).

THREATS

One technique of negotiation is to threaten the other party in an effort to induce settlement. Is it ever improper for the lawyer to threaten to bring civil action if settlement is not agreed to by the other party? New York County Opinion 438 (1954) suggests that it is proper to suggest the alternative of suit to promote settlement and avoid litigation if the last sentence of Canon 29 is kept in mind. "He should strive at all times to uphold the honor and to maintain the dignity of the profession and to improve not only the law but the administration of justice." Is this a useful guide? Does it make a difference if the lawyer has no intention to sue? See New York County Opinion 306 (1933).

Frequently the tortious act of a defendant is at the same time the violation of a criminal statute. May the lawyer for the claimant threaten the institution of criminal proceedings if the civil claim is not settled?

MATTER OF GELMAN

Supreme Court of New York, Appellate Division, 1930.
230 App.Div. 524, 245 N.Y.S. 416.

Disciplinary proceedings instituted by the Association of the Bar of the City of New York, New York County Lawyers' Association and Bronx County Bar Association.

DOWLING, P. J. . . . The supplemental petition, . . . charges misconduct, in that in October, 1925, respondent, in behalf of certain clients, commenced an action in the Municipal Court of the City of New York to recover for personal injuries and property damages resulting from an automobile accident, and that under date of October 23, 1925, he wrote the defendant, Emanuel R. Miccione, as follows: . . . "Up to the present time I have not received an answer to the summons, and I am, therefore, in a position to enter judgment against you by default. If I am put to the trouble of proceeding against you personally on the judgment referred to, I will be compelled to institute criminal proceedings against you for failing to cover your taxicab by proper insurance policy under the law. I have been more than lenient with you and will refuse to tolerate any more of your nonsense. . . ."

. . . Respondent urges that this letter was written with a view to getting the defendant, a taxicab driver and owner, to turn the matter over to his insurance carrier, respondent being of the belief that the owner was covered, but had simply neglected to refer the claim to the insurance company. Respondent interprets the letter as simply giving notice that a prosecution for the violation of a penal statute would follow if it developed that there was no insurance. We think the letter presents the alternative of payment or criminal prosecution. As Miccione was in fact insured, respondent had no occasion to make good his threat to institute criminal proceedings. . . .

We are of the opinion that the letter in question was improper, and that in writing and sending it respondent was guilty of unprofessional conduct. This court has heretofore expressed its disapproval of using threats of criminal prosecution as a means of forcing a settlement of civil claims. . . .

Respondent has been guilty of a violation of the principle which condemns any confusion of threats of criminal prosecution with the enforcement of civil claims. For this misconduct he should be severely censured.

NOTES

(1) In New York City Opinion 299 (1934) a lawyer proposed settlement in a letter and ended with these words: "Are you familiar with Section _____ of the Penal Law?" The Committee concluded that this was obviously a threat of criminal prosecution and professionally improper. See Code of Professional Responsibility, DR 7–105. If defendant has violated a criminal law, why is such threat improper? If a settlement results in these cases can it be set aside?

In extreme cases the attorney's threat of criminal prosecution may amount to the crime of extortion. See People v. Beggs, 178 Cal. 79 (1918).

(2) "On the criminal side the Magistrates' Courts are well worthy of mention as aids to the poor man. This is due largely to the fact that more and more matters are prosecuted criminally than was once the case . . . it is astonishing how many cases that are essentially civil are adjusted through the elasticity of the magistrates' summons system of case. The informal way such summonses issue and the informal way that they are heard are primarily responsible for this and the magistrates' district court is a forum of untold value to scores of thousands of poor persons with a grievance to air if not an actual right invaded. . . ." Report of Joint Committee for the Study of Legal Aid of the Association of the Bar of the City of New York and the Welfare Council of New York City, p. 58 (1928).

(3) How about the threat of the prosecutor in a criminal action, express or implied, to charge a more serious crime if the accused does not plead guilty to a lesser offense? See Chapter IX, Section 1A, page 363, infra.

CONCILIATION

In addition to negotiation of settlements and the actual trial of a lawsuit the lawyer should not overlook other possibilities of dispute resolution. Third parties may be used as mediators or conciliators and also as arbitrators. The latter situations makes use of a "judge" selected generally by the parties whose function it is to decide as a judge with no attempt on his part to bring about a bargained settlement. The mediator or conciliator, on the other hand, is not given the power to decide. His role is that of endeavoring to bring the parties to a voluntary negotiated settlement. Each process has this in common—the resolution of disputes short of a judicial trial.

Some judges have always regarded conciliation and the encouragement of compromise as a part of their duty or at least of their opportunity, as is well brought out in an article. Frank H. Randall, Conciliation as a Function of the Judge, 18 Ky.L.J. 330 (1930). These are the concluding paragraphs:

> "Experience and investigation permit the conservative statement that some judges consistently do all in their power to bring about conciliation and others do very little, though practically all are acquiescent and sympathetic if settlement is suggested by counsel. But on the whole, little is done in comparison with possible accomplishment.
>
> "The widespread use of conciliation in foreign countries for hundreds of years, and the persistent attempts in one form or another in the United States show that it is a matter to be taken care of. The demand will be met either by independent tribunals or by the more extended and consistent employment of the method of conciliation by the judges of our present courts. The power is theirs. The opportunity is theirs."

In some countries conciliation has long been a part of the official machinery. Smith, The Danish Concilation System, 11 J.Am.Jud. Soc. 85 (1927). See Chapter IV, page 217 supra. See also Chapter VII, Section 5, page 329, infra.

CHAPTER NOTES

(1) *The Lawyer and His Client*

A.B.A. Canon 8 calls for the encouragement of compromise, closing with the statement: "Whenever the controversy will admit of fair adjustment, the client should be advised to avoid or end the litigation." Similarly, provisions in a retainer agreement which hamper or bar settlement by the clients are invalid. See Drinker, Legal Ethics 102 (1953). Yet the opinion has been expressed that it is proper for a lawyer to advise against even a reconciliation of husband and wife, if he believes the reconciliation to be opposed to the best interests of his client. ABA Opinion 82 (1932). Although the lawyer may have the laboring oar in the negotiations leading to a settlement it is clear that the decision is the client's as to whether a compromise offer is to be accepted. See Code of Professional Responsibility, EC 7–7.

One of the unavoidable areas of conflict between attorney and client arises when it becomes necessary to set the fee for legal services. (See

Chapter XII, page 443, infra) A special problem is seen with reference to charges for services as a negotiator of a dispute. How should these be valued if the lawyer is not on retainer? Generally speaking, the lawyer feels more justified in charging a larger fee and the amount is more easily set if the case goes to court. An even larger fee is in order if an appeal is necessary. Obviously no argument can be made that the attorney should advise court action, rather than settlement, for this reason and yet his views are persuasive as to whether the case should be litigated and this is true whether the dispute to be settled is in the field of criminal law, personal injury, divorce, labor relations, or any other. If in the attorney's best judgment, following a careful evaluation of the prospects in court and an assessment of the costs of both alternatives, litigation is inadvisable and an out-of-court settlement between the disputants is reached, what factors should enter into the setting of the fee? Is the fact that costly litigation was avoided relevant? See A.B.A. Canon 12 and Code of Professional Responsibility, DR 2–106. Does a contingent fee contract operate to discourage out-of-court settlements? Such contracts generally make specific provision for higher percentages if the case goes to court.

In many of the different bargaining situations there is the danger of conflict between the lawyer's duty to a single client and his obligation to other clients where the lawyer, but not his immediate client, will have future negotiations with the same representative of the other party. This may be true in the settlement of personal injury claims with an insurance adjuster, the settlement of tax disputes with the Internal Revenue Service, in plea bargaining with a public prosecutor, and, in fact, whenever the attorney may have future relations, on behalf of other clients, with the same attorney for the other party. Is the lawyer under an obligation to settle the immediate dispute on the best possible terms even though by so doing he acquires a reputation as an unreasonable negotiator and possibly impairs his effectiveness in negotiations for other clients? Is the same problem present when the attorney has several concurrent separate cases and has an opportunity for a "wholesale" settlement? One court condemned the settlement of a group of personal injury cases on a lump sum basis, saying: "The trading of so many releases for a fixed sum, to be distributed as the attorney thinks best, leads inevitably to the situation where some client has failed to receive the consideration which the merits of his case warranted." Matter of Glucksman, 230 App.Div. 185 (1930). The broader problem suggests itself: Is the lawyer's obligation to negotiate the best possible settlement in a particular case ever in conflict with his desire for a general professional reputation?

Does an examination of the different bargaining situations in this chapter suggest that there is a logical line dividing the fields where the lawyer is the exclusive representative from those where he is not? Are problems of unlawful practice of law posed? Is there a distinction to be drawn between representing a party in the settlement of a dispute, where the alternative is court action, and representing a party in drawing up a commercial contract? Do you picture areas other than those referred to in this Chapter where negotiation is an important process? Is the lawyer a significant factor in those areas? Is it likely that some of the present-day methods of dispute settlement will in the future be supplanted by negotiation and other less formal procedures, as witness the changes in the field of labor relations?

See Chapter XI, page 425 infra, for a discussion of other conflicts of interest in the case of settlements by the lawyer for a liability insurance company.

(2) *The Lawyer and Third Persons*

Is the lawyer as negotiator subject to fewer restraints in forcefully urging his client's position than the lawyer as advocate in court? Do you agree with the observations of Judge Hincks in In re Sacher as set forth on page 285 of the casebook? Does the advocate's responsibility as an officer of the court have a counterpart in the process of negotiation outside of court? What should be the standards of the profession towards exaggeration in claim or in statement, of concealment of the facts, of threats and bombast? If the party himself in a commercial negotiation can engage in puffing, short of fraud, and not be subject to liability, should a lawyer representing him be under any more restriction? Are we still in the stage when haggling is expected to begin with inflated claims on each side? Is the earned reputation of a lawyer for candor and fairness as influential in negotiation as it is in court?

The attorney for the estate of a decedent has information that leads him to believe that certain real property in the estate would be reasonably valued at $100 per acre. The Internal Revenue Agent is suggesting a figure of $200 for estate tax valuation. At the opening of negotiations should the attorney come up with an amount substantially less than $100 for bargaining purposes? Would your answer be different if the attorney had many cases before the Internal Revenue Service and would likely have many more in the future? Does this suggest any conflict of interests between the attorney's present client and other clients?

A.B.A. Opinion 314 (1965) reads, in part:

". . . For example, what is the duty of a lawyer in regard to disclosure of the weaknesses in his client's case in the course of negotiations for the settlement of a tax case?

"Negotiation and settlement procedures of the tax system do not carry with them the guarantee that a correct tax result necessarily occurs. The latter happens, if at all, solely by reason of chance in settlement of tax controversies just as it might happen with regard to other civil disputes. In the absence of either judicial determination or of a hypothetical exchange of files by adversaries, counsel will always urge in aid of settlement of a controversy the strong points of his case and minimize the weak; this is in keeping with Canon 15, which does require 'warm zeal' on behalf of the client. Nor does the absolute duty not to make false assertions of fact require the disclosure of weaknesses in the client's case and in no event does it require the disclosure of his confidences, unless the facts in the attorney's possession indicate beyond reasonable doubt that a crime will be committed. A wrong, or indeed sometimes an unjust, tax result in the settlement of a controversy is not a crime. . . ."

A.B.A. Canon 9 states: "A lawyer should not in any way communicate upon the subject of controversy with a party represented by counsel; much less should he undertake to negotiate or compromise the matter with him, but should deal only with his counsel. It is incumbent upon the lawyer most particularly to avoid everything that may tend to mislead a party not represented by counsel, and he should not undertake to advise him as to the law." See 1 A.L.R.3rd 1113 (1965) for a collection of cases involving Canon 9. See also Code of Professional Responsibility, DR 7–104. Is there any less obligation not to misrepresent when the other party is represented by counsel? Why the absolute prohibition against a direct negotiation with a party represented by counsel? ABA Opinion 75 (1932) holds that the lawyer should seek to dissuade his client from negotiating directly with the other party, citing the first part of Canon 16. In Carpenter v. The State Bar, 210 Cal. 520 (1930), the attorney for a defendant prepared and had executed by the parties an agreement of settlement of the pending litigation, in the absence of the attorney for the plaintiff and without informing the plaintiff of an affirmance of a decision in her favor. For this misconduct, he was suspended from practice.

Is an attorney justified in representing a personal injury claimant in negotiations with defendant's insurance company even though he has advised the claimant that his case is weak and that an actual law suit will not be filed due to contributory negligence?

In addition to the lawyer's duties to his client, to adverse parties, and to the judicial system generally, what other interests of society are at stake in the negotiation process? Do you find that these interests vary with each of the settings referred to in this Chapter?

(3) *Impediments to Settlement*

What are some of the impediments to out-of-court settlements? Ill advised techniques, of course, loom large in any analysis of this question. Frequently, however, it is the attitude of clients with unconcealed animosity towards each other. Curtis, It's Your Law (1959) pp. 3, 4, expresses the view that litigated suits are in part justified to satisfy peacefully such feelings. Do you agree? Should the lawyer endeavor to assuage such feelings as a prelude to settlement? Some lawyers are temperamentally unfit for negotiation, viewing any opening compromise offers as a sign of weakness and a disservice to his client and are convinced that the opening offer must come from opposing counsel. Can an effective answer be made to this philosophy?

For some perceptive observations on the barriers to settlement see *Games Lawyers Play*, 10 Trial L.Guide 223 (1966). The author discusses the psychological and financial pressures on the trial lawyer which cause him to block settlements that might well be to the best interests of his client. He argues that trial lawyers frequently attach too much importance to success in court and engage in unnecessary trials despite the fact that litigation might be uneconomic in a particular case due to a high risk of loss or may be unprofitable in the long run because of continually increasing costs of litigation.

Unreasonable refusals to settle are obviously impediments to settlements. Can anything be done to discourage such refusals? Geller, *Unreasonable Refusal to Settle and Calendar Congestion—Suggested Remedy*, 34 N.Y.S.B.J. 477 (1962), suggests a method of encouraging settlement: If the gap between defendant's offer and the plaintiff's asking figure cannot be narrowed by negotiation and a trial results, plaintiff may recover attorney's fees from defendant if the verdict equals or exceeds plaintiff's figure. If the verdict is not in excess of defendant's offer, defendant recovers attorney's fees. Do you find anything objectionable in Justice Geller's proposal? Does it go beyond cure of unreasonable refusals?

Is an oral settlement enforceable? Langlois v. Langlois, 5 App.Div.2d 75 (1956), dealt with an oral settlement of a tort claim in judge's chambers and a subsequent refusal by the plaintiff to execute a release. Plaintiff claimed his agreement was an executory accord which was required to be in writing under New York Law. The court held, instead, that it was intended as a superseding agreement and was enforceable even though oral. See Note, *Compromise and Settlement—Superseding Agreement—Settlement of Tort Claims in Judge's Chambers*, 22 Albany L.Rev. 366 (1958). For an excellent and thorough analysis of the finality of voluntary settlements and the reasons for which they are sometimes set aside see Dobbs, *Conclusiveness of Personal Injury Settlements: Basic Problems*, 41 No.Car.L.Rev. 665 (1963).

SPAULDING v. ZIMMERMAN

Supreme Court of Minnesota, 1962.
263 Minn. 346, 116 N.W.2d 704.

[A young man of twenty was injured in a collision between an automobile in which he was a passenger and another automobile, and an action for the injuries was brought by the injured man's guardian against the drivers of both the automobiles. The injured man's family physician and two specialists examined him. At the request of one of the defendants a fourth physician made an examination and he found an aneurysm of the aorta, which had escaped the notice of the other physicians, and he reported the grave condition to the lawyers of both defendants. When the case was called for trial the two sides had the information given them by their respective medical examiners. An agreement of settlement for $6,500 was reached, and the counsel for the plaintiff presented to the court a petition for approval of the settlement in which the plaintiff's injuries were described as found by two of the injured man's physicians and as set out in their affidavits. The court made an order approving the settlement.

Two years later the injured man had a physical checkup for the army reserve. In this examination, by the same family physician, the aneurysm of the aorta was discovered, and the condition in incipient form was confirmed by a reexamination of X-rays taken shortly after the accident. Immediate surgery was performed.

Shortly afterward the injured man, who had attained his majority, brought an action for additional damages against the same defendants due to the more serious injuries, including the aorta aneurysm, which he charged resulted from the accident. The trial judge made an order vacating the earlier settlement and in an accompanying memorandum stated:

"By reason of the failure of plaintiff's counsel to use available rules of discovery, plaintiff's doctor and all his representatives did not learn that defendants and their agents knew of its existence and possible serious consequences. Except for the character of the concealment in the light of plaintiff's minority, the Court would, I believe, be justified in denying plaintiff's motion to vacate, leaving him to whatever questionable remedy he may have against his doctor and against his lawyer. . . . There is no doubt that during the course of the negotiations, when the parties were in an adversary relationship, no rule required or duty rested upon defendants or their representatives to disclose this knowledge. However, once the agreement to settle was reached, it is difficult to characterize the parties' relationship as adversary. At this point all parties were interested in securing Court approval. . . .

"When the adversary nature of the negotiations concluded in a settlement, the procedure took on the posture of a joint application to the Court, at least so far as the facts upon which the Court could and must approve settlement is concerned. . . . To hold that the concealment was not of such character as to result in an unconscionable advantage over plaintiff's ignorance or mistake, would be to penalize innocence and incompetence and reward less than full performance of an officer of the Court's duty to make full disclosure to the Court when applying for approval in minor settlement proceedings."

On appeal the order of the trial court vacating the prior order approving the settlement was affirmed.]

GALLAGHER, J. . . . The principles applicable to the court's authority to vacate settlements made on behalf of minors and approved by it appear well established. With reference thereto, we have held that the court in its discretion may vacate such a settlement, though it is not induced by fraud or bad faith, where it is shown that in the accident the minor sustained separate and distinct injuries which were not known or considered by the court at the time settlement was approved; . . . and even though the releases furnished therein purported to cover both known and unknown injuries resulting from the accident. . . .

From the foregoing it is clear that in the instant case the court did not abuse its discretion in setting aside the settlement which it had approved on plaintiff's behalf while he was still a minor. . . .

While no canon of ethics or legal obligation may have required them [defendants' counsel] to inform plaintiff or his counsel with respect thereto, or to advise the court therein, it did become obvious to them at the time, that the settlement then made did not contemplate or take into consideration the disability described. This fact opened the way for the court to later exercise its discretion in vacating the settlement. . . .

NOTES

(1) Was the Court accurate in stating in the principal case that there was no obligation of disclosure on the defendants' counsel although it set aside the settlement? Was not the upsetting of the settlement to the injury of the defendant a sanction for the breach of a duty to disclose?

(2) Is there need for special protection of claimants from claim agents and defense lawyers who may press hard for low settlements? In Brotherhood of Railroad Trainmen v. Virginia ex rel. Virginia State Bar, 377 U.S. 1, 3–4 (1964) Mr. Justice Black mentioned two companion evils:

"It soon became apparent to the railroad workers, however, that simply having these federal statutes on the book was not enough to assure that the workers would receive the full benefit of the compensatory damages Congress intended they should have. Injured workers or their families often fell prey on the one hand to persuasive claims adjusters eager to gain a quick and cheap settlement for their railroad employers, or on the other to lawyers either not competent to try these lawsuits against the able and experienced railroad counsel or too willing to settle a case for a quick dollar."

In the *Spaulding* case above there was no such speed or pressure, yet the court vacated the settlement. Do the ordinary rules of law as to fraud, overreaching, protection of minors and so on, give to the claimants all the protection they should fairly have? Or should specific rules be developed, as a common law rule on the effect of settlement of civil cases parallelling the constitutional rule as to confessions in criminal cases that a claimant is entitled to the advice of counsel before making a settlement; or that the burden of proof is on the defendant to show that the settlement was fair under all the circumstances; or would such rules encourage excessive claims?

Consider Garrett v. Moore-McCormack Co., 317 U.S. 239 (1942), where the court held that the federal rule as to the release executed by a seaman should be applied in a state court action on a federal law claim. Mr. Justice Black stated:

"We hold, therefore, that the burden is upon one who sets up a seaman's release to show that it was executed freely, without deception or coercion, and that it was made by the seaman, with full understanding of his rights. The adequacy of the consideration and the nature of the medical and *legal advice available* to the seaman at the time of signing the release are relevant to an appraisal of this understanding." (Emphasis added.)

Chapter VII

THE ADVOCATE

SECTION 1. THE NATURE OF A TRIAL

REPORT OF THE JOINT CONFERENCE ON
PROFESSIONAL RESPONSIBILITY

1958 A.A.L.S. Pro. 187, 188, 44 A.B.A.J. 1159, 1160 (1958).

The Lawyer's Role as Advocate in Open Court

The lawyer appearing as an advocate before a tribunal presents, as persuasively as he can, the facts and the law of the case as seen from the standpoint of his client's interest. It is essential that both the lawyer and the public understand clearly the nature of the role thus discharged. Such an understanding is required not only to appreciate the need for an adversary presentation of issues, but also in order to perceive truly the limits partisan advocacy must impose on itself if it is to remain wholesome and useful.

In a very real sense it may be said that the integrity of the adjudicative process itself depends upon the participation of the advocate. This becomes apparent when we contemplate the nature of the task assumed by an arbiter who attempts to decide a dispute without the aid of partisan advocacy.

Such an arbiter must undertake, not only the role of judge, but that of representative for both of the litigants. . . .

These, then, are the reasons for believing that partisan advocacy plays a vital and essential role in one of the most fundamental procedures of a democratic society. . . . In whatever form adjudication may appear, the experienced judge or arbitrator desires and actively seeks to obtain an adversary presentation of the issues. Only when he has had the benefit of intelligent and vigorous advocacy on both sides can he feel fully confident of his decision.

Viewed in this light, the role of the lawyer as a partisan advocate appears not as a regrettable necessity, but as an indispensable part of a larger ordering of affairs. The institution of advocacy is not a concession to the frailties of human nature, but an expression of human insight in the design of a social framework within which man's capacity for impartial judgment can attain its fullest realization. . . .

It is small wonder, then, that failure generally attends the attempt to dispense with the distinct roles traditionally implied in adjudication. What generally occurs in practice is that at some early point a familiar pattern will seem to emerge from the evidence; an accustomed label is waiting for the case and, without awaiting further proofs, this label is promptly assigned to it. . . . What starts as a preliminary diagnosis designed to direct the inquiry tends, quickly and imperceptibly, to become a fixed conclusion, as all that confirms the diagnosis makes a strong imprint on the mind, while all that runs counter to it is received with diverted attention.

An adversary presentation seems the only effective means for combatting this natural human tendency to judge too swiftly in terms of the familiar that which is not yet fully known. The arguments of counsel hold the case, as it were, in suspension between two opposing interpretations of it. While the proper classification of the case is thus kept unresolved, there is time to explore all of its peculiarities and nuances. . . .

When we take into account the preparations that must precede the hearing, the essential quality of the advocate's contribution becomes even more apparent. . . .

The matter assumes a very different aspect when the deciding tribunal is compelled to take into its own hands the preparations that must precede the public hearing. . . .

NOTES

(1) "A suit [in which there are no effective adversaries for the parties] is collusive because it is not in any real sense adversary. It does not assume the 'honest and actual antagonistic assertion of rights' to be adjudicated—a safeguard essential to the integrity of the judicial process and one which we have held to be indispensable to adjudication of constitutional questions by this Court." U. S. v. Johnson, 319 U.S. 302, 305 (1943).

(2) "Our system is one where counsel are zealously committed to, and often identified with, one side, and where the judges of fact are limited in their ability to grasp facts, exposed to prejudice, and much influenced by counsel skillful in leading them. These conditions greatly affect the advocate's duties and responsibilities as one concerned in the administration of justice. They leave him in the open field of every-day responsibility, unsheltered by any professional immunity, and answerable to public judgment for whatever he does, or tries to do, for his client." Warner, *The Responsibilities of the Lawyer*, 19 A.B.A. Rep. 319, 328, (1896). See also Chapter XIV, p. 502, infra.

(3) To what extent should the adversary process be availed of to resolve disputes in our competitive society? Consider the problems involved in a university disciplining its students or a church, political party, trade union or fraternal organization seeking to apply sanctions to its members. In Section 5, infra, alternatives to the adversary system are considered and in Chapter VI, supra, the role of the lawyer as negotiator is discussed.

(4) The adversary system is sometimes contrasted with the inquisitorial system, especially in the preparation and trial of criminal cases. The adversary system lays stress on the zeal and self interest of the parties and of

their lawyers. The inquisitorial system places primary reliance on the competence, thoroughness and fairness of the public tribunal and its representatives. See discussion, Chapter IV, Section 3, A Glance at Other Systems, supra p. 213.

(5) Under both adversary and inquisitorial systems a public trial is one of the means whereby society seeks protection for itself and for individuals. A balance must be struck between "efficiency" in the public interest and "due process" for the individual. For an interesting discussion of both systems and the procedural pitfalls they share see Morrissey, *Escobedo's European Ancestors*, 52 A.B.A.J. 723 (1966).

(6) See Chapter III, page 173, supra, for a discussion of "Free Press v. Free Trial" and Chapter III, page 177, supra, for a discussion of "Television in the Courtroom."

EDMUND M. MORGAN,[*] FOREWORD, MODEL CODE OF EVIDENCE, AMERICAN LAW INSTITUTE[**]

Pages 3-4 (1942).

Thoughtful lawyers realize that a lawsuit is not, and cannot be made, a scientific investigation for the discovery of truth. The matter to be investigated is determined by the parties. They may eliminate many elements which a scientist would insist upon considering. The court has no machinery for discovering sources of information unknown to the parties or undisclosed by them. It must rely in the main upon data furnished by interested persons. The material event or condition may have been observed by only a few. The capacities and stimuli of each of these few for accurately observing and remembering will vary. The ability and desire to narrate truly may be slight or great. The trier of fact can get no more than the adversaries are able and willing to present. The rules governing the acceptable content of the data and the methods and forms of presenting them must be almost instantly applied in the heat and hurry of the trial. Prompt decision on the merits is imperative, for justice delayed is often justice denied. Sometimes a wrong decision quickly made is better than a right decision after undue procrastination. "Some concession must be made to the shortness of human life." The trier must assume that the data presented are complete, and the litigants must be satisfied with a determination of the preponderance of probability. If the data leave the mind of the trier in equilibrium, the decision must be against the party having the burden of persuasion. No scientist would think of basing a conclusion upon such data so presented. The court is not a scientific body. It is composed of one or more persons skilled in the law, skilled in the general art of investigation, but not necessarily skilled in the field which the dispute concerns, acting either alone or

---

[*] The late Professor Morgan taught for many years at Harvard; later at Vanderbilt Law School.

[**] Copyright 1946. Reprinted with the permission of the American Law Institute.

with a body of men not necessarily trained in investigation of any kind. Its final determination is binding only between the parties and their privies. It does not pronounce upon the facts for any purpose other than the adjustment of the controversy before it. Consequently there must be a recognition at the outset that nicely accurate results cannot be expected; that society and the litigants must be content with a rather rough approximation of what a scientist might demand. And it must never be forgotten that in the settlement of disputes in a court room, as in all other experiences of individuals in our society, the emotions of the persons involved—litigants, counsel, witnesses, judge and jurors—will play a part. A trial cannot be a purely intellectual performance.

All this is not to say that the rules for conducting the investigation of the facts cannot be, or need not be, rational. Quite the contrary.

NOTE

"Some evidence may be excluded which could have helped to establish the facts. Yet, surely, a trial has purposes other than to lay reality bare. A trial is a part of government's teaching apparatus. Social values of the greatest importance receive expression in the courtroom. To reach a decision in accordance with the truth is only one value which, in some circumstances, may have to bow before others." Paulsen, *The Exclusionary Rule and Misconduct by the Police*, 50 Crim.L.C. & P.S. 255 (1961).

SIR JOHN MACDONELL, HISTORICAL TRIALS *

Pages 15, 86 (1927).

I come to the questions which twenty centuries have reiterated and which are still fresh. Was it a fair trial? Was Socrates guilty? Was the defence a sophism? Did he corrupt the youth? Was the result a judicial error or a judicial murder? I do not believe that to these questions there ever will be one answer. There will always be those who prize order and the interests of the community above all else; who make the safety of the State the supreme law; and they will answer as did Hegel, as many others have done since: "It was a good deed, a necessary deed; Socrates must die that the people might live and be strong." That was the opinion of the majority of his fellow citizens; and there is no reason to believe that they repented, at all events until long afterwards. . . .

. . . [F]ear brings back the primitive conception of the function of courts; not necessarily, or indeed often, personal fear, but fear of changes; fear on the part of the upholders of the old order; fear of the effects of the discoveries of new truths; fear of emerging into the full light. Where such fear is justice cannot be; a court becomes

---

* With the permission of the Clarendon Press, Oxford.

an instrument of power; judges are soldiers putting down rebellion; a so-called trial is a punitive expedition or a ceremonial execution—its victim a Bruno, a Galileo, or a Dreyfus.

NOTES

(1) The student will no doubt think of other and more recent examples of political trials—e. g., after the assumption of power by Fidel Castro in Cuba. It is interesting in this connection to remember the criticism of the verdict at Nuremberg by the late Senator Robert Taft in the face of the inevitable political penalty to be paid by him. See Paston, *Superior Orders As Affecting Responsibility for War Crimes* (1946).

(2) "In periods of generally received moral systems, the contrast between legal results and strict ethical requirements will appeal only to individuals. In periods of free individual thought in morals and ethics, and especially in an age of social and industrial transition, this contrast is greatly intensified and appeals to large classes of society. Justice, which is the end of law, is the ideal compromise between the activities of each and the activities of all in a crowded world. The law seeks to harmonize these activities and to adjust the relations of every man with his fellows so as to accord with the moral sense of the community. When the community is at one in its ideas of justice, this is possible. When the community is divided and diversified, and groups and classes and interests understanding each other none too well, have conflicting ideas of justice, the task is extremely difficult. It is impossible that legal and ethical ideas should be in entire accord in such a society. The individual looks at cases one by one and measures them by his individual sense of right and wrong. The lawyer must look at cases in gross, and must measure them largely by an artificial standard. He must apply the ethics of the community, not his own. If discretion is given him, his view will be that of the class from which he comes. If his hands are tied by law, he must apply the ethics of the past as formulated in common law and legislation. In either event, judicial and individual ethical standards will diverge. And this divergence between the ethical and the legal, as each individual sees it, makes him say with Luther, 'Good jurist, bad Christian'." Pound, *The Causes of Popular Dissatisfaction With the Administration of Justice*, 29 A.B.A.Rep. 395, 398–99 (1906).

(3) ". . . [I]t is also important to realise that neither speed, nor cheapness nor universality are the ultimate ends of litigation. The ultimate end is justice and the only foundation upon which a scheme of this kind, or any other scheme for the improvement of litigation, can be founded is the knowledge that justice, when it comes, will be the best and nearest approach to the truth and to the right assessment of liability that human wisdom and skill can give. Nothing short of that will give prestige or respect to a system of litigation or dispensation in any country." The Hon. Quintin Hogg * Debate in the House of Commons on the Legal Aid and Advice Act, 1949, 465 Hansard, Col. 1379, quoted in Eric Sachs, *Legal Aid* 39 (1945), Eyre & Spottiswoode, publishers.

---

* As Lord Hailsham this barrister later gave up a promising career in the House of Commons but went on to become Chairman of the Conservative Party.

ROSCOE POUND, THE CAUSES OF POPULAR DISSATISFACTION WITH THE ADMINISTRATION OF JUSTICE

29 Am.Bar Ass'n Rep. 395, 404 (1906)

A no less potent source of . . . [dissatisfaction with the administration of justice] lies in our American exaggerations of the common law contentious procedure. The sporting theory of justice, the "instinct of giving the game fair play," as Professor Wigmore has put it, is so rooted in the profession in America that most of us take it for a fundamental legal tenet. But it is probably only a survival of the days when a lawsuit was a fight between two clans in which change of venue had been taken to the forum. So far from being a fundamental fact of jurisprudence, it is peculiar to Anglo-American law; and it has been strongly curbed in modern English practice. With us, it is not merely in full acceptance, it has been developed and its collateral possibilities have been cultivated to the furthest extent. Hence in America we take it as a matter of course that a judge should be a mere umpire, to pass upon objections and hold counsel to the rules of the game, and that the parties should fight out their own game in their own way without judicial interference.

HUTCHESON, REVIEW OF WIGMORE, THE PRINCIPLES OF JUDICIAL PROOF

17 A.B.A.J. 817, 819 (1931).

The book makes it clear how the problems of judicial proof are made more problematical by the dramatic conditions under which they are adduced. All preparation for judicial proof looks toward, and all such proof is finally presented in a trial, an action in form dramatic in every case, and in fact overwhelmingly so in many of them; especially in criminal cases to which public interest attaches is this dramatic feature present and operative. It affects the witnesses, the lawyers, the litigants, the triers themselves. It is this—that the conclusions of the triers do not come as the result of cold and careful reasoning upon data coolly, carefully and in a wholly non-partisan way supplied—which gives the intensely dramatic character to a trial. These conclusions are reached always in the atmosphere of drama, often under the pressure of emotional stress, and the book makes clear that it is rare that the verdict in a criminal trial, and it is of these trials that a great part of the book treats, is wholly free from the influences, the feelings, the antagonisms, which litigants have been able to arouse and to inject into a case.

ERIC BENTLEY, VIETNAM THE STATE OF OUR FEELINGS

The Columbia University Forum, Summer, 1967. Col. 1, page 10

Now, however much they are backed up with reason and truth, stands are emotional. However much can be said for any cause by way of fact and by way of argument, it is still a question why . . . in the end we decided to invest so much emotion, so much of ourselves, in that cause. I come here to the subject of commitment. To be committed is not to favor the idea of commitment, it is to *make* commitments—and stand by them.

SHEPPARD v. MAXWELL

Supreme Court of the United States, 1966.
384 U.S. 333, 86 S.Ct. 1507, 16 L.Ed.2d 600.
(The case appears supra p. 175).

NOTE

The constitutional status of television, the "hottest" of the media, in the courtroom was discussed in Estes v. State of Texas, 381 U.S. 532 (1965), supra p. 177.

THE ART

GEOFFREY LAWRENCE,[*] THE ART OF ADVOCACY

50 A.B.A.J. 1121 (1964).

The art of advocacy is one of the oldest of the arts of civilization. You can go back to the great orators of classical times: Demosthenes in fifth-century Athens; Cicero in Imperial Rome; Quintilian in Rome, perhaps the greatest and most practiced technician of them all, who said there were three qualities which an orator should display —he should instruct, he should move and he should delight.

Too often today we limit ourselves to the first of these, mere instruction. That is not enough. There are occasions when you must move people. You must move the court. You must move the jury. There are occasions also when, to rivet and fix their attention, you must delight them.

The study of this art of persuasion in the trial courts is something quite different from the study of the law itself. It was once

---

[*] Sir Geoffrey Lawrence is a Queen's Counsellor with more than 30 years' experience at the Bar. The quotation is from an address before the Section of Judicial Administration during the 1964 annual meeting of the American Bar Association.

said that the qualities you need for success at the Bar are high spirits, a good sense of humor, capacity for hard work, immense vitality and a sense of good fellowship, and if to all those you could add a little knowledge of the law, so much the better.

JOHN BUCHAN,* THE JUDICIAL TEMPERAMENT, IN HOMILIES AND RECREATIONS
Pages 211–213 (1926).

The specific qualities of the advocate are, I think, universally understood. You will find them analyzed by a succession of competent authorities from Cicero downwards. The root of the talent is simply the power to persuade—a power which is shared by such diverse characters as saints and company promoters, Abraham Lincoln or Mr. Gladstone and the soap-box orator at the street corner. This power depends upon knowledge of human nature, and it is applied both to the intellect and to the passions of the hearers. The legal advocate must make both appeals or he fails in the highest walks of advocacy. He has to deal with juries of average men, and he must lay his mind alongside theirs and speak their own language. It used to be said of a recent English Chief Justice that he succeeded largely because his mind was more average than that of the average juryman. On that side, the art, whether it be spontaneous or nicely calculated, is based upon an understanding of human nature and the capacity to arouse the more obvious human emotions. It is no more than a superior form of demagogy.

But the advocate has also to deal with the Bench, and there a subtler art is needed. Knowledge of human nature is again the first requirement, but it is a more sophisticated type of human nature. There must, of course, be a certain appeal to the intellect, but advocacy is rarely a cold-blooded impersonal dialectic. The temperament of the judge must be considered. The Bench has its work to get through and it looks to the Bar for assistance, and that advocate will be the best verdict-getter who divines most shrewdly what kind of assistance this or that judge requires.

Advocacy, therefore, is a subtle and varied art, and at its best it will cover an almost infinite range of human nature. But consider what it is. It is primarily a psychological appeal and not the dry light of reason. There is nothing judicial about it; nay, the judicial is at a discount. That is why the very great advocate is very rarely a great judge, and, if he is, it is because of the possession of qualities which were not revealed in his advocacy.

---

* As Lord Tweedsmuir this fine lawyer and writer was known to many Americans during his term as Governor-General of Canada.

SECTION 2. THE ZEAL OF THE ADVOCATE

Introduction. Read again the extract from the Report of the Joint Conference on Professional Responsibility, supra p. 272. The section on the Lawyer's Role as Advocate in Open Court concludes: When advocacy is thus viewed, it becomes clear by what principle limits must be set to partisanship. The advocate plays a role well when zeal for his client's cause promotes a wise and informed decision of the case. He plays his role badly, and trespasses against the obligations of professional responsibility, when his desire to win leads him to muddy the headwaters of decision, when, instead of lending a needed perspective to the controversy, he distorts and obscures its true nature.

NOTE

For a perceptive study see E. Wayne Thode, *The Ethical Standard for the Advocate,* 39 Texas L.Rev. 575 (1961).

MEASURE OF ZEAL—ONE EXTREME

WILLIAM FORSYTHE, HORTENSIUS

Page 389 (3d Ed., 1879).

The most highly coloured picture of the devotion which an advocate is supposed to owe to his client is that drawn by Lord Brougham in the well-known and striking passage that occurs in his defence of Queen Caroline before the House of Lords. "I once before took occasion to remind your lordships, which was unnecessary, but there are many whom it may be needful to remind, that an advocate, by the sacred duty which he owes his client, knows in the discharge of that office but one person in the world, that client and none other. To save that client by all expedient means, to protect that client at all hazards and costs, to all others, and among others to himself, is the highest and most unquestioned of his duties; and he must not regard the alarm, the suffering, the torment, the destruction which he may bring upon any other. Nay, separating even the duties of a patriot from those of an advocate, and casting them, if need be, to the wind, he must go on reckless of the consequences, if his fate it should unhappily be to involve his country in confusion for his client's protection."

NOTES

(1) To this passage, the author appended the following footnote:

"It will be interesting to quote, with reference to this passage, an extract from a letter I received from Lord Brougham in 1859. He says—

"'I wish to mention to you, in reference to what you discuss in chapter 10 on the duties and rights of an advocate, and where you refer to what has been so often the subject of dispute, my statement in the Queen's case. The real truth is, that the statement was anything rather than a deliberate and well-considered opinion. It was a menace, and it was addressed chiefly to George IV, but also to wiser men, such as Castlereagh and Wellington. I was prepared, *in case of necessity*, that is, in case the Bill passed the Lords, to do two things—first, to resist it in the Commons *with the country at my back*; but next, if need be, to dispute the King's title, to show he had forfeited the crown by marrying a Catholic, in the words of the Act 'as if he were naturally dead.' What I said was fully understood by Geo. IV; perhaps by the Duke and Castlereagh, and I am confident it would have prevented them from pressing the Bill beyond a certain point.'"

(2) In Third Great Western Turnpike Road Co. v. Loomis, 32 N.Y. 127, 133 (1865), the court quoted this "atrocious but memorable declaration" by Lord Brougham, and said "Such a proposition shocks the moral sense. . ."

The setting of Lord Brougham's famous speech is well shown in J. B. Atlay, 1 The Victorian Chancellors Chap. XI, (1906).

(3) See Costigan, *The Full Remarks on Advocacy of Lord Brougham and Lord Chief Justice Cockburn at the Dinner to M. Berryer on November 8, 1864*, Copyright © 1931, California Law Review, Inc. Reprinted by Permission. Lord Chief Justice Cockburn said: "My noble and learned friend, Lord Brougham, whose words are the words of wisdom, said that an advocate should be fearless in carrying out the interests of his client; but I couple that with this qualification and this restriction—that the arms which he wields are to be the arms of the warrior and not of the assassin. It is his duty to strive to accomplish the interests of his clients per fas, but not per nefas; it is his duty, to the utmost of his power, to seek to reconcile the interests he is bound to maintain, and the duty it is incumbent upon him to discharge, with the eternal and immutable interests of truth and justice."

MEASURE OF ZEAL—THE OTHER EXTREME

THE NEW YORK TIMES

Dec. 14, 1949, pp. 1, 9. Sofia, Bulgaria, Dec. 13.

Traicho Kostov, former Bulgarian Vice Premier, again denied in the Supreme Court in Sofia today that he was guilty of charges of espionage or treason. . . .

Lueben Diukmejiev, Mr. Kostov's defense counsel, an elderly, white-haired Sofia lawyer, set the pattern for the defense of the accused this morning when he made a long exposition of the duties of a defense lawyer in a Socialist state as distinct from that in a Western "bourgeois" state. He rejected the idea of a lawyer's defending a criminal by scoring technical points once he knew the criminal was guilty.

"In a Socialist state there is no division of duty between the judge, prosecutor and defense counsel," he said. "The defense must assist the prosecution to find objective truth in a case."

He apologized for defending Mr. Kostov, as did all other defense counsel, but pointed out that under the Constitution all accused had a right to a defense.

Mr. Diukmejiev said Mr. Kostov had asked him to point out two facts in connection with the charge that Mr. Kostov was an agent and ally of Marshal Tito of Yugoslavia.

The first was that it was Mr. Kostov who presented an anti-Tito report at the Bucharest meeting that expelled Marshal Tito from the Communist Information Bureau.

"This, of course," counsel explained, "is hardly a serious argument, as Mr. Kostov was presenting a report only in behalf of the Central Committee of the Bulgarian Communist Party."

The second point was that at the congress of the Yugoslav Communist party in June, 1948, Marshal Tito had said Yugoslav Communists had always believed that Mr. Kostov and an official named Gechev (police chief who was allegedly a British agent and had spared Mr. Kostov's life in return for Mr. Kostov's signed declaration to co-operate with the police) were agents for some foreign power.

"Marshal Tito," according to the defense counsel, "was only covering up his tracks for the day when Mr. Kostov would be arrested, so that he could prove Mr. Kostov had not been his agent."

Mr. Diukmejiev concluded: "If Traicho Kostov finds words to show he recognizes his crimes, then I beg this may be taken in his favor." . . .

AND A FOOTNOTE

THE NEW YORK TIMES, April 4, 1956, p. 1. Headline:

"Bulgaria Clears Name of Kostov,
Vindicates Leader Executed in 1949."

[ed. note.: The above article does not state what happened to Kostov's lawyer.]

IN RE METZGER

Supreme Court of the Territory of Hawaii, 1931.
31 Haw. 929 (Sup.Ct. 1931).

[In the course of a trial for murder, the defendant's lawyer, the present respondent, secured a continuance of a case while he was cross-examining the hand-writing expert for the state. During the continuance, respondent got from the clerk the samples of writing which the witness identified as coming from the same hand. Then, disclosing his plan to disinterested attorneys who found no fault with it, he simulated one of the exhibits on another blank. He had a witness present while he did it, and it was carefully but secretly marked so as to distinguish it from the original. On returning to court when the trial was resumed, he returned to the clerk the simulated copy, not disclosing to him the simulation, and refusing to take back his receipt with the explanation that there would be further transactions. Then in the midst of his continued cross-examination of the expert he asked the clerk for "the papers". The clerk handed him the papers, including the simulated copy, and these were presented to the witness. The copy was used in the cross-examination of the expert.

The present proceeding is an information by the attorney general charging the lawyer with misconduct. The majority of the court found the respondent's conduct was improper, and he was suspended for ten days.]

PERRY, CHIEF JUSTICE. . . . The plan had been carefully devised. His express purpose, as he admitted at the hearing in this court in answer to a question by a member of the court, was, in saying what he said and in doing what he did, to deceive the witness into thinking that he was handing him the genuine exhibit "E." The plan devised and followed was well calculated to accomplish that purpose; and succeeded. . . . When, after a lengthy examination and a lengthy cross-examination upon the handwriting of the letter, the envelope and the genuine card, the clerk, in answer to the cross-examining attorney's request, produced the letter and a card, the witness had a right to believe, and could only believe, that the card was the genuine exhibit "E." The presentation by the respondent to the witness of a card as exhibit "E" was a deliberate misrepresentation. . . .

There can be no doubt that it was the right and the duty of the respondent, who was entrusted with the defense of two men who were on trial for their lives, to expose if he could what he believed to be a lack of ability and a lack of credibility or accuracy on the part of the witness who had testified as an expert on handwriting; but there was a limitation upon that right and that duty and the limitation was that the test and the exposure must be accomplished by fair and lawful means, free from falsehood and misrepresentation. . . .

BANKS, J., [dissenting.] Metzger's right to impeach by every proper means Bailey's opinion that the letter, envelope and card were written by the same hand it seems to me must be conceded. Indeed it was not only his right to do this but his duty to do so—his duty to his clients, to the jury and to the court. . . . His purpose was not the evil one of misleading the jury as to a fact which he knew existed but the laudable one of exposing what he believed to be an erroneous opinion. This was in the interest of justice and not against it. . . .

I do not think that his treatment of the witness was unfair. . . . I think the ethical quality of everything that Metzger did in carrying out the plan he devised for testing the accuracy of Bailey's opinion must be judged by the motive that actuated him to make the test, *unless what he did was otherwise inherently wrong.*

I cannot agree that Metzger did anything wrong and I therefore most respectfully dissent from the majority opinion.

NOTE

. . . "It will thus be seen that respondent has not been remiss to his clients in his representation of them. In fact, his breaches of ethics result from the opposite attitude—he has been overzealous in his efforts on their behalf to the unwarranted extent that he has made serious departures from ethical conduct on their behalf. Where this results in deliberate falsification for the purpose of obtaining more than the client is entitled to, the seriousness of the charge is not lessened because it was done to further a client's interests. Giving effect to all that was established in the record, we conclude that, while it has not been shown that respondent has demonstrated unfitness to remain a member of the bar, to impress the gravity of his breaches of ethics both on himself and as an example to others, suspension from practice is required.

"Respondent is suspended from practice for a period of three years. All concur." In re Ander, 22 App.Div.2d 14, 15, 253 N.Y.S.2d 323, 325 (First Dep't., 1964).

IN RE SACHER

United States Court of Appeals, Second Circuit, 1953.
206 F.2d 358.

AUGUSTUS N. HAND, CIRCUIT JUDGE. This is an appeal from an order disbarring the respondent for professional misconduct while the jury was being selected and during the course of the trial of the communist leaders, who had been indicted under the "Smith Act," 18 U.S.C.A. § 2385, for advocating the overthrow of the government of the United States by force and violence, United States v. Dennis, 2 Cir., 183 F.2d 201, affirmed 341 U.S. 494, 71 S.Ct. 857, 95 L.Ed. 1137. The present proceeding was commenced by the service of an order to show cause issued upon a petition by the Association of the Bar of the City of New York and the New York County Lawyers' Association. On the trial before the District Court sitting without a jury the only evidence introduced was the record of the trial and the preliminary proceedings in the Dennis case—the respondent offered no testimony on his behalf. In a carefully considered opinion Judge Hincks held that the instances of misconduct shown by this record required Sacher's disbarment, although the judge stated: "I find in the entire record no intimation that his conduct was tainted by venality or lack of fidelity to the interests of his clients,—offenses which demonstrate a moral turpitude wholly absent here. His fault, rather, seems to have stemmed from a temperament which led to such excess of zeal in representing his clients that it obscured his recognition of responsibility as an officer of the court. Thus the very qualities which in my judgment make him professionally unfit to remain a member of this Bar might well be unobjectionable in commercial fields where competitive effort is not subject to the restraints required of an officer of the Court. For instance, in negotiations . . . I should expect that he would be a trustworthy and highly effective representative. . . ."

Paragraph 15 of the petition of the Bar Associations charged 36 instances of improper conduct, of which the court held 28 had been proved, requiring disbarment. Two of the specifications were discussed in detail by the District Court as evidencing particularly serious misconduct and have been emphasized on this appeal by the respondent as influencing the discipline imposed. One related to the continuation of a cross-examination by Sacher which the court permitted under what the respondent knew to be a misapprehension of facts which he failed to correct. . . . We agree with the court below that his failure to correct the trial judge's misapprehension was a violation of his professional duty. . . .

In any event disbarment was decreed on other independent grounds which we believe fully justified the order. Two types of conduct alleged in Paragraph 16 of the Bar Associations' petition were each held to require that the respondent be no longer allowed to practice before the court. This paragraph charged that Sacher "persistently, in disregard of the repeated warnings and orders of the Court, argued without permission; [and] refused to desist from argument and comment" and that he made "insolent, sarcastic, impertinent and disrespectful remarks to the Court and conducted himself in a provocative manner." For a few examples of respondent's conduct see our opinion in United States v. Sacher, 2 Cir., 182 F.2d 416, at 423–24, aff'd 343 U.S. 1, 72 S.Ct. 451, 96 L.Ed. 717. . . .

Basically the respondent's argument is that in view of his previous unblemished record disbarment is too severe a discipline to impose for conduct in part brought on by the demands of an unusual and important trial which took place in an atmosphere of hostility toward the defendants. . . .

The purpose of striking an attorney from the rolls of a court is not to punish him but to protect the court itself and relieve the public of a member of the legal profession, who is unfit to serve as such, in order to maintain the respect due the court by insuring that attorneys, who are "officers of the court," are of good professional character. See Matter of Rouss, 221 N.Y. 81, 85, 116 N.E. 782. Because the consequences of disbarment are necessarily severe, it is a measure to be exercised only for compelling reasons. See Ex parte Wall, 107 U.S. 265, 288, 2 S.Ct. 569, 27 L.Ed. 552. In the case at bar we think that the proved instances of unprofessional conduct, constantly repeated in the face of the court's admonitions, and continuing during a trial of extended duration, clearly demonstrated a lack of respect for the court and constituted a serious obstruction to the administration of justice. It is evident that the respondent either was unable to comprehend his obligations to a court of law or was unwilling to fulfill them when he felt it inexpedient to do so. Even if a less severe measure of discipline might have been imposed, we do not find any abuse of discretion in disbarring the respondent from practice such as was found to exist in In re Doe, 2 Cir., 95 F.2d 386. See In re Chopak, 2 Cir., 160 F.2d 886, 887, certiorari denied 331 U.S. 835, 67 S.Ct. 1516, 91 L.Ed. 1848.

Order affirmed.

CLARK, CIRCUIT JUDGE (dissenting). . . . so we have the result—surely anomalous and not duplicated elsewhere in the precedents—of absolute disbarment of a lawyer whose conduct has no taint of "venality or lack of fidelity to the interests of his clients," but only an "excess of zeal in representing his clients" or qualities "unobjectionable in commercial fields" or making him in negotiations "a trustworthy and highly effective representative." There must be something topsy-turvey when in "our contentious craft"—to use the Supreme Court's apt expression—a lawyer loses his profession permanently for displaying those very qualities most often associated with it. I do not believe that can be the law.

NOTES

(1) On appeal to the Supreme Court, the judgment was reversed. In a per curiam decision the Court said, "At the time the District Court made its decision in this case, the contempt judgment was under review on appeal, and it did not know and could not know that petitioner would be obliged to serve, as he did, a six months' sentence for the same conduct for which it disbarred him. In view of this entire record and of the findings of the courts below, we are of the opinion that permanent disbarment in this case is unnecessarily severe. The judgment is reversed and the case remanded to the District Court for further consideration and appropriate action not inconsistent with this opinion." Two justices dissented. Sacher v. Association of the Bar of the City of New York, 347 U.S. 388 (1954).

(2) For the treatment accorded another lawyer for the defense in the same prosecution of leaders of the Communist Party, see In re Isserman, 9 N.J. 269 (1952). Isserman was disbarred from practice before the courts of New Jersey. See also In re Isserman, 345 U.S. 286 (1952), in which he was disbarred from practice before the Supreme Court of the United States. The latter decision was reversed in In re Isserman, 348 U.S. 1 (1954).

(3) Lawyers have in the past been subject to discipline for impugning the integrity of a court and undermining public confidence in the judiciary in this fashion. They have also been disciplined for obstructing the administration of justice in a particular case. Garrison v. Louisiana, 379 U.S. 64 (1964), imposed limits on the "impugning" rule so far as a criminal proceeding against an attorney for public criticism of judges is concerned. The court held that truthful criticism of the manner in which public officials, including judges, conducted their business was absolutely privileged against criminal prosecution and that even false statements were privileged unless made knowingly or with reckless disregard for the truth. The court relied heavily on New York Times Co. v. Sullivan, 376 U.S. 254 (1964), where similar restrictions were placed on the right of public officials to recover damages in a civil defamation action. Is there any reason to believe disciplinary proceedings against attorneys who criticize judges will not be subject to the same constitutional limitations as those imposed in *Garrison* and *N. Y. Times*?

(4) Is there a distinction between the right of attorneys generally to criticize courts and their decisions and the right of an attorney of record in a pending case to criticize? In re Sawyer, 360 U.S. 622 (1959), reversed an attorney's suspension from practice for "impugning the integrity" of a judge presiding over a Smith Act trial, the suspended attorney serving as defense counsel. Justice Brennan, writing the majority opinion, emphasized that lawyers, whether of record or not, were free to criticize the law as unfair and a judge as in error without thereby impugning the integrity of the judge. Four dissenting justices would uphold the suspension on the ground that defense counsel's speech impaired the administration of justice in the pending case. Justice Brennan conceded that in some instances "remarks made during the course of a trial might tend to such obstruction where remarks made afterwards would not." (p. 636).

THE NEED FOR RESTRAINTS

The necessity for limitations on the zeal of the advocate can, perhaps, be indicated by a comparison of our economic system with our legal system. The capitalist system of economic organization and the adversary system of administration of justice are similar in that both have competition as a basic element. In the 1930's when the New Deal was in full swing, an opponent of Mr. Roosevelt made the comment on his proposals for life-long security for the individual: "The capitalist system is a hell of a system. And it just won't work if you try to take all the hell out of it." The further comment might be added: "And it just won't work if you leave all the hell in it."

Both comments can be applied to the adversary system in the administration of justice. The competitive element is valuable in law as well as in business for the stimulus it gives. But no such idea, valuable though it is, can be pushed to its logical extreme. It meets limitations derived from other elements and other ideas.

The adversary system calls for loyal effort by a lawyer in behalf of his client. It will destroy itself unless it develops other affirmative obligations as well as restraints which are needful for the effective performance of its role in the administration of justice.

NOTES

(1) For a challenging statement of the duty of the lawyer see Curtis, *The Ethics of Advocacy,* 4 Stan.L.Rev. 3, (1951):

> "I want first of all to put advocacy in its proper setting. It is a special case of vicarious conduct. A lawyer devotes his life and career to acting for other people. So too does the priest, and in another way the banker. The banker handles other people's money. The priest handles other people's spiritual aspirations. A lawyer handles other people's troubles.
>
> "But there is a difference. The loyalty of a priest or clergyman runs not to the particular parishioner . . . but to his church; and the banker looks to his bank. . . . So too when a lawyer works for the government. His loyalties hang on a superior peg. . . . Not so the lawyer in private practice. His loyalty runs to his client. He has no other master."

(2) For a reply see Drinker, *Some Remarks on Mr. Curtis' "The Ethics of Advocacy,"* 4 Stan.L.Rev. 349 (1952).

(3) For a fuller statement of the views of Mr. Curtis, in a chapter which discusses the advocate's position and loyalty, see Curtis, It's Your Law (1954) Chap. I, "The Advocate."

PREPARATION

The lawyer's devotion to his client calls for something more difficult than courage and vigor at the trial. It calls for thorough and effective preparation of the case before trial. The following statements are from a trial judge and a trial lawyer.

"The effect which preparation or lack of preparation has on the result is, of course, hard to measure with any degree of accuracy, because of the many other factors, and is matter of opinion in the particular case. During the years 1926 and 1927 I sat in the trial parts only, and made procedural and other notes on almost every case. Examination of these notes, I was surprised to find, discloses that out of 33 cases tried in the second year, where one or more lawyers impressed me as below standard in this respect, in nearly 82% of the instances where I criticized plaintiff's counsel, and in nearly 85% of those where it was defendant's counsel, the lack of preparation was in my opinion directly responsible for a result unfavorable to the client." Philip James McCook, Trials and the Art of Advocacy (1933).

"The first essential is to prepare the case. This may be done by the trial lawyer himself, but because of lack of time it generally devolves upon tried and trusted younger men of capacity. . . . I once talked to a Federal judge who had tried a long and very complicated criminal case under the Sherman Act. . . . The judge criticized the chief defense counsel because his case was 'over-prepared.' I told the judge there was no such animal—that it was easy to over-try a case, but impossible to over-prepare a case." Emory R. Buckner, The Lawyer in Court, 27 A.B.A.J. 5, 6 (1941).

APPEAL TO EMOTION

The Statement of the Joint Conference of the American Bar Association and the Association of American Law Schools on the lawyer's role as advocate, which is quoted at the beginning of the chapter supra p. 272, opens, "The lawyer appearing as an advocate before a tribunal presents, as persuasively as he can, the facts and the law of the case as seen from the standpoint of his client's interest." Professor Morgan, in the excerpt from his writings which follows supra p. 274, notes that ". . . it must never be forgotten that in the settlement of disputes in a court room, as in all other experiences of individuals in our society, the emotions of the persons involved—the litigants, counsel, witnesses, judge and jurors—will play a part. A trial cannot be a purely intellectual performance."

We now consider more specifically what feelings may be appealed to, what methods may be used to stir the feelings, and where the answers to these questions are to be found—in rules of law or in the standards of the profession. Advocacy being a part of the general experience of mankind, we may assume that when the appeal is made to feelings generally shared and approved, it is more apt to be upheld. When the appeal is to emotions which our ideals seek to allay rather than to inflame, it may be condemned.

JEROME MICHAEL, THE BASIC RULES OF PLEADING

5 Record Ass'n. Bar City N.Y. 175, 199 (1950).

At this point I am going to say something which you may find very shocking. Judge Coleman is supposed to submit an issue to the jury if, as the judges say, the jury can decide reasonably either way. But to say that I can decide an issue of fact reasonably either way is to say, I submit, that I cannot, by the exercise of reason, decide the question. That means that the issue which we typically submit to juries is an issue which the jury cannot decide by the exercise of its reason.

The decision of an issue of fact in cases of closely balanced probabilities, therefore, must, in the nature of things, be an emotional rather than a rational act; and the rules regulating that stage of a trial which we call the stage of persuasion, the stage when lawyers sum up to a jury, recognize that distinction. Time and again, when an objection is made to a summation, the Appellate Court will say in effect: "Counsel, in summation to the jury, do not have to be logical. They have to be logical in proof, but they do not have to be logical in argument."

The point is beautifully made by an old Tennessee case in which the plaintiff's counsel, when summing up to the jury, began to weep, and he wept very copiously. The lawyer for the defendant objected and asked the trial judge to stop him from weeping. Weeping is not a form of argument, is it; not rational argument? Well, the Supreme Court of Tennessee said: "It is not only counsel's privilege to weep for his client; it is his duty to weep for his client." (Laughter)

That makes the point, don't you see, that I am trying to make. We have rules of evidence that are designed to preserve the rational character of the state of a trial when propositions are being proved and disproved. We have rules regulating the stage of persuasion, the stage of argumentation, which are of such a character that irrational considerations may be urged upon the tribunal. Every lawyer who has ever summed up to a jury may not be fully aware of this, but I am sure he has some sense of it.

You see, there are three states of a controversy: pleading, proof and persuasion. Theoretically, those three states are supposed to be isolated from one another. You plead, you prove, and then you persuade. However, everyone knows that rhetorical processes accompany logical processes throughout the trial. That is why we say of some lawyers that they flirt with juries. We all know what that means. When do they begin to flirt? Well, just as soon as they see a juror, they begin to flirt. That indicates that they recognize that in the last analysis it is rhetorical considerations and not logical considerations which are important.

NOTES

(1) For a vivid discussion of "the power of appeals to the biases and prejudices of the jurors", see Frank, J., in Skidmore v. Baltimore & O. R. Co., 167 F.2d 54, 61–64 (2d Cir. 1948).

(2) The difficulties in securing a fair trial when public emotions are aroused is shown in a series of case illustrations. Arthur Garfield Hays, Trial by Prejudice (1933). There continue to be many examples: e. g., Sheppard v. Maxwell, 384 U.S. 333 (1966) Supra p. 175.

NEW YORK CENT. R. R. CO. v. JOHNSON

Supreme Court of the United States, 1929.
279 U.S. 310, 49 S.Ct. 300, 73 L.Ed. 706.

MR. JUSTICE STONE delivered the opinion of the Court.

[Actions for personal injuries alleged to have been caused by the negligent operation of the petitioner's trains. In the federal district court, the plaintiffs recovered judgments, and the judgments were affirmed by the Circuit Court of Appeals. The Supreme Court granted petitions for certiorari.]

. . . All material allegations of the complaint were denied, including those specially setting up the cause and nature of respondent's injuries. In the course of the cross-examination of respondents' witnesses, petitioner's counsel elicited the fact that, following the accident, one of respondent's physicians had administered a treatment usually given for syphilis. He asked other questions tending to show, had favorable answers been received, that she had exhibited symptoms recognized to be those of this disease; that the Wasserman test for syphilis, which had been applied to her by her physician with negative results, was not necessarily conclusive as to its non-existence; that other more reliable tests had not been applied; that the disease might cause the paralysis complained of and the treatment for it produce the other symptoms exhibited by respondent. . . .

In the closing argument petitioner's counsel denied any belief that respondent was afflicted with the disease and disclaimed any purpose to show that her present condition was due to it. He then for the first time suggested, although there was no evidence to support it, that her condition was caused by the administration by one of her physicians, of a specific for syphilis in consequence of a mistaken diagnosis.

Two counsel for respondents participated in the closing argument. The first, who preceded counsel for petitioner, made the following statements to the jury, to which, at several points, objection was made, overruled, and an exception noted:

"But, gentlemen, the vilest defense made in this case, a defense which would bar that girl from all society, intimated in this case that she had the syphilis. That is the defense in this case, that she had syphilis. . . .

"Gentlemen of the jury, they would charge her with a disease which would brand her as bad as a leper and exclude her from the society of decent people. That is the kind of a defense that is in this case, and I resent it. I resent the New York Central coming into this town and saying that that girl has the syphilis and trying to make this jury believe that she has the syphilis. . . . [Counsel further expanded upon and exploited this text.]" . . .

In this condition of the record, the repeated statements of counsel that syphilis was the defense, coupled with the vituperative language which we have quoted and the statements that the petitioner had charged respondent with indecency, made in the face of testimony of respondent's own witness that the disease was frequently transmitted by the use of drinking cups or other innocent means, was not fair comment on the evidence or justified by the record. . . . Their obvious purpose and effect were improperly to influence the verdict by their appeal to passion and prejudice. . . .

Such a bitter and passionate attack on petitioner's conduct of the case, under circumstances tending to stir the resentment and arouse the prejudice of the jury, should have been promptly suppressed. . . . The failure of the trial judge to sustain petitioner's objection or otherwise to make certain that the jury would disregard the appeal, could only have left them with the impression that they might properly be influenced by it in rendering their verdict, and thus its prejudicial effect was enhanced. . . . That the quoted remarks of respondent's counsel so plainly tended to excite prejudice as to be ground for reversal, is, we think, not open to argument. The judgments must be reversed, with instructions to grant a new trial. . . .

As there must be a new trial, attention should be directed to other objectionable conduct by respondent's counsel in the course of the trial; their repeated assertion, without supporting evidence, that the defense was a "claim agent defense"; references to petitioner as an "eastern railroad"; and statements that the railroad had "come into this town" and that witnesses and records had been "sent on from New York" for the trial of the cause. Such remarks of counsel, and others of similar character, all tending to create an atmosphere of hostility toward petitioner as a railroad corporation located in another section of the country, have been so often condemned as an appeal to sectional or local prejudice as to require no comment. . . .

Reversed.

NOTES

(1) In a cross-claim by an air line against an airplane manufacturer, a verdict for the manufacturer was set aside because, "the policy of obstruction and confusion that was pursued by trial counsel for Douglas in this litigation deprived United of a fair trial . . . improper insinuations and assertions both during the course of the trial and in summation . . . were deliberately calculated to mislead the jury." De Vito v. United Air Lines, 98 F.Supp. 88, 100, 105 (D.C.N.Y.1951).

(2) In McCarthy v. Spring Valley Coal Co., 232 Ill. 473 (1908), an action for personal injuries, the court reversed a judgment for the plaintiff: "The statement to the jury that the appellee had a wife and five children was manifestly improper. Its only object could have been to enhance the damages by getting before the jury, in this improper and unprofessional manner, facts calculated to arouse their sympathy, which counsel knew could not in any legitimate way be brought to their attention. . . ."

But it has been said: ". . . A competent trial lawyer not only can, but practically must—it is one of the skills his wage scale depends upon—deliberately violate and evade the prohibitive rules. . . . The most drastic enforcement of the rules fails to blot out color spilled upon the fact picture before the rules can be invoked." Nelles, *Commonwealth v. Hunt*, 32 Col.L.Rev. 1128, 1137 (1932).

THE SUBTLETIES OF PERSUASION

HICKS, ARGUMENTS AND ADDRESSES OF JOSEPH HODGES CHOATE

Page 166 (1926).

In Martinez v. Del Valle, the plaintiff sued for $50,000 damages for breach of promise and seduction. Joseph H. Choate was the defense attorney and the opening portion of his closing argument follows: "I must congratulate you, gentlemen of the jury, on your prospect of a speedy release. I don't know how experienced you have heretofore been in these matters of breach of promise and seduction. It is my first venture, and I confess an unpleasant and disagreeable duty, and the painful incidents of the trial have weighed upon me, as I believe they have upon you. A few hours more, fortunately limited by the wise rule of the Court to five hours in all! We are apt, we lawyers, to run along alike the brook, forever, my learned friend, especially has been engaged in cases where it seemed as if the case never could end because of the seeming impossibility of terminating his speech.

"I want, in the first place, gentlemen, to put you on your guard against a most natural sympathy with a woman of the appearance presented by this fair plaintiff. There are some feelings that no man is proof against, and I think one of them is sympathy, compassion, pity, human feeling for a woman who presents herself as she has in this case. For one, I confess that I pity her with all my heart. I would not place a feather's weight of calumny or injustice upon her—so far as my duty to my client would permit, I would have shielded her from that torrent of evidence which she has herself poured out here. Some of you gentlemen while she was on the stand—especially you, Mr. Foreman, and your immediate neighbors of the panel—have been exposed to the full blaze of her charms at short range for a very long time; you can't but have been sensible of it. . . . I have a right to caution you against this most natural human sympathy. It has been said to me many times during the progress of this trial, 'Mr. Choate, you have a good case—a perfectly clear case—but there's one obstacle in it that you can't overcome, and that is that there is a beautiful woman in the case against you, which will be too much for any jury.' Now, gentlemen, I know you are sworn to try this case upon your oaths, and I know that I need only mention this danger to have you steel your hearts and your consciences against it, so that the men of New York and the women of New York shall not say that there is no chance for justice for a man against a beautiful woman.

"I want to warn you, too, against the seductive eloquence and power of the learned counsel whom she has enlisted in her cause—

one of the veterans of our bar, a gentleman of whose talents and achievements the whole profession is proud, in all the branches of what I may call sexual litigation without a peer or a rival, from his long experience. Gentlemen, you can no more help being swayed by his eloquence than the rocks and the trees could help following the lyre of Orpheus. But remember that it is one of the essential elements of a case like this that the fair plaintiff should succeed in enlisting the sympathies of some brave and gallant champion at the bar. If she could persuade him, as she seems to have done here, of the merits of her case she knew full well that he would enlist in it with an ardor which no money could buy, a combination of pity and of eloquence that would bare any facts that might be brought before the jury.

"In presenting the facts of my case I first ask your attention to a remark that fell from the plaintiff under oath upon the stand that she had not brought this suit for money. 'Not one cent' did she desire at your hands, not one; but that her sole object was to establish her character. Ah, gentlemen, I think if that was her object the case might well stop here. Has not her character been established in a way that no further progress of the case or of time can ever wipe out? We sit here trying cases like this under the telescopic eye of the whole world. The trumpet-tongued press takes up every word, and it is read next morning throughout the land. Now with pain and sorrow, I say has not this lady, by her own evidence and her sister's, established her character? Her case depends upon her sworn word alone, and what is her picture as painted by herself?

"She said that it was her misfortune from nine years old to 20 to be . . . brought up in the very house of impurity, exposed not only to impure approaches but to constant threats of violence and murder, in case she dared to pursue the ordinary courses and fate of women and contract a marriage. While this family was without means, while this singular stepfather was without occupation or resources he quietly acquiesced in all expenses being paid by the female members of his family without ever asking whence the money came. That family was without religion, without church, without God. Thus you find her at the time she met the defendant—not a mere, inexperienced young girl but already an adept in the ways of New York life."

NOTE

For the cross-examination of the plaintiff in this case, see, Wellman, Art of Cross-Examination 205–262 (1936). See also Lake, How to Win Lawsuits Before Juries 274 (1954).

APPEALS TO BROADER SOCIAL AND POLITICAL FEELINGS

CHARLES YALE HARRISON, CLARENCE DARROW *
Pages 92-97 (1931).

In May, 1898, the woodworkers of Oshkosh, Wisconsin, went on strike. They demanded an increase of wages, the abolition of female and child labor, the recognition of their organization, and a weekly pay-day. The strike continued for fourteen weeks and was conducted by George Zentner and Michael Troiber, both of Oshkosh, and Thomas I. Kidd, General Secretary of the Amalgamated Woodworkers International Union, whose headquarters were in Chicago. Zentner and Troiber, in the course of the strike, acted as captains of pickets. At the moment when the strikers seemed assured of success, Kidd, Zentner and Troiber were arrested, charged with conspiracy to injure the business of the Payne Lumber Co., the largest manufacturer of sashes, doors and blinds involved in the strike and operating in fourteen states. Under the laws of Wisconsin no indictment was necessary, but the defendants were eventually brought to trial upon a complaint filed by the District Attorney and the case was tried in the Municipal Court of Oshkosh, which is a court of general criminal jurisdiction in Wisconsin.

The International Union in Chicago appealed to Darrow to defend the strikers. He accepted the case, remembered that he was the son of a woodworker. . . .

Kidd, under direct examination by Darrow, testified that workers were receiving as low as eighty and ninety cents a day and that children as young as ten and eleven years were working in the factory. In denying that the action of the International Union in undertaking to organize the workers was a conspiracy, Darrow offered proof that the movement for unionization originated in Oshkosh when certain militant workers gathered in one another's homes and discussed their poor wages and the growing use of female and child labor which was rapidly displacing men.

When Payne was being cross-examined by Darrow, it was brought out that the Oshkosh factory was worth more than a million dollars, that the low wages charged by Kidd were substantially correct, and that all efforts for mediation were scornfully spurned by the millionaire manufacturer. Payne did not reply to a letter listing the demands of the workers for the reason that "it was such an unbusinesslike letter." A specific charge against Troiber stated that during the strike he had committed assault and battery upon a strikebreaker who was returning from one of the mills.

* With the permission of the Author.

Finally all the evidence was in and Darrow summed up before the jury:

"Whatever its form, this is really not a criminal case. It is but an episode in the great battle for human liberty, a battle which was commenced when the tyranny and oppression of man first caused him to impose upon his fellows and which will not end so long as the children of one father shall be compelled to toil to support the children of another in ease and luxury. . . .

"So long as they rob childhood of its life and joy you will find other conspirators to take the place of these as fast as jail doors shall close upon them. If other conspirators should be wanting, I should be ashamed of this country. The counsel may argue as they please about the minor details of the case but deep in your hearts and mine is the certain knowledge that this is but a phase of the great social question that moves the world. These employers are using this court of justice to destroy what little is left of that spirit of independence and manhood which they have been slowly crushing from the breasts of those who toil for them."

In these opening remarks Darrow employed an appeal which seems to run through his summations in subsequent labor cases: that criminal charges in labor cases are subterfuges, that labor cases are historical events of tremendous importance, that the jurors in rendering their verdict are faced with tasks of great social responsibility, that labor cases are part of the age-long struggle between the powerful few who own and the disinherited mass which must endlessly toil. . . .

". . . I know you will be told that I am a labor agitator, a Socialist, Anarchist. . . . It may be that you think I am wild and insane when I look abroad over this fair land of ours and see wealth upon one hand and poverty and misery and want upon the other. . . . I believe that the world is filled with wrong. I believe that men are imperfect, I believe that institutions are imperfect. . . . I feel there is injustice now. No man ever entered this struggle for human liberty without measuring the cost, and the jail is one of the costs that must be measured with the rest; and if you see fit to send my clients there, they will take their punishment like men. . . . I appeal to you, not for Thomas I. Kidd, but . . . the long, long line reaching back through the ages . . . of despoiled and downtrodden people of the earth. . . .

"It is fallen to your lot, gentlemen, to be leading actors in one of the great dramas of human life. For some mysterious reason Providence has placed in your charge for today, aye for ages, the helpless toilers, the hopeless men, the despondent women and suffering children of the world; it is a great, a tremendous trust, and I know you will do your duty bravely, wisely, humanely and well; that you will render a verdict in this case which will be a milestone in the history of the world, and an inspiration and hope to the dumb, despairing millions whose fate is in your hands."

NOTES

(1) The records of trials show that at times the advocate seeks to identify his case with great issues merely as a means of gaining the sympathy of the particular tribunal and of winning his case. At other times, however, he seeks the same identification for the essentially political purpose of dramatizing and making vivid the great issues for the multitude. Should there be a distinction between these purposes in the degree of approbation or condemnation by the profession and the courts?

(2) In Hardaway v. State, 99 Miss. 223 (1911), the conviction of a Negro for the unlawful sale of intoxicating liquor was reversed because "In his closing argument to the jury the acting district attorney, over the protest of appellant, and unrebuked by the court, appealed to race prejudice by suggesting to the jury that they believe the state witness instead of appellant, for the reason that the state witness was a white man and appellant [the sole witness in his own behalf] was a Negro." The court said, quoting Tannehill v. State, 159 Ala. 51 (1909), "It is the duty of the court to see that the defendant is tried according to the law and the evidence, free from any appeal to prejudice or other improper motive, and this duty is emphasized when a colored man is placed upon trial before a jury of white men." For a lengthy annotation on "Counsel's appeal to racial, religious, social, or political prejudices or prejudice against corporations as ground for a new trial or reversal," see Note, 78 A.L.R. 1438 (1932).

SECTION 3. CANDOR

Introduction. In the trial of a case the prevailing spirit has been that of a contest between two parties, each of whom will bring forward only so much as is favorable to his side.

There are important forces in favor of fuller disclosure. The modern discovery practice and the pre-trial conference facilitate the ascertainment by each side of the other's case. The standards of the profession, and even the rules of law call for disclosure in certain situations. A less tangible matter is the encouragement given by the court to candor by the advocates.

Candor is important to the judge, for if he is not informed of the facts and the law at the time of the hearing, he has not the material essential to the decision. The judge can get this information only with the aid of counsel. Candor is also important to the adversary. If he does not know ahead of time the facts or grounds of the case, he is handicapped in preparation; and if he is a shaper, he is prevented from shaping the case to meet his needs.

To say that candor is a requirement of the administration of justice is not to answer the question of how the individual lawyer meets his responsibility to his client, to the system of justice and to himself in a specific situation. We shall explore some of these situations and learn from them but the full dimensions of professional responsibility can be tested only in the course of each career at the bar.

CODE OF PROFESSIONAL RESPONSIBILITY *

EC 7-19

Our legal system provides for the adjudication of disputes governed by the rules of substantive, evidentiary and procedural law. . . . the advocate, by his zealous preparation and presentation of facts and law, enables the tribunal to come to the hearing with an open and neutral mind and to render impartial judgments. The duty of a lawyer to his client and his duty to the legal system are the same: to represent his client zealously within the bounds of law. . . .

EC 7-23

The complexity of law often makes it difficult for a tribunal to be fully informed unless the pertinent law is presented by the lawyers in the cause. . . .

EC 7-26

The law and Disciplinary Rules prohibit the use of fraudulent, false or perjured testimony or evidence. A lawyer who knowingly participates in introduction of such testimony or evidence is justly subject to discipline. A lawyer should, however, present any evidence his client desires to have presented unless he knows, or from facts within his knowledge should know, that such testimony or evidence is false, fraudulent, or perjured.

NOTES

(1) Is the lawyer's duty to inform the tribunal with respect to facts at issue put the same way as his duty to inform with respect to relevant law? See discussion, infra, beginning at p. 306.

(2) Professor Mazor of the University of Utah notes that the concept of the lawyer as professional agent is not of great antiquity. "Law without lawyers is a tenet of a utopian credo. . . . The visionary future, the anthropological past, and the recurrent attempt to create lawyerless procedures reveal how deep seated is the belief that juristic acts are intensely personal." Mazor, *Power and Responsibility in the Attorney-Client Relation*, 20 Stan.L.Rev. 1120 (1968).

Regarding the "personal" nature of juristic acts do we in fact assume, although we may not say so, that the client in availing himself of the services of the lawyer-agent and of the system of justice must be prepared to

---

* Copyright 1969 by the American Bar Association. Reprinted with permission.

surrender some advantages which he might claim if he were alone before the tribunal?

(3) The reader will recall the statement by Mr. Charles P. Curtis quoted in Note 1, supra p. 288, that the loyalty of the lawyer in private practice runs to his client. "He has no other master." Compare another response:

". . . When Mr. Curtis intimates that in his opinion a lawyer's duty to his client is higher than that to the court, he ignores the established principle of privileged communications. . . . It was for this reason that the lawyer could not tell the police officers where his client had telephoned him that he was hiding. When the police officers asked the lawyer, there was no necessity for him to lie. He should have said, 'If I knew, my duty as a lawyer would forbid my telling you.' Throughout his article Mr. Curtis gives the impression that a lawyer may say or do things on behalf of his client which it would be wholly improper for him to do or say on his own behalf, and that the successful and happy lawyer is one who may use almost any subterfuge or trickery in order to win his case. Nothing could be farther from the truth. The files of the Ethics Committees . . . are full of opinions construing Canon 15. . . . These opinions are unanimous in holding that the last two sentences of the Canon mean just what they say: 'The office of attorney does not permit much less does it demand of him for any client, violation of law or any manner of fraud or chicane. He must obey his own conscience and not that of his client.'" Drinker, *Some Remarks on Mr. Curtis' "The Ethics of Advocacy"*, 4 Stan.L.Rev. 349, 350–51 (1952).

EARL WARREN, OBSERVATION: THE ADVOCATE AND THE ADMINISTRATION OF JUSTICE IN AN URBAN SOCIETY *

47 Tex.L.Rev. 615 (1968).

A free adversary process before independent judges and within a fair legislative process will in most instances find the right rule. The things that are most important go on in the courtroom. The search for truth, the interpretation of rules, and the manner in which the business of the courts is dispatched determine the nature and quality of law as it operates on society. It has been my belief for many years that the most serious problem today in the administration of justice is the manner in which we handle judicial work. . . .

The unfortunate aspect of this great perception is that the gaming theory of law is, after more than sixty years, still with us. Despite the wide adoption of the Federal Rules of Civil Procedure, with their effective discovery mechanisms, the view is still widely held that the law suit belongs to the lawyers; that the judge is an umpire to be

---

* [From an address given by Chief Justice Warren at the cornerstone-laying ceremonies of the Roscoe Pound-American Trial Lawyers Law Center at Cambridge, Massachusetts.]

called upon at the will of the lawyers; that concealment and surprise are proper weapons in the lawyer's arsenal of tricks; that truth and justice will somehow better emerge from ignorance of opposing viewpoints than from a knowledge of them.

In actuality, the "exaggerated contentious procedure" is at the heart of the malfunctioning of our urban courts. The sparring of the litigants; the tactics employed for delay; the use of the courts as lever in settlement, all demean the adversary process and reduce it to a trade carried on by men expert, not at the law, but at calculated bargaining. Only when the courts are properly called upon to furnish a genuine forum for disputed facts and doubtful legal questions will the adversary process reach its full strength, and the advocate find his proper place in the courts.

IDENTITY OF CLIENT

NEW YORK COUNTY OPINION 259 (1958)

Question. 1. An attorney is retained to represent the defendant in a criminal prosecution. The defendant when arraigned, and before retaining the attorney, and without any advice from the attorney, employed an alias. The attorney, when employed, knows the true name of the defendant.

In the opinion of the Committee, is it the duty of the lawyer to disclose to the Court or to the prosecuting attorney's office the true name of the defendant, or is it proper for the attorney to represent the defendant under the name which the defendant assumed and without disclosing the true state of facts to the authorities?

2. A employs an attorney in connection with the purchase of certain real estate. For reasons undisclosed to the attorney, A desires to acquire title under an assumed name which he has adopted solely for the purposes of the one transaction. A has opened a bank account under such assumed name and is ready and able to pay all the sums of money to be paid in connection with the transaction. Is it proper for the attorney to represent A while A is acting under such assumed name without disclosing such fact to the sellers or their attorneys?

Answer. The Committee is of the opinion that the paramount duty of a lawyer, with certain recognized exceptions, not involved in the question, is to preserve inviolate the confidential disclosures made to him by his client. Consequently, without his client's consent, he cannot with professional propriety make any of the disclosures indicated in the . . . inquiries.

Answering the specific questions:

1. In the opinion of the Committee it is not the duty of the attorney to make the disclosure; and in the opinion of a majority of the

Committee, it is not improper for him to represent the client notwithstanding the facts assumed. As to 2 . . . it is the opinion of the Committee that the danger of injuries to others by the use of the assumed name are such that the attorney ought not to participate in any of the transactions unless the name of the client is disclosed, and such disclosure ought to be so made that it will relieve the respective transactions of such danger according to the circumstances of the respective cases.

NOTES

(1) Does it make any difference in situation No. 1, supra, whether the defendant told his attorney of the change of name or the attorney knew this independently? What are the "recognized exceptions" to the rule against disclosure to which the Committee refers? Are answers No. 1 and No. 2 consistent? If not, what explanation do you offer?

(2) "In presenting a matter to a tribunal, a lawyer shall disclose: . . . Unless privileged or irrelevant, the identities of the clients he represents and of the persons who employed him." Code of Professional Responsibility DR 7–106(B) (2).

(3) Even though the client prefers to remain unidentified and the lawyer accordingly claims the privilege to refuse such identification a court may require disclosure:

"In our opinion, there is no competent reason why the Supreme Court should uphold the claim of confidential relationship between appellant and his clients to the point of sealing their identity where the safe and proper custody of a child is involved . . . . The Supreme Court's overriding concern with the welfare of the infant as a ward of the court overbalances any interest of technical claim on the appellant's part with respect to the confidential relationship between him and his clients." Tierney v. Flower, 32 App.Div.2d 392, 395, 302 N.Y.S.2d 640, 643 (1969).

(4) See also Chapter XII, Section 3 infra, Confidential Communications.

SOURCE OF IMPORTANT EVIDENCE

KINGSLAND v. DORSEY

Supreme Court of the United States, 1949.
338 U.S. 318, 70 S.Ct. 123, 94 L.Ed. 123.
Rehearing denied 338 U.S. 939, 70 S.Ct. 341, 94 L.Ed. 579.

Back in 1926 the Hartford-Empire Co. conceived and executed a scheme to prepare and publish over the signature of an apparently disinterested labor leader, an article to be published and then used in support of the company's pending patent application. Such a dissertation, entitled, "Introduction of Automatic Glass Working Machinery; How Received by Organized Labor," was prepared. It purported to be authorized by one Clarke, president of a glass workers' union. It was published in a trade journal and then presented to the Patent Office as recognition by a "reluctant witness" of the success of the device under consideration. Several years later, involved in litigation testing the validity of its patent Hartford-Empire took steps to suppress evidence of the real authorship of the Clarke essay. It made a gift of $8,000 to Clarke, who had told investigators employed by Hartford-Empire's adversary that he had written the article and would so testify if called upon as a witness. Ultimately, this Court reviewed the actions of Hartford-Empire and held that the sum total of acts attributable to it constituted a fraud on the Patent Office and the federal courts. Hazel-Atlas Glass Co. v. Hartford-Empire Co., 322 U.S. 238, 64 S.Ct. 997, 88 L.Ed. 1250, reversing Hartford-Empire Co. v. Hazel-Atlas Glass Co., 3 Cir., 137 F.2d 764. See also United States v. Hartford-Empire Co., D.C., 46 F.Supp. 541.

Dorsey was one of counsel for Hartford-Empire in the 1926 patent application and, shortly following our decision in Hazel-Atlas, supra, proceedings to suspend or exclude him from further practice before the Patent Office were commenced under 35 U.S.C. § 11, 35 U.S.C.A. § 11. Identical but separate proceedings were instituted against three other members of the patent bar involved in the transactions. All were disbarred. Only the Dorsey case is here.

Dorsey was charged with gross misconduct in that, as particularized in the notice which instituted the proceeding, he ". . . participated in the preparation of [the Clarke] article and/or the presentation thereof to the United States Patent Office during the prosecution of said patent application knowing that said article was not written by said William P. Clarke, and with the purpose of deceiving the Patent Office as to the authorship of said article and influencing the action of the Patent Office on said application. . . ."

A view of the facts least favorable to Dorsey indicates that he inspected and criticized a few details of an early draft of the Clarke article and that later, with knowledge that it had been prepared by a Hartford-Empire employee, he submitted it to the Patent Office as being what on its face it purported to be. This is the long and the short of the case against Dorsey. The case against Hartford-Empire, however, included much in which Dorsey is not shown to have had even a consenting part. In two respects only are his actions urged to be wrongdoing; first, in that he deceived the Patent Office as to the real author, and second (not charged in the notice but advanced here), that Dorsey represented it as the work of a "reluctant witness." . . .*

PER CURIAM. Acting under the provisions of § 487 of the Revised Statutes, 35 U.S.C. § 11, 35 U.S.C.A. § 11, the Commissioner of Patents found after hearings that petitioner, an attorney, had been

* The statement of facts is taken from the dissenting opinion.

Ch. 7 CANDOR 303

guilty of gross misconduct, and entered an order barring him from practice before the United States Patent Office. Pursuant to authority granted by the same provisions, the District Court reviewed the Commissioner's order. Concluding that the hearings had been fairly conducted after due notice of charges and that there was substantial evidence to support the findings and action of the Commissioner, the District Court affirmed the order. 69 F.Supp. 788. The Court of Appeals reversed, D.C.Cir., 173 F.2d 405, 410. A majority of that court thought the notice of charges inadequate and the proceedings before the Commission unfair. . . . Judge Edgerton, dissenting, thought the hearings had been fairly conducted and "the result just." *

The statute under which the Commissioner acted represents congressional policy in an important field. It relates to the character and conduct of "persons, agents, or attorneys" who participate in proceedings to obtain patents. We agree with the following statement made by the Patent Office Committee on Enrollment and Disbarment that considered this case: "By reason of the nature of an application for patent, the relationship of attorneys to the Patent Office requires the highest degree of candor and good faith. In its relation to applicants, the Office . . . must rely upon their integrity and deal with them in a spirit of trust and confidence . . . ." It was the Commissioner, not the courts, that Congress made primarily responsible for protecting the public from the evil consequences that might result if practitioners should betray their high trust. . .

The judgment of the Court of Appeals is reversed, and that of the District Court affirmed. It is so ordered.

MR. JUSTICE JACKSON, whom MR. JUSTICE FRANKFURTER joins, dissenting. . . . The worst that can be said of Dorsey is that he took advantage of this loose practice [of the Patent Office] to use a trade journal article as evidence, without disclosing that it was ghost-written for the ostensible author. . . .

I should suppose that, so far as the law is concerned, one may as effectively father statements by adoption as by conception and that sincerely subscribing to what another has written for him does not constitute legal deceit or grounds for disbarment, impeachment or other penalty. And in this case, not only is there no claim that the Clarke article contained one false statement, but there is no denial that, whoever was the scribe, Clarke believed and knowingly adopted as his own every word of it.

I should not like to be second to anyone on this Court in condemning the custom of putting up decoy authors to impress the guileless,

---

* In the Court of Appeals, Judge Edgerton, dissenting, said: "Appellant represented it [the Clarke article] to the Patent Office as the disinterested work of Clarke. This representation was false and appellant knew it was false. This false representation was highly material. As appellant himself says, 'It was Clarke's name that gave [the article] its status.'"

a custom which as the court below cruelly pointed out flourishes even in official circles in Washington. Nor do I contend that Dorsey's special adaptation of the prevailing custom comports with the highest candor. . . . But has any man before Dorsey ever been disciplined or even reprimanded for it? And will any be hereafter? . . .

FULL CONTROVERSY

UNITED STATES v. CHICAGO, MILWAUKEE, ST. PAUL & PACIFIC R. CO.

Supreme Court of the United States, 1931.
282 U.S. 311, 51 S.Ct. 159, 75 L.Ed. 359.

The property of an insolvent railroad corporation was sold by equity receivers and the sale was confirmed by the court, with the proviso that the conveyance should not be made to the new corporation organized pursuant to the reorganization plan until the Interstate Commerce Commission had authorized the issuance of the securities provided for in the plan. The plan provided that the stockholders of the old corporation might participate in the reorganization by depositing their stock together with $32 for each share of common stock and $28 for each share of preferred stock; and that $4 per share of the fund so created were to be used, so far as was necessary, for the compensation of the reorganization managers, counsel and depositaries.

The plan further provided that the fees and disbursements to be paid out of the $4 fund to the counsel and depositaries should be fixed by the reorganization managers in their discretion. When application was made to the Interstate Commerce Commission for approval of the plan, the Commission entered an order approving it, with the proviso that payments should not be made out of the $4 fund until authorized by order of the court or of the Commission. The reorganization plan then proceeded, with the execution of deeds of the property to the new corporation and the issuance of its securities.

Thereafter an equity suit was brought which attacked the Commission's proviso mentioned above as beyond the authority of the Commission and asked that its enforcement be enjoined. The Supreme Court affirmed a decree of the District Court which found the proviso was invalid and accordingly enjoined its enforcement.

Three justices dissented.

OPINION OF MR. JUSTICE STONE. I think the judgment should be reversed and the order of the Interstate Commerce Commission upheld as one within its statutory authority. But even if it be assumed that the condition attached to the order was an improper one, it would seem that the respondent is now estopped to challenge it. . . .

So far as appears, not until appellee filed the present petition did it disclose any purpose to disregard the condition upon which the order depended. In the meantime it had taken full advantage of the benefits of the order. . . .

If appellee were unable or unwilling to comply with the order as made, equity and good conscience required, at least, either disclosure of that fact to the District Court before securing the transfer of the railroad property to it; application, upon full statement of the facts, to the Commission to exercise the jurisdiction, which it had reserved, to approve a modified plan; or prompt initiation of the present proceedings to test the validity of the order before a situation had been created prejudicial to the public interest and to the Commission's performance of its duties. Instead, appellee adopted a course of conduct consistent throughout only with its apparent purpose to comply with the order; and now, without tendering any excuse for the belated disclosure of its real purpose, it asks relief from the condition only after it has enjoyed benefits which it cannot be said would have been granted without the condition. Neither this Court nor the court below is acting any the less as a court of equity because its powers are invoked to deal with an order of the Interstate Commerce Commission. The failure to conform to those elementary standards of fairness and good conscience which equity may always demand as a condition of its relief to those who seek its aid, seems to require that such aid be withheld from this appellee. See Davis v. Wakelee, 156 U.S. 680, 15 S.Ct. 555. . . .

Mr. Justice Holmes and Mr. Justice Brandeis concur in this opinion. The Chief Justice took no part in the consideration or decision of this case.

NOTES

(1) In Swaine, The Cravath Firm, Vol. II, 418–431 (1948), there is a detailed outline of the Milwaukee case and the statement that the dissenters were in error as to the facts. In Lowenthal, The Investor Pays (1933), there is a critical discussion of the case. In several reviews of the latter book the lawyer's participation in receiverships at that time is described. See Review by Foster, 43 Yale L.J. 352 (1933); Review by Flynn, 33 Col.L.Rev. 1080 (1933); Review by Weiner, 47 Harv.L.Rev. 719 (1934).

(2) In an annulment action the lawyer for the petitioner husband so artfully framed his questions to his client on the witness stand as to secure answers which were literally true but which concealed from the court the pendency of the separation suit brought by the wife. In censuring the lawyer, the court said: "We hold that in the circumstances of this case the appellant was under an active duty to see to it that the pendency of the separation suit be brought to the notice of the court. . . ." Matter of Heimsoth, 255 N.Y. 409 (1931). See also People ex rel. Healy v. Case, 241 Ill. 279 (1909).

(3) On the duty of a receiver to inform the federal court of a pending state proceeding see Harkin v. Brundage, 276 U.S. 36 (1928).

FACTS AND LAW

IN RE GREENBERG

Supreme Court of New Jersey, 1954.
15 N.J. 132, 104 A.2d 46.

[Respondent had been delegated by his law office to prepare a petition for certification, draft the brief and argue the appeal in the Supreme Court of a tort case against the Lehigh Valley Railroad Company. In his preparation he made use of a statement of facts and brief used before the lower court by a New York lawyer who had appeared *pro hac vice*. Unfortunately these papers stated matters of fact which respondent would have seen were not supported by the record, if he had examined it himself.

Disciplinary proceedings were instituted against respondent and an order to show cause was issued, which came on for hearing before the Supreme Court.]

VANDERBILT, C. J.

The respondent in his brief and in his oral argument in Shellhammer v. Lehigh Valley Railroad Company, 14 N.J. 341, 102 A.2d 602, 605 (1954), contended that:

"it is shown by 'uncontroverted evidence' that an interval of 15 to 20 minutes had elapsed between the all-clear signal, followed by the air-brake test . . . and the actual starting of the train by . . . defendant's engineer; . . ."

[The trial judge found]

"The Court's preargument examination of the record revealed no ground whatever for the statement that between 15 to 20 minutes intervened between the giving of the all-clear signal and the movement of the train. . . ."

[I]t is so obvious as not to require the citation of authorities that the work of our appellate courts cannot go on satisfactorily if we cannot rely on the representations of counsel to us both as to the facts and as to the law. . . . The facts of a case are or should be peculiarly within the knowledge of the counsel who are arguing the appeal and there is great likelihood of error by the court and of consequent injustice to the parties, if counsel do not adequately present the facts of the case.

Similarly, if counsel is responsible, as he is under the Canons of Ethics, for making known to the court any decisions in the State adverse to his cause in the event his opponent fails to cite them, it necessarily follows that he is even more responsible for citing authorities which cannot conceivably be taken to stand for the proposition for which he cites them, although as in the matter of presenting facts he is permitted to argue freely every inference that can be legitimately drawn from the cases he cites provided he does not misrepresent to the court the contents of such cases. . . .

These problems have never, to our knowledge, come before our courts in a disciplinary matter, but they are of transcendent importance in the administration of justice. In view of our findings with reference to the good faith of the respondent, it would be manifestly unfair to impose discipline on him. Nevertheless, the case should serve as a warning to all that the bar is expected to live up in full measure to its professional obligations in the delicate and difficult process of molding the law of the state . . . .

The order to show cause is discharged . . . .

NOTE

"In his representation of a client, a lawyer shall not: . . . Knowingly make a false statement of law or fact." Code of Profesional Responsibility DR 7-102(A) (5).

"In presenting a matter to a tribunal, a lawyer shall disclose: Legal authority in the controlling jurisdiction known to him to be directly adverse to the position of his client and which is not disclosed by opposing counsel." Code of Professional Responsibility DR 7-106(B) (1).

The Code follows American Bar Association Opinion 280 (1949).

In what respects, if any, does Chief Justice Vanderbilt modify this position in setting forth the standards for the bar and courts in New Jersey? Can you perceive any difficulty in applying the ABA standard on disclosure of adverse law? See Tunstall, *Ethics in Citation: A Plea for Reinterpretation of a Canon*, 35 A.B.A.J. 5 (1949).

SAMUEL WILLISTON, LIFE AND LAW

Pages 271-272 (1940).

"The lawyer must decide when he takes a case whether it is a suitable one for him to undertake and after this decision is made, he is not justified in turning against his client by exposing injurious evidence entrusted to him. . . . [D]oing something intrinsically regrettable, because the only alternative involves worse consequences, is a necessity in every profession."

Williston's autobiography tells of one of his early cases which illustrates the difficulties involved in this type of situation. Williston's client was sued in a financial matter. Williston at once went through his letter file painstakingly, sorting and collating it. As the trial approached, the plaintiff's lawyers did not demand to see the correspondence or ask for its production. Williston states that he did not feel bound to disclose the correspondence. At the close of the trial in the course of the remarks the Chief Justice stated as a reason for his decision a supposed fact which Williston knew to be unfounded. He had in front of him a letter showing the Judge's error. Williston says: "Though I have no doubt of the propriety of my behavior in keeping silent, I was somewhat uncomfortable at the time."

NEW YORK COUNTY OPINION 309 (1933)

Question: In an action, on behalf of an infant three years of age, for injuries sustained by falling off a porch owned by the defendant, due to the alleged negligence of the defendant, where there is no eye witness known to the plaintiff's attorney and thereafter when the case came to trial the infant's case was dismissed on motion of the defendant's attorney, on the ground that the infant plaintiff was unable to make out a sufficient case of circumstantial evidence. During the presentation of the plaintiff's case, said attorney for the defendant had an eye witness to said accident actually present in the court and did not mention said fact, either to the plaintiff's attorney or to the court and kept the court in ignorance of the fact that a person did exist who actually saw said accident, and was present in court. Was the failure of the defendant's attorney to disclose said information to the court improper professional conduct?

Answer: In the opinion of the Committee the conduct of the defendant's attorney is not professionally improper. The fact of infancy does not call for a different reply.

NOTE

The Code of Professional Responsibility does not set forth a duty to disclose adverse facts as it does to disclose relevant adverse law. Why should this distinction prevail?

OTHER SITUATIONS IN WHICH DUTY TO CLIENT MAY CONFLICT WITH DUTY TO DISCLOSE

HENRY S. DRINKER, LEGAL ETHICS *

Pages 122–30 (1953).

From the earliest times the Common Law judges have reiterated the principle, derived apparently from the ecclesiastical law, that the state has an interest in the marital status of its citizens which precludes their being divorced by agreement, and have thrown doubt on the validity of a divorce in the obtaining of which there has been cooperation on their part.

The lawyer's duty to his client requires him to secure for the client the legal redress that the client wants, provided this can be done by proper legal means. His duty to the court requires him not to misrepresent any facts or to mislead the court. Is there an additional duty by the lawyer to the state and to the court, as its instru-

---

* With permission of the publisher, Columbia University Press.

ment, in divorce cases which may conflict with his obligation to his client?

It would seem clear that a lawyer owes no duty to the state in which he practices to refrain from advising a client to go to another state in order to take advantage of laws more favorable to the redress which the client desires. Thus, in its Opinion 12, a majority of the New York County Committee held it not improper for a New York lawyer to advise a client that a New York decree prohibiting marriage with the co-respondent did not preclude her going to Connecticut and there contracting a marriage which would be recognized as valid in New York and not punishable there as a contempt of court. The Committee disapproved, however, the lawyer's having gone there with the client and "giving her away," as "likely to be misunderstood" and tending to "diminish public respect for the profession."

Similarly in its Opinion 100 a majority of the County Committee held it not improper for the lawyer for a deserted New York wife to enter into an agreement with the husband's lawyer that she make a bona fide and actual change of domicile to another state where desertion was a valid ground for divorce, he to go there and accept service and make her a substantial payment in settlement of all claims for future maintenance, with a substantial fee for her lawyer. . . .

In a later Opinion 289, the County Committee said: Where an action for divorce has been commenced on valid grounds, facilitation of the decree by the party at fault is not in itself improper. Nor is a New York attorney to be criticized for participating in the lawful dissolution in another jurisdiction of the marriage of a New York citizen, merely because the grounds are not sufficient to obtain a divorce in New York.

These decisions were based on the assumption that the Full Faith and Credit Clause would make the decree of the foreign court binding in New York. It does not follow that a lawyer may properly participate in procuring a Mexican mail-order divorce, manifestly invalid in the United States, and which can be used by his client only to misrepresent married status.

Manufacture of or connivance in procuring ground for divorce. Clearly a lawyer may not originate or participate in a scheme to make it appear to the court that a ground for divorce has occurred when this is not the fact. Such is the case in the so-called "hotel divorces," prevalent in jurisdictions where adultery is the only ground for divorce, and based on the principle that intercourse will be presumed from apparently uninhibited opportunity.

Deliberate neglect to allege or prove a defense. A more difficult question arises where the statutory ground for the divorce relied on may be dependent on the non-consent of the plaintiff. Is there a "desertion" where the defendant, although leaving with no intent to return, goes away with the expressed or silent approval and satisfaction of the plaintiff? In a divorce proceeding based on such a "desertion," is defendant or his lawyer bound to tell this to the court, or under any duty to tell of defendant's rebuffed offer to return, the latter, if known, being a bar to the divorce?

After the decision of the New York Appellate Division holding that plaintiff's adultery was by way of defense only, the New York City and County Committees held it proper for a lawyer to accept employment to secure a divorce on the ground of adultery though knowing that his client had also committed adultery. It would seem to follow that the lawyer owes no duty to the state to disclose independent defenses to a divorce action.

Agreement to make no defense, or to withdraw a defense. In an early opinion, Opinion 81, the New York City Committee, although sanctioning an agreement, disclosed to the court, by the parties to a divorce relative to alimony, counsel fees, and custody of children, stated flatly that a lawyer should not countenance an agreement not to defend a matrimonial action. In a later opinion, however, Opinion 314, this Committee modified the above statement, holding that a lawyer who, on behalf of a husband, had filed an answer denying adultery and alleging connivance and procurement, might properly agree with the other side, "in the absence of fraud or collusion," to withdraw the defense or suffer a default in consideration of the wife's waiving all alimony and counsel fees. . . .

The New York County Committee, in its Opinion 54, approved an agreement by counsel for the wife, sued for divorce, to bring an action for annulment and accept a fixed sum in lieu of alimony and counsel fees, the husband to discontinue the divorce action, provided the agreement be disclosed to the court in both cases. . . .

In a later opinion, also, Opinion 230, the same Committee approved an agreement, communicated to the court, by the wife's lawyer with the husband for an uncontested annulment, for adequate cause, the husband to pay all expenses.

Despite these decisions, the New York County Committee, in its Opinion 205, stated flatly that an agreement not to defend a divorce action was against public policy and should not be made or countenanced by a lawyer.

Furnishing otherwise unobtainable evidence of actual facts constituting a ground for divorce. A distinction may well be drawn between the prior instigation of or connivance in the acts relied on as a ground for divorce, and the facilitation of proving such acts after they have unquestionably occurred. If the willingness of both parties to secure a divorce absolutely precluded each of them, under the law, from getting it, the participation of a lawyer in facilitating proof might be considered improper. However, despite statements in some opinions to the contrary, it is not believed that the "collusion" doctrine is carried so far; or that this type of cooperation by a lawyer has ever been characterized as unprofessional.

In its Opinion 86, a majority of the New York County Committee held it not improper for the wife's lawyer to accept the husband's agreement to furnish, in consideration of a satisfactory money settlement, witnesses to flagrant acts by him, the agreement being fully disclosed to the court and the parties being told that the court might not agree. . . .

The propriety of the lawyer's conduct in cases within these last three subdivisions would appear to depend on the nature of the particular case. Where the offense relied on as ground for the divorce is clear, flagrant, and indefensible, the proposed settlement between the parties fair and reasonable, and the stipulated cooperation by the defendant merely to eliminate nuisance value, the disclosure of all the facts to the court affords adequate protection against fraudulent "collusion." Where, however, the situation is such as to indicate the possibility that purchased evidence may be manufactured, the lawyer should resolve the doubt by declining to have a part in the arrangement. While the decisions by the two New York Committees are on their face difficult to reconcile, it is believed that, as a practical matter, they may well have been influenced by the above considerations. . . .

Designating lawyer for the other side. The American Bar Association, the Michigan Committee, and the two New York Committees have held that the lawyer for one spouse should not recommend a lawyer for the other, or prepare the pleadings or papers or testimony for the other or act for or give legal advice to the other in any respect, and that disclosure to the court, even before the decree, would not make this proper. . . .

Apparently the decisions which would insulate the parties and their respective lawyers completely from one another are based on the fiction that the interests of parties to a divorce suit are necessarily and always antagonistic to one another and on the further assumption that this was necessary to secure proper protection for the interest of the state in preserving their marital status. It would, however, seem very questionable as to whether such protection is needed in a bona fide case, where it is clear that the wife honestly wants the divorce and is not coerced into it by an obviously dominant husband, where the allowance proposed by him is reasonable, and where the lawyer suggested to her by the husband or by his lawyer has not theretofore represented the husband. It is manifest that such suggestion is but natural and occurs all the time in uncontested cases. To condemn it where it is openly disclosed would seem both futile and unnecessary.*

---

* This does not, however, mean that in cases so flagrant as Staedler v. Staedler, 6 N.J. 380 (1951) (where the husband's regular lawyer managed the whole proceedings) the court should not call a halt, as it there did, suspending the lawyer for a year. [Author's footnote].

Acceptance of compensation from the other side. It is not considered unethical or apparently as indicating "collusion" for the wife's lawyer to be paid by the husband. In fact many divorce statutes provide for this, as well as for alimony. There can seem to be no impropriety in a bona fide agreement to this effect, or in an agreement, disclosed to the court, with regard to property, alimony, counsel fees, and custody of children.

The upshot of the foregoing would seem to be:

Collusion involving deliberate distortion of the facts constituting the ground of the divorce, or connivance in inducing defendant to commit acts constituting such ground is obviously improper.

Cooperation with the other side in facilitating proof of acts theretofore committed without such connivance is not necessarily so, but where involving a money payment will be viewed with suspicion and should be fully disclosed to the court.

The mere fact that the more affluent of the parties agrees to make a payment to the other on account of counsel fees and other expenses and a lump sum or allowance is not improper where this is likewise disclosed to the Court. . . .

NOTES

(1) Does the reader agree with the underlying assumptions of Mr. Drinker? The principal assumptions seem to be two: first, that the community's attitude toward marriage and divorce has been changing, and the legal rules do not yet embody the new attitude; second, that the lawyer must not participate in a deception of any kind, but it is at least arguable that he may participate in a fiction which is known to the court to be a fiction. If the reader agrees with the basic assumptions, does he agree with the application of them by the bar association committees or by the author in the various situations described?

See also, Drinker, *Problems of Professional Ethics in Matrimonial Litigation,* 66 Harv.L.Rev. 443 (1953).

(2) A woman client comes to Lawyer "A" seeking a divorce. Her husband has agreed to a consent decree on grounds of adultery (the only grounds available in the jurisdiction), although in fact no such act was committed. Lawer "A" knows this. The client asks "A" to take the case. How should lawyer "A" respond? For the response of a sample of New York City lawyers see Carlin, Lawyers' Ethics 200 (1966).

A. B. A. OPINION 287 (1953)

[Two inquiries were dealt with in this opinion. In the first one a lawyer had procured a divorce for a husband on the ground of the wife's desertion in a proceeding in which the wife was represented by counsel and knew of the evidence to be presented by the husband. Three months after the entry of the decree the husband returned to his lawyer and told him that his testimony on which the decree was given was false, for the desertion had not continued as long as he testified or as long as was necessary under the law. His former wife now threatens to disclose the fact to the court unless he provides for her support. What is the duty of the lawyer to the court and to his client?

In the second case a lawyer represented a convicted criminal who came before the court for sentence. The clerk of the court indicated to the court that the convicted man had no previous criminal record, and the court stated that for this reason he would be put on probation. The lawyer knew, either through his investigation or from his client, that the client had a criminal record. The inquiries were: (1) On these facts is it the duty of the lawyer to disclose the facts to the court? (2) If the convicted man, on inquiry from the court, had made a false statement, what would be the duty of the lawyer? (3) If the judge asked the lawyer whether his client had a criminal record, what should the lawyer do?]

The Opinion of the Committee is stated by MR. DRINKER, MESSRS. JACKSON, FREDERIC M. MILLER and SHACKELFORD MILLER concurring: . . . Canon 37 provides that it is the duty of a lawyer to preserve his client's confidences, which duty outlasts the lawyer's employment. . . .

The reason and the purpose of the rule embodied in Canon 37 were thus summarized in two of this Committee's opinions. In Opinion 91 we said:

> "The reason for the rule lies in the fact that it is essential to the administration of justice that there should be perfect freedom of consultation by client with attorney without any apprehension of a compelled disclosure by the attorney to the detriment of the client. . . ."

Canon 37 recognizes and specifies conditions under which the privilege is not applicable, the second paragraph providing that the announced intention of a client to commit a crime is not included within the confidences which he is bound to respect, and states that he may properly make such disclosure as may be necessary to prevent the criminal act or to protect those against whom it is threatened. . . .

In the case submitted to us, the communication by the client to the lawyer that he had committed perjury was made to the lawyer in his professional capacity, when seeking advice as to what to do, and is within the letter and the spirit of Canon 37, which would apply unless controlled by some other Canon or consideration.

Canon 41 provides as follows:

> "When a lawyer discovers that some fraud or deception has been practiced, which has unjustly imposed upon the court or a party, he should endeavor to rectify it; at first by advising his

client, and if his client refuses to forego the advantage thus unjustly gained, he should promptly inform the injured person or his counsel, so that they may take appropriate steps."

We do not believe that Canon 41 was directed at a case such as that here presented but rather at one in which, in a civil suit, the lawyer's client has secured an improper advantage over the other through fraud or deception. . . .

A more forcible argument for an exception to Canon 37 is found in Canon 29, which provides:

"The counsel upon the trial of a cause in which perjury has been committed owe it to the profession and to the public to bring the matter to the knowledge of the prosecuting authorities."

On its face this provision would apparently make it the duty of the lawyer to disclose his client's prior perjury to the prosecuting authorities. However, to do so in this case would involve the direct violation of Canon 37.

Accordingly, it is essential to determine which of the Canons controls. . . .

We do not consider that either the duty of candor and fairness to the court, as stated in Canon 22, or the provisions of Canons 29 and 41 above quoted are sufficient to override the purpose, policy and express obligation under Canon 37.

In the case stated the lawyer should urge his client to make the disclosure, advising him that this is essential to secure for him any leniency in the event of the court's finding out the truth. He should also advise him to tell his wife that he proposes to do so, and thus avoid further blackmail. If the client will not take this advice, the lawyer should have nothing further to do with him, but despite Canons 29 and 41, should not disclose the facts to the court or to the authorities. Compare also Opinion 268.

Turning to the second inquiry, relative to the convicted client up for sentence, whose lawyer sees the court put him on probation by reason of the court's misinformation as to his criminal record, known to the lawyer: If the client's criminal record was communicated by him to his counsel when seeking professional advice from him, Canon 37 would prevent its disclosure to the court unless the provisions of Canons 22, 29 and 41 require this. If the court asks the defendant whether he has a criminal record and he answers that he has none, this, although perhaps not technical perjury, for the purposes of the present question amounts to the same thing. Despite this, we do not believe the lawyer justified in violating his obligation under Canon 37. He should, in due course, endeavor to persuade the client to tell the court the truth and if he refuses to do so should sever his relations with the client, but should not violate the client's confidence. . . .

If the fact of the client's criminal record was learned by the lawyer without communication, confidential or otherwise, from his client, or on his behalf, Canon 37 would not be applicable, and the only problem would be as to the conflicting loyalties of the lawyer on the one hand to represent his client with undivided fidelity and not to divulge his secrets (Canon 6), and on the other to treat the court in every case in which he appears as counsel with the candor and fairness (Canon 22) which the court has the right to expect of him as its officer. In this case we deem the following considerations applicable.

If the court asks the lawyer whether the clerk's statement is correct, the lawyer is not bound by fidelity to the client to tell the court what he knows to be an untruth, and should ask the court to excuse him from answering the question, and retire from the case, though this would doubtless put the court on further inquiry as to the truth.

Even, however, if the court does not directly ask the lawyer this question, such an inquiry may well be implied from the circumstances, including the lawyer's previous relations with the court. The situation is analogous to that discussed in our Opinion 280 where counsel knows of an essential decision not cited by his opponent and where his silence might reasonably be regarded by the court as an implied representation by him that he knew of no such authority. If, under all the circumstances, the lawyer believes that the court relies on him as corroborating the correctness of the statement by the clerk or by the client that the client has no criminal record, the lawyer's duty of candor and fairness to the court requires him, in our opinion, to advise the court not to rely on counsel's personal knowledge as to the facts of the client's record. . . .

If the lawyer is quite clear that the court does not rely on him as corroborating, by his silence, the statement of the clerk or of his client, the lawyer is not, in our opinion, bound to speak out.

Opinion concurring in part and dissenting in part by William B. Jones. . . . I think that Canon 37 applies to all information received by the lawyer, whether or not directly from the client, when the information is received in the course of the lawyer's professional employment and as a result of the confidential relationship existing because of that employment. . . .

Dissenting opinion concurred in by Wilbur M. Brucker and William H. White.

We can not subscribe to the majority opinion. Canon 29 expressly provides:

> "The counsel upon the trial of the cause in which perjury has been committed owe it to the profession and to the public to bring the matter to the knowledge of the prosecuting authorities."

No good reason exists for ignoring the plain and unmistakable mandate of the Canon. Canon 29 is based upon sound public policy which singles out perjury because perjury strikes at the roots of our American system of jurisprudence. . . . No exception is made in Canon 29 as to the manner in which the knowledge of perjury is acquired by the lawyer. No longer is a trial supposed to be a "Game" to be played by unscrupulous laymen with lawyers as mere pawns. Canon 29 seeks to make a trial an organized search for the truth,— charging the lawyers with the duty of seeing that no litigant prevails through perjury.

In addition, Canon 41 deals another blow at perjury and emphasizes the duty of a lawyer to report perjury to the court, . . . As if Canon 29 and Canon 41 were not enough, Canon 15 provides: "The office of attorney does not permit, much less does it demand of him, for any client, violation of law or any manner of fraud or chicane. He must obey his own conscience and not that of his client." Also, Canon 22 requires the utmost "candor and fairness" on the part of the lawyer in all his dealings with the court. In view of all these positive admonitions, how can a lawyer expect to remain passive when willful and deliberate perjury, fraud and deception have been committed or are being committed in the course of a trial? . . .

The *method* by which the lawyer brings the true information to the knowledge of the court is a mere detail. Whether the lawyer asks for a recess to advise privately with his client about disclosing the truth, or whether the lawyer makes the suggestion to his client in open court, is merely a choice of procedure. In our opinion the lawyer's duty under these circumstances is to see that his client reveals the truth to the court about his criminal record, and if the client refuses, the lawyer's duty to do so becomes mandatory under Canons 29 and 41. . . .

NOTE

A guardian's attorney, upon being informed by his client that he has misappropriated his ward's estate, should do everything possible to see that his client reports the misappropriation and makes full restitution. Unless these steps are taken, the attorneys should not continue to represent the client. Canon 37 applies, however, and he must preserve his client's confidence. A.B.A. Informal Opinion 778. 51 A.B.A.J. 444 (1965).

SECTION 4. WITNESSES

THE LAWYER AS WITNESS

WEIL v. WEIL

Supreme Court, Appellate Division, First Department, 1953.
283 App.Div. 33, 125 N.Y.S.2d 368.

PER CURIAM. After trial of framed issues of adultery plaintiff wife, who was found guilty of one of the charges, claims error in the admission of evidence and unfairness in the trial as a result of tactics of the husband's trial counsel.

The wife brought the action for separation. The husband counterclaimed for divorce in an amended and supplemental answer specifying two adulteries. One adultery is alleged to have occurred in New York City with one of the lawyers for the wife, during the pendency of the action. At the close of the husband's proof the charge of adultery in Italy was dismissed. The trial proceeded with respect to the issue of the alleged New York City adultery.

The lawyer who tried the case for the husband had personally directed the investigation, and was personally present during the shadowing and the "raid" which produced the evidence of the alleged New York City adultery. He testified at length as a witness with respect to his observations in such investigation including the "raid". As a consequence of the lawyer's activity and testimony, developed before the jury, his participation as overall strategist, investigator and witness must have been impressed upon the jury.

The record demonstrates that his integrity, credibility and professional status were intertwined inseparably with the issues of the case upon which the jury was obliged to make a finding.

The Canons of Professional Ethics provide:

"When a lawyer is a witness for his client, except as to merely formal matters, such as the attestation or custody of an instrument and the like, he should leave the trial of the case to other counsel. Except when essential to the ends of justice, a lawyer should avoid testifying in Court on behalf of his client."

(Canon 19).

The Canons further provide:

"It is improper for a lawyer to assert in argument his personal belief in his client's innocence or in the justice of his cause." (Canon 15).

Assuming that the lawyer's active personal participation in the pre-trial investigation was nothing worse than undignified, it established the likelihood of his becoming a witness upon the trial. Even if he had not testified as a witness, the repeated reference to his presence at events described by witnesses procured and examined by him emphasized that he personally vouched for their testimony. When the implication of such voucher was made manifest by his taking the stand the lawyer staked his oath and his word against his client's adversary. In the absence of compelling necessity that was improper. The record shows that the trial lawyer's word and his oath were in issue. Especially in a case involving such delicate issues, charged with high emotional pressure, the trial was not a fair one regardless of cumulative proof.

There is no showing, except for an *ipse dixit*, of the necessity of counsel becoming a witness or of the prospective witness acting as counsel.

For the reasons set forth we might be moved to consider on those grounds alone the granting of a new trial in the interests of fairness and in the interests of maintaining the dignity of the judicial tribunal and of the profession. See Flamm v. Nobel, 274 App.Div. 1037, 86 N.Y.S.2d 253; Cherry Creek Nat. Bank v. Fidelity & Casualty Co., 207 App.Div. 787, 791, 202 N.Y.S. 611, 614. But there was more in this trial for which the trial lawyer was largely responsible. Unfairness in the offer of rejected evidence in combination with errors in the admission of evidence had the effect, on the particular facts, of debasing the verdict. . . .

It will be recalled that the New York City adultery was alleged to have occurred with a lawyer who had represented the wife. This lawyer had been employed by a firm of lawyers. One of the partners of that firm was called to the stand and permitted to testify that the lawyer was no longer an employee. Effort was made to offer a paper bearing the signatures of the wife and the partner. The fact that the law firm waived all compensation for its services was presented to the jury in a question by the lawyer for the husband, to which question objection was of course sustained. Then, to top it off, counsel asked in open court for a waiver of the privilege between attorney and client, which was declined. Commentary is not required. . . .

The circumstances mentioned render the trial in this case an unfair one and therefore require a reversal of the interlocutory judgment and the granting of a new trial upon the framed issue of the alleged New York City adultery. . . . It is mandatory that the issues be presented clearly and free of a murky atmosphere of prejudice, irrelevant suggestion, and the displacement of clients by counsel. . . .

Judgment reversed and a new trial ordered in accordance with the opinion herein.

COHN, J., dissents in a dissenting opinion in which DORE, J., concurs.

COHN, JUSTICE (dissenting). . . . Though the practice of a trial counsel becoming a witness in his client's behalf is not to be encouraged (Canon of Professional Ethics No. 19) the witness, however, is not disqualified. At times it may even be an attorney's duty to testify in order to prevent a miscarriage of justice. Hughes v. Wilson Sullivan Co., Inc., 261 App.Div. 39, 40, 24 N.Y.S.2d 534, 535.

It has repeatedly been held that testimony of a trial attorney offered in behalf of his own client is competent. The weight of such testimony is, of course, for the jury; questions of his interest, partiality and bias are to be considered in weighing his testimony. . . .

The fact that defendant's attorney was a witness for his own client should furnish no basis whatever for upsetting the verdict. His testimony as to the occurrences of June 15, 1952 was wholly cumulative since three other witnesses had previously given proof of the same facts. Defendant's attorney endeavored to refrain from taking the witness stand by asking his adversary to concede that his testimony would be of similar import to that of the previous witnesses. Such concession was refused. In his zeal for his client's cause, counsel then felt that it was his duty to testify. Such conduct could hardly be characterized as unfair or prejudicial. . . .

NOTES

(1) See the very detailed DR 5–102 in the Code of Professional Responsibility; also Note, *The Ethical Propriety of an Attorney's Testifying in Behalf of his Own Client*, 38 Iowa L.Rev. 139 (1952).

(2) As to the duty of a lawyer to withdraw from a case in which he learns his partner will be a material witness, see A.B.A. Opinion 50 (1931). See also, In re Estate of Benson, 153 Neb. 824 (1951).

HICKMAN v. TAYLOR

Supreme Court of the United States, 1947.
329 U.S. 495, 67 S.Ct. 385, 91 L.Ed. 451.

[The plaintiff in a suit in a federal district court against tug owners to recover for the death of a seaman in the sinking of the tug filed interrogatories directed to the defendants, requesting that exact copies of all statements of members of the crew be disclosed. The district court ordered that the memoranda of defendants' counsel containing statements of facts by witnesses either be produced or submitted to the court for determination of those portions which should be revealed to the plaintiff. When the defendants and their counsel refused to comply, they were adjudged in contempt. The Supreme Court of the United States held that the order of the district court was erroneous.]

MR. JUSTICE MURPHY. . . . the memoranda, statements and general impressions in issue in this case fall outside the scope of the attorney-client privilege and hence are not protected from discovery on that basis. . . . But the impropriety of invoking that privilege does not provide an answer to the problem before us. . . .

Here is simply an attempt, without purported necessity or justification, to secure written statements, private memoranda and personal recollections prepared or formed by an adverse party's counsel in the course of his legal duties. As such, it falls outside the arena of discovery and contravenes the public policy underlying the orderly prosecution and defense of legal claims. . . .

Historically, a lawyer is an officer of the court and is bound to work for the advancement of justice while faithfully protecting the rightful interests of his clients. In performing his various duties, however, it is essential that a lawyer work with a certain degree of privacy, free from unnecessary intrusion by opposing parties and their counsel. . . . This work is reflected, of course, in interviews, statements, memoranda, correspondence, briefs, mental impressions, personal beliefs, and countless other tangible and intangible ways—aptly though roughly termed by the Circuit Court of Appeals in this case as the 'work product of the lawyer.' Were such materials open to opposing counsel on mere demand, much of what is now put down in writing would remain unwritten. . . . The effect on the legal profession would be demoralizing. And the interests of the clients and the cause of justice would be poorly served.

MR. JUSTICE JACKSON, concurring. Every lawyer dislikes to take the witness stand and will do so only for grave reasons. This is partly because it is not his role; he is almost invariably a poor witness. But he steps out of professional character to do it. He regrets it; the profession discourages it.

NOTES

(1) In the principal case the Court protected the work product of defendant's counsel from discovery by opposing counsel. Should similar protection be extended to statements obtained by those working in conjunction with counsel?

In admiralty suits brought by two seamen against the United States for personal injuries plaintiffs sought discovery of statements of prospective or possible witnesses taken by the Federal Bureau of Investigation. The government resisted, partly on the grounds laid down in *Hickman v. Taylor*, supra. The trial court ruled against the government. The Circuit Court reversed: " . . no valid distinction can be based on the fact that in the one case trial counsel does all the work of preparation for trial, including the interviewing of witnesses, while in the other case he is assisted by others employed by him or by his client. . . . In either situation the rationale of the opinion in the Hickman case requires that the same showing of good cause for the production of such statements of witnesses should be made by the adverse party seeking copies of them." Alltmont v. United States, 177 F.2d 971, 976 (3d Cir., 1949), cert. denied 339 U.S. 967 (1950).

(2) Should protection against discovery extend to the reports of experts employed by a party or his attorney? See discussion of this and other issues raised by Hickman v. Taylor in Note, *Attorney's Work-Product Privilege in the Federal Courts*, 42 St. John's L.Rev. 560 (1968).

A DECEITFUL CLIENT

GEBHARDT v. UNITED RAILWAYS COMPANY OF ST. LOUIS

Supreme Court of Missouri, 1920.
220 S.W. 677, 9 A.L.R. 1076.

SMALL, C. Appeal from the circuit court of the city of St. Louis.

Suit for $15,000 for personal injuries. The jury found for defendant. The court granted a new trial to plaintiff on the ground that the court erred in admitting testimony on behalf of defendant, from which order defendant appealed. The testimony, so improperly admitted as contended for by respondent's learned counsel, was that of the witness Charles Fensky, who was the original attorney for plaintiff, and one Grant Gillespie, who testified, in effect, that plaintiff told them in each other's presence that she was not on the car, as stated in her petition, and consequently was not injured by the defendant; . . .

We have no doubt that the testimony of the witness Fensky was entirely proper. It is true that after a crime has been committed the accused or guilty person may freely consult and even disclose his guilt to his attorney, in order to prepare his defense. In such circumstances, the law puts the seal of secrecy upon such communications. But neither under our statute, R.S.Mo.1909, sec. 6362, nor at common law, of which said statute is simply declaratory, can a person employ an attorney for the purpose of aiding and abetting him in the commission of a future crime or fraud, and thereby seal the lips of his lawyer to secrecy and thus prevent the exposure or detection of such crime or fraud. The privileged communication may be a shield of defense as to crimes already committed, but it cannot be used as a sword or weapon of offense to enable persons to carry out contemplated crimes against society. The law does not make a law office a nest of vipers in which to hatch out frauds and perjuries. This case was first set for trial on the 20th of October, 1914, and it was not only the right, but it was the duty, of Attorney Fensky, when he found, upon examining his client before the trial, that the case had no foundation in fact and could not be successfully maintained without perjury, to at once withdraw from the case, as he did, and to prevent the consummation of the contemplated crime and fraud by testifying to the facts as related to him by the plaintiff. Such communication was not privileged. . . .

[The order of the trial court sustaining plaintiff's motion for a new trial was reversed.]

NOTES

(1) "Deceit by an attorney may be punished as a contempt if the deceit is an abuse of the functions of his office (Bowles v. United States, 50 F.2d 848, 851; United States v. Ford, 9 F.2d 990), and that apart from its punishable quality if it had been the act of someone else. . . . There is a privilege protecting communication between attorney and client. The privilege takes flight if the relation is abused. A client who consults an attorney for advice that will serve him in the commission of a fraud will have no help from the law. He must let the truth be told." Cardozo, J., in Clark v. United States, 289 U.S. 1, 12, 15 (1933). On the use of false evidence as ground for discipline, see 14 A.L.R. 868, note (1921).

(2) To the Disbarment Committee of the Supreme Court of Louisiana, which rendered advisory opinions on legal ethics, the following situation was stated: The attorney for an administratrix, who was the widow of the deceased, learned from his client that the deceased had left property standing in the name of a third person. The administratrix intended not to include this property among the listed assets of the estate, in order to conceal its existence from the heir, who was a son of the deceased by an earlier marriage. The lawyer asked whether he could properly disclose the existence of the property to the heir. The Committee expressed the opinion "that the attorney should use all proper means at his command to persuade the client to disclose the assets and account for them in due course of administration. But if expostulation should fail, then his duty to the court and to the profession would require him to disclose the facts within his knowledge to those adversely interested, to prevent the consummation of the wrong which otherwise might be perpetrated. If resort to the latter alternative should prove necessary, he should at once sever his connection as attorney for the administratrix, and make known to the legal heir his rights in the property concealed." Advisory Opinion No. 4, 4 Tulane L.Rev. 586 (1930).

(3) In Matter of Hardenbrook, 135 App.Div. 634 (1909), affirmed 199 N.Y. 539 (1910), it appeared that an attorney discovered on the first day of a trial that his client had testified falsely, but he continued with the case. He was disbarred. ". . . if an attorney with knowledge of the fact that the testimony upon which his client is seeking to sustain a claim before the court is false and known to his client to be false, so that his client in giving the testimony is guilty of perjury, insists upon the truth of the testimony and endeavors to procure a verdict in his client's favor, it is certainly deceit and malpractice. . . ."

(4) How do you distinguish the above positions on the duty of the lawyer to disclose to the proper authority his client's perjury from that of the majority of the American Bar Association Committee in its Opinion 287, p. 313 supra (the lawyer who knows of his client's prior criminal record is not required to disclose this fact to the sentencing court)?

(5) See Gardner, *The Crime or Fraud Exception to the Attorney-Client Privilege*, 47 A.B.A.J. 708 (1961).

(6) See discussion in Chapter XII, Section 3, Confidential Communications, infra p. 454.

NEW YORK CITY OPINION 62 (1926)

Question: Prior to an examination in supplementary proceedings *A*, a judgment debtor, discloses in professional confidence to *B*, his attorney, the fact that he made a payment to a third party which might be regarded as in fraud of the judgment creditor. *B* has absolute knowledge that the client's statement is true. At the examination *A*, in the presence of *B*, as attorney of record, denies the fact of payment. *B* confers with *A* privately for the purpose of inducing him to correct his testimony. This *A* flatly refuses to do. What is the proper professional course for *B* to pursue?

Answer: In the opinion of the Committee, the right to disclose the confidential communication is a question of law, and the Committee does not assume to define the limits of the client's privilege. It is, however, of the opinion that the attorney should ask the Court to permit him to withdraw. If he is asked the reason, he should assert the reason as founded upon a confidential communication from his client, and if the Court then requires the disclosure, the attorney may properly make it to the Court.

NOTES

(1) "The client is not entitled to have a lawyer who will permit a witness or a client to testify to something which the lawyer himself does not believe to be true. I know that many lawyers—and some of the best reputation—say 'That is my client's story and he has a right to tell it. It is not for me to pass upon its truth. That is for the jury or for the court.' . . .

"I wish most emphatically to disagree with this attitude. I think that if the lawyer thinks that his client or a witness is not telling the truth he should not be a party to what he believes to be perjury, and should not be a party to polluting our courts of justice with this poison, which is doing more right now in New York City to infect the administration of justice than any other one thing. . . ." Buckner, *The Trial of Cases*, 15 A.B.A.J. 271, 273 (1929).

(2) Assume you are assigned to defend a person charged with an offense which carries a capital penalty. You have made your preparation and have entered upon the trial after having pleaded your client innocent. Your client now comes to you and says, "My conscience will be easier if I tell you that I really did commit the crime of which I am charged. However, you are doing a good job for me and of course I want you to continue to try to get me off." What action do you take when next you appear in court?

See Chapter XI, Section 1, infra p. 411.

THE LAWYER AND WITNESSES FOR HIS SIDE

EUSTACE CULLINAN AND HERBERT W. CLARK, PREPARATION FOR TRIAL OF CIVIL ACTIONS *

Pages 24–26 (2d Ed. 1953).

Witnesses should be interviewed separately. When the stories of his witnesses differ in details or on material points, an attorney will sometimes assemble them and have each listen to the other's recitals in the hope of ironing out the conflicts. It is a mistake to do so. Opposing counsel are almost certain to bring out the facts that the witnesses met and rehearsed their tales together and will shout about a school for witnesses. . . .

There is a good deal of loose talk about "coaching" witnesses. Of course, an honest lawyer does not suggest, encourage or wink at perjury or suppression of the truth, or permit it to occur in his case if he can possibly prevent it. Sometimes he will find that his job is rather to *prevent* the witness from hiding or stretching the truth.

But it is fair and right for an attorney to go over the testimony of a witness, to cross-examine in advance his own witness, and to point out to him traps and pitfalls into which he may be lured by opposing counsel. Artful cross-examination may sometimes make a truthful witness look like a liar. Witnesses should be warned to beware of a suave cross-examiner who in friendly fashion puts words in their mouths and gets them to agree. It is well to alert witnesses to watch their tempers, to tell them not to resent questions, and not to make statements in anger that cannot be justified on cross-examination, not to make smart answers or bandy wisecracks with the cross-examiner. All this is just another way of advising the witness to tell the truth and stick to it and to answer questions directly and then to stop. So many witnesses seem to feel that it is up to them to win the case for their side. Many a trial lawyer has been surprised, not to say startled, by statements which his own witnesses make on cross-examination; statements that go beyond the truth and make a hurtful impression on judge and jury.

NOTE

See also, Osborn, The Problem of Proof 177–180 (2d ed. 1926).

---

* Prepared for the Committee on Continuing Legal Education of the American Law Institute collaborating with the American Bar Association.

COMPENSATION OF WITNESSES

NEW YORK COUNTY OPINION 110 (1917)

Question: A lawyer has a contingent arrangement for the prosecution of an action, in which there is but one witness with knowledge of the substantial facts. This witness declines to testify unless compensated for his time and attendance at a rate in excess of the legal fees. The client refuses to accede to the demand of the witness. (a) Can the attorney properly advise his client to pay the witness the amount of his demand? . . .

Answer: In the opinion of the Committee,—The first question (a) should be answered in the negative. A lawyer should not advise his client to pay money to unseal the lips of a witness. The Committee deems it desirable to call attention in this connection to the following judicial decisions: "The payment of a sum of money to a witness 'to tell the truth' is as clearly subversive of the proper administration of justice as to pay him to testify to what is not true." (Matter of Robinson, 151 App.Div. 589, 136 N.Y.S. 548.) It has been held that a contract to pay a witness who resides within the State, and is amenable to process therein, an amount in excess of the legal fees for attending as a witness and testifying only as to the facts within his knowledge, is contrary to public policy and void. (Clifford v. Hughes, 139 App.Div. 730, 124 N.Y.S. 478; see also Cowles v. Rochester Folding Box Co., 81 App.Div. 414, 80 N.Y.S. 811; Neece v. Joseph, 95 Ark. 552, 129 S.W. 797, 30 L.R.A.,N.S., 278.) But it seems that the payment of the actual expenses and a reasonable compensation for time lost to persons in impoverished circumstances (Matter of Schapiro, 144 App.Div. 1, 9, 128 N.Y.S. 852), and perhaps to others (Matter of Robinson, 151 App.Div. 589, 600, 136 N.Y.S. 548), is not necessarily improper when there is no attempt to influence the testimony of the witness. Such payment should be disclosed to the jury as bearing on the credibility of the witness. (Green v. Metropolitan Street Ry. Co., 60 App.Div. 317, 70 N.Y.S. 123.) (The payment of expert witnesses, being permitted by law, is not considered by the Committee as involved in the question.) . . .

NOTE

See Code of Professional Responsibility, DR 7–109(C).

IN RE O'KEEFE

Supreme Court of Montana, 1914.
49 Mont. 369, 142 P. 638, L.R.A.1915A, 514.

[Proceedings for the disbarment of a lawyer. The facts assumed by the court were that John Flynn had brutally assaulted E. E. McIntosh, with John and Anne Nakladahl as the only witnesses to the assault. The Nakladahls, who were transients, demanded a guaranty of $250 out of any judgment McIntosh might recover from Flynn, as a condition of their testifying fully as to the affair. The present respondent, who had filed an action for McIntosh against Flynn, gave the written guaranty demanded.]

Mr. Justice Sanner delivered the opinion of the court.

. . . He [respondent] presents, by way of justification, however, one legal and various fact considerations to which we shall advert.

His fact considerations are that the Nakladahls had threatened, if compelled to testify, to forget what had happened, . . . that he never intended to pay them anything, and so worded his letter as to advise anyone of the involuntary character of the promise contained therein; that he had no intention or purpose to procure the Nakladahls to testify falsely or to in any wise color their testimony, but was actuated solely with the desire to protect the rights of his client by insuring their testimony to the truth necessary for the establishment of his cause; that he felt this to be a right and proper discharge of his duty to his client; . . . [that upon the trial of the cause of McIntosh v. Flynn] all these letters were produced in court, read to the jury, and the circumstances connected with the writing of the same were fully disclosed to the judge presiding and to the jury sitting in the cause; that prior to the trial respondent, supposing Judge Utter would preside at the trial, made a similar disclosure to Judge Utter; that upon the trial respondent announced, in the presence of the Nakladahls, his intention not to pay them any part of the money promised . . .; that the testimony given upon the trial of said cause by the Nakladahls was the truth, and nothing but the truth, and that it never was the intent or purpose of the respondent that any other testimony than the truth should be given by them . . . .

The legal consideration presented by the respondent is that, in view of the facts above recited, he is entitled to be entirely acquitted and discharged of the accusation, for the reason that the writing of these letters for the purpose of securing truthful testimony is not an act of malpractice nor any infraction of legal ethics. . . . A sufficient answer, we think, is stated by the commissioner in his report upon this aspect of the case: "An attorney's duty to his client is a solemn obligation, but it has never been held to be greater than the law itself. However just an attorney may believe his client's claim to be, he may not liquidate it by force of arms, by bribery or any other unlawful means. . . . An expert may be paid large sums for his testimony without it being considered bribery, but the theory of the law as to expert witnesses and witnesses testifying to matters of unscientific fact is not the same. . . ."

The material question is what effect such promises are calculated to produce upon a witness or upon his testimony, and it cannot be gainsaid that this effect is not in the direction of plain, unvarnished truth. In such matters the exigencies of any given cause must yield to the larger demands of public good, and we decline to hold that it is proper in this state for an attorney to buy testimony, whether true or false. . . .

[The attorney was suspended for thirty days.]

NOTES

(1) In Matter of Schapiro, 144 App.Div. 1 (1911), it appeared that a lawyer had made an agreement with a physician that he would be paid as much as was paid to the chief attorney in a case at which the physician was to testify. The physician testified at the trial that there was no understanding as to what he would be paid for testifying, and the lawyer allowed the case to go to the jury upon this testimony. In the disbarment proceedings the lawyer testified that the physician had stated that unless he was given the promise of compensation he would testify in a way damaging to the plaintiff and it was for this reason the agreement was made. The lawyer was disbarred.

(2) If a lawyer promises a witness a sum of money in order to procure his testimony, and if the lawyer at the time of his promise intends not to perform it (the O'Keefe case), or later repudiates it or refuses to perform (the Schapiro case), is the latter element in mitigation or in aggravation of his offense?

(3) How do you reconcile the strict rules against bribing witnesses in civil cases with the practice of district attorneys who promise to seek easier sentences in return for testifying for the state in a criminal matter? See discussion of "plea bargaining," in Chapter IX, infra, beginning at p. 363.

INTERVIEWING ADVERSE WITNESS OR OPPOSITE PARTY

A.B.A. OPINION 117 (1934)

We are asked if it is unethical for an attorney who has a claim against the owner of a store in favor of a person injured by falling upon a slippery floor in the store to interview the clerks employed there who were the only witnesses to the accident. The lawyer informs the clerks so interviewed that he represents the claimant and intends to call them as witnesses if their testimony would be helpful to his client.

. . . We see no impropriety in a bona fide attempt to ascertain the truth as to the condition of the floor by questioning the clerks in the store who are supposed to have knowledge of the essential facts, provided no deception is practiced in obtaining their statements and they are informed that the person interviewing them is the attorney for the claimant or represents him. . . .

In the opinion of the committee, therefore, no impropriety is involved in seeking interviews with the employees as set forth in the inquiry.

A.B.A. OPINION 187 (1938)

A letter carrier was injured when struck by an automobile driven by the wife of the owner and an action was instituted against husband and wife. The accident occurred on or near the premises of the defendants. Prior to the trial of the case, but after the employment of counsel by defendants, counsel for the plaintiff visited the scene of the accident with a policeman who had arrived shortly after it occurred. While there, he interviewed the wife about the facts. He contends that his action was proper under Canon 39, since the wife was a prospective witness, but his opposing counsel contends that his action is condemned by Canon 9. The opinion of the Committee has been requested.

. . . Canon 9 reads in part as follows:

"A lawyer should not in any way communicate upon the subject of controversy with a party represented by counsel; much less should he undertake to negotiate or compromise the matter with him, but should deal only with his counsel."

Canon 39, as amended September 30, 1937, reads in part as follows:

"A lawyer may properly interview any witness or prospective witness for the opposing side in any civil or criminal action without the consent of opposing counsel or party."

Considered separately, the two Canons might well be construed as producing different results when applied to the situation presented; but, when read together, any apparent conflict is resolved. Though the wife is undoubtedly a prospective witness for her husband in the pending action, she is likewise a party represented by counsel. Since Canon 9 expressly condemns any communication with her "upon the subject of controversy," Canon 39 must necessarily be construed to refer only to witnesses who are not adverse parties represented by counsel.

It is clear from the earlier opinions of this committee that Canon 9 is to be construed literally and does not allow a communication with an opposing party, without the consent of his counsel, though the purpose merely be to investigate the facts.

Ch. 7 *ALTERNATIVES TO THE ADVERSARY SYSTEM* 329

SECTION 5. ALTERNATIVES TO THE ADVERSARY SYSTEM

Introduction. In considering whether the adversary method is appropriate in the settlement of a controversy three aspects may usefully be distinguished. One is the nature of the process. It assumes that the parties are sharply at issue and that a clearcut decision in favor of one or the other may be reached. A second is the role of the lawyer in the process and the frame of mind developed. The role of the lawyer is that of a partisan representative, not at all a friend of the court in aiding it to reach the golden mean, a result fair to all parties to the controversy. The third is the nature of the controversy and its appropriateness to settlement by rigorous application of rules of law.

In Chapter I, Section 6, we noted the recent emphasis by the United States Supreme Court on the right to counsel as an important goal for society and responsibility of the legal profession. The trend is continuing toward greater emphasis on and wider enforcement of this right, e. g., the right of the juvenile, In re Gault, supra, Chapter I p. 48.

In this Section we consider whether there are alternatives or limits to the adversary system, as the lawyer knows it, and if so, when and under what circumstances they come into play.

MADERA v. BOARD OF EDUCATION OF THE CITY OF NEW YORK

United States Court of Appeals, Second Circuit, 1967.
386 F.2d 778.

[A 14-year old student in the seventh grade of Junior High School was suspended by his principal for behavioral difficulties. According to regular procedure the District Superintendent called a Guidance Conference to which the boy's parents were invited. The parents sought and obtained legal help from the Legal Services Unit of Mobilization for Youth, Inc. However, the attorney was informed that he could not attend the Conference under a ruling of the Superintendent of Schools:

"Inasmuch as this is a guidance conference for the purpose of providing an opportunity for parents, teachers, counselors, supervisors, et. al., to plan educationally for the benefit of the child, attorneys seeking to represent the parent or child may not participate."

The district court enjoined the Conference. "The right to a hearing is a due process requirement of such constitutional significance as to void application of defendants' 'no attorneys provision'." 267 F.Supp. 356, 373. The Board of Education appealed.]

MOORE, CIRCUIT JUDGE. First, the Guidance Conference is not a criminal proceeding: thus the counsel provision of the Sixth Amendment and the cases thereunder are inapplicable. Second, there is no showing that any attempt is ever made to use any statement at the Conference in any subsequent criminal proceeding. . . . Therefore . . . the issue is one of procedural "due process" in its general sense, free from the "specifics" of the Fifth and Sixth Amendments. . . .

The right to representation by counsel is not an essential ingredient to a fair hearing in all types of proceedings. . . . The Guidance Conference is clearly not an adjudication. . . . What due process may require before a child is expelled . . . or is remanded to a custodial school or other institution which restricts his freedom to come and go as he pleases is not before us.

Appellees here argue that the presence of the lawyer is necessary because it is he "who has the communicative skill to express the position of the student's parents when—because of lack of education, inarticulateness, or simply awe at the array of highly educated and articulate professionals in whose presence they find themselves—they may themselves be unable to do so." Actually, the trial record supports the view, despite some testimony to the contrary, that the social worker, who is allowed to attend . . . would provide more adequate counsel to the child or the parents than would a lawyer.

. . . Judgment reversed; injunction vacated and complaint dismissed.

Certiorari to the United States Supreme Court was subsequently denied, 390 U.S. 1028 (1968).

NOTES

(1) What does the court mean when it says the Guidance Conference is "clearly not an adjudication?" Can you think of other situations when you, as the *adjudicator* would prefer to have counsel excused? Is it in the interests of the *parties* to have counsel prohibited in the situation described in *Madera?* What are the reasons why the superintendent welcomes the social worker but wishes to exclude the lawyer?

(2) The attorneys for appellees in *Madera* argued that the lawyer is necessary because he can speak for those who for one reason or another cannot express themselves effectively. Is this a proper thumbnail sketch of the traditional role of the advocate in the adversary system? Does it suggest a new and important role for the advocate in Urban America?

JOHN P. DAWSON, A HISTORY OF LAY JUDGES *

Page 5 (1960).

For us adjudication that carries full authority can be organized only by the state. Tribunals can of course be created by consent of litigants but there are serious questions still as to how far they can exclude or displace the judicial agencies created by the state. . . . We think of arbitration as "private." Arbitration tribunals may ultimately depend on state-created agencies to enforce their decisions and the decisions themselves when rendered may have consequences that state officials must recognize, but the consequences are attributed to private consent. The same is true of discipline or grievance committees and other tribunals set up by membership groups. Though the adjectives used may be different, similar modes of analysis are used to explain courts or commissions created for settlement of international disputes. In this respect our thinking has been pervaded by a political theory of the omnipresent state. Nowhere more than in adjudication does the state's monopoly seem exclusive.

NATHAN P. FEINSINGER, UNIVERSITY OF WISCONSIN CENTER FOR TEACHING AND RESEARCH IN DISPUTES SETTLEMENT **

1968 Wis.L.Rev. 349.

I. INTRODUCTION

In general, there are two methods of disputes settlement. One is by agreement of the parties to a dispute. The other is by the use of force. Agreement may be achieved by the give and take of face-to-face negotiations between or among the parties alone or with the assistance of a "neutral" selected by them. The neutral exercises only such authority as the parties may confer upon him, ranging from merely "sitting in" on meetings as an observer, to issuing a "final and binding" award on the merits of the dispute. Between these extremes, there are various other devices, voluntary in character, likewise designed to achieve a peaceful settlement. A device widely used today is the "fact finding" procedure, under which the neutral makes findings of fact, with or without formal recommendations.

A definition of terms may be helpful at this point. There is a surprising lack of understanding, even among lawyers, as to (1) the difference between the mediation process and the process of arbitration, and (2) the difference between voluntary and compulsory arbitration. The mediation process is wholly voluntary, the neutral, the mediator, seeking to bring the parties together, using the technique, art, or skill of persuasion. Voluntary arbitration is a procedure, again

---

* Copyright by the Harvard University Press.

** Copyright by the University of Wisconsin. Reprinted with permission.

based on an agreement of the parties, authorizing a neutral, here called an arbitrator, to render a final and binding decision or award. Compulsory arbitration is a procedure imposed by law requiring the parties to submit their dispute to an arbitrator or to a panel of arbitrators or, in the case of a labor dispute, to a "labor court." . . .

Mediation is increasingly important as a method of settling disputes of all kinds. Accordingly, a comprehensive understanding of the mediation process is a necessary part of the equipment of the lawyer and the judge. In the case of the lawyer, mediation may be viewed as an additional tool for use in his clients' behalf. Next, the mediation process differs from settlements by compromise in that the former involves the services of a neutral third party. The judges also have an interest. Traditionally, many judges have felt that a settlement in certain cases, with the judge's assistance, is in the best interest of all concerned. The pretrial conference is regarded by some judges and attorneys as an appropriate occasion to attempt to reach a settlement through mediation. Due to their respected position in the community, judges are from time to time called upon to perform the function of a mediator in a case and may do so where they deem it to be in the public interest. In addition, the modern judge's need for understanding the mediation process used in collective bargaining and in strike situations may be illustrated by reference to the New York transit dispute of 1965. . . .

In that case, the court imposed a penalty of fine and imprisonment on the president of the Transit Workers Union of America, thereby seriously handicapping the efforts of the parties to reach a settlement. This unfortunate result might have been avoided without loss of judicial dignity and prestige by suspending the sentence and directing the union president to rejoin the negotiations. If, in this case, the judge made a considered choice between what he believed were competing values—the public interest in supporting the dignity and prestige of the court as compared with the public interest in achieving a settlement of the strike—that is one thing. But if he acted without consideration of the impact of his sentence on the negotiations, that is another, and one which illustrates the need for greater understanding and knowledge of the mediation process. . . .

W. WILLARD WIRTZ, COLLECTIVE BARGAINING: LAWYER'S ROLE IN NEGOTIATIONS AND ARBITRATIONS

34 A.B.A.J. 547, 551 (1948).

It may even be seriously questioned whether the basic approach of the adversary system of advocacy—the trial by half-truths—does not place too much strain on a continuing relationship. It is all right, in court litigation, for first one advocate and then the other to present a skillfully devised assortment of carefully selected facts and precedents and leave it then to the judge to find his way between a Scylla and Charybdis of fractional verities. The two advocates are probably well matched in this art; they speak the same language as does the judge; and the only consequence of his being in fact deceived is that the spoils may be unfairly divided.

None of this protection is present in arbitration proceedings. The advocates are usually not well matched, and the arbitrator frequently knows much less about the subject matter than does anyone else in the room. Worst of all is the fact that if he errs in this weighing of fact and fiction, the parties are going to have to live together with his error. If the mistake is serious enough, it may well start a chain reaction of disputes which are the product only of the arbitrator's misunderstanding. Giving an arbitrator a distorted account involves a risk which need not be calculated in ordinary liquidation litigation.
. . .

NOTES

(1) "A problem may also be resolved not by the application of law (although equally not in violation of law) but by a process of adjustment—an extralegal or metajuridical means. Thus certain heirs may renounce their rights in an estate, or their conflicting claims may be compromised without resort to litigation. The unification of Germany might be brought about without reference to the Potsdam Agreements by a negotiated settlement acceptable to all concerned. But the results may have legal effect and be in legal form. In other words, the solution arrived at without utilizing law may itself provide the law of the case, just as in a commercial arbitration where the arbitrators are authorized to make a fair compromise." Jessup, Transnational Law 6 (1956) Yale University Press.

(2) "As Lord Justice Denning of the Court of Appeals has said, "some lawyers find solutions for every difficulty while other lawyers find difficulties for every solution." Id., at 7. Which type of lawyer thrives in the traditional, "fight-to-the-end" adversary situation? Which type would you prefer to have representing you in an arbitration dispute with an old customer?

(3) "The mediating form-free arbitrator and his opposite number, the stiffly literal judge, are equally threats to effective collective bargaining. The first may dissipate the benefits of careful negotiation and draftsmanship by disregarding the contract in the resolution of disputes. The second may dissipate those benefits by projecting into the agreement incongruent meaning, foreign to the thinking of those who created it." Fuller, Collective Bargaining and the Arbitrator's Rule 8, 51 (1962). Professor Fuller's observation is quoted in a comprehensive Note, *A Study of Labor Arbitration— The Values and the Risks of the Rule of Law*, 1967 Utah L.Rev. 223, 247. It is pointed out that approximately 94 per cent of all collective bargaining contracts contain arbitration clauses.

(4) See also discussion of Conciliation in Chapter IV, Section 3, and Chapter VI, Section 2, supra.

Chapter VIII

THE LAWYER AND THE LEGISLATURE

Introduction. The relationship between the lawyer and the legislature is a close one. This is not surprising. It would be paradoxical if lawyers did not have a significant impact on the branch of government where laws are enacted. On the national scene lawyer legislators outnumber nonlawyers and at the state and local levels they frequently appear as members of legislative bodies. (See Chapter X, Sec. 1, Political Leadership, page 378 infra). The advocate in court must of necessity make frequent use of legislative materials and law schools have been accused of dereliction in overemphasizing case law and not bringing home to students the importance of statutes. The present chapter speaks of the lawyer's connection with the legislature in two other respects—as a lobbyist and as the representative of a client before a legislative investigating committee.

The term "lobbying" has connotations of unethical, if not illegal, activity to many. This was even more clearly the view in an earlier era when bribery, corruption, secrecy and conflicts of interest in the legislative arena were more common than they are today. It is no doubt for this reason that courts have traditionally been hostile to contracts for the services of a lobbyist, often irrespective of the methods of lobbying contemplated, legal or illegal. Today it is recognized that the lobbyist, often a lawyer, is necessary to the legislative process if those who make laws in a complicated society are to be adequately informed. The modern attitude is reflected in these words from a 1950 Congressional committee investigating lobbying: "Every democratic society worthy of its name must have some lawful means by which individuals and groups can lay their needs before government. One of the central purposes of government is that people should be able to reach it . . . with maximum impact and possibility of success. This is, fundamentally, what lobbying is about."

The lobbyist serves a number of important functions in the democratic process of enacting laws. Election of the legislator on a geographical basis does not take into account the fact that individuals may also relate to distinct economic, social, business and other groups that transcend geographical lines, groups that want to be heard in the legislature. Their lobbyists are in a position to make these special views known to elected legislators. They supply factual information, advance policy arguments, draft and analyze bills, and perform other services in the process of helping to educate the legislator. Many of these functions obviously call for the skills of a lawyer. At the same time the lobbyist assists in publicizing the legislative process and is often instrumental in increasing public interest in the affairs of government. When the means are proper the lobbyist in a society as complex as today's can be said to be indispensable in improving the quality of legislation.

It is at the point of means, however, that the critical questions arise in the area of lobbying and it is to these questions that this chapter is addressed. The temptations not to cut square corners can be great when the stakes are high, as they frequently are with legislation, and the methods of lobbying have been frequently investigated and have been subjected to various kinds of regulation. Laws against bribery and other corrupt practices are obvious examples of such regulation. Statutes requiring the registration of lobbyists and the divulging of information as to their activities are widespread. The invalidation of many lobbying contracts has been previously mentioned. Indirect pressure, such as the use of the tax laws, is another form of control.

Lawyers, in addition, are subject to professional restrictions not applicable to other lobbyists although the guidelines here are perhaps less clear than in the courtroom. These too will be examined in this Chapter. Major topics to be considered will include the relationship between private and public interest and the problem of who represents the latter. Also to be studied is the question of whether personal contacts, outside the legislative chamber and the committee room, are proper and whether the influence of the lobbyist should go beyond arguments on the merits. Comparison of the lawyer's adversary role in court and his function before the legislature raises other questions obviously pertinent to our present study of the lawyer as a lobbyist.

Reference to the lawyer as an advocate suggests the second of the two major divisions of this Chapter—the lawyer as the representative of a client before a legislative investigating committee. There is much evidence that in this setting the role of the legislature itself changes substantially with an inexorable impact upon the witnesses called to testify as well as upon their lawyer representatives. The function of the latter becomes far different from that of the legislative lobbyists.

The justification for legislative investigation is the need for information to assist in future legislation as well as the need to inquire into the operation and execution of laws on the books. On both grounds the courts have upheld the constitutionality of legislative investigations and there have been many committees over the years engaged in such activities, especially in Congress. The great majority of these have gone about their work with little public fanfare. A few, however, have made headlines and the names of their chairmen have become household words. The activities of others have become highly controversial with sharp attacks from both liberals and conservatives, dependent upon the subject of the particular investigation. The controversies have often centered on the abuses of power of some committees, particularly with reference to procedures and the right of witnesses. Too often the investigation has become tantamount to a criminal trial with few of the courtroom safeguards. One concern has been that of representation by counsel in such proceedings and a definition of the lawyer's role. Section 2 of this Chapter will focus on that problem.

SECTION 1. THE LOBBYIST

JULIUS COHEN, THE GOOD MAN AND THE ROLE OF REASON IN LEGISLATIVE LAW

41 Corn.L.Qu. 386, 395 (1956).

The average courtroom lawyer would undoubtedly be shocked at the suggestion that the practice of law ought to be geared to the standard set by the shysters and ambulance-chasers, merely because shysterism and ambulance-chasing persist. There should be no difference with respect to those who view the legislative process in practice in the darkest possible light.

Now, granted that the legislative process involves the struggle over competing group interests in which irrational *and* rational forces are at work, in which legislative machinery may be manipulated for good *and* evil ends, and in which motivations are for private *and* public gain, what should be the nature of the lawyer's representational role in the legislative forum? Ideally, his function would parallel that of the lawyer in the judicial forum performing in the highest traditions of his profession. There, though he represents private clients before the court, he serves in a higher public capacity as an officer of the court. Here, too, his public duty as an officer of the legislature would transcend his immediate duty to his clients. He would lend his talents primarily to the task of helping policy-makers strike a proper balance between private group needs and the welfare of the community. Because present legislative procedures for independent fact-finding are woefully inadequate, he would bring to the legislative forum the best evidentiary materials that could be gathered for predicting the consequences of a policy proposal. He would, by logical analysis, endeavor to determine whether the consequences would be in harmony with the existing system of values; he would explore the need for correcting the existing system when it is not in tune with the basic aspirations of the community. Precedent and analogy would play an important role in helping to develop a sense of proportion and perspective, and a critical eye would search out and expose errors and the various types of "crooked thinking" that might be employed by the unscrupulous to influence legislative policy makers. Discounting institutional differences, this is essentially the pattern of the lawyer's role in the judicial arena whenever the court is called upon to legislate judicially—when it is asked, for example, to rule on questions concerning the meaning or the constitutionality of a statute. One of the distinguishing factors is that in the judicial forum, salient policy issues are too often beclouded by impressive legal jargon and symbolism; in the legislative forum, the insulation of legal symbolism is more apt to be stripped off, and the policy considerations more likely to be laid bare. In addition, a lawyer appearing before a court is usually *representing* his client; but before a legislative body, he is apt to be *lobbying* for his client. But to the extent that lobbying involves alerting legislators to problems that might need attention in the legislative forum it is salutary. Petitioning for redress of grievances is, after all, a right that is granted under the Constitution. To the extent that it involves *private* hearings on the merits or demerits of pending proposals, it serves the useful function of bringing to the attention of policy makers information that could shed significant light on policy proposals. The difficulty, of course, with such a procedure is that all competing views are not given an equal chance to be heard. For private hearings require access to policy makers, and too often this is a privilege that is not accorded equally to all who knock at private legislative doors.

Besides the preparation of rigorous arguments for the justification or criticism of a policy proposal, the legislative lawyer should acquaint himself with the intricacies of legislative machinery, procedures, and sources of power. Without such knowledge, the most convincing argument could go for naught. A lack of knowledge of machinery, of "know-how," could well mean the loss of a battle, no matter how meritorious or just the particular cause might be. He must, for example, know who the real legislative judges of a policy issue would be, so as to know whom to persuade; he must have a keen sense of timing; he must be skilled in devising parliamentary strategy for use by a friendly Congressman or Senator; he must know enough about legislative draftsmanship to make sure that the policy that is sought will not be perverted or otherwise defeated by improper legislative language; finally, he must be adept in the art of compromise, of knowing how best to reach a position not as good as the one hoped for, but considerably better than if the opposition forces clearly had their way.

All this, of course, is an account of the *ideal* view of the lawyer's representational role in the legislative forum. What are the practical difficulties in fulfilling this role? There are, indeed, many. The pressure for quick decision, the low level of competence of many legislators, the elements of bias and prejudgment, the factor of manipulation, the unwillingness of many to recognize the relationship between immediate and long-range goals, the impatience with the tedium of rigorous analysis, the high-pitched, volatile emotionalism that often pervades the legislative scene all combine to discourage anyone inspired to stride forth in the role of the idealist. Other factors becloud the scene from a practical point of view. First of all, to amass rigorous empirical data in support of a legislative cause requires financial resources that only the more wealthy clients can afford to make available; the less affluent, accordingly, must suffer. Secondly, there are too many areas—especially those involving social behavior—in which reliable information is unavailable concerning consequences of proposed legislative action—areas in which conjecture and hunch must, of necessity, hold sway. This latter difficulty—one that is born out of the limitations of human knowledge—must be borne with patience and resignation. It provides some small measure of comfort to know that even one of the most gifted of minds was obliged to confide:

> "The simplest problems which come up from day to day seem to me to be quite unanswerable as soon as I try to get below the surface. Each side, when I hear it, seems to me right till I hear the other." *

What then must the less gifted lawyer do under such circumstances? Perhaps he is left with no other recourse save that of presenting the justification for his cause as an hypothesis, and adducing whatever evidence, however slim, is available to sustain its plausibility. He would push his case to the hilt, and so would his adversary; out of the heat of conflict might emerge some basis upon which the policy maker could fashion a reasonably intelligent guess.

These, then, are some of the practical limitations upon the role of reason in the practice of legislative law. They are often discouraging to the idealist, but no more so than is the trial of a complicated issue of fact by a jury. To be sure, there are many shadows on the legal horizon, but where there are shadows there must also be some light. All is not unreason in the making of legislative law. Moreover, whatever the role that unreason plays it must, at the very least, give the idealist good reason for being.

NOTES

(1) The importance and influence of lawyers in the legislative process is emphasized in Hoffmann, *The Lawyer as a Lobbyist*, 1963 Univ. of Ill. Law Forum 16. See also Milbraith, The Washington Lobbyists (1963); Horsky, The Washington Lawyer (1952); Cong.Quarterly Service, Legislators and the Lobbyists, Second Ed., May 1968. ". . . . The legislative body is not a maker of the rule so much as a sort of court before whom the different interests, each appear arguing its own point of view. . . ." Chamberlain, Book Review, 17 A.B.A.J. 685 (1931).

(2) The American Law Institute, noted primarily for its Restatements of the Law, is coming to play an increasingly important role in legislation. For an account of this trend by its Director see Wechsler, *The Course of*

---

* Learned Hand, Democracy: Its Presumptions and Realities, Perspectives U.S.A. 7 (1953).

the Restatements, 55 A.B.A.J. 147 (1969). Bar Association groups at all levels are active proponents of legislative changes, particularly with reference to judicial administration. The American Judicature Society has also been successful in effecting similar changes in the laws of many states. The National Conference of Commissioners on Uniform State Laws has a long record of success in advocating changes in the statutory laws of all states. Over 200 uniform laws on numerous subjects have been proposed by the Conference. The lobbying burden of this program is assumed for the most part by Commissioners in each state. Sec. 18 of the By-Laws of the National Conference provides: "It shall be the duty of the Commissioners from each state to endeavor . . . (b) To procure the enactment by the legislature of the state of such acts recommended by the National Conference as are deemed by the Commissioner suitable and practicable for enactment therein and to report to the Secretary the reasons for their conclusion that any such acts are unsuitable or impracticable for enactment in the State." Handbook of the National Conference of Commissioners on Uniform State Laws 255 (1965). What is the obligation of a Commissioner in a particular state who has an important client opposed to a proposed Uniform Act?

(3) For an informative study of the legislative process and the influence of lobbyists see Eidenberg and Morey, An Act of Congress (1969). (The story of the enactment of the Elementary and Secondary Education Act of 1965).

A. THE PROFESSIONAL STANDARD

CANONS OF PROFESSIONAL ETHICS

No. 26

A lawyer openly, and in his true character, may render professional services before legislative or other bodies, regarding proposed legislation and in advocacy of claims before departments of government, upon the same principles of ethics which justify his appearance before the Courts; but it is unprofessional for a lawyer so engaged to conceal his attorneyship, or to employ secret personal solicitations, or to use means other than those addressed to the reason and understanding, to influence action.

CODE OF PROFESSIONAL RESPONSIBILITY *

EC 8–4

Whenever a lawyer seeks legislative or administrative changes, he should identify the capacity in which he appears, whether on behalf of himself, a client, or the public. A lawyer may advocate such changes on behalf of a client even though he does not agree with them. But when a lawyer purports to act on behalf of the public, he should espouse only those changes which he conscientiously believes to be in the public interest.

* Copyright 1969 by the American Bar Association. Reprinted with permission.

CHARLES A. HORSKY, THE WASHINGTON LAWYER
Page 49 (1952).

A client may arrive in your office, anxious to oppose or favor a bill. Hearings may have been set, and he wants to appear, and wants you to help him to get ready. There is work for you to do.

Conversation will bring out, painfully or promptly as the case may be, why he takes the position he does, and a general flavor of the reasons he can advance. You are then in a position at once similar to but at the same time very different from that of a lawyer preparing a witness for a trial. True, you don't have to worry about the rules of evidence, but you become more keenly aware of the fact that opinion evidence and sweeping conclusions and generalizations are poor substitutes for carefully circumscribed and documented statements, charts, and graphs. You also know that even though you need not fear greatly that irrelevant material will be excluded, your witness will have only a limited amount of time in which to present a position, and time spent on irrelevancies is simply time wasted. You explore the possibility of reasons other than the ones your client has thought of. You imagine all possible arguments on the other side, and determine which ones to try to meet, which ones to ignore, and which ones to try to skate over lightly. And when all of that is done, you make sure that your client understands what you have prepared, agrees with it, and can answer—you hope—such questions as the committee may put to him. . . .

Thus far, we would no doubt all agree that the Washington lawyer is largely exercising the normal skills and abilities of the profession—draftsmanship, marshaling of facts, distillation of issues and arguments as well as resolution of purely legal issues. Let us pursue his activities into areas where his work may be less directly legal. Either in connection with some of the activities already described, or independent of them, a Washington lawyer may be brought directly into legislative activity. Let us say that on some particular measure in which a client is interested the lines have begun to be drawn in Congress. Some of the members are known to be on the client's side. Others are doubtful. The lawyer visits, and seeks to persuade, the doubtful ones who are important, using, let us assume for the moment—to avoid a problem we must face later—the same sort of arguments he has made, or would have made, in a public hearing. . . .

. . . No doubt the non-public nature of this sort of lawyer's work lends itself to the ready suspicion that it is not legal work at all, but influence-peddling or worse. But let us stick to our assumption, and try to see whether a line can or should be drawn between the proper and the improper in relation to what we have thus far described.

The direct guide is none too helpful. Canon 26 of the Canons of Professional Ethics of the American Bar Association . . . has had no pertinent official interpretation.

One matter is clear: an attorney who engages in any of the activities we have described, cannot, with propriety, conceal his attorneyship. This is plainly and rightfully condemned. But there clarity ends. What is the significance of the phrase in the first section of the Canon that the lawyer may render professional services "before legislative . . . bodies"? Does the reference to "bodies" mean to exclude all contact with the individual member of Congress? . . .

We get no help from the second "thou shalt not" section of the Canon. Its clauses are in the disjunctive, and there is an unqualified ban on "secret personal solicitations." Does "secret" mean to prohibit everything except appearances before committees? Specifically, does it prohibit a discussion with a member of Congress in his office, at which the lawyer attempts to persuade him by reasoned arguments? Does the word "personal" in the phrase "secret personal solicitations" mean that it bans only those non-public contacts where personal influence or favors, and not the merits, are the basis of the appeal?

The latter interpretation certainly sounds more reasonable, but if it is to be accepted it means that the whole clause simply duplicates the clause which immediately follows it—that no means shall be used "other than those addressed to the reason and understanding." For that matter, what does that mean? Literally, it means that a lawyer must close his eyes to the fact that lawmaking is a political process— unless "reason and understanding" implies that a lawyer may attempt to make clear to the members of Congress the political facts of life.

In truth, the Canon is either so strict as to be impossible, or so vague as to be useless. Washington lawyers do all of these things, and in my opinion properly so. Both the public and the non-public aspects of such work call for his legal abilities, and for the wisdom, understanding and judgment that can come only from experience in many cases, many victories and defeats, over many years. . . .

Vague as the ethical standards may be, there is clearly a line that no lawyer should pass. Fundamentally, there can be no more basis for a lawyer to obtain the vote of a member of Congress on the basis of friendship, or on the basis of past, present or future favors, than there is for a lawyer to obtain a vote from a judge or a juror on the same basis. The lawyer stands on a different footing from his client. John Smith, the voter, and also the man who favors H.R. 10,000, can with propriety tell his Congressman that the price of Smith's next vote or his next campaign contribution is the Congressman's own vote for H.R. 10,000. It may be poor citizenship; it may move the Congressman to vote against, rather than for, H.R. 10,000. But it is the essence of democracy, it seems to me, that voters should be able to tell a member of Congress what they want, and to tell the member that if he disagrees, he will lose that voter's support in the next campaign.

The Washington lawyer, or any other lawyer, for that matter, is not the voter. He is retained, and paid, for professional advice and services. But when he is retained, or paid, for his influence or alleged influence over a member of Congress, regardless of the merits of the issue, he is no longer acting as a lawyer. . . .

NOTES

(1) Can Canon 26 be interpreted to permit the kind of lobbying espoused by Horsky, i. e., private contacts by lawyer with legislators to advance arguments on the merits? Canon 26 also contains the clause, "upon the same principles of ethics which justify his appearance before the Courts." Does this justify the lobbyist in assuming the role of an adversary? What does this clause suggest with reference to the ex parte call on the legislator?

If a lawyer has been a political supporter of a legislator do you agree that this fact may not be used by the lawyer in obtaining the legislator's vote? Is this view realistic? Is it improper for a lawyer lobbyist to take a legislator to dinner? Is it bribery to promise political support to the legislator if he votes for a bill? If the non-lawyer lobbyist is under no such restrictions does not this impair the effectiveness of the lawyer lobbyist? Can the lawyer circumvent the canons by serving as a non-lawyer in activities, such as lobbying, where many non-lawyers serve?

(2) From 1946 to 1967 twenty-three former United States Senators and ninety former Congressmen, most of them lawyers, had registered as lobbyists under the Federal Regulation of Lobbying Act. (Legislators and the Lobbyists, Cong.Quarterly Sen. 2d Ed., p. 45, May, 1968). Are these lobbyists under any special ethical restrictions? Is the following statement of Senator Douglas applicable to the ex-legislator lobbyist?

"There is a final abuse against which officials should guard. That is the practice for leading members of government to resign and then almost immediately appear as well-paid legal representatives of private agencies which are doing business with the government. Confidential advisors to Presidents, for example, have done this. The practice has been most marked, however, in the case of certain regulatory agencies . . .

"But what, someone may ask is wrong with such practices? Are not these men of ability and should they not be allowed to exercise their talents in order to provide for their families? Furthermore, by serving with the public agency they have been able to acquire almost unique information and knowledge. Since this was acquired by their own efforts should they not be allowed to use it for their own profit?

"Such defenses miss the real point. These men are hired not merely for their ability and knowledge, but also for their influence. Those who engage them believe that their past connections and present friendships will help the private employer to obtain more favorable action than would otherwise be possible. Tacitly, therefore, but not less surely, these men sell their real or supposed influence. . . ." Ethics in Government 55 (1952).

See Code of Professional Responsibility EC 9–3; A.B.A. Op. 26 (1930). Cf. Federal Conflict of Interest Act of 1962 with reference to former employees of the executive branch of the federal government, page 374 infra.

LOUIS D. BRANDEIS, THE OPPORTUNITY IN THE LAW

39 Am.L.Rev. 555, 560 (1905).

For nearly a generation the leaders of the bar with few exceptions have not only failed to take part in any constructive legislation designed to solve in the interest of the people our great social, economic, and industrial problems, they have failed likewise to oppose legislation prompted by selfish interests. They have often gone further in disregard of public interest. They have, at times, advocated as lawyers legislative measures which as citizens they could not approve, and have endeavored to justify themselves by a false analogy. They have erroneously assumed that the rule of ethics to be applied to a lawyer's advocacy is the same where he acts for private interests against the public as it is in litigation between private individuals. . . .

. . . [T]he lawyer recognizes that in trying a case his prime duty is to present his side to the tribunal fairly and as well as he can, relying upon his adversary to present his case fairly and as well as he can. As the lawyers on the two sides are usually reasonably well matched, the judge or jury may ordinarily be trusted to make such a decision as justice demands.

But when lawyers act upon the same principle in supporting the attempts of their private clients to secure or to oppose legislation, a very different condition is presented. In the first place, the counsel selected to represent important private interests possesses usually ability of a high order, while the public is often inadequately represented or wholly unrepresented. That presents a condition of great unfairness to the public. As a result many bills pass in our legislatures which would not have become law if the public interest had been fairly represented; and many good bills are defeated which if supported by able lawyers would have been enacted. Lawyers have, as a rule, failed to consider this distinction between practice in the court involving only private interests and practice before the legislature or city council where public interests are involved. Some men of high professional standing have even endeavored to justify their course in advocating professionally legislation which in their character as citizens they would have voted against.

NOTES

(1) The author of the foregoing article, after a distinguished career at the bar, became the target of perhaps the most bitter criticism ever directed against a Supreme Court appointee. See Frank, *The Legal Ethics of Louis D. Brandeis,* 17 Stan.L.Rev. 683 (1965), for a fascinating account of the background of this controversy and a discussion of the twelve specific counts of ethical unfitness leveled against Justice Brandeis by the minority report of the Senate Judiciary Committee.

(2) As a lawyer are there any ethical restrictions on your accepting a retainer from a tobacco company to defeat a bill which would limit advertising of cigarettes? Assume that your personal views are in opposition to cigarette advertising and that they have been frequently expressed. Are these views relevant to your decision whether to accept the retainer? Are you as a lawyer ethically obligated to refuse an offered retainer to seek by constitutional amendment to limit *Gideon v. Wainwright* (supra page 39) to capital cases? Do the Canons or the Code of Professional Responsibility cover these situations? See Canons of Professional Ethics No. 26; Code of Professional Responsibility, EC 8–4. Cf. the conflicting duties of the lawyer-legislator, Chapter X, Section 1, page 385, note (4), infra.

(3) Must a lawyer refuse to appear before a legislative committee on behalf of a client while a member of his firm is serving in the legislature? A.B.A. Opinion 296 (1959) so concluded, adding: "A full disclosure before the committee would not alter this ruling nor would it be changed by the fact that the member of the Legislature would not share in the fee received thereby." This ruling was modified somewhat in A.B.A. Opinion 306 (1962) after it was pointed out that the earlier opinion had had the effect of cutting down on the number of lawyers in the legislatures, particularly in the smaller states, and had deterred younger lawyers employed by law firms from running for the legislature.

(4) *The "judicial lobbyist." Briefs amicus curiae.* This Chapter explores the lawyer's role in attempting to improve the law as a legislative lobbyist. Even better known is his function as an advocate of a party in "educating" a court with reference to the law of a particular controversy. The lawyer's sights may be colored in either instance by the welfare of his client but his stated objectives are to change (or preserve) the law for the better, clearly a proper professional function. The fact of his bias before the court is obvious if his adversary role is kept in mind and should be equally clear when he becomes a legislative lobbyist on behalf of a client. Development of the brief amicus curiae, however, has raised questions with reference to the lawyer's duties in endeavoring to influence judge-made law in this fashion. The early amicus curiae was literally a "friend of the court," called upon to assist, with no special interest in the case. The shift in modern times from neutral adviser to "lobbyist" before the court is well described in Krislov, *The Amicus Curiae Brief: From Friendship to Advocacy,* 72 Yale L.Jour. 694 (1963). Is there danger that lawyer involvement in this kind of brief writing on behalf of pressure groups, a common practice today, can harm rather than assist the court? Should there be greater concern over the conflict between client interest and public interest in the modern brief amicus curiae than in a brief filed by an attorney for his client-litigant? Is legislative lobbying any different?

B. THE LEGAL STANDARD

STATUTORY REGULATION

FEDERAL REGULATION OF LOBBYING ACT

60 Stat. 842, 2 U.S.C.A. § 267 (1946).

(a) Any person who shall engage himself for pay or for any consideration for the purpose of attempting to influence the passage or defeat of any legislation by the Congress of the United States, shall, before doing anything in furtherance of such object, register with the Clerk of the House of Representatives and the Secretary of the Senate and shall give to those officers in writing and under oath, his name and business address, the name and address of the person by whom he is employed, and in whose interest he appears or works, the duration of such employment, how much he is paid and is to receive, by whom he is paid or is to be paid, how much he is to be paid for expenses, and what expenses are to be included. . . . The provisions of this section shall not apply to any person who merely appears before a committee of the Congress of the United States in support of or opposition to legislation; . . .

(b) All information required to be filed under the provisions of this section with the Clerk of the House of Representatives and the Secretary of the Senate shall be compiled by said Clerk and Secretary, acting jointly, as soon as practicable after the close of the calendar quarter with respect to which such information is filed and shall be printed in the Congressional Record.

NOTE

In United States v. Harriss, 347 U.S. 612 (1954), the constitutionality of this act was upheld by a divided court against the claims of indefiniteness and interference with First Amendment freedoms to speak, publish and petition the Government. Chief Justice Warren explained the purpose of the act in these words (page 625):

"Present-day legislative complexities are such that individual members of Congress cannot be expected to explore the myriad pressures to which they are regularly subjected. Yet full realization of the American ideal of government by elected representatives depends to no small extent on their ability to properly evaluate such pressures. Otherwise the voice of the people may all too easily be drowned out by the voice of special interest groups seeking favored treatment while masquerading as proponents of the public weal. This is the evil which the Lobbying Act was designed to help prevent.

"Toward that end, Congress has not sought to prohibit these pressures. It has merely provided for a modicum of information from those who for hire attempt to influence legislation or who collect or spend funds for that purpose. It wants only to know who is being hired, who is putting up the money, and how much. . . .

"Under these circumstances, we believe that Congress at least within the bounds of the Act as we have construed it, is not constitutionally forbidden to require the disclosure of lobbying activities. To do so would be to deny Congress in large measure the power of self-protection. . . ."

The 1946 Act has been the subject of much criticism, primarily on the ground that it failed to correct many of the abuses of lobbying. The United States Senate in 1967 passed legislation to strengthen the Act but this was defeated in the House. For an account of the 1967 efforts see *Legislators and the Lobbyists*, Cong.Quarterly Serv., 2d Ed. p. 18, May, 1968. A good analysis of the 1946 Act is seen in Note, *Improving the Legislative Process: Federal Regulation of Lobbying*, 56 Yale L.Jour. 304 (1947).

THE FEDERAL INCOME TAX

The Internal Revenue Service until 1963 denied income tax deductions for expenses incurred in efforts to influence legislation despite the fact that many businesses found that representation before a legislative body was both "ordinary and necessary." The United States Supreme Court in upholding the Regulations, refused to distinguish between "proper" and "improper" forms of lobbying. Cammarano v. United States, 358 U.S. 498 (1959). In 1962, Section 162(e) was added to the Internal Revenue Code permitting the deduction of the cost of appearances before legislative bodies and related activities if the business taxpayer has a direct interest. Interpretation of the term "direct interest" may possibly limit the deductibility of some lobbying expenses. Deductions are still denied for expenditures made in an attempt to influence the general public with respect to legislative matters. Charitable organizations may not engage in substantial lobbying activities if they wish to retain an exempt status under Internal Revenue Code Section 501(a)(3) and probably most efforts to influence legislation are collective. What do these restrictions under the tax laws suggest with reference to Congressional policy on lobbying? See Weaver, Taxes and Lobbying—The Issue Resolved, 31 Geo.Wash.L.Rev. 938 (1963).

ILLEGAL CONTRACTS

TRIST v. CHILD

Supreme Court of the United States, 1875.
21 Wall. 441.

Appeal from the Supreme Court of the District of Columbia, the case being thus:

N. P. Trist having a claim against the United States for his services, rendered in 1848, touching the treaty of Guadaloupe Hidalgo—a claim which the government had not recognized—resolved, in 1866–7 to submit it to Congress and to ask payment of it. And he made an agreement with Linus Child, of Boston, that Child should take charge of the claim and prosecute it before Congress as his agent and attorney. As a compensation for his services it was agreed that Child should receive 25 per cent. of whatever sum Congress might allow in payment of the claim. If nothing was allowed, Child was to receive nothing. His compensation depended wholly upon the contingency of success. Child prepared a petition and presented the claim to Congress. Before final action was taken upon it by that body Child died. His son and personal representative, L. M. Child, who was his partner when the agreement between him and Trist was entered into, and down to the time of his death, continued the prosecution of the claim. By an act of the 20th of April 1870, Congress appropriated the sum of $14,559 to pay it. The son thereupon applied to Trist for payment of the 25 percent. stipulated for in the agreement between Trist and his father. Trist declined to pay. Hereupon Child applied to the Treasury Department to suspend the payment of the money to Trist. Payment was suspended accordingly, and the money was still in the treasury.

Child, the son, now filed his bill against Trist, praying that Trist might be enjoined from withdrawing the $14,559 from the treasury until he had complied with his agreement about the compensation, and that a decree might pass commanding him to pay to the complainant $5000, and for general relief.

The defendant answered the bill, asserting, with other defences going to the merits, that all the services as set forth in their bill were "of such a nature as to give no cause of action in any court either of common law or equity."

The case was heard upon the pleadings and much evidence. A part of the evidence consisted of correspondence between the parties. It tended to prove that the Childs, father and son, had been to see various members of Congress, soliciting their influence in behalf of a bill introduced for the benefit of Mr. Trist, and in several instances obtaining a promise of it. There was no attempt to prove that any kind of bribe had been offered or ever contemplated; . . .

MR. JUSTICE SWAYNE delivered the opinion of the court.

The court below decreed to the appellee the amount of his claim, and enjoined Trist from receiving from the treasury "any of the money appropriated to him" by Congress, until he should have paid the demand of the appellee. . . .

Was the contract a valid one? It was, on the part of Child, to procure by lobby service, if possible, the passage of a bill providing for the payment of the claim. The aid asked by the younger Child of Trist, which indicated what he considered needful, and doubtless proposed to do and did do himself, is thus vividly pictured in his letter to Trist of the 20th February, 1871. After giving the names of several members of Congress, from whom he had received favorable assurances, he proceeds: "Please write to your friends to write to any member of Congress. Every vote tells, and a simple request may secure a vote, he not caring anything about it. Set every man you know at work. Even if he knows a page, for a page often gets a vote." . . .

The question now before us has been decided in four American cases. They were all ably considered, and in all of them the contract was held to be against public policy, and void. We entertain no doubt that in such cases, as under all other circumstances, an agreement express or implied for purely professional services is valid. Within this category are included, drafting the petition to set forth the claim, attending to the taking of testimony, collecting facts, preparing arguments, and submitting them orally or in writing, to a committee or other proper authority, and other services of like character. All these things are intended to reach only the reason of those sought to be influenced. They rest on the same principle of ethics as professional services rendered in a court of justice, and are no more exceptionable. But such services are separated by a broad line of demarcation from personal solicitation, and the other means and appliances which the correspondence shows were resorted to in this case. There is no reason to believe that they involved anything corrupt or different from what is usually practiced by all paid lobbyists in the prosecution of their business. . . .

The agreement in the present case was for the sale of the influence and exertions of the lobby agent to bring about the passage of a law for the payment of a private claim, without reference to its merits, by means which, if not corrupt, were illegitimate, and considered in connection with the pecuniary interest of the agent at stake, contrary to the plainest principles of public policy. No one has a right, in such circumstances, to put himself in a position of temptation to do what is regarded as so pernicious in its character. The law forbids the inchoate step, and puts the seal of its reprobation upon the undertaking.

If any of the great corporations of the country were to hire adventurers who make market of themselves in this way, to procure the passage of a general law with a view to the promotion of their private interests, the moral sense of every right-minded man would instinctively denounce the employer and employed as steeped in corruption, and the employment as infamous. . . .

The elder agent in this case is represented to have been a lawyer of ability and high character. The appellee is said to be equally worthy. This can make no difference as to the legal principles we have considered, nor in their application to the case in hand. The law is no respecter of persons.

Decree reversed, and the case remanded, with directions to dismiss the bill.

NOTES

(1) Was the contract invalid because the fee was to be contingent or because personal solicitation, not on the merits, was contemplated? Would either element alone have been sufficient to invalidate the contract? Is there any reason why contingent fees for lobbying should be disapproved, in contrast to contingent fees for representation of clients in court? If the contract to use personal influence is invalid what of the act of using influence? Is a lawyer lobbyist under different restrictions in this respect from the non-lawyer lobbyist?

(2) "Save for a few states where lobbying is prohibited, any person may lobby. If he appears in his own interest no restrictions are placed upon his activities save by general standards of the criminal law or by bribery and corrupt practice statutes. If the lobbyist appears as representative of another he may be required to register and disclose the interest he represents.

"The only sanction that has been effective to date in the control of lobying practices has been the refusal of courts to enforce lobbying contracts. Unfortunately, most of the decisions seem to be based upon popular distrust of lobbying activity. Courts generally have refused to enforce these contracts. A growing minority however has restricted the decisions to those cases where the agreement contemplates illegal conduct or provides for contingent fees. It would seem where neither of these elements occur a lobbying contract should be enforced as readily as claims for attorney's services." Horack, Cases and Materials on Legislation 370, (1940).*

See, Restatement of Contracts, §§ 559 and 563; N.Y.C. Opinion 315 (1934).

* With the permission of the publisher, Callaghan and Company.

THE LEGISLATOR HIMSELF

JOHN W. SMITH, REGULATION OF NATIONAL AND STATE LEGISLATIVE LOBBYING

43 Univ.Det.L.Jour. 663, 690 (1966).

What is needed most for the effective regulation of lobbying is high quality legislators, well educated in the meaning of partial and incomplete and slanted presentations and appeals other than to reason. With highly educated solons great things are possible, with ill-formed legislators little public good can come, for as Herbert Spencer, in an obscure passage, observes:

> "Unquestionably among monstrous beliefs one of the most monstrous is that for a simple handicraft, such as shoe-making, a long apprenticeship is needful, the sole thing which needs no apprenticeship is making a nation's laws!"

The kingpin to effective regulation is not a formal control mechanism at all, rather it is the legislator himself. Formal regulations can at best be but an adjunct. These formal regulations present alternate possibilities for screening out the more obvious cases of wrongdoing. The devices have faults individually and collectively and no one should be relied upon. Registration provisions are inadequate, in part because of defective definitions, incomplete coverage, information required, inadequate attention paid to enforcement of the requirements for filing, incomplete publicity given to the filed data, and lack of enforcement of sanctions against wrong-doers. Tax policies are also by themselves inadequate because they cannot possibly be sufficiently broad in coverage to reach all possible types of informal contacts and modern lobbying, much of which is not conducted on a face-to-face basis. Investigations are also inadequate because they expose only the more blatant cases of wrong-doing, and seldom result in any long-term reform. Court control likewise is limited, for it is also after the fact disclosure, and is severely limited by the amount of case work brought to its attention, and is decided upon criteria not always compatible with the values held by legislators.

If the quality of legislators is the most effective curb on the improper activities of lobbying, then internal legislative reforms are the best secondary line of defense. Lessened dependence upon interest group information could be achieved by several routes, including supplying the legislature with more competent professional assistance, both to committees and individual members.

SECTION 2. THE LEGISLATIVE INVESTIGATING COMMITTEE

ROBERT K. CARR, THE HOUSE COMMITTEE ON UN-AMERICAN ACTIVITIES

Pages 294-306 (1952).

There has been continuous controversy over the issue of the rights to be enjoyed by persons appearing before the committee. In part, this controversy reflects the absence of an established pattern for the conduct of hearings by Congressional committees generally. Moreover, many of the specific criticisms directed against the Un-American Activities Committee could almost as easily have been made against virtually every investigating committee which has dealt with controversial subject matter. There has been a tendency to take all such committees to task for their failure to grant to witnesses the procedural rights which are customarily extended in the criminal courts. The need for procedural reform in the conduct of Congressional investigations is undeniable. But the fact remains that up to the present there has been no general agreement as to the rights that a Congressional committee should extend to its witnesses, and few if any specific committees have ever gone so far as to grant their witnesses the same status they would enjoy in a courtroom. . . .

. . . There has been more controversy over the right of witnesses before the committee to enjoy the assistance of counsel than over any other single procedural issue. . . . the Un-American Activities Committee showed itself reluctant to recognize this right on anything but a very narrow base. While there were moments when the committee seemed to be close to denying a witness any right to counsel, it was generally willing to allow a witness to be accompanied by counsel if he insisted upon it. But it extended this right very grudgingly in many instances; it frequently cast reflections upon witnesses because of their insistence upon enjoyment of the right; it attempted to discredit particular attorneys appearing before it; and it confined counsel to the narrow role of advising a client only with respect to his constitutional rights. . . .

. . . The committee has also upon a number of occasions shown considerable interest in the private communications between a witness and his counsel and has not hesitated to encroach upon what is generally recognized, in judicial procedure at least, to be a confidential relationship. . . .

. . . From time to time attorneys appearing before the committee have asked for permission to question their clients or to cross-examine other witnesses, but invariably these requests have been denied. . . .

. . . In the final analysis, an attorney representing a witness before the Un-American Activities Committee can do virtually nothing for him beyond advising him what his chances are of avoiding a successful prosecution for contempt if he refuses to answer certain questions put to him. It should be repeated again that virtually the same statement can be made about attorneys and witnesses appearing before any Congressional committee. But because the Un-American Activities Committee has personalized its hearings to a degree seldom reached by other committees of Congress, the inability of counsel to render to a witness the kind of assistance he could give were his client a defendant in a court trial becomes a serious matter.

NOTES

(1) One of the most controversial of all Congressional investigating committees was The House Un-American Activities Committee (HUAC), recently renamed The House Internal Security Committee. It inspired a number of excellent studies of Congressional investigations in addition to that of Professor Carr: Symposium, *Legislative Investigations: Safeguards for Witnesses,* 29 Notre Dame Lawyer 157 (1953); Symposium, *Congressional Investigations,* 18 Univ.Chi.L.Rev. 421 (1951); Maslow, *Fair Procedure in Congressional Investigations: A Proposed Code,* 54 Colum.L.Rev. 839 (1954); Taylor, Grand Inquest (1955); Beck, Contempt of Congress (1959); Barth, Government by Investigation (1955).

(2) A significant study and report of Congressional investigations, prompted by HUAC, was made by the American Bar Association. ABA Special Committee on Individual Rights as Affected by National Security, Whitney North Seymour, Chairman 79 A.B.A.Rep. 329 (1954). The Report considered broadly the need for legislative investigations, their history and constitutional basis, and their abuses. With respect to the latter it found frequent invasions of the individual's right to privacy and a long list of "procedural" abuses such as vagueness of the resolution authorizing the investigation, one-man control of the hearings, misuse of executive sessions, combining of the "prosecuting" and "adjudicating functions," injury to reputations of third persons, misuse of confidential committee files, excessive publicity through televising and broadcasting of hearings, and denial of basic rights to witnesses, including notice of the purpose of the investigation, effective right to counsel, right to make statements for the record, and right to an accurate transcript. The Report concluded that the most serious abuse was the failure of Congress to devise rules to govern its committees. It proposed a uniform Code of Investigative Procedure for all Congressional investigating committees, emphasizing that Congressional responsibility was, in the final analysis, the key to elimination of the abuses. The House of Delegates adopted, with two amendments, the committee's proposed Code. 79 A.B.A.Rep. 123 (1954); 40 A.B.A.J. 900 (1954). No overall action was taken by Congress pursuant to this proposal although some committees have adopted rules for their guidance.

(3) HUAC has also created work for the courts. It was inevitable that attacks on the constitutional authority for the investigations would be made and that claims would be urged that the constitutional rights of witnesses had been violated and the doctrine of separation of powers ignored. Several

of these cases reached the United States Supreme Court in the late 50's and 60's. See McKay, *Congressional Investigations and the Supreme Court,* 51 Calif.L.R. 267 (1963); Shapiro, *Judicial Review: Political Reality and Legislative Purpose: The Supreme Court's Supervision of Congressional Investigations,* 15 Vand.L.Rev. 535 (1962); Alfange, *Congressional Investigations and the Fickle Court,* 30 U.Cin.L.Rev. 113 (1961); Redlich, *Rights of Witnesses Before Congressional Committees: Effects of Recent Supreme Court Decisions,* 36 N.Y.U.L.Rev. 1126 (1961); Note, *Congressional Investigations: Imbroglio in the Court,* 8 Wm. & Mary L.Rev. 400 (1967).

(4) For an excellent analysis of the lawyer's "several roles" in representing a client before a Congressional investigating committee see Rauh and Pollitt, *Right to and Nature of Representation Before Congressional Committees,* 45 Minn.L.Rev. 853 (1961).

The A.B.A. Report, referred to in Note (2), recommended the following with reference to the right to counsel:

"1. Counsel should be allowed to accompany him to all hearings, both public and private. . . .

"2. Counsel should be allowed to interpose proper objections to questions or to any failure to follow procedural requirements and to submit legal memoranda in support of his objections.

"3. Counsel should be allowed to advise the witness as to his rights before the committee.

"4. Counsel should be allowed to ask clarifying questions of the witness and to cross-examine adverse witnesses, subject to control of the length of the interrogation by a majority of the members present to prevent abuse. It is recognized that some counsel may attempt to abuse the right to cross-examine and try to impede the progress of the investigation. If this occurs, the committee may withdraw the right of oral cross-examination in a particular case and require that questions asked of adverse witnesses be handled by written interrogatories given to the chairman or counsel of the committee and propounded by him to the witness. This device, with all the others which are available, should be a sufficient sanction to prevent abuse."

LEGISLATIVE INVESTIGATION v. JUDICIAL TRIAL

ALLEN B. MORELAND, CONGRESSIONAL INVESTIGATIONS AND PRIVATE PERSONS

40 So.Calif.L.Rev. 189, 268 (1967).

When a witness is summoned before a congressional committee, there are few statutory procedural privileges available to him. He is more or less dependent upon the rules of the particular committee before which he is appearing. There is, for example, no statutory or common law right for a witness to have advice of counsel; to have witnesses called on his behalf; to cross-examine other witnesses or present preliminary written or oral statements to the committee. Since an investigation is not a "trial," the committee is under no compulsion to make the hearing public or to make a speedy inquiry into the matter under investigation. In practice these procedural privileges have been extended progressively to witnesses even though no statute or rule of law requires them.

Some observers advocate the enactment of uniform rules of procedure. In most cases the advocates for change recommend rules designed to make a congressional investigative proceeding more like court procedure. While there are some changes which could be made in procedure which would result in a nearer approximation of the safeguards afforded to witnesses by courts of law, reform in this direction will of necessity fall short of equating the two.

There are many points in common between courts and congressional investigating committees. However, there are vast differences, and rules of procedure, to be meaningful, must be related to the basic objectives to be accomplished. For instance, in a court the issues are confined to the narrow limits of the pleadings; there are rigid rules of evidence which control the admission of testimony; the court is a disinterested party, leaving to the adversary parties the burden of introducing evidence pro and con; every factor and bit of evidence which could effect the verdict has to be introduced affirmatively on the record. In this process, cross-examination is utilized by both sides to establish the credibility of the source of information. Finally, a court proceeding looks forward to a definitive verdict or judgment, subject only to an appeal procedure which eventually results in a final disposition of the case.

A congressional inquiry in aid of legislation is not limited to a particular case. It seeks to anticipate all cases and situations which may arise concerning the proposed legislation. In such a circumstance, rules of procedure, especially as to evidence, approximating the strictness of those in a court of law, could result in a paralysis of the information-gathering mission of the congressional committees. Further, the committee is a political body, which, with the best of motives, could not be a disinterested party to the proceedings. Finally congressional inquiries are designed to develop a body of information from which general propositions may be drawn to be used in the legislative arena.

NOTE

This article has stressed the differences between investigating committees and courts. Many commentators have spoken of the similarities. What are they? Does the committee hearing involve a contest? Is it an adversary proceeding? Does the hearing result in a judgment? Does the attorney for a witness have a responsibility beyond that owed to his client? Should the attorney urge all objections on behalf of his client, as he would in a criminal trial, or is it his duty to cooperate in furthering the investigation? Does your answer depend upon the attorney's views as to the propriety of the investigation and the questioning?

Chapter IX

THE GOVERNMENT LAWYER

Introduction. The increase of government activities at all levels, national and state and local, has brought a corresponding increase in the controversies between the government and the citizen. It is no coincidence that The 1967 Lawyer Statistical Report of the American Bar Foundation (page 21) shows 40,992 government lawyers (city, county, state and federal) in 1966, compared with 21,273 similarly employed in 1948.

The wide varieties in the controversies between citizens and their government include: (1) nonlitigated matters (as government contracts, and purchase of land), and litigated cases; (2) court cases and cases before administrative tribunals; (3) civil cases and criminal cases (as suit for taxes or prosecution for tax frauds). In all instances the lawyer may be the representative of the government or of the citizen.

In some matters involving the government there may be a peculiar duty on the citizen. The outstanding example is the duty in the self-assessment of taxes to make a full and fair return of matters bearing on tax liability. For the most part, however, it is the government that is under a special duty. The recent expansion of government activities has been accompanied by an increased emphasis by the courts on the civil rights of the citizen in his relations with government and its representatives.

This section chooses for primary consideration the public prosecutor. After calling attention to the ever present question whether to prosecute at all and the very common problem of when to agree on a plea to a lesser offense than that charged ("plea bargaining"), consideration is given to some of the problems that arise in the conduct of the prosecution. Reference is made to the special restraints and duties on a representative of the government and the question is asked as to whether such restraints and duties should be imposed not merely on the prosecutor but on other government lawyers as well. In examining the reasons for these special obligations consider the following elements:

(1) The government is usually not concerned with winning a particular case because of the money involved in that case, as is a private client, but is more concerned with the rule of law to be established and the consequent general effect.

(2) The history of our country reveals a continuing concern with the protection of the citizen against the excesses of governmental of-

ficials. The Declaration of Independence listed the wrongs perpetrated by George III, the Bill of Rights and the Reconstruction Amendments made more explicit the limitations on government, and the recent expansion of governmental activities has been accompanied by an increased emphasis by the courts on the civil rights of the citizen in his relations with government and its representatives.

(3) Often or usually the risk and burden on the citizen from loss of the case are much greater than in ordinary civil litigation, involving as they do life or liberty as well as property, and also a grievous stigma.

(4) Usually, the government lawyer, especially the lawyer for the United States, has much greater resources at his command in the preparation and presentation of a case; and always the cost of preparation and trial puts a special burden on the individual involved which is not felt by the government.

(5) The government lawyer commands greater confidence and respect from a jury and from the public than a lawyer in private employment.

(6) The government desires and needs the respect and confidence of the people, which would be impaired should the government lawyer act unfairly.

(7) (Would the reader add any other factor?)

JACK B. WEINSTEIN, SOME ETHICAL AND POLITICAL PROBLEMS OF A GOVERNMENT ATTORNEY *

18 Maine L.Rev. 155, 157 (1966).

There is a core of knowledge and skills common to lawyers, whether they are practitioners, government officials, law teachers, or judges. One of the great joys of our profession is that our training permits us to advise diverse clients in disparate fields and to move from government to private work with comparative ease. We can learn what we need of economics to try an antitrust suit, of psychiatry to try a homicide case, and of bureaucracy to help our clients get re-elected. . . .

. . . I shall only note here that my experience in government has convinced me of the importance of theoretical training in the law school. The lawyers who are essential when a new and difficult legal problem is presented are those who have been trained to think critically—not necessarily those with the greatest practical experience. Most intelligent lawyers can learn rather quickly the detailed practice in special fields. I do not undervalue, of course, the sense of propor-

---

* Copyright 1966 by University of Maine School of Law. Reprinted with permission. Judge Weinstein was formerly Professor of Law at Columbia University and later County Attorney of Nassau County, New York.

tion and knowledge of alternatives that come with maturity and experience. The Nassau County Attorney's office was, fortunately, nicely balanced with sound, experienced men aware of the limitations of government authority, and bright young law graduates who thought anything was possible. . . .

. . .

The bothersome problems of a government attorney are not so much the legal-technical ones of what can be done, or how to do it, but what should be done. As Edmund Burke put it in his plea to Parliament on behalf of the American colonies in 1775, "The question with me is . . . not what a lawyer tells me I may do, but what humanity, reason, and justice tells me I ought to do". . . .

Governments and their attorneys have a duty to help individuals and to try to build a better society. The persnickety law official who keeps his shoes clean by stepping around the mudholes of politics and public policy neglects the most important and exciting aspect of his office. He conceives of his office as a slot machine handing out opinions and acting with mechanical exactitude; he fails to grasp its more useful, complex and flexible function in meeting social problems. . .

As in private practice, the attorney must tell his client when he is wrong. The attorney is never the mere hireling of government or of anyone else. He is an independent professional and must stand on what he thinks is right.

One good current illustration of this need for the lawyer to stand fast is in the area of reapportionment. The present position is quite clear: one-man-one-vote applies not only to state legislatures but to local legislative bodies. . . .

. . . This same firm position needs to be taken by government attorneys in other instances, as in the local school desegregation cases or as Attorney General Flowers did in Alabama recently when local authorities refused to enforce the penal law in a civil-rights killing. . . .

Energy and resources are, of course, limited. And no one can fight every battle at once. It has been aptly observed that while, on the one hand, "no good society can be unprincipled," on the other hand, "no viable society can be principle-ridden." For "[o]ur democratic . . . government exists in this Lincolnian tension between principles and expediency." For example, partly because of other commitments and partly because it seemed inexpedient to take on too many political and social struggles at one time, my office never seriously came to grips with the bail problem. We did, however, help reform the jail by instituting civil service for jailors and by providing for an appointive head of the correction department to replace an elective sheriff.

. . . In my opinion, it is important that the county attorney and state's attorney—as is the case with the Attorney General of the

United States—be appointed, rather than elected. This view was, as you may recall, the conclusion of the Hoover Commission, in connection with its appraisal of the department of justice and government attorneys in the United States government. . . .

An example of the advantages of the United States Department of Justice concept and centralization of legal services is that the Attorney General of the United States was recently able to set up a commission to coordinate crime control. He could utilize a large legal staff, the FBI, and correction and penal experts, since they are all within his department. . . .

. . .

I have already suggested in my remarks some of the ethical difficulties of the county attorney caused by the heightened responsibility he has as a lawyer for reform of the administration of justice and law. Let me now emphasize one further aspect of this problem caused by the multiplicity of services he renders, the many departments he represents, and the fact that he represents the people as well as government. The private lawyer can, within broad limits, attempt to get the best possible result—from his single client's point of view—letting the adversary system provide justice. What, however, of the public attorney?

He is torn in a number of ways. Let me give you some examples. Shortly after I took office, one of our negotiators presented me with a proposed settlement in a condemnation case, which was approximately one-third of the value of the land we had taken as indicated by our appraiser's reports. The condemnees were not represented by an attorney. What should I have done? I talked to them on the telephone and discovered that they were an elderly couple who had bought their property many years before and who had no idea of how much it had increased in value. In an extended conversation, I finally convinced them that they were entitled to much more than they wanted. But should I have insisted on paying more than I had to?

In another case, the award of the court seemed to me to be too large by several millions of dollars. The condemnation resolutions adopted by the Board of Supervisors, our local legislative body, were exceedingly and unusually favorable to the condemnee, but there was no evidence of fraud. A reversal on the ground of excessiveness of the award was unlikely. What was a proper course of action? I instituted an extensive collateral attack on the award on the ground that the favorable provision was illegal, over the opposition of our Board of Supervisors. We used every procedural device in the book and some created especially for the case. It was clear that we would throw all the County's enormous resources into this litigation. After numerous motions and appeals, when it became obvious that the dispute might go on for many years, the matter was settled with a saving to the county of some million dollars. Once I told my classes procedure should never be used for delay. Now I wonder, are there exceptions?

Somewhere in between those two cases lie the bulk of matters where we insisted that the claimant take somewhat less than our appraisals showed the land to be worth. Condemnees settled and waived interest in order to avoid a long delay before trial and receipt of their money. Is this technique justified even though it saves the taxpayers money? A more appropriate procedure, in my opinion, would be for the County to obtain more thorough and reliable appraisals; they should be revealed to the condemnee, and he should then be tendered the full appraised value plus interest as a matter of due. . . .
. . .

There are instances where the position of one of the departments is completely contrary to the position that the attorney feels is legally defensible. In such cases the county attorney should, I believe, represent the side he considers to be correct. Special independent counsel should be provided to represent the other side. Such an appointment was made by Chief Justice Stone when he was Attorney General of the United States; he himself argued against the special counsel.
. . .

One of the most important functions of the government's lawyer is to provide a bridge or neutral meeting ground between opposing forces so that the viable compromises which are the hallmark of a functioning democracy can be developed. If the government's attorney is to fulfill this role, there must be no doubt in anyone's mind about his good faith and integrity.

I conclude by repeating that, while the government's attorney is a political figure, he operates within a framework of professional and ethical responsibility that limits what he can and should do. There is no inconsistency between sound ethics and good politics. Indeed, government service, while it furnishes some of the hardest ethical problems, affords a lawyer many of the greatest opportunities for professional fulfillment.

AMERICAN BAR FOUNDATION, THE LEGAL PROFESSION IN THE UNITED STATES

Page 11 (1965).

PUBLIC LAW PRACTICE

About 40,000 American lawyers are employees of governmental agencies. They may be thought of as engaged in the practice of public law. One of the longest established, and certainly the most widely encountered, types of public attorney is the public prosecutor (variously called the district attorney, the county attorney, the state solicitor, and other titles). Each of the more than 3,000 counties in the

United States has a district attorney. His principal responsibility is prosecution of criminal cases. In most areas of the country he is also corporation counsel for the county government, and in this respect performs functions that are substantially similar to those performed by a private law firm for its corporate clients. The district attorney's responsibility for enforcement of the criminal law makes him a key figure in local politics. His duties as corporation counsel likewise draw him deeply into public affairs: He must give legal advice on tax and other revenue measures, bond issues, contracts for the purchase of goods and services by public agencies, matters relating to public employees, the regularity and validity of local regulatory measures, and a host of other problems of local government.

The office of the district attorney varies in size according to the size and complexity of the community in which it is located. In rural counties, the district attorney has no staff and he is very often only a part-time official; in metropolitan areas, he heads a staff that may include over a hundred lawyers and correlative numbers of supporting clerical, secretarial, and technical assistants. The number and type of legal problems and legal operations with which the district attorney's office is concerned rivals, and often exceeds, the practice of the largest private law firms in the same community.

The expansion in the number and complexity of governmental agencies, especially in the last half century, has required them to employ more and more lawyers to assist and guide them in their operations. Each city has a corporation counsel; each state has an attorney general with a staff of attorneys who provide legal assistance to a wide variety of agencies of the state government; each autonomous local unit of government, such as water districts, park districts, port and bridge authorities and sewer districts, has its own attorneys, as do the autonomous or semi-autonomous regulatory agencies of the state and federal government.

The Attorney General of the United States is the chief legal officer of the United States and is in charge of the Department of Justice. (Like other members of the President's Cabinet, he is appointed by the President, with the consent of the Senate, and serves at his pleasure.) The Department of Justice is organized in divisions of special responsibility including criminal, antitrust, tax, and civil rights divisions, and a civil division, which is responsible for the general business of the government. The department employs hundreds of lawyers having a wide range of special skills. Subordinate to the Attorney General are the United States Attorneys for the respective federal judicial districts across the country. The United States Attorneys are responsible in their districts for enforcement of federal criminal laws and for handling the federal government's legal business that must be discharged on a local basis.

The Department of Justice has supervision of the Federal Bureau of Investigation, which is the federal government's investigatory arm, and the Federal Bureau of Prisons, which operates the federal prison system and its parole service. In this respect the Attorney General of the United States has a broader responsibility than his state counterpart. The attorneys general of the states usually have no responsibility for the administration of either the state police or the state prison system; these are autonomous agencies whose chief administrative officers report directly to the governor of the state. Hence, the Attorney General of the United States is the public official closest to being a minister of justice in the continental sense. Nevertheless, because our government is a federation, the authority and responsibility of the Attorney General of the United States is limited to matters within the jurisdiction of the federal government. This limitation explains, for example, why the Attorney General of the United States, and for that matter the President, has no general legal authority to intervene in the civil rights conflicts that have arisen in some of the states.

Not all, not even most, of the lawyers who are in the service of the United States are in the Department of Justice. All agencies and tribunals of the federal government, some of which have been referred to specifically, have their own legal staffs. Moreover, the military establishment, which is by far the largest federal agency, has a complex legal staff of its own. This staff includes legal counsel to the Secretary of Defense and to the Secretaries of the Army, Navy, and Air Force, and the Judge Advocate General offices of each of the three branches of service, which provide legal counsel to the services and administer the system of military law and justice that applies to members of the armed forces.

NOTE

For the history of the Department of Justice see Cummings and McFarland, Federal Justice (1937). A description of the Department's present organization and range of activities is seen in Huston, The Department of Justice (1967).

For a study of the offices of Attorney-General and Solicitor-General of England with an account of the office of The Director of Public Prosecutions of England, see Edwards, The Law Officers of the Crown (1964).

In Anglo-American Criminal Justice, Professor Delmar Karlan describes the quite different methods employed in the administration of the criminal law in England and the United States. The ends in the two countries, as Lord Chief Justice Parker states in a Foreword, are the same: "efficient law enforcement and the protection of individual liberty." (p. XII).

SECTION 1. THE PROSECUTOR

A. THE DECISION TO PROSECUTE AND PLEA BARGAINING

KENNETH CULP DAVIS, DISCRETIONARY JUSTICE *

Page 224 (1969).

The enormous and much abused power of prosecutors not to prosecute is almost completely uncontrolled, even though I can find no reason to believe that anyone planned it that way—or that anyone would. Prosecutions are often withheld, sometimes on the basis of political, personal, or other ulterior influence, without guiding rules as to what will or will not be prosecuted, without meaningful standards stemming from either legislative bodies or from prosecutors themselves, through decision secretly made and free from criticism, without supporting findings of fact, unexplained by reasoned opinions, and free from any requirement that the decisions be related to precedents. Futhermore, decisions of a top prosecutor are usually unsupervised by any other administrative authority, and decisions not to prosecute are customarily immune to judicial review. . . .

Prosecutors, in my opinion, should be required to make and to announce rules that will guide their choices, stating as far as practicable what will and what will not be prosecuted, and they should be required otherwise to structure their discretion. Even the Antitrust Division of the Department of Justice, whose subject matter is far more difficult than that of most prosecutors, can and should issue guidelines or rules to guide most of its enormous discretionary power.

CHARLES D. BREITEL, CONTROLS IN CRIMINAL LAW ENFORCEMENT

27 U.Chi.L.Rev. 427 (1960).

The thesis of this discussion is that the presence and expansion of discretion in crime control is both desirable and inevitable in a modern democratic society. The thesis is that discretion may not be eliminated, except at intolerable cost—and this is true at every level—police, prosecutor, grand jury, petty jury, court, probation, correction, and parole. The question then is not how to eliminate or reduce discretion, but how to control it so as to avoid the unequal, the arbitrary, the discriminatory, and the oppressive.

* Copyright 1969 by Louisiana State University Press.

ROBERT H. JACKSON, THE FEDERAL PROSECUTOR *

24 Journ.Am.Jud.Soc. 18 (1940).

There is a most important reason why the prosecutor should have, as nearly as possible, a detached and impartial view of all groups in his community. Law enforcement is not automatic. It isn't blind. One of the greatest difficulties of the position of prosecutor is that he must pick his cases, because no prosecutor can even investigate all of the cases in which he receives complaints. . . .

. . . What every prosecutor is practically required to do is to select the cases for prosecution and to select those in which the offense is the most flagrant, the public harm the greatest, and the proof the most certain.

If the prosecutor is obliged to choose his cases, it follows that he can choose his defendants. Therein is the most dangerous power of the prosecutor: that he will pick people that he thinks he should get, rather than pick cases that need to be prosecuted. . . .

The qualities of a good prosecutor are as elusive and as impossible to define as those which mark a gentleman. And those who need to be told would not understand it anyway. A sensitiveness to fair play and sportsmanship is perhaps the best protection against the abuse of power, and the citizen's safety lies in the prosecutor who tempers zeal with human kindness, who seeks truth and not victims, who serves the law and not factional purposes, and who approaches his task with humility.

NOTE

Remedies for failure to prosecute. In State v. Langley, 214 Or. 445 (1958), cert. denied 358 U.S. 826, a district attorney was convicted, fined and removed from office for failure to enforce gambling laws. A later disciplinary proceeding against him by the state bar was dismissed for want of proof of moral turpitude. In re Langley, 230 Or. 319 (1962). See Comment, *Private Prosecution: A Remedy for District Attorneys' Unwarranted Inaction,* 65 Yale L.J. 209 (1955).

PLEA BARGAINING

ALBERT W. SCHULER, THE PROSECUTOR'S ROLE IN PLEA BARGAINING **

36 U.Chi.L.Rev. 50 (1968).

Today, roughly ninety per cent of all defendants convicted of crime in both state and federal courts plead guilty rather than ex-

---

* This Address by the then Attorney General of the United States was delivered at the Second Annual Conference of United States Attorneys, 1940.

** Copyright 1968 by University of Chicago. Reprinted with permission.

ercise their right to stand trial before a court or jury. Behind this statistic lies the widespread practice of plea bargaining—the exchange of prosecutorial and judicial concessions for pleas of guilty.

The guilty-plea system has grown largely as a product of circumstance, not choice. The volume of crime has increased in recent decades, and the criminal law has come to regulate areas of human activity that were formerly beyond its scope. At the same time, the length of the average felony trial has substantially increased, and a constitutional revolution led by the United States Supreme Court has diverted a major share of judicial and prosecutorial resources from the trial of criminal cases to the resolution of pre-trial motions and post-conviction proceedings. These developments have led in a single direction; there is today an administrative crisis of major proportions in our criminal courts.

. . . Only the guilty-plea system has enabled the courts to process their caseloads with seriously inadequate resources. . . .

As recently as the 1920's, the legal profession was largely united in its opposition to plea bargaining. As America's dependency on pleas of guilty increased, however, attitudes changed. The American Bar Association and the President's Commission on Law Enforcement and the Administration of Justice are among the prestigious observers who have given plea bargaining the remarkably good press that it enjoys today. Most of these observers recognize that the guilty-plea system is in need of reform, but the legal profession now seems as united in its defense of plea negotiation as it was united in opposition less than a half-century ago.

. . .

When a prosecutor grants concessions in exchange for a plea of guilty, he may be acting in any—or all—of several different roles. First, the prosecutor may be acting as an administrator. His goal may be to dispose of each case in the fastest, most efficient manner in the interest of getting his and the court's work done.

Second, the prosecutor may be acting as an advocate. His goal may be to maximize both the number of convictions and the severity of the sentences that are imposed after conviction. In this role, the prosecutor must estimate the sentence that seems likely after a conviction at trial, discount this sentence by the possibility of an acquittal, and balance the "discounted trial sentence" against the sentence he can insure through a plea agreement. Were a prosecutor to adopt this role to the exclusion of all others, he would accept a plea agreement only when its assurance of conviction outweighed the loss in sentence severity it might entail.

Third, the prosecutor may act as a judge. His goal may be to do the "right thing" for the defendant in view of the defendant's social circumstances or in view of the peculiar circumstances of his crime—

with the qualification, of course, that the "right thing" will not be done unless the defendant pleads guilty.

Fourth, the prosecutor may act as a legislator. He may grant concessions because the law is "too harsh," not only for this defendant but for all defendants.

NOTES

(1) Are any of the roles described by Alschuler improper usurpations of authority? Isn't the prosecutor's promise of leniency, whether with reference to dismissing or reducing charges or recommending a lighter sentence, tantamount to a threat of harsher treatment if the defendant does not waive his constitutional right to a trial, by pleading guilty? Is there anything improper in the use of such threats? See Comment, *Official Inducements to Plead Guilty*, 32 U.Chi.L.Rev. 167 (1964), discussing the requirements of a knowing and voluntary waiver by defendant. Is the prosecutor's exercise of discretion in plea bargaining any different from his discretion whether to charge in the first instance? What are the major advantages of plea bargaining? What disadvantages do you perceive? See Newman, Conviction, The Determination of Guilt or Innocence Without Trial (1966); The President's Commission on Law Enforcement and Administration of Justice, The Challenge of Crime in a Free Society 134–136 (1967) and Task Force Report: The Courts, 108–119 (1967).

(2) If most defendants are convicted through pleas of guilty, many of these negotiated, the discretionary power of the prosecutor again looms large. What safeguards might be erected? Is defense counsel particularly important? Should the judge be fully advised of the agreement? See A.B. A. Project on Minimum Standards for Criminal Justice, Standards Relating to Pleas of Guilty 60–69 (Approved Draft 1968), approved February 1968, 2 Crim.L.Rep. 2419, 2422 (1968); Note, *Guilty Plea Bargaining: Compromises by Prosecutors to Secure Guilty Pleas*, 112 U.Pa.L.Rev. 865, 882–895 (1964). (An extensive Appendix to this note sets forth the plea bargaining practices of the chief prosecuting officers in some of the most populous counties of thirty-one states.)

Federal Rules of Criminal Procedure, Rule 11, 18 U.S.C.A., provides that the trial judge may not accept a guilty plea "without first addressing the defendant personally and determining that the plea is made voluntarily with understanding of the nature of the charge and the consequences of the plea. . . . The court shall not enter a judgment upon a plea of guilty unless it is satisfied that there is a factual basis for the plea." McCarthy v. United States, 394 U.S. 459 (1969), interpreted this Rule strictly in a plea bargaining situation.

(3) Defendant pleads guilty after the prosecutor assures him that he will recommend a lenient sentence if the judge requests a recommendation. No such recommendation is requested by the judge and the prosecutor, from past experience, is aware that this particular judge rarely asks for advice in sentencing. The prosecutor actually intended to recommend leniency had he been asked. Is the prosecutor's conduct improper? After receiving the maximum sentence would defendant have any recourse? Would it make a difference if he were represented by counsel? See Dillon v. United States,

307 F.2d 445 (9th Cir. 1962). Would your answer be different if the prosecutor had expected the judge to request a recommendation? Suppose the prosecutor actually makes a recommendation for leniency but this is ignored by the judge. Suppose the prosecutor had promised the defendant he would "see to it that the minimum sentence was imposed".

B. THE PROSECUTION

"The United States wins its case whenever justice is done one of its citizens in the courts." (Inscription carved in the walls outside the office of the United States Attorney General)

REPORT OF THE JOINT CONFERENCE ON PROFESSIONAL RESPONSIBILITY

44 ABAJ 1159, 1218 (1958); 1958 A.A.L.S. Proc. 187, 201 (1958).

Two positions of public trust require special mention. The first of these is the office of public prosecutor. The manner in which the duties of this office are discharged is of prime importance, not only because the powers it confers are so readily subject to abuse, but also because in the public mind the whole administration of justice tends to be symbolized by its most dramatic branch, the criminal law.

The public prosecutor cannot take as a guide for the conduct of his office the standards of an attorney appearing on behalf of an individual client. The freedom elsewhere wisely granted to partisan advocacy must be severely curtailed if the prosecutor's duties are to be properly discharged. The public prosecutor must recall that he occupies a dual role, being obligated, on the one hand, to furnish that adversary element essential to the informed decision of any controversy, but being possessed, on the other, of important governmental powers that are pledged to the accomplishment of one objective only, that of impartial justice. Where the prosecutor is recreant to the trust implicit in his office, he undermines confidence, not only in his profession, but in government and the very ideal of justice itself.

BERGER v. UNITED STATES

Supreme Court of the United States, 1935.
295 U.S. 78, 55 S.Ct. 629, 79 L.Ed. 1314.

[Harry Berger was convicted of conspiracy to utter counterfeit notes purporting to have been issued by federal reserve banks, the conviction was affirmed by the Circuit Court of Appeals for the Second Circuit (73 F.2d 278), and defendant brings certiorari.]

MR. JUSTICE SUTHERLAND delivered the opinion of the Court.

That the United States prosecuting attorney overstepped the bounds of that propriety and fairness which should characterize the conduct of such an officer in the prosecution of a criminal offense is clearly shown by the record. He was guilty of misstating the facts in his cross-examination of witnesses; of putting into the mouths of such witnesses things which they had not said; of suggesting by his questions that statements had been made to him personally out of court, in respect of which no proof was offered; of pretending to understand that a witness had said something which he had not said and persistently cross-examining the witness upon that basis; of assuming prejudicial facts not in evidence; of bullying and arguing with witnesses; and, in general, of conducting himself in a thoroughly indecorous and improper manner. . . .

The trial judge, it is true, sustained objections to some of the questions, insinuations and misstatements, and instructed the jury to disregard them. But the situation was one which called for stern rebuke and repressive measures and, perhaps, if these were not successful, for the granting of a mistrial. It is impossible to say that the evil influence upon the jury of these acts of misconduct was removed by such mild judicial action as was taken.

The prosecuting attorney's argument to the jury was undignified and intemperate, containing improper insinuations and assertions calculated to mislead the jury. A reading of the entire argument is necessary to an appreciation of these objectionable features. The following is an illustration: A witness by the name of Goldie Goldstein had been called by the prosecution to identify the petitioner. She apparently had difficulty in doing so. The prosecuting attorney, in the course of his argument, said (italics added):

"Mrs. Goldie Goldstein takes the stand. She says she knows Jones, *and you can bet your bottom dollar she knew Berger.* She stood right where I am now and looked at him and was afraid to go over there, and when I waved my arm everybody started to holler, 'Don't point at him.' You know the rules of law. Well, it is the most complicated game in the world. I was examining *a woman that I knew knew Berger and could identify him*, she was standing right here looking at him, and I couldn't say, 'Isn't that the man?' Now, imagine that! But that is the rules of the game, and I have to play within those rules."

The jury was thus invited to conclude that the witness Goldstein knew Berger well but pretended otherwise; and that this was within the personal knowledge of the prosecuting attorney. . . .

The United States Attorney is the representative not of an ordinary party to a controversy, but of a sovereignty whose obligation to govern impartially is as compelling as its obligation to govern at all; and whose interest, therefore, in a criminal prosecution is not that it shall win a case, but that justice shall be done. As such, he is in a peculiar and very definite sense the servant of the law, the twofold aim of which is that guilt shall not escape or innocence suffer. He may prosecute with earnestness and vigor—indeed, he should do so. But, while he may strike hard blows, he is not at liberty to strike foul ones. It is as much his duty to refrain from improper methods calculated to produce a wrongful conviction as it is to use every legitimate means to bring about a just one.

It is fair to say that the average jury, in a greater or less degree, has confidence that these obligations, which so plainly rest upon the prosecuting attorney, will be faithfully observed. Consequently, improper suggestions, insinuations and, especially, assertions of personal knowledge are apt to carry much weight against the accused when they should properly carry none. The court below said that the case against Berger was not strong; and from a careful examination of the record we agree. . . .

In these circumstances prejudice to the cause of the accused is so highly probable that we are not justified in assuming its non-existence. If the case against Berger had been strong, or, as some courts have said, the evidence of his guilt "overwhelming," a different conclusion might be reached. . . . Moreover, we have not here a case where the misconduct of the prosecuting attorney was slight or confined to a single instance, but one where such misconduct was pronounced and persistent, with a probable cumulative effect upon the jury which cannot be disregarded as inconsequential. A new trial must be awarded. . . .

Judgment reversed.

NOTES

(1) An allusion or an appeal may get its unfair and prejudicial effect from the spirit and emotion of the time and place. In commenting on the argument of the prosecuting attorney to a jury in war time, Chief Justice Stone said: "In his closing remarks to the jury he indulged in an appeal wholly irrelevant to any facts or issues in the case, the purpose and effect of which could only have been to arouse passion and prejudice. . . . At a time when passion and prejudice are heightened by emotions stirred by our participation in a great war, we do not doubt that these remarks addressed to the jury were highly prejudicial, and that they were offensive to the dignity and good order with which all proceedings in court should be conducted." Viereck v. United States, 318 U.S. 236, 248 (1943).

But cf. Commonwealth v. Sacco, 255 Mass. 369 (1926).

Compare these words of Judge Learned Hand:

". . . [T]he position of a public officer, charged with the enforcement of a law is different from one who must decide a dispute. If there is a fair doubt, his duty is to present the case for the side which he represents, and leave decision to the court, or the administrative tribunal, upon which lies the responsibility of decision. If he surrenders a plausible construction, it will, at least it may, be surrendered forever; and yet it may be right. . . . [S]uch rulings need not have the detachment of a judicial, or semi-judicial decision, and may properly carry a bias . . ." Fishgold v. Sullivan Drydock & Repair Corp., 154 F.2d 785, 789 (2d Cir. 1946), affirmed 328 U.S. 275 (1946).

(2) For a discussion of forensic misconduct on the part of the prosecuting attorney see, *The Nature and Consequences of Forensic Misconduct in the Prosecution of a Criminal Case*, 54 Col.L.Rev. 946 (1954).

(3) In People v. Wilkes, 44 Cal.2d 679 (1955), the prosecuting attorney in oral argument made reference to the failure of defendant to call his wife as a witness, she being best able to establish a claimed alibi. In reversing for this statement by the prosecutor the California Supreme Court pointed out that similar tactics had been repeatedly denounced by earlier decisions but there had been no previous reversal under the doctrine of "non-prejudicial error." Is it permissible for the prosecuting attorney to engage in improper conduct on the assumption that there will probably be no reversal in the particular instance? Compare the responsibility of defense counsel in this regard or of counsel in civil cases.

(4) See Freedman, *The Professional Responsibility of the Prosecuting Attorney*, 55 Geo.L.J. 1030 (1967), and Braun, *Ethics in Criminal Cases: A Response*, 55 Geo.L.J. 1048 (1967), for a dialogue as to the line which the prosecutor must work out between proper strategy and unethical conduct in several areas of particular difficulty. An especially helpful consideration of the problems of the prosecutor and of counsel for the defense is found in Schwartz, Cases and Materials on Professional Responsibility and The Administration of Criminal Justice (1962).

(5) For a description of the demands of the district attorney's office in the most densely populated county in the country (King's County, N. Y.) see Silver, in Listen to Leaders in Law 197 (1963). Preparation and trial by the United States Attorney's Office is described by Whitney North Seymour Jr., *Why Prosecutors Act Like Prosecutors*, 11 Record Ass'n Bar City N. Y. 302 (1956).

(6) Chapter III, Section 2c, pages 173–178 supra, deals with the limitations upon prosecutors as well as upon other attorneys with reference to release of information to the news media concerning trials. See Reardon, *The Fair Trial—Free Press Standards*, 54 A.B.A.J. 343 (1968); Code of Professional Responsibility DR 7–107.

(7) *The duty to disclose.*

Mooney v. Holohan, 294 U.S. 103 (1935) established the proposition that the knowing use by the prosecutor of perjured testimony to obtain a conviction violated due process. Subsequent cases extended this principle to deliberate suppression of evidence favorable to the defendant. Questions have remained as to the effect of the prosecutor's failure to disclose the known existence of exculpatory evidence in other instances. In Brady v. Maryland, 373 U.S. 83 (1963), Justice Douglas, by dictum in the majority opinion, extended the Mooney principle with these words: "We now hold that the suppression by the prosecution of evidence favorable to an accused upon request violates due process where the evidence is material either to guilt or to punishment, irrespective of the good faith or bad faith of the prosecution."

In Giles v. Maryland, 386 U.S. 66 (1967), it was not clear whether a majority of the court was prepared to go that far.

Constitutional rights to a fair trial have not been the only weapons of defense counsel in extracting evidence from reluctant prosecutors. Chief Justice Roger J. Traynor discusses the development of rights to criminal discovery in two excellent articles, *Ground Lost and Found in Criminal Discovery*, 39 N.Y.U.L.Rev. 228 (1964), and *Ground Lost and Found in Criminal Discovery in England*, 39 N.Y.U.L.Rev. 749 (1964). The American Bar Association Project on Minimum Standards for Criminal Justice, Discovery and Procedure Before Trial (Tent.Draft 1969), proposes more liberal discovery practices in criminal cases.

As to the ethical obligations of a prosecutor to disclose evidence favorable to the defendant see Code of Professional Responsibility EC 7-13 and DR 7-103. Under the adversary theory is there any obligation in a civil action or upon defense counsel in a criminal action to educate the other party? See *Spaulding v. Zimmerman* (Chapter VI, page 269 supra.)

(8) Many prosecutors, state and federal, have been critical of United States Supreme Court decisions during the 1960's, decisions which greatly expanded the legal rights of criminal suspects. For a reasoned analysis of this new challenge to the prosecutor, contrasting his responsibility with that of defense counsel, see Evelle J. Younger (District Attorney of Los Angeles County), *Prosecution Problems*, 53 A.B.A.J. 695 (1967).

(9) It might be helpful at this point to summarize the reasons for the frequent assertion that the public prosecutor is under ethical, as well as legal, restraints different from those that govern defense counsel. Include the suggestions found in this Chapter as well as others that occur to you. Do you find the same considerations relevant to government lawyers other than prosecutors? See next Section.

C. THE PROSECUTOR AND PRIVATE PRACTICE

A number of opinions of the American Bar Association Committee on Professional Ethics have dealt with the matter of private practice by a prosecuting attorney during his term of office. This is permitted in many jurisdictions but questions arise as to conflicting interests with reference to certain kinds of representation. Canon 6 has been most frequently invoked. Compare Code of Professional Responsibility EC 8-8. How would you answer the following questions that have been put to the A.B.A. Committee? What part does consent (see Canon 6) play in these cases? Assume in each instance that the prosecutor is permitted to engage in some private practice. See also Chapter XI, Section 2, page 414 infra.

1. May a state prosecuting attorney represent defendants before federal courts, boards and bureaus in matters involving federal laws? (A.B.A. Opinion 262 (1944)).

2. Is it ethical for a United States Attorney or an Assistant United States Attorney to practice on the civil side of the Federal Courts? (A.B.A. Opinion 278 (1948)).

3. A prosecuting attorney investigates an automobile collision to determine whether a prosecution is warranted. He determines it is not. May he later represent any of the parties in the accident in a civil suit to recover damages from the person concerning whom the criminal investigation was made? (A.B.A. Opinion 135 (1935)).

4. Is it ethical for a lawyer who becomes a state attorney general to continue to be a member of a private law firm or to allow his name to be used as a part of the name of the law firm? May the firm accept professional employment which requires dealings with the state? May the attorney general ethically recommend the firm to those he deals with in his official position? Would it make a difference if he had severed connections with the firm? (A.B.A. Opinion 192 (1939)).

5. May a prosecuting attorney in one county accept employment to obtain a pardon or parole of one convicted of a crime in another county? (A.B.A. Opinion 118 (1934)).

6. May a public prosecutor in one state defend an accused person in another state? (A.B.A. Opinion 30 (1931)).

7. The answer to this should be clear: May one member of a firm defend a person who is being prosecuted by another member of the same firm in the latter's capacity as prosecuting attorney? (A.B.A. Opinion 16 (1929)).

8. What of the prosecutor's ethical responsibilities after he leaves office? May he defend cases that originated while he was in office? (A.B.A. Opinion 134 (1935)). See Canon 36, as well as Canon 6; Code of Professional Responsibility EC 9–3. Compare Chapter VIII (The Lawyer and the Legislature) page 342 supra. See page 374 infra with reference to the Federal Conflict of Interest Act of 1962.

SECTION 2. OTHER GOVERNMENT LAWYER ROLES

ESTHER LUCILLE BROWN, LAWYERS, LAW SCHOOL AND THE PUBLIC SERVICE *

Pages 7, 78, 85 (1948).

[T]he private lawyer of the future can ill afford, as Professor Walter Gellhorn has cogently argued, to be unaware of what the government lawyer must know. "The fact that government is today a business partner or competitor or cherished customer cannot be overlooked by those who expect to serve business as legal advisers." To no inconsiderable degree legislatures are hearing bodies before whom

* Copyright 1948 by Russell Sage Foundation. Reprinted with permission.

the different interests appear, each arguing its own point of view. Administrative proceedings, furthermore, and their attendant negotiations and litigations are not unilateral. When government law is in the making, private lawyers share in forming the product. So far beyond the offices of the government does the work of government now extend that even legislation, decision, and administration go forward in hundreds of non-official law offices the nation over. The enlarged participation of the private practitioner in governmental matters in the last generation leads to the supposition that prospective private lawyers, currently attending professional schools, will have practices largely colored by the same factors that will determine the activities of the government lawyer.

. . .

So exceedingly important is the question of the lawyer's participation in policy-making that some detailed consideration must be given to it. Policy is effectuated by attorneys on several levels and in a variety of ways. The policy-making function is most obvious when the general solicitor of a department or agency or the chief counsel of a bureau acts in an advisory capacity to administrative officials. But policy is made pervasively and continuously, although less conspicuously, on lower levels. It is made through the drafting of legislation, regulations, and executive orders; through interpretation of statutory and administrative law; through reviewing of work done by bureaus and divisions; and through the litigatory and administrative process. It is also made as the result of fortuitous circumstances whereby a lawyer, upon a particular occasion or in a particular agency, is given broad opportunity for planning and even administration which at another time or in another agency would be decisively denied him.

. . .

Much of the most influential work of the attorney as policymaker is done in the role of legal and policy adviser to administrative officials. The importance of this role is sometimes overlooked, because it varies greatly from agency to agency and because the advisory function is often exercised in so informal or highly personalized a way that little appears about it in annual reports or other published form.

Since a swarm of legal problems surrounds almost every question with which administrators and policy-makers are faced, they are likely to turn constantly to counsel for advice. They inquire if there *is* a legal aspect to the problem; they want to know *what* they can do in regard to a particular situation, and *how* it can be done. They frequently expect counsel to sit at the conference table at which questions of policy are decided. In such a close relationship the attorney almost inevitably comes, sometimes perhaps without realizing it, to express approval or disapproval of administrative policy. Even when he does not create, he at least strongly influences, policy.

NOTES

(1) In *The Responsibilities of the Legal Profession*, 54 A.B.A.J. 121 (1968), Justice William J. Brennan, Jr. describes the movement within the government of increasing numbers of outstanding young lawyers "away from the more traditional legal positions of prosecutor, tax specialist and the like toward fields such as civil rights or the 'war on poverty,' international relations, the Peace Corps and criminal justice." Justice Brennan urges the private sector of the bar, in its own self interest and in the interest of the public, to devise better ways of enabling lawyers to combine consecutive periods of full-time private service and governmental service and at the same time to continue "the search for imaginative new ways by which the lawyer can serve the public interest, while continuing in private practice, in a more substantial and concentrated fashion than has traditionally been true of spare-time activities."

(2) For a suggestion that more governmental agencies should occasionally retain outside counsel see Rostow, *The Lawyer and His Client*, 48 A.B.A.J. 146, 147 (1962). Dean Rostow argues that governmental legal staffs would be stimulated by the occasional participation of distinguished outside lawyers in their cases and that "more lawyers would gain the inestimable advantage of viewing the world in the perspective of governmental interests." Can you envision conflicts of interest that might arise under such practice?

(3) Beresford, *Lawyers, Science, and the Government*, 33 G.W.L.Rev. 181 (1964), discusses lawyers in government who work with scientists and suggests the optimum training for such lawyers. See also Bilder, *The Office of the Legal Adviser: The State Department Lawyer and Foreign Affairs*, 56 Am.J.Int'l.L. 633 (1962); Hoffman, Government Lawyer (1956); Carlock in Listen to Leaders in Law 257 (1963). Chapter X, Section 1 page 378 infra describes lawyers as legislators and political officials. Chapter XIV page 502 infra is devoted to the lawyer as a judge.

IN RE A. AND B., ATTORNEYS-AT-LAW

Supreme Court of New Jersey, 1965.
44 N.J. 331, 209 A.2d 101.

PER CURIAM.

A complaint was filed with the County Ethics Committee charging respondents with violation of Canon 6 of the Canons of Professional Ethics in that while serving as municipal attorneys, they also were attorneys for and served conflicting interests of certain land and building developers whose projects were located in the same municipality. The Committee did not make a presentment but at our request filed a report. We issued an order to show cause. . . .

Dual representation is particularly troublesome where one of the clients is a governmental body. So, an attorney may not represent both a governmental body and a private client merely because disclosure was made and they are agreeable that he represent both interests. As Mr. Justice Hall said in Ahto v. Weaver, 39 N.J. 418, 431, 189 A.2d 27, 34 (1963), "Where the public interest is involved, he may not represent conflicting interests even with consent of all concerned. . . ."

Here, as we have said, we do not find the respondents represented the developers in the developers' dealings with the municipality. Although for this reason there is no literal violation of Canon 6, nonetheless that canon does not exhaust the ethical responsibility of the bar in this area. . . . We all know from practical experience that the very nature of the work of the developer involves a probability of some municipal action, such as zoning applications, land subdivisions, building permits, compliance with the building code, etc.

It is accordingly our view that such dual representation is forbidden even though the attorney does not advise either the municipality or the private client with respect to matters concerning them. The fact of such dual representation itself is contrary to the public interest.

We of course appreciate that the dual representation here involved has not been uncommon. For that reason it would be unfair to adjudge guilt in this, the first proceeding raising the issue before the Court. For that reason no such action will be taken in this matter, and the names of the attorneys concerned will be omitted from the caption.

The order is discharged.

NOTES

(1) May a county attorney who represents the county in civil matters only represent a defendant in a criminal case prosecuted by the district attorney? (A.B.A. Opinion 186 (1938). Cf. A.B.A. Opinion 34 (1931)). Would the situation be different if defendant were an indigent and the bar small? (See A.B.A. Opinion 55 (1931)).

(2) May an attorney who had charge of the legal matters connected with a municipal bond issue, including a successful validation suit, later accept employment by a taxpayer to attack the validity of such bonds? (A.B.A. Opinion 71 (1932)).

THE FEDERAL GOVERNMENT LAWYER AND POST-EMPLOYMENT RESTRICTIONS

The Federal Conflict of Interest Act of 1962, 76 Stat. 1119, 18 U.S.C.A. §§ 201–218 (1964), deals broadly with conflict of interest in the executive branches of the federal service. For former government employees, section 207 of the Act is specific on two sets of matters. On matters in which "he participated personally and substantially" as an employee he is disqualified forever. On matters which were "under his official responsibility . . . at any time within a period of one year prior to the termination of such responsibility", he is disqualified for one year from appearing personally before any federal court or agency. The statute places no bar on appearance as to new matters before any government agency. Nor does the statute deal explicitly with the disqualification of a firm with which the government employee becomes associated.

It has been assumed that the statute does not seek to occupy the whole field and that "major responsibility for regulations and for administrative enforcement of regulations, in the field of conflict of interest is vested in the individual departments and agencies." Manning, p. 271, note (1) infra.

Should the statute be implemented and filled out by common law principles and professional standards, which may well be more exacting than the statute alone? The courts may find that the statute, dealing only with specific matters in a limited way, leaves the rest of the field to be developed in accordance with the usual principles that apply to lawyers. Cf. United States v. Standard Oil Co. of New Jersey, 136 F.Supp. 345 (1955).

The states are free to develop their conflict of interest principles according to the standards they deem appropriate. The federal statute, however, will probably be influential in helping the states to shape their own standards.

NOTES

(1) The federal statute is excellently discussed against the background of the earlier federal legislation in Manning, Federal Conflict of Interest Law (1964), and Perkins, *The New Federal Conflict of Interest Law*, 76 Harv.L.Rev. 1113 (1963). Both Dean Manning and Mr. Perkins were active in the influential study and report of the Special Committee on the Federal Conflict of Interest Laws of the Association of the Bar of the City of New York, "Conflict of Interest and Federal Service" (1960).

(2) A prominent firm specializing in tax cases sends out an announcement stating that a named member of the firm "has withdrawn from the firm to become Commissioner of Internal Revenue." Any impropriety? Would the area of dissemination of the announcement be material? See Chapter II, Section 6, page 123 supra with reference to announcement cards.

Chapter X

PUBLIC RESPONSIBILITY

Introduction. No aspect of the lawyer's professional life has received more attention during the past decade than the discharge of his public responsibilities. This focus is due in large part to the social upheaval of our times. Many segments of society are insisting upon change, often in violent terms, and demands to respond have been addressed to the courts, the legislatures, governmental officials and the public generally. In this process the lawyer is called upon to furnish leadership, not only in combating disruption, but, more importantly, in devising and implementing positive solutions to society's ills. The dimensions of the task are such as to require the sustained effort of the profession. Law school graduates of recent years have made it clear that they will not be satisfied with less.

The major portion of this book is devoted to the responsibility of the lawyer as a private practitioner. It speaks of his duties to clients and to the courts, duties that in many respects are prescribed by canons, by court decisions, and by disciplinary committee reports. This is not to say that the guide lines in private practice are invariably clear and free from dispute. We have had much evidence to the contrary. But when we turn to the broader public responsibilities of the lawyer it is at once apparent that canons, court decisions, and committee reports are almost never to be found. No code tells the lawyer what he must do, if anything, beyond effective representation of clients and faithful discharge of his role as an officer of the court. No touchstone tells him where to start or where to leave off. In this area legal sanctions disappear and the "law" of "obedience to the unenforceable" takes over.

Certain propositions may be set out as axiomatic prior to consideration of the lawyer's world beyond practice. Few will quarrel with the conclusion that competent practice is a basic responsibility of the private practitioner and that responsible private practice is an important form of public service. The administration of justice under our system of law depends upon the faithful performance of this role. The very definition of a profession must include the concept of public service and the lawyer who competently represents clients within the confines of his court role has discharged an important public responsibility whether his activities stop at this point or go beyond. It might be said in fact that the lawyer who renders incompetent service to client or court renders the greatest public disservice. The new Code of Professional Responsibility spells out competency as a basic responsibility (Canon 6) in contrast to the veiled reference of the older Canons. (See Chapter XII, Section 4, page 456 infra).

But what of the lawyer's opportunities and responsibilities beyond private practice? Here we turn to the lawyer as a holder of public office, whether elective or appointive. We next examine his participation outside the political sphere in an almost unlimited field of public concerns, as an individual lawyer or as a member of a law or lay group. We see him here as an educator and as a prime mover in the resolution of public discontent primarily through improvement in the law. We conclude with a look at the more obvious areas of lawyer concern but at the same time areas of broad public interest. These include improvement of the administration of justice and the extension of professional knowledge.

Before these subjects are taken up, however, it is well to be explicit on two matters with the student reader. First, you may well feel almost resentful toward the chapter and toward us, your teacher and the editors. You know that a primary obligation on you is to make adequate provision for those dependent on you. You will meet that obligation through your earnings in practice. So you may plan to postpone attention to the wider and less personal obligations until, say, you have made your first million.

This is a natural feeling. Yet it would be most unfortunate if the inclination were carried into decision, unfortunate for the community, local or national or international, to which you can direct some of your time in public activities. Dean Pound reminded the lawyers of Oklahoma that:

"There have been eras of liberalization and of growth [in improving the administration of justice and meeting the needs of a changed social order]. In such periods it has happened often that some of the prime movers were lawyers. Yet it should be observed that usually they were young lawyers, not the veteran leaders of the bar." *

It would be unfortunate, too, for you as an individual. Interests and powers left unused shrivel and atrophy. Keep them alive by use, knowing as you do that these interests and powers will be directed to constantly changing conditions.

The second personal matter is the choices of the field and the type of activities. With so many areas of opportunity there is the temptation to emulate the fabled rider who, after a few too many drinks at a tavern, jumped on his horse and rode off in all directions. Choices have to be made of the field of special interest and work. And choices have to be made, too, of the type of activity. Some lawyers lack the qualities fitting them for elective political office, though admirably suited to bar organization activity or to legal work for the poor. The choices made may depend on the particular opportunities

---

* Roscoe Pound, *The Legal Profession and the Law*, 18 Rep. Oklahoma State Bar Ass'n 179, 193–194 (1924).

which are open or can be made to open, and on the individual's primary interests as well as on his assessment of his major abilities.

As you go through this chapter bear in mind these two personal matters. At the end come to a decision, very tentative though it is, on the areas and activities through which you hope to make your contributions.

SECTION 1. POLITICAL LEADERSHIP

HEINZ EULAU AND JOHN D. SPRAGUE, LAWYERS IN POLITICS *

Pages 11–15 (1964).

No occupational group stands in more regular and intimate relation to American politics than the legal profession. Lawyers make up a large proportion of American politicians at all levels and in all branches of government, in the political parties, and in other political organizations. . . .

That lawyers have an almost complete monopoly of public offices connected with law enforcement and with the administration of law in the courts is not surprising. But they are also prominent as an occupational group in the executive and legislative arenas of government. This has been true from the earliest days of the republic. Of the fifty-two signers of the Declaration of Independence, twenty-five were lawyers, as were thirty-one of the fifty-five members serving in the Continental Congress. Of the thirty-six American presidents, twenty-three have been lawyers. Between 1877 and 1934, 70 per cent of American presidents, vice-presidents, and cabinet members were lawyers. Of a total of 995 elected governors in all American states between 1870 and 1950, 46 per cent were practicing lawyers.

In the legislative branches, the ascendancy of the legal profession is equally marked. Of 175 members serving in the Senate of the United States between 1947 and 1957, 54 per cent were lawyers. In the seventy-first through the seventy-fifth Congresses, from 61 to 76 per cent of the members of the Senate and from 56 to 65 per cent of the members of the House of Representatives belonged to the legal profession. Between 1925 and 1935, of a total of 12,689 persons serving in the lower houses of thirteen selected states and in the upper houses of twelve, 28 per cent were lawyers by occupation. A survey of all 7,475 American state legislators serving in 1949 showed that 22 per cent were lawyers. . . .

. . .

* Copyright 1964 by the Bobbs-Merrill Co. Reprinted by permission.

The conventional explanation of the lawyer's dominance in politics is, as Alexis de Tocqueville put it long ago, that "scarcely any question arises in the United States which does not become, sooner or later, a subject of judicial debate. In contrast to the mother country, where the final locus of political power, as the outcome of the struggle between Crown and Parliament, was acknowledged in the latter's legal sovereignty, in the United States the political power of the legislature was inhibited by constitutional limitations." But if the power of the legislature is limited, who is in a better position than the lawyer to know whether the Constitution has been violated? . . .

ALBERT BLAUSTEIN AND CHARLES PORTER, THE AMERICAN LAWYER

Pages 97–105 (1954).*

Why are so many lawyers found in federal and state legislative assemblies? A few generalized answers seemed indisputable. First, lawyers are more strongly attracted to public service as legislative candidates than are other professionals generally. This is particularly true of young lawyers outside the metropolitan areas. The personal characteristics and inclinations that cause men to seek legal training are such as will also pull them into active political affairs. . . .

Second, candidacy for the state legislature is, in many parts of the country, a traditional form of professional advertising, and of course a perfectly legitimate one. Even the unsuccessful candidate brings his name to the attention of prospective clients. If he wins, the lawyer attains valuable standing in his community and has exceptional opportunities to meet persons of state-wide political and business influence. . . .

Added to these two factors is the further consideration that attendance at a legislative session works no particular hardship on a lawyer's practice.

It would be unrealistically cynical, however, to account for the prevalence of lawyers in legislative positions entirely in terms of their greater availability as candidates. Beyond doubt, the most important single factor is the marked tendency Americans have always shown to choose lawyers for positions of high political responsibility. To couple this well-established public preference with some other public attitudes is to suggest, says Harry W. Jones, this paradox: "The public is often severely critical of lawyers *as lawyers*, but it has a marked preference for them as public officials." . . .

* Copyright 1954 by the University of Chicago. Reprinted by permission.

The role which lawyers have played in local government in this country has not been glorious, declares Murray Seasongood, an eminent lawyer who has long led the fight for good government in Cincinnati and Hamilton County, Ohio, in reporting on this subject for the Survey of the Legal Profession.

Local government is, he maintains, the most important segment of governmental administration in our nation. Its financial requirements are huge; it is the branch of government which most directly and most frequently affects the ordinary citizen. Though commonly referred to as the "lowest" level of government, it is so in the sense that the foundation is the lowest part of a building—and the most important. . . .

These observations should be rather obvious, but to the American lawyer, Seasongood holds, they are not. His record of participation in local political affairs seems to indicate a lack of understanding, callous indifference, or sometimes actual hostility. With few exceptions, lawyers have not busied themselves with the functioning of local government. . . .

Singling out the law schools for sharpest attack, Seasongood points out that, while some of them give courses in legal ethics, not one gives courses in public legal duties. In perhaps half of the law schools there is no course on the law of municipal corporations, and in only a very few of these is such a course required.

NOTE

For a comparison of influence of lawyers in the U.S.S.R., see Barry and Berman, *The Soviet Legal Profession*, 82 Harv.L.Rev. 1 (1968) pp. 32–33:

"Unlike American lawyers, who are well represented in the leadership groups of political and business organizations and in government bodies at all levels, Soviet jurists are almost entirely unrepresented in the formal and informal centers of political power in Soviet society. None of the members of the Politburo of the Communist Party has ever been a jurist—except for Lenin, who can hardly be said to have 'represented' the legal profession. As of 1968, in the Central Committee of the Party, with its 195 members and 165 candidate members, only Procurator General Rudenko (a full member) was from the legal profession, and in the Central Auditing Commission, with its 79 members, only Supreme Court President Gorkin was from the legal profession. . . .

"Yet, . . . jurists participate actively in the work of the higher legislative and administrative agencies—not as members but as staff advisors, consultants, or members of subordinate divisions appointed to assist those agencies. . . ."

KENNETH B. KEATING,* LETTER TO EDITOR OF THE CORNELL LAW FORUM

Summer 1968 (p. 3).

I have spent over half of my adult life in public service in one form or another. As a result, I have had to deal with many questions of public interest that go far beyond and are far different from anything which I studied while attending law school. As the years have gone by, I have seen the role of government in the life of every citizen become ever more pervasive and the increase in scientific knowledge add new complexities to every public question. At times, I had the disturbing feeling that we were about to be overwhelmed by the sheer immensity of this new "knowledge" and the difficulty of our social problems. Nevertheless, I found that my training at the law school had given me an irreplaceable tool with which to deal with this mountain of new "knowledge" and allegedly insoluble social problems.

The tool, of course, is what is generally referred to as legal analysis or the legal method. Its greatest virtue is that it teaches one to ask the pertinent, or should I say impertinent question. Too often I have seen what parades as expertise is nothing more than conclusions based upon questionable assumptions and undisclosed prejudice. Knowledge of the legal method gained in law school, enabled me to distinguish between the truth, half-truth, or outright falsity in many fields of knowledge outside of the law.

Still, I do think that law school education until recently tended to forget that, great as it is, the legal method is only a tool. Great legal minds created logical-legal systems that had the simplicity, symmetry and beauty of a great work of art. But, somehow, these systems often lost touch with reality, with the people's sense of justice.

. . .

A divorce of the law from the great social problems of the day is dangerous both to the law and the public good. It was in this failure to apply the legal method to practical problems of every day law practice or to the urgent social problems of the day that for a long time threatened to make law school education and the rule of law as well an irrelevancy.

Happily, I see a surging revitalization of law school programs in the areas of the criminal law and international law as well as the addition of strong new programs in urban affairs, civil rights and civil liberties in our law schools today. Welcoming this trend as I do, it must not come at the expense of a thorough grounding in the methods of legal analysis.

---

* Ambassador to India, Formerly Judge of the New York Court of Appeals, Formerly United States Senator, Formerly United States Representative. Copyright 1968 by the Cornell Law Forum. Reprinted by permission.

ARTHUR T. VANDERBILT,* MEN AND MEASURES IN THE LAW **

Pages 45-46 (1949).

No class in our society has been more generous with its time and the use of its capacity for leadership in social enterprises than the lawyers. They are always to be found in key positions on the boards of colleges and hospitals and in the forefront of community drives. But too many of the ablest of them have shrunk from public office-holding, from party leadership, and from posts of influence in the formation of public opinion and even from active participation in the affairs of the organized bar. The reasons are known to all. First of all, successful lawyers are very busy men; like all professional men they render personal service and much of their work cannot be delegated. Time is a most important element in their lives. Even more controlling, the lawyer is subject to the same pressures to escape his duties as a citizen as are all other men. His family, and particularly the women of the family, are likely to oppose his getting in what is often called a "dirty game." They forget that it is only through politics that a democratic, representative government can be run, and that it is the acts of the men who run our government more than any others that determine whether we shall have peace or war, prosperity or depression. The stakes are high enough, it would seem, to merit anyone's attention. Fortunately for our country, family and social aversion to participation in public affairs disappears in the face of war. Then lawyers render yeoman service. Even though in each war the military started by claiming that lawyers were worth "a dime a dozen," it is significant that the value of their services was soon recognized whenever the capacity for independent thinking was a requisite. But why must patriotism always be thought of solely as a wartime virtue?

The objections to a lawyer's activity in the interest of the public do not come solely from his family and friends. The leaders of many industries deem it necessary to keep out of politics, officially at any rate, and they often expect their lawyers to do so too. The attitude of many clients, particularly in the larger communities, toward the politics of their attorneys has had its baleful influence. They prefer their lawyers not to be active politically, but at the same time to have political contacts if they should be needed in furtherance of the clients' affairs. They look with favor, therefore, on law firms made up of members of both political parties so that the partnership may have a foot in each camp. Not only the ethics but the effectiveness of this

---

* See Chapter I, page 14 supra.

** Part of the William W. Cook Foundation Lectures. Copyright 1949 by the Regents of the University of Michigan. Reprinted by permission of A. A. Knopf, publisher.

point of view may be questioned, but the fact that it represents a widespread opinion of clients in selecting lawyers cannot be gainsaid. The greatest deterrent, however, that confronts the lawyer who would do his duty in public life is one that is shared by many other citizens. It is the feeling that politics and government are so complicated that nothing that he, as an individual, can do would possibly count. We have come in recent years to talk so much about society collectively that the individual, whether he be lawyer or layman, is likely to feel a sense of frustration as to his capacity for personal achievement in public affairs. The greatest need of our age and for us individually as lawyers, I have no hesitancy in saying, is for us to recapture the conviction that controlled the action of men in earlier crises in society and in the law, that the actions of individual men can be made to count and that we do have within us the power to work out solutions of social problems by dint of reason and resolution.

LAWYERS IN FOREIGN AFFAIRS *

New York Times, Jan. 6, 1969, p. 46.

By naming two distinguished lawyers—William P. Rogers and Elliot L. Richardson—to head the State Department, President-elect Nixon keeps alive a long, American tradition of lawyers in key foreign policy posts. There has been a characteristic legalism in American diplomacy which has made an important contribution to the growth of international law, the creation of the United Nations and the League of Nations, and the search for institutional methods to resolve international rivalry and conflict.

Inherently, however, this tradition also includes a certain rigidity and insensitivity to the depth of cultural differences between societies and to the social and ideological sources of international conflict. Law functions within a structure of shared assumptions; its starting point is the acceptance, by all parties, of the legitimacy of the legal structure and of the values it embodies.

Everyone understands that this shared value commitment and belief in the adjudication of conflict does not exist in more than a fragmentary manner in international society. Nevertheless, the legal habit of mind has sometimes led the United States to discount these difficulties, even to assume for itself and its own policies an international legitimacy which other states were unwilling to concede. Along with this has gone a trust in formal arrangements and alliances which the social and political realities have not at all times justified.

George Kennan commented on the influence of lawyers on American policy nearly 20 years ago in his "American Diplomacy 1900–1950." He noted that Americans find it "improbable that people

* Copyright 1969 by The New York Times. Reprinted by permission.

should have positive aspirations, and ones that they regard as legitimate, more important to them than the peacefulness and orderliness of international life." As a result this country too often is baffled that conflicts and interests are pursued "unreasonably," or that others interpret our commitment to international order as a calculated rationalization of American self-interest.

More recently Arthur Schlesinger Jr. has found much the same legacy of legalism in the American view that there must be "a single durable structure of world security, which must everywhere be protected against aggression; if aggression were permitted to go unpunished in one place this would lead to a general destruction of the system of world order." He argues that this state of mind, often reflected in the statements of Secretary Rusk and President Johnson, contributed heavily to this country's errors in Vietnam.

To criticize this aspect of American diplomatic thinking is not, of course, to condemn it. This country's quest for international law and for institutions of order and adjudication has had profoundly constructive effects on the world as well. But as a new period of change and challenge in international affairs begins, the assumptions as well as the programs of American foreign policy need reappraisal. Secretary Rogers and Under Secretary Richardson should take critical account of the weaknesses, as well as the strengths, of the tradition they bring to the Department of State.

NOTES

(1) Can you suggest reasons other than those set forth above why lawyers have historically occupied and continue to occupy such a high percentage of political offices? Is it arguable that lawyers have been too prominent in American political life? If it is true that there has been a dearth of lawyers in local government, why should this be so? Has your law training equipped you for political office? Is there any way in which it might have better equipped you? Is there any reason why it should?

A critic of the legal profession once asserted that, although a high percentage of those in political life had law degrees, few of our political leaders and statesmen during the twentieth century had been outstanding in the private practice of law. Consider the Presidents of this country as well as the defeated candidates for President, other political leaders, and American statesmen since 1900 and ask yourself whether you agree. Can you prepare a list of names to refute the criticism?

(2) For a study of the bar of one state indicating that there is no homogeniety in the legal profession with reference to political involvement see Bromall, *Lawyers in Politics: An Exploratory Study of the Wisconsin Bar,* 1968 Wis.L.Rev. 751 (1968). This study indicates that there are many variables with reference to the recruitment of lawyers into politics among which are early experiences, performance in law school, professional environment, etc. Would the reasons likely to attract a country lawyer to politics be the same as those which attract a city lawyer?

(3) On the political and public leadership of the American Bar, see Hurst, The Growth of American Law—The Law Makers (1950), pp. 352–375.

(4) *Conflicting Interests.* It frequently happens that the lawyer who holds public office and who had previously been engaged in private practice will find conflicting duties to the public and to clients, past or present. Former Senator Paul H. Douglas recites an extreme example of nineteenth century conflict of interest in his book, Ethics in Government * 15 (1952):

. . . "Webster was the defender, on the floor of the Senate, of the Second Bank of the United States, which was seeking a renewal of its charter and which was being opposed by President Andrew Jackson. As the bank struggle reached its climax in 1833, Webster kept somewhat aloof from it but on December 21st wrote Nicholas Biddle, the President of the Bank, as follows: 'Sir:—Since I have arrived here I have had an application to be concerned professionally against the Bank which I have declined of course, although I believe my retainer has not been renewed, or refreshed as usual. If it be wished that my relation to the Bank should be continued it may be well to send me the usual retainers.'

"This letter, which has seldom been surpassed for its essential blackmail, brought the desired result. The retainer was 'refreshed' and Webster girded on the sword of his oratory to do battle for his employer.

. . .

. . . "I do not mention this to besmirch the memory of Daniel Webster for in many ways that gentleman served our country well. But I do so to show the great moral progress which we have made during the last century. For on the basis of personal knowledge, I am confident that there could not now be such wholesale corruption of Congress as took place in connection with Mr. Biddle's machinations. . . ."

Acknowledging that Senator Douglas is correct as to today's Congress what should the lawyer-legislator do when the legislature considers matters affecting his clients? Should he disclose the relationship and abstain from voting? Is there a counterpart to the judge's disqualifying himself? (Chapter XIV, page 525 infra.) See Malone, *The Lawyer and His Professional Responsibilities,* 17 Wash. & Lee L.Rev. 191, 206 (1960).

Kirby, Congress and the Public Trust (1970), is the report of The Association of the Bar of the City of New York Special Committee on Congressional Ethics of which Professor Kirby was the Executive Director. The book shows the extent to which the lawyers in Congress continue in law practice and makes recommendations on the subject of the lawyer-legislator, including the specific one that the Member of Congress should refrain from the practice of law.

The ABA Code of Professional Responsibility address itself to some of the problems. See EC 8–8; EC 2–12.

Report of the Joint Conference on Professional Responsibility:

"Special fiduciary obligations are also incumbent on the lawyer who becomes a representative in the legislative branch of government, especially

---

* Part of the Godkin Lectures. Copyright 1952 by the President and Fellows of Harvard College. Reprinted by permission of the Harvard University Press.

where he continues his private practice after assuming public office. Such a lawyer must be able to envisage the moral disaster that may result from a confusion of his role as legislator and his role as the representative of private clients. The fact that one in this position is sometimes faced with delicate issues difficult of resolution should not cause the lawyer to forget that a failure to face honestly and courageously the moral issues presented by his position may forfeit his integrity both as lawyer and as legislator and pervert the very meaning of representative government." 44 A.B.A.J. 1159, 1218 (1958); 1958 A.A.L.S.Proc. 187, 201 (1958).

"There is a sense in which the lawyer must keep his obligations of public service distinct from the involvements of his private practice. This line of separation is aptly illustrated by an incident in the life of Thomas Talfourd. As a barrister Talfourd had successfully represented a father in a suit over the custody of a child. Judgment for Talfourd's client was based on his superior legal right, though the court recognized in the case at bar that the mother had a stronger moral claim to custody than the father. Having thus encountered in the course of his practice an injustice in the law as then applied by the courts, Talford later as a member of Parliament secured the enactment of a statute that would make impossible a repetition of the result his own advocacy had helped to bring about. Here the line is clearly drawn between the obligation of the advocate and the obligation of the public servant." 44 A.B.A.J. 1159, 1162 (1958); 1958 A.A.L.S.Proc. 187, 194 (1958).

See Rauh, Conflict of Interest in Congress, U. of Chi. Conference on Conflict of Interest, No. 17, p. 1, in Conference Series (1961); Perkins, Conflict of Interest in the Executive Branch, ibid p. 67. In 1967 the Illinois legislature passed an extensive Governmental Ethics Act (Smith-Hurd Illinois Annotated Statutes, chap. 127, Secs. 601–101 through 607–101.) This act pertains to legislators, other elected state officials, judges, candidates for these positions, and also non-elected officers and employees, whether lawyers or non-lawyers. Other states have enacted similar legislation.

SECTION 2. LEADERSHIP IN PUBLIC AFFAIRS

ADDRESS OF JOHN W. GARDNER [*] BEFORE THE A.B.A. SECTION ON INDIVIDUAL RIGHTS AND RESPONSIBILITIES, Aug. 5, 1968.

The possibilities for the lawyer interested in community service are enormous in scope and variety precisely because he brings to the assignment such extraordinary potentialities as negotiator, advocate, planner, organizer, appraiser of the legality of administrative actions, student of constitutional questions, drafter of legislation and so on.

The possible fields of interest that lie before him cover every major area of social concern—poverty, civil rights, education, employment, health, transportation, air and water pollution, police-community relations, and housing. He can interest himself in any of a

---

[*] Formerly President of the Carnegie Corporation and Secretary of Health, Education and Welfare.

variety of groups whose legal rights have been inadequately protected, including tenants, consumers, welfare recipients, the mentally ill and juvenile delinquents.

The most readily visible challenge to the lawyer is of course to insure that legal services be available as a matter of right. The idea of legal aid is well-established. Federally-funded neighborhood legal services are now familiar and reasonably well-accepted. But we have a long way to go. . . .

Provision of the voluntary services of high priced lawyers is a necessary but inadequate response. Eventually, as in the health field, there will have to be innovations in the delivery of services that reduce unit cost, make better use of highly trained professionals and eliminate needlessly complicated and costly legal procedures. Such innovations might include use of sub-professionals and para-professionals, standardization of certain routine legal transactions, and so on.

Provision of legal services is the challenge that is on your doorstep. A world of even greater challenge lies beyond.

. . .

. . . I am not simply asking you to give more time to the ethics committee of your bar association or more time to philanthropic work in the community. I am asking you to remember that lawyers wrote *The Federalist Papers,* and lawyers drafted the Constitution. I am asking you to reflect on the fact that lawyers are probably better equipped than any other profession to think about the design of human institutions, and the process by which they are redesigned without bloodshed.

The possibilities for such redesign cover the total range of our social institutions. I'm going to mention only a few that seem to me of special pertinence to this audience.

First, modernization of our governmental institutions. We need a major overhaul of the Federal Government. The relations between the Federal Government and State and local government and the private sector are in an exciting period of transition, a period in which significant innovation is possible. The modernization of State and local government is a crying need. . . .

Second, an overhaul of our tax structure and reexamination of the allocation of resources to the various levels of government. . .

Third, the design of institutional arrangements to foster participation. Grass roots participation is a healthy and growing reaction against distant and anonymous government decrees that affect one's life. . . .

Fourth, the development and operation of effective grievance procedures. Nothing is more certain than that current interest in ombudsman procedures will grow. This interest feeds on the impatience of all classes of society with the invisible processes of bureaucracy. . . .

Fifth, the design of planning mechanisms that will make possible comprehensive planning at Federal, regional, State, metropolitan area and city levels.

Sixth, reform in the organization and administration of the courts.
. . .

In closing, let me say that I'm well aware of the size and scope of the chores that I've placed before you. In order to cope with those assignments, I should like to see both individuals and firms engage in tithing with respect to the time available for community purposes. I know the difficulties inherent in such a proposal. I know that for lawyers time is money. Time is your stock in trade. I know that you already contribute to charity. You give time to your bar association, to your service as court appointed counsel, and to civic and charitable activities.

Even so, I believe that something in the nature of tithing should be tried.

I don't know whether I should try to strengthen the argument by appealing to your self-interest. . . .

But I do not take a dim view of self-interest as a motive. Of all the things that motivate people, I find it one of the most satisfactory to work with. For one thing, it is admirably consistent. It's always there. Other motives wax and wane; it only waxes.

First of all, as every alert senior partner knows, many of the ablest young lawyers are determined to engage in some kind of significant community service. Their restlessness is not a passing mood. They know what they want. In order to hold the best young people today, the firm had better come to terms with their public services impulses. One practical means, by the way, of encouraging those young men who take seriously their responsibility to the community is for the firm to include in its periodic review of the individual's performance his services to the community.

A more fundamental point of self-interest is that the practice of law depends heavily on the framework of order and of orderly procedure that is being so directly challenged today. The legal profession cannot flourish while the society rattles to pieces. It is in the elementary self-interest of lawyers to prevent the disintegration of their society.

Now one of the great and classic weaknesses of rules for virtuous behavior is that they are very easily gotten around. Thus, in tithing, some men will seek to perform their entire duty by sitting on the boards of distinguished charities of which their clients are chairmen. But I hope that many will take on the large and difficult tasks I have talked about today. If self-interest does not command them, perhaps some higher impulse will come to the rescue.

In the long perspective of history, you and I are on the stage for a very brief moment—and then gone. I assume none of us wants it said that in our short time of effective public influence we did anything but the best we could possibly do. That is how I feel and I know it's how you feel. In the long run a man doesn't have to fear the judgment of the world so much as he has to fear his verdict on himself. We don't want it said that in our time we trifled with our country's future, or ran away from the tough problems, or were pygmies when our country needed giants.

Maybe in the light of eternity we are all pygmies, but in our own eyes, our stature will depend on how seriously we try.

COUNCIL ON LEGAL EDUCATION FOR PROFESSIONAL RESPONSIBILITY, INC., EDUCATIONAL VALUES IN CLINICAL EXPERIENCE FOR LAW STUDENTS

Vol. II, No. 1, September 1969, page 4.

The law student in the clinical legal experience also should learn the distinction between 1) that which the lawyer has a special power for accomplishing as a lawyer, and, 2) that which the lawyer has to accomplish as a citizen using all the powers at his command. In the first category there are those things which the lawyer can do to influence reform directly by virtue of his work as a lawyer. These involve work on the substance, the doctrine, and the procedure of the law in the course of providing legal service. They include special efforts to improve the machinery of justice in those instances where the organized bar and its closely related institutions undertake reform. In the second category there are those reform activities, including the machinery of justice but also extending into the economy and social institutions, where the lawyer is effective as a citizen with standing because he has achieved in his own profession.

Clinical legal education should help to make the future lawyer sensitive to the broad issues going beyond the immediate case. It should give him practice in how to act as a lawyer in making constructive change in justice in the course of his professional work. It should make him aware that he has another role as an active and responsible citizen of the community at large. The first is professional. The second is political. The two roles are complementary. They are not identical or interchangeable.

RALPH NADER, CRUMBLING OF THE OLD ORDER, LAW SCHOOLS AND LAW FIRMS *

161 The New Republic 20 (October 11, 1969).

For decades, the law school curriculum reflected with remarkable fidelity the commercial demands of law firm practice. Law firm determinants of the content of courses nurtured a colossal distortion in priorities both as to the type of subject matter and the dimension of its treatment. What determined the curriculum was the legal interest that came with retainers. Thus, the curriculum pecking order was predictable—tax, corporate, securities and property law at the top and torts (personal injury) and criminal law, among others, at the bottom. Although in terms of the seriousness of the legal interest and the numbers of people affected, torts and criminal law would command the heights, the reverse was true, for the retainers were not as certain nor as handsome. Courses on estate planning proliferated, there were none for environmental planning until a few years ago. Other courses dealt with collapsible corporations, but the cupboard was bare for any student interested in collapsing tenements. Creditors' rights were studied deeply; debtors' remedies were passed by shallowly. Courses tracking the lucre and the prevailing ethos did not embrace any concept of professional sacrifice and service to the unrepresented poor or to public interests being crushed by private power. Such service was considered a proper concern of legal charity, to be dispensed by starved legal aid societies.

The generations of lawyers shaped by these law schools in turn shaped the direction and quality of the legal system. They came to this task severely unequipped except for the furtherance of their acquisitive drives. Rare was the law graduate who had the faintest knowledge of the institutionalized illegality of the cities in such areas as building and health code violations, the endemic bribing of officialdom, the illegalities in the marketplace, from moneylending to food. Fewer still were the graduates who knew anything of the institutions that should have been bathed in legal insight and compassion—hospitals, schools, probate and other courts, juvenile and mental institutions and prisons. Racialism, the gap between rich and poor, the seething slums—these conditions were brought to the attention of law firms by the illumination of city riots rather than the illumination of concerned intellects.

. . . . Law as prevention, law as incorporator of highway and vehicle engineering facts and feasibilities was almost totally ignored. The emphasis was on legal impact after crashes occurred, so as to assign liabilities and determine damages between drivers. . . .

---

* Copyright 1969 by Harrison-Blaine, N. J. Reprinted by permission.

Possibly the greatest failure of the law schools—a failure of the faculty—was not to articulate a theory and practice of a just deployment of legal manpower. With massive public interests deprived of effective legal representation, the law schools continued to encourage recruits for law firms whose practice militated against any such representation even on a sideline, *pro bono* basis. Lawyers labored for polluters, not anti-polluters, for sellers, not consumers, for corporations, not citizens, for labor leaders, not rank and file, for, not against, rate increases or weak standards before government agencies, for highway builders, not displaced residents, for, not against, judicial and administrative delay, for preferential business access to government and against equal citizen access to the same government, for agricultural subsidies to the rich but not food stamps for the poor, for tax and quota privileges, not for equity and free trade. None of this and much more seemed to trouble the law schools. Indeed, law firms were not even considered appropriate subjects of discussion and study in the curriculum. The legal profession—its organization, priorities and responsibilities—were taken as given. As the one institution most suited for a critical evaluation of the profession, the law school never assumed this unique role. Rather, it serviced and supplied the firms with fresh manpower selected through an archaic hierarchy of narrow worthiness topped by the editors of the school's law review. In essence it was a trade school.

The strains on this established legal order began to be felt with *Brown vs. Board of Education* in 1954. *Brown* rubbed the raw nerves of the established order in public. The mounting conflict began to shake a legal order built on deception and occult oppression. The ugly scars of the land burned red. Law students began to sense, to feel, to participate, and to earn scars of their own. Then came the Kennedy era with its verbal eloquence, its Peace Corps—overseas and later here. Then came Vietnam and Watts, Newark and the perturbation became a big-league jolt. Law students began to turn away from private practice, ... Those who went directly to the firms were less than enthusiastic. The big corporate firms in New York and Washington began to detect early signs that their boot camps were not responding to the customary Loreleis of the metropolitan canyons. Starting salaries began to reflect the emergence of a seller's market. Almost two years ago, the big New York Cravath firm set a starting salary of $15,000 a year and many firms followed. Still the law graduate detour continued. The big firms began to promise more free time to engage in *pro bono* work—the phrase used to describe work in the public interest such as representing indigents. The young graduates were still dissatisfied—first over the contraction of the promises and second over the narrow interpretation given to *pro bono* work.

At the same time, more new or alternative career roles in public service began to emerge. Neighborhood Legal Services, funded by

OEO, was manned by 1,800 young lawyers around the country at last count. The draft is driving many graduates into VISTA programs. There are more federal court clerkships available. And the growth of private, public-service law institutions . . . are not only providing such career roles but articulating their need throughout the country.

Meanwhile back at the law schools, student activism has arrived. . . . New courses in environmental, consumer and poverty law are being added to the lists. The first few weeks of the present school year indicate that the activists' attention is turning to the law firms that are now coming on campus to recruit. In an unprecedented move, a number of detailed questionnaires, signed by large numbers of students, are going out to these firms. The questions range far beyond the expected areas of the firms' policies on minority and women lawyers, and *pro bono* work. They include inquiries about the firms' policies on containing their clients' ambitions, on participation in law-reform work, on conflict of interest issues, on involvement in corporate client and political activity, and on subsidizing public-interest legal activity. . . .

The responses which the firms give to these questionnaires, and whatever planned response the students envisage for those firms who choose not to reply, will further sharpen the issues and the confrontations. The students have considerable leverage. They know it is a seller's market. They know how vulnerable these very private firms are to effective public criticism. Status is crucial to these firms. Status is also a prime attraction for competent law school graduates. . . .

The struggle of the established law firms to portray themselves as merely legal counselors affording their corporate clients their right to legal representation is losing ground. So too is their practice of hiding behind their responsibility to those clients, and not taking the burden of their advocacy as the canons of ethics advise them to do wherever the public interest is importantly involved. Either they are technical minions or they bear the responsibility attendant upon their status as independent professionals.

Clearly, there is need for a new dimension to the legal profession. This need does not simply extend to those groups or individuals who cannot afford a lawyer. It extends to the immense proliferation of procedural and substantive interests which go to the essence of the kind of society we will have in the future, but which have no legal representation. The absence of remedy is tantamount to an absence of right. The engineer of remedies for exercising rights is the lawyer.

The yearning of more and more young lawyers and law students is to find careers as public-interest lawyers who, independent of government and industry, will work on these two major institutions to further the creative rule of law. The law, suffering recurrent and deepening breakdowns, paralysis and obsolescence, should no longer tolerate a retainer astigmatism which allocates brilliant minds to trivial or harmful interests.

WILLIAM J. BRENNAN, JR., THE RESPONSIBILITIES OF THE LEGAL PROFESSION *
54 A.B.A.J. 121 (1968).

. . . For all these reasons, it seems to me unquestionable that the lawyer in America is uniquely situated to play a creative role in American social progress. Indeed, I would make bold to suggest that the success with which he responds to the challenges of what is plainly a new era of crisis and of promise in the life of our nation may prove decisive in determining the outcome of the social experiments on which we are embarked.

I would remind that in past periods of acute national need the response of the profession has fallen disappointingly short. Justice Stone (as he then was) in 1934 returned—in the words of his biographer—"an unvarnished indictment of lawyers' neglect of public duties". "Steadily," he said, "the best skill and capacity of the profession has been drawn into the exacting and highly specialized service of business and finance" with the consequence that "at its worst it has made the learned profession of an earlier day the obsequious servant of business and tainted it with the morals and manners of the market place in its most anti-social manifestations."

The record of the profession was not, of course, entirely a blemished one in that era; the great reform measures of the New Deal were in significant part also the product of lawyers. Yet, the lesson which Mr. Justice Stone rightly, I think, drew was that a more affirmative, responsible and progressive attitude on the part of the profession as a whole might have averted the crisis which evoked those measures.

The lesson remains timely, although the critical problems today are quite different. The focus has shifted from the abuses of concentrated economic power and the vagaries of cycles of boom and bust. Society's overriding concern today is with providing freedom and equality of rights and opportunities, in a realistic and not merely formal sense, to all the people of this nation: justice, equal and practical, to the poor, to the members of minority groups, to the criminally accused, to the displaced persons of the technological revolution, to alienated youth, to the urban masses, to the unrepresented consumers—to all, in short, who do not partake of the abundance of Amer-

---

* Copyright 1969 by the American Bar Association. Reprinted by permission.

ican life. To be sure, it is our very success in overriding the cruder privations and injustices of an earlier day—massive unemployment, rural backwardness, institutional segregation, overt police brutality—that has brought to the fore the current problems. But that they were formerly obscured by even greater wrongs does not make the remaining issues of injustice and inequality trivial or tractable.

Who will deny that despite the great progress we have made in recent decades toward universal equality, freedom and prosperity, the goal is far from won and ugly inequities continue to mar the national promise? Much, surely, remains to be done. Lawyers obviously cannot do it all, but their potential contribution is great. Yet, it is doubtful whether the legal profession is at present fully capable of assuming, or entirely disposed to assume, the full measure of its responsibilities.

This pessimistic note may come as a surprise in light of the conspicuous role which lawyers have played in recent efforts to attack the problems I have mentioned; one need only mention, as examples, the recent burgeoning in legal aid, neighborhood legal services and public defender activities. What these efforts reveal, however, is a growing and rather ominous cleavage in the profession. The burden of the new quest for justice has been assumed very largely (though not exclusively) by government lawyers, law professors and young men associated with public defender or neighborhood law offices or civil rights organizations. The practicing bar has remained largely aloof—where it has not been affirmatively obstructive, as in some unduly literal and inflexible applications of the Canons of Ethics to novel methods of affording legal representation to disadvantaged individuals. Mr. Justice Stone's warning thirty-three years ago was prophetic: "Our Canons of Ethics for the most part are generalizations designed for an earlier era."

NOTES

(1) The address of Justice Stone (later Chief Justice), referred to by Justice Brennan in the preceding article, was delivered at the dedication of the Law Quadrangle of the University of Michigan on June 15, 1934, and has become a classic in this field. See Stone, *The Public Influence of the Bar*, 48 Harv.L.Rev. 1 (1934).

(2) For an appraisal of lawyers, see A. A. Berle, Jr., *Modern Legal Profession*, 9 Encyc.Soc.Sci., p. 340 (1933). For a sympathetic consideration of the qualities developed and the opportunities offered by the practice of law, see Louis D. Brandeis, *The Opportunity in the Law*, 39 Am.L. Rev. 555 (1905). See also, Woodrow Wilson, *The Lawyer and the Community*, 35 A.B.A.Rep. 419 (1910).

Orison S. Marden, former President of the American Bar Association, urged corporate counsel to become more sensitive to their public responsibilities. *The Corporate Lawyer Today*, 35 N.Y.State Bar Jour. 317 (1965). Is there evidence today that lawyers and law firms are heeding to an increasing extent these suggestions?

E. Blythe Stason in *Why a Profession?*, 21 La.L.Rev. 153 (1960), speaks of public responsibility in terms of "statesmanship as distinguished from craftsmanship." See also John W. Wade, *Public Responsibilities of the Learned Professions*, 21 La.L.Rev. 130 (1960), comparing the professions of law and medicine with respect to the obligation to society.

Whitney North Seymour, in the Twenty-fifth Annual Benjamin Cardozo Lecture, had this to say:

> "The breadth of the lawyer's obligations does not rest alone on logic. No lawyer who tries to serve the public interest through the organized bar or otherwise, first says to himself: 'I must do this to justify my exclusive franchise.' Rather his sense of professional and public responsibility is an almost instinctive by-product of his whole background and training for the profession. With good luck, he is nourished on it from the moment he chooses the profession; the great law teachers, who themselves chose the profession because it was much more than a way to make a living, weave the sense of duty into their teaching, and many lawyers and judges emphasize it in their lives." The Obligations of the Lawyer to his Profession 14 (1968).

(3) Are there explanations other than "duty" for lawyer participation in community affairs? See Harrison Tweed, One Lawyer's Life, in Listen To Leaders In Law, 324–325 (1963):

> "I am convinced that what leads the lawyer to give of his talents, beyond what has been called 'client serving,' to some form of work of value to the community is a search for variety and a spirit of adventure more than it is a sense of duty or a desire to perform professional or public obligation. To put it in another way, the impulse does not come from the conscience of lawyers as much as from their common sense. It is not a compulsion to do good in the interest of others, but rather to live one's own life to the full. . . .
>
> "The lawyer who seeks opportunities for this fuller life will have no difficulty in finding them."

(4) The Peace Corps opened opportunities for lawyers to perform much needed legal services abroad in developing countries. See Robert Sargent Shriver, Jr., *Peace Corps Lawyers: Building Emerging African Societies*, 49 A.B.A.J. 456 (1963). For an account of young lawyers' activities in poverty areas of this country see *Advocates of Change, Lawyers as Vista Volunteers*, 14 Stud.Lawyer Jour. 7 (Oct. 1968).

REPORT OF THE JOINT CONFERENCE ON PROFESSIONAL RESPONSIBILITY

44 A.B.A.J. 1159, 1217 (1958); 1958 A.A.L.S.Proc. 187, 199 (1958).

The Lawyer and Legal Reform

There are few great figures in the history of the bar who have not concerned themselves with the reform and improvement of the law. The special obligation of the profession with respect to legal reform rests on considerations too obvious to require enumeration. Certainly it is the lawyer who has both the best chance to know when the law is working badly and the special competence to put it in order.

Where the lawyer fails to interest himself in the improvement of the law, the reason does not ordinarily lie in a lack of perception. It lies rather in a desire to retain the comfortable fit of accustomed ways, in a distaste for stirring up controversy within the profession, or perhaps in a hope that if enough time is allowed to pass, the need for change will become so obvious that no special effort will be required to accomplish it.

The lawyer tempted by repose should recall the heavy costs paid by his profession when needed legal reform has to be accomplished through the initiative of public-spirited laymen. Where change must be thrust from without upon an unwilling bar, the public's least flattering picture of the lawyer seems confirmed. The lawyer concerned for the standing of his profession will, therefore, interest himself actively in the improvement of the law. In doing so he will not only help to maintain confidence in the bar, but will have the satisfaction of meeting a responsibility inhering in the nature of his calling.

The Lawyer as Citizen

Law should be so practiced that the lawyer remains free to make up his own mind how he will vote, what causes he will support, what economic and political philosophy he will espouse. It is one of the glories of the profession that it admits of this freedom. Distinguished examples can be cited of lawyers whose views were at variance from those of their clients, lawyers whose skill and wisdom made them valued advisers to those who had little sympathy with their views as citizens.

Broad issues of social policy can and should, therefore, be approached by the lawyer without the encumbrance of any special obligation derived from his profession. To this proposition there is, perhaps, one important qualification. Every calling owes to the public a duty of leadership in those matters where its training and experience give it a special competence and insight. The practice of his profession brings the lawyer in daily touch with a problem that is at best imperfectly understood by the general public. This is, broadly speaking, the problem of implementation as it arises in human affairs. Where an objective has been selected as desirable, it is generally the lawyer who is called upon to design the framework that will put human relations in such an order that the objective will be achieved. For that reason it is likely to be the lawyer who best understands the difficulties encountered in this task.

A dangerously unreal atmosphere surrounds much public discussion of economic and political issues. The electorate is addressed in terms implying that it has only to decide which among proferred objectives it considers most attractive. Little attention is paid to the question of the procedures and institutional arrangements which these objectives will require for their realization. Yet the lawyer knows that the most difficult problems are usually first encountered in giving workable legal form to an objective which all may consider desirable in itself. Not uncommonly at this stage the original objective must be modified, redefined, or even abandoned as not being attainable without undue cost.

Out of his professional experience the lawyer can draw the insight needed to improve public discussion of political and economic issues. Whether he considers himself a conservative or a liberal, the lawyer should do what he can to rescue that discussion from a world of unreality in which it is assumed that ends can be selected without any consideration of means. Obviously if he is to be effective in this respect, the lawyer cannot permit himself to become indifferent and uninformed concerning public issues.

J. J. CAVANAUGH, THE LAWYER IN SOCIETY *

Page 12 (1963).

Ideas for social reform or progress are often stated in beguiling terms, and the popular temptation is to rush these ideas into legislation in the first bloom of enthusiasm. The lawyer in the legislature, and lawyers outside it, are well aware that the goal is often too sweeping in statement and too indifferent to side-effects. Even with legislation popularly supported and without significant opposition there needs to be a conservative definition of the purpose, a careful choosing of sanctions, and a minimizing of the disruptive effects. If we decide to legislate on the problem of excessive interest rates for the loaning of money, it is not enough to forbid the charging of excessive rates. To be considered are the question of what is excessive; the question of how the rate is to be calculated; the question of what punishment shall follow from a violation of the statute; the question of when the new law shall become effective; the question of whether it shall be permanently effective until repealed; the question of whether violations shall be policed (creating a new government bureau) or the law left to haphazard enforcement by the complaints of victims; the question of whether punishment shall vary with the degree of violation; the question of whether the appropriate sanction might not be a steeply graduated tax on all interest income above designated rates, thus using an existing bureau, the tax agency, as enforcer of the new provisions; and so on. It is this elaboration of definitions, alternatives, conditions, and purposes which frequently exasperates the non-legal, non-technical mind. Yet the lawyer is usually doing no more than making feasible and practically workable the reform or progress popularly endorsed. Without this careful at-

* Copyright 1963 by Philosophical Library Inc. Reprinted by permission.

tention to the details of implementation, the grand plan would be successfully attacked by its enemies, thrown out by the courts as too general for enforcement, or enforced by the courts but with court interpretations which themselves would write the details of the statute at a cost of prolonged litigation. . . .

NOTE

Does the lawyer's training qualify him and should his public responsibilities lead him to at least speak out on the merits of important social, economic and political issues of the day? Should he become involved in professional and lay action groups looking to the solution of such problems? Does he have the qualification and the duty to work further towards their resolution? Does law school analytical training in the solution of private problems assist in the solution of the larger problems of society? How might that training be improved? Do other disciplines better train for the solution of these larger problems? As the practice of law becomes more specialized will the lawyer's role in public leadership likely be lessened? Consider these questions with reference to each of the following issues:

(a) Changes in the electoral college. (The House of Delegates of the American Bar Association on February 13, 1967, adopted the report of its Commission on Electoral College Reform, placing the Association on record as favoring a constitutional amendment to provide for the direct election of the President of the United States. See 53 A.B.A.J. 219 (1967)).

(b) Civil rights legislation and decisions.

(c) Federal aid to education.

(d) The war on poverty.

(e) The report of the National Advisory Commission on Civil Disorders to the President of the United States (March 1, 1968) relating to efforts to help "identify and reduce, or eliminate, the underlying and triggering causes of rioting and disorders in our cities." See Report of Institute jointly sponsored by The Section of Individual Rights and Responsibilities of the American Bar Association and The Lawyers' Committee for Civil Rights Under Law, appointed by The President of the United States, "What Lawyers Can Do In Response to the Report of the Commission on Civil Disorders," (May 20, 1968.)

(f) Federal gun registration.

(g) United States involvement in the Viet Nam war.

(h) Revision of the Selective Service system.

(i) The needs of law enforcement v. the rights of an accused.

(j) Race relations. (In August, 1968, the House of Delegates of the American Bar Association adopted the following resolution proposed by its Section of Individual Rights and Responsibilities: "We declare it to be the responsibility of the individual lawyer and of the organized profession to be forceful advocates for full legal recognition of equality before the law and equality of opportunity. We declare further that it is one of the lawyer's responsibilities to help through orderly processes to achieve such equality." See 54 A.B.A.J. 1028 (1968)).

THE ORGANIZED BAR

ROBERT E. MATHEWS, PROBLEMS ILLUSTRATIVE OF THE RESPONSIBILITIES OF MEMBERS OF THE LEGAL PROFESSION *

Pages 238–241. (Second Revised Edition, 1968).

[I]t has been the occasional practice for hundreds of years for courts to invite or to permit contributions of disinterested opinion in connection with pending controversial litigation where issues of substantial public interest were at stake. Characteristically individuals and private or philanthropic institutions have been those whose opinions were contributed, but of late, Bar associations in this country have come to sense the opportunities here offered to make known to the courts their views as to the principles of law whose acceptance, regardless of views of the parties, would most further the welfare of the country. Undoubtedly it was an eminent New York lawyer, partner in the great firm of Root and Clark whose devotion to the preservation of constitutional values and the conservation of our democratic institutions, who was first and foremost in the initiation of this trend. His name is Grenville Clark.

It was back in 1938 that he made the suggestion that the organized bar had both an opportunity and a responsibility to take a position in defense of basic civil rights. . . .

. . . Arthur T. Vanderbilt, then President of the American Bar Association, and Frank J. Hogan, President-Elect, called on Mr. Clark and asked him to be Chairman of a Committee on The Bill of Rights, which they had decided to sponsor for the Association. Thus was the Committee established.

. . .

. . . Inspired and encouraged by the national Committee, many state and city bar associations set up similar committees, the sum-total of whose efforts has never been estimated. In any event, a significant pattern was established for the participation in litigation by the organized bar on behalf of a principle of law as distinguished from the partisan interest of a client. While there can be no measurable criteria as to the weight given briefs of this sort, the quality of those submitted by this Committee and the distinction and competence of the lawyers who sponsored them, can hardly have failed to have made a significant impression.

. . .

It was undoubtedly an outgrowth of this trend that led, in 1966, to the establishment, by unanimous vote of the House of Delegates,

---

* Copyright 1968 by Robert E. Mathews. Reprinted by permission.

of the Section of Individual Rights and Responsibilities. Grenville Clark had been a member of the organizing committee and Dean Jefferson B. Fordham, of the University of Pennsylvania Law School, was the first chairman (55 A.B.A.J. 1155, 1966).

EUGENE V. ROSTOW, THE LAWYER AND HIS CLIENT *
48 A.B.A.J. 146, 150 (1962).

What I have in mind, however, would go farther. The American Bar Association's Committee on the Bill of Rights is authorized, under certain circumstances, to appear in court as amicus curiae, or as counsel of record, where "vital issues of civil liberties are deemed to be involved". State and local bar associations have similar powers, exercised either through committees, or through the governing bodies of those associations. We do not hesitate to go to court or before legislatures in the name of the Bar itself, to protest against what we regard as the unauthorized practice of law, or to seek tax privileges for our period of retirement. I do not criticize such programs, but they hardly exhaust our capacity for collective action. Why should we not be as vigorous in maintaining some of the more affirmative canons of our code of ethics as we are in protecting our economic interests? The troubled history of our law during the last twenty years, and the prospects of trouble ahead, require, I suggest, a more sustained effort not only by lawyers, but by their professional organizations.

. . . What I envision is the development of vigilance and the habit of action, on the part of our national, state and local bar associations, in the interest of protecting and helping to develop those constitutional guaranties which distinguish free societies from tyrannies. Programs of this kind would include the making of studies and the publication of reports—a field in which the Association of the Bar of the City of New York has provided such notable leadership in recent years. It would also, and in my view indispensably include court appearances, and appearances before legislative committees, to put the weight and prestige of the Bar itself into the process through which our law evolves. I do not suggest that the American Bar Association's Committee on the Bill of Rights acquire a monopoly of representation in civil liberties cases—Heaven forbid. Nor do I have in mind that it replace the individual lawyers, and civil associations, who now carry so much of the load, and carry it, on the whole, so well. What I do propose is that such agencies of our national, state and local bar associations emerge as forceful participants in this area of law, whose content is of such far-reaching significance to the character and quality of our legal system, and that they do so on a continuing basis.

* Copyright 1962 by the American Bar Association. Reprinted by permission.

JAMES C. DAVIS, THE ORGANIZED BAR'S RESPONSIBILITY TO IMPROVE INTERRACIAL RELATIONS *

54 A.B.A.J. 551, 553 (1968).

What then, should be the role of the organized Bar in achieving solution of these interracial problems? Of course, we must support all proper measures for the maintenance of law and order, but we cannot solve these questions with our heads in the sand. We ourselves must believe, and we must exert the full force of our efforts to make others realize, that law and order cannot be maintained by suppressive and repressive efforts alone. The white majority must come to realize that suppression of the symptoms of riot and disorder will afford no permanent solution. We must lead the way to a full realization of the true nature of the underlying causes of such symptoms and the urgent necessity for the development of workable means for their removal.

We must lead the Negro citizen at the same time to realize that there is understanding and appreciation by the white majority of these causes and that the majority will face up to its responsibility for their removal. The Negro, in the mass, must be given hope. The absence of hope has been a material cause of riots.

What specific aids can the organized Bar bring to the solution of these problems? We can start with the profession itself. We can remove all restrictions, if any still remain, on the admission of Negro lawyers to our professional societies on a basis of complete equality with their white contemporaries. We can eliminate the bars to the employment of competent Negro lawyers by white law firms. If the leadership of lawyers is to be effective, it must include both white and Negro lawyers acting together in equality.

At the national and state levels we can utilize the influence of the organized Bar to bring public authorities to the realization that our interracial problems cannot be solved without large-scale government assistance. The white majority must accept this cost. The organized Bar must provide the leadership to obtain that acceptance. The provision of such assistance is not the breaking of new ground. In the depth of the great depression, when our white majority was faced with economic and social distress comparable to that now facing the Negro minority, neither the federal nor the state governments hesitated to act. What measures are now required may be debated, but the need for effective measures should not be. . . .

* Copyright 1968 by the American Bar Association. Reprinted by permission.

WILLIAM T. GOSSETT, "LET US RESPOND TO DISCONTENT . . ."

Presidential Address at Philadelphia, Pa.
American Bar News Vol. 13, No. 9 (1968) p. 3.

But the times are not placid. The overwhelming fact we face is that our society is not a peaceful one. Deeply rooted and widespread movements of social protest question the efficacy of the law as an instrument of social justice. . . . This is apparent from the frequent assertions that the law is being used as a device to frustrate the legitimate aspirations of those seeking to participate more fully in the benefits of American society.

It would be an obvious oversimplification to suggest that lawyers alone can produce fundamental solutions to problems of such magnitude. Yet the legal order is an inherent and highly relevant factor, and the lawyer's contribution to such solutions could be of enormous importance. Indeed, it is no exaggeration to say that the situation presents challenges to the wisdom and ingenuity of lawyers that in many respects are unprecedented; and in terms of obligations and opportunities for leadership in social and legal engineering, our profession has a special competence and a compelling responsibility.

The utilization of that competence and the profession-wide rising to this responsibility must constitute our major associative effort this year. There is no side-stepping it. There is no delaying it. We have no alternative.

I propose as President of the ABA to do all I can this coming year to mobilize the great resources and the prestige of the Association and the profession as a whole in a united effort, first, to support and facilitate by all available means the firm and resolute enforcement of the law against all violators, especially those who would destroy our institutions by violent action, and second, to open to the restless and the deprived among our people full participation in the lawful procedures that are the only effective means of social change.

But let us not be frightened by manifestations of discontent. Discontent is not a scare-word in America. It is a brave word. It is not a negative word. It is a positive word. This land was settled by the discontented. Its independence, its nationhood and, indeed, its constitution—all of them born in this historic city—were conceived and created in response to discontent. And almost every significant measure of social, economic and even juristic progress that we have achieved in the crowded years since has come about in an almost continuing response to discontent.

Let us who occupy positions of leadership in a powerful and disciplined profession use our formidable resources to turn in our time the discontent that wracks our society into yet another constructive chapter in the contribution of our profession to the nation's progress.

Let us respond to discontent—not ignore it. Let us direct it into creative channels—not contest it.

. . .

NOTE

Is the obligation of an attorney to speak out on public issues different from that of the bar association to which he belongs? Lewis F. Powell, Jr., former President of the American Bar Association, stated that "the prevailing view is that the Association must follow a policy of noninvolvement in political and emotionally controversial issues—however important they may be—unless they relate directly to the administration of justice." Powell, *The President's Page,* 51 A.B.A.J. 101 (1965). Are the views of Mr. Gossett, a later President of the American Bar Association, consistent with those of Mr. Powell? Should the fact that membership in the American Bar Association is voluntary make a difference in this regard? Would a state integrated bar have a lesser or a greater responsibility to take a position on such subjects? How broad is the concept of "administration of justice?" Which, if any, of the issues detailed in the Note page 398 supra would Mr. Powell include within the meaning of that phrase? See Bowman, *What Price "Effectiveness",* 55 A.B.A.J. 251, (1969), for a later comment on the obligation of bar associations to speak out. Is the range of public activity of the organized bar limited by the views of the justices of the Supreme Court of the United States in *Lathrop v. Donohue,* supra p. 158, as to what is an appropriate activity of an integrated bar?

SECTION 3. LAW ADMINISTRATION

Introduction. The preceding section has pointed up the opportunities afforded members of the legal profession to educate the public and to mold public opinion. In so doing lawyers play essential roles in helping to resolve many areas of discontent. Reform of the law is perhaps the weapon most frequently employed in the resolution of society's problems and here it is that the lawyer is uniquely equipped to take the laboring oar. By training and experience lawyers should also be the first to observe deficiencies in the administration of justice and should not leave to outsiders improvements in the system. Bar associations and other lawyer groups have properly placed emphasis on these objectives. See Chapter III, Section 2B; Chapter XIV, Section 4.

Improvement in the administration of justice must be undertaken along several fronts. Greater availability of legal services to all segments of society has come increasingly to be recognized as an imperative. This must be a high priority item for the profession and for its individual members. See Chapter II. Upgrading of the judiciary requires the constant attention of lawyers to the problems of selection, tenure and retirement of judges. See Chapter XIV, Section

3. Admission to and discipline of the profession, as well as general improvement of the profession itself, are matters of great public importance requiring the services of many individual lawyers. See Chapter XIII, Section 2.

Finally, competent and faithful representation of clients by individual attorneys is perhaps the most vital ingredient of the administration of justice under our system and the lawyer's role here is obvious. He is not only architect and repairman but the principal actor as well. On his shoulders falls the responsibility for establishing and maintaining public confidence in our system of administering justice. This responsibility and its importance are well stated in the Preamble to the Canons of Professional Ethics of the American Bar Association.

"In America, where the stability of Courts and of all departments of government rests upon the approval of the people, it is peculiarly essential that the system for establishing and dispensing Justice be developed to a high point of efficiency and so maintained that the public shall have absolute confidence in the integrity and impartiality of its administration. The future of the Republic, to a great extent, depends upon our maintenance of Justice pure and unsullied. It cannot be so maintained unless the conduct and the motives of the members of our profession are such as to merit the approval of all just men."

REPORT OF THE JOINT CONFERENCE ON PROFESSIONAL RESPONSIBILITY

44 A.B.A.J. 1159, 1162 (1958); 1958 A.A.L.S. Proc. 187, 194 (1958).

The Lawyer's Opportunities and Obligations of Public Service
Private Practice as a Form of Public Service

Private practice is a form of public service when it is conducted with an appreciation of, and a respect for, the larger framework of government of which it forms a part, including under the term government those voluntary forms of self-regulation already discussed in this statement. It is within this larger framework that the lawyer must seek the answer to what he must do, the limits of what he may do.

Thus, partisan advocacy is a form of public service so long as it aids the process of adjudication; it ceases to be when it hinders that process, when it misleads, distorts and obfuscates, when it renders the task of the deciding tribunal not easier, but more difficult. Judges are inevitably the mirrors of the bar practicing before them; they can with difficulty rise above the sources on which they must depend in reaching their decision. The primary responsibility for preserving adjudication as a meaningful and useful social institution rests ultimately with the practicing legal profession.

Where the lawyer serves as negotiator and draftsman, he advances the public interest when he facilitates the processes of voluntary self-government; he works against the public interest when he obstructs the channels of collaborative effort, when he seeks petty advantages to the detriment of the larger processes in which he participates.

Private legal practice, properly pursued, is, then, itself a public service. This reflection should not induce a sense of complacency in the lawyer, nor lead him to disparage those forms of public service that fall outside the normal practice of law. On the contrary, a proper sense of the significance of his role as the representative of private clients will almost inevitably lead the lawyer into broader fields of public service.

The Lawyer as a Guardian of Due Process

The lawyer's highest loyalty is at the same time the most intangible. It is a loyalty that runs, not to persons, but to procedures and institutions. The lawyer's role imposes on him a trusteeship for the integrity of those fundamental processes of government and self-government upon which the successful functioning of our society depends.

All institutions, however sound in purpose, present temptations to interested exploitation, to abusive short cuts, to corroding misinterpretations. The forms of democracy may be observed while means are found to circumvent inconvenient consequences resulting from a compliance with those forms. A lawyer recreant to his responsibilities can so disrupt the hearing of a cause as to undermine those rational foundations without which an adversary proceeding loses its meaning and its justification. Everywhere democratic and constitutional government is tragically dependent on voluntary and understanding cooperation in the maintenance of its fundamental processes and forms.

It is the lawyer's duty to preserve and advance this indispensable cooperation by keeping alive the willingness to engage in it and by imparting the understanding necessary to give it direction and effectiveness. This is a duty that attaches not only to his private practice, but to his relations with the public. In this matter he is not entitled to take public opinion as a datum by which to orient and justify his actions. He has an affirmative duty to help shape the growth and development of public attitudes toward fair procedures and due process.

Without this essential leadership, there is an inevitable tendency for practice to draft downward to the level of those who have the least understanding of the issues at stake, whose experience of life has not taught them the vital importance of preserving just and proper forms of procedure. It is chiefly for the lawyer that the term "due process" takes on tangible meaning, for whom it indicates what is allowable and what is not, who realizes what a ruinous cost is incurred when its demands are disregarded. For the lawyer the insidious dangers contained in the notion that "the end justifies the means" is not a matter of abstract philosophic conviction, but of direct professional experience. If the lawyer fails to do his part in educating the public to these dangers, he fails in one of his highest duties.

JEROME FRANK, * BOTH ENDS AGAINST THE MIDDLE
100 U.Pa.L.Rev. 20, 27 (1951).

No one can quarrel with lawyers who maintain that our profession should interest itself in moral problems not directly germane to our profession—for instance, those relating to housing or medical care. But a moral problem directly affecting the work of the courts is uniquely our responsibility, since lawyers alone have the skills requisite to its solution, so far as it can be solved. If we do not put our own house in order, we will look like meddlesome busybodies when we go about telling other professions how to run theirs.

CODE OF PROFESSIONAL RESPONSIBILITY **
EC 8–1

Changes in human affairs and imperfections in human institutions make necessary constant efforts to maintain and improve our legal system. This system should function in a manner that commands public respect and fosters the use of legal remedies to achieve redress of grievances. By reason of education and experience, lawyers are especially qualified to recognize deficiencies in the legal system and to initiate corrective measures. Thus they should participate in proposing and supporting legislation and programs to improve the system, without regard to the general interests or desires of clients or former clients.

EC 9–1

Continuation of the American concept that we are to be governed by rules of law requires that the people have faith that justice can be obtained through our legal system. A lawyer should promote public confidence in our system and in the legal profession.

---

* Judge Frank served on the U.S. Court of Appeals for the second circuit from 1941 until his death in 1957. Prior to that time he had held many public offices, including that of Chairman of the Securities and Exchange Commission. He was a discerning critic of the legal process.

** Copyright 1969 by the American Bar Association. Reprinted with permission.

EC 8-6

. . . Adjudicatory officials, not being wholly free to defend themselves, are entitled to receive the support of the bar against unjust criticism. While a lawyer as a citizen has a right to criticize such officials publicly, he should be certain of the merit of his complaint, use appropriate language, and avoid petty criticisms, for unrestrained and intemperate statements tend to lessen public confidence in our legal system. Criticisms motivated by reasons other than a desire to improve the legal system are not justified.

NOTES

(1) Perhaps no opinions of the United States Supreme Court have ever been subjected to as much lay and professional criticism and censure throughout the South as those beginning with Brown v. Board of Education, 347 U.S. 483 (1954). For a hard-hitting indictment of the official organ of the Alabama State Bar, alleging failure to present but one side of the problems of race and civil rights, see Frankel, *The Alabama Lawyer, 1954-64: Has the Official Organ Atrophied?*, 64 Colum.L.Rev. 1243 (1964). Professor Frankel, now Judge Frankel, analyzes a ten-year series of one-sided articles in The Alabama Lawyer which refer to May 17, 1954, the date of the *Brown* decision, as "Black Monday," which proclaim that Supreme Court decisions like *Brown* are not the "law of the land", and which deal with "Negro inferiority", and "the Supreme Court's communistic, atheistic, nihilistic destruction of the Constitution." The author's concern is not so much that these views are wrong but rather the complete failure of the official state bar journal to at any time present the other side, a failure which he charges evidences a lack of professional responsibility of the members of the bar. Do you agree? If a state bar publication in another state had devoted its pages exclusively to a defense of the United States Supreme Court decision in this field, could it be subject to similar charges? Suppose The Alabama Lawyer had printed nothing with reference to these decisions?

Compare the action of a Grievance Committee of the State Bar of Texas which reprimanded a prosecuting attorney in the office of the District Attorney of Dallas County, finding that he had violated Canon 1 of the Canons of Ethics. The reprimand read: "He indiscriminately and indiscretly disseminated criticisms of the Supreme Court of the United States rather than submit his grievances in a proper manner to the proper authorities. By doing so, he failed to maintain a respectful attitude toward the Supreme Court of the United States" 31 Texas Bar Journal 835 (1968). The attorney in this case, through newspaper and television interviews, had been particularly critical of the Supreme Court's opinion in Witherspoon v. Illinois, 389 U.S. 1035 (1968).

The Supreme Court of the United States had this to say in Konigsberg v. State Bar of California, 353 U.S. 252, 269 (1957): "Citizens have a right under our constitutional system to criticize governmental officials and agencies. Courts are not, and should not be, immune to such criticism." In the *Konigsberg* case admissions to the State Bar of California had been denied to an applicant who had been highly critical of the United States Supreme

Court. The Supreme Court, in reversing the judgment of the California Supreme Court upholding the action of the Committee of Bar Examiners, concluded that an inference of bad moral character could not rationally be drawn from such writings. (See Chapter XIII, page 498 infra, for the sequel to *Konigsberg*.)

(2) The criticisms of the United States Supreme Court during the 1950's and 1960's were accompanied by occasional proposals to deprive that court of some of its power. Chief Justice Earl Warren addressed himself to some of these proposals at the dedication of the new Duke Law School Building, 1963 Duke L.J. 387, 393–394 * (1963):

"In December of last year, a committee of state legislators, acting through the Council of State Governments, recommended to the Legislatures of all the States of the Union that they adopt a never-before-used alternative route (under Article V) to amend the Constitution of the United States in three respects: 1. To take away from the federal courts all jurisdiction in state legislative apportionments; 2. To establish a court composed of the 50 Chief Justices of the States, with power to overrule the Supreme Court of the United States in cases involving federal-state relationships, and 3. To change the amending process so as to practically supplant the Congress of the United States in favor of the Legislatures of the States.

"It must be apparent to all that these proposed Constitutional Amendments would radically change the character of our institutions.

"I shall not at this time argue the merits or demerits of any of these proposals. I merely point out that, if adopted, they would make profound changes in the judiciary, the relationship between the federal and state Governments, and even the stability of the United States Constitution.

"I suppose there are some, perhaps many, in this audience who have never heard of these proposals. And that is not surprising because so little public mention has been made of them. Yet in 24 States of the Union, one or both Houses of the Legislature have adopted one or two or even all three of these proposals. It has been accomplished with little or no debate and with practically no recognition by the Bar of America.

"In preparation of this occasion, I researched the publications in the Supreme Court Library and in the Library of Congress. This included all the law reviews in the country, all the legal periodicals and the publications of all the legal societies. The net result of that search was one article in the *Yale Law Journal* for April by Professor Charles L. Black of that Law School. Not another recognition of these drastic changes in our Government was to be found in any of these legal publications which are designed to alert, not only the members of the Bar, but the public at large to the legal problems confronting us. If proposals of this magnitude had been made in the early days of the Republic, the voices of the lawyers of that time would have been heard from one end of our land to the other. The great debate would be resounding in every

---

* Copyright 1963 by Duke Law Journal. Reprinted by permission.

legislative hall and in every place where scholars and statesmen gather. Surely the problems of America are as great today as they were in those days. Surely the Constitution should be as precious to us now as it was then. If lawyers are not to be the watchmen for the Constitution, on whom are we to rely?"

SECTION 4. THE EXTENSION OF PROFESSIONAL KNOWLEDGE

In many professions it is accepted that there is a duty on the part of the individual professional man to make public information that he has acquired in his research, or developed through reflection and practice, which would be of substantial benefit to other members of the profession. Almost every important medical journal has reports by physicians on methods employed by them in treating patients. Similarly, the university scientist has a duty to make public promptly the findings from his research and studies. Sir Francis Bacon wrote with particular reference to the duty of the lawyer when he said:

"I hold every man a debtor to his profession; from the which as men of course do seek to receive countenance and profit, so ought they of duty to endeavor themselves by way of amends to be a help and ornament thereunto. This is performed in some degree by the honest and liberal practice of a profession, when men shall carry a respect not to descent into any course that is corrupt and unworthy thereof, and preserve themselves free from the abuses wherewith the same profession is noted to be infected: but much more is this performed if a man be able to visit and strengthen the roots and foundation of the science itself; thereby not only gracing it in reputation and dignity, but also amplifying it in perfection and substance. . . ." *

Is there such a duty on the lawyer and on other professional men? In so far as the lawyer's knowledge is derived from his knowledge of a particular client's case, and its confidential character is an element in the protection to which the client is entitled, professional duty to his client must prevail over professional duty to give this knowledge to the public. The question might also be asked whether a client who has paid a large fee to an attorney to develop tax savings arrangements on his behalf would be uncomplaining if similar arrangements were published or used by the attorney in serving a competitor, especially if a smaller fee were charged. Is the attorney's situation in such case different from that of the doctor who has developed more efficient methods of diagnosis while treating one of his patients? A

---

* The quotation is taken from the Preface to his Maxims of the Law in which he explains his purpose in writing the book.

similar conflict may arise as to, say, the chemical engineer, where there is a conflict between the duty of the professional man to give to the public the benefit of his research and the duty of the employee of a business to keep business secrets. The years since World War II have witnessed much University soul-searching with reference to secrecy of classified research under governmental defense contracts and the conflicts this may engender. See Walter Gellhorn, Security, Loyalty and Science (1950).

To the doctor human bodies are alike and it is perhaps easier in his profession to make public valuable generalized information than it is in the legal profession. On many matters, however, the individual lawyer will develop a "know-how" which could be given to other members of the profession without the slightest injury to his client. The Joint Committee on Continuing Legal Education of the American Law Institute and the American Bar Association publishes a monthly magazine, The Practical Lawyer, devoted to the passing on of professional information in the field of law. Many state bar associations sponsor institutes and programs designed to share professional knowledge both procedural and substantive. Certainly lawyers do profit immensely from the experiences, fortunate and unfortunate, of their predecessors and their contemporaries—witness, for example, the growth through the centuries of the form of settlement or will used by the English solicitor. See Kales, The Will of an English Gentleman of Moderate Fortune, 19 Green Bag, 214 (1907). Consider the growth of the corporate mortgage, with new provisions being widely added as they were upheld or as the need for them was demonstrated, as well as the development of the percentage lease and the multitude of estate planning devices. Is there an obligation on the part of United States government attorneys to permit defense counsel in antitrust actions to make use of the government computer facilities?

It has been suggested that the existence of a group sense of a duty to disclose and pass on for the benefit of humanity the personal knowledge and skill in the field acquired by individual members (except as the fair obligation to the client or patient may forbid) is a mark of a profession. Is this statement too strong? Does it apply to the lawyer?

Part Three

THE CLIENT AND THE LAWYER

Chapter XI

THE ESTABLISHMENT OF THE RELATIONSHIP

SECTION 1. A CASE OFFERED

THE FREEDOM OF THE INDIVIDUAL AND THE OBLIGATION OF THE GROUP.

The American lawyer has no professional obligation to accept every case tendered him. The Code of Professional Responsibility, EC 2–26 states:

> A lawyer is under no obligation to act as adviser or advocate for every person who may wish to become his client; but in furtherance of the objective of the bar to make legal services fully available, a lawyer should not lightly decline proffered employment. The fulfillment of this objective requires acceptance by a lawyer of his share of tendered employment which may be unattractive both to him and the bar generally.

This independence of choice is in contrast with the obligation of the English barrister to accept on tender of a proper fee a retainer in a case which merits the judgment of a court, an obligation which had its origin in the example set by Erskine's acceptance of the representation of the revolutionary, Thomas Paine, in the prosecution for his publication of The Rights of Man.

The freedom of the American lawyer may conflict with two accepted principles. One is the moral right of every person to legal representation when needed; the other is the legal right of every person accused of crime to be represented by counsel. The conflict is tempered by increasing recognition, by the bar and by government, of the social obligation to develop methods by which every person may have the services of a lawyer when needed.

NOTES

(1) "Many generations of students have been taught to follow Erskine's famous words in which he justified his unpopular defence of Tom Paine:

> From the moment that any advocate can be permitted to say that he will or will not stand between the Crown and the subject arraigned in the court where he daily sits to practice, from that moment the liberties of England are at an end.

It is easier, pleasanter and more advantageous professionally for barristers to advise, represent or defend those who are decent and reasonable and likely to succeed in their action or their defence than those who are unpleasant, unreasonable, disreputable, and have an apparently hopeless case. Yet it would be tragic if our legal system came to provide no reputable defenders, representatives or advisers for the latter. And that would be the inevitable result of allowing barristers to pick and choose their clients." Lord Morris of Borth-Gest, in Rondel v. Worsley, [1969] 1 A.C. 189, 275.

(2) The English rule stated in Note (1) applies to barristers. It does not extend to solicitors who are the office lawyers through whom the barrister is retained. See Megarry, Lawyers and Litigants in England 76 (1962).

SOME HYPOTHETICAL CASES

Let the reader consider the cases below and determine whether because of their nature or because of what the client said or desired, he would decline to take the case at all or would decline to do what the client desired or would withdraw.

First Case. A man indicted as a subversive person asked you to defend him at his trial. (Assume he is charged with subversion as a communist or as a fascist, whichever you dislike the most.) After you indicate you may represent him, he expresses his warm thanks and tells you that your success in securing an acquittal will have a resounding effect in aiding the revolutionary cause, for court cases are among the most striking ways of winning publicity for the cause. He goes on to say that after the acquittal he will desire your aid in so planning the affairs of the party that it will remain within the law without impairing the efficacy of the revolutionary plans. Finally, he tells you that after the acquittal he will wish you to aid him in concealing any illegal activities so they will not be discovered.

Second Case. A professional gambler, who has long been suspected of bribing athletes to throw games, is indicted for such bribery. He asks you to defend him in the criminal trial. He tells you that the fee will be a large one and will be made up of contributions from many other gamblers; for if this case is won, the gamblers expect they will not be disturbed for a long time. He goes on to say that he wishes you to investigate the laws on gambling and bribery in the various states so as to find one or more states in which bribing players is not a crime, and then to help him plan his activities so they will be within the law. Finally, he states that if you cannot plan his activities so they will be legal, he wishes wour help in devising ways by which his acts in your state, though illegal, will not be discovered.

Third Case. A business man has been indicted for fraud in making his tax returns. He asks you to defend him at the criminal trial. He goes on to say that he will later wish your aid in so planning his business as to reduce taxes as much as possible. Finally, he says that he would like you to help him devise ways of concealing his assets so that the amount of his net worth at the end of the taxable year will be impossible to ascertain.

In answering these questions remember that you do not have to take a case unless you want to. Each of us takes a case, as the Canons state, "on his own responsibility". In the office the lawyer's work is affirmative, as he is helping to plan for the future. In that situation our control over our client and our share in administering the law are at their greatest.

You may hear it said, or at least intimated, that the responsibility of a lawyer for work in his office is no different from that of the advocate, so that he may represent a client in his office in any matter in which he might later defend him in court. This is grotesquely wrong. Would anyone in his senses say that because a lawyer may as advocate defend a man accused of murder, he may therefore have the privilege to help the client plan the murder?

NOTES

(1) "No matter where we turn in an analysis of lawyers at work, we find power to choose and accompanying responsibility for choices made. . . . A great office lawyer uses legal sources as an artist uses pigments, to accomplish a design. He can not evade moral responsibility for the worth of that design. In the words of the 1958 report of the Joint Conference on Professional Responsibility:

> 'The reasons that justify and even require partisan advocacy in the trial of a cause do not grant license to the lawyer to participate as legal adviser in a line of conduct that is unmoral, unfair, or of doubtful legality. In saving himself from this unworthy involvement, the lawyer cannot be guided solely by an unreflective inner sense of good faith; he must be at pains to preserve a sufficient detachment from his client's interests so that he remains capable of a sound and objective appraisal of the propriety of what his client proposes to do.'

Reason and learning are not enough; in his office as in court, the lawyer must 'possess the resolution necessary to carry into effect what his intellect tells him ought to be done.'" Jones, *Law and Morality in the Perspective of Legal Realism*, 61 Colum.L.Rev. 799, 806–807 (1961).

(2) A lawyer retained by a gambling organization to advise and represent the members and their subordinates was disbarred. "A highly neces-

sary function, the defense of those charged with crime, is prostituted into the furtherance of crime itself." In re Mogel, 18 App.Div.2d 203, 238 N.Y.S. 2d 683 (1963).

(3) "A lawyer shall not accept employment on behalf of a person if he know or it is obvious that such person wishes to:

(1) Bring a legal action, conduct a defense, or assert a position in litigation, or otherwise have steps taken for him, merely for the purpose of harassing or maliciously injuring any person.

(2) Present a claim or defense in litigation that is not warranted under existing law, unless it can be supported by good faith argument for an extension, modification, or reversal of existing law." Code of Professional Responsibility, DR 2–109.

SECTION 2. LOYALTY

GLASSER v. UNITED STATES

Supreme Court of the United States, 1942.
315 U.S. 60, 62 S.Ct. 457, 86 L.Ed. 680.

[Glasser, Kretske and another were found guilty upon an indictment charging them with a conspiracy to defraud the United States. Glasser sought to have his conviction set aside on the ground he had been denied the effective assistance of counsel. At the trial Glasser had retained Stewart as his associate counsel, and Kretske indicated a desire to discharge the lawyer who had entered an appearance for him. The trial judge then asked Stewart to act as counsel for Kretske, too. Kretske assented to this, but Glasser remained silent. After some demur on the ground there was some inconsistency in the defenses of the two men, Stewart accepted the appointment by the court as counsel for Kretske, too. He represented both of them throughout the trial and was the most active of the array of counsel for the various defendants. The conviction of Glasser was reversed by the Supreme Court of the United States.]

MR. JUSTICE MURPHY delivered the opinion of the Court. . . .

The guarantees of the Bill of Rights are the protecting bulwarks against the reach of arbitrary power. Among those guarantees is the right granted by the Sixth Amendment to an accused in a criminal proceeding in a federal court "to have the Assistance of Counsel for his defense" . . .. Even as we have held that the right to the assistance of counsel is so fundamental that the denial by a state court of reasonable time to allow the selection of counsel of one's own choosing, and the failure of that court to make an effective appointment of counsel, may so offend our concept of the basic requirements of a fair hearing as to amount to a denial of due process of law contrary to the Fourteenth Amendment, Powell v. Alabama, 287 U.S. 45, 53 S. Ct. 55, 77 L.Ed. 158, 84 A.L.R. 527 (1932), so we are clear that the "Assistance of Counsel" guaranteed by the Sixth Amendment contemplates that such assistance be untrammeled and unimpaired by a court order requiring that one lawyer shall simultaneously represent conflicting interests. If the right to the assistance of counsel means less than this, a valued constitutional safeguard is substantially impaired.

There is yet another consideration. Glasser wished the benefit of the undivided assistance of counsel of his own choice. We think that such a desire on the part of an accused should be respected. Irrespective of any conflict of interest the additional burden of representing another party may conceivably impair counsel's effectiveness.

To determine the precise degree of prejudice sustained by Glasser as a result of the court's appointment of Stewart as counsel for Kretske is at once difficult and unnecessary . . . .. Of equal importance with the duty of the court to see that an accused has the assistance of counsel is its duty to refrain from embarrassing counsel in the defense of an accused by insisting, or indeed, even suggesting that counsel undertake to concurrently represent interests which might diverge from those of his first client, when the possibility of that divergence is brought home to the court.

GRIEVANCE COMMITTEE OF THE BAR OF HARTFORD COUNTY v. ROTTNER

Supreme Court of Errors of Connecticut, 1964.
152 Conn. 59, 203 A.2d 82.

[In 1959 a senior member of a law firm was consulted by a man, Twible, on bringing a suit against three persons responsible for Twible's temporary commitment to a mental hospital and the lawyer declined to take the case. In 1962 two junior members of the law firm represented Twible in petty collection matters, and one of them was engaged late in July of that year in another collection matter in securing a default judgment on his behalf. On July 31 of that year still another member of the firm was asked by another person, O'Brien, to bring suit against Twible for assault and battery. The latter member of the firm, after disclosing to O'Brien the representation of Twible and ascertaining that Twible was not a client on a retainer basis, agreed to represent O'Brien. The next day he brought suit against Twible while the collection matter being handled by the junior members of the firm was still pending, and he had Twible's home attached. Several months later the senior members of the firm learned of the matter about the time Twible filed a complaint against the firm with the grievance committee of the bar association. At the hearing before the committee all members of the firm were present, and after the hearing the senior members permitted the firm's appearance in both the matters for and against Twible to continue. On presentment to the Superior Court by the grievance committee the two senior members of the firm were found guilty of a violation of the Canons of Professional Ethics. The court reprimanded the firm members and ordered them to withdraw from both the cases for and against Twible and to repay all retainers without liability by the clients for services rendered by the firm. The defendants appealed.]

COMLEY, ASSOCIATE JUSTICE . . . The [trial] court found such violations to exist apart from any consideration of the existence of a conflict of interest. In other words the court concluded that a firm may not accept any action against a person whom the firm is presently representing even though there is no relationship between the two cases. In arriving at this conclusion the court cited an opinion of the New York County Lawyers' Association which states in part: "While under the circumstances . . . there may be no actual conflict of interest . . . 'maintenance of public confidence in the Bar requires an attorney who has accepted representation of a client to decline, while representing such client, any employment from an adverse party in any matter even though wholly unrelated to the original retainer.' " . . .

We feel that this rule should be rigidly followed by the legal profession. When a client engages the services of a lawyer in a given piece of business he is entitled to feel that until that business is finally disposed of in some manner, he has the undivided loyalty of the one upon whom he looks as his advocate and his champion. If, as in this case, he is sued and his home attached by his own attorney, who is representing him in another matter, all feeling of loyalty is necessarily destroyed, and the profession is exposed to the charge that it is interested only in money. . . .

This determination is sufficient to support the judgment and to render unnecessary a discussion of the specific canons which the court found were violated by the defendants. There is no error.

NOTE

"A lawyer who receives a commission (whether delayed or not) from a title insurance company or guaranty fund for recommending or selling the insurance to his client, or for work done for the client or the company, without either fully disclosing to the client his financial interest in the transaction, or crediting the client's bill with the amount thus received, is guilty of unethical conduct. Such conduct would be a direct violation of *Canon 38*." American Bar Association, Opinion 304, 48 A.B.A.J. 383 (1962).

T. C. & THEATRE CORP. v. WARNER BROS. PICTURES

United States District Court, S.D.New York, 1953.
113 F.Supp. 265.

[A motion picture producer, Universal, had been a defendant in a federal anti-trust proceeding, and in that proceeding it retained Cooke as one of its lawyers. After the anti-trust proceeding ended a motion picture theater owner brought an action against Universal for damages inflicted by the same monopolistic activities, and the motion picture theater owner retained Cooke as one of its counsel in the case. Universal made a motion in the latter case to disqualify Cooke from having any part as lawyer in the case so long as Universal was defendant.]

. . .

WEINFELD, DISTRICT JUDGE.

Universal seeks to disqualify Cooke from now acting as attorney against it upon two separate grounds: (1) that the causes of action asserted by the plaintiff against Universal are based substantially on the identical charges made against it and the other distributor-defendants in the Paramount case, so that as present counsel for the plaintiff he will necessarily be called upon to prove against Universal, his former client, the very charges against which he had earlier defended it. Cooke's disqualification is urged irrespective of any showing that actual confidential information relating to the case had been received by him during the former representation; (2) that, in fact, matters of confidence were disclosed to Cooke while he acted as Universal's counsel in the Paramount litigation which are related to the issues at bar; and that his current representation of the plaintiff involves, or may involve, the disclosure or use of such confidences. . . .

A lawyer's duty of absolute loyalty to his client's interests does not end with his retainer. He is enjoined for all time, except as he may be released by law, from disclosing matters revealed to him by reason of the confidential relationship. Related to this principle is the rule that where any substantial relationship can be shown between the subject matter of a former representation and that of a subsequent adverse representation, the latter will be prohibited.

This salutory principle is summed up in Canon 6 of the Canons of Professional Ethics adopted by the American Bar Association, which, in part, provides:

> "The obligation to represent the client with undivided fidelity and not to divulge his secrets or confidences forbids also the subsequent acceptance of retainers or employment from others in matters adversely affecting any interest of the client with respect to which confidence has been reposed."

It is upon this Canon that movant places its principal reliance. I agree that if Cooke's present retainer by T. C. falls within this Canon, he is disqualified to represent it.

I am not in accord with Mr. Cooke that Universal is required to show that during the Paramount litigation it disclosed matters to him related to the instant case. Rather, I hold that the former client need show no more than that the matters embraced within the pending suit wherein his former attorney appears on behalf of his adversary are substantially related to the matters or cause of action wherein the attorney previously represented him, the former client. . . .

To compel the client to show, in addition to establishing that the subject of the present adverse representation is related to the former, the actual confidential matters previously entrusted to the attorney and their possible value to the present client would tear aside the protective cloak drawn about the lawyer-client relationship. For the Court to probe further and sift the confidences in fact revealed would require the disclosure of the very matters intended to be protected by the rule. It would defeat an important purpose of the rule of secrecy—to encourage clients fully and freely to make known to their attorneys all facts pertinent to their cause. . . . In cases of this sort the Court must ask whether it can reasonably be said that in the course of the former representation the attorney might have acquired information related to the subject of his subsequent representation. If so, then the relationship between the two matters is sufficiently close to bring the later representation within the prohibition of Canon 6. In the instant case I think this can be said. . . .

A government suit, while primarily in the public interest, if successful, also accrues to the immediate benefit of those injured by the wrongful conduct. . . .

The defendants and their counsel were not unaware of the importance of the decree to possible future triple damage suits. For example, while the appeal was pending, Cooke in a letter to his client, Universal, stressed the importance of the decree, stating ". . . the decree, if unreversed, makes you prima facie guilty of violating the Sherman Act, in triple damage suits . . . .". . .

In sum, enough appears to show that Mr. Cooke's present representation deals with matters as to which his former client reposed confidence in him. Hence, I hold that Mr. Cooke is disqualified from acting as counsel for the plaintiff in this case in any capacity so long as Universal is a party defendant, and the motion is granted to this extent. This disposition makes it unnecessary to consider the second ground for the motion to disqualify, based on Canon 37.

NOTES

(1) The duty of unimpaired loyalty with its corollary principle as to conflicting interest applies to representatives and fiduciaries broadly. See Restatement, Second, Trusts, § 170; Restatement, Restitution, §§ 190–201.

(2) A client is entitled to the lawyer's devotion unimpaired by differing interest. Is the client entitled as well to objectivity of judgment unimpaired

by identity of interest of the lawyer with the client? The length to which the preservation of objectivity has been guarded is told in the biography of a law firm. "Cravath early came to believe that in most cases the client is best advised by a lawyer who maintains an objective point of view and that such objectivity may be impeded by any financial interest in the client's business or any participation in its management. Accordingly he made it the policy of the firm that neither its partners nor its associates should hold any equity securities of any client, or serve as a director of a corporate client, or have a financial interest, direct or indirect, in any transaction in which the firm was acting as counsel. Occasionally, more frequently in recent years, clients have insisted upon exceptions permitting partners to occupy directorships and own qualifying equity securities, but the exceptions have been few." Robert T. Swaine, The Cravath Firm, Vol. II, pp. 9–10 (1948).

(3) On the variety of sanctions which may be invoked, see Note, *Sanctions for Attorney's Representation of Conflicting Interests*, 57 Colum.L.Rev. 994 (1957)

CONSENT OF BOTH PARTIES

DRINKER, LEGAL ETHICS

Pages 120–21 (1953).

Canon 6 forbids the representation of conflicting interests "except by express consent of all concerned given after a full disclosure of the facts."

. . . The Canon does not sanction representation of conflicting interests in every case where such consent is given, but merely forbids it *except* in such cases. The American Bar Association has acquiesced in the numerous decisions of its Ethics Committee construing the exception as not exclusive, and consent as unavailable where the public interest is involved. There are, also, certain cases in which such representation is improper or at least unwise even with consent. There are, however, not infrequently cases in which it is highly desirable and to the advantage of everyone concerned that the same lawyer should, at the desire of both parties, represent them both. Where it is or becomes apparent that they should have independent counsel, the lawyer should so advise them.

In order that mutual consent be effective, full disclosure must, of course, be made and the effect of the dual relationship fully explained to both parties. Also, all parties concerned must consent, a majority not being enough.

If, at the time the duality of representation is suggested, the lawyer has it distinctly understood with both that in the event such a conflict develops he is to represent one of them, this would seem to amount both to a consent in advance by the other under Canon 6 and to a waiver of any privilege under Canon 37. Even so, the lawyer will often be wise not to allow himself to be put in the position of representing conflicting interests or of being subject to the charge of betraying professional confidence.

NOTES

(1) In Eisemann v. Hazard, 218 N.Y. 155 (1916), in which the court was almost evenly divided, the opinion of the majority states: "It is not always improper or unlawful for an attorney at law to represent conflicting interests. Adverse interests, if they are to be adjusted, may be represented by the same counsel, though the cases in which this can be done are exceptional, and never entirely free from danger of conflicting duties."

(2) "*Question:* A and B come into the office of C, an attorney, and A employs him to draft a deed conveying certain property to B. Before the deed is drawn, C discovers that the title to the property is defective. Should he divulge this fact to B, who has had nothing to do with his employment?

"*Answer:* In the opinion of the Committee, the question implies that B reposes trust and confidence in C as a lawyer; and in effect that the lawyer is asked to represent both parties. Therefore, in the opinion of the Committee, C should disclose the defect to both A and B. If C is not acting for B, the Committee is of the opinion that C should only continue to act for A after advising B to secure separate counsel." New York County Opinion 90 (1916).

W. E. BASSETT CO. v. H. C. COOK CO.

United States District Court, D.Connecticut, 1962.
201 F.Supp. 821 affd. per curiam 302 F.2d 268.

[Attorney A, who represented Corporation X in a protracted controversy with Corporation Y, joined a firm one member of which had formerly represented Corporation Y in the same controversy. Aware of the possible conflict of interest the lawyers in the firm agreed that A would be permitted to continue in the case as his own without any participation by his new partners, and A so conducted the case at arm's length from his new partners. The trial judge, learning of the situation, on his own motion, held a hearing on the matter of disqualification.]

ANDERSON, CHIEF JUDGE. . . . [The facts are]: first, that Mr. Cuningham and Mr. Dunham became partners; second, that Mr. Dunham had represented the defendant the H. C. Cook Company and advised it concerning some of the most important issues in this case. These facts require Mr. Cuningham's disqualification in the present action. . . .

That the defendants raised no objection until the plaintiff's Rule 34 motion of November 16, 1961 has little or no bearing on the matter, because the court has a duty over and above that of counsel to see that the integrity and good name of the bar and of the administration of the law are upheld. The court is satisfied that Mr. Cuningham, Mr. Dunham and the other partners of Cooper, Dunham, Dearborn and Henninger made every effort to comply with Canons 6 and 37 as they honestly interpreted them.

It is by no means a case of irresponsible conduct or contumacy on the part of any of them. . . .

Circumstances have now been created which, with Mr. Cuningham remaining in the case, will inevitably lead to suspicion and distrust in the minds of the defendants and the opportunity for misunderstanding on the part of the public which will lead to a lack of confidence in the bar. . . .

Attorney Cuningham is ordered to disappear as counsel for the plaintiff and to disassociate himself from the case.

NOTES

(1) ". . . [A]ll authorities agree that all members of a partnership are barred from participating in a case from which one of the partners is disqualified. . . . And once a partner is thus vicariously disqualified for a particular case, the subsequent dissolution of the partnership cannot cure his ineligibility to act as counsel in that case. . . . Such a result . . . is necessary to facilitate maximum disclosure of relevant facts on the part of clients. Once the partnership is dissolved, however, the inference from access to receipt of information, in a new case having no relationship to the old partnership, becomes logically less compelling and should therefore become rebuttable legally, lest the chain of disqualification becomes endless." Clark, C. J., in Laskey Bros. v. Warner Bros. Pictures, 224 F.2d 824, 826–27 (1955).

(2) Limits on disqualification because of conflict of interests when a lawyer moves from one firm to another might be set by looking to the substance of the matter in either the first or the second firm. If the first firm was so compartmentalized and its members so insulated that the moving party did not have, and could not reasonably have had, any knowledge or responsibility as to the matter in question handled by the first firm, then the rule might be that the second firm is not disqualified from participation in the matter on the other side. Such a principle appears to have been the basis of the decision in United States v. Standard Oil Co., 136 F.Supp. 345 (1955). There a lawyer who had been employed in one division of the Treasury left the Department of the Treasury and joined a firm, with which he worked on a matter in which a different division of the Treasury had been concerned during his employment. It may also be the basis of the limits set on disqualification in the Federal Conflict of Interests Act of 1962 to matters in which "he participated personally and substantially" and to those "under his official responsibility." See Chapter IX, page 374 supra.

Conversely, if after the move the second firm takes all steps to insulate the moving partner or the rest of the firm, as the case may be, from one another as to the matter, the disqualification might not be imposed.

(3) The principal case is criticized in Note, *Unchanging Rules in Changing Times: The Canons of Ethics and Intra-Firm Conflicts of Interest*, 73

Yale L.J. 1058 (1964). "The social values of mobility from government service into private practice and of mobility among private firms, the harsh effects of depriving clients of counsel, and the impracticability of the current firm disqualification rule as evidenced by its wide disregard, argue for modification of the present rule." Id. at 1074.

MURPHY v. WASHINGTON AMERICAN LEAGUE BASEBALL CLUB, INC.

United States Court of Appeals, D.C.Circuit, 1963.
324 F.2d 394, 116 U.S.App.D.C. 362.

[The Washington baseball team of the American League moved to Minnesota over the objection of a stockholder owning or controlling over 40 per cent of the corporate stock. The board of directors then voted substantial salary increases to most of its own members and to some employees. The minority stockholder brought suit to challenge the increases. At the trial it was shown the move to Minnesota was a profitable one, and the payment of salaries more commensurate with those paid by other baseball companies had become possible. The trial judge denied a motion for a preliminary injunction and the petitioner appealed.]

WASHINGTON, CIRCUIT JUDGE. . . . Appellant's main contention is that since the board voted salary increases to most of its members, the rule against self-dealing vitiates the board's action as a matter of law. We cannot agree. In a closely-held corporation, where the directors are officers and majority stockholders, self-dealing on salary questions may be inevitable as a practical matter, and does not render the board's action void. Whether the board's action is voidable depends on all the circumstances, including a consideration of the reasonableness of its action.

We think the District Court was amply justified in denying the preliminary injunction against payment of the salary increases.

. . . A serious question has thus been raised, however, upon which we think we should comment. Counsel for the corporation, as we have noted, represents appellee Eugene V. Young, and has filed a joint answer for the corporation and Young, defending the challenged transactions on the merits. He has also filed materials on their joint behalf resisting on the merits the motion for a preliminary injunction. The record shows that the corporation has authorized the payment from the corporate treasury of the expenses and counsel fees of the individual defendants.

We said in Milone v. English, 113 U.S.App.D.C. 207 at 210, 306 F.2d 814 at 817 (1962), in words which seem as applicable to stockholders' derivative suits as to union litigation:

> "The treasury of a union is not at the disposal of its officers to bear the cost of their defense against charges of fraudulently

depriving the members of their rights as members. It is clear the complaint in this case charged individual officer defendants with conduct which was seriously detrimental to the interests of the International and to the rights of its members. And in deciding whether or not union funds may be used to defend such a suit the final outcome of the charges is not determinative; for if the charges have substance a sound resolution may be prevented by the very fact of dual representation during the process leading to a decision with respect to the charges. Different counsel would be required in this process. In other words, counsel who are chosen by and represent officers charged with the misconduct, and who also represent the union, are not able to guide the litigation in the best interest of the union because of the conflict in counsel's loyalties. In such a situation it would be incumbent upon counsel not to represent both the union and the officers."

. . . As to the propriety of the corporation's paying the legal expenses and counsel fees of the individual defendants in the present litigation, we think final settlement of this question must await the termination of the suit.*

. . . For these reasons, the order of the District Court will be affirmed without prejudice. . . .

NOTE

"A lawyer employed or retained by a corporation or similar entity owes his allegiance to the entity and not to a stockholder, director, officer, employee, representative, or other person connected with the entity. In advising the entity, a lawyer should keep paramount its interests and his professional judgment should not be influenced by the personal desires of any person or organization. Occasionally a lawyer for an entity is requested by a stockholder, director, officer, employee, representative, or other person connected with the entity to represent him in an individual capacity; in such case the lawyer may serve the individual only if the lawyer is convinced that differing interests are not present." Code of Professional Responsibility EC 5–18.

LIQUIDATION AND REORGANIZATION

A liquidation or reorganization case, whether a petty bankruptcy or a railroad receivership, may involve numerous interests, and so is particularly apt to present conflicting interests.

The contending groups are in three main classes, which may be divided into subclasses. They are the creditors, including secured creditors, creditors claiming priority, and general creditors. Then

---

* For a general discussion of the whole subject, see Washington & Bishop, Indemnifying The Corporate Executive (1963). (note by the court)

there are the various groups of stockholders. In addition there are the management groups, which will include the promoters and bankers of the business, the officers and directors of the corporation. Finally, there are the liquidators, and the reorganizers with their bankers.

A conflict of interests may arise at the inception of the case, which may be instituted in the name of one person though actually at the instigation and for the purposes of another. Then there is the selection of the personnel for liquidation proceedings, as, the liquidator, the attorney for the liquidator, and the protective committees. During the running of the liquidation, there are various questions, including what claims shall be enforced or resisted. At the sale or reorganization, there is the question of time and method and upset price. Finally, there is the problem of fees: who shall be paid, and for what services.

Some of the recurring questions involve: the selection of the liquidator; who may be the attorney for the liquidator; and what relation the attorney for the liquidator may have to the attorneys for other interests. Then there is the question whether a lawyer may represent different claimants in the same proceeding, or may acquire a claim against or an interest in the business in liquidation. The cases noted below illustrate a few of the problems.

NOTES

(1) May a lawyer who is a trustee in bankruptcy be represented by his own firm as attorneys for the trustee? The American Bar Association Committee in Opinion No. 271 (1946), 33 A.B.A.J. 161 (1947) stated this is proper, since under the Bankruptcy Act, as amended, the appointment must have the approval of the court and the fees are subject to the approval of the court to which the trustee makes his accounting. The committee stated the same principle applies to receivers.

(2) In a reorganization, may the attorney for junior claimants, as general creditors or common stockholders, represent senior claimants, as bondholders or preferred stockholders? No. ". . . the equity owner is peculiarly ill-suited to represent the mortgagee in these situations because of their historic clash of interests." Douglas, J., in Woods v. City National Bank & Trust Co., 312 U.S. 262, 265 (1941).

(3) May the attorney for a receiver participate indirectly in the purchase of the property of the receivership estate? In Tracy v. Willys Corporation, 45 F.2d 485 (1930), the facts were that an automobile company was in receivership and a member of the firm of lawyers who were counsel for the receiver negotiated a sale of the property of the company to a syndicate, taking title in himself though in fact as trustee for the syndicate. Two days later he became in effect a member of the syndicate under what the court found was from the start an expectation and intention on both sides. Through this participation the lawyer made a profit of nearly half a million dollars. The counsel for the receiver who had already received an allowance of compensation for earlier services sought an allowance for their

services in the sale. The record indicated that the lawyer in charge had conducted the reorganization sale with great skill, though the sales price was only enough to pay the creditors and to give a considerable interest to the preferred stockholders, with nothing for the common stockholders. On objection by special counsel for the preferred stockholders the court denied further compensation to the firm, saying "where property is to be sold by a receiver, neither he nor his counsel can be substantially interested as purchasers." Observe the transaction took place in the 1920s when the courts were less sensitive than they are now to the dangers in such a situation. If today you were counsel for the preferred stockholders or for the common stockholders of such a company, would you ask for further relief than that sought and given in the principal case, say, return to the receivership estate of the profits from the conflict of interests transaction made by the attorney personally, or by all the syndicate members who were parties to or beneficiaries of the conflict of interests sale?

(4) May the attorney for a liquidator purchase certificates of interest in the property in liquidation? In the liquidation of an insolvent estate the trustee issued first mortgage certificates. The attorneys for the trustee purchased some of the certificates on the open market at 16 cents on the dollar. The certificates yielded much more. In the final accounting of the trustee other certificate holders objected to the allowance of attorneys' fees and urged that the attorneys for the trustee should surrender to the trust estate their profits made through the purchase of the certificates. Without passing on the question of attorneys' fees, the court held that the profits made through the purchase of the certificates should be surrendered, saying ". . . the attorneys in no event may keep the certificates and the profits, but must account therefore to the trust estate as upon a constructive trust . . .". In re Bond & Mortgage Guarantee Co., 303 N.Y. 423 (1952).

THE LAWYER FOR A LIABILITY INSURANCE COMPANY

A liability insurance policy ordinarily provides that the insurance company will hold the insured harmless against liability incurred to third parties within the monetary limits fixed by the policy, that the company will provide a lawyer to represent the insured in any claim or action covered by the policy, and that the insured will cooperate with the insurance company in the defense against the claims or actions. On the face of it the arrangement violates the standards of the profession of law.

One standard violated is the prohibition against representing conflicting interests. The insured, who is the named defendant in a claim or action and whom the lawyer represents, is interested in the settlement of the controversy without liability to him regardless of the cost to the insurance company. The insurance company, which chooses and pays the lawyer, is interested in making money for itself by paying as little as practicable in settlement or after trial.

Another standard of the profession which is violated is the condemnation of a lay intermediary which interposes itself between the client and the lawyer. In the case of liability insurance the insurance company is a lay intermediary which furnishes and pays the lawyer for the insured. A major reason for the condemnation of the lay intermediary is the possibility of conflicting interests discussed above.

Yet liability insurance is a socially useful institution, and the provision of a lawyer by the insurance company for the protection of the insured and the company is an essential element in it. Liability insurance is approved, without the professional standards as to conflicting interests being entirely set aside. So it is incumbent on lawyers to take account of the difficulties inherent in their dual representation and to consider what limitations on their relationship with the two parties, the insurance company and the insured, are wise so that the insurance may best serve its purposes. A few illustrations of acute conflicts of interests are given below.

Changing Sides. One obvious limitation is the prohibition against changing sides. If a lawyer has investigated a claim at the instance of an insurance company he may not later represent the claimant, whether the investigation was made by him or through a claim agent. A more usual case is that of the lawyer who is generally employed by a particular insurance company in claims and actions against its insured. A case is tendered to the lawyer by an injured person against a defendant who is insured by that insurance company. It is the practice of the bar for a lawyer so situated to refuse the tendered case.

Conflict of Interest During the Representation; Settlement of the Case. The insurance company may be under a duty to give weight to the interests of the insured as well as its own in determining whether to settle a case. The courts vary in the measure of duty they state is owed by the insurer. Some say the insurer may give paramount consideration to its own interests; others that it must give paramount consideration to the interests of the insured; still others that it should give equal consideration to the two interests. See Farmers Insurance Exchange v. Henderson, 82 Ariz. 335, 313 P.2d 404 (1957).

A much more troubling question is the professional duty of the lawyer as contrasted with the legal duty of the insurance company. If one client, the insurance company, fails to give the consideration to the interest of the other, the insured, which the law requires, what is the professional duty of the lawyer? Certainly, it would appear to be the duty of the lawyer not only to inform the insurance company of the measure of its legal duty to the insured in the matter of settlement, but to use his best influence to see to it that this duty to the insured is fully complied with. It may happen that the insurance company officials fail to give such consideration to the interests of the insured as the law and fairness require. In other types of cases the lawyer will ordinarily be controlled by the wishes of his client as to settlement. But here he has two clients, one of whom he believes is acting unfairly toward the other. To make the question more difficult it is obvious that the unfair client is one who retained him in the case, who is paying his fee, and who will be a continuing source of legal work unless it becomes dissatisfied with his services or his attitude. The insured is his client in the case only because of the insurance company's choice and is not apt ever to retain the lawyer who, through the company's choice, represented him in this unpleasant incident.

Failure of the Insured to Cooperate. At times the insured may fail to give the cooperation in the defense that the policy calls for. This is usually an intra-family case, as one in which a father who was the driver of an automobile when his son was injured is sued by the son. The father desires that the son recover a judgment against him, since as the father hopes the judgment will be paid by the insurance company. What are the duties of the lawyer?

There may be no legal liability on the insurance company to indemnify the insured or to provide counsel for him when the insured fails to give the cooperation called for by the policy. Yet if the insurance company fails to defend the action and a large judgment is given for the plaintiff, the company runs the danger of having a court find in a later action that there was no such failure of the insured to cooperate as the policy required, so the insurance company must indemnify the insured. If the insurance company defends the actions without any sort of disclaimer, it runs another danger of waiving its defense based on the insured's lack of cooperation. Clearly, it is the duty of the lawyer to inform the insurance company on all these matters and to advise it on the appropriate course of action to take.

Similarly, the insured needs advice and counsel on each aspect mentioned. Should the lawyer retained by the insurance company give this advice and counsel? Or must he not inform the insured that he needs independent counsel and then withdraw from the case? Withdrawal is a step of some difficulty. If the lawyer for the insurance company has appeared in a legal proceeding as counsel for the insured defendant, he may not withdraw without good cause and without permission granted by the court. (See p. 434 infra.) It has been held that mere direction by the insurance company that he withdraw as representative is not by itself adequate reason for the court to grant the permission. Thomas v. Douglas, 2 A.D.2d 885 (1955). In any event a lawyer who has become the attorney for the insured may not withdraw except at a time and under conditions which leave ample opportunity for the insured to retain new counsel to protect his interests.

A related question is, may the lawyer who was counsel of record for the insured in an action brought against him by the injured party be the counsel for the insurance company in an action between the insured and the company over the issue of lack of cooperation by the insured and consequent loss of his right of indemnity? It would appear most unwise for the same lawyer who had represented the insured to appear against him in another phase of the same general controversy. If this is so, do the legal principle and the professional standard as to privileged communications between lawyer and client apply to the lawyer first designated by the company to represent the insured so he may not inform the lawyer now representing the insurance company on the issue of loss of the right of indemnity, of any of his communications with the insured?

A Fraudulent Claim. If the insurance company is of the opinion that the claim presented by the insured is a fraudulent one, the problems discussed above as to the lawyer designated to represent the insured take on an aggravated form.

The broad privilege of the lawyer designated by an insurance company to represent the insured is dealt with at some length in Opinion No. 282 of the American Bar Association, 36 A.B.A.J. 733 (1950). See also Drinker, Legal Ethics 114–18 (1953).

SECTION 3. COMMENCEMENT, PROTECTION AND TERMINATION

LAWRENCE v. TSCHIRGI

Supreme Court of Iowa, 1953.
244 Iowa 386, 57 N.W.2d 46.

[An old man had married three times. In 1943 his divorced second wife consulted a lawyer in an effort to protect her children from the efforts of the third wife to obtain some of her husband's property for herself, though apparently with no mention of employment when her former husband died. In 1945 and 1946 the children of the second marriage consulted the lawyer for the same purpose. In 1946 the two children, both mature persons, signed an "Agreement for Contingent Fee" under which they retained the lawyer to look after their interests in their father's estate on his death, and they agreed to pay him 25 per cent of the money or property so received. In 1948 the father died.]

GARFIELD, JUSTICE. This is a suit in equity by an attorney for a declaratory judgment . . . that a written contract by which defendants agreed to pay plaintiff 25 per cent of what they realized from their father's estate is valid and to determine and recover the amount due thereunder. Following trial the court held the contract is valid . . . . Plaintiff's total fee amounts to $44,468.18 in addition to expense money. Defendants have appealed. . . .

The defense to plaintiff's suit is that the attorney fee contract was made while a confidential relation existed between plaintiff and defendant without a full and fair disclosure of the facts on which the contract was predicated, it exacts an unreasonable and exorbitant fee and is oppressive . . . . .

The trial court found against defendants on all issues except he found the relation of attorney and client existed between plaintiff and defendants at the time the contract was made. . . .

It is important to determine at the outset whether the fee contract was made, as defendants contend and the trial court found, during the existence of an attorney-client relationship between plaintiff and defendants or, as plaintiff argues, at the inception thereof. It is more difficult for an attorney to enforce such a contract if made during the existence of the relationship rather than at its inception. . . .

Where such contracts made during the existence of the attorney-client relationship are not regarded as void they are viewed with suspicion and closely scrutinized by the courts, as are all dealings between trustee and cestui. There is a presumption of unfairness or invalidity attaching to a contract for compensation made after the relationship has been established and the burden is on the attorney to show it was fairly and openly made, that the client was fully informed concerning it and understood its effect. . . .

No formal contract is necessary to create the relation of attorney and client. Nor is payment of a fee necessary. The contract may be implied from conduct of the parties. . . .

We have no doubt an attorney-client relation existed between plaintiff and defendants for at least several months before the fee contract was made. . . .

Under the authorities above cited it is our duty to view this contract with suspicion and scrutinize it closely. It is presumed to be unfair. The burden is on plaintiff to show it was fairly made, that defendants were fully informed concerning it and understood its effect. We think plaintiff has failed to discharge this burden. . . .

. . . For acting as attorney in the matters specified plaintiff was to receive 25 per cent of what defendants realized from their father's estate regardless of whether there was litigation or plaintiff benefited them in any way. Under this contract defendants could retain only three fourths of what they might have received from their father's estate if plaintiff had not acted as their attorney. It seems to us the contract is one-sided.

Nor is it shown satisfactorily that defendants were fully informed concerning the contract and understood its effect. . . .

Defendants received no independent advice before signing the fee contract. Plaintiff did not give his clients such advice regarding it as a disinterested attorney could be expected to give them or such advice as plaintiff should have given them if the proposed contract were between them and a strange attorney. . . .

In Edler v. Frazier, supra, 174 Iowa 46, 156 N.W. 182, on which plaintiff strongly relies, and in other Iowa decisions he cites, the contract for fees was made at the inception of the attorney-client relation when the attorney was free to deal at arm's length. As we have indicated and as Edler v. Frazier recognizes, at page 52 of 174 Iowa, page 184 of 156 N.W., a different rule applies where, as here, the contract is made after such a relation has been in existence. . . .

Many precedents which refuse to enforce a contract for attorney fees point out that the decision does not deny the right to recover the reasonable value of the services rendered if the attorney seeks to avail himself of that right. There is no evidence before us from which we could determine the reasonable value of plaintiff's services nor has plaintiff asserted a claim therefor. Our decision is without prejudice to any right plaintiff may have to recover the reasonable value of his services.

For decree dismissing plaintiff's petition in harmony with this opinion the cause is—

Reversed and remanded.

NOTES

(1) "[T]he trial court, or this court, has power, at any stage of the case to require an attorney, one of its officers, to show his authority to appear." Pueblo of Santa Rosa v. Fall, 273 U.S. 315, 319, 47 S.Ct. 106 (1927).

(2) Controversies over the existence of the relationship of lawyer and client ordinarily do not involve the broad question whether and when the relationship began or ended. They involve narrower questions as to the application of specific protective rules. Is the following principle wise? Each incident of the relation will begin as soon as, and will continue as long as, it is important and useful for the effectiveness of the relationship and the protection of the parties to it.

(3) The privileged character of a confidential communication to an attorney may arise from merely preliminary negotiations, even though no employment actually results. Thorp v. Goewey, 85 Ill. 611 (1877); Hanson v. Kline, 136 Iowa 101, 113 N.W. 504 (1907) (dictum); but cf. Kitz v. Buckmaster, 45 App.Div. 283, 61 N.Y.S. 64 (1899) (communication held not privileged where there was no pretense or intention of engaging the attorney in his professional capacity).

Similarly, the presumption that an attorney has exercised undue influence in transactions between himself and a client may be indulged, even after the actual termination of the employment. Bingham v. Sheldon, 101 App. Div. 48, 91 N.Y.S. 917 (1905); Barrett v. Ball, 101 Mo.App. 288, 73 S.W. 865 (1903); Kline v. Charles, 124 S.W. 347 (Ky.1910); Hill v. Hall, 191 Mass. 253, 77 N.E. 831 (1906).

HERRON v. STATE FARM MUTUAL INS. CO.

Supreme Court of California, 1961.
56 Cal.2d 202, 14 Cal.Rptr. 294, 363 P.2d 310.

[Some lawyers brought this action against a liability insurance company and its agent for intentional interference with contractual relations. The complaint alleged that the Halversons were injured in an automobile accident because of the negligence of a person insured by the defendant insurance company, that their claim was reasonably worth $60,000 and that the Halversons retained the plaintiffs as their lawyers under a contingent fee contract for one third of the net amount of the recovery. The plaintiffs notified the defendant company of the retainer and conducted an investigation costing $1,250. The defendants by telling the Halversons that they did not need a lawyer and that a satisfactory settlement would be made induced them to discharge the plaintiffs. The conduct of defendant was maliciously designed to injure plaintiff's rights and violated the rules of the National Conference Committee on Adjustors of which the defendant company is a member, which provide in part that an insurance company will not deal directly with any claimant represented by a lawyer without the consent of the lawyer. The plaintiffs asked for judgment for $20,000 or one third of the amount of the settlement, whichever is the lesser, and for $25,000 punitive damages. The defendants demurred, and the trial court sustained the demurrer.]

GIBSON, CHIEF JUSTICE.

. . . An action will lie for the intentional interference by a third person with a contractual relationship either by unlawful means or by means otherwise lawful when there is a lack of sufficient justification. . . . There is no valid reason why this rule should not be applied to an attorney's contingent fee contract. . . .

Our conclusion that intentional interference with a contingent fee contract may give rise to liability is supported by cases from several jurisdictions. . . . Cases relied upon by defendants, such as Herbits v. Constitution Indemnity Co., 279 Mass. 539, 181 N.E. 723, 724–725, and Krause v. Hartford Acc. & Indem. Co., 331 Mich. 19, 49 N.W.2d 41, 44–45, which involve settlements by clients without the consent of their attorneys, are distinguishable. In none of them were the clients induced, as a means of obtaining the settlements, to repudiate the contracts with their attorneys and to refuse to pay them. In the present case plaintiffs do not complain because there may have been a settlement but because defendants induced the Halversons to repudiate the contract and deprive plaintiffs of its benefits.

Whether an intentional interference by a third party is justifiable depends upon a balancing of the importance, social and private, of the objective advanced by the interference against the importance of the interest interfered with, considering all circumstances including the nature of the actor's conduct and the relationship between the parties. . . . see Rest., Torts, § 767; Prosser on Torts (2d ed. 1955), pp. 735 et seq. Justification is an affirmative defense and may not be considered as supporting the trial court's action in sustaining a demurrer unless it appears on the face of the complaint. . . .

The conduct of an insurance company in inducing an injured person to repudiate his contract with an attorney may be detrimental not only to the interests of the attorney but also to the interests of the client since, as we have seen, the client, in addition to being deprived of the aid and advice of his attorney, may also be liable for the full contract fee. Defendants argue that the policy of the law is to encourage settlement, that an insurance company has a legal duty to effect a settlement of a claim against its insured in an appropriate case (Comunale v. Traders & General Ins. Co., 50 Cal.2d 654, 658 et seq., 328 P.2d 198, 68 A.L.R.2d 883) and that furtherance of the actor's own economic interests will justify an intentional interference with a contractual relationship in some circumstances where his interests are threatened by the contract. However, these considerations standing alone cannot justify inducing the Halversons to repudiate the contract and to deprive plaintiffs of its benefits. So far as appears from the complaint, no cause for the dismissal of plaintiffs existed, no efforts were made to negotiate with them, and there is no indication that State Farm could not have protected its interests and obtained a satisfactory settlement without interfering with the contract.

The judgment is reversed with directions to overrule the demurrer.

NOTE

The rule of the principal case is the prevailing one. There is some disagreement. Walsh v. O'Neil, 350 Mass. 586, 215 N.E.2d 915 (1966).

MATTER OF KROOKS

Court of Appeals of New York, 1931.
257 N.Y. 329, 178 N.E. 548.

O'BRIEN, J. Fanny E. Krooks owned real estate assessed at $25,000, title to which the city of New York acquired by condemnation. By written contract, she retained William W. Conrad as her attorney to take such proceedings as might be necessary "in connection with the collection of any award or the payment of any compensation resulting from the condemnation," and by that contract she agreed to pay him all moneys in excess of $38,000 "which may be paid to me or my assigns as a result of said proceedings." On this record a finding could properly be made that Mr. Conrad faithfully performed services as her attorney and that he acted with such energy and skill that the justice at Special Term before whom the condemnation proceeding was conducted stated in a memorandum that the sum of $46,500 was awarded by him for the Krooks property. Two days after the publication of that memorandum Mrs. Krooks canceled her retainer and on the following day instituted this proceeding to set aside the written agreement and to determine the attorney's lien. The application in so far as it sought to set aside the agreement was denied. Without taking evidence in relation to the value of the attorney's services, the lien was fixed "at the amount set forth in said agreement of retainer of October 22, 1929, to wit, the sum over and above $38,000, which may be paid to the said Fanny E. Krooks, or her assigns, as a result of said condemnation proceedings."

A client may at any time for any reason which seems satisfactory to him, however arbitrary, discharge his attorney. (Tenney v. Berger, 93 N.Y. 524, 529; Matter of Dunn, 205 N.Y. 398, 402; Matter of Paschal, 77 U.S. 483, 496.) Even in the presence of a definite agreement the client's right persists. Cancellation by him cannot constitute a breach of contract, for implied in every such agreement is the right to discharge. . . .

The client's right to control her retainer does not permit her to cheat her attorney. (Matter of Levy, 249 N.Y. 168, 170.) If the attorney shall be paid the reasonable value of his services, no cheating will occur. The contract has been canceled and its terms cannot establish the standard for compensation. . . . Quantum meruit is the rule to apply. (Matter of City of New York, 219 N.Y. 192.)

The order of the Appellate Division and that of the Special Term should be reversed, without costs to either party, and the matter remitted to the Special Term with directions to take testimony in relation to the value of the attorney's services and to fix the lien therefor.

CRANE, J., dissents upon the ground that there was substantial compliance with the contract.

NOTES

(1) The principle is often stated but rarely applied that when an attorney's power is coupled with an interest he cannot be discharged by the client. What is meant by the phrase, "coupled with an interest", is not clear. A contingent fee contract does not give such an interest, even when coupled with a provision for assignment of the agreed proportion of the cause of action. O'Connell v. Superior Court, 2 Cal.2d 418, 41 P.2d 334 (1935).

(2) The cases are in disagreement on the measure of recovery of a lawyer who has been discharged by his client without fault. See Annot., 136 A.L.R. 231, 1942. The rule that the lawyer may recover the full amount agreed on though he has not rendered the full services is a great discouragement of the client's continued freedom of choice of his lawyer and is not consistent with the maintenance of the confidence of the client in his lawyer which is at the heart of the relationship. See Drinker, Legal Ethics 175–76 (1953).

(3) "A decision by a lawyer to withdraw should be made only on the basis of compelling circumstances and in a matter pending before a tribunal he must comply with the rules of the tribunal regarding withdrawal. A lawyer should not withdraw without considering carefully and endeavoring to minimize the possible adverse effect on the rights of his client and the possibility of prejudice to his client as a result of his withdrawal. Even when he justifiably withdraws, a lawyer should protect the welfare of his client by giving due notice of his withdrawal, suggesting employment of other counsel, delivering to the client all papers and property to which the client is entitled, cooperating with counsel subsequently employed, and otherwise endeavoring to minimize the possibility of harm. Further, he should refund to the client any compensation not earned during the employment." Code of Professional Responsibility EC 2–32. See also DR 2–110.

A CONFESSED KILLER

In TUCKIAR v. THE KING, 52 Commonw.L.R. 335 (1934), the lawyer representing an aboriginee on trial for murder received a confession of guilt which the lawyer immediately communicated to the judge. After a verdict of guilty of murder he repeated the confession in open court, and the confession was given wide publicity. The High Court of Australia severely condemned the lawyer's action. "Indeed, counsel seems to have taken a course calculated to transfer to the Judge the embarrassment which he appears so much to have felt. . . . He had a plain duty, both to his client and to the Court, to press such rational considerations as the evidence fairly gave rise to in favor of complete acquittal or conviction of manslaughter only." Because counsel's action and the consequent publicity made a fair trial impossible, the High Court directed a judgment of acquittal.

Chapter XII

SOME CONSEQUENCES OF THE RELATIONSHIP

SECTION 1. CONTROL OVER THE CASE

BONNIFIELD v. THORP

United States District Court, D. Alaska, 1896.
71 Fed. 924.

[In an action at law brought by two co-plaintiffs, the defendant failed to answer in time and an order of default was entered. The defendant made a motion to vacate the default and in support of the motion submitted an affidavit of his counsel. The affidavit stated, among other things, that after the time to answer had expired the defendant's counsel requested one of the three counsel of record for the plaintiffs to agree to extend the time for answering but the request was refused. The defendant's counsel then saw the plaintiff Bonnifield who signed a stipulation extending the time.]

DELANEY, DISTRICT JUDGE. While the courts are vested with a large discretion in determining applications of this character, its exercise must be confined to the limits prescribed by statute, which, so far as this court is concerned, are laid down in section 102, pp. 242, 243, Hill's Code Or. This section provides that the court may, in its discretion, "relieve a party from a judgment, order or other proceeding, taken against him through his mistake, inadvertence, surprise, or excusable neglect." The only testimony submitted in support of the application is the affidavit of one of the attorneys for the defendant.

[The court first considered whether the plaintiff Bonnifield was represented by the counsel of record for the plaintiffs.]

There is no principle of practice better settled in our American law than that an appearance in court by an attorney for a client carries with it the presumption of authority to appear. . . .

The practice is also well settled that the authority for an attorney to appear cannot be called into question except by a motion directly for that purpose, based upon affidavits, showing, in the first instance, prima facie a want of authority; and, upon the hearing, such want must be established by clear and positive proofs. . . . In the absence of some such proceeding, directly challenging the authority, the court will not hear or inquire into the question of the authority of the attorney for his appearance. . . .

This brings us to the consideration of the stipulation made on the 24th of December, 1895, by and between Bonnifield, as plaintiff, and the attorneys for the defendant, extending the time to answer. The court has no doubt whatever that this stipulation must be disregarded. The line of demarcation between the respective rights and powers of an attorney is clearly defined. The cause of action, the claim or demand sued upon, the subject-matter of the litigation, are within the exclusive control of the client; and the attorney may not impair, compromise, settle, surrender, or destroy them without the client's consent. . . . But all the proceedings in court to enforce the remedy, to bring the claim, demand, cause of action, or subject-matter of the suit to hearing, trial, determination, judgment, and execution, are within the exclusive control of the attorney. "All acts, in and out of court, necessary or incidental to the prosecution or management of the suit, and which affect the remedy only, and not the cause of action," are to be performed by the attorney. . . .

The rule now under consideration has been followed by the courts of the Pacific states, and the supreme court of California has declared the rule in the following language:

"A party to an action may appear in his own proper person or by attorney, but he cannot do both. If he appears by attorney, he must be heard through him; and it is indispensable to the decorum of the court and the due and orderly conduct of a cause that such attorneys shall have the management and control of the action, and his acts go unquestioned by any one except the party he represents. So long as he remains the attorney of record, the court cannot recognize any other as having the management of the case. If the party, for any cause, becomes dissatisfied with his attorney, the law points out a remedy. He may move the court for leave to change his attorney. Until that has been done, the client cannot assume control of the case." . . . Commissioners v. Younger, 29 Cal. 147. . . .

A stipulation extending the time to answer is certainly one of the proceedings in or incident to the progress of a cause pending in court; and, as Bonnifield was represented by attorneys when the stipulation was made, his action cannot be recognized by the court. Additional force is given to the importance of this rule when it is considered that Bonnifield has a coplaintiff. . . .

It follows from these views that the motion to vacate the default must be denied, and the plaintiffs will have judgment in accordance with the demand of the summons and complaint.

NOTES

(1) An admission of counsel in the course of a trial is binding on his client. "The power of the court to act in the disposition of a trial upon the facts conceded by counsel is as plain as its power to act upon the evidence produced." Oscanyan v. Arms Co., 103 U.S. 261, 263 (1880). However, a statement by counsel must be clear and unambiguous to be accepted as evi-

dence against the client's interest. Rhoades, Incorporated v. United Air Lines, Inc., 340 F.2d 481 (3rd Cir., 1965).

(2) As noted in the principal case the client retains control of the subject-matter of the litigation. Even where a compromise settlement proposed by plaintiff's attorney has been approved by the court, a motion to vacate the settlement will be granted upon the client's request if it appears that the client at no time consented to the settlement and was not consulted by the attorney with respect thereto. Fasano v. City of New York, 22 App.Div.2d 799, 254 N.Y.S.2d 133 (1964). However, the client may ratify his lawyer's unauthorized compromise or settlement of the client's claim. Yarnall v. Yorkshire Worsted Mills, 370 Pa. 93, 87 A.2d 182 (1952).

ANDREWES v. HAAS

Court of Appeals of New York, 1915.
214 N.Y. 255, 3 A.L.R. 458, 108 N.E. 423.

CARDOZO, J. The plaintiff is a member of the bar. He complains that the defendants refused to prosecute an action in which they had retained him as their lawyer. The agreement was, he says, that they would sue for $180,000, and pay him twenty-five per cent of the amount recovered. He drafted a complaint for them, but there the action stopped. The defendants refused to go on with it. They were advised and became convinced, as they now allege in their answer, that the action was without merit. Because of their refusal to proceed with it the plaintiff says that they owe him $45,000. In opening his case he declined to prove the value of his services up to the time when the case was halted; he took his stand upon the ground that he was entitled to the profits that would have come to him if his clients had pressed the case to a successful conclusion. At the close of his opening the complaint was dismissed.

The employment of a lawyer to serve for a contingent fee does not make it the client's duty to continue the lawsuit and thus increase the lawyer's profit. The lawsuit is his own. He may drop it when he will. Even an express agreement to pay damages for dropping it without his lawyer's consent, would be against public policy and void. (Matter of Snyder, 190 N.Y. 66, 69.) . . . The notion that such a thing is possible betrays a strange misconception of the function of the legal profession and of its duty to society. When the defendants abandoned the action, they became liable to the plaintiff for the value of the services then rendered. That is the measure of their liability and of his right.

We have been referred to cases where clients, after retaining a lawyer for a contingent fee, have continued the litigation through another lawyer, and have been held answerable in damages. (Martin v. Camp, 161 App.Div. 610; Carlisle v. Barnes, 102 App.Div. 573.) We are not required at this time either to approve or to condemn those rulings. They have not passed unchallenged. (Martin v. Camp, supra; Johnson v. Ravitch, 113 App.Div. 810.) In those cases, and in others like them, the clients went on with the lawsuit. Here they abandoned it. We refuse to hold that they were bound to pay their lawyer as if they had gone on with it and won it.

The plaintiff's claim is without merit. The judgment should be affirmed, with costs.

NOTES

(1) "The rule . . . is that the client has a right to discharge the attorney and terminate the relation at any time, even without cause, no matter how arbitrary his action may seem." MacLeod v. Vest Transportation Co., 235 F.Supp. 369, 371 (N.D.Miss., 1964). Should the same rule apply if the lawyer is retained by the client for a fixed period of time?

(2) See also discussion in Chapter XI, Section 3, Commencement, Protection and Termination [of the lawyer-client relationship]. The material begins p. 428 supra.

THE RIGHT OF A LAWYER TO CONTROL THE INCIDENTS OF A TRIAL

CODE OF PROFESSIONAL RESPONSIBILITY *

EC 7-7

In certain areas of legal representation not affecting the merits of the cause or substantially prejudicing the rights of a client, a lawyer is entitled to make decisions on his own. But otherwise the authority to make decisions is exclusively that of the client and, if made within the framework of the law, such decisions are binding on his lawyer. As typical examples in civil cases, it is for the client to decide whether he will accept a settlement offer or whether he will waive his right to plead an affirmative defense. A defense lawyer in a criminal case has the duty to advise his client fully on whether a particular plea to a charge appears to be desirable and as to the prospects of success on appeal, but it is for the client to decide what plea should be entered and whether an appeal should be taken.

CANONS OF PROFESSIONAL ETHICS

No. 24.

As to incidental matters pending the trial, not affecting the merits of the cause or working substantial prejudice to the rights of the client, such as forcing the opposite lawyer to trial when he is under affliction or bereavement; forcing the trial on a particular day to the injury of the opposite lawyer when no harm will result from a trial at a different time; agreeing to an extension of time for signing a

* Copyright 1969 by the American Bar Association. Reprinted with permission.

bill of exceptions, cross interrogatories and the like, the lawyer must be allowed to judge. In such matters no client has a right to demand that his counsel shall be illiberal, or that he do anything therein repugnant to his own sense of honor and propriety.

NOTES

(1) In a criminal case the decision not to lodge an appeal is a personal decision residing in the convicted individual. It is not a matter resting within the exclusive discretion of his counsel whether court-appointed or not. Grubbs v. State of Oklahoma, 239 F.Supp. 1014 (E.D.Okl.1965).

(2) If counsel knew or should have known that any of the essential elements of a cause of action were not present and still advised bringing on the action, she is guilty of unprofessional conduct. The attorney was disbarred. In re Rivette, 21 App.Div.2d 591, 252 N.Y.S.2d 936 (1964).

(3) Control of the incidents of a trial is in the hands of the attorney of record. Where the amount of liability insurance is not likely to be enough to protect an insured defendant from personal liability he may wish to consult his "personal attorney" in addition to the attorney retained by the insurer. In granting a motion by plaintiff to direct the defendant to appear for examination before trial, the court decided that only the attorney of record retained by the insurance company need be served. The "personal attorney" has no official standing even though he had served a notice of appearance. Ratner v. Lehigh Valley R. R. Co., 26 Misc.2d 981, 206 N.Y.S.2d 954 (Sup. Ct.1959).

(4) The federal estate tax return must be filed within 15 months after decedent's death. Failure to file on time subjects the estate to penalties unless "it is shown that failure is due to reasonable cause." I.R.C. Secs. 6075, 6651. Is reliance on an attorney "reasonable cause?" For a negative reply see Estate of Duttenhoffer, 49 T.C. 200 (1967).

SECTION 2. FINANCIAL RELATIONS

A. GIFTS AND CONTRACTS

WEBSTER v. KELLY

Supreme Judicial Court of Massachusetts, 1931.
274 Mass. 564, 175 N.E. 69.

PIERCE, J. This is a bill in equity brought by Hannah M. Webster against the defendant William J. Kelly, hereinafter called the defendant, and his wife, Maud A. Kelly, wherein the plaintiff prays that they be ordered to reconvey the premises described in the bill of complaint. . . .

The circumstances which gave rise to this suit, as they are disclosed by the reports of the masters, in substance are as follows: after the death of her husband on December 24, 1918, the plaintiff, an elderly woman who had become estranged from her adopted son, was in need of "advice in regard to the management of her real estate." She was the owner of her residence, 677 Cambridge Street, in the Brighton district of Boston, and of two apartment houses. The defendant "was a tenant" in one of these apartments. She consulted the defendant for the reason that he was an attorney at law and for several years prior to her husband's death had acted as his counsel in various matters. Her husband had great friendship for the defendant and great confidence in him, and on his dying bed told the plaintiff to consult the defendant in regard to her affairs and that he would look after her affairs properly and competently, both as an attorney and as a friend. The defendant, with the assistance of the adopted son of the plaintiff, succeeded in restoring the apartments to a paying basis and in selling one of them at an advantageous price. In July, 1920, the plaintiff, who had paid the defendant nothing for his services, because he had served her husband as legal adviser without compensation and had helped her since her husband's death, expressed the wish to give him several articles of furniture in her residence and to give him her residence after her death. The defendant assented, but informed her that in the circumstances he ought not to make the will and "suggested that she go to one of the judges of the local court for that purpose." In consequence of this advice she made out a list of the furniture which she desired to leave the defendant and went with it to a judge of the Municipal Court of the City of Boston for the Brighton District. On September 22, 1920, in the presence of the presiding judge of that court and two witnesses, she executed a will which purported to appoint the defendant executor and to give him a large amount of furniture and the house, land and garage described in the bill of complaint. This will remained in the custody of the defendant until the hearing before the master.

When the plaintiff took this will to the defendant she asked him if it was satisfactory and he, having in mind a possible contest of the will, suggested that a deed of the premises would be more effective in carrying out her wishes. The master finds "that the respondent did not instruct or request the complainant to execute such a deed." On October 2, 1920, the plaintiff went alone to the office of said judge of the Boston Municipal Court for the purpose of executing a deed, and the judge "drew a deed" from the plaintiff to John F. Holloran and then drew another deed from Holloran conveying the said premises to the plaintiff "for and during the term of her natural life, with remainder to William J. Kelly . . . in fee." These words were duly executed, acknowledged and recorded. The master finds that the plaintiff, "at the time of the execution of said deeds, intended to give the respondent said house and land after her death for the reason stated in said will; that she had an opportunity to read said deeds before the same were executed and that she neither asked for nor received any information from the respondent or Judge Connelly as to the legal effect of said deeds." He further finds that the said judge "dealt with said deeds as a matter of routine, that he had no reason to suspect that the complainant did not understand what she was doing, and that he was concerned chiefly with satisfying the legal requirements to make said will and deeds effective." After the deed from Holloran was executed, it was delivered by the plaintiff to the defendant and kept by him until introduced in evidence before the master.

In October, 1920, the plaintiff became apprehensive as to her ability to live comfortably upon the income obtainable from ordinary investments and with the advice and assistance of the defendant invested her capital in annuities payable to herself and ceasing at her death. Performing all legal services required in the plaintiff's affairs, the defendant acted as her counsel until about August or September, 1921. The defendant "not . . . on account of said will or deeds or in consideration thereof," loaned the plaintiff in 1922 $10, and in 1924 paid $253.82 for the repair of her residence. On January 19, 1922, the defendant conveyed the remainder interest in the property to his wife, Maud A. Kelly. On the above facts the judge ruled rightly that the relation of attorney and client which here existed required that the defendant before accepting the deed should have used active diligence to see that his client was fully informed of the nature and effect of the transaction proposed and of his own rights and interests in the subject matter involved, and should have seen to it that his client had independent advice in the matter or else should have received from him such advice as he would have been expected to give had the transaction been one between his client and a stranger, and should have seen that his client was so placed as to be enabled to deal with him at arm's length without being swayed by the relation of trust and confidence which existed between them. . . .

In this case, although an independent attorney drafted the will and the deeds, he did so "as a matter of routine." It was the clear duty of the defendant not alone to advise the plaintiff to have independent advice but to see that the advice when given was directed to the significance of her proposed act and that it made clear to her that the legal effect of her deed was to give the defendant a present vested title to the property conveyed as distinguished from a right or title to come into existence at the time of her death. Here, while there is no taint of fraud or chicanery on the part of the defendant, he failed in his duty because, knowing that the plaintiff by her will intended to give him only an estate to take effect at her death, he did not see to it that she was advised and that she understood her deed would not be revocable at her pleasure but in law was a conveyance of a present estate in fee subject to her life enjoyment. The defendants' appeal from the final decree voiding the deed from the plaintiff to John F.

Holloran, the deed from John F. Holloran to the defendant, and the deed from the defendant to Maud A. Kelly is without merit. . . .

[The decree of reconveyance was conditioned on the payment by the plaintiff of the money due the defendant for legal services and expenditures.]

FROST v. BACHMAN

Court of Appeals of New York (1940).
283 N.Y. 744, 28 N.E.2d 969.

[Action by Theodora B. Frost, individually as an executrix of George S. Frost, deceased, against A. Pierre Bachman, as executor of the last will and testament of Charles G. Hensley, deceased, to cancel and annul a contract entered into between the plaintiff and defendant testator, an attorney, who at the time the contract was made was acting as plaintiff's attorney. The contract (prepared by the attorney) was beneficial to him, was based on certain representations made by him therein, and was executed by plaintiff without any independent advice.

On the trial plaintiff offered evidence to establish the relationship of attorney and client at the time the contract was made and the execution of the contract and other evidence from which it might be inferred that she acted without independent advice, and she rested on the theory that the burden of establishing that the contract was fair, just and equitable and free from all the elements of over-reaching was on defendant. Defendant rested without proof, and the complaint was dismissed on the ground that the burden of proof was on plaintiff.

From an order of the Appellate Division, 259 App.Div. 745, 18 N.Y.S.2d 702, reversing a judgment for defendant and granting a new trial on the ground that under the facts in the record the burden was on defendant to establish that the contract was made with full knowledge of all the surrounding circumstances, that it was free in every respect from fraud on the part of defendant's testator or misconception on the part of plaintiff and that all was fair, open, voluntary and well understood by the client, defendant appeals.]

PER CURIAM.

Order affirmed and judgment absolute ordered against appellant on the stipulation with costs in all courts.

All concur except LEHMAN, C. J., and LOUGHRAN and SEARS, JJ.

NOTES

(1) Cf. Liles v. Terry, [1895] 2 Q.B. 679, in which Lord Esher said, ". . . there is a positive rule of equity to the effect that, because the solicitor who acted in relation to the execution of the deed was the husband of the plaintiff's niece [a cestui que trust in remainder under the deed], and

the plaintiff had not the advice of an independent solicitor, therefore the gift which the plaintiff intended to make for the benefit of her niece was invalid; or in other words, according to the authorities by which the rule of equity on the subject is determined, there is in such a case a legal presumption of undue influence by the solicitor which cannot be met or rebutted by any evidence."

(2) "Here, the attorney is not designated a beneficiary in the will but his mother is the sole legatee. Should the same inference arise [of undue influence]? . . . (I)f a benefit in some form is probably to be received by the attorney-draftsman by reason of a substantial bequest to the beneficiary, the inference ought to arise. Human nature and the experience of mankind justify such inference." In re Perssion's Estate, 20 Wis.2d 537, 123 N.W.2d 465 (1963).

(3) The Court of Appeals of the District of Columbia, in subordinating the principle of res judicata in suits on successive notes to the policy of fair dealing between lawyer and clients said: "In a very real sense attorneys are officers of the courts in which they practice; and clients are wards of the court in regard to their relationship with their attorneys . . . Fee contracts between attorney and client are a subject of special interest and concern to the courts. They are not to be enforced upon the same basis as ordinary commercial contracts." Washington, J., in Spilker v. Hankin, 188 F.2d 35, 37–39 (Ct. of Appeals, D.C., 1951).

(4) There is a presumption against the validity of a gift from a client to his attorney. Whipple v. Barton, 63 N.H. 613, 3 A. 922 (1886). See McDonald v. Hewlett, 102 Cal.App.2d 680, 228 P.2d 83 (1951) in which the court gives consideration to such factors as client's mental or physical infirmities, improvidence of gift and delay in revealing fact gift was made.

(5) "The relation between attorney and client is highly fiduciary in its nature and of a most delicate, exacting and confidential character, requiring a very high degree of fidelity and good faith. Attorney-client contacts are in general controlled by the traditional law of contracts with special emphasis on the truly fiduciary nature of the relationship." Williston on Contracts No. 1285 (3rd ed. Taeger, 1967).

(6) Should the "traditional law of contracts" (Williston, supra) apply with respect to the *formation* of a contract of employment between attorney and prospective client? For a case in which plaintiff was unsuccessful in establishing the lawyer-client relationship and therefore unable to avail herself of the "truly fiduciary nature of the relationship" see McGlone v. Lacey, 288 F.Supp. 662 (D.C.S.D.1968).

B. FEES

Introduction. Deciding how much to charge his client and arranging to be paid probably cause a lawyer more pain than anything he does except, perhaps, not being in a position to have the problem at all.

A lawyer's position vis-a-vis his client is a product of history and custom and the lawyer's individual professional standards. The closest we can come to a definition of this position is to call it a "relationship." In part it is a contractual relationship, but in the parlance of the market place in which the lawyer offers his service this connotes a freedom in both parties which is not enjoyed by the lawyer.

Between a lawyer and his client there should be no conflict of interest, and yet there is with respect to fees. The situation is more delicate than perhaps in any of the other professions.

How should the matter be dealt with by the lawyer in private practice? Should he take cover behind the organized bar or some quasi-governmental device for fixing fees? Such a system prevails in some countries, e. g., the English Taxing Office which decides what remuneration is fair and reasonable for interlocutory work by barristers and looks to the Bar and the solicitor profession for agreement upon "market rates." See Joint Statement by the Law Society and the Bar Council (1957). In the United States the private lawyer has remained free to agree with his client on a proper fee, with certain exceptions noted later in this section.

The lawyer has an obligation, founded on the fiduciary principle, to be fair and open in dealing with the client in the matter of charges. This involves not only competent service but keeping good records—to permit full disclosure of the basis of the charge—and a willingness to explain the reasons for a charge. It should seldom if ever be necessary to sue a client for a fee. The lawyer can always decline to serve again if the client fails to live up to his side of this delicate bargain—the lawyer-client relationship.

Fair and proper charges for a lawyer's services is a matter of concern to the profession as well as to the individual lawyer. The professional guidelines in fee-setting are detailed and in some instances, such as the contingent fee, may be supplemented by court rule or statute.

ELEMENTS TO BE CONSIDERED BY THE LAWYER IN FIXING HIS FEES

CODE OF PROFESSIONAL RESPONSIBILITY *

EC 2–17

The determination of a proper fee requires consideration of the interests of both client and lawyer. A lawyer should not charge more than a reasonable fee, for excessive cost of legal service would deter laymen from utilizing the legal system in protection of their rights. Furthermore, an excessive charge abuses the professional relationship between lawyer and client. On the other hand, adequate compensation is necessary in order to enable the lawyer to serve his client effectively and to preserve the integrity and independence of the profession.

* Copyright 1969 by the American Bar Association. Reprinted with permission.

EC 2-18

The determination of the reasonableness of a fee requires consideration of all relevant circumstances, including those stated in the Disciplinary Rules. The fees of a lawyer will vary according to many factors, including the time required, his experience, ability, and reputation, the nature of the employment, the responsibility involved, and the results obtained. Minimum and suggested fee schedules of state and local bar associations provide some guidance on the subject of reasonable fees.

DR 2-106 Fees for Legal Services

(A) A lawyer shall not enter into an agreement for, charge, or collect an illegal or clearly excessive fee.

(B) A fee is clearly excessive when, after a review of the facts, a lawyer of ordinary prudence would be left with a definite and firm conviction that the fee is in excess of a reasonable fee. Factors to be considered as guides in determining the reasonableness of a fee include the following:

(1) The time and labor required, the novelty and difficulty of the questions involved, and the skill requisite to perform the legal service properly.

(2) The likelihood, if apparent to the client, that the acceptance of the particular employment will preclude other employment by the lawyer.

(3) The fee customarily charged in the locality, for similar legal services.

(4) The amount involved and the results obtained.

(5) The time limitations imposed by the client or by the circumstances.

(6) The nature and length of the professional relationship with the client.

(7) The experience, reputation, and ability of the lawyer or lawyers performing the services.

(8) Whether the fee is fixed or contingent.

(C) A lawyer shall not enter into an arrangement for, charge, or collect a contingent fee for representing a defendant in a criminal case.

NOTES

(1) Why do you think the Rule requires that a fee be found to be "clearly excessive" before it will be forbidden?

(2) The fee arrangement is of course a matter of contract. Such a contract for compensation will be enforced, unless it appears to have been pro-

cured by fraud, deceit, overreaching, undue influence or through any other means which would move a court of equity to modify or set it aside. Rodkinson v. Haecker, 248 N.Y. 480, 489, 162 N.E. 493, 496 (1928). But see Matter of Krooks, Chapter XI, p. 432, supra. Who should have the burden of proof on the matters concerning whether a fee contract with a lawyer may be set aside?

(3) Where the lawyer's services under the contract with a client are not completed, should the usual contract rules apply or should the client be allowed to discharge the attorney and force him to seek recovery under the principles of quantum meruit? For a case favoring the client in this situation see Martin v. Camp, 219 N.Y. 170 (1916) cited in Matter of Krooks, supra, p. 432 and Andrewes v. Haas, supra p. 437. Per contra, the rule in Illinois and Pennsylvania would allow the attorney to enforce his rights under the contract where he has substantially performed. Eastman v. Blackledge, 171 Ill.App. 404 (1912), Kent v. Fishblate, 247 Pa. 361, 93 A. 509 (1915). See Note, 54 A.L.R.2d 608 (1957).

(4) A special guardian for decedent's infant granddaughter achieved a settlement with the executors which also benefited decedent's adult grandson. The surrogate allowed the guardian a fee to be charged against and paid out of the grandson's share in the estate. The grandson appealed from allowance of the fee. Held. ". . . an allowance for legal services (in such a situation) . . . may be properly made only in a proceeding or action brought by the attorney to fix and determine his compensation for services to his alleged client; . . . the retainer and compensation of attorneys being a matter of contract, express or implied (Judiciary Law Section 474), it follows that mere benefit resulting from legal services does not justify a fee. . . ." In re Linder's Estate, 17 App.Div.2d 949, 950, 234 N.Y.S.2d 53, 54, 55 (1962).

(5) On the historical development of the right to fees and to sue for them see Sommerich, *The History and the Development of Attorneys' Fees*, 6 Record of Ass'n. Bar City N. Y. 363 (1951); Adams v. Stevens & Cagger, 26 Wend. 451 (N.Y.1841).

TOUCHETT v. E Z PAINTER CORP.

Supreme Court of Wisconsin, 1961.
14 Wis.2d 479, 111 N.W.2d 419.

[An experienced Wisconsin lawyer represented a businessman for five years in enforcing a contract for the payment of royalties from a corporation. During this period seven separate suits were instituted against the corporation including one in the United States District Court for the Eastern District of Wisconsin. The client collected about $75,000 in royalties and was offered, but refused to accept, a settlement in excess of $270,000. Eventually the attorney was replaced and the matter of the fee due him for his professional services became the subject of litigation.

The attorney kept daily time records which were summarized as follows:

In circuit and county courts	23⅓ days
Before court commissioner	6½ days
In supreme court	3 days
In United States courts	2½ days
On other out-of-town business	14½ days
Office work, 1,307 hours, or	217⅚ days
	267⅔ days

He called prominent local attorneys as expert witnesses to testify with respect to the reasonable value of the legal services he had rendered. Taking into account customary charges in the area and the results attained their estimates of a fair value for these services ranged from $28,000 to $29,000. The trial judge awarded the attorney some $18,000 based largely on time spent at the rates suggested in the minimum fee schedule of the Wisconsin Bar Association.

The attorney appealed to the Supreme Court of Wisconsin.]

CURRIE, JUSTICE.

. . . One of the best statements of these factors we have come across is that appearing in Huffman's Estate, 1944, 349 Pa. 59, 64–65, 36 A.2d 640, 643, 151 A.L.R. 1384:

> "The things to be taken into consideration in determining the compensation to be recovered by an attorney are the amount and character of the services rendered, the labor, the time, and trouble involved, the character and importance of the litigation, the amount of money or value of the property affected, the professional skill and experience called for, and the standing of the attorney in his profession; to which may be added the general ability of the client to pay and the pecuniary benefit derived from the services." . . .

The general rule is that a trial court's findings of fact will not be disturbed on appeal unless contrary to the great weight and clear preponderance of the evidence. However, an exception to this rule exists with respect to determinations of the value of legal services. This is because the value of legal services is reviewed on appeal by judges who have expert knowledge as to the reasonable value of legal services. . . .

We are satisfied that the reasonable value of the professional services at issue on this appeal lies within the range of $28,400 to $29,500 covered by the expert testimony of attorneys McLeod, Edgarton, McGalloway and Nuss. It is our considered judgment that $28,512.50 is the total reasonable value of the services rendered by Sutherland to Touchett. The breakdown of this determination is as follows:

20 days in federal courts, the Wisconsin supreme court, and in performing other out-of-town business, at $150 per day	$ 3,000
29⅚ days in circuit and county courts and before court commissioners, at $125 per day	3,729.17
217⅚ days of office work at $100 per day	21,783.33
total:	$28,512.50

In view of this determination, Sutherland is entitled to be paid out of the funds on deposit with the clerk the sum of $28,512.50, less $9,404.10 previously paid by Touchett, or $19,108.40, together with the earnings realized on the sum of $19,108.40 during the period it was on deposit with the clerk. . . .

NOTES

(1) Are there other elements in determining the amount of a fee in addition to those described in the principal case?

> "The pecuniary ability of the client is an element in determining the reasonable value of an attorney's services." French v. Robert S. Abbott Publishing Co., Inc., 223 App.Div. 276 (1928) (two judges dissenting), affirmed 251 N.Y. 586 (1929) (three judges dissenting). See Note, 64 U.S.L.Rev. 169 (1930). Is this consistent with Disciplinary Rule 2–106, supra?

(2) How many chargeable hours can a lawyer count on? The New York State Bar Association has estimated that five hours per day is a safe average. Multiplying this by 250 working days (allowing for weekends and holidays) results in only 1250 chargeable hours in a year. See New York State Bar Association, Fee Consideration and Computation Fact Sheet issued in connection with Conference in New York City (1962).

(3) "I was quite struck by the answer Mr. Crapser gave in his testimony because it is so true. We talk about parts of days, but the truth of the matter is we never get the cases out of our heads. . . . The value of an attorney's services cannot be limited to specified and detailed bills of particulars with a specified amount for each item, as in the case of goods sold, or mere manual services rendered. . . . That is necessarily so, for the real value of an attorney's services may be the result of his thought about the legal questions involved, while away from his office, at home, or elsewhere. An idea thought out in bed at night may be the most valuable part of an attorney's services, and may constitute a solution of the vital question involved in a litigation." Matter of Potts, 213 App.Div. 59, 62, 209 N.Y.S. 655, 657, 659, aff'd 241 N.Y. 593, 150 N.E. 568 (1925).

A SCHEDULE OF FEES

A.B.A. OPINION 302 (1961).

The Habitual Charging of Fees Less Than Those Established by A Minimum Fee Schedule. . . .

The establishment of suggested or recommended minimum fee schedules by bar associations is a thoroughly laudable activity. The evils of fee cutting ought to be apparent to all members of the Bar. . . . Canon 12 . . . admonishes lawyers not to overcharge or to undervalue their services. When members of the Bar are induced to render legal services for inadequate compensation, as a consequence the quality of the service rendered may be lowered, the welfare of the profession injured and the administration of justice made less efficient. . . . Direct or indirect advertising by whatever means, that a lawyer habitually charges less than reasonable or minimum fees would, of course, be objectionable.

Canon 12 provides that in fixing his fees, it is proper for a lawyer to consider a schedule of minimum fees adopted by a bar association "not alone but along with other considerations"; however, it also provides that "no lawyer should permit himself to be controlled thereby or to follow it as his sole guide in determining the amount of the fee." While under the latter clause, this committee has consistently held that minimum fee schedules can only be suggested or recommended and cannot be made obligatory (Opinion 28), it is equally true that the habitual charging of fees less than that established in suggested or recommended minimum fee schedules, or the charging of such fees without proper justification may be evidence of unethical conduct, and the committee accordingly so holds, anything to the contrary in Opinion 190 being hereby overruled.

NOTE

Reference was made supra, p. 444, to the English practice of establishing a scale of fees for certain kinds of legal work. In the United States the law prescribes a *maximum* fee in some fields: e. g. workmen's compensation acts and claims by soldiers against the government. Or courts may establish certain norms for fees and require that a lawyer justify any excess over the norm. See Gair v. Peck, Chapter II, Section 5, supra p. 111.

DIVISION OF FEES

A.B.A. OPINION 854 (1962).

Question: X, who has been injured in an automobile accident, requests attorney A to represent him in making claims for his injuries. A agrees to represent X, but indicates to X that because he does not personally engage in this type practice, he will arrange for attorney B to handle the matter. A and B are not partners. A does not thereafter actively participate in the case and has no further direct relationship with X in respect to X's claims. Nevertheless, A is listed as counsel of record on all papers filed in court in respect of X's claims, and B, who handles X's case, is listed as "of counsel." The fee earned on the case is shared by A and B.

Is it proper for A to receive any share of the fee under the foregoing circumstances?

Answer: In accordance with Canon 34, the Committee has previously taken the position that the proper basis of the sharing of fees between lawyers is either the acceptance or the sharing of professional responsibility, or the sharing of professional services, and that it is not proper for a lawyer to receive compensation for merely recommending another lawyer to his client (see Opinions 123, 127, 500 and 592 of this Committee).

Since A has rendered no professional service to X, he is not entitled to any fee except to the extent that he has shared the responsibility of X's case. A's share in the responsibility of X's case has only been the listing of his name as counsel of record on court papers. In the absence of other participation by A in the case, the described activity constitutes only a very slight "division of . . . responsibility" within the meaning of Canon 34. Accordingly, it is proper for A to receive only an insignificant share of the fee paid by X commensurate with the small quantum meruit value of A's assumption of responsibility.

If a disclosure has not been made to the court of the nominal responsibility assumed by A for the conduct of the case, A, by permitting his name to be listed as counsel of record, and B, by filing papers in court listing A as counsel of record and listing B as "of counsel," have engaged in a misrepresentation to the court, which would appear to constitute a violation of Canon 22.

Of the fifteen members of the Committee present one dissented on the ground that A is not entitled to any part of the fee, and another on the ground that A having been retained by the client and having appeared as attorney of record has thereby assumed full responsibility for the case and therefore any arrangement between A and B as to division of the fee is proper.

NOTES

(1) "Lawyer 'A' refers a matter to Lawyer Jones for which 'A' accepts a one-third referral fee. 'A's' only connection with the case has been to hear the client's story and telephone Jones and inform him that he is sending over the client on the matter in question. 'A' has no further contact with the

client or with Lawyer Jones in this matter. What . . . (would you do) in this situation? . . ."

	Per Cent
Accept fee	67
Take more than one-third	1
Take less than one-third	2
Accept if client's fee is not affected	1
Not accept fee unless some work performed	25
No answer	4
	100

Answers found by Jerome Carlin in interviewing random sample of New York City bar as reported in Carlin, Lawyers' Ethics 200 (1966).

(2) The Code of Professional Responsibility, DR 2–107, sets out a requirement of disclosure to and consent by the client in addition to the requirement in Canon 34 that a division of fees between lawyers shall be in proportion to the services performed and the responsibility assumed by each. Should there be any further requirement in a fee-sharing arrangement in order to protect the client's interests?

What is the policy behind prohibiting fee sharing with a layman? Is it primarily (1) to protect clients; (2) to protect the bar; or (3) for some other purpose?

(3) The Internal Revenue Service found a deficiency of almost $1,000,000 against a taxpayer. In order to contest the deficiency, the taxpayer executed a contract between himself on the one hand and a lawyer and an accountant on the other, agreeing to pay them one-third of the total sum saved him. At the successful close of the matter (a settlement in the amount of $300,000) they presented a bill for some $200,000. The taxpayer refused to pay. The lawyer sued on the contract in his own behalf and as assignee of the accountant. The taxpayer defended on the grounds, inter alia, that the contract violated the provision then in the New York Penal Code prohibiting division of a fee between a lawyer and a layman, and was unenforceable. Reinstating a verdict for the plaintiff lawyer, the Court of Appeals commented favorably on the cooperation of lawyers and accountants in the tax area:

"It is of no consequence that their retainer was effected by a single agreement or that their compensation was to be equal or that it was specified in a lump sum contingency percentage, as long as the fee provided for the accountant was to be for accounting services rendered by him and the fee for the lawyer for legal services which he was to perform." Blumenberg v. Neubecker, 12 N.Y.2d 456, 461, 191 N.E.2d 269, 271 (1963). One judge dissented.

(4) Costs are often awarded to the prevailing party and against the losing party in a lawsuit. In the United States such costs generally do not include lawyer's fees. Why not? Compare the following:

"In England, the costs which the unsuccessful party has to pay consist (in substance) in the expense he has wrongfully made the other party incur; in other words, the unsuccessful party in England has to pay his opponent's lawyer's bill as well as his own. The possibility of having to pay the lawyer's bill of both parties to the action makes a plaintiff think twice before he sues out a writ and a defendant think twice before he defends an action which ought not be defended, and that is a direct deterrent on the number of cases put or kept in suit. . . . There is another reason for adopting the principle of substantial costs . . . (and) that is that it does justice. . . . On what principle of justice can a plaintiff wrongfully run down on a public highway recover his doctor's bill but not his lawyer's bill? And on what principle of justice is a defendant who has been wrongfully haled into court made to pay out of his own pocket the expense of showing that he was wrongfully sued?"

First Report of the Mass. Judicial Council, 11 Mass.L.Q., 63–64 (1925).

THE AMOUNT OF A CONTINGENT FEE

GAIR v. PECK

Court of Appeals of New York, 1959.
6 N.Y.2d 97, 188 N.Y.S.2d 491, 160 N.E.2d 43, cert. den. 361 U.S. 374,

(The case appears at p. 111, supra.)

PROTECTING THE ATTORNEY'S CLAIM FOR FEES

NOTE: ATTORNEY'S RETAINING LIEN OVER FORMER CLIENT'S PAPERS

65 Colum.L.Rev. 296, 298–300 (1965).

. . . At an early date the English courts recognized the right of an unpaid attorney to retain papers and other property given to him by his client in the course of their professional relationship. This right has come to be known as the attorney's "general" or "retaining lien"—"retaining" because the attorney may retain possession but may not satisfy his claim out of the property of the client. No jurisdiction in the United States has rejected the lien although some states have modified its strength by statutes. The federal courts have recognized the right of an attorney to assert a retaining lien in cases based on diversity of citizenship, bankruptcy, condemnation and employer liability.

. . .

Since a retaining lien can attach only to property that comes into the lawyer's possession in the course of and with respect to his employment as an attorney, the lien will not apply to documents received in the capacity of a trustee, or mortgagee, or in connection with transactions that do not concern strictly legal services. However, the distinction between receiving property from a client as an attorney or in other capacities is not always clear. Where the attorney's legal and nonlegal functions merge and become indistinguishable, the lien will probably be upheld. On the other hand, certain materials given in connection with legal services may not be held protected by the lien. If particular property is entrusted to an attorney for a special purpose that is itself nonlegal, the attorney's lien will not apply. Thus an attorney was required to surrender valuables given to him by a female client who has sought merely to deny possession to her estranged spouse. Similarly, the client was able to recover printed forms for the appeal of pending litigation which he had paid for and delivered to his attorney.

The effect of the retaining liens may be illustrated by comparison with the "charging" lien—another major weapon of the attorney seeking to collect his fees from recalcitrant clients. To aid the attorney who does not possess any of his client's papers or property, many states recognize the right to a charging lien which attaches to the judgment produced by the attorney's efforts. The attorney cannot assert a retaining lien against the proceeds of the judgment because it is deemed to be created by law and not capable of being possessed. The major advantage of the charging lien over the retaining lien— its enforceability in court—is balanced by its limitation to obligations incurred by the client during the particular action in which the judgment was awarded. The retaining lien, by contrast, applies to all papers that the attorney has received during the entire period of the attorney-client relationship. Whether the attorney worked on the papers in the period for which he claims money due is immaterial.

NOTES

(1) The charging lien may be enlarged to the extent that it attaches to a cause of action even before judgment. E. g., New York State Judiciary Law, Cons.Laws, ch. 30, sec. 475.

(2) The attorney in certain proceedings, e. g., an assignment for the benefit of creditors or the settlement of an estate, will be allowed a fee as an expense of administration. Such expenses may have priority even over taxes. Abrams v. United States, 274 F.2d 8 (8th Cir. 1960).

(3) "It seems well settled, and without authority to the contrary, that an attorney merely defeating a recovery against his client, a defendant, is not entitled to a lien on the property involved in the litigation." Wessinger v. Sturkie, 77 F.2d 751, 753 (4th Cir. 1935).

(4) ". . . The retaining lien has been characterized by the judiciary as being only of nuisance value to the attorney. In practical application, it has probably been more of a nuisance to the courts than to anyone else. In the absence of statutory guidelines as to how clients should proceed to obtain papers from attorneys' files, judges in most states have been uncertain and inconsistent in their determination of the correct procedure to be followed. Of course, the general practice of the parties is to work out a private arrangement among themselves. Nevertheless, the number of cases requiring judicial settlement is sufficient to merit a legislative resolution that will properly accommodate the conflicting interests of attorney and client. The most desirable solution might be to provide that, when a retaining lien is interposed in answer to a demand for papers by a former client, release of

the lien will be conditioned upon the client's posting bond security in the amount of the attorney's claim, and the merits will be postponed for later determination. The client would thus obtain the papers necessary to his litigation and the attorney, if his claim is valid, would be assured of eventual payment." 65 Colum.L.Rev., supra p. 452 at 308, 09.

SECTION 3. CONFIDENTIAL COMMUNICATIONS

THE PROFESSIONAL STANDARD

CODE OF PROFESSIONAL RESPONSIBILITY *

EC 4–1

Both the fiduciary relationship existing between lawyer and client and the proper functioning of the legal system require the preservation by the lawyer of confidences and secrets of one who has employed or sought to employ him. A client must feel free to discuss whatever he wishes with his lawyer and a lawyer must be equally free to obtain information beyond that volunteered by his client. A lawyer should be fully informed of all the facts of the matter he is handling in order for his client to obtain the full advantage of our legal system. It is for the lawyer in the exercise of his independent professional judgment to separate the relevant and important from the irrelevant and unimportant. The observance of the ethical obligation of a lawyer to hold inviolate the confidences and secrets of his client not only facilitates the full development of facts essential to proper representation of the client but also encourages laymen to seek early legal assistance.

EC 4–2

The obligation to protect confidences and secrets obviously does not preclude a lawyer from revealing information when his client consents after full disclosure, when necessary to perform his professional employment, when permitted by Disciplinary Rules, or when required by law. . . .

DR 4–101

Preservation of Confidences and Secrets of Clients.

(A) "Confidence" refers to information protected by the attorney-client privilege under applicable law, and "secret" refers to other information gained in the professional relationship which the client has requested be held inviolate or the publication of which would be embarrassing or likely to be detrimental to the client.

* Copyright 1969 by the American Bar Association. Reprinted with permission.

(B) Except as permitted by DR 4–101(C) a lawyer shall not knowingly:

(1) Reveal a confidence or secret of his client.

(2) Use a confidence or secret of his client to the disadvantage of that client.

(3) Use a confidence or secret of his client for the advantage of himself or of a third person, unless the client consents after full disclosure.

(C) A lawyer may reveal:

(1) Confidences or secrets with the consent of the client or clients affected, but only after full disclosure to them.

(2) Confidences or secrets when permitted by Disciplinary Rules or required by law or court order.

(3) The intention of his client to commit a crime and the information necessary to prevent the crime.

(4) Confidences or secrets necessary to establish or collect a fee or to defend himself or his employees or associates against an accusation of wrongful conduct. . . .

THE EVIDENTIARY RULE

WIGMORE, TREATISE ON EVIDENCE

Vol. 8, Sec. 2292 (McNaughton, rev. 1961).

(1) Where legal advice of any kind is sought (2) from a professional legal adviser in his capacity as such, (3) the communications relating to that purpose, (4) made in confidence (5) by the client, (6) are at his instance permanently protected (7) from disclosure by himself or by the legal adviser, (8) except the protection be waived.

NOTES

(1) "The words 'confidence' and 'confidences' as used in canons 7 and 37 include more than specific matters of fact or information which come to the lawyer on a confidential basis. They include also intangibles arising from the very nature of the lawyer-client relationship which result from natural discussion of the problems facing the client consideration of the problems by counsel and the advice given thereon, the rationale of the solutions proposed and the legal techniques by which such solutions are arrived at." Marco v. Dulles, 169 F.Supp. 622, 629 (S.D.N.Y.1959), appeal dismissed, 268 F.2d 192 (2d Cir. 1959).

(2) The scope of privileged communications under the professional standard is broader than the scope under the evidentiary rule. However, neither the standard nor the rule extend to matters which the law requires a lawyer to reveal. In a given situation the lawyer may find it painfully difficult to know what is required of him. Consider the following:

" . . . The privilege of confidential communication between client and attorney should be regarded as sacred. It is not to be whittled away by means of specious argument that it has been waived. . . . Here the attorney was compelled to testify against his client under threat of punishment for contempt. Such procedure would have been justified only in case the defendant with knowledge of his rights had waived the privilege in open court or by his statements and conduct had furnished explicit and convincing evidence that he did not understand, desire or expect that his statements to his attorney would be kept in confidence. Defendant's attorney should have chosen to go to jail and take his chances of release by a higher court. This is not intended as a criticism of the action of the attorney. It is, however, a suggestion to any and all attorneys who may have the misfortune to be confronted by the same or a similar problem." Shinn, P. J., concurring in People v. Kor, 129 Cal.App.2d 436, 446–47, 277 P.2d 94, 100–01 (1954).

(3) Is a corporation a "client" within the meaning of the professional standard and the evidentiary rule as to confidential or privileged communications? Is the attorney's "work product privilege" (Hickman v. Taylor, 329 U.S. 495, supra at p. 319), and protection given under the law to trade secrets sufficient protection in the corporate situation? In Radiant Burners, Inc. v. American Gas Ass'n, 320 F.2d 314 (7th Cir. 1963), the question was answered in favor of granting the privilege without regard to the corporate or non-corporate character of the client. The court warned, however, that the attorney-client privilege is not available to allow a corporation to funnel its papers and documents into the hands of its lawyers for custodial purposes and thereby avoid disclosure and that the requisite professional relationship is not established when the corporate client seeks business or personal advice as opposed to legal assistance. Accord. United States v. Bartone, 400 F.2d 459 (6th Cir. 1968), cert. denied 393 U.S. 1027 (1969).

(4) The reader will recall other examples in the casebook where the privilege of the attorney to reveal his client's confidences was at issue: e. g., the lawyer who is disqualified because he might make use of confidences against a former client (T. C. Theatre Corp. v. Warner Bros. Pictures, 113 F.Supp. 265, supra p. 417); the lawyer whose client is up for sentencing before a judge who is misinformed as to the facts (A.B.A.Op. 287, supra p. 311); the lawyer who testifies against a former client who has committed perjury (Gebhardt v. United Railways Company of St. Louis, supra p. 321).

SECTION 4. COMPETENCE AND CARE

Introduction. The standards of competence and care of the lawyer, as his other standards, may be set at different levels according to the several sanctions. (See Chapter III supra.) The law itself may provide a variety of sanctions and a corresponding difference in the level of expertness called for. It may apply one standard in determining the right of an accused to a new trial in a criminal case, yet another in a civil case, and still a third in determining whether the lawyer is under a personal liability to the client. The minimum disciplinary standard and the ethical standard recommended in the Code of Professional Responsibility may be set at different levels. The individual's own standard may vary from lawyer to lawyer as, indeed, they appear to do in the following statements by Messrs. Miller and Drinker when one man was apparently thinking of an especially difficult field of law appropriate only for the expert and the other had in mind the general practitioner.

JOHN S. MILLER, FUNCTIONS AND ETHICAL PROBLEMS OF THE LAWYER IN DRAFTING A WILL

1950 Illinois Law Forum 415, 419, 423 (1950).

Without attempting to formulate the rules [on the ethical obligations of a lawyer in drafting a will], it is submitted that they are based upon three fundamental duties: (1) Loyalty. (2) Integrity. (3) Competency.

One might urge that loyalty alone is a sufficient basis for this ethics; that one cannot be loyal without also being both honest and competent. This may be true. . . .

Indeed, it would be no exaggeration to say that of all the moral obligations of the lawyer who undertakes to prepare a will the obligation of competence is paramount. . . . No lawyer should prepare a will unless he considers himself competent to do so. He should approach this question with a realization that to the client the will is probably the most important document of his life. . . . The property may be the result of a lifetime of effort. Its disposition will have lasting and significant effect both upon those included as beneficiaries and upon those excluded who might naturally expect or hope to be included. . . . If the lawyer doubts his ability to produce the best possible will for the client, he should decline to prepare one.

NOTES

(1) Mr. Drinker has written: "A lawyer should not presume to undertake professional employment for which he is not reasonably competent but should recommend or at least associate a specialist." Drinker, Legal Ethics 139 (1953). What is the bearing of this on the general practitioner? The field of which Mr. Miller wrote may be so complex that the general practitioner is unable to gain an adequate knowledge of it in working on one case without an inordinate amount of study. Other fields may be different. Compare, "Duty of physician or surgeon to advise patient of the possibility or probability of better results from treatment by specialist or by a mode of treatment which he is not qualified to give". 132 A.L.R. 392, Anno. (1941).

(2) If the situation envisioned by Mr. Drinker in note (1) calls for special competence in some profession other than law, is there a comparable duty to recommend or at least associate a collaborator in the other profession? See discussion in Chapter II, Section 7, supra, p. 140, and Blumenberg v. Neubecker, supra p. 451.

TRIMBOLI v. KINKEL

Court of Appeals of New York, 1919.
226 N.Y. 147, 123 N.E. 205, 5 A.L.R. 1385.

CARDOZO, J. This is an action by client against attorney.

In 1906 the plaintiffs retained the defendant to search the title to land in Brooklyn which the plaintiffs were about to buy. The defendant reported that the title was good and marketable. He made up an abstract which he delivered to his clients. This abstract shows that in 1861 title was in Aaron Clark and Harriet A. Anderson as tenants in common. Mr. Clark left a will by which his real estate passed to devisees in fee. Power to sell the land and divide the proceeds was given to the executor. The executor in 1863 conveyed his testator's undivided interest to the co-tenant, Harriet A. Anderson. The grantee in return conveyed to the executor an interest in another parcel. The transaction was not a sale for money, but an exchange. Its nature is disclosed by the deed, which is described in the abstract. Harriet A. Anderson conveyed the land in 1868 to one Frederick W. Grimme, whose title passed thereafter, by mesne conveyances, to the plaintiffs' vendors. The law is settled that a power to sell and distribute the proceeds is not a power to exchange (Woerz v. Rademacher, 120 N.Y. 62, 68; Moran v. James, 21 App.Div. 183, 185; Woodward v. Jewell, 140 U.S. 247, 253). There was, therefore, a flaw in the record title. The defendant made no mention of it to his clients. He made no investigation of the occupation of the land. He supplied no evidence of adverse possession. He let his clients complete the purchase on the assumption that the record title was perfect. In 1910 the plaintiffs made a contract of resale. The purchaser rejected title because of the flaw in the record. The defendant represented the plaintiffs at the closing. Even then he supplied no evidence of adverse possession. He made no claim that title could be sustained upon that ground. His position still was that the record title was sufficient. The purchaser sued for the deposit and expenses of searching title. The sellers defended. They were then represented by new counsel. The purchaser prevailed, and the title was adjudged unmarketable (Turco v. Trimboli, 152 App.Div. 431). This action was then brought to compel the attorney to respond for the damages resulting from his negligence. In defense he has attempted to prove that the defect in the record title has been cured by adverse possession for more than fifty years. The trial judge held that, with this evidence available, there was a marketable title, and that the defendant had not been negligent. The complaint was dismissed upon the merits. The Appellate Division ruled that "the defendant was negligent in passing the title upon the view that the executor's deed was valid." It, therefore, reversed the judgment and ordered a new trial.

We agree with the Appellate Division that negligence was proved. The executor's deed was plainly invalid. It is negligence to fail to apply the settled rules of law that should be known to all conveyancers. . . . In the absence of clear and cogent evidence of adverse possession, the title was unmarketable (Freedman v. Oppenheim, 187 N.Y. 101). That evidence, if it existed, should have been gathered by the defendant, and preserved in fitting form, before title was accepted (Crocker Point Association v. Gouraud, 224 N.Y. 343, 350). Nothing of the kind was done. Mere lapse of time was insufficient without proof of a hostile holding (Simis v. McElroy, 160 N.Y. 156). The defendant does not acquit himself of negligence by showing that evidence could have been collected. He must show that it was collected. Until that duty had been fulfilled, the title was unmarketable.

The question remains whether there is any evidence of damage. . . . [The court found there was evidence of damage and affirmed the order of the Appellate Division.]

NOTES

(1) In this case the defendant, who had been employed to search a title, was held liable for failing to know that a trustee's power to sell is not equivalent to a power to exchange. Is the court employing a standard applicable only to specialists in conveyances or one applicable to ordinary attorneys whenever they handle a conveyance? See further discussion under "Specialist and Generalist," beginning infra p. 461.

(2) Should a lawyer be held liable for failure to know and comply with the law of a state other than one in which he is admitted to the bar? For conflicting views see Fenaille v. Coudert, 44 N.J.L. 286 (1882), and Degen v. Steinbrink, 202 App.Div. 477, 195 N.Y.S. 810 (1922), affirmed 236 N.Y. 669, 142 N.E. 328 (1923). As to the liability of a lawyer for the negligence of an associated lawyer, see Note, 47 Harv.L.Rev. 1056 (1934).

(3) The emphasis has been on the standard of the lawyer. As the tradition of service to clients in law firms spreads to the middle class (group legal services) and to the poor (legal aid) how do we establish and enforce standards of competence for legal service agencies? For one suggestion see Elson, *Accreditation of Legal Service Agencies,* 53 A.B.A.J. 415 (1967).

(4) The theory of an action for professional malpractice by a lawyer may be based upon breach of an attorney's implied promise to use reasonable skill and diligence or upon violation of a duty to employ due care, the violation of which gives rise to a liability in tort. See Note, *Attorney Malpractice,* 63 Colum.L.Rev. 1292 (1963). See also Wade, *The Attorney's Liability for Negligence,* 12 Vand.L.Rev. 755 (1959).

(5) See Code of Professional Responsibility:

"DR 6–101 Failing to Act Competently.

(A) A lawyer shall not:

(1) Handle a legal matter which he knows or should know that he is not competent to handle, without associating with him a lawyer who is competent to handle it.

(2) Handle a legal matter without preparation adequate in the circumstances.

(3) Neglect a legal matter entrusted to him.

DR 6–102 Limiting Liability to Client.

(A) A lawyer shall not attempt to exonerate himself from or limit his liability to his client for his personal malpractice."

If a client believes that his lawyer has indeed taken on a matter beyond his competence and has handled it negligently can the client cite the Code as the standard to which his lawyer must be held? See Preamble to the Code of Professional Responsibility: ". . . nor does it (the Code) undertake to define standards for civil liability of lawyers for professional conduct." What reason do you suggest for this disclaimer?

(6) Beginning in the 1950's some bar associations have established security accounts, either funded with an insurance carrier or self-funded, to meet claims of clients for reimbursement of losses which arise from the conduct of attorneys who are not themselves financially responsible. These client security funds are set up to cover defalcations; not to meet malpractice claims. See Bryan, *Clients' Security Funds Ten Years Later*, 55 A.B.A.J. 757 (1969).

(7) For a discussion of auditing powers and procedures to compel accountability in court for trust money in the possession of attorneys see Blackman v. Hale, 78 Cal.Rptr. 567 (1969).

COMPETENCE OF COUNSEL IN A CRIMINAL CASE

In Chapter I, Section 6, we noted the importance of having counsel in a criminal case.

> "Lawyers to prosecute are everywhere deemed essential to protect the public's interest in an orderly society. Similarly, there are few defendants charged with crime, few indeed, who fail to hire the best lawyers they can get to prepare and present their defenses. . . . The right of one charged with crime to counsel may not be deemed fundamental and essential in fair trials in some countries, but it is in ours." Justice Black writing for the Court in Gideon v. Wainwright, 372 U.S. 335, 344 (1963).

Does "counsel" mean, by implication, "competent counsel" and if so, to what standards shall the courts look in enforcing the right? Does it make any difference if a criminal defendant chooses his own counsel—and thereby makes him his agent—or if counsel is appointed by the court? These are difficult questions which the courts have tried to answer as they arose.

NOTES

(1) In a leading case involving the competence of counsel selected by the defendant, two judges differed in the importance of the effective assistance of counsel: "Was the failure of [appellant's] . . . counsel to present evidence of his [client's] alleged previous good character and as to his mental condition due to incompetency or lack of preparation, or was it a part of a well thought out plan of defense? . . . [Appellant] was en-

titled to be competently defended by counsel learned in the law. Though questions of degrees of competency and learning may always be present there is assuredly a level below which the courtroom performance of counsel representing a defendant in a capital case may not sink or the Fourteenth Amendment will be encountered . . . nor should it be deemed to be a pertinent distinction that the defendant's counsel is selected by himself or by members of his family or his friends rather than appointed by the court." Biggs, Chief Judge. ". . . There is, however, . . . 'a vast difference between lacking the effective assistance of competent counsel and being denied the right to have the effective assistance of competent counsel'. It is the latter only for which the state is responsible, the former being normally the sole responsibility of the defendant who selected his counsel . . .". Maris, Circuit Judge. United States ex rel. Darcy v. Handy, 203 F.2d 407, 416–17, 26 (3d Cir. 1953), cert. denied, 346 U.S. 865 (1953).

(2) "Court-appointed counsel generally are held to a very high standard of professional duty to a client, whereas retained counsel in criminal cases have been allowed to proceed in the most negligent and reckless manner without the helpless defendant having any recourse." Polur, *Retained Counsel, Assigned Counsel: Why the Dichotomy?* 55 A.B.A.J. 254 (1969).

(3) What should be the significance of the fact that counsel for accused is of his own choosing? For consideration of this and other matters relating to the setting aside of a criminal conviction because of incompetency of counsel, see discussion following report of Lunce v. Overlade, 244 F.2d 108 (7th Cir. 1957) in 7 A.L.R.2d 1384 (1960).

(4) Does establishment of this "fundamental and essential" right in criminal proceedings in state courts as well as in the federal courts (*Gideon*) imply the need to develop higher and more uniform standards of competence on the part of counsel for the defense?

SPECIALIST AND GENERALIST

A mark of our times is the swift development of the natural sciences and derivative technologies. There have been accompanying developments of the social sciences, and of a popular insistence that government take a more active role in economic and social matters.

Inevitably, these immense and continuing developments in knowledge and in attitude find their reflection in law and its practice. If anyone doubts it, let him consider the changes in economic and social life, in government and in law, during the past fifty years. Then let him seek to project the even swifter developments that are pretty certain over the next fifty years.

A result of these developments is that no lawyer can now have an adequate working knowledge of the law on all the subjects that naturally come into the office of the general practitioner. Nor can a lawyer acquire an adequate working knowledge of the law on all these subjects in a length of time that will make practicable a fee for services that is fair to the client and fair to the lawyer. Yet the client is entitled to adequate representation for a fair fee, and the lawyer is required by his professional standards as well as by the rules of law to be competent in the matters which he undertakes to handle. The client is entitled, too, to something more from lawyers than answers on specialized questions of law. He needs wise counsel on his problems as an integrated whole, a matter which the specialist who focuses on a particular aspect of it may overlook.

There are three points of impact of the needs for the specialist as well as the generalist that call for mention here. One is the lawyer in practice: How will the lawyer see to it that the combined needs of the client are met? Another is the organized bar: what methods will the bar support and develop to further the needed cooperation of the specialist and the generalist? A third is the law student: what will and should he do because of these developments? Some comments and questions are offered for the consideration of the reader.

The Lawyer in Practice. The large corporate law office is essentially an example of the group practice of law, with specialized resources within it, to which the general practitioner in the firm may resort when the needs of the client call for it. The solo practitioner or member of a small firm is in a very different situation. He may associate a specialist when needed in a particular case. Yet there are difficulties in the way. The client, not accustomed as is the patient in medicine to the calling of a specialist, may lose all confidence in his lawyer because of this admission of lack of omniscience in law. Then there is the problem of fee-splitting, and the danger of the specialist taking over the client. How should the practitioner deal with the matter?

The Organized Bar. The American Bar Association after an earlier abortive effort has taken up consideration of the problem. (1) Should the organized bar make the public aware that there is need for the specialist as well as the generalist in law; and will such action by the bar be injurious to and resented by the generalist? (2) Should methods be adopted to qualify and identify dependable specialists in various fields of practice through training, testing, and certification? (3) Should the association of generalist and specialist be facilitated by a system for making dependable specialists known to the generalist? (4) What measures are called for to protect the several interests involved, as, the client from needless or excessive charges, the generalist from excessive claims and publicity by the specialist, the generalist from having his client taken away by the specialist who is associated in a matter?

The Law Student. The law school, the law student, and the young lawyer have interlocking problems, which can be indicated in terms of the law student. How much specialization should the student seek to develop in the law school years? What are the ends of specialization of intensive work or specialization in law school: knowledge of the particular area or the development of intellectual power for use in any field? Who should point toward specialization in law school or later, and who toward general practice; and does the answer to this question turn on such personal elements, as, temperament, abilities, opportunities? Does the law school have a duty or an opportunity to aid the development of specialized knowledge and ability and, it may be, to revive the breadth of view of the generalist as well as the specialist, in the years of practice; and may this be done most effectively in cooperation with the organized bar?

NOTES

(1) Former Dean Russell D. Niles in an article citing much of the literature on the question of specialization in the law suggests that before the profession grants further recognition to specialists it should agree on the following rules of practice:

"a) A lawyer should be under a duty to recommend or associate a specialist when required for competent handling of a client's problem;

b) When a client's lawyer has associated a specialist with him or has referred his client to a specialist, the specialist must advise the client to return to the forwarding lawyer and must decline to accept employment from the client for matters outside his specialty even if the client refuses to return to his original lawyer;

c) A specialist should be allowed to make his special competence known to other lawyers but not to the public as a means of attracting clients directly." Niles, *Ethical Prerequisites to Certification of Special Proficiency*, 49 A.B.A.J. 83, 84 (1963).

(2) In the article noted above Dean Niles points out that the medical profession generally recognizes the validity of Rules "a" and "b" but that there is no rule against a physician making his special competence known directly to the public. What reasons can you suggest for making this distinction between the two professions?

(3) If the specialist is practicing before a federal tribunal, Dean Niles' Rule "c" may be desired by the local bar but unenforceable. See Silverman v. State Bar of Texas, 405 F.2d 410 (5th Cir., 1969).

(4) "A strong movement is underway in the American Bar Association and in several states to establish legal specialties comparable to medical specialties. The Section of General Practice is vitally interested in this movement and intends to make oral and written presentations to various ABA and state committees which are dealing with the establishment of legal specialties. The Section will emphasize to such committees the importance of the lawyer in general practice, both to the public and to the profession.

"The Section will also point out to such committees that any plan of certifying specialists involves extremely complex questions regarding methods of certifying, qualifications necessary to obtain certification, and whether certificated specialists will be entitled to serve the public or will be limited to serving other lawyers.

"The Section of General Practice takes the position that lawyers conversant in many fields of law are best able to identify legal problems, to act as counselors in the broad sense of the word, and to refer particular problems to specialist attorneys when advisable. In this area and others, such as the development of various kinds of group legal service, general practitioners need someone to represent their veiwpoint." From a letter dated August 23, 1968, to ABA members sent out in behalf of the Section of General Practice.

(5) For perspective on specialization and on the use of specialists in other professions by lawyers see Cheatham, A Lawyer When Needed, (1963), especially Chapter 5.

(6) Why does the Code of Professional Responsibility DR 2–105(A) authorize a lawyer who is admitted to practice as a proctor in admiralty or a patent lawyer to state his specialty on his letter head or shingle and deny such a privilege to other lawyers?

(7) Code of Professional Responsibility DR 2–102(A) (6) authorizes publication of law lists. A publisher of one such list rates lawyers "a", "b" or "c" according to reputed legal ability. Also, in the biographical section of this list lawyers may state that they practice in such areas as accounting law, antitrust and trade association law, estate planning, federal taxation, etc. Do such listings raise problems relating to claims of special competence which call for attention by the bar? See Harnsberger, *Publication of Specialties and Legal Ability Rating in Law Lists*, 49 A.B.A.J. 33 (1963).

(8) To what extent does recognition of specialization in a branch of the practice of law imply certification of competence therein? How might such special competence be determined? What special training might be required and should such training be assumed by law schools or conducted by bar associations as continuing legal education?

SECTION 5. INJURIES TO THIRD PARTIES

WAUGH v. DIBBENS

Supreme Court of Oklahoma, 1916.
61 Okl. 221, 160 P. 589, L.R.A.1917B, 360.

Opinion by RITTENHOUSE, C. . . . Le Roy E. Waugh brought an action against the Guthrie Gas, Light, Fuel & Improvement Company for injuries alleged to have been received on account of an explosion. After the petition was filed the defendant served notice to take depositions before Hon. J. C. Strang, judge of the county court of Logan county, at which hearing the plaintiff, Le Roy E. Waugh, was sworn as a witness and testified to certain matters. When asked as to the name of the physician, living in Missouri, who attended him during his injuries, he refused to testify, whereupon Frank Dale, attorney for the company, requested and procured an order punishing him for contempt. The defendant was subsequently discharged by this court in Ex parte Waugh, 40 Okl. 188, 137 P. 105, . . . this action was brought against J. C. Strang, who was the judge of the county court of Logan county, and issued the commitment and Frank Dale, who was the attorney for the company, . . . asking judgment in the sum of $16,347, for an alleged false imprisonment, occasioned by his refusal to testify in the original action.

[The trial judge found for the defendants, without letting the case go to the jury, and the plaintiff appealed.]

We now come to the question of the liability of an attorney for an alleged false imprisonment. . . . It became material in the trial of the damage suit to ascertain the facts connected with the plaintiff's injuries, and the company through its attorney was attempting to elicit from the witness the name of the physician who attended him during his confinement resulting from such injuries, this the witness refused to answer, whereupon the attorney requested that he be punished for contempt. There was no evidence of bad faith or malicious motive. Anderson et al. v. Canaday, 37 Okl. 171, 131 P. 697, L.R.A.1915A, 1186, Ann.Cas.1915B, 714. He was merely representing his client in his capacity as an attorney at law, requesting an order which he was entitled to have, but which was held to be void because the order for commitment failed to show the question propounded to the witness, and that such question was pertinent and material to the issue in the action for damages. Upon a thorough examination of the authorities, we are convinced that the general rule is that attorneys at law, in the exercise of their proper functions as such, are not liable for their acts, if such acts are made in good faith and pertinent to the matter in question, and when in the course of a judicial proceeding a witness refuses to answer a question which is pertinent and material to the issue involved, and the attorney requests that such witness be punished for contempt, the attorney is not liable in damages for false imprisonment. . . .

NOTES

(1) May an attorney be liable in an action for slander because of words spoken in the course of a trial? ". . . in such a case the words alleged to have been spoken by the defendant . . . in his capacity as counsel, to the effect that plaintiff had in his possession money which he had collected for and which belonged to defendants, had reference to the subject matter of inquiry before the court, and if they had reference or relation to the case on trial, then they are strictly within the rule of privilege and whether they were true or false, or whether they were spoken maliciously or in good faith, are questions altogether immaterial,—being privileged no action will lie against the defendant." Maulsby v. Reifsnider, 69 Md. 143, 164, 14 A. 505, 511 (1888). See also, Gregoire v. Biddle, 177 F.2d 579 (2d Cir. 1949), cert. den. 339 U.S. 949 (1950).

(2) The immunity of the lawyer from personal liability for damages in an action for defamation is not a bar to professional discipline. In People v. Green, 9 Colo. 506, 13 P. 514, 524, 526 (1887), the court said: "He enjoys this privilege by virtue of his license as an attorney. The gist of the complaint in this proceeding is that the respondents have abused this privilege, and that they are unfit persons to hold the license of this court, and to exercise and enjoy the rights and privileges which it confers."

(3) However, a lawyer will be allowed great leeway in making motions highly critical of the court (Blankenbaker v. State, 201 Ind. 142, 166 N.E. 265 (1929)) or of the application of law by the court or of court procedure (In re Sawyer, 360 U.S. 622 (1959), or even of individual judges (Garrison v. Louisiana, 379 U.S. 64 (1964), Chapter VII, page 287 supra.

Do disciplinary proceedings against attorneys deter free and open discussion of essentially public matters? Should such proceedings be subject to constitutional limitations as in the area of civil and criminal defamation? Cf. Holt v. Com. of Virginia, 381 U.S. 131 (1965).

(4) As to the exemption of an attorney from service of process while in attendance in connection with a suit, see Lamb v. Schmitt, 285 U.S. 222 (1932); Thornton, A Treatise on Attorneys at Law, Secs. 73, 74; 71 A.L.R. 1399 (1914), anno. 1931.

LUCAS v. HAMM

Supreme Court of California, 1961.
56 Cal.2d 583, 15 Cal.Rptr. 821, 364 P.2d 685.

GIBSON, C. J. Plaintiffs who are beneficiaries under the will of Eugene H. Emmick, deceased, brought this action for damages against Hamm, an attorney at law who had been engaged by the testator to prepare the will. They have appealed from a judgment of dismissal entered after an order sustaining a general demurrer to the second amended complaint without leave to amend.

The allegations . . . are summarized as follows: Defendant agreed with the testator for a consideration, to prepare a will and codicils thereto by which plaintiffs were to be designated as beneficiaries of a trust . . . and were to receive 15% of the residue. . . . Defendant, in violation of instructions and in breach of his contract, negligently prepared testamentary instruments containing phraseology that was invalid by virtue of . . . sections . . . of the Civil Code relating to restraints on alienation and the rule against perpetuities. (footnote omitted) . . . After the death of the testator the instruments were admitted to probate. Subsequently defendant, as . . . counsel of record for the executors, advised plaintiffs in writing that the residual trust provision was invalid and that plaintiffs would be deprived of the entire amount to which they would have been entitled if the provision had been valid unless they made a settlement with the blood relatives of the testator under which plaintiffs would receive a lesser amount than that provided for them by the testator.

[They settled for $75,000 less than they would have received under the will.]

It was held in Buckley v. Gray, 110 Cal. 339, 42 P. 900, 31 L.R. A. 862, that an attorney who made a mistake in drafting a will was not liable for negligence or breach of contract to a person named in the will . . . The court stated that an attorney is liable to his client alone . . . and it was reasoned that there could be no recovery for mere negligence where there was no privity by contract or otherwise between the defendant and the person injured. . . . The court further concluded that there could be no recovery on the theory of a contract for the benefit of a third person, because the contract with the attorney was not expressly for the plaintiff's benefit and the testatrix only remotely intended the plaintiff to be benefited as a result of the contract. . . . For the reasons hereinafter stated the case is overruled.

The reasoning underlying the denial of tort liability in the Buckley case, i. e., the stringent privity test, was rejected in Biakanja v. Irving, 49 Cal.2d 647, 648–650, 320 P.2d 16, 65 A.L.R.2d 1358, where we held that a notary public who, although not authorized to practice law, prepared a will but negligently failed to direct proper attestation was liable in tort to an intended beneficiary who was damaged because of the invalidity of the instrument. It was pointed out that since 1895, when Buckley was decided, the rule that in the absence of privity there was no liability for negligence committed in the performance of a contract had been greatly liberalized. . . . In restating the rule it was said that the determination whether in a specific case the defendant will be held liable to a third person not in privity is a matter of policy and involves the balancing of various factors, among which are the extent to which the transaction was intended to affect the plaintiff, the foreseeability of harm to him, the degree of certainty that the plaintiff suffered injury, the closeness of the connection between the defendant's conduct and the injury and the policy of preventing future harm. . . . The same general principle must be applied in determining whether a beneficiary is entitled to bring an action for negligence in the drafting of a will when the instrument is drafted by an attorney rather than by a person not authorized to practice law.

[The court went on to excuse the attorney from liability because of the difficulty of interpreting the rules relating to perpetuities and restraints on alienation noting that "these closely akin subjects have long perplexed the courts and the bar" and quoting Professor Gray in The Rule Against Perpetuities (4th ed. 1942) at page xi: "There is something in the subject which seems to facilitate error." The court said that it would not be proper in the circumstances to hold that defendant failed to use such skill, prudence and diligence as lawyers of ordinary skill and capacity commonly exercise.]

Affirmed.

Certiorari to the United States Supreme Court was denied. 368 U.S. 987 (1962).

NOTES

(1) In Lucas v. Hamm would liability have attached if the attorney had held himself out as a specialist in the drafting of wills rather than as a general practitioner?

(2) Testatrix retained a lawyer to draw a will. She told him she wanted her estate to go to her children. She also told him she was going to marry soon after. The lawyer drew a will leaving everything to the children. It did not refer to the prospective husband except to name him executor. The lawyer neglected to tell her that under California law a will executed before marriage is void as to the surviving spouse unless the spouse is provided for in the will or it shows an intent not to provide for him. Ten days after executing the above will Testatrix married. Some seven months thereafter, she died, her will was admitted to probate and the widower claimed a portion of the estate as a post-testamentary spouse.

Alleging these facts, testatrix's children brought an action for negligence against the attorney. The attorney answered with a general demurrer. The court ruled that the complaint stated a cause of action. "The duty thus recognized in *Lucas* [v. Hamm, Supra] stems from the attorney's undertaking to perform legal services for the client but reaches out to protect the intended beneficiary. We impose this duty because of the relationship between the attorney and the intended beneficiary; public policy requires that the attorney exercise his position of trust and superior knowledge responsibly so as not to affect adversely persons whose rights and interests are certain and forseeable." Hyer v. Flaig, 74 Cal.Rptr. 225, 229, 449 P.2d 161, 165 (1969).

(3) In Investment Corporation of Florida v. Buchman, 208 So.2d 291 (Fla.App., 1968), a case involving possible liability of an accountant for acting negligently with respect to parties not in privity with him, the court compares the approach of Judge Cardozo in Ultramares Corporation v. Touche, 255 N.Y. 170 (1931), with that of the California Supreme Court in Biakanja v. Irving, the case involving a notary public cited in the principal case, Lucas v. Hamm, supra. Judge Cardozo drew back from allowing negligence, (as distinguished from fraud) as a basis for liability to persons not in privity with the offending professional. In contrast, The California court allowed recovery by a beneficiary under a will against the notary public.

A possible intermediate ground is to allow a jury to infer fraud from grossly negligent failure on the part of the accountant or other professional. This position was adopted by a later New York Court in State Street Trust Co. v. Ernst, 278 N.Y. 104, 15 N.E.2d 416 (1938).

The court in the 1968 Florida case (Investment Corporation of Florida v. Buchman, supra) opts for this intermediate position of potential liability for an accountant. See discussion in Note, 23 Univ. of Miami L.Rev. 256 (1968).

(4) As to the possible liability of lawyers as well as accountants and others for false registration statements in connection with securities, see Securities Act of 1933, sec. 11, U.S.C.A. Tit. 15, § 77K.

Part Four

PERSONNEL OF THE PROFESSION

Chapter XIII

THE LAWYER: EDUCATION, ADMISSION, DISCIPLINE

SECTION 1. LEGAL EDUCATION

HOLMES, HUGHES, CARDOZO ON LEGAL EDUCATION
OLIVER WENDELL HOLMES, THE USE OF LAW SCHOOLS

(1886), in Collected Legal Papers 36–37, 47–48 (1920).

A law school does not undertake to teach success. That combination of tact and will which gives a man immediate prominence among his fellows comes from nature, not from instruction; and if it can be helped at all by advice, such advice is not offered here. It might be expected that I should say, by way of natural antithesis, that what a law school does undertake to teach is law. But I am not ready to say even that, without a qualification. It seems to me that nearly all the education which men can get from others is moral, not intellectual. The main part of intellectual education is not the acquisition of facts, but learning how to make facts live. Culture, in the sense of fruitless knowledge, I for one abhor. The mark of a master is, that facts which before lay scattered in an inorganic mass, when he shoots through them the magnetic current of his thought leap into an organic order, and live and bear fruit. But you cannot make a master by teaching. He makes himself by aid of his natural gifts.

Education, other than self-education, lies mainly in the shaping of men's interests and aims. If you convince a man that another way of looking at things is more profound, another form of pleasure more subtle than that to which he has been accustomed—if you make him really see it—the very nature of man is such that he will desire the profounder thought and the subtler joy. So I say the business of a law school is not sufficiently described when you merely say that it is to teach law, or to make lawyers. It is to teach law in the grand manner, and to make great lawyers.

CHARLES EVANS HUGHES, SOME OBSERVATIONS ON LEGAL EDUCATION AND DEMOCRATIC PROGRESS

Page 25 (1920).

The service of the law school is that of method and cooperation, of standards and ideals. It does not supply brains or tact, or any substitute for either. It can give but a modicum of legal learning, less now, relatively, than ever. The best informed among us can know but a small part of the law, . . . He [the law student returning from law school to his State] sees at once, if he did not appreciate it before, that little has counted in his preparation but method and self-discipline.

And in this feeling of bewilderment and sense of the only path to mastery, there is nothing new. How did the masters arrive in the absence of great law schools? . . . There is only one answer. The great lawyer has always been a great teacher and his best pupil is himself.

BENJAMIN N. CARDOZO, LAW AND THE UNIVERSITY

47 Law Quarterly Review 19 (1931).

I was reading a while ago some words of Dr. Alfred Whitehead, formerly of Cambridge and now of Harvard University, that gave me food for thought. A university, he wrote, is a place where one is to teach learning imaginatively, and so indeed it is. . . . Well, now, that is quite as true of law as it is of anything else. Conspicuously it is true of the creative process by which day by day and hour by hour the body of the law renews itself at the hands of its disciples. . . . We are trying to teach law and to study it scientifically, and yet imaginatively too,—feeling our way to a new sense of its significance, of the forces that have brought it into being, of the processes that are keeping it alive, and of the ends that it must serve and foster if its high potencies are not to fail.

NOTE

(1) For a history of legal education, see Harno, Legal Education in the United States (1953)

TO ASSURE THAT REPRESENTATION IS EFFECTIVE

WARREN E. BURGER, A CHALLENGE TO CURRENT LEGAL EDUCATION, ADDRESS AT THE ANNUAL MEETING OF PHI ALPHA DELTA LAW FRATERNITY, WASHINGTON, D. C. (1968).

Since we are a professional legal brotherhood, one of our first concerns has been—and rightly so—the making of better lawyers to serve Mankind in a period when the next imperative after peace among nations is the pursuit of peace within our own society. We have called this "law and order," but some people now seek to give that good phrase a sinister twist and make it mean something oppressive. If we say the goal of society must be the maintenance of order under the rule of law with justice, I trust no one can distort that concept into something that it is not. An ordered society which is based on justice is something more than one in which lawbreakers are punished and streets are safe places. It is also a society in which the ruthless and greedy are restrained from exploiting the weak; it is a society in which the simple and even the foolish are protected by rules of law from oppression by the superior cunning of other elements.

. . . Today you lawyers are more important to the functioning of an organized society than even the police or the courts who are the coercive instruments. This is true because you, as lawyers, can exercise the function of peace makers—providing the lubricants which reduce the frictions of our complex society.

The instrument we have chosen in this country to train and educate lawyers to perform this crucial function is, then, a vital part of our total social mechanism. That instrument, of course, is the Law School, sometimes a free-standing institution, but more often part of a university complex.

To be sure that my point will emerge clearly from the underbrush of all that I say, I will, at the outset, state my thesis. It is this: THE MODERN LAW SCHOOL IS FAILING IN ITS BASIC DUTY TO PROVIDE SOCIETY WITH PROBLEM-ORIENTED AND PEOPLE-ORIENTED COUNSELORS AND ADVOCATES TO MEET THIS BROAD SOCIAL NEED. This failure is represented largely by the fallacy of Langdell's case method of study and the fallacy of Langdell is the failure of the Law Schools. . . .

As I proceed to make my case you will note that I will borrow the techniques of the Law teacher and employ the professorial technique of hyperbolic shock power to sharpen my points.

But even as I castigate the worthy professors for hiding their heads in academic sands for 40 years and more, I am bound to pay tribute to them for teaching superbly so many of the technical skills of our craft which make today's law graduate a most sophisticated technician in legal analysis and legal principle. As new Law Clerks come into my office each year I marvel at the vast store of knowledge they possess on legal rules and the opinions of appellate courts. Note that I do not use the term "cases"; you will soon see why.

The shortcoming of today's graduate lies not in a deficient knowledge of law but in little if any training in dealing with *facts*— the stuff of which cases are made. It is a rare law graduate, for example, who knows how to ask questions—*single* questions, one at a time in order to develop facts in evidence. And a lawyer who cannot do that cannot begin to do his tasks properly.

Professor Langdell was almost guilty of a form of fraud in the very naming of his system. It is miscalled the "case" method of study. It should have been called the *opinion* method or the *appellate* method. This is very important because students thought they were dealing with *cases* when they were really dealing with *opinions* and *appeals,* and there is an enormous difference. The difference is illustrated in part by the truism, well known among judges, that almost any good lawyer can make a passable appellate judge but only a few can make good trial judges. . . .

In appellate opinions, with few exceptions, the facts are determined, but in the trial courts the facts, again with few exceptions, are the "whole ball game." To rely on appellate opinions as the prime teaching tool not only deprives the student of a chance to learn how to deal with facts but, what is more serious, he fails to learn that "cases" are essentially facts. . . .

In retrospect one could hardly conceive a system of legal education farther removed from the realities of life than the case method. Although the analogy is less than perfect, we may shed light on the problem by asking whether we could train doctors simply by having them do autopsies for 5 years in medical school and perhaps wind up with one course on how to examine and question and diagnose a *live patient.* . . .

Would we of the legal profession not say at once that a doctrine like *res ipsa loquitur* should govern when a man holds himself out as a doctor without having done real life acts as part of his training —if he relied solely on reading books and listening to lectures—to learn how to be a doctor? Today the education of a doctor is approximately 20–25% books and classrooms and 75–80% clinical, by which is meant the direct observation of sick people with the doctor who must make the diagnosis and either treat or perform surgery on the patient. In addition, he observes surgical procedures, assists in operations, and gradually learns to take part in surgery. In this clinical process he spends roughly 80% of his time with practicing doctors as his teachers. . . .

Yet today in a vast number of courtrooms good cases are being bungled by inadequately trained lawyers and needy people suffer because lawyers are licensed with very few exceptions without the slightest inquiry into their capacity to perform the practical functions of a counselor or an advocate. . . . [T]he basic fault still rests with the Law School for its failure to teach in real life terms when it has the students in a captive audience.

NOTE

Are the qualities mentioned in the "shock" discussion above essential for lawyers? Are they capable of being developed in law school? Are the law faculties as now constituted capable, the most capable, means of developing the qualities? Granted that the large corporate offices give excellent apprenticeship training for their own special purposes, is there need for other methods of apprenticeship training for law graduates who do not have that specialized opportunity?

TO RAISE THE SIGHTS

SAMUEL D. THURMAN, EDUCATION FOR PROFESSIONAL RESPONSIBILITY

Proceedings of the Association of American Law Schools 63, 70–72 (1962).

Law schools have become increasingly derelict, I believe, in offering and requiring broad gauge courses that raise the sights of students above the intricacies of today's many technical subjects; derelict in setting before students at an early date the goals of the profession. The cries of crowded curricula have often drowned out the protests of those who feel there is great value in seeing to it that law students continue to study legal history with its focus on the lives and examples of the great men of the law and the past glories of the profession. Students are occasionally, but perhaps far too infrequently, brought into effective contact with today's leaders of the profession, today's lawyers who have caught the vision of professional responsibility. . . .

Ways should be found to see that law students are familiar with the great biographies of the law, possibly by required readings at some stage, maybe prior to entrance into law school. It is a rare student who would not gain great insight into the unlimited potential of a lawyer by reading Mason's "Life of Brandeis." Such reading would do much to make clear the distinction between a competent craftsman and a lawyer.

We cannot assume that law students will do such reading especially in view of the heavy demands made upon their time in what appear to them to be more practical courses. We fail students when we do not bring dramatically home to them in some fashion the lives of those who in the past have made the profession great and the lives of those who today continue that tradition. We do not adequately train for professional responsibility if students are not required to study and analyze carefully how such men solved the complex problems that have confronted lawyers in all periods of time.

Far from being less important, the need to train students to think big has become increasingly critical in a world of specialization. The law student concentrating in a narrow area of the law must have his sights raised not only within the law itself but with reference to all areas of learning and it is incumbent upon the law schools to devise ways and means of accomplishing this objective. The increasing fragmentation of human knowledge goes on apace while our crying need is to bring human knowledge, human knowledge of all kinds, together. The much referred to gap between the sciences and the humanities must be narrowed by men trained to think big if the humanists are ever to understand what it is that makes scientists tick and if scientists are to be made aware of the price mankind is paying, the price in things that have made life worthwhile in the past, perhaps life itself, for his scientific progress.

At an earlier period perhaps we could assume that an incidental by-product of a more leisurely law school training would be education for professional responsibility. The pace was slower in individual courses, the curriculum itself had far fewer competing demands. Today we can no longer indulge in the assumption that students will somehow or other become steeped in the greatness of their profession. Positive steps should be taken to re-introduce into law school programs more exposure to the lives of those who best exemplify the highest ideals of the profession and thus insure "the habitual vision of greatness."

CONTINUING LEGAL EDUCATION

The years immediately following graduation from law school are inevitably a period of education in the practical side of the profession. In the large offices, where much of the work is done by, and where future members of the firm will be drawn from, the younger staff, there is excellent apprenticeship training. In many small offices there is given an equally good apprenticeship training in the technical aspects together with an understanding of the attitude of the professional man toward accepting and dealing with clients. The requirement of a period of apprenticeship following graduation from law school is imposed in some states, with indifferent success.

The Committee on Continuing Legal Education of the American Law Institute collaborating with the American Bar Association "has as its primary function the organizing and conduct of institutes and lectures on important subjects of the law. Such projects are conducted under the sponsorship of state and local bar associations and other lawyer organizations." Much of the Committee's work can be of great aid to the young lawyer as well as to his older colleagues in the profession.

The Practicing Law Institute, of New York City, offers numerous courses and monographs, which do much to give the young members of the bar an understanding of the elements of general practice as well as of practice in several specialized areas.

There remain a considerable number of young lawyers who may have no adequate apprenticeship training but who nonetheless start out early to practice for themselves. The common remark that they must learn on their early cases is a grievous admission of the needless and irreparable sufferings they may bring to their clients, usually the poor, who have trusted them as adequately prepared members of the bar. It is a satisfaction to know that their difficulties and the plight of their clients are mitigated by the friendliness and cooperation which characterize the profession of law, so the younger lawyer may frequently draw on his older colleagues for suggestions and advice.

Despite the efforts sketched above the legal profession in the United States of America does less in a systematic way to bridge the gap between school and practice, it is believed, than does the legal profession in any other comparable nation, and it does less than any other comparable profession in this nation.

Two suggestions from this sketch will suggest themselves to the reader. One is that the law student must consider the first years of practice as a part of the period of legal education, no less truly than the university years, and he should give thoughtful consideration to the methods of his continuing self-education in this period. The second is that the methods of bridging the gap deserves the continuing attention of the law schools and of the organized profession.

NOTES

(1) "An imposed apprenticeship period survives in five states. But even in those states there are few who agree in support of its utility. To a large extent it operates haphazardly, the young lawyers receiving little guidance and most of them becoming embittered by a sense of economic exploitation and hardship. . . .

"The decline of the clerkship does not appear to represent a rejection of the value of genuine law office experience. Indeed, a survey in New Jersey, where the clerkship has been heavily attacked, showed that practice was considered the best teacher of every skill a lawyer needs, except legal research. As Dean Stason has written: 'Let us concede, however, that the law graduate needs practical training that he does not and cannot now get in the law schools, that he needs it before he can be really competent to serve clients. How can this be provided without sacrificing the values inherent in the academic training now offered in our better law schools?'" O'Toole, *"Realistic Legal Education,"* 54 A.B.A.J. 774, 775 (1968).

(2) "If it were made clear that . . . the aim of legal education has to be the cultivation of the mind for a lifetime of presently undetermined activity, and not to train apprentices, the curriculum and teaching procedures in law schools might achieve considerably greater clarity. In this light, moreover, the institutional apparatus of legal education and professional apprenticeship might be substantially reworked. It would be the function of law schools to pursue general and frankly theoretical analysis of legal processes and institutions. It would be the function of technical training institutes to impart relevant practical skills that can be made the subject of formal instruction, as some post-graduate and continuing legal education programs are now in fact doing. And it would be the function of established professionals to provide the training in those practical and idiosyncratic arts that can best be learned on the job, whatever kind of professional job it is." Hazard, Challenges to Legal Education, The Path of Law from 1968: Proceedings and Papers at the Harvard Law School Convocation 185, 189.

(3) State bar associations, particularly when membership is compulsory and therefore finances are adequate, have been active in offering post law school training for their members. The California State Bar is a notable example. See Stumpf, *Preventive Law and Continuing Legal Education*, 38 S.Cal.L.Rev. 381 (1965). Most of the continuing legal education effort so far has been directed to improving the competency of the generalist lawyer faced with an ever-expanding body of law. An important problem for the profession is continuing education leading to certification as a specialist in some branch or field of law. (See Chapter XII, Section 4, pages 455ff, supra). If the profession accepts the responsibility of designating specialists (which it has not yet done), it will have to decide how to train and test for competence.

TWO LAW STUDENTS (SMITH AND JONES), TWO TEACHERS (DOE AND ROE), AND LEGAL EDUCATION

(1970 AND AFTER).

SMITH: Mr. Doe, I should like to introduce myself. I am John Smith, a beginning third year man with pretty poor grades. No one here seems to think I am worth anything. This summer I worked for a good small firm and they thought my work was great. Last year you and Mr. Roe said you would be glad to talk over methods of study with us. This is Mr. Henry Jones. He said he would like to come along and ask some questions. He is on the student committee on the curriculum.

DOE: The first two or three things I have to say are beyond dispute. The first one has been put this way: "All education is self-education. University education is self-education under guidance." The important word is self-education. Guidance can be of some aid, but you seek guidance in the wrong thing, in the rules of law. You should seek guidance on how you can develop your abilities.

SMITH: What is the second thing?

DOE: A man can gain more from a process when he understands its purpose and methods. Try to gain some understanding of legal education and its elements. You are a part of legal education, indeed, the most important part. In university education you students are the principals. We teachers are mere auxiliaries who exist because of you.

ROE: I don't agree.

DOE: The third suggestion is closely connected to the other two. The student should give thought to his own methods of study. There is no one best method for all students or even for the same student in all courses.

SMITH: What would you suggest we do?

DOE: I remind you of the purpose of careful study of cases. Justice Frankfurter said lawyers are "experts in relevance." Analysis is directed to making you experts in relevance.

JONES: Be more specific, if you can.

DOE: In most cases, there are three kinds of questions: (1) the formal issue, that is how under our system of procedure does the question arise; (2) the rule-of-law question; (3) the fundamental question. Take the very short case of *Frost v. Bachman*, (supra p. 442). The formal question or issue was a motion for judgment on the pleadings, and in whose favor the judgment should be granted. The rule-of-law question was, who has the burden of going forward with the evidence when a client attacks a transaction with his lawyer on the ground of unfairness. A purpose of procedure is to put the element in controversy before the tribunal in clear form. The rules of substantive law are distillates of the views of the courts and the legislatures on what justice and wisdom call for, expressed in a form which is readily applicable.

JONES: So the fundamental question or issue in the *Frost* case, you would say, is what does wisdom and good sense call for when a client attacks a transaction with his lawyer.

DOE: When you look first for the formal issue it adds greatly to the sharpness and clarity of the decision.

JONES: In class some professors ask us about the second, the rule-of-law, and usually ignore the other two.

DOE: Let there be variety in the thoroughness and detail with which you read and brief the cases. With so many courses and so many cases it is impossible to read all cases with the desired thoroughness. Students usually read and brief all cases with the same thinness and inadequacy. It would be wiser for them to read some of the cases even more summarily, just enough to enable them to follow the class discussion, so as to make time to read a few cases with all the care they will give to a decision relevant in practice next year.

SMITH: Have you any other suggestions for us?

DOE: Yes, my major suggestion on methods of study is "Organization". When you leave here, you students have at least pretty good powers of analysis. You are weakest in your power of organization. Yet you will have to organize ideas and facts all the time. Remember the words of Holmes:

> "The mark of a master is, that facts which before lay scattered in an inorganic mass, when he shoots through them the magnetic current of his thought leap into an organized order and live and bear fruit."

The difference between a good brief and a poor brief, between a good letter and a poor letter, Mr. Smith, even between a good examination answer and a poor one, is largely a matter of organization.

JONES: You don't give us any practice.

DOE: No, but we give you the opportunity right at hand in every course, which you can organize for yourself. The casebooks give the material in an order designed for teaching purposes, not for clarity in exposition or for ease in understanding. There are major gaps in the subject, some of them filled in by class discussion.

SMITH: But what is the use of our making these organizations?

DOE: One reason is to enable you to get a useable understanding of the law of the field. If you see the subject merely case after case like beads in a box, you have no working understanding of the law of the field. You need to see the cases or rather the principles—the legal pushes and pulls they illustrate—in a coherent form.

JONES: Oh, I see. What you want are summaries.

DOE: Not at all. There are two things wrong with the usual student summary. The first is that the student simply follows the order of the class discussion instead of shooting "through them the magnetic current of his thoughts". A second thing wrong is the excessive time it takes.

But your comment threw me off the track. The first reason for organizing a course for yourself is to gain an understanding of the law of the field. The second reason is much more important. It is the best, or at least the most readily available, way for you to develop your powers of organization. Organization is a way of putting relevant things together and irrelevant ones off to one side. All your life you will have to organize ideas, either as an aid to understanding them, or to making others understand them.

SMITH: You mean that the kind of organization we can make here is the kind we will use all through our professional work.

ROE: No. You will organize ideas for different purposes. Here in law school you are organizing for the purpose of gaining a better understanding yourself, which you can later apply in dealing with new cases. Much of your work in practice will be devoted to convincing others, as, in a brief, a conference, a letter. In dealing with others the first commandment is, put yourself in his place. Consider what the other person needs to know about the matter and make an organization which will be clearest and most convincing for him. A very common error is to assume that the person we are addressing has the same background for understanding that we have.

SMITH: You said that summaries take up too much time to write out. Mine did. What else can I do by way of organization?

DOE: I suggest—yes, insist—that you try a tabular organization something like this:

    I.

        A.

        B.

            1.

            2.

            3.

                a.

                b.

    II.

    III.

    Etc.

Use each of the coordinate headings for coordinate ideas. Put under each number or letter a page reference to the places in your notes where the matter is dealt with. You will probably find that under I, A, 2, c, you have some such page numbers as 34, 63, 41, 36. Under III, B, 1, b, you may have 34, 97, 73. Class discussion brings up the same idea or related ideas at many different places.

JONES: That looks pretty mechanical to me.

DOE: An artist would agree with you. There are some gifted men who refuse, and wisely so, to follow such a system. They do not want to fetter their intuition and insight.* But give the system a try. It is universal in briefs. You may think of it as the highly detailed table of contents of the text book you would write with your present knowledge of the subject. Gaps, as well as relationships, will be clearer to you. It did not fetter the work of such a gifted and imaginative man as Dean Wigmore. Look at the detailed and nicely organized table of contents of a chapter of his treatise on evidence, say, the chapter on privileged communications. An excellent judge urged this system of skeleton outline.**

SMITH: I thought the first thing you would discuss is the case system.

ROE: The case system is primarily a system of study, not a system of teaching.

It has the great advantage for teaching purposes that it deals with actual situations in which the student can readily envisage himself as an actor. It has something of the advantage in interest that the individual illustration has over the general proposition, that the drama or the novel or the biography has over history or philosophy.

JONES: In looking up discussions of legal education I came across the report of the 1966 Meeting of the Association of American Law Schools. One address was by Mr. Oscar Schachter who, I understand, has had a distinguished legal career with the United Nations. Much of what he has to say in criticism of lawyers and legal education, if I may say so, Mr. Doe, applies to your suggestions to us.*

DOE: The best justification I can give for my insistence on analysis and organization is from Alfred North Whitehead:

"Necessary technical excellence can only be acquired by habits of study that are apt to damage those energies of mind which should guide the technical skill. This is the chief fact about education and the source of most of its difficulties."

---

* ". . . many honest and sensible judgments . . . express an intuition of experience which outruns analysis and sums up many unnamed and tangled impressions; impressions which may lie beneath consciousness without losing their worth." Holmes, J., in Chicago, B. & Q. Ry. v. Babcock, 204 U.S. 585, 598 (1907).

** Dore, *Expressing the Idea—The Essentials of Oral and Written Argument*, 9 The Record of N.Y.C.B.A. 413 (1954).

* "Lawyers, by and large, are not in the intellectual vanguard; they do not seem to be particularly well equipped with new approaches and techniques relevant to the world I have described. At best, they are the present day classicists, skilled in verbal analysis, in structured argumentation, in close reading of documents. . . . For the most part, their emphasis is on words, on abstractions, on a highly limited slice of the real world." Remarks, Proceedings, Asso. Am. L. Schools, (1966), II, 157, 159.

As Whitehead indicated technical excellence is necessary but we must go beyond technical excellence to the "energies of mind" which should guide it.

SMITH: We have taken up enough of your time.

DOE: Don't go yet. You come to law school believing your sole aim is to learn law and to develop the intellectual qualities you will need in practice. Your three years here should be years of fully rounded development. The profession of law is a demanding one, and the broadly moral demands are greater than the intellectual ones. You will be dealing all your life not so much with law as with people and their problems in the context of law, so you should develop the best you can your abilities to deal with people.

JONES: What are these moral qualities you speak of? Legal ethics?

DOE: No, that is a very small part of it. They tell a story of Lord Birkenhead when he was a roistering young barrister. He and Winston Churchill were together at a meeting where the speaker pontificated: "Character will always tell." In a stage whisper he said, "Winnie, there is no future for us." When he became Lord Chancellor he took a broader view and asked which of the two characters indicated by his title he should exemplify—whether he should be sober as a judge or drunk as a lord.

SMITH: Which did he choose?

JONES: What are these elements of a lawyer's character?

DOE: I will mention only two or three. You will be dealing with other people, so they include understanding and sympathy and tact. You will be dealing with uncertainties, so you will need imagination and judgment. Some action must be taken—to do nothing is to do something—so you will need the qualities of decision and perseverance which turn judgment into action. I do not depreciate the intellectual qualities to which we devote most of our attention, yet the other qualities are the more important.

SMITH: What in the world can a student do to help develop these personal qualities? There is no opportunity in study or class.

DOE: Yes, there is. I told you not to think of character narrowly. A man's character develops out of the situations and responsibilities he meets. This is a rigorous place. One quality which this rigor may help you to develop is accuracy—accuracy in reading, in understanding, and in expression. Another quality is intelligent industry, which you will certainly need.

SMITH: I hadn't thought of those qualities as going to a man's character. But I suppose they do.

DOE: There is another quality which you can develop and strengthen here. A favorite of mine is Sir William Osler, a Canadian, who probably had a greater influence on medical education than any other man in American history. In a talk he made to the graduating class of a medical school he discussed the quality most important for a physician. The quality he singled out is the one which gave its name to the address, and to a volume of his essays which I strongly recommend to you. He was a classicist and he used a Latin word "Aequanimitas". I do not know how you would translate it: equanimity, poise, composure, steadiness. However you may translate the word, the quality is needed no less in law than in medicine. Steadiness, and also its twin quality, readiness. You will be the spokesman for others, and you must be ready to speak up in court or in conference no matter what the difficulties. Something can be done here to develop these companion qualities, steadiness and readiness.

SMITH: Maybe, Professor X was right. He said he would be rigorous with us to see if we could stand up under difficulties.

ROE: More difficult to bear are your fellow students and their titter at mistakes. Do not let that abominable sound intimidate you. Their laughter comes not from a sense of superiority but from a sense of relief that they are not making the mistake. Each one says to himself, "There, but for the Grace of God spake I." Don't turn yourselves, even temporarily, into humbled men without spring and drive. Express your ideas and put your questions with the same readiness and directness which you will show within a year in a courtroom or in your law office.

SMITH: But how does a man get and keep the qualities you discuss?

DOE: We all need and get strength from outside ourselves. What is called for is the strength to do the decent and difficult thing in a strenuous profession. And do not think a social conscience is a substitute for an individual conscience. The shyster has often sought to conceal his professional weakness under the cover of lofty social views.

SMITH: Again, how do I develop and keep those qualities?

DOE: Men are affected by widely varying influences. Some, by religion and the guide and support it gives in individual conduct. Others are strengthened by identification with something here on earth: with the profession and its long history; with the part the profession plays in the solution of current social problems; with our great predecessors in the profession, for the influence of example through biography can be potent.

You have put some general questions to Mr. Roe and me. Now I want to ask you some questions. Have you read a book all the way through since you entered law school?

SMITH: What kind of a book?

DOE: Any kind of a book other than the tired businessman's fare. A book which has substance, delineates character, stirs the imagination: philosophy, history, biography, novel, drama, poetry. Listen to this passage from a talk by Judge Learned Hand to a group of young Philadelphia lawyers: *

"I venture to believe that it is as important to a judge called upon to pass on a question of constitutional law, to have at least a bowing acquaintance with Acton and Maitland, with Thucydides, Gibbon and Carlyle, with Homer, Dante, Shakespeare and Milton, with Machiavelli, Montaigne and Rabelais, with Plato, Bacon, Hume and Kant as with the books which have been specifically directed to the subject. For in such matters everything turns upon the spirit in which he approaches the questions before him. The words which he must construe are empty vessels into which he can pour nearly anything he will. Men do not gather figs of thistles, nor supply institutions from judges whose outlook is limited by parish or class."

SMITH: I have to go to class.

DOE: We haven't yet given Jones a chance to ask his questions. Let us meet again, say next Thursday at noon at the faculty club.

. . . .

Thursday noon.

JONES: Mr. Doe, as I listened last week to you reading that list from Judge Hand's address, I caught the name of only one writer of this century whom he—that is you—mentioned. Are not writers of this century even more important? We are lawyers of the next half century, not of antiquity or of mediaeval times.

ROE: Judge Hand had in mind the lasting problems of human society.

JONES: Mr. Roe, I do have some questions to ask you and Mr. Doe and I hope you will not think me impertinent. Has any other school of the university changed so little in its methods in the last century as the law school of Langdell and the 1870s?

ROE: That is a rhetorical question. We have a good method with actual cases handed us by the courts. What else should we do?

JONES: Chief Justice Burger says "the case system" is a misnomer. It should be called "the appellate opinion system". When lawyers talk to me about their cases I observe they never mention the law. They refer to three things: facts, people, society. Chief Justice

---

* Hand, *Sources of Tolerance*, 79 U. Pa.L.Rev. 1, 12 (1930) reprinted Hand, The Sources of Liberty 66, 81 (1962).

Burger says actual cases are based, of course, on facts. The most difficult part of practice is to dig out the facts, say to go back the fourth time on a Sunday afternoon to find at last the witness who noted the engineer failed to blow the whistle at a crossing, or to go over the facts of a proposed merger and to present them in the most effective way. The strong business schools spend thousands of dollars digging up the complex facts of business cases. You law teachers have too easy a time with the appellate opinions handed you by the courts.

ROE: That does not show how we are to teach the digging up of facts in a law case.

JONES: At least to deal with a complex record, or, better still, to deal with a case as it was in the lawyer's office would carry the student farther back into the processes of business or of law. The second aspect lawyers mention is people. I agree with Mr. Doe on the importance of learning how to deal with people. Professor Harrop Freeman has a casebook, "Legal Interviewing and Counseling". In the Foreword Dean Erwin Griswold of Langdell's old school said the Freeman book on how to deal with troubled human beings might come to rank as a pioneer with Langdell's first casebook on appellate court cases on Contracts.

ROE: I will look it up.

JONES: The third aspect they mention is society. (I wish I could find a better word.) No one now sticks to the cases alone.* There are the social factors, "the energizing forces" as Chief Justice Stone called them, that have come to be recognized.

ROE: When I was in practice I would rather have a case in point by our supreme court than all the social factors put together. You are trying to turn the law schools into advanced schools of social studies, to clutter up casebooks with non-legal materials.

JONES: I heard a justice of the Supreme Court of the United States say he never saw any non-legal materials. Mr. Roe, we all know that at the founding of our government, the Founding Fathers drew on what they thought to be the principles of political science. What other social studies have been drawn on?

DOE: When the social studies forced themselves on the attention of the law, the first one to be used was economics. In recent years the emphasis has shifted to sociology. The federal government now employs many men trained in these disciplines. I expect that much increased attention will be given to psychology and psychiatry as aids in understanding the individual.

---

* See Patterson, *The Case Method In American Legal Education: Its Origins and Objectives*, 4 J.Leg.Ed. 1 (1951).

ROE: And what of philosophy and ethics, not to go into literature and the arts and the immense developments in the natural sciences. Doe, you and Jones bring to mind Dean Prosser's satire, "The Ten Year Law School." *

SMITH: Can not the university make better use of the students' years. The university should decide first on its objectives of its seven years for men of law.

ROE: I like the McDougal-Lasswell article because it begins with that question as to the law school and offers its answers.*

JONES: How did the American university system develop with its sharp separation of the college years from the professional school years?

DOE: The credit goes to the colleges which established themselves firmly before the professions entered the universities. When the professional schools later joined the universities, they accepted this vested interest of four college years.

SMITH: Is this a wise system?

DOE: It is open to question. Dean Landis mentioned "a seven year continuum", something like three years in college, two years in law school, another year back in college or graduate school, and the last year in law school. In the 1920's and 1930's there were efforts at integration but they fell through. One difficulty was that the college and graduate schools courses were not developed with the toughness and at the level of law school men. As one student put it: "To go back to the college courses after two years of law school is like cutting soft butter with a knife."

SMITH: Why do you question the wisdom of the 4–3 plan?

DOE: One reason is that the college subjects—philosophy, ethics, government, history, literature—are more fundamental. For understanding they call for greater maturity than the first year and a half in law school. In that law school period the emphasis is on "the art of the relevant", that is the art of the relevant primarily in terms of the law itself. If after a year and a half of demanding law school

---

* Prosser, *The Ten Year Curriculum*, 6 J.Leg.Ed. 149 (1953).

* "A first indispensable step toward the effective reform of legal education is to clarify ultimate aim. We submit this basic proposition: if legal education in the contemporary world is adequately to serve the needs of a free and productive commonwealth, it must be conscious, efficient and systematic *training for policy-making.* . . . None who deal with law, however defined, can escape *policy* when policy is defined as the making of important decisions which affect the distribution of values." Lasswell & McDougal, *Legal Education and Public Policy: Professional Training in the Public Interest*, 52 Yale L.J. 203, 206, 207 (1943).

work the students were to go back to the more fundamental subjects, they could deal with them on a higher plane. And if after a treatment of the college and graduate school subjects—a treatment which could be more fundamental because of the greater maturity of the students—the students returned to law school, they would demand a more fundamental consideration of legal problems by us in the law school.

SMITH: I should like to raise another subject. What role should the students have in the government of the law school?

JONES: I like to recall that the great law school of the Middle Ages, the university of Bologna, was essentially a guild of students.* They hired and fired and fined the professors.

ROE: If you are going to take on responsibility then as with every responsibility you must prepare yourself by reading and reflection.

SMITH: The last thing I wish to raise is the law school and the poor. The law school and its "successful" graduates have been concerned with the law for the rich and the comfortable, not with law as it is applied or misapplied to the poor and the disadvantaged, especially the Negro. It is astounding that the law schools have given so little attention to these other groups.

DOE: We do something through the legal aid societies and the legal aid clinics.

SMITH: Is there something more than case by case representation, say attention to the shortcomings of the law which bears harshly on the poor? If students had had a role in law school government, more might have been done earlier.

JONES: This discussion, I must say, is unsatisfying. It is wholly in terms of method and structure, how to study law, the place of students in university government, and how to bring law and the social studies together. Isn't there anything more to it all than that?

DOE: I have to go and get ready for a class. Obviously, we ought to meet again next week. Same time, same place? Before I go I'd like to offer an answer to Jones' last question. The unit to be kept in mind in all the law school's work is the individual student, not course or curriculum, method or structure. It is what is caught, not what is taught, that matters. In the address Mr. Jones referred to last time Mr. Oscar Schachter made the point as to the teacher. Certainly he would apply it no less to the student.*

"My third and last suggestion stems from the first point in my 'diagnosis'; the deeply divided, diversified world with its

---

* See Cowen, *Student Participation in Law School Administration*, 13 J.Leg. Ed. 214 (1960).

* Remarks, Proceedings, Asso. Am. L. Schools (1966) II, 157, 161–162.

enormous barriers to understanding. For this, we need something more than methodology or history. We are in the realm of the intangibles: sympathy, identification, heroism, tragedy, pride. These are the factors best perceived through literary and humanistic studies but surely they are not entirely foreign to law school studies. . . . The task of breaking out of the professional grooves does not require interdisciplinary courses—or for that matter, new courses. The challenge, if I may call it that, can be met mainly by the law teacher. It is he who must take a wide and searching look elsewhere and apply in his own courses the insights and ideas learned outside of the law."

SECTION 2. ADMISSION AND DISCIPLINE

Introduction. Admission to the bar is a two step process. One step is directed to inquiring into and testing the intellectual abilities of the applicant. A few states give to a few schools "the diploma privilege", that is the acceptance of a law degree from those schools as satisfaction of the intellectual requirements. Most states call for a bar examination.

The boards of bar examiners have joined to create the National Conference of Bar Examiners, which has adopted a "Code of Recommended Standards for Bar Examiners".* The Code is included in "The Bar Examiners Handbook" (1968), prepared and annotated under the sponsorship of the Conference by Mr. Robert A. Sprecher of the Chicago Bar as editor-in-chief. On the nature of the examination the Code provides:

"16. *Purpose of Examination:* The bar examination should test the applicant's ability to reason logically, to analyze accurately the problems presented to him, and to demonstrate a thorough knowledge of the fundamental principles of law and their application. The examination should not be designed primarily for the purpose of testing information, memory or experience. . . .

18. *Questions:* The major portion of the bar examination should consist of questions in the form of hypothetical fact problems requiring essay answers."

The second step is an inquiry into the moral qualities. Each state has its committees on character and fitness which make inquiry into these qualities. The actions of these committees, as with the actions of their parallel committees for the discipline of lawyers already ad-

---

* See Sullivan, *The Professional Associations and Legal Education*, 4 J. Leg.Ed. 401, 419 (1952).

mitted, have given rise to a good many questions. One set of questions concerns the required or the appropriate tribunals and methods for the inquiry. A more troublesome set of questions involves the nature of the conduct which may bar admission or bring discipline. Such conduct can usefully be divided into two broad categories. The first category includes the ordinary financial frailties of man; the second deals with heterodox political activities and allegiances. The former category is by far the larger in the number of cases involved; the latter has drawn the greater attention because of the decisions in the field by the Supreme Court of the United States. The latter category is part of numerous controversies involving civil rights and the privileges and protection of the heterodox in varied settings. (See T. Emerson, D. Haber, and N. Dorsen, Political and Civil Rights in the United States (3d ed. 1967), especially vol. I, pp. 262–285). For the lawyer, the controversy has extended to the right of silence when his actions or beliefs are inquired into in proceedings for either admission or discipline.

In the middle part of the 20th century, most of the cases involved Communism and the furtive connection of applicants or lawyers with Communist associations. In the latter part of the century, the cases concerned disorder used as an expression of social and political dissent. Some demonstrators were moved by anger and resentment at what they believed to be continuing denials of legal rights and equal privileges to disadvantaged groups and they used these striking measures to gain publicity for their causes and to effect changes. Many may well have been led on by a sense of personal frustration and the willingness to express that sense on the institution at hand. A few were actuated by hatred of the whole political and social structure, "the establishment", and by a determination to overthrow it and to replace it with anarchy or some one of the several forms of Communism marked by names of leaders, Stalin, Trotsky, Mao. The measures used by the demonstrators varied as did their purposes, ranging upward in violence as sit-down, shout-down, knock-down, burn-down, shoot-down. The use of the measures poses questions as to both justice and order, change and stability. What of the lawyer or the law student who has a share in them?

NOTES

(1) "A state can require high standards of qualification such as good moral character or proficiency in its law, before it admits an applicant to the bar, but any qualification must have a rational connection with the applicant's fitness or capacity to practice law." Mr. Justice Black in Schware v. Board of Bar Examiners, 353 U.S. 232, 239 (1957). The educational requirement of graduation from an "accredited" law school, defined as one approved by the American Bar Association, is valid. Hackin v. Lockwood, 361 F.2d 499 (9th Cir.), cert. denied 385 U.S. 960 (1966).

(2) The system for determination of character employed in two New York judicial departments was attacked as violating the First and Four-

teenth Amendments. A New York statute provided that a candidate for admission to the bar who had passed the bar examination should be admitted if the court

> "shall be satisfied that such person possesses the character and general fitness requisite for an attorney and counsellor-at-law"

A Rule directed that no person should be admitted

> "unless he shall furnish saisfactory proof to the effect: (1) that he believes in the form of the government of the United States and is loyal to such government . . ."

The character committees prescribed detailed questionnaires for the candidates. The majority of a United States District Court of three judges, speaking through Judge Friendly, upheld the system, though calling for some modifications in the questionnaires. Judge Motley, dissenting, stated that the statute on its face was valid but invalid in its application, and the Rule was invalid on its face and in its application. Law Students Civil Rights Research Council, Inc. v. Wadmond, 299 F.Supp. 117 (S.D.N.Y.1969). Cert. granted, U. S. Law Week Jan. 13, 1970. Comment, 23 Vand.L.Rev. 131 (1969).

HALLINAN v. COMMITTEE OF BAR EXAMINERS

Supreme Court of California In Bank, 1966.
65 Cal.2d 447, 55 Cal.Rptr. 228, 421 P.2d 76.

[Petitioner, Terence Hallinan, sought review of the action of the Committee of Bar Examiners in refusing to certify him for admission to practice law in California. He had passed the bar examination, but the Committee refused to certify him for admission on the ground he did not meet the statutory requirement "of good moral character". The principal ground for the Committee's action was the petitioner's violations of the law in planned civil rights activities.]

PETERS, JUSTICE. . . .

The findings of the Board of Governors of the State Bar or of a committee such as respondent, while given great weight, are not binding upon this court. . . . In disciplinary proceedings this court examines and weighs the evidence and passes upon its sufficiency. . . . Any reasonable doubt encountered in the making of such an examination should be resolved in favor of the accused. . . . These rules are equally applicable to admission proceedings.

There are some distinctions between admission proceedings and disciplinary proceedings, the essential one being that in the former the burden is upon the applicant to show that he is morally fit, whereas in the latter the burden is upon the State Bar to prove that an attorney is morally unfit. . . .*

---

* Stricter substantive and procedural requirements necessary to sustain an adverse decision in a disciplinary proceeding are frequently rationalized on the theory that an attorney has a vested property *right* in maintaining a practice already established, whereas an applicant for admission seeks

Since commission of an act constituting "moral turpitude" is a statutory ground for disbarment (Bus. & Prof. Code, § 6106) and is perhaps the most frequent subject of inquiry in disciplinary proceedings, it may readily be seen that, insofar as the scope of inquiry is concerned, the distinction between admission and disciplinary proceedings is today more apparent than real.**

Fundamentally, the question involved in both situations is the same—is the applicant for admission or the attorney sought to be disciplined a fit and proper person to be permitted to practice law, and that usually turns upon whether he has committed or is likely to continue to commit acts of moral turpitude. At the time of oral argument the attorney for respondent frankly conceded that the test for admission and for discipline is and should be the same. We agree with this concession. Therefore, in considering the kinds of acts which would justify excluding a candidate for admission we may look to acts which have been relied upon to sustain decisions to disbar or suspend individuals previously admitted to practice. . . .

The findings of the respondent disclose that the conclusion that petitioner "has a fixed and dominant propensity for lawlessness whenever violation of the law suits his purposes of the particular moment" was predicated on evidence relating to two distinct subjects of inquiry by the hearing committee: first, petitioner's participation in and attempts to justify certain acts of "civil disobedience" committed for the purpose of vindicating the civil rights of minority groups, particularly Negroes. Petitioner's participation in such acts of civil disobedience has resulted in various admitted and intentional violations of the criminal law for some of which he has been prosecuted and convicted. The second area of inquiry at the hearings concerned petitioner's alleged habitual and continuing resort to fisticuffs to settle per-

---

merely to be accorded a *privilege.* (See Note, 65 Yale L.J. 873.) . . .

It seems somewhat difficult to maintain that an individual, like petitioner, who has invested considerable time, energy and expense in obtaining a legal education and who has demonstrated the requisite intellectual qualities and technical proficiencies does not thereby acquire at least the semblance of a right to be admitted to the profession similar to the right of an attorney already admitted to practice. In any event, opinions of the United States Supreme Court and of our court which characterize a claim for admission to the bar as a claim of a right entitled to the protections of procedural due process (Willner v. Committee on Character and Fitness, 373 U.S. 96, 102, 83 S.Ct. 1175, 10 L. Ed.2d 224; In re Summers, 325 U.S. 561, 568, 65 S.Ct. 1307, 89 L.Ed. 1795; see also Woodard v. State Bar, 16 Cal.2d 755, 757, 108 P.2d 407) make it impossible for us to regard admission to the profession as a mere privilege. [Footnote by the Court]

** Moreover, in Schware v. Board of Bar Examiners, 353 U.S. 232, 242, 77 S.Ct. 752, 1 L.Ed.2d 796, the United States Supreme Court appears to treat "moral turpitude" as the relevant criterion in reviewing a decision to refuse admission, even though the New Mexico statute, like our own statute, required a showing of good moral character on the part of the applicant. And in Moura v. State Bar, 18 Cal.2d 31, 32, 112 P.2d 629, this court used "good moral character" as the standard in a disbarment case. [Footnote by the Court] sonal differences. We discuss these two matters and their legal consequences separately.

First, as to petitioner's activities in connection with civil disobedience. His first arrest in this connection, so far as the record shows, occurred in 1960 while he was in England. At that time he participated in a peace demonstration in London allegedly involving "about a hundred thousand people." . . . Petitioner was formally charged with "blocking a footpath" and fined one pound on his plea of *nolo contendere*.

After returning to the United States, petitioner's growing interest in the civil rights movement caused him to apply for membership in the Student Non-Violent Coordinating Committee (SNCC), an organization formed to carry out civil rights activities in the south. As a member of this organization he spent the summer of 1963 assisting in efforts to register Negroes to vote in Mississippi and to desegregate public facilities in that state. During this period, because of these activities, petitioner was twice arrested by local authorities in Mississippi, first for loitering, and subsequently for littering public areas. Neither arrest resulted in a conviction or even a trial. On both occasions petitioner was released from jail after intervention, after the first arrest, by the Attorney General of the United States, and, after the second, by the National Council of Churches.

When petitioner returned to San Francisco from Mississippi he became a member of the Congress of Racial Equality (CORE), the National Association for the Advancement of Colored People (NAACP), the Ad Hoc Committee to End Racial Discrimination, an organization affiliated with the United Freedom Movement, and helped to organize the W.E.B. DuBois Club, which is composed of young Socialists. As a member of these groups he expanded his participation in activities calculated to obtain civil rights for Negroes by direct action in the form of picketing and "sitting-in" at various business establishments in San Francisco believed to follow discriminatory business or hiring practices. . . .

As a result of petitioner's two arrests on "auto row" he was twice tried and twice convicted on separate charges. . . . At the time of the hearing before the committee an appeal from the latter judgment of conviction was pending.

The so-called "auto row" "sit-ins" were the result of charges by the NAACP that certain automobile dealers adhered to and refused to negotiate about their claimed discriminatory hiring practices. At the first demonstration, on March 14, 1964, the demonstrators, including petitioner, entered the premises of the Cadillac agency, sat down and sang and clapped. The police arrived and the officer in charge read an order to the demonstrators requesting and directing them to leave the building in an orderly manner. Some of the demonstrators, but not petitioner, complied with the order. Those who remained in the building went limp and were carried out by the police and deposited in a patrol wagon. The only resistance offered by these demonstrators was passive. . . .

Petitioner did not deny his participation in these acts of civil disobedience, but justified his conduct by certain moral and political considerations. . . .

Petitioner agreed that the traditional methods of securing changes in the law by instituting legal proceedings or petitioning the Legislature are preferable to attempting to do so through direct action in the form of civil disobedience. He also stated, however, that "Unfortunately part of the progress of moving the legislature to do things has proved to be the necessity for some people committing acts of civil disobedience or sitting-in and picketing and singing and doing whatever you do. . . . that is, without the kind of direct activity and showing of feelings and so on, you won't get the legislature passing the laws. But unless you get the legislature passing the laws and changing the laws, then there is really no objective in all the mass civil disobedience and mass demonstrations and picket lines and everything else. . . .

"I think somebody in the southern part of the United States has an obligation—as a lawyer—has a duty, to disobey some of those laws that are really unconstitutional and that persecute people on the basis of their race and everything else. . . . And it's only because of the activities, particularly of the Negro people, but a lot of their white supporters too, that a lot of those laws have been passed and that now it is possible to begin, but only to begin, talking about settling these things legally and in court, and not have to demonstrate and so on about it."

Does this type of evidence adequately support the refusal of respondent to certify petitioner for admission? We think not.

Preliminarily, we note that every intentional violation of the law is not, ipso facto, grounds for excluding an individual from membership in the legal profession. . . .

Whether these activities involve moral turpitude is dependent upon the issues involved and the motivation of the violator. Of course, we do not mean to condone disobedience of the law in any form; we mean only to express strong doubt that the leaders of current civil rights movements are today or will in the future be looked upon as persons so lacking in moral qualifications that they should for that reason alone be prevented from entering their chosen profession.*

---

* In United States v. Francioso (2d Cir. 1947) 164 F.2d 163, the court was called upon to interpret the phrase "good moral character" as contained in the Nationality Act (8 U.S.C.A. § 707, subd. (a) (3)) and stated that it established as a test whether "the moral feelings, now prevalent generally in this country" would "be outraged" by the conduct in question.

To the extent that acts of civil disobedience involve violations of the law it is altogether necessary and proper that the violators be punished. But criminal prosecution, not exclusion from the bar, is the appropriate means of punishing such offenders. The purposes of investigation by the bar into an applicant's moral character should be limited to assurance that, if admitted, he will not obstruct the administration of justice or otherwise act unscrupulously in his capacity as an officer of the court. . . . We do not believe that petitioner's participation in the civil disobedience here shown can be characterized as involving moral turpitude. If we were to deny to every person who has engaged in a "sit-in" or other form of nonviolent civil disobedience, and who has been convicted therefor, the right to enter a licensed profession, we would deprive the community of the services of many highly qualified persons of the highest moral courage. This should not be done.

[The court found that the other charges against the petitioner lacked substance and it ordered the Committee of Bar Examiners to certify him as qualified to practice law. McCOMB, JUSTICE, dissenting.]

DISCIPLINARY PROCEEDINGS: THE FIRST STAGE

There are two stages in disciplinary proceedings. The first is the screening stage at which it is determined whether the lawyer's acts call for court consideration. Most complaints, based as they are on mere misunderstanding between clients and lawyers, stop here. The administration of this stage is entrusted by many courts to bar associations. If the bar association on inquiry finds the lawyer's actions warrant it, the bar association may present the matter to the court. The report immediately following indicates the nature of the work of an excellent grievance committee with a good staff to aid it.

COMMITTEE ON GRIEVANCES, THE ASSOCIATION OF THE BAR OF THE CITY OF NEW YORK, REPORT

Supplement, The Record, 1962–63, pp. 32–41.

The obligation of the Committee on Grievances is twofold: first, to protect the public against misconduct by attorneys, and, second, to protect attorneys against unjustified accusations.

The Committee, which maintains offices at the House of the Association, receives complaints against attorneys from a great variety of sources including other attorneys, clients, judges, law enforcement

---

See also In re Hatch, supra, 10 Cal.2d 147, 151, 73 P.2d 885, 887, where it is stated that "'The concept of moral turpitude depends upon the state of public morals, and may vary according to the community or the times.'" [Footnote by the Court].

agencies and other bar associations. The Committee may also commence investigations on its own motion by reason of newspaper articles and similar information. . . .

All complaints within the Committee's purview are initially evaluated by a member of the staff. Those involving fee disputes not amounting to fraud or overreaching, requests for advice, misunderstanding of the law or of the duty of the attorney, or other allegations not involving misconduct are closed without further investigation. In such instances, the complainant is advised of the action taken and the reason therefor. The attorney complained of is not called upon to answer the complaint and may never know of its existence.

No file concerning any complaint, however, no matter how trivial, can be finally closed without a member of the Committee having reviewed the same. . . .

Complaints which, upon initial evaluation, present a *prima facie* case of misconduct are further investigated. The attorney involved may in the first instance be asked for an explanation. The Committee recognizes that a visit to its offices is time consuming and may be an unnecessary burden upon a busy practitioner. Therefore, he is usually requested to submit his explanation in writing. Personal interviews are scheduled where complaints involve complicated transactions requiring personal discussion; where the written explanation submitted is insufficient or unresponsive; and when requested by the attorney concerned.

Whenever required, the staff conducts interviews of material witnesses and obtains relevant evidence. . . .

Upon the completion of its investigation, the staff again evaluates the matter. Where the complaint is found unwarranted or where there is insufficient evidence to support it, both the complainant and the attorney involved are notified accordingly. As noted earlier, a committee member reviews every file before the matter is finally closed.

Complaints involving conviction for a crime involving moral turpitude, not amounting to a felony under New York Law, are referred directly to the Association's Executive Committee for prosecution in the Court . . .

All complaints not otherwise disposed of under the procedures heretofore discussed are scheduled for hearings before the Committee on Grievances. . . . At the hearing the respondent is entitled to be represented by counsel, to call witnesses in his own behalf and to cross-examine witnesses called by the Committee staff.

The hearing is non-public, and is conducted in accordance with ordinary courtroom procedures. The testimony is taken under oath and the entire proceeding is recorded. Upon completion of the proof, the Committee retires in executive session to consider its decision.

The Committee disposes of all cases before it in one of three ways. If the charges are found not sustained, it dismisses. Where a charge is found sustained but mitigating circumstances or like considerations exist, the Committee may admonish the respondent. . . . Charges of a more serious nature, which the Committee finds sustained, are reported to the Association's Executive Committee with a recommendation that they be prosecuted in the Court.

The general character and behavior of a respondent is always a major factor in the Committee's determination, as the main object of disciplinary proceedings is to protect the public and not to punish.

It will be recognized that many matters, lacking merit as complaints, must nevertheless be given considerable attention since the Committee performs an important function in explaining to members of the public complications arising in the handling of their cases not attributable to misconduct by their attorneys; in easing personality conflicts; and, in general, in promoting a better understanding between the public and the Bar. These, and other matters which do not involve true grievances against attorneys, may not be summarily dismissed, if this Committee is to do its part in improving the stature of the profession.

Peter H. Kaminer,
Chairman.

NOTE

In 1967 the American Bar Association created a Special Committee on the Evaluation of Disciplinary Enforcement, now under the chairmanship of former Justice Tom C. Clark. The Committee, after circulating a preliminary draft of its report for criticisms and suggestions, expects to submit its final report to the Association in 1970.

THE SECOND STAGE

IN RE ROUSS

Court of Appeals of New York, 1917.
221 N.Y. 81, 116 N.E. 782.

CARDOZO, J. In 1912 the appellant, Jacob Rouss, was the attorney for one Eugene Fox. Fox, a member of the police force in the city of New York, had been brought before a magistrate on the charge of collecting bribes from the keeper of a disorderly house. The keeper of the house, one George A. Sipp, had been served with a subpoena, or at least there had been to his knowledge an attempt to serve him. Rouss and Sipp's attorney entered into an arrangement that Sipp for a money consideration would keep without the state. The money was paid; Sipp fulfilled his bargain; and Fox was discharged. Indictments were later found against five inspectors of police for conspiracy to obstruct justice through the suppression of Sipp's testimony. On the trial of those indictments, Rouss was a witness for the people. His testimony as there given is in substance a confession of guilt. Charges of professional misconduct were afterward preferred against him. To these charges he makes answer that he is immune from discipline by force of section 584 of the Penal Law, which says that:

"No person shall be excused from attending and testifying before any court . . . for a violation of any of the provisions of this article [article 54, defining and punishing conspiracy], for the reason that the testimony . . . may tend to convict him of a crime or to subject him to a penalty or forfeiture; but no person shall be prosecuted or subjected to any penalty or forfeiture for or on account of any transaction, matter or thing concerning which he may so testify . . ."

The question is whether disbarment is a penalty or forfeiture within the meaning of that statute.

Membership in the bar is a privilege burdened with conditions. A fair private and professional character is one of them. Compliance with that condition is essential at the moment of admission; but it is equally essential afterwards. . . . Whenever the condition is broken the privilege is lost. To refuse admission to an unworthy applicant is not to punish him for past offenses. The examination into character, like the examination into learning, is merely a test of fitness. To strike the unworthy lawyer from the roll is not to add to the pains and penalties of crime. The examination into character is renewed; and the test of fitness is no longer satisfied. For these reasons courts have repeatedly said that disbarment is not punishment. . . . Even pardon will not elude it. Pardon blots out the offense and all its penalties, forfeitures, and sentences; but the power to disbar remains. Matter of an Attorney, 86 N.Y. 563. We do not need to inquire now whether the power is so essential and inherent that the Legislature may not take it away. . . . At least we will not hold it to have been taken away by words of doubtful meaning. We will not declare, unless driven to it by sheer necessity, that a confessed criminal has been intrenched by the very confession of his guilt beyond the power of removal.

The problem before us, let it be recalled, is one solely of statutory construction. There is no question of constitutional right. . . .

We think that section 584 of the Penal Law was designed to give an immunity as broad as the constitutional privilege, and no broader. . . .

The order of disbarment should be affirmed.

IN RE HALLINAN

Supreme Court of California In Bank, 1954.
43 Cal.2d 243, 272 P.2d 768.

TRAYNOR, JUSTICE.

Vincent W. Hallinan was charged by indictment with violating section 145(b) of the Internal Revenue Code, 26 U.S.C. § 145(b) by "willfully and knowingly fil[ing] false and fraudulent income tax returns." The jury found him guilty as charged on five counts of the indictment. The court sentenced him to 18 months imprisonment on each count, the sentences to run concurrently, and fined him $50,000. He did not appeal, and the time for appeal has now elapsed. The State Bar filed with this court a certified copy of the indictment and judgment of conviction, contending that it calls for Hallinan's disbarment under sections 6101 and 6102 of the Business and Professions Code. These sections provide for the summary disbarment of attorneys who are convicted of "a felony or misdemeanor, involving moral turpitude . . . ." Hallinan objects to the entry of an order of disbarment and moves that the proceeding be dismissed on the grounds that he is being deprived of equal protection of the laws, that the term "moral turpitude" in sections 6101 and 6102 is too vague, uncertain, and indefinite to meet the requirements of due process of law, and that in any event the crime proscribed by section 145(b) does not involve moral turpitude.

Hallinan has not made the required showing of discrimination to sustain his contention that he is being denied equal protection of the laws. . . .

. . . Although the problem of defining moral turpitude is not without difficulty . . . it is settled that whatever else it may mean, it includes fraud and that a crime in which an intent to defraud is an essential element is a crime involving moral turpitude. It is also settled that the related group of offenses involving intentional dishonesty for purposes of personal gain are crimes involving moral turpitude. . . . The fraudulent acquisition of another's property is but another form of theft in this state. Pen.Code, § 484. We see no moral distinction between defrauding an individual and defrauding the government, United States ex rel. Berlandi v. Reimer, supra, 113 F.2d 429, 430–431, and an attorney, whose standard of conduct should be one of complete honesty, McGregor v. State Bar, 24 Cal.2d 283, 288–289, 148 P.2d 865, who is convicted of either offense is not worthy of the trust and confidence of his clients, the courts, or the public, and must be disbarred, since his conviction of such a crime would necessarily involve moral turpitude.

Conversely, if a conviction for any crime can be had without proof of facts showing moral turpitude, an attorney convicted of such a crime cannot be summarily disbarred under section 6101 and 6102 of the Business and Professions Code. . . .

Since section 145(b) is a United States statute, we must accept the interpretation given it by the United States courts. . . .

These courts have definitely held that an intent to defraud is not an essential element of section 145(b) and that a conviction under that section does not necessarily involve moral turpitude. . . .

. . . Although every conviction for violating section 145(b) may not involve moral turpitude, some convictions may. In such cases discipline or disbarment should be imposed by non-summary procedures. Bus. & Prof. Code, § 6106 et seq., . . . This court has inherent power over the admission, suspension, and disbarment of attorneys . . . and in the exercise thereof can initiate disciplinary proceedings on its own motion, and, in so doing, it may adopt "any suitable process or mode of proceeding . . .." Code Civ.Proc. § 187, . . .

The motion to dismiss is denied and the matter is referred to the Board of Governors of the State Bar for a hearing, report, and recommendation on the question whether the facts and circumstances surrounding the commission of the offense of which Vincent W. Hallinan was convicted involved moral turpitude or other misconduct warranting disbarment or suspension.

SHENK, SCHAUER, and SPENCE, JJ., concur.

CARTER, J., did not participate herein.

KONIGSBERG v. STATE BAR OF CALIFORNIA

Supreme Court of the United States, 1961.
366 U.S. 36, 81 S.Ct. 997, 6 L.Ed.2d 105.

MR. JUSTICE HARLAN delivered the opinion of the Court.

This case, involving California's second rejection of petitioner's application for admission to the state bar, is a sequel to Konigsberg v. State Bar, 353 U.S. 252, 77 S.Ct. 722, 1 L.Ed.2d 810, in which this Court reversed the State's initial refusal of his application.

Under California law the State Supreme Court may admit to the practice of law any applicant whose qualifications have been certified to it by the California Committee of Bar Examiners. Cal. Bus. & Prof.Code § 6064. To qualify for certification an applicant must, among other things, be of "good moral character," Id., § 6060 (c), and no person may be certified "who advocates the overthrow of the Government of the United States or of this State by force, violence, or other unconstitutional means . . .." Id., § 6064.1. The Committee is empowered and required to ascertain the qualifications of all candidates. Id., § 6046. Under rules prescribed by the Board of

Governors of the State Bar, an applicant before the Committee has "the burden of proving that he is possessed of good moral character, of removing any and all reasonable suspicion of moral unfitness, and that he is entitled to the high regard and confidence of the public."

. . .

On remand [after the reversal of the State's denial of his application] petitioner moved the California Supreme Court for immediate admission to the bar. The court vacated its previous order denying review and referred the matter to the Bar Committee for further consideration. At the ensuing Committee hearings Konigsberg introduced further evidence as to his good moral character (none of which was rebutted), reiterated unequivocally his disbelief in violent overthrow, and stated that he had never knowingly been a member of any organization which advocated such action. He persisted, however, in his refusals to answer any questions relating to his membership in the Communist Party. The Committee again declined to certify him, this time on the ground that his refusals to answer had obstructed a full investigation into his qualifications. The California Supreme Court, by a divided vote, refused review, and also denied Konigsberg's motion for direct admission to practice. . . . We again brought the case here. . . .

Petitioner's contentions in this Court in support of reversal of the California Supreme Court's order are reducible to three propositions: (1) the State's action was inconsistent with this Court's decision in the earlier *Konigsberg* case; (2) assuming the Committee's inquiries into Konigsberg's possible Communist Party membership were permissible, it was unconstitutionally arbitrary for the State to deny him admission because of his refusals to answer; and (3) in any event, Konigsberg was constitutionally justified in refusing to answer these questions.

Consideration of petitioner's contentions as to the effect of this Court's decision in the former *Konigsberg* case requires that there be kept clearly in mind what is entailed in California's rule, comparable to that in many States, that an applicant for admission to the bar bears the burden of proof of "good moral character"—a requirement whose validity is not, nor could well be, drawn in question here.

Under such a rule an applicant must initially furnish enough evidence of good character to make a prima facie case. The examining Committee then has the opportunity to rebut that showing with evidence of bad character. Such evidence may result from the Committee's own independent investigation, from an applicant's responses to questions on his application form, or from . . . Committee interrogation of the applicant himself. . . .

We think it clear that the Fourteenth Amendment's protection against arbitrary state action does not forbid a State from denying admission to a bar applicant so long as he refuses to provide unprivileged answers to questions having a substantial relevance to his qualifications.

The judgment of the Supreme Court of California is Affirmed.

[Four justices dissented in two opinions.]

NOTES

(1) In In re Anastaplo, 366 U.S. 82 (1961) the Supreme Court, by a 5–4 vote, upheld the right of a state (Illinois) to deny admission to an applicant as to whom there was strong and uncontroverted evidence of good moral character but who, as a libertarian and relying on the First Amendment, refused to cooperate with the Committee on Character and Fitness in answering questions about his political views and associations.

(2) In bar admission proceedings procedural due process is essential and this includes the right of confrontation. Willner v. Committee on Character and Fitness, 373 U.S. 96 (1963).

SPEVACK v. KLEIN

Supreme Court of the United States, 1967.
385 U.S. 511, 87 S.Ct. 625, 17 L.Ed.2d 574.

[Petitioner Spevack, a member of the New York Bar, was served with a *subpoena duces tecum* by the grievance committee of the Association of the Bar of the City of New York and the New York County Lawyers' Association. He refused to produce the demanded financial records and refused to testify at a subsequent judicial inquiry into his fitness to practice law on the ground that production of the records and his testimony would tend to incriminate him. The Appellate Division of the New York Supreme Court ordered petitioner disbarred and the Court of Appeals affirmed. The Supreme Court granted certiorari.]

Mr. Justice Douglas announced the judgment of the Court and delivered an opinion in which The Chief Justice, Mr. Justice Black and Mr. Justice Brennan concur.

. . . We said in Malloy v. Hogan [378 U.S. 1 (1964)]:

"The Fourteenth Amendment secures against State invasion the same privilege that the Fifth Amendment guarantees against federal infringement—the right of a person to remain silent unless he chooses to speak in the unfettered exercise of his own will, and to suffer no penalty . . . for such silence." 378 U.S. at 8, 84 S.Ct., at 1493.

In this context "penalty" is not restricted to fine or imprisonment. It means as we said in Griffin v. California, 386 U.S. 609, 85

S.Ct. 1229, 14 L.Ed.2d 106, the imposition of any sanction which makes assertion of the . . . privilege "costly." Id. at 614. . .

The threat of disbarment and loss of professional reputation, and of livelihood are powerful forms of compulsion. . . .

Reversed.

[The Court specifically overruled Cohen v. Hurley, 366 U.S. 117 (1961).]

MR. JUSTICE FORTAS, concurring in the judgment.

I agree that Cohen v. Hurley . . . should be overruled. But I would distinguish between a lawyer's right to remain silent and that of a public employee who is asked questions specifically, directly, and narrowly relating to the performance of his official duties . . ..

MR. JUSTICE HARLAN, with whom MR. JUSTICE CLARK and MR. JUSTICE STEWART join, dissenting. . . . What is done today will be disheartening and frustrating to courts and bar associations throughout the country in their efforts to maintain high standards at the bar. . . .

It cannot be claimed that the purposes served by the New York rules at issue here, comprehensively aimed at ambulance chasing and its attendant evils, are unimportant or unrelated to the protection of legitimate State interests. . . . A state may require evidence of good character, and may place the onus of its production upon the applicant. Konigsberg v. State Bar of California, 366 U.S. 36 . . ..

[Mr. Justice White dissented in a separate opinion.]

NOTES

(1) Does the principal case overrule the Konigsberg case above? See Niles and Kaye, *Spevack v. Klein: Milestone or Millstone in Bar Discipline?*, 53 A.B.A.J. 1121 (1967); Brown, *Lawyers and the Fifth Amendment: A Dissent*, 40 A.B.A.J. 404 (1954).

(2) Due process to which a lawyer is entitled in disciplinary proceedings was held to require that a lawyer be informed at the commencement of the proceedings of the nature of the charges against him and that a lawyer could not be disbarred on the basis of charges added during the pendency of the proceedings even though given opportunity to answer them. In re Ruffalo, 390 U.S. 544 (1968).

(3) In granting a petition of an attorney for reinsatement the court said: "All that we can require is a showing of rehabilitation and of present moral fitness. . . . Rehabilitation is of course a 'state of mind.' . . . The law looks with favor upon the regeneration of erring attorneys and should not place unnecessary burdens upon them." Peters, J., in Resner v. State Bar of California, 67 Cal.2d 799, 812, 433 P.2d 748 (1967).

Chapter XIV

THE JUDGE

SECTION 1. THE QUALITIES OF THE JUDGE

Introduction. This chapter deals with the personnel and structure of the judiciary and with its relationship to the bar. It leaves to other courses a consideration of how judges, especially appellate judges, reach their decision in the various fields of law. See Cardozo, The Nature of the Judicial Process (1921), p. 512 infra.

HARRY W. JONES, THE TRIAL JUDGE—ROLE ANALYSIS AND PROFILE, THE COURTS, THE PUBLIC, AND THE LAW EXPLOSION *

Pages 136, 144 (1965).

In any sizeable community there will be many lawyers of complete financial probity and genuinely first rate professional skill and acumen. Some of these able men would be very bad trial judges. It has been a central thesis of this essay that the role of the trial judge calls for uncommon qualities of personality and character. The demands and strains of his courtroom task require unusual emotional stability, exceptional firmness and serenity of temperament, and not infrequently great intellectual and psychic endurance. . . .

Courtroom decorum has to be maintained with a firm hand if cases are to be tried fairly and expeditiously, and as a case proceeds the trial judge is called upon to make many rulings that are of great strategic and tactical importance for the outcome of the litigation. These rulings, characteristically, have to be made by the trial judge "from the hip," that is, under the pressures of the trial and without opportunity for extended consultation of the formal authorities in the law books. Many trial judges who have later moved up to high appellate courts have spoken gratefully of the more relaxed pace and opportunity for reflection they found in appellate work after years of the hurly-burly of trial court proceedings. It is as if a teacher had suddenly been translated from a classroom assignment in a problem high school to the relative tranquility of a post as assistant superintendent of schools. . . .

In his relations with jurymen, witnesses, and litigants, the trial judge has to be empathetic and endlessly patient. As a sentencing official, his action must be compassionate without being mushyheaded,

---

* Copyright 1965 by The American Assembly, Columbia University. Reprinted by permission.

and his demeanor must be at once sensitive and austere. These are not attributes that can be measured on a quantitative scale or in any precisely objective way. But they are essential to performance of the role in accordance with the best traditions of common law adjudication.

NOTES

(1) "Avoiding a catastrophic choice is essential, but it is not enough. A judge need not be vicious, corrupt, or witless to be a menace in office. Mediocrity can be in the long run as bad a pollutant as venality, for it dampens opposition and is more likely to be tolerated. Judicial office today demands the best possible men, not those of merely average ability who were gray and undistinguished as lawyers and who will be just as drab as judges." Rosenberg, *The Qualities of Justices—Are they Strainable?*, 44 Texas L.Rev. 1063, 64 (1966).

(2) "When I became a judge I thought I had worked on just about every kind of case known to man or beast. The factual backgrounds, of course, were different, but the hundreds of appeals that I argued in various appellate courts covered a pretty wide range and I felt that all this experience was going to prove very helpful. What was my amazement to find that in the entire four years of my experience as a district judge I seemed always to be working on something that I knew absolutely nothing about. Patent cases, admiralty cases, special issues formulated by the Supreme Court, regulations of the Securities and Exchange Commission and the Interstate Commerce Commission, interpretations of the Wage and Hour Law, the Portal-to-Portal Law and so on and so on." Medina, *Some Reflections on the Judicial Function*, 38 A.B.A.J. 107, 09 (1952).

(3) "A judge should possess *knowledge;* and so far as he lacks that, he should go out to see that he obtains it. Knowledge, as I use it, is made intentionally an all-inclusive word. It will necessarily mean many things: complete understanding of the actual case and its growth and development and the parties before the court; familiarity with the background elements, including for so many of our cases the history of our government and the economic and political background of the debated issues; and an understanding of other wisdoms and disciplines, even—spare the word for the vehemence it has aroused—psychology. In short, the judge needs to be an educated man, educated not merely in the particular case, but in all that concerns the governmental institution which gives meaning and authority to his acts. Of course in one sense I am giving you very little beyond what all of us conceive for the ideal judge. In another, however, I am urging what I think can give a judge the wisdom and insight to exercise the situation-sense that the hard, but vital, case demands. And I am also warning against easy substitutes, however abstractly labeled, for the intellectual labor of acquiring knowledge and using it. There is no automation or IBM to provide answers, and the judge must know that and act on his own and all alone." Clark, The Limits of Judicial Objectivity* 13–14 (Am.U.1962).

* This is an excerpt from the Second Annual Edwin A. Mooers Lecture given by Judge Charles E. Clark at the Washington College of Law, The American University. Judge Clark of the United States Court of Appeals, Second Circuit, was formerly Dean of the Yale Law School.

MAURICE ROSENBERG, THE QUALITIES OF JUSTICES—ARE THEY STRAINABLE? *
44 Texas L.Rev. 1063, 67, 68, 70, 75, 76 (1966).

[In order to ascertain those qualities which trial judges themselves deem most important for success in their vocation, Professor Maurice Rosenberg of Columbia Law School asked 144 trial judges of varied experience to choose from 23 listed attributes those which they considered most essential. Surprisingly, the veteran judges and the novices were in agreement on the order of the six qualities of highest priority:

(1) Moral courage

(2) Decisiveness

(3) Reputation for fairness and uprightness

(4) Patience

(5) Good health, physical and mental

(6) Consideration for others.]

A striking feature of these highest ranking attributes is that they tend to focus upon the personality or person of the candidate—what he is rather than what he has done, his innate or intrinsic qualities rather than his "external" attainments. They are more concerned with temperament, disposition, character, and attitude than with background, training, or formal achievement. Except for good health, they tend to be subjective and difficult to recognize and measure. Furthermore, they are qualities that do not relate uniquely to the law, its study or its practice, and are not peculiar to lawyers or judges. They do not clearly differentiate those who are best equipped to be trial judges from other persons of virtue. Finally, they are not the kinds of qualities likely to erupt in a person for the first time after he reaches the bench—even granting the possibility that experience in judging may at times sharpen an existing capacity for decisiveness, courage, patience, and considerateness. . . .

[The two groups of trial judges were similarly in agreement in regard to what they felt to be the least significant of the listed qualities:

(23) Past honorable partisan political activity

(22) Higher earnings in practice than as a judge

(21) Active in civic and community affairs

(20) Experience in supervision of subordinates

(19) Well above average law school record

(18) Active in professional associations and work.]

---

* Copyright 1966 by The Texas Law Review. Reprinted with permission.

The highest scoring group, we have seen, is composed of attributes that are largely personal and subjective; the lowest rated tend to be impersonal and more objective. Between the two groups appear attributes of each type. High on the list of qualities of secondary importance were punctuality and good professional repute, both of the hard-to-measure type; but also present was trial experience, a matter that lends itself to quantitative assessment. Far down on the list were subjective qualities such as sense of humor, appearance, industriousness, dignity, and the most objective item of all: age . . . the judges' relative lack of sympathy for an age limit of sixty on appointments to the bench contrasts with strong views in bar-association and judicial-selection circles favoring the limit.

Like their check-list answers, the judges' additional answers heavily stressed homely virtues and humane qualities. These write-in entries were made in response to a survey question that followed the list of twenty-three attributes and asked the judge to insert additional "important attributes for a lawyer under consideration for the trial bench." The leading responses were compassion, patience, humility, integrity, and common sense. One judge summed up the qualities as "simple love for humanity"; another wrote "compassion for human error, weakness and fallibility." "Patience" appeared several times and so did "humility," for which one judge offered the straight-faced translation, "He should not have a super ego." . . .

[Since the early 1960's the Mayor's Committee on the Judiciary, comprised predominantly of lawyers, has been charged with recommending lawyers for appointment to judicial vacancies in New York City.]

"Character" was identified (by the Committee) as the most important personal qualification, and it was defined as moral vigor or ethical firmness and imperviousness to corrupting or venal influences. Next came "patience," the capacity to exercise forbearance under provocation, that is, to suffer fools gladly (or at least calmly) whether they are counsel or witnesses. Humility and tolerance were named as hallmarks of this quality and were defined as the capacity to listen with a mind intent on understanding the ideas or arguments being advanced and with an appreciation that "the certainties of today may become the superstitions of tomorrow." The Committee equated patience to the more common term, "judicial temperament."

"Zeal and capacity for work" came next on the Committee's list. These were termed the key to a judge's efficient and proper administration of his judicial functions. "Common sense" was chosen as a quality to look for because of the importance to a judge of the ability to make practical and reasonable judgments. Finally, the memorandum included "tact"—a sensitivity to the feelings of others and a capacity to deal with others without giving offense. It is no coincidence, of course, that the attributes picked by the Committee very closely resemble those contained in the injunction to the mayor "to select persons who are especially qualified for the court's work by reason of their character, personality, tact, patience and common sense."

HARRY W. JONES, THE TRIAL JUDGE—ROLE ANALYSIS AND PROFILE, THE COURTS, THE PUBLIC, AND THE LAW EXPLOSION
Page 138 (1965).

As claimants, defendants, and accused persons pass before him, a trial judge meets and has to put up with many more scoundrels, cheats, and liars than most other men encounter in their vocations. His work is not calculated to make him excessively optimistic concerning the natural inclinations of human nature. The lawyers who appear as counsel before him are often incompetent or barely competent, and the trial judge of first-rate intellectual and professional attainments has the good craftsman's proper impatience with shoddy work and wishes that the sorry advocates before him would get on with their business. It is hard for an able man to suffer fools gladly when they are certified members of his own profession. Sometimes the trial judge has the even more painful awareness that one of his fellow professionals of the practicing bar is trying to mislead him into acceptance of a fraudulent claim or defense or trying to badger him into some error that will cause the reversal of the trial court judgment on appeal. And, all the while, the conscientious trial judge is striving to maintain unbroken concentration on a flow of complex and conflicting evidence that may extend over many days.

NOTES

(1) The significance in the administration of justice of "the eight cardinal judicial virtues—the virtues of independence, of courtesy and patience, of dignity and a sense of humor, of openmindedness, of impartiality, of thoroughness and decisiveness, of an understanding heart and of social consciousness" are discussed and made vivid with illustrations in Bernard L. Shientag, The Personality of the Judge, Third Annual Cardozo Lecture, Association of the Bar of the City of New York, 20 (1944).

(2) See Canons of Judicial Ethics No. 34. Reference is made to these Canons and to the American Bar Association reformulation in Chapter III, Section 2, Note (2) p. 166 supra.

(3) The "qualities of justices" (to borrow from Rosenberg) noted above are important but are they somehow too static to satisfy the needs of the contemporary scene? Our judges must be truthful men—not just interpret the law truthfully. They must be just men—not just dispense justice honorably and impartially. Then the qualities they sense and understand can be sensed and understood by those who stand before them.

(4) "It is only by confidence in our ability to reach truth by our own individual thinking, that we are capable of accepting truth from outside." Schweitzer, C. T. Campion, tr., Out of My Life and Thought 173 (Mentor ed. 1949). Copyright, Holt, Rinehart and Winston, Inc., 1933, 1949, 1961.

SECTION 2. THE FUNCTION OF THE JUDGE

A. THE TRIAL JUDGE

HARRY W. JONES, THE TRIAL JUDGE—ROLE ANALYSIS AND PROFILE, THE COURTS, THE PUBLIC, AND THE LAW EXPLOSION

Pages 125, 130 (1965).

Aristotle was surely right when he said that members of the public look upon the judge as "living justice," that is, as the personification of the legal order. For better or worse, it is the trial judge upon whom this representative responsibility falls in our society. He is the law for most people and most legal purposes. Whenever a trial judge fails in probity, energy, objectivity, or patience, his failure is observable and cannot but impair public fidelity to law. This is true even and particularly of the minor magistrate in a police court or a small-claims tribunal. He may be at the bottom of the judicial totem pole, but it is there that the exposure is often greatest and strains of the judge's role manifest for all to see. . . .

What of the other preconception that underlies public discounting of the importance of the trial judge's role as an adjudicative official? What merit is there in the suggestion that the center of gravity of American adjudication is really in the appellate courts and that the determinations of trial judges are provisional only and subject to ready correction on appeal? The realities of the American judicial system have been obscured, in scholarly writing as in public discussion, by the stubborn persistence of what the late Judge Jerome Frank called the "upper-court myth," the notion that everything will be all right in the house of justice so long as appeals from trial-court decisions are freely available and the upper courts manned by judges of wisdom, experience, and professional competence. In this view, which has been contributed to by the almost exclusive preoccupation of American legal education with the reported opinions of appellate courts, the trial-court stage of a civil suit or criminal prosecution seems a mere preliminary bout; the main event will not begin until the case reaches the appellate court of last resort. Political scientists have absorbed the upper-court myth as uncritically as their scholarly brothers in the law schools. For every book or article analyzing the functioning of the trial courts as agencies of government and large-scale public administration, there are a dozen or more given to charting the batting averages of individual justices of the Supreme Court of the United States on this or that issue of constitutional law or to developing the logical or policy subtleties of striking pieces of rhetoric in Supreme Court opinions.

The extent to which the upper-court myth distorts the relative significance of trial-court functioning and appellate-court functioning is manifest even if we put aside, for the moment, the assembly-line operations of police courts, traffic courts, small claims courts, and the like and consider only the traditional and substantial civil and criminal cases that are heard, as of first instance, in trial courts of general jurisdiction. It is a safe guess that at least 90 per cent of even these blue ribbon controversies are determined and controlled, as to practical outcome, by rules of law applied and facts "found" at the trial-court stage, as against 10 per cent at most that are controlled in result by what happens to them in the appellate courts. It is in the appellate courts that precedents are forged for the future and statutes given their authoritative interpretation and effect, but, as concerns the ultimate adjudicative fate of litigated controversies, the trial courts outweigh the appellate courts by at least nine to one.

EDWARD L. BARRETT, CRIMINAL JUSTICE: THE PROBLEM OF MASS PRODUCTION, THE COURTS, THE PUBLIC AND THE LAW EXPLOSION

Page 87 (1965).

If one enters the courthouse in any sizeable city and walks from courtroom to courtroom, what does he see? One judge, in a single morning, is accepting pleas of guilty from and sentencing a hundred or more persons charged with drunkenness. Another judge is adjudicating traffic cases with an average time of no more than a minute per case. A third is disposing of a hundred or more other misdemeanor offenses in a morning, by granting delays, accepting pleas of guilty, and imposing sentences.

Wherever the visitor looks at the system, he finds great numbers of defendants being processed by harassed and overworked officials. Police have more cases than they can investigate. . . .

Suddenly it becomes clear that for most defendants in the criminal process, there is scant regard for them as individuals. They are numbers on dockets, faceless ones to be processed and sent on their way. The gap between the theory and the reality is enormous.

REPORT OF THE JOINT CONFERENCE ON PROFESSIONAL RESPONSIBILITY

1958 A.A.L.S. Pro. 187, 188, 44 A.B.A.J. 1159, 1160 (1958).

It is only through the advocate's participation that the hearing may remain in fact what it purports to be in theory: a public trial of the facts and issues. Each advocate comes to the hearing prepared to present his proofs and arguments, knowing at the same time that his arguments may fail to persuade and that his proofs may be rejected as inadequate. It is a part of his role to absorb these possible disappointments. The deciding tribunal, on the other hand, comes to the hearing uncommitted. It has not represented to the public that any fact can be proved, that any argument is sound, or that any particular way of stating a litigant's case is the most effective expression of its merits.

The matter assumes a very different aspect when the deciding tribunal is compelled to take into its own hands the preparations that must precede the public hearing. In such a case the tribunal cannot truly be said to come to the hearing uncommitted, for it has itself appointed the channels along which the public inquiry is to run. If an unexpected turn in the testimony reveals a miscalculation in the design of these channels, there is no advocate to absorb the blame. The deciding tribunal is under a strong temptation to keep the hearing moving within the boundaries originally set for it. The result may be that the hearing loses its character as an open trial of the facts and issues, and becomes instead a ritual designed to provide public confirmation for what the tribunal considers it has already established in private.

NOTES

(1) "In an athletic contest, the referee or umpire occupies a most inconspicuous position during the contest. The trial judge on the bench high above the trial arena occupies the most conspicuous place in the courtroom. The jurors watch him constantly. He is in charge of everything. He opens the Court and runs it. He decides all questions of law. He tells both jurors and lawyers when to stand, sit, leave and return. He tells the jurors when not to consider certain things. When he talks, everyone remains quiet and listens. In most instances, the judge is garbed in a black robe. He creates the impression of quiet dignity. He speaks with authority and finality. Every time the judge moves his head, arms or body the jurors watch him. They look at his face. In the minds of the jurors, the judge is supreme. He can do no wrong. Jurors seek to avoid the displeasure of the judge. They are reluctant to decide questions of fact contrary to what they believe the views of the judge to be. Most of all, if the judge criticizes or condemns counsel, jurors join with the judge in his condemnation. The lawyer then has two strikes against him and his chances of winning are remote." Conner, The Trial Judge, his Facial Expressions, Gestures and General Demeanor—Their Effect on the Administration of Justice, Trial Lawyer's Guide 1965, 257 (1965).

(2) "I have in the past—I am glad to say it is now the dim and distant past—seen a jury rendered so inimical by the conduct of the judge that they have returned a verdict in the teeth of the evidence. Juries are fairminded. They strongly object to any form of persecution rather than prosecution and thus if the judge indicates too strong a view against an accused person, they are quite likely to return a verdict which may be regarded as against the judge rather than in favour of the prisoner. On the other hand, if the jury decide that the judge has conducted the trial fairly, they will perform their duty equally fairly, and will not shrink from returning a verdict which is in conflict with their sympathies but in accordance with justice." Sir Laurence

A. Byrne, *The Judge's Role in Administering Justice*, 22 Federal Probation 12, 13 (March 1958).

(3) "While a courtroom is not a laboratory for the scientific pursuit of truth, a trial judge is surely not confined to an account, obviously fragmentary, of the circumstances of a happening, here the meagre testimony of Johnson, when he has at his command the means of exploring them fully, or at least more fully, before passing legal judgment. A trial is not a game of blind man's buff; and the trier of the facts upon which he is to pronounce the law—need not blindfold himself by failing to call an available vital witness simply because the parties, for reasons of trial tactics, choose to withhold his testimony.

"Federal judges are not referees at prize-fights but functionaries of justice. See Herron v. Southern Pacific Co., 283 U.S. 91, 95; Quercia v. United States, 289 U.S. 466, 469. As such they have a duty of initiative to see that the issues are determined within the scope of the pleadings, not left to counsel's chosen argument." Justice Frankfurter dissenting in part in Johnson v. United States, 333 U.S. 46, 53–54, (1947).

(4) "In nonjury as in jury cases, a substantial part of the bar prefers to have the judge sit patiently while the evidence comes in and then at the end of the trial summarize the testimony which he believes. This seems the sounder practice in the great bulk of trials. But in cases of public significance, Edmund Burke admonished us: 'It is the duty of the Judge to receive every offer of evidence, apparently material, suggested to him, though the parties themselves through negligence, ignorance, or corrupt collusion, should not bring it forward'. A judge is not placed in that high situation merely as a passive instrument of parties. He has a duty of his own, independent of them, and that duty is to investigate the truth." Wyzanski, *A Trial Judge's Freedom and Responsibility*, 65 Harv.L.Rev. 1281, 93, 94, (1952). Copyright, Harvard Law Review Association.

(5) See further discussion of the role of advocate and judge in the adversary process in Chapter VII, supra, particularly Section 1, The Nature of a Trial.

U. S. v. MARZANO

United States Court of Appeals, Second Circuit, 1945.
149 F.2d 923.

[From the transcript of the trial, the judge questioning two witnesses:

The Court: Listen to the oath very carefully. I am going to give it to you.

The Witness: Your Honor, I refuse—

The Court: No. Do you solemnly swear that the testimony you shall give in this case shall be the truth, the whole truth and nothing but the truth, so help you God?

The Witness: I swear.

Q. What is your full name? A. Vincent Tessalone.

Q. You pleaded guilty here to both indictments? A. That is why I refuse to answer.

Q. You have pleaded guilty and are awaiting sentence by me, aren't you? A. Yes, sir.

Q. Do you know the defendant Alfonso Marzano? A. I do.

Q. How long do you know him? A. All my life.

Q. Are you related to him? A. No, sir.

Q. What do you mean by "all your life"? How old are you? A. Since I was a kid.

Q. How old are you? A. 45.

Q. Did you have any conversation with this defendant about narcotics? A. I refuse to answer, your Honor.

Q. Why? A. I am already under sentence.

The Court: I direct you to answer. A. I never did.

Q. What? A. I do not get that.

Q. Did you ever have any talks with the defendant Marzano about narcotics? A. I do not remember.

Q. You do not remember? A. I do not know nothing about him.

Q. What is it you remember? A. I never did talk to him.

Q. Never talked to him? A. No.

Q. Did you ever discuss narcotics with him? A. I never did.

Q. Drugs? A. No, sir.

Q. Are you telling the truth? A. I am. . . .

By the Court: Q. You are awaiting sentence? Do you know you are awaiting sentence by me? You know I am going to sentence you? A. Yes, sir.

Q. You know that? A. Yes, sir.

Q. Anything you want to change about your testimony, anything here—

Mr. Solomon: I object.

The Court: Overruled.

Mr. Solomon: I want to get this on the record. I object as to your Honor stating to this witness in words or substance, "You know I am going to sentence you," because in my opinion—

The Court: I do not care anything about your opinion. Do not express it.

Mr. Solomon: I object to it on the ground that it tends to influence this man in giving testimony, because it may be under threat. That is my humble opinion.

Q. Have you told the truth here? A. Yes, sir. I do not know anything else about the man.]

L. HAND, J. (at p. 926) . . .

Moreover, even if the jury were not as likely as seems to us to be the case, to have so understood what took place, the judge was exhibiting a prosecutor's zeal, inconsistent with that detachment and aloofness which courts have again and again demanded, particularly in criminal trials. Despite every allowance he must not take on the role of a partisan; he must not enter the lists; he must not by his ardor induce the jury to join in a hue and cry against the accused. Prosecution and judgment are two quite separate functions in the administration of justice; they must not merge. . . .

Judgment reversed; new trial ordered.

NOTES

(1) In the principal case what if it were the defense counsel instead of the prosecution, who seemed to need the court's help? Would this warrant such active participation by the trial judge? Had the judge not been so blatantly coercive in his technique, should a new trial have been granted merely because the trial judge took charge of examining this key witness?

(2) A judge may properly intervene in a trial . . . to promote expedition, and prevent unnecessary waste of time, or to clear up some obscurity, but he should bear in mind that his undue interference, impatience, or participation in the examination of witnesses, or a severe attitude on his part toward witnesses . . . may tend to prevent the proper presentation of the cause, or the ascertainment of the truth in respect thereto. . . Canons of Judicial Ethics No. 15.

B. THE APPELLATE JUDGE

BENJAMIN J. CARDOZO, THE NATURE OF THE JUDICIAL PROCESS *

Pages 10, 19–21 (1921).

. . . What is it that I do when I decide a case? To what sources of information do I appeal for guidance? In what proportions do I permit them to contribute to the result? In what proportions ought they to contribute? If a precedent is applicable, when do I refuse to follow it? If no precedent is applicable, how do I reach the rule that will make a precedent for the future? If I am seeking logical consistency, the symmetry of the legal structure, how far shall I seek it? At what point shall the quest be halted by some discrepant custom, by some consideration of the social welfare, by my own or the common standards of justice and morals? Into that strange compound which is brewed daily in the caldron of the courts, all these ingredients enter in varying proportions. I am not concerned to in-

---

* Copyright 1921 by the Yale University Press. Reprinted with permission.

quire whether judges ought to be allowed to brew such a compound at all. I take judge-made law as one of the existing realities of life. . . .

In a system so highly developed as our own, precedents have so covered the ground that they fix the point of departure from which the labor of the judge begins. Almost invariably, his first step is to examine and compare them. If they are plain and to the point, there may be need of nothing more. *Stare decisis* is at least the everyday working rule of our law. I shall have something to say later about the propriety of relaxing the rule in exceptional conditions. But unless those conditions are present, the work of deciding cases in accordance with precedents that plainly fit them is a process similar in its nature to that of deciding cases in accordance with a statute. It is a process of search, comparison, and little more. Some judges seldom get beyond that process in any case. Their notion of their duty is to match the colors of the case at hand against the colors of many sample cases spread out upon their desk. The sample nearest in shade supplies the applicable rule. But, of course, no system of living law can be evolved by such a process, and no judge of a high court, worthy of his office, views the function of his place so narrowly. If that were all there was to our calling, there would be little of intellectual interest about it. The man who had the best card index of the cases would also be the wisest judge. It is when the colors do not match, when the references in the index fail, when there is no decisive precedent, that the serious business of the judge begins. He must then fashion law for the litigants before him. In fashioning it for them, he will be fashioning it for others.

NOTES

(1) See Canons of Judicial Ethics No. 20, Influence of Decisions upon the Development of the Law.

(2) "First, what are the practical, political limits within which the Supreme Court exercises its august authority to set aside the actions of the other branches of the Government of the United States or of a State as inconsistent with the Constitution? Second, what are the moral limits of the power that this great responsibility entails?" Wechsler, *The Courts and the Constitution*, 65 Col.L.Rev. 1001 (1965).

C. EXTRAJUDICIAL FUNCTIONS

ARTHUR T. VANDERBILT, JUDGES AND JURORS: THEIR FUNCTIONS, QUALITIES AND SELECTION *

Page 12 (1956).

In addition to these judicial tasks throughout the centuries judges have been entrusted with other governmental assignments. Historically this is clearly seen in the activities of the early common law

---

* Copyright 1969 by the American Bar Association. Reprinted with permission.

judges as statesmen and advisers to the King, and in the participation of the Lord Chancellor to this day in the English cabinet. In early America this pattern was duplicated; Chief Justice Jay of the Supreme Court was called upon by President Washington to act as Ambassador to England to conduct the negotiation of a treaty with that country. In more recent years when impartiality and independence of party was required Justice Roberts headed the Pearl Harbor Commission and Justice Jackson served as the American Prosecutor of the Nazis at Nuremberg. Such tasks are not properly a part of the judicial function and may even be said to derogate from the judge's proper performance of his duties.

THE NEW YORK TIMES, EDITORIAL *

June 15, 1969, Sec. 4, at 16, Col. 1.

The Honor of the Court

The Judicial Conference under the leadership of Chief Justice Earl Warren has moved with commendable swiftness and sensitivity to protect the good name of the Federal judiciary. In setting forth strict new rules against outside earnings and in providing for full financial disclosure, the Conference has adopted a standard of behavior more rigorous than that required of members of the executive branch . . .

The new rules make explicit the standards most judges have followed on their own initiative. Judges are not to serve as directors of banks and corporations, not to engage in the practice of law by managing trusts and estates, and not to accept retainers from foundations and other institutions. The underscoring of these restraints is all to the good.

In one respect, however, the new code seems unnecessarily stringent. By barring all outside compensation, it would prevent judges from earning money by writing or by lecturing at law schools. Outside activities of this kind, provided the payment is reasonably modest, could involve no conceivable conflict of interest and might improve a judge's work by deepening his insight into changing trends in law and society.

Judges have to guard themselves at all times against even the appearance of impropriety but they can exercise appropriate self-discipline without retreating into monastic isolation. Since the new code provides that a judge can apply to the judicial council of his own circuit for permission to accept outside compensation in specific instances, the Judicial Conference might well consider giving a blanket exemption for writing and lecturing on the law. . . . Although

---

* Copyright 1969 by The New York Times. Reprinted with permission.

the Conference's power to discipline a judge is undefined, it would be a rare judge who would ignore the censure of his colleagues.

There remains the problem of Supreme Court justices over which the Judicial Conference has no authority. . . .

NOTES

(1) Consider Chief Justice Warren's role as Chairman of the Commission which investigated the assassination of President Kennedy. Was his service useful to the Court? To the Country?

(2) See Hurst, The Growth of American Law—The Law Makers (1950), Chap. 9, "Social Functions of the Courts."

(3) The undesirability of calling on judges of the Courts of the United States to perform tasks, perhaps political as well as controversial, in executive departments and agencies of the federal government, was the subject of commentary in a report of the Committee on the Judiciary of the United States Senate. The portion of the report dealing with the matter is reprinted under the title, *Independence of Judges: Should They Be Used for Non-Judicial Work?*, in 33 A.B.A.J. 792 (1947). This question was answered in the negative by the action of Justice Fortas in withdrawing his name from consideration as Chief Justice of the United States.

(4) To what extent is it desirable for judges to educate the public about the meaning of their opinions? See the following Letter to the Editor which appeared in The Wall Street Journal, July 3, 1968:

Washington

Editor, The Wall Street Journal:

I have read with interest the editorial of June 20, "The Alternate Legislature."

In the case to which you refer, a man was refused the purchase of a house solely because he was a Negro. He eventually brought his case to the Supreme Court, relying upon a law, 42 U.S.C.A. § 1982, written and passed by Congress, that says:

"All citizens of the United States shall have the same right, in every State and Territory, as is enjoyed by white citizens thereof to inherit, purchase, lease, sell, hold, and convey real and personal property."

The Supreme Court held (1) that this law means what it says, and (2) that Congress had Constitutional power to pass it. You say this made the Court a "legislature."

What would the Court have been if it had held (1) that the law does not mean what it says, or (2) that Congress did not have power to pass it?

I add only that Congress, having enacted 42 U.S.C.A. § 1982, remains free to amend it at any time.

Potter Stewart,
Associate Justice, U. S. Supreme Court

SECTION 3. SELECTION AND TENURE OF JUDGES

CAREER JUDICIARY

E. BLYTHE STASON, JUDICIAL SELECTION AROUND THE WORLD

41 J.Am.Jud.Soc'y 134, 137–38 (1958).

Since the French system of judicial selection and tenure has been copied throughout most of continental Europe, we can afford to take a careful look at it. We find that the judiciary in France is entirely separate from the practicing branch of the profession. Young men at the time of finishing law school choose either to go into the active practice of the law or into the "magistrature." If they decide upon the latter, they must pass competitive examinations; and thereafter as vacancies arise they enter upon their judicial duties and do so at a fairly early age, spending their lives in public service, starting at the lower ranks and progressing from time to time in accordance with their ability and especially according to their good fortune in obtaining promotion through the Ministry of Justice. Down to 1934 the appointment and promotion of all judges was left to the more or less complete discretionary power of the Minister, but in 1934 dissatisfaction with that system brought about a change, and since that date the task has been handled by a judiciary commission of five members, all judges, including the president of the Court of Cessation; two associate judges of that court, selected by the court; a president of a court of appeal selected by the presidents of the courts of appeal; and one other judge, selected by the trial courts. This commission, with a representative of the Ministry sitting with it but without vote, submits a list of three names for each judicial vacancy from which the Minister of Justice must make his selection. The list is prepared from the total roster of judges plus the neophytes who have passed the competitive examinations. . . .

The French system is followed with modifications in Italy, Belgium, and, indeed, in most of the continent of Europe as well as in certain other countries of the world. . . .

NOTE

"The system of a judicial civil service has much to commend it. So far as original appointment is concerned, it provides a notable safeguard against favoritism in nomination; and the esprit de corps engendered has certainly given to France a body of judges distinguished by their learning and technical competence. Its weaknesses, it may be argued, are twofold. The very fact that it is a civil service tends to make it both conservative in outlook and excessively formalistic in method; it tends to emphasize the procedural rather than the substantive side of law. And the fact that promotion is an internal matter tends to deprive it of the services of men who come to the problems of the law with a knowledge of the world outside the courts and therefore something of the statesman's insight. A system like the French may produce judges to rival Story in eminence or Willes in learning; it will hardly produce judges with the breadth of outlook of Mansfield or Marshall. And it may be argued that in the process of adjusting law to life the power to produce and use men of the stamp of Mansfield and Marshall is essential to the full success of a judicial system." Laski,* Judiciary, 8 Encyclopedia of the Social Sciences 464, 466 (1937). Copyright, The Macmillan Company.

POLITICAL APPOINTMENT

E. BLYTHE STASON, JUDICIAL SELECTION AROUND THE WORLD

41 Am.Jud. Soc'y 134, 136, 138 (1958).

The Lord Chancellor is principal judicial officer in the British Government. He is a member of the Cabinet. He presides as Speaker in the House of Lords. He is the Custodian of the Great Seal. He is the presiding judge of England's highest tribunal, the House of Lords. He is a member of the Judicial Committee of the Privy Council. When vacancies occur in the membership of the High Court of Justice, these vacancies are filled on recommendation of the Lord Chancellor. Not only does he fill vacancies on the High Court, but all of the county courts of England, fifty-six in number and certain of the London local courts are under his supervision, and the judges of these courts also are appointed and may be removed by him. It is obvious, therefore, that the Lord Chancellor's position is one of very great power and influence. He holds his own appointment from the King or Queen, but long custom has established the practice that the monarch merely confirms the recommendation made by the Prime Minister. The Lord Chancellor is therefore a political officer in a very real sense, for a change of government usually results in appointment of a new Lord Chancellor thus to represent the views of the prevailing party.

However, the traditions of the Bench and the Bar in England are such that the Lord Chancellor's appointments to the bench can be said to be uniformly non-political in character. Tradition commands that when an appointment is to be made to the British bench only the best in the way of judicial ability will be accepted, and once the appointment is made the independence of the judge is assured.

It is sometimes true that the Lord Chancellor confers with the Prime Minister concerning the appointments, but the choice is entirely his own. . . .

---

* Harold Laski is best known as a political writer and as a contributor to political thinking in Great Britain, particularly in the Labour Party. His book, The American Democracy includes a chapter on "The Professions in America."

JOEL B. GROSSMAN, LAWYERS AND JUDGES, THE ABA AND THE POLITICS OF JUDICIAL SELECTION

Pages 24, 27, 62 (1965).

The constitutional responsibility for selecting justices of the [United States] Supreme Court, "by and with the advice and consent of Senate," rests with the President.

. . . Of the three levels of federal courts, the President's latitude for choice is greatest with regard to nominations to the Supreme Court and least (but not nonexistent) concerning nominees to the District Courts. With rare exceptions Presidents have considered Supreme Court appointments to be their personal prerogative, and senators of the same party as the President have always considered District Court appointments to fall within their sphere of responsibility. Nominations to the Courts of Appeals and (formerly) nonconstitutional courts appear to "go either way," depending on the case at hand. . . .

[Since 1946 with the formation of the Special Committee on the Judiciary the American Bar Association has played an active role in the selection of Federal Judges.]

The Committee on Federal Judiciary (as it was later named) has become the major instrument in the postwar campaign of the American Bar Association to exert a direct influence on the selection of specific persons as federal judges. From the inception of this Committee in 1946 until the present, the American Bar Association has sought (and to a large degree achieved) public and official approval for the right of the organized bar to be consulted in the actual selection of judges. Its successful campaign to achieve this goal marks the first time in American history that the legal profession has been accorded that privilege at the federal level.

NOTE

". . . In nine states, Puerto Rico, and the federal system, judges are appointed by the Governor (or President) with the consent of the legislature. In Puerto Rico, the Governor has recently voluntarily appointed a nominating commission to furnish him with recommendations for his judicial appointments. In four states judges are appointed by the legislature itself . . ." The Association of the Bar of the City of New York, Report of the Special Committee on the Constitutional Convention, Selection of Judges 4 (1967).

ELECTION OF JUDGES

RUSSELL D. NILES, THE POPULAR ELECTION OF JUDGES IN HISTORICAL PERSPECTIVE

21 Record of the Ass'n.Bar City N.Y. 523, 526–27 (1963).

The [New York Constitutional] Convention of 1846 was the first where delegates were elected on the basis of near-universal suffrage. Unlike its predecessors, it was not dominated by the old landed aristocracy, and the politicians, lawyers and judges who were identified with them. Of the 127 delegates, 45 were lawyers, or "lawyers and farmers"; a goodly number were merchants, mechanics and farmers. A major object of reform was the appointive judiciary. The specific grievance concerned the judges themselves, since the tenant farmers needed a sympathetic judiciary to void the oppressive leases. But, more generally, the delegates were caught up in the spirit of the day. All privileges, and all appointive systems which took control from the people, were to be condemned. Even qualifications for admission to the bar were attacked as creating a "privileged class."

. . .

[T]he spirit of reform carried the day. Despite the fact that only Mississippi elected its superior court judges, the New York Convention was completely persuaded by the following argument: "Abolish the appointing power, and you will have no more scrambling to get on nominating committees. You will elect good men to office, and politicians by trade will not exhaust their patriotism in serving on committees without pay." To combine the words of two nineteenth century critics of the reformed system, the popular election of judges "floated in on the rush of the stream of revolution," "not for any assigned cause, but purely upon a political theory." All judges and all public officers were to be elected.

The consequences of the decision in New York to abandon the appointive system in all courts of superior jurisdiction had an immediate profound influence in many other states. In 1846, only a few states had experimented with the elective system in their inferior courts. Mississippi alone had adopted an elective system for all judges. By 1856, however, 15 of the 29 states had swung over to popular election of judges—seven in the year 1850. Thereafter, as new states were admitted to the Union, all accepted the popular election of some or all of their judges up until the admission of Alaska.

NOTES

(1) "Today thirty-four states use the elective system for selecting judges in whole or in part. In sixteen of these states ballots without party designations are used, which tends to reduce the political aspects of the contest." The Association of the Bar of the City of New York, Special Committee on the Constitutional Convention, Selection of Judges, 4 (1967).

(2) "[P]eoples' judges, that is, the judges of the lower courts, are elected by popular vote. Judges of the higher courts are elected by the Soviet representative assemblies; namely, the regional and supreme Soviets. Judges may be removed from office prior to the conclusion of their terms by recall by the constituency. Although elected, the Soviet judge works under the control of the federal Ministry of Justice, the Ministry of Justice of the Republic, and the so-called Regional Bureaus of the Ministry of Justice attached to Regional Soviets. All of these administrative agencies are authorized, among other things, to check by means of inspection the correctness of the application of laws by the peoples' courts in trying criminal and civil cases [and] to submit to the Commissar for Justice cases which are proven by inspection to have been decided by the peoples' courts 'against the law'." Stason, *Judicial Selection Around the World*, 41 J.Am.Jud.Soc'y. 134, 140 (1958).

(3) ". . . Most American judges have always gone on the bench by *appointment*—not by election. This is true because of the almost universal provision that in case of a vacancy caused by death or resignation, the governor may appoint someone to fill out the the remainder of the term. This is the way most vacancies occur, and so a majority of the judges even in the elective states have become judges by appointment, not election.

"In ten years, 1948–1957, more than 56 per cent, 242 out of 434, of the justices of courts of last resort in 36 so-called *elective* states went on to the bench by appointment. Three such courts were composed entirely of appointed judges. Four states had over an 80 per cent average and ten *elective* states had 60 to 80 per cent of their judges appointed.

"An equivalent study of trial courts has not yet been undertaken, but specific instances indicate a similar condition. Eight years ago, 70 of the 78 judges then sitting in the Los Angeles Superior Court had gone on by appointment. Two thirds of the general trial judges now sitting in New Mexico were appointed; 19 of the 41 Colorado district judges in 1963; 29 of 36 Philadelphia Common Pleas judges from 1896 to 1937; 42 per cent of the Wisconsin circuit judges up to 1953; three-fourths of the Minnesota district judges sitting in 1941; 66 per cent of all Texas judges between 1940 and 1962—all these are *appointed* judges in so-called *elective* states.

"If to the number of judges formally appointed by governors to fill vacancies, is added those *de facto* appointees whose names are selected by political party leaders to run without opposition or on coalition tickets so that the voters have no choice, the percentage is even higher." Winters and Allard, *Two Dozen Misconceptions About Judicial Selection and Tenure*, 48 J.Am.Jud.Soc. 138, 139–40 (1964).

APPOINTMENT FROM A PANEL

In 1913 Professor Albert M. Kales of Northwestern University Law School developed a plan, based on merit, for the selection and tenure of judges. The American Judicature Society, founded in 1913 to promote reform in the judiciary, campaigned vigorously for the adoption of the Kales plan. In 1937 the House of Delegates of the American Bar Association endorsed the essential elements of the plan, and in 1940 Missouri became the first state to adopt the merit plan, using it for the selection and tenure of all appellate judges and for the trial judges of the City of St. Louis and for Jackson County (Kansas City). The Kales plan, which became commonly known as the American Bar or Missouri Plan, was later accepted by Alaska, Iowa, Nebraska and Arizona, and with modifications in California and Illinois, and by the cities of Denver, Tulsa and Cleveland and by Dade County, Florida.

Basically, the Missouri Plan provides for:

1) nomination of prospective candidates for vacant judicial offices by a nominating commission composed of representatives of the lay public, the bar and the bench.

2) appointment of judges by the governor from a list of candidates submitted by the nominating commission.

3) opportunity for the public, after a stipulated period of time, to determine by popular vote whether or not to retain the judge in office. The judge runs solely on his record—he is unopposed and the ballot is non partisan.

NOTE

A 1965 survey of the Missouri bar conducted by a team of political scientists with the assistance of grants from the Social Science Research Council and the Research Center of the University of Missouri showed the following:

"Of the 1,233 respondents who replied to the questionnaire, 61 per cent favor the [Missouri] plan, 16 per cent prefer nonpartisan elections, 12 per cent partisan elections and 11 per cent have other suggestions or expressed no opinion. The results [of personal interviews with over 200 state lawyers] show that the consequences of the plan about which most lawyers agree are that the plan recruits better judges than popular election does. The major reason advanced for this result is that able lawyers are more willing to seek a judgeship under a system that spares them the rigors, expense and uncertainties of election campaigns. Most lawyers also agree that the independence judges enjoy under the plan encourages them to make decisions based on the merits of cases, rather than subjecting them to pressures elective judges must often face. About two thirds of the attorneys see these as results of the plan, while only about one tenth of them do not.

"The allegations concerning the merit plan about which the Missouri Bar is most uncertain are those relating to the role that 'politics' plays in choosing judges. The lawyers are almost evenly divided on the issue of whether the plan has succeeded for the most part in taking 'politics' out of the selection of judges. Thirty-eight per cent say it has, while 41 per cent feel it has not. More than half the lawyers in the state agree, moreover, that the plan substitutes Bar politics and gubernatorial politics for the traditional politics of party leaders and machines, compared to about one fifth of the Bar that thinks this result has not occurred." Watson, *Missouri Lawyers Evaluate the Merit Plan for Selection and Tenure of Judges*, 52 A.B.A.J. 539, 540–42 (1966).

REPORT OF THE ASSOCIATION OF THE BAR OF THE CITY OF NEW YORK, SPECIAL COMMITTEE ON THE CONSTITUTIONAL CONVENTION, SELECTION OF JUDGES

Pages 5–9 (1967).

Arguments for the Elective System

(1) The elective system assures the selection of judges representative of all groups in the community—ethnic, religious, racial and age; this is important to foster faith in the judicial process by these groups.

(2) Courts must reflect to some degree social changes in the community; because of popular participation in it, the political process is better able to select men aware of and sensitive to these changes.

(3) Politics can never be eliminated from selection of any government officer. Appointive authorities, including Presidents and Governors, are generally the leaders of their own political parties; nominating commissions and bar associations are all subject to their own kind of political pressures.

(4) It is important to support party government because in the long run it will produce better candidates; any appointive system weakens party government.

Arguments for the Nominating Commission and Appointive System

(1) The appointive system with a judicial nominating commission greatly minimizes political influence.

(2) The electorate participates in a limited degree and is not informed concerning elected judicial candidates or their qualifications.

. . . In New York State a poll was taken in 1954 which showed that only 1% of the voters in a rural upstate county, as well as in New York City, could remember the name of the newly-elected Chief Judge of the Court of Appeals.

(3) The elective system is essentially a system of choice by political party officials. . . .

(4) Political ties often continue after election. . . .

(5) Many able lawyers are unwilling to become judicial candidates under the elective process.

(6) The appointive system can produce a balanced as well as qualified judiciary. . . .

(7) The nominating commission system maximizes independence of the judicial branch.

It was noted above that one of the arguments made for an elective system is the notion that it is essential to the separation of powers—i. e., that under an appointive process the executive branch will be unduly influential over the judicial branch.

On the contrary, it would appear that the nominating commission system would help to assure the independence of the judiciary by narrowly limiting the choice which can be made by the appointive power. Moreover, if judges are given life tenure as in the federal judiciary and as recommended herein, they would be uniquely independent of the executive branch.

NOTES

(1) In spite of the arguments in favor of the nominating commission and appointive system New York still retains the elective system. What reasons can you suggest?

(2) "Two successive Mayors of the City of New York have voluntarily created a judicial nominating commission, known as the Mayor's Committee on the Judiciary, which recommends names to him for vacancies on the Criminal Court and Family Court of New York City and, where vacancies occur between elections, on the Civil Court. Mayor Lindsay has strongly urged that this system be given constitutional status and be extended to other courts." Report of the Association of the Bar of the City of New York, Special Committee on the Constitutional Convention, Selection of Judges 8–9 (1967).

(3) A detailed study of the methods of selecting judges in common law and civil law countries is available in Haynes, The Selection and Tenure of Judges (1944).

TENURE AND RETIREMENT OF JUDGES

THE ASSOCIATION OF THE BAR OF THE CITY OF NEW YORK, REPORT OF THE SPECIAL COMMITTEE ON THE CONSTITUTIONAL CONVENTION, REMOVAL OF JUDGES

Pages i–v (1967).

The subject of removal of judges has received much attention in recent years from bench, bar and legislatures. A number of states have proposed or are considering proposing constitutional amendments relating to the problem. The American Bar Association at its general meeting in Miami last August authorized a comprehensive study of the subject. The United States Senate has been holding hearings on the problem. The American Bar Association Journal and the Journal of The American Judicature Society have carried numerous pertinent articles in the last three years.

The problem is to devise a fair and effective means to deal with judges and justices who cannot properly discharge their duties because of their age, incompetency, arbitrariness, judicial misconduct, extrajudicial misconduct or other breaches of judicial ethics.

The traditional method of impeachment has been found to be an inadequate solution. Impeachment is a legislative action generally brought by the lower house and tried by the upper house, with conviction requiring a two-thirds vote. Impeachment proceedings are cumbersome, often political, with no right of appeal . . . in the history of this country, only eight judges have been tried by the United States Senate and only four have been impeached. It has been reported that the average length of these trials was 16 to 17 days. . . .

. . . There have been various proposals suggested or adopted to meet the problem of removal and to avoid the impeachment process. Compulsory retirement at a fixed age has been suggested. While this is a help, it does not deal with judges who should be retired early for reasons other than age. Removal by action of the executive branch has been criticized because of the threat to judicial independence. In some states the problem has been treated as one of bar discipline. The Ohio and Wisconsin Supreme Courts have vested bar association grievance committees with authority to consider complaints for judicial misconduct. But this practice has been criticized as vesting too much authority in the organized bar. Further, it does not appear to be a satisfactory arrangement for practicing lawyers to present and try charges against their judges.

There are two additional methods which have been adopted for handling the problem of removal and retirement. . . . One may be called the 'Special Court System' and another the 'Commission System'.

[In 1948] New York created the Court on the Judiciary . . . Under this . . . provision, a judge or justice of the courts of superior jurisdiction in the state "may be removed for cause or retired for mental or physical disability preventing the proper performance of his judicial duties after due notice and hearing by a court on the judiciary." . . .

The Court on the Judiciary is composed of the Chief Judge of the Court of Appeals, the Senior Associate Judge of the Court of Appeals, and one justice of each of the four Appellate Divisions selected by the majority of the justices of each of the Appellate Divisions . . . .

The Chief Judge may convene the Court on the Judiciary upon his own motion and must convene it upon written request by the Governor, by a presiding justice of the Appellate Division or by a majority of the Executive Committee of the New York State Bar Association. . . .

In the more than seventeen years since creation of the Court it has been convened three times. The first, in 1959, resulted in a dismissal of the charges with censure. The other two cases resulted in removal from office.

A number of other states have adopted some variation of this "Special Court" plan either by constitutional amendment or by statutory enactment. These states include Alabama, Texas, Louisiana,

New Jersey, Illinois and Alaska, and similar proposals are presently before the legislatures in Kansas, Ohio and Oklahoma. In addition, the American Bar Association in 1962 endorsed a model judicial article which includes such a "Special Court System". . . .

[The California Commission on Judicial Qualifications established in 1960] consists of nine members: five judges appointed by the Supreme Court . . . two laymen . . . appointed by the Governor with the consent of the Senate; and two lawyers appointed by the Board of Governors of the State Bar, which is an integrated bar. . . .

The Commission has authority to investigate and conduct proceedings against any California judge. . . . The duty of the Commission is to recommend to the Supreme Court for removal from judicial office any judge found by the Commission to be guilty of willful misconduct in office, willful and persistent failure to perform his duties, habitual intemperance or disability of a permanent character seriously interfering with the performance of his duties.

The Commission employs an executive secretary and a legal stenographer. It meets regularly. It has jurisdiction to receive complaints from any source. . . .

. . . As of the end of 1964 the Commission received 344 complaints against judges. Of these, 118 required investigation, . . . As a result of action taken by the Commission, 26 judges have resigned or retired. It is interesting to note that over the same four-year period there were more than 1000 judges in California. . . .

Any system for removal or compulsory retirement of judges involves a delicate balance with the need to maintain judicial independence. In the view of the Committee, the best way to preserve this balance is to keep the removal process within control of judges themselves. It should be a prime objective of any system to assure against the possibility of removal or discipline merely because a judge or justice has rendered unpopular decisions. The less the executive or legislative branches have the ultimate determination, the more likely judicial independence will be maintained. In this respect both New York's Court on the Judiciary and California's Commission (dominated by the Judiciary) serve the public interest well. . . .

NOTES

(1) For a discussion of retirement practices see Major, *Why Not Mandatory Retirement for Federal Judges?*, 52 A.B.A.J. 29 (1966).

(2) In addition to tenure as a judge, there is the question of tenure in a case. For a thorough discussion of the latter subject see Frank, *Disqualification of Judges*, 56 Yale L.J. 605 (1947). See also *Disqualification of Judges for Bias in the Federal Courts*, 79 Harv.L.Rev. 1435 (1965).

GLENN R. WINTERS, THE MERIT PLAN FOR JUDICIAL SELECTION AND TENURE—ITS HISTORICAL DEVELOPMENT

7 Duquesne L.Rev. 61, 77-78 (1968).

I think the ultimate pattern of merit selection and tenure probably will turn out to be nomination by a commission and appointment for life or good behavior, the issue of good behavior being determined by a California-type Judicial Qualifications Commission. There have been suggestions, and the plans enacted in Idaho and pending in Indiana are so drafted, that a single commission may serve both the nominating and the disciplinary function. I am wary of that, because I can see the possibility, even though remote, that the commission might some day decide to oust A in order to turn around and install B in his place. I do not think that ought to be possible; the two functions should be in separate hands. . . .

I predict that by the end of the decade of the '70's merit selection and tenure will have taken over to the point that the general level of the judiciary, in terms of intelligence, integrity, legal ability and quality of performance will be such that problems of judicial personnel will have receded into the background and will have been supplanted by who knows what new crises that now lie below the horizon.

SECTION 4. COURT ORGANIZATION AND ADMINISTRATION
THE ADMINISTRATION OF JUSTICE

HAROLD MEDINA, PROCEDURAL REFORM AND THE ACHIEVEMENT OF JUSTICE *

11 Wash. & Lee L.Rev. 141 (1954).

At one time or another probably every single member of the community has meditated upon the subject of the difference between law and justice. Hidden behind the quips and jokes about lawyers and judges and the administration of justice generally there is a deep-seated feeling, ranging anywhere from mere suspicion to deep conviction, that somehow or other the vast mills of the law grind out judgments and statutes and practices and procedures which essentially fail to achieve justice. I venture to say that there are few sufferings more poignant than those of the man who knows in his soul that he is in the right but who comes out of an altercation with society or with his neighbors or from a lawsuit with a decision against him.

---

* Copyright 1954 by the School of Law, Washington & Lee University. Reprinted with permission.

It is bad enough when one of us feels that he has been unjustly dealt with by his friends or his business associates or his adversaries in the ebb and flow of life. But the experience is devastating when the injustice, whether real or fancied, has been or seems to have been perpetrated by the very system supposedly designed by organized society for our protection.

Some of this is due, of course, to the fallibility of the human animal. It is possible for a person to think he is right when in fact he is wrong; it is possible for juries and for judges to make mistakes. And no amount of tinkering with the rules of the game and the formulation of the laws and improving the procedures for the administration of justice will ever wholly eliminate the possibility of error.

What I wish to emphasize here at the outset is the downright suffering of the person unjustly dealt with by society. Here, I believe, is the origin and the source of all the speculation on the subject of law and justice. And I am talking about what goes on in the mind of the ordinary person, whether he be a businessman or a mechanic or a college professor or a manicurist. . . .

There is no such thing as achieving justice by the process of merely trying to be fair in particular situations. . . .

. . . To avoid confusion and chaos there had to be ways of doing things in administering laws. To the insiders who were the only ones who understood such matters these masses of procedural technicalities have always been a happy hunting ground. Of course the initiates never denied that the merits of the case and the application of the governing rule of substantive law were matters of first importance. But the merits had a way of getting lost in the fog. . . .

The undoubted fact is that lawyers and judges like to play with these things and, when they have once mastered the intricacies of any particular system of procedure, it is only human nature for them to perpetuate their monopoly, if they can. . . .

But the people who were thrown out of court on one technicality after another must have suffered the tortures of the damned. . . . And I verily believe that of all the instances where justice has fallen short of its mark, perhaps a majority have been due to defects and shortcomings in matters of procedure.

The subject of this lecture is the discussion of some of the more important of these procedural inadequacies, especially those which are hardly ever given formal treatment in the traditional curriculum of the typical American law school. These are indeed earthy subjects, as you shall see. They are tough, thorny, and difficult of solution. Their importance will be self-evident. That is why I am preaching the gospel about them.

First in importance is the selection of judges and the making of provisions for their tenure, compensation and retirement. A corrollary subject is the selection of jurors, providing them with suitable quarters and accommodations, and the formulation of methods designed to obtain general jury panels which represent a true cross section of the community. Next, the business management of the courts, by court integration, Judicial Councils and by the establishment of an administrative officer or director or executive assistant to the Chief Justice. Fourth, judicial regulation of procedure by giving the rule-making power to the highest court of a state and taking it away from the legislature.

NOTES

(1) Judge Medina writes eloquently about the suffering of the *person* unjustly dealt with by society. Sometimes classes of persons find themselves in the same position; then society is indeed in trouble: "In many of the cities which experienced disorders last summer, there were recurring breakdowns in mechanisms for processing, prosecuting and protecting arrested persons. These resulted mainly from long-standing structural deficiencies in the criminal court systems, and from the failure of communities to anticipate and plan for the emergency demands of civil disorders. In part, because of this, there were few successful prosecutions for serious crimes committed during the riots. In those cities where mass arrests occurred many arrestees were deprived of basic legal rights." Report of the National Advisory Commission on Civil Disorders, Summary, Chapter 13, "The Administration of Justice Under Emergency Conditions" (1968).

(2) See Chapter X, Section 3, page 403–409 supra, on the role of lawyers in improving the administration of justice.

ADMINISTRATIVE FUNCTIONS OF THE JUDGE

A portrayal of the average American trial judge of today as one who presides over the day's cases and returns home to his library, pipe and slippers overlooks the formidable judicial burden of court administration. The necessity of attacking the logjam of cases which choke the calendars of most courts in our metropolitan centers, while assuring each litigant his day in court with the attending due process guarantees, is one of the crucial problems of recent years. One solution is to increase substantially the number of judges and courthouses. Even if this should occur with dependable regularity judges will still be responsible for the proper administration of their courts.

JOSEPH D. TYDINGS,* A FRESH APPROACH TO JUDICIAL ADMINISTRATION

50 J.Am.Jud. Soc'y 46–48 (1966).

I suggest that before the courts—and I speak here of both federal and state courts—can begin to overcome the problems of congestion and delay three important steps must be taken:

First, each court system must have a supervising judge with the power and personnel to make and implement administrative decisions.

Second, each court system must establish procedures to collect and analyze detailed current information about all relevant aspects of the court's operations.

Third, each court system must have adequate physical facilities, competent clerical personnel, and office procedures that promote the efficient administration of justice.

Let me elaborate upon these three prerequisites for sound judicial administration.

First, judicial efficiency and centralized administration of a court system are inseparable. In the judicial process there are a number of necessary and important decisions that are not judicial decisions in the traditional sense. They are, rather, determinations affecting the efficient administration of the court. Control of the docket, the assignment of judges to cases, and the use of supporting personnel are all related elements of a total administrative picture. At present, too often these matters are regulated by the inertia of the system rather than by conscious choice. Administrative decisions must be made quickly, on a day-to-day basis. They are best placed in the hands of a single judge having the power to enforce his administrative judgment.

Second, in order to make effective use of a sound administrative framework, the judge discharging administrative duties must have at his disposal current and meaningful data that will allow him to make informed decisions. In too many of our courts today statistics are compiled unsystematically and too late to allow the court to control the flow of cases in an intelligent way. Modern science has devised methods of collecting and analyzing information and making it available almost instantaneously. Only a few courts have begun to take advantage of these techniques, but these few courts have found modern methods an indispensable tool in a program to reduce backlog and delay. Availability of information places control of the calendar in the hands of the court rather than in the hands of the litigants or their attorneys.

---

* United States Senator from the State of Maryland.

NOTES

(1) After adoption of a new constitution in 1947 and the appointment of a new supreme court headed by Chief Justice Arthur T. Vanderbilt, New Jersey began a continuing process of reform of its courts and the administration of justice within the state. "New Jersey did not come up with some novel remedy. All that was done was to take over and apply to court administration, lock, stock and barrel, the principles of business management which have been America's great contribution to our own and the world's social and economic well-being. . . . The business of the courts is very big business indeed. The stuff of that business is of course litigation. . ." Justice William J. Brennan, *The Congested Calendars in Our Courts—the Problem Can Be Solved*, 38 Chic.Bar Record 103 (1956).

(2) The notion that courts should be adminstered like a business was put strongly by the then Chief Justice of the United States. Vinson, *The Business of Judicial Administration: Suggestions to the Conference of Chief Justices*, 35 A.B.A.J. 893 (1949). Can you perceive any problems in applying an approach borrowed from business administration to the obvious problems of court administration?

(3) For a comprehensive discussion of court reform and related administrative challenges see Finley, *Judicial Administration: What is This Thing Called Legal Reform?* 65 Col.L.Rev. 569 (1965).

(4) Chief Justice Taft, addressing the Judicial Section of the American Bar Association in 1921, said, "Judges are men and are not so keenly charged with the duty of constant labor that the stimulus of an annual inquiry into what they are doing may not be helpful. With such mild visitation they are likely to cooperate much more readily in an organized effort to get rid of business and do justice than under the go-as-you-please system. . . ." 21 J.Am.Jud.Soc'y 195 (1937).

(5) A Model State Judicial Article has been drafted which is a composite of experience derived from Alaska, Hawaii, New Jersey and Puerto Rico. The full text appears in Holt, *The Model State Judicial Article in Perspective*, 47 J.Am.Jud.Soc'y 30 (1963).

ADMINISTRATIVE SUPPORT

HENRY P. CHANDLER, THE FEDERAL JUDICIAL ADMINISTRATION FROM THE STANDPOINT OF THE ADMINISTRATIVE OFFICE
Conference on Judicial Administration

16 Conference Series 3–6 (University of Chicago, 1956).

The title of the administrator in the federal judicial system is Director of the Administrative Office of the United States. . . . It recognizes that the courts themselves have the primary responsibility for their administration as well as the sole responsibility for their judicial decisions. So the head of the Administrative Office in the federal system is not to be regarded as the administrator of the courts.

He is the chief of an office with various functions designed to give material and moral support to the courts. . . .

A function which all judicial administrative offices have in common is to furnish information to the judicial authorities concerning the currency of the calendars and to aid in overcoming congestion and delay in the disposition of cases. The federal Administrative Office does this but a good deal else. It gives a proportionately large amount of attention to procuring appropriations for the operation of the courts and to allocating and supervising the expenditure of the funds appropriated. . . .

To . . . two bodies—the Judicial Conference of the United States and the judicial councils of the circuits . . . including not only all the federal judges but representatives of the bar, who meet annually for discussion, and to their committees, the Administrative Office supplies information, and, when requested, as it frequently is, conducts research and renders reports on problems under consideration. But the policies of the Judicial Conference of the United States and of the judicial councils of the circuits are for determination by those bodies, and the Administrative Office acts only as an executive agent. . . .

NOTES

(1) Court administrators are beginning to specialize and develop standards like any respectable bureaucracy. See Klein, *The Position of the Trial Court Administrator in the States*, 50 J.Am.Jud.Soc'y. 278 (1967).

(2) Can the computer help? See Ellenbogen, *Automation in the Courts*, 50 A.B.A.J. 665 (1964).

(3) For a good over-all description of the court system in the United States, problems of court administration and some proposed solutions see The Courts, The Public and The Law Explosion (The American Assembly, Harry W. Jones, ed.,) op. cit. supra p. 502.

(4) "This interaction of trial and appellate machinery, this appellate administration, and this intellectual process of appellate judgment are of the greatest public importance. Yet they are not bruited about, even in the current lively discussions on modernizing the law. Is it that ancestral pictures of bewigged and berobed justice stand as a barrier against inquiry, working a black spell, intimidating us into the silence that comes over children in the presence of the aloof and unfamiliar? Or do we rationalize that the dignity of the appellate courts depends on their mystery? If so, we do not honor them, for the implication hovers in such a premise that whatever dignity attends the judicial process emanates not from its exacting demands on mind and integrity but from its secrecy. We may even do them injury, for in modern times that which operates in an aura of mystery may eventually find itself suspect rather than respected." Traynor, Some Open Questions on the Work of State Appellate Courts, Conference on Judicial Administration, (University of Chicago) supra p. 530, at 72.

JUDICIAL EDUCATION

We noted in Section 3, Selection and Tenure of Judges, the prevalence of a career judiciary in countries of the civil law tradition. The Anglo-American tradition is to select judges from the practice or from teaching positions. Although this method of selecting judges makes for a strong and independent judiciary, it means that judges may go on the bench with little understanding of the judicial process and with no apprenticeship in the role and function of a trial or appellate judge.

Before 1956 the only training available to judges in the United States was on-the-job. In that year a summer Seminar for Appellate Judges was inaugurated at New York University which has been attended by a number of judges of state supreme courts and of the United States courts of appeals. The curriculum includes opinion writing, the nature of the appellate process and some material in substantive areas of the law presented from the judge's point of view. Members of the United States Supreme Court have served as Seminar leaders.

More recently programs for federal and state trial judges have been offered. There is now a National College of Trial Judges at the University of Nevada sponsored by the National Conference of State Trial Judges of the Section of Judicial Administration of the American Bar Association.

For descriptions of these and other efforts to bridge the gap between practice or teaching and service on the bench see Karlen, Judicial Education, 52 A.B.A.J. 1049 (1966); Rosenberg, Judging Goes to College, 52 A.B.A.J. 342 (1966); Leflar, Continuing Legal Education for Appellate Judges, 15 Buf.L.Rev. 370 (1965).

NOTE

Is the rush toward continuing education an admission that the tradition of selecting judges without regard to their educational background is in error or are we merely improving an otherwise preferable system?

EPILOGUE

A student using this book in the 1970's and 1980's will in his practice reach far into the twenty-first century.

"The Past Is Prologue". So much of the past as is set down in this book is but prologue to his fifty years in the law, the working span of a practitioner. What will the profession offer him in opportunity and challenge? Let the reader, first, put himself fifty years ago and from that point of view try to see the past half century with all its incredible changes. Let him next shift his point of view to his own day and peer ahead. As he does so, he will take note of the greatly increased number of scientists and engineers at work, those true revolutionaries. He will take note, too, of the rising expectations of classes and peoples all over the world. He will take heart as he remembers the continuing need of organized society for law and for men of law, a need increasing in his time as science and technology bring people closer together.

We are in the midst of a series of revolutions: a revolution of production, one aspect of which is the affluent society; a revolution of millions of agricultural workers no longer needed on the farms; a revolution of distribution which has done much for the middle classes but not nearly so much for the disadvantaged; a revolution in the roles of the law. The latter revolution has given to government a large part in the regulation of business. It has given to the law, through the Bill of Rights, an active role in the protection of the citizen, especially the political dissenter, against government itself.

The most striking fact in the history of Europe of the nineteenth century, it has been said, is that Great Britain had no Revolution. Instead, it had a series of little revolutions which in sum added up to enormous social change.

An eloquent little book by Mr. John Gardner, "Self-Renewal" urges the importance, even the necessity, of self-examination and self-renewal so that individuals and institutions may play their full part in changing times. For no institution is this critical self-examination and determined self-renewal more important than for the bar whose system of precedent encourages it to look to the past.

By self-renewal, to which it is hoped this book may contribute, the reader throughout his life can continue to achieve his individual and professional and social objectives. By self-renewal he will continue as well to contribute to those little revolutions which it is the function of his profession to bring about thereby maintaining stability and at the same time achieving change through law.

APPENDIX

CODE OF PROFESSIONAL RESPONSIBILITY *

Table of Contents

	Page
PREAMBLE AND PRELIMINARY STATEMENT	539

CANON 1. A LAWYER SHOULD ASSIST IN MAINTAINING THE INTEGRITY AND COMPETENCE OF THE LEGAL PROFESSION 541

Ethical Considerations 541

Disciplinary Rules 542
- DR 1-101 Maintaining Integrity and Competence of the Legal Profession 542
- DR 1-102 Misconduct 542
- DR 1-103 Disclosure of Information to Authorities 543

CANON 2. A LAWYER SHOULD ASSIST THE LEGAL PROFESSION IN FULFILLING ITS DUTY TO MAKE LEGAL COUNSEL AVAILABLE 543

Ethical Considerations 543
- Recognition of Legal Problems 543
- Selection of a Lawyer: Generally 545
- Selection of a Lawyer: Professional Notices and Listings 545
- Financial Ability to Employ Counsel: Generally 547
- Financial Ability to Employ Counsel: Persons Able to Pay Reasonable Fees 547
- Financial Ability to Employ Counsel: Persons Unable to Pay Reasonable Fees 549
- Acceptance and Retention of Employment 550

Disciplinary Rules 551
- DR 2-101 Publicity in General 551
- DR 2-102 Professional Notices, Letterheads, Offices, and Law Lists 551
- DR 2-103 Recommendation of Professional Employment 554
- DR 2-104 Suggestion of Need of Legal Services 555
- DR 2-105 Limitation of Practice 555
- DR 2-106 Fees for Legal Services 556
- DR 2-107 Division of Fees Among Lawyers 556
- DR 2-108 Agreements Restricting the Practice of a Lawyer 557
- DR 2-109 Acceptance of Employment 557
- DR 2-110 Withdrawal from Employment 557

CANON 3. A LAWYER SHOULD ASSIST IN PREVENTING THE UNAUTHORIZED PRACTICE OF LAW 558

Ethical Considerations 558

Disciplinary Rules 560
- DR 3-101 Aiding Unauthorized Practice of Law 560
- DR 3-102 Dividing Legal Fees with a Non-Lawyer 560
- DR 3-103 Forming a Partnership with a Non-Lawyer 560

---

* Adopted by the American Bar Association at annual meeting in Dallas, Texas, on Aug. 12, 1969. Copyrighted by American Bar Association. Published with permission.

CODE OF PROFESSIONAL RESPONSIBILITY

	Page
CANON 4. A LAWYER SHOULD PRESERVE THE CONFIDENCES AND SECRETS OF A CLIENT	560
Ethical Considerations	560
Disciplinary Rules	561
DR 4–101 Preservation of Confidences and Secrets of a Client	561
CANON 5. A LAWYER SHOULD EXERCISE INDEPENDENT PROFESSIONAL JUDGMENT ON BEHALF OF A CLIENT	563
Ethical Considerations	563
Interests of a Lawyer That May Affect His Judgment	563
Interests of Multiple Clients	565
Desires of Third Persons	567
Disciplinary Rules	568
DR 5–101 Refusing Employment When the Interests of the Lawyer May Impair His Independent Professional Judgment	568
DR 5–102 Withdrawal as Counsel When the Lawyer Becomes a Witness	568
DR 5–103 Avoiding Acquisition of Interest in Litigation	568
DR 5–104 Limiting Business Relations with a Client	569
DR 5–105 Refusing to Accept or Continue Employment if the Interests of Another Client May Impair the Independent Professional Judgment of the Lawyer	569
DR 5–106 Settling Similar Claims of Clients	569
DR 5–107 Avoiding Influence by Others Than the Client	569
CANON 6. A LAWYER SHOULD REPRESENT A CLIENT COMPETENTLY	570
Ethical Considerations	570
Disciplinary Rules	571
DR 6–101 Failing to Act Competently	571
DR 6–102 Limiting Liability to Client	571
CANON 7. A LAWYER SHOULD REPRESENT A CLIENT ZEALOUSLY WITHIN THE BOUNDS OF THE LAW	571
Ethical Considerations	571
Duty of the Lawyer to a Client	573
Duty of the Lawyer to the Adversary System of Justice	576
Disciplinary Rules	580
DR 7–101 Representing a Client Zealously	580
DR 7–102 Representing a Client Within the Bounds of the Law	580
DR 7–103 Performing the Duty of Public Prosecutor or Other Government Lawyer	581
DR 7–104 Communicating with One of Adverse Interest	581
DR 7–105 Threatening Criminal Prosecution	581
DR 7–106 Trial Conduct	581
DR 7–107 Trial Publicity	582
DR 7–108 Communication with or Investigation of Jurors	584
DR 7–109 Contact with Witnesses	584
DR 7–110 Contact with Officials	584

CODE OF PROFESSIONAL RESPONSIBILITY

Page

CANON 8. A LAWYER SHOULD ASSIST IN IMPROVING THE LEGAL SYSTEM 585

Ethical Considerations 585

Disciplinary Rules 586
    DR 8–101 Action as a Public Official 586
    DR 8–102 Statements Concerning Judges and Other Adjudicatory Officers 587

CANON 9. A LAWYER SHOULD AVOID EVEN THE APPEARANCE OF PROFESSIONAL IMPROPRIETY 587

Ethical Considerations 587

Disciplinary Rules 588
    DR 9–101 Avoiding Even the Appearance of Impropriety 588
    DR 9–102 Preserving Identity of Funds and Property of a Client 588

DEFINITIONS 589

*

CODE OF PROFESSIONAL RESPONSIBILITY

With amendments to February 24, 1970

PREAMBLE AND PRELIMINARY STATEMENT

Preamble [1]

The continued existence of a free and democratic society depends upon recognition of the concept that justice is based upon the rule of law grounded in respect for the dignity of the individual and his capacity through reason for enlightened self-government.[2] Law so grounded makes justice possible, for only through such law does the dignity of the individual attain respect and protection. Without it, individual rights become subject to unrestrained power, respect for law is destroyed, and rational self-government is impossible.

Lawyers, as guardians of the law, play a vital role in the preservation of society. The fulfillment of this role requires an understanding by lawyers of their relationship with and function in our legal system.[3] A consequent obligation of lawyers is to maintain the highest standards of ethical conduct.

In fulfilling his professional responsibilities, a lawyer necessarily assumes various roles that require the performance of many difficult tasks. Not every situation which he may encounter can be foreseen,[4] but fundamental ethical principles are always present to guide him. Within the framework of these principles, a lawyer must with courage and foresight be able and ready to shape the body of the law to the ever-changing relationships of society.[5]

The Code of Professional Responsibility points the way to the aspiring and provides standards by which to judge the transgressor. Each lawyer must find within his own conscience the touchstone against which to test the extent to which his actions should rise above minimum standards. But in the last analysis it is the desire for the respect and confidence of the members of his profession and of the society which he serves that should provide to a lawyer the incentive for the highest possible degree of ethical conduct. The possible loss of that respect and confidence is the ultimate sanction. So long as its practitioners are guided by these principles, the law will continue to be a noble profession. This is its greatness and its strength, which permit of no compromise.

Preliminary Statement

In furtherance of the principles stated in the Preamble, the American Bar Association has promulgated this Code of Professional Responsibility, consisting of three separate but interrelated parts: Canons, Ethical Considerations, and Disciplinary Rules.[6] The Code is designed to be adopted by appropriate agencies both as an inspirational guide to the members of the profession and as a basis for disciplinary action when the conduct of a lawyer falls below the required minimum standards stated in the Disciplinary Rules.

Obviously the Canons, Ethical Considerations, and Disciplinary Rules cannot apply to non-lawyers; however, they do define the type of ethical conduct that the public has a right to expect not

---

[1] The footnotes are intended merely to enable the reader to relate the provisions of this Code to the ABA Canons of Professional Ethics adopted in 1908, as amended, the Opinions of the ABA Committee on Professional Ethics, and a limited number of other sources; they are not intended to be an annotation of the views taken by the ABA Special Committee on Evaluation of Ethical Standards. Footnotes citing ABA Canons refer to the ABA Canons of Professional Ethics, adopted in 1908, as amended.

[2] *Cf.* ABA Canons, Preamble.

[3] "[T]he lawyer stands today in special need of a clear understanding of his obligations and of the vital connection between those obligations and the role his profession plays in society." *Professional Responsibility: Report of the Joint Conference,* 44 A.B.A.J. 1159, 1160 (1958).

[4] "No general statement of the responsibilities of the legal profession can encompass all the situations in which the lawyer may be placed. Each position held by him makes its own peculiar demands. These demands the lawyer must clarify for himself in the light of the particular role in which he serves." *Professional Responsibility: Report of the Joint Conference,* 44 A.B.A.J. 1159, 1218 (1958).

[5] "The law and its institutions change as social conditions change. They must change if they are to preserve, much less advance, the political and social values from which they derive their purposes and their life. This is true of the most important of legal institutions, the profession of law. The profession, too, must change when conditions change in order to preserve and advance the social values that are its reasons for being." Cheatham, *Availability of Legal Services: The Responsibility of the Individual Lawyer and the Organized Bar,* 12 U.C.L.A.L. Rev. 438, 440 (1965).

[6] The Supreme Court of Wisconsin adopted a Code of Judicial Ethics in 1967. "The code is divided into standards and rules, the standards being statements of what the general desirable level of conduct should be, the rules being particular canons, the violation of which shall subject an individual judge to sanctions." In re Promulgation of a Code of Judicial Ethics, 36 Wis.2d 252, 255, 153 N.W. 2d 873, 874 (1967).

The portion of the Wisconsin Code of Judicial Ethics entitled "Standards" states that "[t]he following standards set forth the significant qualities of the ideal judge . . . ." *Id.,* 36 Wis.2d at 256, 153 N.W.2d at 875. The portion entitled "Rules" states that "[t]he court promulgates the following rules because the requirements of judi-

CODE OF PROFESSIONAL RESPONSIBILITY

only of lawyers but also of their non-professional employees and associates in all matters pertaining to professional employment. A lawyer should ultimately be responsible for the conduct of his employees and associates in the course of the professional representation of the client.

The Canons are statements of axiomatic norms, expressing in general terms the standards of professional conduct expected of lawyers in their relationships with the public, with the legal system, and with the legal profession. They embody the general concepts from which the Ethical Considerations and the Disciplinary Rules are derived.

The Ethical Considerations are aspirational in character and represent the objectives toward which every member of the profession should strive. They constitute a body of principles upon which the lawyer can rely for guidance in many specific situations.[7]

The Disciplinary Rules, unlike the Ethical Considerations, are mandatory in character. The Disciplinary Rules state the minimum level of conduct below which no lawyer can fall without being subject to disciplinary action. Within the framework of fair trial,[8] the Disciplinary Rules should be uniformly applied to all lawyers,[9] regardless of the nature of their professional activities.[10] The Code makes no attempt to prescribe either disciplinary procedures or penalties [11] for violation of a Disciplinary Rule,[12] nor does it undertake to define standards for civil liability of lawyers for professional conduct. The severity of judgment against one found guilty of violating a Disciplinary Rule should be determined by the character of the offense and the attendant circumstances.[13] An enforcing agency, in applying the Disciplinary Rules, may find interpretive guidance in the basic principles embodied in the Canons and in the objectives reflected in the Ethical Considerations.

---

cial conduct embodied therein are of sufficient gravity to warrant sanctions if they are not obeyed . . . ." *Id.*, 36 Wis.2d at 259, 153 N.W.2d at 876.

[7] "Under the conditions of modern practice it is peculiarly necessary that the lawyer should understand, not merely the established standards of professional conduct, but the reasons underlying these standards. Today the lawyer plays a changing and increasingly varied role. In many developing fields the precise contribution of the legal profession is as yet undefined." *Professional Responsibility: Report of the Joint Conference*, 44 A.B.A.J. 1159 (1958).

"A true sense of professional responsibility must derive from an understanding of the reasons that lie back of specific restraints, such as those embodied in the Canons. The grounds for the lawyer's peculiar obligations are to be found in the nature of his calling. The lawyer who seeks a clear understanding of his duties will be led to reflect on the special services his profession renders to society and the services it might render if its full capacities were realized. When the lawyer fully understands the nature of his office, he will then discern what restraints are necessary to keep that office wholesome and effective." *Id.*

[8] "Disbarment, designed to protect the public, is a punishment or penalty imposed on the lawyer. . . . He is accordingly entitled to procedural due process, which includes fair notice of the charge." In re Ruffalo, 390 U.S. 544, 550, 20 L.Ed.2d 117, 122, 88 S.Ct. 1222, 1226 (1968), *rehearing denied*, 391 U.S. 961, 20 L.Ed.2d 874, 88 S.Ct. 1833 (1968).

"A State cannot exclude a person from the practice of law or from any other occupation in a manner or for reasons that contravene the Due Process or Equal Protection Clause of the Fourteenth Amendment. . . . A State can require high standards of qualification . . . but any qualification must have a rational connection with the applicant's fitness or capacity to practice law." Schware v. Bd. of Bar Examiners, 353 U.S. 232, 239, 1 L.Ed.2d 796, 801-02, 77 S.Ct. 752, 756 (1957).

"[A]n accused lawyer may expect that he will not be condemned out of a capricious self-righteousness or denied the essentials of a fair hearing." Kingsland v. Dorsey, 338 U.S. 318, 320, 94 L.Ed. 123, 126, 70 S.Ct. 123, 124-25 (1949).

"The attorney and counsellor being, by the solemn judicial act of the court, clothed with his office, does not hold it as a matter of grace and favor. The right which it confers upon him to appear for suitors, and to argue causes, is something more than a mere indulgence, revocable at the pleasure of the court, or at the command of the legislature. It is a right of which he can only be deprived by the judgment of the court, for moral or professional delinquency." Ex parte Garland, 71 U.S. (4 Wall.) 333, 378-79, 18 L.Ed. 366, 370 (1866).

See generally Comment, *Procedural Due Process and Character Hearings for Bar Applicants*, 15 Stan.L.Rev. 500 (1963).

[9] "The canons of professional ethics must be enforced by the Courts and must be respected by members of the Bar if we are to maintain public confidence in the integrity and impartiality of the administration of justice." In re Meeker, 76 N.M. 354, 357, 414 P.2d 862, 864 (1966), *appeal dismissed*, 385 U.S. 449 (1967).

[10] *See* ABA Canon 45.

"The Canons of this Association govern all its members, irrespective of the nature of their practice, and the application of the Canons is not affected by statutes or regulations governing certain activities of lawyers which may prescribe less stringent standards." ABA Comm. on Professional Ethics, OPINIONS, No. 203 (1940) [hereinafter each Opinion is cited as "ABA Opinion"].

Cf. ABA Opinion 152 (1936).

[11] "There is generally no prescribed discipline for any particular type of improper conduct. The disciplinary measures taken are discretionary with the courts, which may disbar, suspend, or merely censure the attorney as the nature of the offense and past indicia of character may warrant." Note, 43 Cornell L.Q. 489, 495 (1958).

[12] The Code seeks only to specify conduct for which a lawyer should be disciplined. Recommendations as to the procedures to be used in disciplinary actions and the gravity of disciplinary measures appropriate for violations of the Code are within the jurisdiction of the American Bar Association Special Committee on Evaluation of Disciplinary Enforcement.

[13] "The severity of the judgment of this court should be in proportion to the gravity of the offenses, the moral turpitude involved, and the extent that the defendant's acts and conduct affect his professional qualifications to practice law." Louisiana State Bar Ass'n v. Steiner, 204 La. 1073, 1092-93, 16 So.2d 843, 850 (1944) (Higgins, J., concurring in decree).

"Certainly an erring lawyer who has been disciplined and who having paid the penalty has given satisfactory evidence of repentance and has been rehabilitated and restored to his place at the bar by the court which knows him best ought not to have what amounts to an order of permanent disbarment entered against him by a federal court solely on the basis of an earlier criminal record and without regard to his subsequent rehabilitation and present good character . . . . We think, therefore, that the district court should reconsider the appellant's appli-

CODE OF PROFESSIONAL RESPONSIBILITY

CANON 1

A Lawyer Should Assist in Maintaining the Integrity and Competence of the Legal Profession

ETHICAL CONSIDERATIONS

EC 1-1 A basic tenet of the professional responsibility of lawyers is that every person in our society should have ready access to the independent professional services of a lawyer of integrity and competence. Maintaining the integrity and improving the competence of the bar to meet the highest standards is the ethical responsibility of every lawyer.

EC 1-2 The public should be protected from those who are not qualified to be lawyers by reason of a deficiency in education [1] or moral standards [2] or of other relevant factors [3] but who nevertheless seek to practice law. To assure the maintenance of high moral and educational standards of the legal profession, lawyers should affirmatively assist courts and other appropriate bodies in promulgating, enforcing, and improving requirements for admission to the bar.[4] In like manner, the bar has a positive obligation to aid in the continued improvement of all phases of pre-admission and post-admission legal education.

EC 1-3 Before recommending an applicant for admission, a lawyer should satisfy himself that the applicant is of good moral character. Although a lawyer should not become a self-appointed investigator or judge of applicants for admission, he should report to proper officials all unfavorable information he possesses relating to the character or other qualifications of an applicant.[5]

EC 1-4 The integrity of the profession can be maintained only if conduct of lawyers in violation of the Disciplinary Rules is brought to the attention of the proper officials. A lawyer should reveal voluntarily to those officials all unprivileged knowledge of conduct of lawyers which he believes clearly to be in violation of the Disciplinary Rules.[6] A lawyer should, upon request, serve on and assist committees and boards having responsibility for the administration of the Disciplinary Rules.[7]

EC 1-5 A lawyer should maintain high standards of professional conduct and should encourage fellow lawyers to do likewise. He should be temperate and dignified, and he should refrain from all

---

cation for admission and grant it unless the court finds it to be a fact that the appellant is not presently of good moral or professional character." In re Dreier, 258 F.2d 68, 69–70 (3d Cir. 1958).

[1] "[W]e cannot conclude that all educational restrictions [on bar admission] are unlawful. We assume that few would deny that a grammar school education requirement, before taking the bar examination, was reasonable. Or that an applicant had to be able to read or write. Once we conclude that *some* restriction is proper, then it becomes a matter of degree—the problem of drawing the line. . . . .

"We conclude the fundamental question here is whether Rule IV, Section 6 of the Rules Pertaining to Admission of Applicants to the State Bar of Arizona is 'arbitrary, capricious and unreasonable.' We conclude an educational requirement of graduation from an accredited law school is not." Hackin v. Lockwood, 361 F.2d 499, 503–04 (9th Cir. 1966), *cert. denied*, 385 U.S. 960, 17 L.Ed.2d 305, 87 S.Ct. 396 (1966).

[2] "Every state in the United States, as a prerequisite for admission to the practice of law, requires that applicants possess 'good moral character.' Although the requirement is of judicial origin, it is now embodied in legislation in most states." Comment, *Procedural Due Process and Character Hearings for Bar Applicants*, 15 Stan.L.Rev. 500 (1963).

"Good character in the members of the bar is essential to the preservation of the integrity of the courts. The duty and power of the court to guard its portals against intrusion by men and women who are mentally and morally dishonest, unfit because of bad character, evidenced by their course of conduct, to participate in the administrative law, would seem to be unquestioned in the matter of preservation of judicial dignity and integrity." In re Monaghan, 126 Vt. 53, 222 A.2d 665, 670 (1966).

"Fundamentally, the question involved in both situations [i.e. admission and disciplinary proceedings] is the same—is the applicant for admission or the attorney sought to be disciplined a fit and proper person to be permitted to practice law, and that usually turns upon whether he has committed or is likely to continue to commit acts of moral turpitude. At the time of oral argument the attorney for respondent frankly conceded that the test for admission and for discipline is and should be the same. We agree with this concession." Hallinan v. Comm. of Bar Examiners, 65 Cal.2d 447, 453, 421 P.2d 76, 81, 55 Cal. Rptr. 228, 233 (1966).

[3] "Proceedings to gain admission to the bar are for the purpose of protecting the public and the courts from the ministrations of persons unfit to practice the profession. Attorneys are officers of the court appointed to assist the court in the administration of justice. Into their hands are committed the property, the liberty and sometimes the lives of their clients. This commitment demands a high degree of intelligence, knowledge of the law, respect for its function in society, sound and faithful judgment and, above all else, integrity of character in private and professional conduct." In re Monaghan, 126 Vt. 53, 222 A.2d 665, 676 (1966) (Holden, C. J., dissenting).

[4] "A bar composed of lawyers of good moral character is a worthy objective but it is unnecessary to sacrifice vital freedoms in order to obtain that goal. It is also important both to society and the bar itself that lawyers be unintimidated—free to think, speak, and act as members of an Independent Bar." Konigsberg v. State Bar, 353 U.S. 252, 273, 1 L.Ed.2d 810, 825, 77 S.Ct. 722, 733 (1957).

[5] See ABA Canon 29.

[6] ABA Canon 28 designates certain conduct as unprofessional and then states that: "A duty to the public and to the profession devolves upon every member of the Bar having knowledge of such practices upon the part of any practitioner immediately to inform thereof, to the end that the offender may be disbarred." ABA Canon 29 states a broader admonition: "Lawyers should expose without fear or favor before the proper tribunals corrupt or dishonest conduct in the profession."

[7] "It is the obligation of the organized Bar and the individual lawyer to give unstinted cooperation and assistance to the highest court of the state in discharging its function and duty with respect to discipline and in purging the profession of the unworthy." *Report of the Special Committee on Disciplinary Procedures*, 80 A.B.A.Rep. 463, 470 (1955).

illegal and morally reprehensible conduct.[8] Because of his position in society, even minor violations of law by a lawyer may tend to lessen public confidence in the legal profession. Obedience to law exemplifies respect for law. To lawyers especially, respect for the law should be more than a platitude.

EC 1-6 An applicant for admission to the bar or a lawyer may be unqualified, temporarily or permanently, for other than moral and educational reasons, such as mental or emotional instability. Lawyers should be diligent in taking steps to see that during a period of disqualification such person is not granted a license or, if licensed, is not permitted to practice.[9] In like manner, when the disqualification has terminated, members of the bar should assist such person in being licensed, or, if licensed, in being restored to his full right to practice.

DISCIPLINARY RULES

DR 1-101 Maintaining Integrity and Competence of the Legal Profession.

(A) A lawyer is subject to discipline if he has made a materially false statement in, or if he has deliberately failed to disclose a material fact requested in connection with, his application for admission to the bar.[10]

---

[8] *Cf.* ABA Canon 32.

[9] "We decline, on the present record, to disbar Mr. Sherman or to reprimand him—not because we condone his actions, but because, as heretofore indicated, we are concerned with whether he is mentally responsible for what he has done.

"The logic of the situation would seem to dictate the conclusion that, if he was mentally responsible for the conduct we have outlined, he should be disbarred; and, if he was not mentally responsible, he should not be permitted to practice law.

"However, the flaw in the logic is that he may have been mentally irresponsible [at the time of his offensive conduct] . . ., and, yet, have sufficiently improved in the almost two and one-half years intervening to be able to capably and competently represent his clients. . . .
. . .

"We would make clear that we are satisfied that a case has been made against Mr. Sherman, warranting a refusal to permit him to further practice law in this state unless he can establish his mental irresponsibility at the time of the offenses charged. The burden of proof is upon him.

"If he establishes such mental irresponsibility, the burden is then upon him to establish his present capability to practice law." In re Sherman, 58 Wash.2d 1, 6–7, 354 P.2d 888, 890 (1960), *cert. denied.* 371 U.S. 951, 9 L.Ed.2d 499, 83 S.Ct. 506 (1963).

[10] "This Court has the inherent power to revoke a license to practice law in this State, where such license was issued by this Court, and its issuance was procured by the fraudulent concealment, or by the false and fraudulent representation by the applicant of a fact which was manifestly material to the issuance of the license." North Carolina ex rel. Attorney General v. Gorson, 209 N.C. 320, 326, 183 S.E. 392, 395 (1936), *cert. denied,* 298 U.S. 662, 80 L.Ed. 1387, 56 S.Ct. 752 (1936).

See also Application of Patterson, 318 P.2d 907, 913 (Or. 1957), *cert. denied,* 356 U.S. 947, 2 L.Ed.2d 822, 78 S.Ct. 795 (1958).

(B) A lawyer shall not further the application for admission to the bar of another person known by him to be unqualified in respect to character, education, or other relevant attribute.[11]

DR 1-102 Misconduct.

(A) A lawyer shall not:

  (1) Violate a Disciplinary Rule.

  (2) Circumvent a Disciplinary Rule through actions of another.[12]

  (3) Engage in illegal conduct involving moral turpitude.[13]

---

[11] *See* ABA Canon 29.

[12] In *ABA Opinion* 95 (1933), which held that a municipal attorney could not permit police officers to interview persons with claims against the municipality when the attorney knew the claimants to be represented by counsel, the Committee on Professional Ethics said:

"The law officer is, of course, responsible for the acts of those in his department who are under his supervision and control." *Opinion 85. In re Robinson,* 136 N.Y.S. 548 (affirmed 209 N.Y. 354–1912) held that it was a matter of disbarment for an attorney to adopt a general course of approving the unethical conduct of employees of his client, even though he did not actively participate therein.

". . . . 'The attorney should not advise or sanction acts by his client which he himself should not do.' *Opinion 75.*"

[13] "The most obvious non-professional ground for disbarment is conviction for a felony. Most states make conviction for a felony grounds for automatic disbarment. Some of these states, including New York, make disbarment mandatory upon conviction for *any* felony, while others require disbarment only for those felonies which involve moral turpitude. There are strong arguments that some felonies, such as involuntary manslaughter, reflect neither on an attorney's fitness, trustworthiness, nor competence and, therefore, should not be grounds for disbarment, but most states tend to disregard these arguments and, following the common law rule, make disbarment mandatory on conviction for any felony." Note, 43 Cornell L.Q. 489, 490 (1958).

"Some states treat conviction for misdemeanors as grounds for automatic disbarment . . .. However, the vast majority, accepting the common law rule, require that the misdemeanor involve moral turpitude. While the definition of moral turpitude may prove difficult, it seems only proper that those minor offenses which do not affect the attorney's fitness to continue in the profession should not be grounds for disbarment. A good example is an assault and battery conviction which would not involve moral turpitude unless done with malice and deliberation." *Id. at 491.*

"The term 'moral turpitude' has been used in the law for centuries. It has been the subject of many decisions by the courts but has never been clearly defined because of the nature of the term. Perhaps the best general definition of the term 'moral turpitude' is that it imports an act of baseness, vileness or depravity in the duties which one person owes to another or to society in general, which is contrary to the usual, accepted and customary rule of right and duty which a person should follow. 58 C.J.S. at page 1201. Although offenses against revenue laws have been held to be crimes of moral turpitude, it has also been held that the attempt to evade the payment of taxes due to the government or any subdivision thereof, while wrong and unlawful, does not involve moral turpitude. 58 C.J.S. at page 1205." Comm. on Legal Ethics v. Scheer, 149 W.Va. 721, 726–27, 143 S.E.2d 141, 145 (1965).

CODE OF PROFESSIONAL RESPONSIBILITY

(4) Engage in conduct involving dishonesty, fraud, deceit, or misrepresentation.

(5) Engage in conduct that is prejudicial to the administration of justice.

(6) Engage in any other conduct that adversely reflects on his fitness to practice law.[14]

DR 1-103 Disclosure of Information to Authorities.

(A) A lawyer possessing unprivileged knowledge of a violation of DR 1-102 shall report such knowledge to a tribunal or other authority empowered to investigate or act upon such violation.[15]

(B) A lawyer possessing unprivileged knowledge or evidence concerning another lawyer or a judge shall reveal fully such knowledge or evidence upon proper request of a tribunal or other authority empowered to investigate or act upon the conduct of lawyers or judges.[16]

CANON 2

A Lawyer Should Assist the Legal Profession in Fulfilling Its Duty to Make Legal Counsel Available

ETHICAL CONSIDERATIONS

EC 2-1 The need of members of the public for legal services [1] is met only if they recognize their legal problems, appreciate the importance of seeking assistance,[2] and are able to obtain the services of acceptable legal counsel.[3] Hence, important functions of the legal profession are to educate laymen to recognize their legal problems, to facilitate the process of intelligent selection of lawyers, and to assist in making legal services fully available.[4]

Recognition of Legal Problems

EC 2-2 The legal profession should assist laymen to recognize legal problems because such problems may not be self-revealing and often are not

---

"The right and power to discipline an attorney, as one of its officers, is inherent in the court. . . . This power is not limited to those instances of misconduct wherein he has been employed, or has acted, in a professional capacity; but, on the contrary, this power may be exercised where his misconduct outside the scope of his professional relations shows him to be an unfit person to practice law." In re Wilson, 391 S.W.2d 914, 917-18 (Mo. 1965).

[14] "It is a fair characterization of the lawyer's responsibility in our society that he stands 'as a shield,' to quote Devlin, J., in defense of right and to ward off wrong. From a profession charged with these responsibilities there must be exacted those qualities of truth-speaking, of a high sense of honor, of granite discretion, of the strictest observance of fiduciary responsibility, that have, throughout the centuries, been compendiously described as 'moral character'". Schware v. Bd. of Bar Examiners, 353 U.S. 232, 247 L.Ed.2d 796, 806, 77 S.Ct. 752, 761 (1957) (Frankfurter, J., concurring).

"Particularly applicable here is Rule 4.47 providing that 'A lawyer should always maintain his integrity; and shall not willfully commit any act against the interest of the public; nor shall he violate his duty to the courts or his clients; *nor shall he, by any misconduct, commit any offense against the laws of Missouri or the United States of America, which amounts to a crime involving acts done by him contrary to justice, honesty, modesty or good morals*; nor shall he be guilty of any other misconduct whereby, for the protection of the public and those charged with the administration of justice, he should no longer be entrusted with the duties and responsibilities belonging to the office of an attorney.' " In re Wilson, 391 S.W.2d 914, 917 (Mo. 1965).

[15] *See* ABA Canon 29; *cf.* ABA Canon 28.

[16] *Cf.* ABA Canons 28 and 29.

[1] "Men have need for more than a system of law; they have need for a system of law which functions, and that means they have need for lawyers." Cheatham, *The Lawyer's Role and Surroundings*, 25 Rocky Mt.L.Rev. 405 (1953).

[2] "Law is not self-applying; men must apply and utilize it in concrete cases. But the ordinary man is incapable. He cannot know the principles of law or the rules guiding the machinery of law administration; he does not know how to formulate his desires with precision and to put them into writing; he is ineffective in the presentation of his claims." Cheatham, *The Lawyer's Role and Surroundings*, 25 Rocky Mt.L.Rev. 405 (1953).

[3] "This need [to provide legal services] was recognized by . . . Mr. [Lewis F.] Powell [Jr., President, American Bar Association, 1963-64], who said: 'Looking at contemporary America realistically, we must admit that despite all our efforts to date (and these have not been insignificant), far too many persons are not able to obtain equal justice under law. This usually results because their poverty or their ignorance has prevented them from obtaining legal counsel.' " Address by E. Clinton Bamberger, Association of American Law Schools 1965 Annual Meeting, Dec. 28, 1965, in Proceedings, Part II, 1965, 61, 63-64 (1965).

"A wide gap separates the need for legal services and its satisfaction, as numerous studies reveal. Looked at from the side of the layman, one reason for the gap is poverty and the consequent inability to pay legal fees. Another set of reasons is ignorance of the need for and the value of legal services, and ignorance of where to find a dependable lawyer. There is fear of the mysterious processes and delays of the law, and there is fear of overreaching and overcharging by lawyers, a fear stimulated by the occasional exposure of shysters." Cheatham, *Availability of Legal Services: The Responsibility of the Individual Lawyer and of the Organized Bar*, 12 U.C.L.A.L. Rev. 438 (1965).

[4] "It is not only the right but the duty of the profession as a whole to utilize such methods as may be developed to bring the services of its members to those who need them, so long as this can be done ethically and with dignity." ABA Opinion 320 (1968).

"[T]here is a responsibility on the bar to make legal services available to those who need them. The maxim, 'privilege brings responsibilities,' can be expanded to read, exclusive privilege to render public service brings responsibility to assure that the service is available to those in need of it." Cheatham, *Availability of Legal Services: The Responsibility of the Individual Lawyer and of the Organized Bar*, 12 U.C.L.A.L.Rev. 438, 443 (1965).

"The obligation to provide legal services for those actually caught up in litigation carries with it the obligation to make preventive legal advice accessible to all. It is among those unaccustomed to business affairs and fearful of the ways of the law that such advice is often most needed. If it is not received in time, the most valiant and skillful representation in court may come too late." *Professional Responsibility: Report of the Joint Conference*, 44 A.B.A.J. 1159, 1216 (1958).

CODE OF PROFESSIONAL RESPONSIBILITY

timely noticed.[5] Therefore, lawyers acting under proper auspices should encourage and participate in educational and public relations programs concerning our legal system with particular reference to legal problems that frequently arise. Such educational programs should be motivated by a desire to benefit the public rather than to obtain publicity or employment for particular lawyers.[6] Examples of permissible activities include preparation of institutional advertisements [7] and professional articles for lay publications [8] and participation in seminars, lectures, and civic programs. But a lawyer who participates in such activities should shun personal publicity.[9]

EC 2-3 Whether a lawyer acts properly in volunteering advice to a layman to seek legal services depends upon the circumstances.[10] The giving of advice that one should take legal action could well be in fulfillment of the duty of the legal profession to assist laymen in recognizing legal problems.[11] The advice is proper only if motivated by a desire to protect one who does not recognize that he may have legal problems or who is ignorant of his legal rights or obligations. Hence, the advice is improper if motivated by a desire to obtain personal benefit,[12] secure personal publicity, or cause litigation to be brought merely to harass or injure another. Obviously, a lawyer should not contact

---

[5] "Over a period of years institutional advertising of programs for the benefit of the public have been approved by this and other Ethics Committees as well as by the courts. . . .

"To the same effect are opinions of this Committee: *Opinion 179* dealing with radio programs presenting a situation in which legal advice is suggested in connection with a drafting of a will; *Opinions 205* and *227* permitting institutional advertising of lawyer referral plans; *Opinion 191* holding that advertising by lawyer members of a non-bar associated sponsored plan violated *Canon 27*. The Illinois Ethics Committee, in its *Opinion 201*, sustained bar association institutional advertising of a check-up plan . . .

"This Committee has passed squarely on the question of the propriety of institutional advertising in connection with a legal check-up plan. Informal Decision C–171 quotes with express approval the Michigan Ethics Committee as follows:

As a public service, the bar has in the past addressed the public as to the importance of making wills, consulting counsel in connection with real estate transactions, etc. In the same way, the bar, as such, may recommend this program, provided always that it does it in such a way that there is not suggestion of solicitation on behalf of any individual lawyer."
ABA Opinion 307 (1962).

[6] "We recognize a distinction between teaching the lay public the importance of securing legal services preventive in character and the solicitation of professional employment by or for a particular lawyer. The former tends to promote the public interest and enhance the public estimation of the profession. The latter is calculated to injure the public and degrade the profession.

"Advertising which is calculated to teach the layman the benefits and advantages of preventive legal services will benefit the lay public and enable the lawyer to render a more desirable and beneficial professional service. . . ."
ABA Opinion 179 (1938).

[7] "[A bar association] may engage in a dignified institutional educational campaign so long as it does not involve the identification of a particular lawyer with the check-up program. Such educational material may point out the value of the annual check-up and may be printed in newspapers, magazines, pamphlets, and brochures, or produced by means of films, radio, television or other media. The printed materials may be distributed in a dignified way through the offices of persons having close dealings with lawyers as, for example, banks, real estate agents, insurance agents and others. They may be available in lawyers' offices. The bar association may prepare and distribute to lawyers materials and forms for use in the annual legal check-up." *ABA Opinion* 307 (1962).

[8] "A lawyer may with propriety write articles for publications in which he gives information upon the law . . . ." ABA Canon 40.

"The newsletters, by means of which respondents are alleged to have advertised their wares, were sent to the officers of union clients represented by their firm. . . . They contain no reference to any cases handled by the respondents. Their contents are confined to rulings of boards, commissions and courts on problems of interest to labor union, together with proposed and completed legislation important to the Brotherhood, and other items which might affect unions and their members. The respondents cite Opinion 213 of the Committee on Professional Ethics and Grievances as permitting such practice. After studying this opinion, we agree that sending of newsletters of the above type to regular clients does not offend Canon 27." In re Ratner, 194 Kan. 362, 371, 399 P.2d 865, 872–73 (1965).

Cf. ABA Opinion 92 (1933).

[9] *Cf. ABA Opinions* 307 (1962) and 179 (1938).
"There is no ethical or other valid reason why an attorney may not write articles on legal subjects for magazines and newspapers. The fact that the publication is a trade journal or magazine, makes no difference as to the ethical question involved. On the other hand, it would be unethical and contrary to the precepts of the Canons for the attorney to allow his name to be carried in the magazine or other publication . . . as a free legal adviser for the subscribers to the publication. Such would be contrary to *Canons 27* and *35* and Opinions heretofore announced by the Committee on Professional Ethics and Grievances. (See *Opinions 31, 41, 42,* and *56*)." *ABA Opinion* 162 (1936).

[10] *See* ABA Canon 28.

[11] This question can assume constitutional dimensions: "We meet at the outset the contention that 'solicitation' is wholly outside the area of freedoms protected by the First Amendment. To this contention there are two answers. The first is that a State cannot foreclose the exercise of constitutional rights by mere labels. The second is that abstract discussion is not the only species of communication which the Constitution protects; the First Amendment also protects vigorous advocacy, certainly of lawful ends, against governmental intrusion. . . .

"However valid may be Virginia's interest in regulating the traditionally illegal practice of barratry, maintenance and champerty, that interest does not justify the prohibition of the NAACP activities disclosed by this record. Malicious intent was of the essence of the common-law offenses of fomenting or stirring up litigation. And whatever may be or may have been true of suits against governments in other countries, the exercise in our own, as in this case of First Amendment rights to enforce Constitutional rights through litigation, as a matter of law, cannot be deemed malicious." NAACP v. Button, 371 U.S. 415, 429, 439–40, 9 L.Ed.2d 405, 415–16, 422, 83 S.Ct. 328, 336, 341 (1963).

[12] *See* ABA Canon 27.

CODE OF PROFESSIONAL RESPONSIBILITY

a non-client, directly or indirectly, for the purpose of being retained to represent him for compensation.

EC 2-4 Since motivation is subjective and often difficult to judge, the motives of a lawyer who volunteers advice likely to produce legal controversy may well be suspect if he receives professional employment or other benefits as a result.[13] A lawyer who volunteers advice that one should obtain the services of a lawyer generally should not himself accept employment, compensation, or other benefit in connection with that matter. However, it is not improper for a lawyer to volunteer such advice and render resulting legal services to close friends, relatives, former clients (in regard to matters germane to former employment), and regular clients.[14]

EC 2-5 A lawyer who writes or speaks for the purpose of educating members of the public to recognize their legal problems should carefully refrain from giving or appearing to give a general solution applicable to all apparently similar individual problems,[15] since slight changes in fact situations may require a material variance in the applicable advice; otherwise, the public may be misled and misadvised. Talks and writings by lawyers for laymen should caution them not to attempt to solve individual problems upon the basis of the information contained therein.[16]

Selection of a Lawyer: Generally

EC 2-6 Formerly a potential client usually knew the reputations of local lawyers for competency and integrity and therefore could select a practitioner in whom he had confidence. This traditional selection process worked well because it was initiated by the client and the choice was an informed one.

EC 2-7 Changed conditions, however, have seriously restricted the effectiveness of the traditional selection process. Often the reputations of lawyers are not sufficiently known to enable laymen to make intelligent choices.[17] The law has become increasingly complex and specialized. Few lawyers are willing and competent to deal with every kind of legal matter, and many laymen have difficulty in determining the competence of lawyers to render different types of legal services. The selection of legal counsel is particularly difficult for transients, persons moving into new areas, persons of limited education or means, and others who have little or no contact with lawyers.[18]

EC 2-8 Selection of a lawyer by a layman often is the result of the advice and recommendation of third parties—relatives, friends, acquaintances, business associates, or other lawyers. A layman is best served if the recommendation is disinterested and informed. In order that the recommendation be disinterested, a lawyer should not seek to influence another to recommend his employment.[19] A lawyer should not compensate another person for recommending him, for influencing a prospective client to employ him, or to encourage future recommendations.[20]

Selection of a Lawyer: Professional Notices and Listings

EC 2-9 The traditional ban against advertising by lawyers, which is subject to certain limited exceptions, is rooted in the public interest. Competitive advertising would encourage extravagant, artful, self-laudatory [21] brashness in seeking business and

---

[13] "The Canons of Professional Ethics of the American Bar Association and the decisions of the courts quite generally prohibit the direct solicitation of business for gain by an attorney either through advertisement or personal communication; and also condemn the procuring of business by indirection through touters of any kind. It is disreputable for an attorney to breed litigation by seeking out those who have claims for personal injuries or other grounds of action in order to secure them as clients, or to employ agents or runners, or to reward those who bring or influence the bringing of business to his office. . . . Moreover, it tends quite easily to the institution of baseless litigation and the manufacture of perjured testimony. From early times, this danger has been recognized in the law by the condemnation of the crime of common barratry, or the stirring up of suits or quarrels between individuals at law or otherwise." In re Ades, 6 F.Supp. 467, 474–75 (D. Mary. 1934).

[14] "Rule 2.
"§a. . . .
"[A] member of the State Bar shall not solicit professional employment by
"(1) Volunteering counsel or advice except where ties of blood relationship or trust make it appropriate." Cal. Business and Professions Code § 6076 (West 1962).

[15] "Rule 18 . . . A member of the State Bar shall not advise inquirers or render opinions to them through or in connection with a newspaper, radio or other publicity medium of any kind in respect to their specific legal problems, whether or not such attorney shall be compensated for his services." Cal.Business and Professions Code § 6076 (West 1962).

[16] "In any case where a member might well apply the advice given in the opinion to his individual affairs, the lawyer rendering the opinion [concerning problems common to members of an association and distributed to the members through a periodic bulletin] should specifically state that this opinion should not be relied on by any member as a basis for handling his individual affairs, but that in every case he should consult his counsel. In the publication of the opinion the association should make a similar statement." *ABA Opinion* 273 (1946).

[17] "A group of recent interrelated changes bears directly on the availability of legal services. . . . [One] change is the constantly accelerating urbanization of the country and the decline of personal and neighborhood knowledge of whom to retain as a professional man." Cheatham, *Availability of Legal Services: The Responsibility of the Individual Lawyer and of the Organized Bar*, 12 U.C.L.A.L. Rev. 438, 440 (1965).

[18] *Cf.* Cheatham, *A Lawyer When Needed: Legal Services for the Middle Classes*, 63 Colum.L.Rev. 973, 974 (1963).

[19] *See* ABA Canon 27.

[20] *See* ABA Canon 28.

[21] " 'Self-laudation' is a very flexible concept; Canon 27 does not define it, so what course of conduct would be said to constitute it under a given state of facts would no doubt vary as the opinions of men vary. As a famous English judge said, it would vary as the length of the chancellor's foot. It must be in words and tone that will 'offend the traditions and lower the tone of our profession.' When it

CODE OF PROFESSIONAL RESPONSIBILITY

thus could mislead the layman.[22] Furthermore, it would inevitably produce unrealistic expectations in particular cases and bring about distrust of the law and lawyers.[23] Thus, public confidence in our legal system would be impaired by such advertisements of professional services. The attorney-client relationship is personal and unique and should not be established as the result of pressures and deceptions.[24] History has demonstrated that public confidence in the legal system is best preserved by strict, self-imposed controls over, rather than by unlimited, advertising.

---

does this, it is 'reprehensible.' This seems to be the test by which 'self-laudation' is measured." State v. Nichols, 151 So.2d 257, 259 (Fla. 1963).

[22] "Were it not for the prohibitions of . . . [Canon 27] lawyers could, and no doubt would be forced to, engage competitively in advertising of all kinds in which each would seek to explain to the public why he could serve better and accomplish more than his brothers at the Bar.

"Susceptible as we are to advertising the public would then be encouraged to choose an attorney on the basis of which had the better, more attractive advertising program rather than on his reputation for professional ability.

"This would certainly maim, if not destroy, the dignity and professional status of the Bar of this State." State v. Nichols, 151 So.2d 257, 268 (Fla. 1963) (O'Connell, J., concurring in part and dissenting in part).

[23] Cf. ABA Canon 8.

[24] "The prohibition of advertising by lawyers deserves some examination. All agree that advertising by an individual lawyer, if permitted, will detract from the dignity of the profession, but the matter goes deeper than this. Perhaps the most understandable and acceptable additional reasons we have found are stated by one commentator as follows:

" '1. That advertisements, unless kept within narrow limits, like any other form of solicitation, tend to stir up litigation, and such tendency is against the public interest.

" '2. That if there were no restrictions on advertisements, the least capable and least honorable lawyers would be apt to publish the most extravagant and alluring material about themselves, and that the harm which would result would, in large measure, fall on the ignorant and on those least able to afford it.

" '3. That the temptation would be strong to hold out as inducements for employment, assurances of success or of satisfaction to the client, which assurances could not be realized, and that the giving of such assurances would materially increase the temptation to use ill means to secure the end desired by the client.

" 'In other words, the reasons for the rule, and for the conclusion that it is desirable to prohibit advertising entirely, or to limit it within such narrow bounds that it will not admit of abuse, are based on the possibility and probability that this means of publicity, if permitted, will be abused.' Harrison Hewitt in a comment at 15 A.B.A.J. 116 (1929) reproduced in Cheatham, Cases and Materials on the Legal Profession (2d Ed., 1955), p. 525.

"Of course, competition is at the root of the abuses in advertising. If the individual lawyer were permitted to compete with his fellows in publicity through advertising, we have no doubt that Mr. Hewitt's three points, quoted above, would accurately forecast the result." Jacksonville Bar Ass'n v. Wilson, 102 So.2d 292, 294-95 (Fla. 1958).

EC 2-10 Methods of advertising that are subject to the objections stated above [25] should be and are prohibited.[26] However, the Disciplinary Rules recognize the value of giving assistance in the selection process through forms of advertising that furnish identification of a lawyer while avoiding such objections. For example, a lawyer may be identified in the classified section of the telephone directory,[27] in the office building directory, and on his letterhead and professional card.[28] But at all times the permitted notices should be dignified and accurate.

EC 2-11 The name under which a lawyer conducts his practice may be a factor in the selection process.[29] The use of a trade name or an assumed name could mislead laymen concerning the identity, responsibility, and status of those practicing thereunder.[30] Accordingly, a lawyer in private practice should practice only under his own name, the name of a lawyer employing him, a partnership name composed of the name of one or more of the lawyers practicing in a partnership, or, if permitted by law, in the name of a professional legal corporation, which should be clearly designated as such. For many years some law firms have used a firm name retaining one or more names of deceased or retired partners and such practice is not improper if the firm is a bona fide successor of a firm in which the deceased or retired person was a member, if the use of the name is authorized by law or by contract, and if the public is not misled thereby.[31] However, the name of a partner

---

[25] See ABA Canon 27.

[26] Cf. ABA Opinions 309 (1963) and 284 (1951).

[27] Cf. ABA Opinions 313 (1964) and 284 (1951).

[28] See ABA Canon 27.

[29] Cf. ABA Opinion 303 (1961).

[30] See ABA Canon 33.

[31] Id.

"The continued use of a firm name by one or more surviving partners after the death of a member of the firm whose name is in the firm title is expressly permitted by the Canons of Ethics. The reason for this is that all of the partners have by their joint and several efforts over a period of years contributed to the good will attached to the firm name. In the case of a firm having widespread connections, this good will is disturbed by a change in firm name every time a name partner dies, and that reflects a loss in some degree of the good will to the building up of which the surviving partners have contributed their time, skill and labor through a period of years. To avoid this loss the firm name is continued, and to meet the requirements of the Canon the individuals constituting the firm from time to time are listed." ABA Opinion 267 (1945).

"Accepted local custom in New York recognizes that the name of a law firm does not necessarily identify the individual members of the firm, and hence the continued use of a firm name after the death of one or more partners is not a deception and is permissible. . . . The continued use of a deceased partner's name in the firm title is not affected by the fact that another partner withdraws from the firm and his name is dropped, or the name of the new partner is added to the firm name." Opinion No. 45, Committee on Professional Ethics, New York State Bar Ass'n, 39 N.Y.St.B.J. 455 (1967).

Cf. ABA Opinion 258 (1943).

who withdraws from a firm but continues to practice law should be omitted from the firm name in order to avoid misleading the public.

EC 2-12 A lawyer occupying a judicial, legislative, or public executive or administrative position who has the right to practice law concurrently may allow his name to remain in the name of the firm if he actively continues to practice law as a member thereof. Otherwise, his name should be removed from the firm name,[32] and he should not be identified as a past or present member of the firm; and he should not hold himself out as being a practicing lawyer.

EC 2-13 In order to avoid the possibility of misleading persons with whom he deals, a lawyer should be scrupulous in the representation of his professional status.[33] He should not hold himself out as being a partner or associate of a law firm if he is not one in fact,[34] and thus should not hold himself out as a partner or associate if he only shares offices with another lawyer.[35]

EC 2-14 In some instances a lawyer confines his practice to a particular field of law.[36] In the absence of state controls to insure the existence of special competence, a lawyer should not be permitted to hold himself out as a specialist [37] or as having special training or ability, other than in the historically excepted fields of admiralty, trademark, and patent law.[38]

---

[32] Cf. ABA Canon 33 and *ABA Opinion* 315 (1965).

[33] Cf. *ABA Opinions* 283 (1950) and 81 (1932).

[34] See *ABA Opinion* 316 (1967).

[35] "The word 'associates' has a variety of meanings. Principally through custom the word when used on the letterheads of law firms has come to be regarded as describing those who are employees of the firm. Because the word has acquired this special significance in connection with the practice of the law the use of the word to describe lawyer relationships other than employer-employee is likely to be misleading." In re Sussman and Tanner, 241 Ore. 246, 248, 405 P.2d 355, 356 (1965).

According to *ABA Opinion* 310 (1963), use of the term "associates" would be misleading in two situations: (1) where two lawyers are partners and they share both responsibility and liability for the partnership; and (2) where two lawyers practice separately, sharing no responsibility or liability, and only share a suite of offices and some costs.

[36] "For a long time, many lawyers have, of necessity, limited their practice to certain branches of law. The increasing complexity of the law and the demand of the public for more expertness on the part of the lawyer has, in the past few years—particularly in the last ten years—brought about specialization on an increasing scale." *Report of the Special Committee on Specialization and Specialized Legal Services*, 79 A.B.A.Rep. 582, 584 (1954).

[37] "In varying degrees specialization has become the *modus operandi* throughout the legal profession. . . . American society is specialization conscious. The present Canons, however, do not allow lawyers to make known to the lay public the fact that they engage in the practice of a specialty. . . ." Tucker, *The Large Law Firm: Considerations Concerning the Modernization of the Canons of Professional Ethics*, 1965 Wis.L.Rev. 344, 348-49 (1965).

[38] See ABA Canon 27.

EC 2-15 The legal profession has developed lawyer referral systems designed to aid individuals who are able to pay fees but need assistance in locating lawyers competent to handle their particular problems. Use of a lawyer referral system enables a layman to avoid an uninformed selection of a lawyer because such a system makes possible the employment of competent lawyers who have indicated an interest in the subject matter involved. Lawyers should support the principle of lawyer referral systems and should encourage the evolution of other ethical plans which aid in the selection of qualified counsel.

Financial Ability to Employ Counsel: Generally

EC 2-16 The legal profession cannot remain a viable force in fulfilling its role in our society unless its members receive adequate compensation for services rendered, and reasonable fees [39] should be charged in appropriate cases to clients able to pay them. Nevertheless, persons unable to pay all or a portion of a reasonable fee should be able to obtain necessary legal services,[40] and lawyers should support and participate in ethical activities designed to achieve that objective.[41]

Financial Ability to Employ Counsel: Persons Able to Pay Reasonable Fees

EC 2-17 The determination of a proper fee requires consideration of the interests of both client and lawyers.[42] A lawyer should not charge more than a reasonable fee,[43] for excessive cost of legal service would deter laymen from utilizing the legal system in protection of their rights. Furthermore, an excessive charge abuses the professional relationship between lawyer and client. On the other hand, adequate compensation is necessary in order to enable the lawyer to serve his client effectively and to preserve the integrity and independence of the profession.[44]

EC 2-18 The determination of the reasonableness of a fee requires consideration of all relevant circumstances,[45] including those stated in the Disciplinary Rules. The fees of a lawyer will vary according to many factors, including the time required, his experience, ability, and reputation, the

---

[39] See ABA Canon 12.

[40] Cf. ABA Canon 12.

[41] "If there is any fundamental proposition of government on which all would agree, it is that one of the highest goals of society must be to achieve and maintain equality before the law. Yet this ideal remains an empty form of words unless the legal profession is ready to provide adequate representation for those unable to pay the usual fees." *Professional Representation: Report of the Joint Conference*, 44 A.B.A.J. 1159, 1216 (1958).

[42] See ABA Canon 12.

[43] Cf. ABA Canon 12.

[44] "When members of the Bar are induced to render legal services for inadequate compensation, as a consequence the quality of the service rendered may be lowered, the welfare of the profession injured and the administration of justice made less efficient." ABA Opinion 302 (1961). Cf. ABA Opinion 307 (1962).

[45] See ABA Canon 12.

nature of the employment, the responsibility involved, and the results obtained. Suggested fee schedules and economic reports of state and local bar associations provide some guidance on the subject of reasonable fees.[46] It is a commendable and long-standing tradition of the bar that special consideration is given in the fixing of any fee for services rendered a brother lawyer or a member of his immediate family.

EC 2-19 As soon as feasible after a lawyer has been employed, it is desirable that he reach a clear agreement with his client as to the basis of the fee charges to be made. Such a course will not only prevent later misunderstanding but will also work for good relations between the lawyer and the client. It is usually beneficial to reduce to writing the understanding of the parties regarding the fee, particularly when it is contingent. A lawyer should be mindful that many persons who desire to employ him may have had little or no experience with fee charges of lawyers, and for this reason he should explain fully to such persons the reasons for the particular fee arrangement he proposes.

EC 2-20 Contingent fee arrangements[47] in civil cases have long been commonly accepted in the United States in proceedings to enforce claims. The historical bases of their acceptance are that (1) they often, and in a variety of circumstances, provide the only practical means by which one having a claim against another can economically afford, finance, and obtain the services of a competent lawyer to prosecute his claim, and (2) a successful prosecution of the claim produces a *res* out of which the fee can be paid.[48] Although a lawyer generally should decline to accept employment on a contingent fee basis by one who is able to pay a reasonable fixed fee, it is not necessarily improper for a lawyer, where justified by the particular circumstances of a case, to enter into a contingent fee contract in a civil case with any client who, after being fully informed of all relevant factors, desires that arrangement. Because of the human relationships involved and the unique character of the proceedings, contingent fee arrangements in domestic relation cases are rarely justified. In administrative agency proceedings contingent fee contracts should be governed by the same considerations as in other civil cases. Public policy properly condemns contingent fee arrangements in criminal cases, largely on the ground that legal services in criminal cases do not produce a *res* with which to pay the fee.

EC 2-21 A lawyer should not accept compensation or any thing of value incident to his employment or services from one other than his client without the knowledge and consent of his client after full disclosure.[49]

EC 2-22 Without the consent of his client, a lawyer should not associate in a particular matter another lawyer outside his firm. A fee may properly be divided between lawyers[50] properly associated if the division is in proportion to the services performed and the responsibility assumed by each lawyer[51] and if the total fee is reasonable.

EC 2-23 A lawyer should be zealous in his efforts to avoid controversies over fees with clients[52] and should attempt to resolve amicably any differences on the subject.[53] He should not sue a client for a fee unless necessary to prevent fraud or gross imposition by the client.[54]

---

[46] *Id.*
"[U]nder . . . [*Canon 12*], this Committee has consistently held that minimum fee schedules can only be suggested or recommended and cannot be made obligatory . . . ." *ABA Opinion* 302 (1961).

"[A] compulsory minimum fee schedule is contrary to *Canon 12* and repeated pronouncements of this committee." *ABA Opinion* 190 (1939).

Cf. ABA Opinions 171 (1937) and 28 (1930).

[47] *See* ABA Canon 13; *see also* Mackinnon, Contingent Fees for Legal Services (1964) (A report of the American Bar Foundation).

"A contract for a reasonable contingent fee where sanctioned by law is permitted by *Canon 13*, but the client must remain responsible to the lawyer for expenses advanced by the latter. 'There is to be no barter of the privilege of prosecuting a cause for gain in exchange for the promise of the attorney to prosecute at his own expense.' (Cardozo, C. J. in Matter of Gilman, 251 N.Y. 265, 270–271.)" *ABA Opinion* 246 (1942).

[48] *See* Comment, *Providing Legal Services for the Middle Class in Civil Matters: The Problem, the Duty and a Solution,* 26 U.Pitt.L.Rev. 811, 829 (1965).

[49] *See* ABA Canon 38.
"Of course, as . . . [Informal Opinion 679] points out, there must be full disclosure of the arrangement [that an entity other than the client pays the attorney's fee] by the attorney to the client . . . ." *ABA Opinion* 320 (1968).

[50] "Only lawyers may share in . . . a division of fees, but . . . it is not necessary that both lawyers be admitted to practice in the same state, so long as the division was based on the division of services or responsibility." *ABA Opinion* 316 (1967).

[51] *See* ABA Canon 34.
"We adhere to our previous rulings that where a lawyer merely brings about the employment of another lawyer *but renders no service and assumes no responsibility in the matter,* a division of the latter's fee is improper. (*Opinions 18 and 153*).

"It is assumed that the bar, generally, understands what acts or conduct of a lawyer may constitute 'services' to a client within the intendment of *Canon 12*. Such acts or conduct invariably, if not always, involve 'responsibility' on the part of the lawyer, whether the word 'responsibility' be construed to denote the possible resultant legal or moral liability on the part of the lawyer to the client or to others, or the onus of deciding what should or should not be done in behalf of the client. The word 'services' in *Canon 12* must be construed in this broad sense and may apply to the selection and retainer of associate counsel as well as to other acts or conduct in the client's behalf." *ABA Opinion* 204 (1940).

[52] *See* ABA Canon 14.

[53] *Cf. ABA Opinion* 320 (1968).

[54] *See* ABA Canon 14.
"Ours is a learned profession, not a mere money-getting trade. . . . Suits to collect fees should be avoided. Only where the circumstances imperatively require, should resort be had to a suit to compel payment. And where a lawyer does resort to a suit to enforce payment of fees

EC 2-32 A decision by a lawyer to withdraw should be made only on the basis of compelling circumstances [73], and in a matter pending before a tribunal he must comply with the rules of the tribunal regarding withdrawal. A lawyer should not withdraw without considering carefully and endeavoring to minimize the possible adverse effect on the rights of his client and the possibility of prejudice to his client [74] as a result of his withdrawal. Even when he justifiably withdraws, a lawyer should protect the welfare of his client by giving due notice of his withdrawal,[75] suggesting employment of other counsel, delivering to the client all papers and property to which the client is entitled, cooperating with counsel subsequently employed, and otherwise endeavoring to minimize the possibility of harm. Further, he should refund to the client any compensation not earned during the employment.[76]

DISCIPLINARY RULES

DR 2-101 Publicity in General.[77]

(A) A lawyer shall not prepare, cause to be prepared, use, or participate in the use of, any form of public communication that contains professionally self-laudatory statements calculated to attract lay clients; as used herein, "public communication" includes, but is not limited to, communication by means of television, radio, motion picture, newspaper, magazine, or book.

(B) A lawyer shall not publicize himself, his partner, or associate as a lawyer through newspaper or magazine advertisements, radio or television announcements, display advertisements in city or telephone directories, or other means of commercial publicity,[78] nor shall he authorize or permit others to do so in his behalf [79] except as permitted under DR 2-103.

This does not prohibit limited and dignified identification of a lawyer as a lawyer as well as by name [80]:

(1) In political advertisements when his professional status is germane to the political campaign or to a political issue.

(2) In public notices when the name and profession of a lawyer are required or authorized by law or are reasonably pertinent for a purpose other than the attraction of potential clients.[81]

(3) In routine reports and announcements of a bona fide business, civic, professional, or political organization in which he serves as a director or officer.

(4) In and on legal documents prepared by him.

(5) In and on legal textbooks, treatises, and other legal publications, and in dignified advertisements thereof.

(C) A lawyer shall not compensate or give any thing of value to representatives of the press, radio, television, or other communication medium in anticipation of or in return for professional publicity in a news item.[82]

DR 2-102 Professional Notices, Letterheads, Offices, and Law Lists.

(A) A lawyer or law firm shall not use professional cards, professional announcement cards,

---

[73] See ABA Canon 44.
"I will carefully consider, before taking a case, whether it appears that I can fully represent the client within the framework of law. If the decision is in the affirmative, then it will take extreme circumstances to cause me to decide later that I cannot so represent him." Thode, *The Ethical Standard for the Advocate*, 39 Texas L.Rev. 575, 592 (1961) (from "A Proper Oath for Advocates").

[74] *ABA Opinion* 314 (1965) held that a lawyer should not disassociate himself from a cause when "it is obvious that the very act of disassociation would have the effect of violating *Canon 37*."

[75] ABA Canon 44 enumerates instances in which ". . . the lawyer may be warranted in withdrawing on due notice to the client, allowing him time to employ another lawyer."

[76] *See* ABA Canon 44.

[77] *Cf.* ABA Canon 27; *see generally ABA Opinion* 293 (1957).

[78] *Cf. ABA Opinions* 133 (1935), 116 (1934), 107 (1934), 73 (1932), 59 (1931), and 43 (1931).

[79] "There can be no justification for the participation and acquiescence by an attorney in the development and publication of an article which, on its face, plainly amounts to a self-interest and unethical presentation of his achievements and capabilities." Matter of Connelly, 18 App.Div. 2d 466, 478, 240 N.Y.S.2d 126, 138 (1963).
"An announcement of the fact that the lawyer had resigned and the name of the person to succeed him, or take over his work, would not be objectionable, either as an official communication to those employed by or connected with the administrative agency or instrumentality [that had employed him], or as a news release.
"But to include therein a statement of the lawyer's experience in and acquaintance with the various departments and agencies of the government, and a laudation of his legal ability, either generally or in a special branch of the law, is not only bad taste but ethically improper.
"It can have but one primary purpose or object: to aid the lawyer in securing professional employment in private practice by advertising his professional experience, attainments and ability." *ABA Opinion* 184 (1938).
Cf. ABA Opinions 285 (1951) and 140 (1935).

[80] "The question is always . . . whether under the circumstance the furtherance of the professional employment of the lawyer is the primary purpose of the advertisement, or is merely a necessary incident of a proper and legitimate objective of the client which does not have the effect of unduly advertising him." *ABA Opinion* 290 (1956).
See ABA Opinion 285 (1951).

[81] *See ABA Opinions* 299 (1961), 290 (1956), 158 (1936), and 100 (1933); *cf. ABA Opinion* 80 (1932).

[82] "Rule 2.
. . . .
"[A] member of the State Bar shall not solicit professional employment by . . . .
"(4) The making of gifts to representatives of the press, radio, television or any medium of communication in anticipation of or in return for publicity." Cal.Business and Professions Code § 6076 (West 1962).

CODE OF PROFESSIONAL RESPONSIBILITY

office signs, letterheads, telephone directory listings, law lists, legal directory listings, or similar professional notices or devices,[83] except that the following may be used if they are in dignified form:

(1) A professional card of a lawyer identifying him by name and as a lawyer, and giving his addresses, telephone numbers, the name of his law firm, and any information permitted under DR 2-105. A professional card of a law firm may also give the names of members and associates. Such cards may be used for identification [84] but may not be published in periodicals, magazines, newspapers,[85] or other media.[86]

(2) A brief professional announcement card stating new or changed associations or addresses, change of firm name, or similar matters pertaining to the professional office of a lawyer or law firm, which may be mailed to lawyers, clients, former clients, personal friends, and relatives.[87] It shall not state biographical data except to the extent reasonably necessary to identify the lawyer or to explain the change in his association, but it may state the immediate past position of the lawyer.[88] It may give the names and dates of predecessor firms in a continuing line of succession. It shall not state the nature of the practice except as permitted under DR 2-105.[89]

(3) A sign on or near the door of the office and in the building directory identifying the law office. The sign shall not state the nature of the practice, except as permitted under DR 2-105.

(4) A letterhead of a lawyer identifying him by name and as a lawyer, and giving his addresses, telephone numbers, the name of his law firm, associates, and any information permitted under DR 2-105. A letterhead of a law firm may also give the names of members and associates,[90] and names and dates relating to deceased and retired members.[91] A lawyer may be designated "Of Counsel" on a letterhead if he has a continuing relationship with a lawyer or law firm, other than as a partner or associate. A lawyer or law firm may be designated as "General Counsel" or by similar professional reference on stationery of a client if he or the firm devotes a substantial amount of professional time in the representation of that client.[92] The letterhead of a law firm may give the names and dates of predecessor firms in a continuing line of succession.

(5) A listing of the office of a lawyer or law firm in the alphabetical and classified sections of the telephone directory or directories for the geographical area or areas in which the lawyer resides or maintains offices or in which a significant part of his clientele resides [93] and in the city directory of the city in which his or the firm's office is located; [94] but the listing may give only the name of the lawyer or law firm, the fact he is a lawyer, addresses, and telephone numbers.[95] The listing shall not be in distinctive form [96] or type.[97] A law firm may have a listing in the firm name separate from that of its members and associates.[98] The listing in the classified section shall not be under a heading or classification other than "Attorneys" or "Lawyers",[99]

---

[83] Cf. ABA Opinions 233 (1941) and 114 (1934).

[84] See ABA Opinion 175 (1938).

[85] See ABA Opinions 260 (1944) and 182 (1938).

[86] But cf. ABA Opinions 276 (1947) and 256 (1943).

[87] See ABA Opinion 301 (1961).

[88] "[I]t has become commonplace for many lawyers to participate in government service; to deny them the right, upon their return to private practice, to refer to their prior employment in a brief and dignified manner, would place an undue limitation upon a large element of our profession. It is entirely proper for a member of the profession to explain his absence from private practice, where such is the primary purpose of the announcement, by a brief and dignified reference to the prior employment.

". . . [A]ny such announcement should be limited to the immediate past connection of the lawyer with the government, made upon his leaving that position to enter private practice." ABA Opinion 301 (1961).

[89] See ABA Opinion 251 (1943).

[90] "Those lawyers who are working for an individual lawyer or a law firm may be designated on the letterhead and in other appropriate places as 'associates'." ABA Opinion 310 (1963).

[91] See ABA Canon 33.

[92] But see ABA Opinion 285 (1951).

[93] See ABA Opinion 295 (1959).

[94] But see ABA Opinion 313 (1964) which says the Committee "approves a listing in the classified section of the city directory for lawyers only when the listing includes all lawyers residing in the community and when no charge is made therefor."

[95] "The listing should consist only of the lawyer's name, address and telephone number." ABA Opinion 313 (1964).

[96] "[A]dding to the regular classified listing a 'second line' in which a lawyer claims that he is engaged in a 'specialty' is an undue attempt to make his name distinctive." ABA Opinion 284 (1951).

[97] "[Opinion 284] held that a lawyer could not with propriety have his name listed in distinctive type in a telephone directory or city directory. We affirm that opinion." ABA Opinion 313 (1964).
See ABA Opinions 123 (1934) and 53 (1931).

[98] "[I]f a lawyer is a member of a law firm, both the firm, and the individual lawyer may be listed separately." ABA Opinion 313 (1964).

[99] See ABA Opinion 284 (1951).

CODE OF PROFESSIONAL RESPONSIBILITY

except that additional headings or classifications descriptive of the types of practice referred to in DR 2-105 are permitted.[100]

(6) A listing in a reputable law list [101] or legal directory giving brief biographical and other informative data. A law list or directory is not reputable if its management or contents are likely to be misleading or injurious to the public or to the profession.[102] A law list is conclusively established to be reputable if it is certified by the American Bar Association as being in compliance with its rules and standards. The published data may include only the following: name, including name of law firm and names of professional associates; addresses [103] and telephone numbers; one or more fields of law in which the lawyer or law firm concentrates;[104] a statement that practice is limited to one or more fields of law; a statement that the lawyer or law firm specializes in a particular field of law or law practice but only if authorized under DR 2-105 (A)(4);[105] date and place of birth; date and place of admission to the bar of state and federal courts; schools attended, with dates of graduation, degrees, and other scholastic distinctions; public or quasi-public offices; military service; posts of honor; legal authorships; legal teaching positions; memberships, offices, committee assignments, and section memberships in bar associations; memberships and offices in legal fraternities and legal societies; technical and professional associations and societies; foreign language ability; names and addresses of references,[106] and, with their consent, names of clients regularly represented.[107]

(B) A lawyer in private practice shall not practice under a trade name, a name that is misleading as to the identity of the lawyer or lawyers practicing under such name, or a firm name containing names other than those of one or more of the lawyers in the firm, except that the name of a professional corporation or professional association may contain "P.C." or "P.A." or similar symbols indicating the nature of the organization, and if otherwise lawful a firm may use as, or continue to include in, its name, the name or names of one or more deceased or retired members of the firm or of a predecessor firm in a continuing line of succession.[108] A lawyer who assumes a judicial, legislative, or public executive or administrative post or office shall not permit his name to remain in the name of a law firm or to be used in professional notices of the firm during any significant period in which he is not actively and regularly practicing law as a member of the firm,[109] and during such period other members of the firm shall not use his name in the firm name or in professional notices of the firm.[110]

---

[100] *See* Silverman v. State Bar of Texas, 405 F.2d 410, (5th Cir. 1968); *but see ABA Opinion* 286 (1952).

[101] *Cf.* ABA Canon 43.

[102] *Cf. ABA Opinion* 255 (1943).

[103] "We are asked to define the word 'addresses' appearing in the second paragraph of Canon 27 . . . .
"It is our opinion that an address (other than a cable address) within the intendment of the canon is that of the lawyer's office or of his residence. Neither address should be misleading. If, for example, an office address is given, it must be that of a bona fide office. The residence address, if given, should be identified as such if the city or other place of residence is not the same as that in which the law office is located." *ABA Opinion* 249 (1942).

[104] "[T]oday in various parts of the country Committees on Professional Ethics of local and state bar associations are authorizing lawyers to describe themselves in announcements to the Bar and in notices in legal periodicals and approved law lists as specialists in a great variety of things. Thus in the approved law lists or professional announcements there appear, in connection with the names of individual practitioners or firms, such designations as 'International Law, Public and Private'; 'Trial Preparation in Personal Injury and Negligence Actions'; 'Philippine War Damage Claims'; 'Anti-Trust'; 'Domestic Relations'; 'Tax Law'; 'Negligence Law'. It would seem that the ABA has given at least its tacit approval to this sort of announcement.
"It is important that this sort of description is not, in New York at least, permitted on letterheads or shingles or elsewhere in communications to laymen. This is subject to the single exception that such announcement to laymen is permitted in the four traditional specialties, Admiralty, Patent, Copyright and Trade-mark." *Report of the Special Committee on Specialization and Specialized Legal Education*, 79 A.B.A. Rep. 582, 586 (1954).

[105] This provision is included to conform to action taken by the ABA House of Delegates at the Mid-Winter Meeting, January, 1969.

[106] *See* ABA Canon 43 and *ABA Opinion* 119 (1934); *but see ABA Opinion* 236 (1941).

[107] *See* ABA Canon 27.

[108] *See* ABA Canon 33; *cf. ABA Opinions* 318 (1967), 267 (1945), 219 (1941), 208 (1940), 192 (1939), 97 (1933), and 6 (1925).

[109] *ABA Opinion* 318 (1967) held, "anything to the contrary in Formal Opinion 315 or in the other opinions cited notwithstanding" that: "Where a partner whose name appears in the name of a law firm is elected or appointed to high local, state or federal office, which office he intends to occupy only temporarily, at the end of which time he intends to return to his position with the firm, and provided that he is not precluded by holding such office from engaging in the practice of law and does not in fact sever his relationship with the firm but only takes a leave of absence, and provided that there is no local law, statute or custom to the contrary, his name may be retained in the firm name during his term or terms of office, but only if proper precautions are taken not to mislead the public as to his degree of participation in the firm's affairs."
Cf. ABA Opinion 143 (1935), New York County Opinion 67, and New York City Opinions 36 and 798; *but cf. ABA Opinion* 192 (1939) and Michigan Opinion 164.

[110] *Cf.* ABA Canon 33.

CODE OF PROFESSIONAL RESPONSIBILITY

(C) A lawyer shall not hold himself out as having a partnership with one or more other lawyers unless they are in fact partners.[111]

(D) A partnership shall not be formed or continued between or among lawyers licensed in different jurisdictions unless all enumerations of the members and associates of the firm on its letterhead and in other permissible listings make clear the jurisdictional limitations on those members and associates of the firm not licensed to practice in all listed jurisdictions;[112] however, the same firm name may be used in each jurisdiction.

(E) A lawyer who is engaged both in the practice of law and another profession or business shall not so indicate on his letterhead, office sign, or professional card, nor shall he identify himself as a lawyer in any publication in connection with his other profession or business.

(F) Nothing contained herein shall prohibit a lawyer from using or permitting the use, in connection with his name, of an earned degree or title derived therefrom indicating his training in the law.

DR 2-103 Recommendation of Professional Employment.[113]

(A) A lawyer shall not recommend employment, as a private practitioner,[114] of himself, his partner, or associate to a non-lawyer who has not sought his advice regarding employment of a lawyer.[115]

(B) Except as permitted under DR 2-103(C), a lawyer shall not compensate or give anything of value to a person or organization to recommend or secure his employment[116] by a client, or as a reward for having made a recommendation resulting in his employment[117] by a client.

(C) A lawyer shall not request a person or organization to recommend employment, as a private practitioner, of himself, his partner, or associate,[118] except that he may request referrals from a lawyer referral service operated, sponsored, or approved by a bar association representative of the general bar of the geographical area in which the association exists and may pay its fees incident thereto.[119]

(D) A lawyer shall not knowingly assist a person or organization that recommends, furnishes, or pays for legal services to promote the use of his services or those of his partners or associates. However, he may cooperate in a dignified manner with the legal service activities of any of the following, provided that his independent professional judgment is exercised in behalf of his client without interference or control by any organization or other person:

(1) A legal aid office or public defender office:

(a) Operated or sponsored by a duly accredited law school.

(b) Operated or sponsored by a bona fide non-profit community organization.

(c) Operated or sponsored by a governmental agency.

(d) Operated, sponsored, or approved by a bar association representative of the general bar of the geographical area in which the association exists.[120]

(2) A military legal assistance office.

(3) A lawyer referral service operated, sponsored, or approved by a bar association representative of the general bar of the geographical area in which the association exists.[121]

(4) A bar association representative of the general bar of the geographical area in which the association exists.[122]

---

[111] See ABA Opinion 277 (1948); cf. ABA Canon 33 and ABA Opinions 318 (1967), 126 (1935), 115 (1934), and 106 (1934).

[112] See ABA Opinions 318 (1967) and 316 (1967); cf. ABA Canon 33.

[113] Cf. ABA Canons 27 and 28.

[114] "We think it clear that a lawyer's seeking employment in an ordinary law office, or appointment to a civil service position, is not prohibited by . . . [Canon 27]." ABA Opinion 197 (1939).

[115] "[A] lawyer may not seek from persons not his clients the opportunity to perform . . . a [legal] check-up." ABA Opinion 307 (1962).

[116] Cf. ABA Opinion 78 (1932).

[117] "'No financial connection of any kind between the Brotherhood and any lawyer is permissible. No lawyer can properly pay any amount whatsoever to the Brotherhood or any of its departments, officers or members as compensation, reimbursement of expenses or gratuity in connection with the procurement of a case.'" In re Brotherhood of R. R. Trainmen, 13 Ill.2d 391, 398, 150 N.E. 2d 163, 167 (1958), quoted in In re Ratner, 194 Kan 362, 372, 399 P.2d 865, 873 (1965).

See ABA Opinion 147 (1935).

[118] "This Court has condemned the practice of ambulance chasing through the media of runners and touters. In similar fashion we have with equal emphasis condemned the practice of direct solicitation by a lawyer. We have classified both offenses as serious breaches of the Canons of Ethics demanding severe treatment of the offending lawyer." State v. Dawson, 111 So.2d 427, 431 (Fla. 1959).

[119] "Registrants [of a lawyer referral plan] may be required to contribute to the expense of operating it by a reasonable registration charge or by a reasonable percentage of fees collected by them." ABA Opinion 291 (1956).

Cf. ABA Opinion 227 (1941).

[120] Cf. ABA Opinion 148 (1935).

[121] Cf. ABA Opinion 227 (1941).

[122] "If a bar association has embarked on a program of institutional advertising for an annual legal check-up and provides brochures and reprints, it is not improper to have these available in the lawyer's office for persons to read and take." ABA Opinion 307 (1962).

Cf. ABA Opinion 121 (1934).

CODE OF PROFESSIONAL RESPONSIBILITY

(5) Any other non-profit organization that recommends, furnishes, or pays for legal services to its members or beneficiaries, but only in those instances and to the extent that controlling constitutional interpretation at the time of the rendition of the services requires the allowance of such legal service activities,[123] and only if the following conditions, unless prohibited by such interpretation, are met:

    (a) The primary purposes of such organization do not include the rendition of legal services.

    (b) The recommending, furnishing, or paying for legal services to its members is incidental and reasonably related to the primary purposes of such organization.

    (c) Such organization does not derive a financial benefit from the rendition of legal services by the lawyer.

    (d) The member or beneficiary for whom the legal services are rendered, and not such organization, is recognized as the client of the lawyer in that matter.

(E) A lawyer shall not accept employment when he knows or it is obvious that the person who seeks his services does so as a result of conduct prohibited under this Disciplinary Rule.

DR 2-104 Suggestion of Need of Legal Services.[124]

(A) A lawyer who has given unsolicited advice to a layman that he should obtain counsel or take legal action shall not accept employment resulting from that advice,[125] except that:

    (1) A lawyer may accept employment by a close friend, relative, former client (if the advice is germane to the former employment), or one whom the lawyer reasonably believes to be a client.[126]

    (2) A lawyer may accept employment that results from his participation in activities designed to educate laymen to recognize legal problems, to make intelligent selection of counsel, or to utilize available legal services if such activities are conducted or sponsored by any of the offices or organizations enumerated in DR 2-103(D)(1) through (5), to the extent and under the conditions prescribed therein.

    (3) A lawyer who is furnished or paid by any of the offices or organizations enumerated in DR 2-103(D)(1), (2), or (5) may represent a member or beneficiary thereof, to the extent and under the conditions prescribed therein.

    (4) Without affecting his right to accept employment, a lawyer may speak publicly or write for publication on legal topics [127] so long as he does not emphasize his own professional experience or reputation and does not undertake to give individual advice.

    (5) If success in asserting rights or defenses of his client in litigation in the nature of a class action is dependent upon the joinder of others, a lawyer may accept, but shall not seek, employment from those contacted for the purpose of obtaining their joinder.[128]

DR 2-105 Limitation of Practice.[129]

(A) A lawyer shall not hold himself out publicly as a specialist [130] or as limiting his practice,[131] except as permitted under DR 2-102(A)(6) or as follows:

    (1) A lawyer admitted to practice before the United States Patent Office may use the designation "Patents," "Patent Attorney," or "Patent Lawyer," or any combination of those terms, on his letterhead and office sign. A lawyer engaged in the trademark practice may use the designation "Trademarks," "Trademark Attorney," or "Trademark Lawyer," or any combination of those terms, on his letterhead and office sign, and a lawyer engaged in the admiralty practice may use the designation "Admiralty," "Proctor in Admiralty," or "Admiralty Lawyer," or any combination of those terms, on his letterhead and office sign.[132]

---

[123] United Mine Workers v. Ill. State Bar Ass'n, 389 U.S. 217, 19 L.Ed.2d 426, 88 S.Ct. 353 (1967); Brotherhood of R.R. Trainmen v. Virginia, 371 U.S. 1, 12 L.Ed.2d 89, 84 S.Ct. 1113 (1964); NAACP v. Button, 371 U.S. 415, 9 L.Ed.2d 405, 83 S.Ct. 328 (1963).

[124] ABA Canon 28.

[125] Cf. ABA Opinions 229 (1941) and 173 (1937).

[126] "It certainly is not improper for a lawyer to advise his regular clients of new statutes, court decisions, and administrative rulings, which may affect the client's interests, provided the communication is strictly limited to such information. . . .

"When such communications go to concerns or individuals other than regular clients of the lawyer, they are thinly disguised advertisements for professional employment, and are obviously improper." ABA Opinion 213 (1941).

"It is our opinion that where the lawyer has no reason to believe that he has been supplanted by another lawyer, it is not only his right, but it might even be his duty to advise his client of any change of fact or law which might defeat the client's testamentary purpose as expressed in the will.

"Periodic notices might be sent to the client for whom a lawyer has drawn a will, suggesting that it might be wise for the client to reexamine his will to determine whether or not there has been any change in his situation requiring a modification of his will." ABA Opinion 210 (1941). Cf. ABA Canon 28.

[127] Cf. ABA Opinion 168 (1937).

[128] But cf. ABA Opinion 111 (1934).

[129] See ABA Canon 45; cf. ABA Canons 27, 43, and 46.

[130] Cf. ABA Opinions 228 (1941) and 194 (1939).

[131] See ABA Opinions 251 (1943) and 175 (1938).

[132] See ABA Canon 27; cf. ABA Opinion 286 (1952).

(2) A lawyer may permit his name to be listed in lawyer referral service offices according to the fields of law in which he will accept referrals.

(3) A lawyer available to act as a consultant to or as an associate of other lawyers in a particular branch of law or legal service may distribute to other lawyers and publish in legal journals a dignified announcement of such availability,[133] but the announcement shall not contain a representation of special competence or experience.[134] The announcement shall not be distributed to lawyers more frequently than once in a calendar year, but it may be published periodically in legal journals.

(4) A lawyer who is certified as a specialist in a particular field of law or law practice by the authority having jurisdiction under state law over the subject of specialization by lawyers may hold himself out as such specialist but only in accordance with the rules prescribed by that authority.[135]

DR 2-106 Fees for Legal Services.[136]

(A) A lawyer shall not enter into an agreement for, charge, or collect an illegal or clearly excessive fee.[137]

(B) A fee is clearly excessive when, after a review of the facts, a lawyer of ordinary prudence would be left with a definite and firm conviction that the fee is in excess of a reasonable fee. Factors to be considered as guides in determining the reasonableness of a fee include the following:

(1) The time and labor required, the novelty and difficulty of the questions involved, and the skill requisite to perform the legal service properly.

(2) The likelihood, if apparent to the client, that the acceptance of the particular employment will preclude other employment by the lawyer.

(3) The fee customarily charged in the locality for similar legal services.

(4) The amount involved and the results obtained.

(5) The time limitations imposed by the client or by the circumstances.

(6) The nature and length of the professional relationship with the client.

(7) The experience, reputation, and ability of the lawyer or lawyers performing the services.

(8) Whether the fee is fixed or contingent.[138]

(C) A lawyer shall not enter into an arrangement for, charge, or collect a contingent fee for representing a defendant in a criminal case.[139]

DR 2-107 Division of Fees Among Lawyers.

(A) A lawyer shall not divide a fee for legal services with another lawyer who is not a partner in or associate of his law firm or law office, unless:

(1) The client consents to employment of the other lawyer after a full disclosure that a division of fees will be made.

(2) The division is made in proportion to the services performed and responsibility assumed by each.[140]

(3) The total fee of the lawyers does not clearly exceed reasonable compensation for all legal services they rendered the client.[141]

---

[133] *Cf. ABA Opinion* 194 (1939).

[134] *See* ABA Canon 46.

[135] This provision is included to conform to action taken by the ABA House of Delegates at the Mid-Winter Meeting, January, 1969.

[136] *See* ABA Canon 12.

[137] The charging of a "clearly excessive fee" is a ground for discipline. State ex rel. Nebraska State Bar Ass'n. v. Richards, 165 Neb. 80, 90, 84 N.W.2d 136, 143 (1957).

"An attorney has the right to contract for any fee he chooses so long as it is not excessive (see Opinion 190), and this Committee is not concerned with the amount of such fees unless so excessive as to constitute a misappropriation of the client's funds (see Opinion 27)." *ABA Opinion* 320 (1968).

Cf. ABA Opinions 209 (1940), 190 (1939), and 27 (1930) and State ex rel. Lee v. Buchanan, 191 So.2d 33 (Fla. 1966).

[138] *Cf.* ABA Canon 13; *see generally* MacKinnon, Contingent Fees for Legal Services (1964) (A Report of the American Bar Foundation).

[139] "Contingent fees, whether in civil or criminal cases, are a special concern of the law. . . .

"In criminal cases, the rule is stricter because of the danger of corrupting justice. The second part of Section 542 of the Restatement [of Contracts] reads: 'A bargain to conduct a criminal case . . . in consideration of a promise of a fee contingent on success is illegal. . . .'" Peyton v. Margiotti, 398 Pa. 86, 156 A.2d 865, 967 (1959).

"The third area of practice in which the use of the contingent fee is generally considered to be prohibited is the prosecution and defense of criminal cases. However, there are so few cases, and these are predominantly old, that it is doubtful that there can be said to be any current law on the subject. . . . In the absence of cases on the validity of contingent fees for defense attorneys, it is necessary to rely on the consensus among commentators that such a fee is void as against public policy. The nature of criminal practice itself makes unlikely the use of contingent fee contracts." MacKinnon, Contingent Fees for Legal Services 52 (1964) (A Report of the American Bar Foundation).

[140] *See* ABA Canon 34 and *ABA Opinions* 316 (1967) and 294 (1958); *see generally ABA Opinions* 265 (1945), 204 (1940), 190 (1939), 171 (1937), 153 (1936), 97 (1933), 63 (1932), 28 (1930), 27 (1930), and 18 (1930).

[141] "*Canon 12* contemplates that a lawyer's fee should not exceed *the value of the services* rendered. . . .
. . . .
"*Canon 12* applies, whether joint or separate fees are charged [by associate attorneys] . . . ." *ABA Opinion* 204 (1940).

CODE OF PROFESSIONAL RESPONSIBILITY

(B) This Disciplinary Rule does not prohibit payment to a former partner or associate pursuant to a separation or retirement agreement.

DR 2-108 Agreements Restricting the Practice of a Lawyer.

(A) A lawyer shall not be a party to or participate in a partnership or employment agreement with another lawyer that restricts the right of a lawyer to practice law after the termination of a relationship created by the agreement, except as a condition to payment of retirement benefits.[142]

(B) In connection with the settlement of a controversy or suit, a lawyer shall not enter into an agreement that restricts his right to practice law.

DR 2-109 Acceptance of Employment.

(A) A lawyer shall not accept employment on behalf of a person if he knows or it is obvious that such person wishes to:

(1) Bring a legal action, conduct a defense, or assert a position in litigation, or otherwise have steps taken for him, merely for the purpose of harassing or maliciously injuring any person.[143]

(2) Present a claim or defense in litigation that is not warranted under existing law, unless it can be supported by good faith argument for an extension, modification, or reversal of existing law.

DR 2-110 Withdrawal from Employment.[144]

(A) In General.

(1) If permission for withdrawal from employment is required by the rules of a tribunal, a lawyer shall not withdraw from employment in a proceeding before that tribunal without its permission.

(2) In any event, a lawyer shall not withdraw from employment until he has taken reasonable steps to avoid foreseeable prejudice to the rights of his client, including giving due notice to his client, allowing time for employment of other counsel, delivering to the client all papers and property to which the client is entitled, and complying with applicable laws and rules.

(3) A lawyer who withdraws from employment shall refund promptly any part of a fee paid in advance that has not been earned.

(B) Mandatory withdrawal.

A lawyer representing a client before a tribunal, with its permission if required by its rules, shall withdraw from employment, and a lawyer representing a client in other matters shall withdraw from employment, if:

(1) He knows or it is obvious that his client is bringing the legal action, conducting the defense, or asserting a position in the litigation, or is otherwise having steps taken for him, merely for the purpose of harassing or maliciously injuring any person.

(2) He knows or it is obvious that his continued employment will result in violation of a Disciplinary Rule.[145]

(3) His mental or physical condition renders it unreasonably difficult for him to carry out the employment effectively.

(4) He is discharged by his client.

(C) Permissive withdrawal.[146]

If DR 2-110(B) is not applicable, a lawyer may not request permission to withdraw in matters pending before a tribunal, and may not withdraw in other matters, unless such request or such withdrawal is because:

(1) His client:

(a) Insists upon presenting a claim or defense that is not warranted under existing law and cannot be supported by good faith argument for an extension, modification, or reversal of existing law.[147]

(b) Personally seeks to pursue an illegal course of conduct.

(c) Insists that the lawyer pursue a course of conduct that is illegal or that is prohibited under the Disciplinary Rules.

(d) By other conduct renders it unreasonably difficult for the law-

---

[142] "[A] general covenant restricting an employed lawyer, after leaving the employment, from practicing in the community for a stated period, appears to this Committee to be an unwarranted restriction on the right of a lawyer to choose where he will practice and inconsistent with our professional status. Accordingly, the Committee is of the opinion it would be improper for the employing lawyer to require the covenant and likewise for the employed lawyer to agree to it." *ABA Opinion* 300 (1961).

[143] *See* ABA Canon 30.
"Rule 13. . . . A member of the State Bar shall not accept employment to prosecute or defend a case solely out of spite, or solely for the purpose of harassing or delaying another . . ." Cal.Business and Professions Code § 6067 (West 1962).

[144] *Cf.* ABA Canon 44.

[145] *See also* Code of Professional Responsibility, DR 5-102 and DR 5-105.

[146] *Cf.* ABA Canon 4.

[147] *Cf.* Anders v. California, 386 U.S. 738, 18 L.Ed.2d 493, 87 S.Ct. 1396 (1967), *rehearing denied*, 388 U.S. 924, 18 L.Ed.2d 1377, 87 S.Ct. 2094 (1967).

CODE OF PROFESSIONAL RESPONSIBILITY

yer to carry out his employment effectively.

(e) Insists, in a matter not pending before a tribunal, that the lawyer engage in conduct that is contrary to the judgment and advice of the lawyer but not prohibited under the Disciplinary Rules.

(f) Deliberately disregards an agreement or obligation to the lawyer as to expenses or fees.

(2) His continued employment is likely to result in a violation of a Disciplinary Rule.

(3) His inability to work with co-counsel indicates that the best interests of the client likely will be served by withdrawal.

(4) His mental or physical condition renders it difficult for him to carry out the employment effectively.

(5) His client knowingly and freely assents to termination of his employment.

(6) He believes in good faith, in a proceeding pending before a tribunal, that the tribunal will find the existence of other good cause for withdrawal.

CANON 3

A Lawyer Should Assist in Preventing the Unauthorized Practice of Law

ETHICAL CONSIDERATIONS

EC 3-1 The prohibition against the practice of law by a layman is grounded in the need of the public for integrity and competence of those who undertake to render legal services. Because of the fiduciary and personal character of the lawyer-client relationship and the inherently complex nature of our legal system, the public can better be assured of the requisite responsibility and competence if the practice of law is confined to those who are subject to the requirements and regulations imposed upon members of the legal profession.

EC 3-2 The sensitive variations in the considerations that bear on legal determinations often make it difficult even for a lawyer to exercise appropriate professional judgment, and it is therefore essential that the personal nature of the relationship of client and lawyer be preserved. Competent professional judgment is the product of a trained familiarity with law and legal processes, a disciplined, analytical approach to legal problems, and a firm ethical commitment.

EC 3-3 A non-lawyer who undertakes to handle legal matters is not governed as to integrity or legal competence by the same rules that govern the conduct of a lawyer. A lawyer is not only subject to that regulation but also is committed to high standards of ethical conduct. The public interest is best served in legal matters by a regulated profession committed to such standards.[1] The Disciplinary Rules protect the public in that they prohibit a lawyer from seeking employment by improper overtures, from acting in cases of divided loyalties, and from submitting to the control of others in the exercise of his judgment. Moreover, a person who entrusts legal matters to a lawyer is protected by the attorney-client privilege and by the duty of the lawyer to hold inviolate the confidences and secrets of his client.

EC 3-4 A layman who seeks legal services often is not in a position to judge whether he will receive proper professional attention. The entrustment of a legal matter may well involve the confidences, the reputation, the property, the freedom, or even the life of the client. Proper protection of members of the public demands that no person be permitted to act in the confidential and demanding capacity of a lawyer unless he is subject to the regulations of the legal profession.

EC 3-5 It is neither necessary nor desirable to attempt the formulation of a single, specific definition of what constitutes the practice of law.[2] Functionally, the practice of law relates to the rendition of services for others that call for the professional judgment of a lawyer. The essence of the professional judgment of the lawyer is his educated ability to relate the general body and philosophy of law to a specific legal problem of a client; and thus, the public interest will be better served if only lawyers are permitted to act in matters involving professional judgment. Where this professional judgment is not involved, non-lawyers, such as court clerks, police officers, abstracters, and many governmental employees, may engage in occupations that require a special knowledge of law in certain areas. But the services of a lawyer are essential in the public interest whenever the exercise of professional legal judgment is required.

EC 3-6 A lawyer often delegates tasks to clerks, secretaries, and other lay persons. Such delegation is proper if the lawyer maintains a direct relationship with his client, supervises the delegated work, and has complete professional responsibility for the work product.[3] This delegation enables a law-

---

[1] "The condemnation of the unauthorized practice of law is designed to protect the public from legal services by persons unskilled in the law. The prohibition of lay intermediaries is intended to insure the loyalty of the lawyer to the client unimpaired by intervening and possibly conflicting interests." Cheatham, *Availability of Legal Services: The Responsibility of the Individual Lawyer and of the Organized Bar*, 12 U.C.L.A.L.Rev. 438, 439 (1965).

[2] "What constitutes unauthorized practice of the law in a particular jurisdiction is a matter for determination by the courts of that jurisdiction." *ABA Opinion* 198 (1939).

"In the light of the historical development of the lawyer's functions, it is impossible to lay down an exhaustive definition of 'the practice of law' by attempting to enumerate every conceivable act performed by lawyers in the normal course of their work." State Bar of Arizona v. Arizona Land Title & Trust Co., 90 Ariz. 76, 87, 366 P.2d 1, 8-9 (1961), modified, 91 Ariz. 293, 371 P.2d 1020 (1962).

[3] "A lawyer can employ lay secretaries, lay investigators, lay detectives, lay researchers, accountants, lay scriveners,

CODE OF PROFESSIONAL RESPONSIBILITY

yer to render legal service more economically and efficiently.

EC 3-7 The prohibition against a non-lawyer practicing law does not prevent a layman from representing himself, for then he is ordinarily exposing only himself to possible injury. The purpose of the legal profession is to make educated legal representation available to the public; but anyone who does not wish to avail himself of such representation is not required to do so. Even so, the legal profession should help members of the public to recognize legal problems and to understand why it may be unwise for them to act for themselves in matters having legal consequences.

EC 3-8 Since a lawyer should not aid or encourage a layman to practice law, he should not practice law in association with a layman or otherwise share legal fees with a layman.[4] This does not mean, however, that the pecuniary value of the interest of a deceased lawyer in his firm or practice may not be paid to his estate or specified persons such as his widow or heirs.[5] In like manner, profit-sharing retirement plans of a lawyer or law firm which include non-lawyer office employees are not improper.[6] These limited exceptions to the rule against sharing legal fees with laymen are permissible since they do not aid or encourage laymen to practice law.

EC 3-9 Regulation of the practice of law is accomplished principally by the respective states.[7] Authority to engage in the practice of law conferred in any jurisdiction is not per se a grant of the right to practice elsewhere, and it is improper for a lawyer to engage in practice where he is not permitted by law or by court order to do so. However, the demands of business and the mobility of our society pose distinct problems in the regulation of the practice of law by the states.[8] In furtherance of the public interest, the legal profession should discourage regulation that unreasonably imposes territorial limitations upon the right of a lawyer to handle the legal affairs of his client or upon the opportunity of a client to obtain the services of a lawyer of his choice in all matters including the presentation of a contested matter in a tribunal before which the lawyer is not permanently admitted to practice.[9]

---

nonlawyer draftsmen or nonlawyer researchers. In fact, he may employ nonlawyers to do any task for him except counsel clients about law matters, engage directly in the practice of law, appear in court or appear in formal proceedings a part of the judicial process, so long as it is he who takes the work and vouches for it to the client and becomes responsible to the client." *ABA Opinion* 316 (1967).

ABA Opinion 316 (1967) also stated that if a lawyer practices law as part of a law firm which includes lawyers from several states, he may delegate tasks to firm members in other states so long as he "is the person who, on behalf of the firm, vouched for the work of all of the others and, with the client and in the courts, did the legal acts defined by that state as the practice of law."

"A lawyer cannot delegate his professional responsibility to a law student employed in his office. He may avail himself of the assistance of the student in many of the fields of the lawyer's work, such as examination of case law, finding and interviewing witnesses, making collections of claims, examining court records, delivering papers, conveying important messages, and other similar matters. But the student is not permitted, until he is admitted to the Bar, to perform the professional functions of a lawyer, such as conducting court trials, giving professional advice to clients or drawing legal documents for them. The student in all his work must act as agent for the lawyer employing him, who must supervise his work and be responsible for his good conduct." *ABA Opinion* 85 (1932).

[4] "No division of fees for legal services is proper, except with another lawyer . . . ." ABA Canon 34. Otherwise, according to *ABA Opinion* 316 (1967), "[t]he Canons of Ethics do not examine into the method by which such persons are remunerated by the lawyer. . . . They may be paid a salary, a per diem charge, a flat fee, a contract price, etc."

See ABA Canons 33 and 47.

[5] "Many partnership agreements provide that the active partners, on the death of any one of them, are to make payments to the estate or to the nominee of a deceased partner on a pre-determined formula. It is only where the effect of such an arrangement is to make the estate or nominee a member of the partnership along with the surviving partners that it is prohibited by *Canon 34*. Where the payments are made in accordance with a pre-existing agreement entered into by the deceased partner during his lifetime and providing for a fixed method for determining their amount based upon the value of services rendered during the partner's lifetime and providing for a fixed period over which the payments are to be made, this is not the case. Under these circumstances, whether the payments are considered to be delayed payment of compensation earned but withheld during the partner's lifetime, or whether they are considered to be an approximation of his interest in matters pending at the time of his death, is immaterial. In either event, as Henry S. Drinker says in his book, Legal Ethics, at page 189: 'It would seem, however, that a reasonable agreement to pay the estate a proportion of the receipts for a reasonable period is a proper practical settlement for the lawyer's services to his retirement or death.' " *ABA Opinion* 308 (1963).

[6] *Cf. ABA Opinion* 311 (1964).

[7] "That the States have broad power to regulate the practice of law is, of course, beyond question." United Mine Workers v. Ill. State Bar Ass'n, 389 U.S. 217, 222 (1967).

"It is a matter of law, not of ethics, as to where an individual may practice law. Each state has its own rules." *ABA Opinion* 316 (1967).

[8] "Much of clients' business crosses state lines. People are mobile, moving from state to state. Many metropolitan areas cross state lines. It is common today to have a single economic and social community involving more than one state. The business of a single client may involve legal problems in several states." *ABA Opinion* 316 (1967).

[9] "[W]e reaffirmed the general principle that legal services to New Jersey residents with respect to New Jersey matters may ordinarily be furnished only by New Jersey counsel; but we pointed out that there may be multistate transactions where strict adherence to this thesis would not be in the public interest and that, under the circumstances, it would have been not only more costly to the client but also 'grossly impractical and inefficient' to have had the settlement negotiations conducted by separate lawyers from different states." In re Estate of Waring, 47 N.J. 367, 376, 221 A.2d 193, 197 (1966).

Cf. ABA Opinion 316 (1967).

CODE OF PROFESSIONAL RESPONSIBILITY

DISCIPLINARY RULES

DR 3-101 Aiding Unauthorized Practice of Law.[10]

(A) A lawyer shall not aid a non-lawyer in the unauthorized practice of law.[11]

(B) A lawyer shall not practice law in a jurisdiction where to do so would be in violation of regulations of the profession in that jurisdiction.[12]

DR 3-102 Dividing Legal Fees with a Non-Lawyer.

(A) A lawyer or law firm shall not share legal fees with a non-lawyer,[13] except that:

(1) An agreement by a lawyer with his firm, partner, or associate may provide for the payment of money, over a reasonable period of time after his death, to his estate or to one or more specified persons.[14]

(2) A lawyer who undertakes to complete unfinished legal business of a deceased lawyer may pay to the estate of the deceased lawyer that proportion of the total compensation which fairly represents the services rendered by the deceased lawyer.

(3) A lawyer or law firm may include non-lawyer employees in a retirement plan, even though the plan is based in whole or in part on a profit-sharing arrangement.[15]

DR 3-103 Forming a Partnership with a Non-Lawyer.

(A) A lawyer shall not form a partnership with a non-lawyer if any of the activities of the partnership consist of the practice of law.[16]

---

[10] Conduct permitted by the Disciplinary Rules of Canons 2 and 5 does not violate DR 3-101.

[11] See ABA Canon 47.

[12] It should be noted, however, that a lawyer may engage in conduct, otherwise prohibited by this Disciplinary Rule, where such conduct is authorized by preemptive federal legislation. See Sperry v. Florida, 373 U.S. 379, 10 L.Ed.2d 428, 83 S.Ct. 1322 (1963).

[13] See ABA Canon 34 and *ABA Opinions* 316 (1967), 180 (1938), and 48 (1931).

"The receiving attorney shall not under any guise or form share his fee for legal services with a lay agency, personal or corporate, without prejudice, however, to the right of the lay forwarder to charge and collect from the creditor proper compensation for non-legal services rendered by the law [sic] forwarder which are separate and apart from the services performed by the receiving attorney." *ABA Opinion* 294 (1958).

[14] See *ABA Opinions* 309 (1963) and 266 (1945).

[15] Cf. *ABA Opinion* 311 (1964).

[16] See ABA Canon 33; cf. *ABA Opinions* 239 (1942) and 201 (1940).

ABA Opinion 316 (1967) states that lawyers licensed in different jurisdictions may, under certain conditions, enter "into an arrangement for the practice of law" and that a lawyer licensed in State A is not, for such purpose, a layman in State B.

CANON 4

A Lawyer Should Preserve the Confidences and Secrets of a Client

ETHICAL CONSIDERATIONS

EC 4-1 Both the fiduciary relationship existing between lawyer and client and the proper functioning of the legal system require the preservation by the lawyer of confidences and secrets of one who has employed or sought to employ him.[1] A client must feel free to discuss whatever he wishes with his lawyer and a lawyer must be equally free to obtain information beyond that volunteered by his client.[2] A lawyer should be fully informed of all the facts of the matter he is handling in order for his client to obtain the full advantage of our legal system. It is for the lawyer in the exercise of his independent professional judgment to separate the relevant and important from the irrelevant and unimportant. The observance of the ethical obligation of a lawyer to hold inviolate the confidences and secrets of his client not only facilitates the full development of facts essential to proper representation of the client but also encourages laymen to seek early legal assistance.

EC 4-2 The obligation to protect confidences and secrets obviously does not preclude a lawyer from revealing information when his client consents

---

[1] See ABA Canons 6 and 37 and *ABA Opinion* 287 (1953). "The reason underlying the rule with respect to confidential communications between attorney and client is well stated in Mecham on Agency, 2d Ed., Vol. 2, § 2297, as follows: 'The purposes and necessities of the relation between a client and his attorney require, in many cases, on the part of the client, the fullest and freest disclosures to the attorney of the client's objects, motives and acts. This disclosure is made in the strictest confidence, relying upon the attorney's honor and fidelity. To permit the attorney to reveal to others what is so disclosed, would be not only a gross violation of a sacred trust upon his part, but it would utterly destroy and prevent the usefulness and benefits to be derived from professional assistance. Based upon considerations of public policy, therefore, the law wisely declares that all confidential communications and disclosures, made by a client to his legal adviser for the purpose of obtaining his professional aid or advice, shall be strictly privileged;—that the attorney shall not be permitted, without the consent of his client,—and much less will he be compelled—to reveal or disclose communications made to him under such circumstances.'" *ABA Opinion* 250 (1943).

"While it is true that complete revelation of relevant facts should be encouraged for trial purposes, nevertheless an attorney's dealings with his client, if both are sincere, and if the dealings involve more than mere technical matters, should be immune to discovery proceedings. There must be freedom from fear of revealment of matters disclosed to an attorney because of the peculiarly intimate relationship existing." Ellis-Foster Co. v. Union Carbide & Carbon Corp., 159 F.Supp. 917, 919 (D.N.J. 1958).

Cf. *ABA Opinions* 314 (1965), 274 (1946) and 268 (1945).

[2] "While it is the great purpose of law to ascertain the truth, there is the countervailing necessity of insuring the right of every person to freely and fully confer and confide in one having knowledge of the law, and skilled in its practice, in order that the former may have adequate advice and a proper defense. This assistance can be made safely and readily available only when the client is free

CODE OF PROFESSIONAL RESPONSIBILITY

after full disclosure,[3] when necessary to perform his professional employment, when permitted by a Disciplinary Rule, or when required by law. Unless the client otherwise directs, a lawyer may disclose the affairs of his client to partners or associates of his firm. It is a matter of common knowledge that the normal operation of a law office exposes confidential professional information to non-lawyer employees of the office, particularly secretaries and those having access to the files; and this obligates a lawyer to exercise care in selecting and training his employees so that the sanctity of all confidences and secrets of his clients may be preserved. If the obligation extends to two or more clients as to the same information, a lawyer should obtain the permission of all before revealing the information. A lawyer must always be sensitive to the rights and wishes of his client and act scrupulously in the making of decisions which may involve the disclosure of information obtained in his professional relationship.[4] Thus, in the absence of consent of his client after full disclosure, a lawyer should not associate another lawyer in the handling of a matter; nor should he, in the absence of consent, seek counsel from another lawyer if there is a reasonable possibility that the identity of the client or his confidences or secrets would be revealed to such lawyer. Both social amenities and professional duty should cause a lawyer to shun indiscreet conversations concerning his clients.

EC 4–3 Unless the client otherwise directs, it is not improper for a lawyer to give limited information from his files to an outside agency necessary for statistical, bookkeeping, accounting, data processing, banking, printing, or other legitimate purposes, provided he exercises due care in the selection of the agency and warns the agency that the information must be kept confidential.

EC 4–4 The attorney-client privilege is more limited than the ethical obligation of a lawyer to guard the confidences and secrets of his client. This ethical precept, unlike the evidentiary privilege, exists without regard to the nature or source of information or the fact that others share the knowledge. A lawyer should endeavor to act in a manner which preserves the evidentiary privilege; for example, he should avoid professional discussions in the presence of persons to whom the privilege does not extend. A lawyer owes an obligation to advise the client of the attorney-client privilege and timely to assert the privilege unless it is waived by the client.

EC 4–5 A lawyer should not use information acquired in the course of the representation of a client to the disadvantage of the client and a lawyer should not use, except with the consent of his client after full disclosure, such information for his own purposes.[5] Likewise, a lawyer should be diligent in his efforts to prevent the misuse of such information by his employees and associates.[6] Care should be exercised by a lawyer to prevent the disclosure of the confidences and secrets of one client to another,[7] and no employment should be accepted that might require such disclosure.

EC 4–6 The obligation of a lawyer to preserve the confidences and secrets of his client continues after the termination of his employment.[8] Thus a lawyer should not attempt to sell a law practice as a going business because, among other reasons, to do so would involve the disclosure of confidences and secrets.[9] A lawyer should also provide for the protection of the confidences and secrets of his client following the termination of the practice of the lawyer, whether termination is due to death, disability, or retirement. For example, a lawyer might provide for the personal papers of the client to be returned to him and for the papers of the lawyer to be delivered to another lawyer or to be destroyed. In determining the method of disposition, the instructions and wishes of the client should be a dominant consideration.

DISCIPLINARY RULES

DR 4–101 Preservation of Confidences and Secrets of a Client.[10]

(A) "Confidence" refers to information protected by the attorney-client privilege under applicable law, and "secret" refers to other information gained in the professional relationship that the client has requested be held inviolate or the disclosure of which would be em-

---

from the consequences of apprehension of disclosure by reason of the subsequent statements of the skilled lawyer." Baird v. Koerner, 279 F.2d 623, 629–30 (9th Cir. 1960). Cf. ABA Opinion 150 (1936).

[3] "Where . . . [a client] knowingly and after full disclosure participates in a [legal fee] financing plan which requires the furnishing of certain information to the bank, clearly by his conduct he has waived any privilege as to that information." ABA Opinion 320 (1968).

[4] "The lawyer must decide when he takes a case whether it is a suitable one for him to undertake and after this decision is made, he is not justified in turning against his client by exposing injurious evidence entrusted to him. . . . [D]oing something intrinsically regrettable, because the only alternative involves worse consequences, is a necessity in every profession." Williston, Life and Law 271 (1940).

Cf. ABA Opinions 177 (1938) and 83 (1932).

[5] See ABA Canon 11.

[6] See ABA Canon 37.

[7] See ABA Canons 6 and 37.
"[A]n attorney must not accept professional employment against a client or a former client which will, or even may require him to use confidential information obtained by the attorney in the course of his professional relations with such client regarding the subject matter of the employment . . . ." ABA Opinion 165 (1936).

[8] See ABA Canon 37.
"Confidential communications between an attorney and his client, made because of the relationship and concerning the subject-matter of the attorney's employment, are generally privileged from disclosure without the consent of the client, and this privilege outlasts the attorney's employment. Canon 37." ABA Opinion 154 (1936).

[9] Cf. ABA Opinion 266 (1945).

[10] See ABA Canon 37; cf. ABA Canon 6.

CODE OF PROFESSIONAL RESPONSIBILITY

barrassing or would be likely to be detrimental to the client.

(B) Except when permitted under DR 4-101(C), a lawyer shall not knowingly:

   (1) Reveal a confidence or secret of his client.[11]

   (2) Use a confidence or secret of his client to the disadvantage of the client.

   (3) Use a confidence or secret of his client for the advantage of himself[12] or of a third person,[13] unless the client consents after full disclosure.

(C) A lawyer may reveal:

   (1) Confidences or secrets with the consent of the client or clients affected, but only after a full disclosure to them.[14]

   (2) Confidences or secrets when permitted under Disciplinary Rules or required by law or court order.[15]

   (3) The intention of his client to commit a crime[16] and the information necessary to prevent the crime.[17]

   (4) Confidences or secrets necessary to establish or collect his fee[18] or to defend himself or his employees or associates against an accusation of wrongful conduct.[19]

(D) A lawyer shall exercise reasonable care to prevent his employees, associates, and others whose services are utilized by him from disclosing or using confidences or secrets of a client, except that a lawyer may reveal the information allowed by DR 4-101(C) through an employee.

---

[11] "§ 6068 . . . It is the duty of an attorney:

. . . .

"(e) To maintain inviolate the confidence, and at every peril to himself to preserve the secrets, of his client." Cal. Business and Professions Code § 6068 (West 1962). Virtually the same provision is found in the Oregon statutes. Ore.Rev.Stats. ch. 9, § 9.460(5).

"Communications between lawyer and client are privileged (Wigmore on Evidence, 3d. Ed., Vol. 8, §§ 2290-2329). The modern theory underlying the privilege is subjective and is to give the client freedom of apprehension in consulting his legal adviser (ibid., § 2290, p. 548). The privilege applies to communications made in seeking legal advice for any purpose (ibid., § 2294, p. 563). The mere circumstance that the advice is given without charge therefore does not nullify the privilege (ibid., § 2303)." *ABA Opinion* 216 (1941).

"It is the duty of an attorney to maintain the confidence and preserve inviolate the secrets of his client . . . ." *ABA Opinion* 155 (1936).

[12] *See* ABA Canon 11.

"The provision respecting employment is in accord with the general rule announced in the adjudicated cases that a lawyer may not make use of knowledge or information acquired by him through his professional relations with his client, or in the conduct of his client's business, to his own advantage or profit (7 C.J.S., § 125, p. 958; Healy v. Gray, 184 Iowa 111, 168 N.W. 222; Baumgardner v. Hudson, D.C.App., 277 F. 552; Goodrum v. Clement, D.C.App., 277 F. 586)." *ABA Opinion* 250 (1943).

[13] *See ABA Opinion* 177 (1938).

[14] "[A lawyer] may not divulge confidential communications, information, and secrets imparted to him by the client or acquired during their professional relations, unless he is authorized to do so by the client (People v. Gerold, 265 Ill. 448, 107 N.E. 165, 178; Murphy v. Riggs, 238 Mich. 151, 213 N.W. 110, 112; Opinion of this Committee, No. 91)." *ABA Opinion* 202 (1940).

Cf. ABA Opinion 91 (1933).

[15] "A defendant in a criminal case when admitted to bail is not only regarded as in the custody of his bail, but he is also in the custody of the law, and admission to bail does not deprive the court of its inherent power to deal with the person of the prisoner. Being in lawful custody, the defendant is guilty of an escape when he gains his liberty before he is delivered in due process of law, and is guilty of a separate offense for which he may be punished. In failing to disclose his client's whereabouts as a fugitive under these circumstances the attorney would not only be aiding his client to escape trial on the charge for which he was indicted, but would likewise be aiding him in evading prosecution for the additional offense of escape.

"It is the opinion of the committee that under such circumstances the attorney's knowledge of his client's whereabouts is not privileged, and that he may be disciplined for failing to disclose that information to the proper authorities. . . . ." *ABA Opinion* 155 (1936).

"We held in *Opinion* 155 that a communication by a client to his attorney in respect to the future commission of an unlawful act or to a continuing wrong is not privileged from disclosure. Public policy forbids that the relation of attorney and client should be used to conceal wrongdoing on the part of the client.

. . . .

"When an attorney representing a defendant in a criminal case applies on his behalf for probation or suspension of sentence, he represents to the court, by implication at least, that his client will abide by the terms and conditions of the court's order. When that attorney is later advised of a violation of that order, it is his duty to advise his client of the consequences of his act, and endeavor to prevent a continuance of the wrongdoing. If his client thereafter persists in violating the terms and conditions of his probation, it is the duty of the attorney as an officer of the court to advise the proper authorities concerning his client's conduct. Such information, even though coming to the attorney from the client in the course of his professional relations with respect to other matters in which he represents the defendant, is not privileged from disclosure. . . . ." *ABA Opinion* 156 (1936).

[16] *ABA Opinion* 314 (1965) indicates that a lawyer must disclose even the confidences of his clients if "the facts in the attorney's possession indicate beyond reasonable doubt that a crime will be committed."

See ABA Opinion 155 (1936).

[17] *See* ABA Canon 37 and *ABA Opinion* 202 (1940).

[18] *Cf. ABA Opinion* 250 (1943).

[19] *See* ABA Canon 37 and *ABA Opinions* 202 (1940) and 19 (1930).

"[T]he adjudicated cases recognize an exception to the rule [that a lawyer shall not reveal the confidences of his client], where disclosure is necessary to protect the attorney's interests arising out of the relation of attorney and client in which disclosure was made.

"The exception is stated in Mechem on Agency, 2d Ed., Vol. 2, § 2313, as follows: 'But the attorney may disclose information received from the client when it becomes necessary for his own protection, as if the client should bring an action against the attorney for negligence or misconduct, and it became necessary for the attorney to

CODE OF PROFESSIONAL RESPONSIBILITY

CANON 5

A Lawyer Should Exercise Independent Professional Judgment on Behalf of a Client

ETHICAL CONSIDERATIONS

EC 5-1 The professional judgment of a lawyer should be exercised, within the bounds of the law, solely for the benefit of his client and free of compromising influences and loyalties.[1] Neither his personal interests, the interests of other clients, nor the desires of third persons should be permitted to dilute his loyalty to his client.

Interests of a Lawyer That May Affect His Judgment

EC 5-2 A lawyer should not accept proffered employment if his personal interests or desires will, or there is a reasonable probability that they will, affect adversely the advice to be given or services to be rendered the prospective client.[2] After accepting employment, a lawyer carefully should refrain from acquiring a property right or assuming a position that would tend to make his judgment less protective of the interests of his client.

EC 5-3 The self-interest of a lawyer resulting from his ownership of property in which his client also has an interest or which may affect property of his client may interfere with the exercise of free judgment on behalf of his client. If such interference would occur with respect to a prospective client, a lawyer should decline employment proffered by him. After accepting employment, a lawyer should not acquire property rights that would adversely affect his professional judgment in the representation of his client. Even if the property interests of a lawyer do not presently interfere with the exercise of his independent judgment, but the likelihood of interference can reasonably be foreseen by him, a lawyer should explain the situation to his client and should decline employment or withdraw unless the client consents to the continuance of the relationship after full disclosure. A lawyer should not seek to persuade his client to permit him to invest in an undertaking of his client nor make improper use of his professional relationship to influence his client to invest in an enterprise in which the lawyer is interested.

EC 5-4 If, in the course of his representation of a client, a lawyer is permitted to receive from his client a beneficial ownership in publication rights relating to the subject matter of the employment, he may be tempted to subordinate the interests of his client to his own anticipated pecuniary gain.

---

show what his instructions were, or what was the nature of the duty which the client expected him to perform. So if it became necessary for the attorney to bring an action against the client, the client's privilege could not prevent the attorney from disclosing what was essential as a means of obtaining or defending his own rights.'

"Mr. Jones, in his Commentaries on Evidence, 2d Ed., Vol. 5, § 2165, states the exception thus: 'It has frequently been held that the rule as to privileged communications does not apply when litigation arises between attorney and client to the extent that their communications are relevant to the issue. In such cases, if the disclosure of privileged communications becomes necessary to protect the attorney's rights, he is released from those obligations of secrecy which the law places upon him. He should not, however, disclose more than is necessary for his own protection. It would be a manifest injustice to allow the client to take advantage of the rule of exclusion as to professional confidence to the prejudice of his attorney, or that it should be carried to the extent of depriving the attorney of the means of obtaining or defending his own rights. In such cases the attorney is exempted from the obligations of secrecy.' " *ABA Opinion* 250 (1943).

[1] *Cf.* ABA Canon 35.

"[A lawyer's] fiduciary duty is of the highest order and he must not represent interests adverse to those of the client. It is also true that because of his professional responsibility and the confidence and trust which his client may legitimately repose in him, he must adhere to a high standard of honesty, integrity and good faith in dealing with his client. He is not permitted to take advantage of his position or superior knowledge to impose upon the client; nor to conceal facts or law, nor in any way deceive him without being held responsible therefor." Smoot v. Lund, 13 Utah 2d 168, 172, 369 P.2d 933, 936 (1962).

"When a client engages the services of a lawyer in a given piece of business he is entitled to feel that, until that business is finally disposed of in some manner, he has the undivided loyalty of the one upon whom he looks as his advocate and champion. If, as in this case, he is sued and his home attached by his own attorney, who is representing him in another matter, all feeling of loyalty is necessarily destroyed, and the profession is exposed to the charge that it is interested only in money." Grievance Comm. v. Rattner, 152 Conn. 59, 65, 203 A.2d 82, 84 (1964).

"One of the cardinal principles confronting every attorney in the representation of a client is the requirement of complete loyalty and service in good faith to the best of his ability. In a criminal case the client is entitled to a fair trial, but not a perfect one. These are fundamental requirements of due process under the Fourteenth Amendment. . . . The same principles are applicable in Sixth Amendment cases (not pertinent herein) and suggest that an attorney should have no conflict of interest and that he must devote his full and faithful efforts toward the defense of his client." Johns v. Smyth, 176 F.Supp. 949, 952 (E.D.Va.1959), *modified,* United States ex rel. Wilkins v. Banmiller, 205 F.Supp. 123, 128 n. 5 (E.D.Pa.1962), *aff'd,* 325 F.2d 514 (3d Cir. 1963), *cert. denied,* 379 U.S. 847, 13 L.Ed.2d 51, 85 S.Ct. 87 (1964).

[2] "Attorneys must not allow their private interests to conflict with those of their clients. . . . They owe their entire devotion to the interests of their clients." United States v. Anonymous, 215 F.Supp. 111, 113 (E.D. Tenn.1963).

"[T]he court [below] concluded that a firm may not accept any action against a person whom they are presently representing even though there is no relationship between the two cases. In arriving at this conclusion, the court cited an opinion of the Committee on Professional Ethics of the New York County Lawyers' Association which stated in part: 'While under the circumstances * * * there may be no actual conflict of interest * * * "maintenance of public confidence in the Bar requires an attorney who has accepted representation of a client to decline, while representing such client, any employment from an adverse party in any matter even though wholly unrelated to the original retainer." See Question and Answer No. 350, N.Y. County L. Ass'n, Questions and Answer No. 450 (June 21, 1956).' " Grievance Comm. v. Rattner, 152 Conn. 59, 65, 203 A.2d 82, 84 (1964).

CODE OF PROFESSIONAL RESPONSIBILITY

For example, a lawyer in a criminal case who obtains from his client television, radio, motion picture, newspaper, magazine, book, or other publication rights with respect to the case may be influenced, consciously or unconsciously, to a course of conduct that will enhance the value of his publication rights to the prejudice of his client. To prevent these potentially differing interests, such arrangements should be scrupulously avoided prior to the termination of all aspects of the matter giving rise to the employment, even though his employment has previously ended.

EC 5-5 A lawyer should not suggest to his client that a gift be made to himself or for his benefit. If a lawyer accepts a gift from his client, he is peculiarly susceptible to the charge that he unduly influenced or overreached the client. If a client voluntarily offers to make a gift to his lawyer, the lawyer may accept the gift, but before doing so, he should urge that his client secure disinterested advice from an independent, competent person who is cognizant of all the circumstances.[3] Other than in exceptional circumstances, a lawyer should insist that an instrument in which his client desires to name him beneficially be prepared by another lawyer selected by the client.[4]

EC 5-6 A lawyer should not consciously influence a client to name him as executor, trustee, or lawyer in an instrument. In those cases where a client wishes to name his lawyer as such, care should be taken by the lawyer to avoid even the appearance of impropriety.[5]

EC 5-7 The possibility of an adverse effect upon the exercise of free judgment by a lawyer on behalf of his client during litigation generally makes it undesirable for the lawyer to acquire a proprietary interest in the cause of his client or otherwise to become financially interested in the outcome of the litigation.[6] However, it is not improper for a lawyer to protect his right to collect a fee for his services by the assertion of legally permissible liens, even though by doing so he may acquire an interest in the outcome of litigation. Although a contingent fee arrangement [7] gives a lawyer a financial interest in the outcome of litigation, a reasonable contingent fee is permissible in civil cases because it may be the only means by which a layman can obtain the services of a lawyer of his choice. But a lawyer, because he is in a better position to evaluate a cause of action, should enter into a contingent fee arrangement only in those instances where the arrangement will be beneficial to the client.

EC 5-8 A financial interest in the outcome of litigation also results if monetary advances are made by the lawyer to his client.[8] Although this assistance generally is not encouraged, there are instances when it is not improper to make loans to a client. For example, the advancing or guaranteeing of payment of the costs and expenses of litigation by a lawyer may be the only way a client can enforce his cause of action,[9] but the ultimate liability for such costs and expenses must be that of the client.

EC 5-9 Occasionally a lawyer is called upon to decide in a particular case whether he will be a witness or an advocate. If a lawyer is both counsel and witness, he becomes more easily impeachable for interest and thus may be a less effective witness. Conversely, the opposing counsel may be handicapped in challenging the credibility of the lawyer when the lawyer also appears as an advocate in the case. An advocate who becomes a witness is in the unseemly and ineffective position of arguing his own credibility. The roles of an advocate and of a witness are inconsistent; the function of an advocate is to advance or argue the cause of another, while that of a witness is to state facts objectively.

EC 5-10 Problems incident to the lawyer-witness relationship arise at different stages; they relate

---

[3] "Courts of equity will scrutinize with jealous vigilance transactions between parties occupying fiduciary relations toward each other. . . . A deed will not be held invalid, however, if made by the grantor with full knowledge of its nature and effect, and because of the deliberate, voluntary and intelligent desire of the grantor. . . . Where a fiduciary relation exists, the burden of proof is on the grantee or beneficiary of an instrument executed during the existence of such relationship to show the fairness of the transaction, that it was equitable and just and that it did not proceed from undue influence. . . . The same rule has application where an attorney engages in a transaction with a client during the existence of the relation and is benefited thereby. . . . Conversely, an attorney is not prohibited from dealing with his client or buying his property, and such contracts, if open, fair and honest, when deliberately made, are as valid as contracts between other parties. . . . [I]mportant factors in determining whether a transaction is fair include a showing by the fiduciary (1) that he made a full and frank disclosure of all the relevant information that he had; (2) that the consideration was adequate; and (3) that the principal had independent advice before completing the transaction." McFail v. Braden, 19 Ill.2d 108, 117-18, 166 N.E.2d 46, 52 (1960).

[4] See State ex rel. Nebraska State Bar Ass'n v. Richards, 165 Neb. 80, 94-95, 84 N.W.2d 136, 146 (1957).

[5] See ABA Canon 9.

[6] See ABA Canon 10.

[7] See Code of Professional Responsibility, EC 2-20.

[8] See ABA Canon 42.

[9] "Rule 3a. . . . A member of the State Bar shall not directly or indirectly pay or agree to pay, or represent or sanction the representation that he will pay, medical, hospital or nursing bills or other personal expenses incurred by or for a client, prospective or existing; provided this rule shall not prohibit a member:

"(1) with the consent of the client, from paying or agreeing to pay to third persons such expenses from funds collected or to be collected for the client; or

(2) after he has been employed, from lending money to his client upon the client's promise in writing to repay such loan; or

(3) from advancing the costs of prosecuting or defending a claim or action. Such costs within the meaning of this subparagraph (3) include all taxable costs or disbursements, costs or investigation and costs of obtaining and presenting evidence." Cal. Business and Professions Code § 6076 (West Supp.1967).

CODE OF PROFESSIONAL RESPONSIBILITY

either to whether a lawyer should accept employment or should withdraw from employment.[10] Regardless of when the problem arises, his decision is to be governed by the same basic considerations. It is not objectionable for a lawyer who is a potential witness to be an advocate if it is unlikely that he will be called as a witness because his testimony would be merely cumulative or if his testimony will relate only to an uncontested issue.[11] In the exceptional situation where it will be manifestly unfair to the client for the lawyer to refuse employment or to withdraw when he will likely be a witness on a contested issue, he may serve as advocate even though he may be a witness.[12] In making such decision, he should determine the personal or financial sacrifice of the client that may result from his refusal of employment or withdrawal therefrom, the materiality of his testimony, and the effectiveness of his representation in view of his personal involvement. In weighing these factors, it should be clear that refusal or withdrawal will impose an unreasonable hardship upon the client before the lawyer accepts or continues the employment.[13] Where the question arises, doubts should be resolved in favor of the lawyer testifying and against his becoming or continuing as an advocate.[14]

EC 5-11 A lawyer should not permit his personal interests to influence his advice relative to a suggestion by his client that additional counsel be employed.[15] In like manner, his personal interests should not deter him from suggesting that additional counsel be employed; on the contrary, he should be alert to the desirability of recommending additional counsel when, in his judgment, the proper representation of his client requires it. However, a lawyer should advise his client not to employ additional counsel suggested by the client if the lawyer believes that such employment would be a disservice to the client, and he should disclose the reasons for his belief.

EC 5-12 Inability of co-counsel to agree on a matter vital to the representation of their client requires that their disagreement be submitted by them jointly to their client for his resolution, and the decision of the client shall control the action to be taken.[16]

EC 5-13 A lawyer should not maintain membership in or be influenced by any organization of employees that undertakes to prescribe, direct, or suggest when or how he should fulfill his professional obligations to a person or organization that employs him as a lawyer. Although it is not necessarily improper for a lawyer employed by a corporation or similar entity to be a member of an organization of employees, he should be vigilant to safeguard his fidelity as a lawyer to his employer, free from outside influences.

Interests of Multiple Clients

EC 5-14 Maintaining the independence of professional judgment required of a lawyer precludes his acceptance or continuation of employment that will adversely affect his judgment on behalf of or dilute his loyalty to a client.[17] This problem arises whenever a lawyer is asked to represent two or more clients who may have differing interests, whether such interests be conflicting, inconsistent, diverse, or otherwise discordant.[18]

EC 5-15 If a lawyer is requested to undertake or to continue representation of multiple clients having potentially differing interests, he must weigh carefully the possibility that his judgment may be impaired or his loyalty divided if he accepts or

---

[10] "When a lawyer knows, prior to trial, that he will be a necessary witness, except as to merely formal matters such as identification or custody of a document or the like, neither he nor his firm or associates should conduct the trial. If, during the trial, he discovers that the ends of justice require his testimony, he should, from that point on, if feasible and not prejudicial to his client's case, leave further conduct of the trial to other counsel. If circumstances do not permit withdrawal from the conduct of the trial, the lawyer should not argue the credibility of his own testimony." *A Code of Trial Conduct: Promulgated by the American College of Trial Lawyers*, 43 A.B.A.J. 223, 224-25 (1957).

[11] *Cf.* Canon 19: "When a lawyer is a witness for his client, except as to merely formal matters, such as the attestation or custody of an instrument and the like, he should leave the trial of the case to other counsel."

[12] "It is the general rule that a lawyer may not testify in litigation in which he is an advocate unless circumstances arise which could not be anticipated and it is necessary to prevent a miscarriage of justice. In those rare cases where the testimony of an attorney is needed to protect his client's interests, it is not only proper but mandatory that it be forthcoming." Schwartz v. Wenger, 267 Minn. 40, 43-44, 124 N.W.2d 489, 492 (1963).

[13] "The great weight of authority in this country holds that the attorney who acts as counsel and witness, in behalf of his client, in the same cause on a material matter, not of a merely formal character, and not in an emergency, but having knowledge that he would be required to be a witness in ample time to have secured other counsel and given up his service in the case, violates a highly important provision of the Code of Ethics and a rule of professional conduct, but does not commit a legal error in so testifying, as a result of which a new trial will be granted." Erwin M. Jennings Co. v. DiGenova, 107 Conn. 491, 499, 141 A. 866, 869 (1928).

[14] "[C]ases may arise, and in practice often do arise, in which there would be a failure of justice should the attorney withhold his testimony. In such a case it would be a vicious professional sentiment which would deprive the client of the benefit of his attorney's testimony." Connolly v. Straw, 53 Wis. 645, 649, 11 N.W. 17, 19 (1881).
But see Canon 19: "Except when essential to the ends of justice, a lawyer should avoid testifying in court in behalf of his client."

[15] *Cf.* ABA Canon 7.

[16] *See* ABA Canon 7.

[17] *See* ABA Canon 6; *cf. ABA Opinions* 261 (1944), 242 (1942), 142 (1935), and 30 (1931).

[18] The ABA Canons speak of "conflicting interests" rather than "differing interests" but make no attempt to define such other than the statement in Canon 6: "Within the meaning of this canon, a lawyer represents conflicting interests when, in behalf of one client, it is his duty to contend for that which duty to another client requires him to oppose."

CODE OF PROFESSIONAL RESPONSIBILITY

continues the employment. He should resolve all doubts against the propriety of the representation. A lawyer should never represent in litigation multiple clients with differing interests,[19] and there are few situations in which he would be justified in representing in litigation multiple clients with potentially differing interests. If a lawyer accepted such employment and the interests did become actually differing, he would have to withdraw from employment with likelihood of resulting hardship on the clients; and for this reason it is preferable that he refuse the employment initially. On the other hand, there are many instances in which a lawyer may properly serve multiple clients having potentially differing interests in matters not involving litigation. If the interests vary only slightly, it is generally likely that the lawyer will not be subjected to an adverse influence and that he can retain his independent judgment on behalf of each client; and if the interests become differing, withdrawal is less likely to have a disruptive effect upon the causes of his clients.

EC 5-16 In those instances in which a lawyer is justified in representing two or more clients having differing interests, it is nevertheless essential that each client be given the opportunity to evaluate his need for representation free of any potential conflict and to obtain other counsel if he so desires.[20] Thus before a lawyer may represent multiple clients, he should explain fully to each client the implications of the common representation and should accept or continue employment only if the clients consent.[21] If there are present other circumstances that might cause any of the multiple clients to question the undivided loyalty of the lawyer, he should also advise all of the clients of those circumstances.[22]

EC 5-17 Typically recurring situations involving potentially differing interests are those in which a lawyer is asked to represent co-defendants in a criminal case, co-plaintiffs in a personal injury case, an insured and his insurer,[23] and beneficiaries of the estate of a decedent. Whether a lawyer can fairly and adequately protect the interests of multiple clients in these and similar situations depends upon an analysis of each case. In certain circumstances, there may exist little chance of the judgment of the lawyer being adversely affected by the slight possibility that the interests will become actually differing; in other circumstances, the chance of adverse effect upon his judgment is not unlikely.

EC 5-18 A lawyer employed or retained by a corporation or similar entity owes his allegiance to the entity and not to a stockholder, director, officer, employee, representative, or other person connected with the entity. In advising the entity, a lawyer should keep paramount its interests and his professional judgment should not be influenced

---

[19] "Canon 6 of the Canons of Professional Ethics, adopted by the American Bar Association on September 30, 1937, and by the Pennsylvania Bar Association on January 7, 1938, provides in part that 'It is unprofessional to represent conflicting interests, except by express consent of all concerned given after a full disclosure of the facts. Within the meaning of this Canon, a lawyer represents conflicting interests when, in behalf of one client, it is his duty to contend for that which duty to another client requires him to oppose.' The full disclosure required by this canon contemplates that the possibly adverse effect of the conflict be fully explained by the attorney to the client to be affected and by him thoroughly understood. . . .

"The foregoing canon applies to cases where the circumstances are such that possibly conflicting interests may permissibly be represented by the same attorney. But manifestly, there are instances where the conflicts of interest are so critically adverse as not to admit of one attorney's representing both sides. Such is the situation which this record presents. No one could conscionably contend that the same attorney may represent both the plaintiff and defendant in an adversary action. Yet, that is what is being done in this case." Jedwabny v. Philadelphia Transportation Co., 390 Pa. 231, 235, 135 A.2d 252, 254 (1957), cert. denied, 355 U.S. 966, 2 L.Ed.2d 541, 78 S.Ct. 557 (1958).

[20] "Glasser wished the benefit of the undivided assistance of counsel of his own choice. We think that such a desire on the part of an accused should be respected. Irrespective of any conflict of interest, the additional burden of representing another party may conceivably impair counsel's effectiveness.

"To determine the precise degree of prejudice sustained by Glasser as a result of the court's appointment of Stewart as counsel for Kretske is at once difficult and unnecessary. The right to have the assistance of counsel is too fundamental and absolute to allow courts to indulge in nice calculations as to the amount of prejudice arising from its denial." Glasser v. United States, 315 U.S. 60, 75-76, 86 L.Ed. 680, 62 S.Ct. 457, 467 (1942).

[21] See ABA Canon 6.

[22] Id.

[23] Cf. ABA Opinion 282 (1950).

"When counsel, although paid by the casualty company, undertakes to represent the policyholder and files his notice of appearance, he owes to his client, the assured, an undeviating and single allegiance. His fealty embraces the requirement to produce in court all witnesses, fact and expert, who are available and necessary for the proper protection of the rights of his client. . . .

". . . The Canons of Professional Ethics make it pellucid that there are not two standards, one applying to counsel privately retained by a client, and the other to counsel paid by an insurance carrier." American Employers Ins. Co. v. Goble Aircraft Specialties, 205 Misc. 1066, 1075, 131 N.Y.S.2d 393, 401 (1954), motion to withdraw appeal granted, 1 App.Div.2d 1008, 154 N.Y.S.2d 835 (1956).

"[C]ounsel, selected by State Farm to defend Dorothy Walker's suit for $50,000 damages, was apprised by Walker that his earlier version of the accident was untrue and that actually the accident occurred because he lost control of his car in passing a Cadillac just ahead. At that point, Walker's counsel should have refused to participate further in view of the conflict of interest between Walker and State Farm. . . . Instead he participated in the ensuing deposition of the Walkers, even took an ex parte sworn statement from Mr. Walker in order to advise State Farm what action it should take, and later used the statement against Walker in the District Court. This action appears to contravene an Indiana attorney's duty 'at every peril to himself, to preserve the secrets of his client' . . ." State Farm Mut. Auto Ins. Co. v. Walker, 382 F.2d 548, 552 (1967), cert. denied, 389 U.S. 1045, 19 L.Ed. 2d 837, 88 S.Ct. 789 (1968).

CODE OF PROFESSIONAL RESPONSIBILITY

by the personal desires of any person or organization. Occasionally a lawyer for an entity is requested by a stockholder, director, officer, employee, representative, or other person connected with the entity to represent him in an individual capacity; in such case the lawyer may serve the individual only if the lawyer is convinced that differing interests are not present.

EC 5-19 A lawyer may represent several clients whose interests are not actually or potentially differing. Nevertheless, he should explain any circumstances that might cause a client to question his undivided loyalty.[24] Regardless of the belief of a lawyer that he may properly represent multiple clients, he must defer to a client who holds the contrary belief and withdraw from representation of that client.

EC 5-20 A lawyer is often asked to serve as an impartial arbitrator or mediator in matters which involve present or former clients. He may serve in either capacity if he first discloses such present or former relationships. After a lawyer has undertaken to act as an impartial arbitrator or mediator, he should not thereafter represent in the dispute any of the parties involved.

Desires of Third Persons

EC 5-21 The obligation of a lawyer to exercise professional judgment solely on behalf of his client requires that he disregard the desires of others that might impair his free judgment.[25] The desires of a third person will seldom adversely affect a lawyer unless that person is in a position to exert strong economic, political, or social pressures upon the lawyer. These influences are often subtle, and a lawyer must be alert to their existence. A lawyer subjected to outside pressures should make full disclosure of them to his client;[26] and if he or his client believes that the effectiveness of his representation has been or will be impaired thereby, the lawyer should take proper steps to withdraw from representation of his client.

EC 5-22 Economic, political, or social pressures by third persons are less likely to impinge upon the independent judgment of a lawyer in a matter in which he is compensated directly by his client and his professional work is exclusively with his client. On the other hand, if a lawyer is compensated from a source other than his client, he may feel a sense of responsibility to someone other than his client.

EC 5-23 A person or organization that pays or furnishes lawyers to represent others possesses a potential power to exert strong pressures against the independent judgment of those lawyers. Some employers may be interested in furthering their own economic, political, or social goals without regard to the professional responsibility of the lawyer to his individual client. Others may be far more concerned with establishment or extension of legal principles than in the immediate protection of the rights of the lawyer's individual client. On some occasions, decisions on priority of work may be made by the employer rather than the lawyer with the result that prosecution of work already undertaken for clients is postponed to their detriment. Similarly, an employer may seek, consciously or unconsciously, to further its own economic interests through the actions of the lawyers employed by it. Since a lawyer must always be free to exercise his professional judgment without regard to the interests or motives of a third person, the lawyer who is employed by one to represent another must constantly guard against erosion of his professional freedom.[27]

EC 5-24 To assist a lawyer in preserving his professional independence, a number of courses are available to him. For example, a lawyer should not practice with or in the form of a professional legal corporation, even though the corporate form is permitted by law,[28] if any director, officer, or stockholder of it is a non-lawyer. Although a lawyer may be employed by a business corporation with non-lawyers serving as directors or officers, and they necessarily have the right to make decisions of business policy, a lawyer must decline to accept direction of his professional judgment from any layman. Various types of legal aid of-

---

[24] *See* ABA Canon 6.

[25] *See* ABA Canon 35.

"Objection to the intervention of a lay intermediary, who may control litigation or otherwise interfere with the rendering of legal services in a confidential relationship, . . . derives from the element of pecuniary gain. Fearful of dangers thought to arise from that element, the courts of several States have sustained regulations aimed at these activities. We intimate no view one way or the other as to the merits of those decisions with respect to the particular arrangements against which they are directed. It is enough that the superficial resemblance in form between those arrangements and that at bar cannot obscure the vital fact that here the entire arrangement employs constitutionally privileged means of expression to secure constitutionally guaranteed civil rights." NAACP v. Button. 371 U.S. 415, 441-42, 9 L.Ed.2d 405, 423-24, 83 S.Ct. 328, 342-43 (1963).

[26] *Cf.* ABA Canon 38.

[27] "Certainly it is true that 'the professional relationship between an attorney and his client is highly personal, involving an intimate appreciation of each individual client's particular problem.' And this Committee does not condone practices which interfere with that relationship. However, the mere fact that the lawyer is actually paid by some entity other than the client does not affect that relationship, so long as the lawyer is selected by and is directly responsible to the client. See Informal Opinions 469 and 679. Of course, as the latter decision points out, there must be full disclosure of the arrangement by the attorney to the client. . . ." *ABA Opinion* 320 (1968).

"[A] third party may pay the cost of legal services as long as control remains in the client and the responsibility of the lawyer is solely to the client. Informal Opinions 469 ad [sic] 679. *See also* Opinion 237." *Id.*

[28] *ABA Opinion* 303 (1961) recognized that "[s]tatutory provisions now exist in several states which are designed to make [the practice of law in a form that will be classified as a corporation for federal income tax purposes] legally possible, either as a result of lawyers incorporating or forming associations with various corporate characteristics."

fices are administered by boards of directors composed of lawyers and laymen. A lawyer should not accept employment from such an organization unless the board sets only broad policies and there is no interference in the relationship of the lawyer and the individual client he serves. Where a lawyer is employed by an organization, a written agreement that defines the relationship between him and the organization and provides for his independence is desirable since it may serve to prevent misunderstanding as to their respective roles. Although other innovations in the means of supplying legal counsel may develop, the responsibility of the lawyer to maintain his professional independence remains constant, and the legal profession must insure that changing circumstances do not result in loss of the professional independence of the lawyer.

DISCIPLINARY RULES

DR 5-101 Refusing Employment When the Interests of the Lawyer May Impair His Independent Professional Judgment.

A) Except with the consent of his client after full disclosure, a lawyer shall not accept employment if the exercise of his professional judgment on behalf of his client will be or reasonably may be affected by his own financial, business, property, or personal interests.[29]

B) A lawyer shall not accept employment in contemplated or pending litigation if he knows or it is obvious that he or a lawyer in his firm ought to be called as a witness, except that he may undertake the employment and he or a lawyer in his firm may testify:

(1) If the testimony will relate solely to an uncontested matter.

(2) If the testimony will relate solely to a matter of formality and there is no reason to believe that substantial evidence will be offered in opposition to the testimony.

(3) If the testimony will relate solely to the nature and value of legal services rendered in the case by the lawyer or his firm to the client.

(4) As to any matter, if refusal would work a substantial hardship on the client because of the distinctive value of the lawyer or his firm as counsel in the particular case.

DR 5-102 Withdrawal as Counsel When the Lawyer Becomes a Witness.[30]

(A) If, after undertaking employment in contemplated or pending litigation, a lawyer learns or it is obvious that he or a lawyer in his firm ought to be called as a witness on behalf of his client, he shall withdraw from the conduct of the trial and his firm, if any, shall not continue representation in the trial, except that he may continue the representation and he or a lawyer in his firm may testify in the circumstances enumerated in DR 5-101(B) (1) through (4).

(B) If, after undertaking employment in contemplated or pending litigation, a lawyer learns or it is obvious that he or a lawyer in his firm may be called as a witness other than on behalf of his client, he may continue the representation until it is apparent that his testimony is or may be prejudicial to his client.[31]

DR 5-103 Avoiding Acquisition of Interest in Litigation.

(A) A lawyer shall not acquire a proprietary interest in the cause of action or subject matter of litigation he is conducting for a client,[32] except that he may:

(1) Acquire a lien granted by law to secure his fee or expenses.

(2) Contract with a client for a reasonable contingent fee in a civil case.[33]

(B) While representing a client in connection with contemplated or pending litigation, a lawyer shall not advance or guarantee financial as-

---

[29] *Cf.* ABA Canon 6 and *ABA Opinions* 181 (1938), 104 (1934), 103 (1933), 72 (1932), 50 (1931), 49 (1931), and 33 (1931).

"New York County [Opinion] 203. . . . [A lawyer] should not advise a client to employ an investment company in which he is interested, without informing him of this." Drinker, LEGAL ETHICS 956 (1953).

"In *Opinions* 72 and 49 this Committee held: The relations of partners in a law firm are such that neither the firm nor any member or associate thereof, may accept any professional employment which any member of the firm cannot properly accept.

"In *Opinion* 16 this Committee held that a member of a law firm could not represent a defendant in a criminal case which was being prosecuted by another member of the firm who was public prosecuting attorney. The Opinion stated that it was clearly unethical for one member of the firm to oppose the interest of the state while another member represented those interests . . . . Since the prosecutor himself could not represent both the public and the defendant, no member of his law firm could either." *ABA Opinion* 296 (1959).

[30] *Cf.* ABA Canon 19 and *ABA Opinions* 220 (1941), 185 (1938), 50 (1931), and 33 (1931); but *cf.* Erwin M. Jennings Co. v. DiGenova, 107 Conn. 491, 498-99, 141 A. 866, 868 (1928).

[31] "This *Canon* [19] *of Ethics* needs no elaboration to be applied to the facts here. Apparently, the object of this precept is to avoid putting a lawyer in the obviously embarrassing predicament of testifying and then having to argue the credibility and effect of his own testimony. It was not designed to permit a lawyer to call opposing counsel as a witness and thereby disqualify him as counsel." Galarowicz v. Ward, 119 Utah 611, 620, 230 P.2d 576, 580 (1951).

[32] ABA Canon 10 and *ABA Opinions* 279 (1949), 246 (1942), and 176 (1938).

[33] *See* Code of Professional Responsibility, DR 2-106(C).

CODE OF PROFESSIONAL RESPONSIBILITY

sistance to his client,[34] except that a lawyer may advance or guarantee the expenses of litigation, including court costs, expenses of investigation, expenses of medical examination, and costs of obtaining and presenting evidence, provided the client remains ultimately liable for such expenses.

DR 5-104 Limiting Business Relations with a Client.

(A) A lawyer shall not enter into a business transaction with a client if they have differing interests therein and if the client expects the lawyer to exercise his professional judgment therein for the protection of the client, unless the client has consented after full disclosure.

(B) Prior to conclusion of all aspects of the matter giving rise to his employment, a lawyer shall not enter into any arrangement or understanding with a client or a prospective client by which he acquires an interest in publication rights with respect to the subject matter of his employment or proposed employment.

DR 5-105 Refusing to Accept or Continue Employment if the Interests of Another Client May Impair the Independent Professional Judgment of the Lawyer.

(A) A lawyer shall decline proffered employment if the exercise of his independent professional judgment in behalf of a client will be or is likely to be adversely affected by the acceptance of the proffered employment,[35] except to the extent permitted under DR 5-105(C).[36]

(B) A lawyer shall not continue multiple employment if the exercise of his independent professional judgment in behalf of a client will be or is likely to be adversely affected by his representation of another client, except to the extent permitted under DR 5-105(C).[37]

(C) In the situations covered by DR 5-105(A) and (B), a lawyer may represent multiple clients if it is obvious that he can adequately represent the interest of each and if each consents to the representation after full disclosure of the possible effect of such representation on the exercise of his independent professional judgment on behalf of each.

---

[34] See ABA Canon 42; cf. ABA Opinion 288 (1954).

[35] See ABA Canon 6; cf. ABA Opinions 167 (1937), 60 (1931), and 40 (1931).

[36] ABA Opinion 247 (1942) held that an attorney could not investigate a night club shooting on behalf of one of the owner's liability insurers, obtaining the cooperation of the owner, and later represent the injured patron in an action against the owner and a different insurance company unless the attorney obtain the "express consent of all concerned given after a full disclosure of the facts," since to do so would be to represent conflicting interests.
See ABA Opinions 247 (1942), 224 (1941), 222 (1941), 218 (1941), 112 (1934), 83 (1932), and 86 (1932).

[37] Cf. ABA Opinions 231 (1941) and 160 (1936).

(D) If a lawyer is required to decline employment or to withdraw from employment under DR 5-105, no partner or associate of his or his firm may accept or continue such employment.

DR 5-106 Settling Similar Claims of Clients.[38]

(A) A lawyer who represents two or more clients shall not make or participate in the making of an aggregate settlement of the claims of or against his clients, unless each client has consented to the settlement after being advised of the existence and nature of all the claims involved in the proposed settlement, of the total amount of the settlement, and of the participation of each person in the settlement.

DR 5-107 Avoiding Influence by Others Than the Client.

(A) Except with the consent of his client after full disclosure, a lawyer shall not:

(1) Accept compensation for his legal services from one other than his client.

(2) Accept from one other than his client anything of value related to his representation of or his employment by his client.[39]

(B) A lawyer shall not permit a person who recommends, employs, or pays him to render legal services for another to direct or regulate his professional judgment in rendering such legal services.[40]

(C) A lawyer shall not practice with or in the form of a professional corporation or association authorized to practice law for a profit, if:

(1) A non-lawyer owns any interest therein,[41] except that a fiduciary representative of the estate of a lawyer may hold the stock or interest of the lawyer for a reasonable time during administration;

(2) A non-lawyer is a corporate director or officer thereof;[42] or

---

[38] Cf. ABA Opinions 243 (1942) and 235 (1941).

[39] See ABA Canon 38.
"A lawyer who receives a commission (whether delayed or not) from a title insurance company or guaranty fund for recommending or selling the insurance to his client, or for work done for the client or the company, without either fully disclosing to the client his financial interest in the transaction, or crediting the client's bill with the amount thus received, is guilty of unethical conduct." ABA Opinion 304 (1962).

[40] See ABA Canon 35; cf. ABA Opinion 237 (1941).
"When the lay forwarder, as agent for the creditor, forwards a claim to an attorney, the direct relationship of attorney and client shall then exist between the attorney and the creditor, and the forwarder shall not interpose itself as an intermediary to control the activities of the attorney." ABA Opinion 294 (1958).

[41] "Permanent beneficial and voting rights in the organization set up to practice law, whatever its form, must be restricted to lawyers while the organization is engaged in the practice of law." ABA Opinion 303 (1961).

[42] "Canon 33 . . . promulgates underlying principles that must be observed no matter in what form of organiza-

(3) **A non-lawyer has the right to direct or control the professional judgment of a lawyer.**[43]

CANON 6

A Lawyer Should Represent a Client Competently

ETHICAL CONSIDERATIONS

EC 6-1 Because of his vital role in the legal process, a lawyer should act with competence and proper care in representing clients. He should strive to become and remain proficient in his practice[1] and should accept employment only in matters which he is or intends to become competent to handle.

EC 6-2 A lawyer is aided in attaining and maintaining his competence by keeping abreast of current legal literature and developments, participating in continuing legal education programs,[2] concentrating in particular areas of the law, and by utilizing other available means. He has the additional ethical obligation to assist in improving the legal profession, and he may do so by participating in bar activities intended to advance the quality and standards of members of the profession. Of particular importance is the careful training of his younger associates and the giving of sound guidance to all lawyers who consult him. In short, a lawyer should strive at all levels to aid the legal profession in advancing the highest possible standards of integrity and competence and to meet those standards himself.

EC 6-3 While the licensing of a lawyer is evidence that he has met the standards then prevailing for admission to the bar, a lawyer generally should not accept employment in any area of the law in which he is not qualified.[3] However, he may accept such employment if in good faith he expects to become qualified through study and investigation, as long as such preparation would not result in unreasonable delay or expense to his client. Proper preparation and representation may require the association by the lawyer of professionals in other disciplines. A lawyer offered employment in a matter in which he is not and does not expect to become so qualified should either decline the employment or, with the consent of his client, accept the employment and associate a lawyer who is competent in the matter.[4]

EC 6-4 Having undertaken representation, a lawyer should use proper care to safeguard the interests of his client. If a lawyer has accepted employment in a matter beyond his competence but in which he expected to become competent, he should diligently undertake the work and study necessary to qualify himself. In addition to being qualified to handle a particular matter, his obligation to his client requires him to prepare adequately for and give appropriate attention to his legal work.

EC 6-5 A lawyer should have pride in his professional endeavors. His obligation to act competently calls for higher motivation than that arising from fear of civil liability or disciplinary penalty.

---

tion lawyers practice law. Its requirement that no person shall be admitted or held out as a practitioner or member who is not a member of the legal profession duly authorized to practice, and amenable to professional discipline, makes it clear that any centralized management must be in lawyers to avoid a violation of this Canon." *ABA Opinion* 303 (1961).

[43] "There is no intervention of any lay agency between lawyer and client when centralized management provided only by lawyers may give guidance or direction to the services being rendered by a lawyer-member of the organization to a client. The language in *Canon 35* that a lawyer should avoid all relations which direct the performance of his duties by or in the interest of an intermediary refers to lay intermediaries and not lawyer intermediaries with whom he is associated in the practice of law." *ABA Opinion* 303 (1961).

[1] "[W]hen a citizen is faced with the need for a lawyer, he wants, and is entitled to, the best informed counsel he can obtain. Changing times produce changes in our laws and legal procedures. The natural complexities of law require continuing intensive study by a lawyer if he is to render his clients a maximum of efficient service. And, in so doing, he maintains the high standards of the legal profession; and he also increases respect and confidence by the general public." Rochelle & Payne, *The Struggle for Public Understanding*, 25 Texas B.J. 109, 160 (1962).

"We have undergone enormous changes in the last fifty years within the lives of most of the adults living today who may be seeking advice. Most of these changes have been accompanied by changes and developments in the law. . . . Every practicing lawyer encounters these problems and is often perplexed with his own inability to keep up, not only with changes in the law, but also with changes in the lives of his clients and their legal problems.

"To be sure, no client has a right to expect that his lawyer will have all of the answers at the end of his tongue or even in the back of his head at all times. But the client does have the right to expect that the lawyer will have devoted his time and energies to maintaining and improving his competence to know where to look for the answers, to know how to deal with the problems, and to know how to advise to the best of his legal talents and abilities." Levy & Sprague, *Accounting and Law: Is Dual Practice in the Public Interest?*, 52 A.B.A.J. 1110, 1112 (1966).

[2] "The whole purpose of continuing legal education, so enthusiastically supported by the ABA, is to make it possible for lawyers to make themselves better lawyers. But there are no nostrums for proficiency in the law; it must come through the hard work of the lawyer himself. To the extent that that work, whether it be in attending institutes or lecture courses, in studying after hours or in the actual day in and day out practice of his profession, can be concentrated within a limited field, the greater the proficiency and expertness that can be developed." *Report of the Special Committee on Specialization and Specialized Legal Education*, 79 A.B.A.Rep. 582, 588 (1954).

[3] "If the attorney is not competent to skillfully and properly perform the work, he should not undertake the service." Degen v. Steinbrink, 202 App.Div. 477, 481, 195 N.Y.S. 810, 814 (1922), *aff'd mem.*, 236 N.Y. 669, 142 N.E. 328 (1923).

[4] *Cf. ABA Opinion* 232 (1941).

CODE OF PROFESSIONAL RESPONSIBILITY

EC 6-6 A lawyer should not seek, by contract or other means, to limit his individual liability to his client for his malpractice. A lawyer who handles the affairs of his client properly has no need to attempt to limit his liability for his professional activities and one who does not handle the affairs of his client properly should not be permitted to do so. A lawyer who is a stockholder in or is associated with a professional legal corporation may, however, limit his liability for malpractice of his associates in the corporation, but only to the extent permitted by law.[5]

DISCIPLINARY RULES

DR 6-101 Failing to Act Competently.

(A) A lawyer shall not:

(1) Handle a legal matter which he knows or should know that he is not competent to handle, without associating with him a lawyer who is competent to handle it.

(2) Handle a legal matter without preparation adequate in the circumstances.

(3) Neglect a legal matter entrusted to him.[6]

DR 6-102 Limiting Liability to Client.

(A) A lawyer shall not attempt to exonerate himself from or limit his liability to his client for his personal malpractice.

CANON 7

A Lawyer Should Represent a Client Zealously Within the Bounds of the Law

ETHICAL CONSIDERATIONS

EC 7-1 The duty of a lawyer, both to his client [1] and to the legal system, is to represent his client zealously [2] within the bounds of the law,[3] which includes Disciplinary Rules and enforceable pro-

---

help in the process of promoting a better tax system. The tax lawyer need not accept his client's economic and social opinions, but the client is paying for technical attention and undivided concentration upon his affairs. He is equally entitled to performance unfettered by his attorney's economic and social predilections." Paul, *The Lawyer as a Tax Adviser*, 25 Rocky Mt. L. Rev. 412, 418 (1953).

[3] *See* ABA Canons 15 and 32.

ABA Canon 5, although only speaking of one accused of crime, imposes a similar obligation on the lawyer: "[T]he lawyer is bound, by all fair and honorable means, to present every defense that the law of the land permits, to the end that no person may be deprived of life or liberty, but by due process of law."

"Any persuasion or pressure on the advocate which deters him from planning and carrying out the litigation on the basis of 'what, within the framework of the law, is best for my client's interest?' interferes with the obligation to represent the client fully within the law.

"This obligation, in its fullest sense, is the heart of the adversary process. Each attorney, as an advocate, acts for and seeks that which in his judgment is best for his client, within the bounds authoritatively established. The advocate does not *decide* what is just in this case—he would be usurping the function of the judge and jury—he acts for and seeks for his client that which he is entitled to under the law. He can do no less and properly represent the client." Thode, *The Ethical Standard for the Advocate*, 39 Texas L.Rev. 575, 584 (1961).

"The [Texas public opinion] survey indicates that distrust of the lawyer can be traced directly to certain factors. Foremost of these is a basic misunderstanding of the function of the lawyer as an advocate in an adversary system.

"Lawyers are accused of taking advantage of 'loopholes' and 'technicalities' to win. Persons who make this charge are unaware, or do not understand, that the lawyer is hired to win, and if he does not exercise every legitimate effort in his client's behalf, then he is betraying a sacred trust." Rochelle & Payne, *The Struggle for Public Understanding*, 25 Texas B.J. 109, 159 (1962).

"The importance of the attorney's undivided allegiance and faithful service to one accused of crime, irrespective of the attorney's personal opinion as to the guilt of his client, lies in Canon 5 of the American Bar Association Canon of Ethics.

"The difficulty lies, of course, in ascertaining whether the attorney has been guilty of an error of judgment, such as an election with respect to trial tactics, or has otherwise been actuated by his conscience or belief that his client should be convicted in any event. All too frequently courts are called upon to review actions of defense counsel which are, at the most, errors of judgment, not properly reviewable on habeas corpus unless the trial is a farce and a mockery of justice which requires the court to intervene. . . . But when defense counsel, in a truly adverse proceeding, admits that his conscience would not permit him to adopt certain customary trial procedures, this extends beyond the realm of judgment and strongly suggests an invasion of constitutional rights." Johns v. Smyth, 176 F.Supp. 949, 952 (E.D.Va.1959), *modified*, United States ex rel. Wilkins v. Banmiller, 205 F.Supp. 123, 128, n. 5 (E.D.Pa.1962), *aff'd*, 325 F.2d 514 (3d Cir. 1963), *cert. denied*, 379 U.S. 847, 13 L.Ed.2d 51, 85 S.Ct. 87 (1964).

"The adversary system in law administration bears a striking resemblance to the competitive economic system. In each we assume that the individual through partisanship or through self-interest will strive mightily for his side, and that kind of striving we must have. But neither system would be tolerable without restraints and modi-

---

[5] *See* ABA Opinion 303 (1961); *cf.* Code of Professional Responsibility, EC 2-11.

[6] The annual report for 1967-1968 of the Committee on Grievances of the Association of the Bar of the City of New York showed a receipt of 2,232 complaints; of the 828 offenses against clients, 76 involved conversion, 49 involved "overreaching," and 452, or more than half of all such offenses, involved neglect. *Annual Report of the Committee on Grievances of the Association of the Bar of the City of New York*, N.Y.L.J., Sept. 12, 1968, at 4, col. 5.

[1] "The right to be heard would be, in many cases, of little avail if it did not comprehend the right to be heard by counsel. Even the intelligent and educated layman has small and sometimes no skill in the science of law." Powell v. Alabama, 287 U.S. 45, 68–69, 77 L.Ed. 158, 170, 53 S.Ct. 55, 64 (1932).

[2] *Cf.* ABA Canon 4.

"At times . . . [the tax lawyer] will be wise to discard some arguments and he should exercise discretion to emphasize the arguments which in his judgment are most likely to be persuasive. But this process involves legal judgment rather than moral attitudes. The tax lawyer should put aside private disagreements with Congressional and Treasury policies. His own notions of policy, and his personal view of what the law should be, are irrelevant. The job entrusted to him by his client is to use all his learning and ability to protect his client's rights, not to

CODE OF PROFESSIONAL RESPONSIBILITY

fessional regulations.[4] The professional responsibility of a lawyer derives from his membership in a profession which has the duty of assisting members of the public to secure and protect available legal rights and benefits. In our government of laws and not of men, each member of our society is entitled to have his conduct judged and regulated in accordance with the law;[5] to seek any lawful objective[6] through legally permissible means;[7] and to present for adjudication any lawful claim, issue, or defense.

EC 7-2 The bounds of the law in a given case are often difficult to ascertain.[8] The language of legislative enactments and judicial opinions may be uncertain as applied to varying factual situations. The limits and specific meaning of apparently relevant law may be made doubtful by changing or developing constitutional interpretations, inadequately expressed statutes or judicial opinions, and changing public and judicial attitudes. Certainty of law ranges from well-settled rules through areas of conflicting authority to areas without precedent.

EC 7-3 Where the bounds of law are uncertain, the action of a lawyer may depend on whether he is serving as advocate or adviser. A lawyer may serve simultaneously as both advocate and adviser, but the two roles are essentially different.[9] In asserting a position on behalf of his client, an advocate for the most part deals with past conduct and must take the facts as he finds them. By contrast, a lawyer serving as adviser primarily assists his client in determining the course of future conduct and relationships. While serving as advocate, a lawyer should resolve in favor of his client doubts as to the bounds of the law.[10] In serving a client as adviser, a lawyer in appropriate

---

fications, and at times without outright departures from the system itself. Since the legal profession is entrusted with the system of law administration, a part of its task is to develop in its members appropriate restraints without impairing the values of partisan striving. An accompanying task is to aid in the modification of the adversary system or departure from it in areas to which the system is unsuited." Cheatham, *The Lawyer's Role and Surroundings*, 25 Rocky Mt. L. Rev. 405, 410 (1953).

[4] "Rule 4.15 prohibits, in the pursuit of a client's cause, 'any manner of fraud or chicane'; Rule 4.22 requires 'candor and fairness' in the conduct of the lawyer, and forbids the making of knowing misquotations; Rule 4.47 provides that a lawyer 'should always maintain his integrity,' and generally forbids all misconduct injurious to the interests of the public, the courts, or his clients, and acts contrary to 'justice, honesty, modesty or good morals.' Our Commissioner has accurately paraphrased these rules as follows: 'An attorney does not have the duty to do all and whatever he can that may enable him to win his client's cause or to further his client's interest. His duty and efforts in these respects, although they should be prompted by his "entire devotion" to the interest of his client, must be within and not without the bounds of the law.'" In re Wines, 370 S.W.2d 328, 333 (Mo. 1963). See Note, 38 Texas L. Rev. 107, 110 (1959).

[5] "Under our system of government the process of adjudication is surrounded by safeguards evolved from centuries of experience. These safeguards are not designed merely to lend formality and decorum to the trial of causes. They are predicated on the assumption that to secure for any controversy a truly informed and dispassionate decision is a difficult thing, requiring for its achievement a special summoning and organization of human effort, and the adoption of measures to exclude the biases and prejudgments that have free play outside the courtroom. All of this goes for naught if the man with an unpopular cause is unable to find a competent lawyer courageous enough to represent him. His chance to have his day in court loses much of its meaning if his case is handicapped from the outset by the very kind of prejudgment our rules of evidence and procedure are intended to prevent." *Professional Responsibility: Report of the Joint Conference*, 44 A.B.A.J. 1159, 1216 (1958).

[6] "[I]t is . . . [the tax lawyer's] positive duty to show the client how to avail himself to the full of what the law permits. He is not the keeper of the Congressional conscience." Paul, *The Lawyer as a Tax Adviser*, 25 Rocky Mt. L. Rev. 412, 418 (1953).

[7] See ABA Canons 15 and 30.

[8] "The fact that it desired to evade the law, as it is called, is immaterial, because the very meaning of a line in the law is that you intentionally may go as close to it as you can if you do not pass it . . . . It is a matter of proximity and degree as to which minds will differ . . . ." Justice Holmes, in Superior Oil Co. v. Mississippi, 280 U.S. 390, 395-96, 74 L. Ed. 504, 508, 50 S.Ct. 169, 170 (1930).

[9] "Today's lawyers perform two distinct types of functions, and our ethical standards should, but in the main do not, recognize these two functions. Judge Philbrick McCoy recently reported to the American Bar Association the need for a reappraisal of the Canons in light of the new and distinct function of counselor, as distinguished from advocate, which today predominates in the legal profession.

". . . In the first place, any revision of the canons must take into account and speak to this new and now predominant function of the lawyer. . . . It is beyond the scope of this paper to discuss the ethical standards to be applied to the counselor except to state that in my opinion such standards should require a greater recognition and protection for the interest of the public generally than is presently expressed in the canons. Also, the counselor's obligation should extend to requiring him to inform and to impress upon the client a just solution of the problem, considering all interests involved." Thode, *The Ethical Standard for the Advocate*, 39 Texas L. Rev. 575, 578-79 (1961).

"The man who has been called into court to answer for his own actions is entitled to fair hearing. Partisan advocacy plays its essential part in such a hearing, and the lawyer pleading his client's case may properly present it in the most favorable light. A similar resolution of doubts in one direction becomes inappropriate when the lawyer acts as counselor. The reasons that justify and even require partisan advocacy in the trial of a cause do not grant any license to the lawyer to participate as legal advisor in a line of conduct that is immoral, unfair, or of doubtful legality. In saving himself from this unworthy involvement, the lawyer cannot be guided solely by an unreflective inner sense of good faith; he must be at pains to preserve a sufficient detachment from his client's interests so that he remains capable of a sound and objective appraisal of the propriety of what his client proposes to do." *Professional Responsibility: Report of the Joint Conference*, 44 A.B.A.J. 1159, 1161 (1958).

[10] "[A] lawyer who is asked to advise his client . . . may freely urge the statement of positions most favorable to the client just as long as there is reasonable basis for those positions." *ABA Opinion 314 (1965)*.

circumstances should give his professional opinion as to what the ultimate decisions of the courts would likely be as to the applicable law.

Duty of the Lawyer to a Client

EC 7-4 The advocate may urge any permissible construction of the law favorable to his client, without regard to his professional opinion as to the likelihood that the construction will ultimately prevail,[11] His conduct is within the bounds of the law, and therefore permissible, if the position taken is supported by the law or is supportable by a good faith argument for an extension, modification, or reversal of the law. However, a lawyer is not justified in asserting a position in litigation that is frivolous.[12]

---

[11] "The lawyer . . . is not an umpire, but an advocate. He is under no duty to refrain from making every proper argument in support of any legal point because he is not convinced of its inherent soundness. . . . His personal belief in the soundness of his cause or of the authorities supporting it, is irrelevant." *ABA Opinion* 280 (1949).

"Counsel apparently misconceived his role. It was his duty to honorably present his client's contentions in the light most favorable to his client. Instead he presumed to advise the court as to the validity and sufficiency of prisoner's motion, by letter. We therefore conclude that the prisoner had no effective assistance of counsel and remand this case to the District Court with instructions to set aside the Judgment, appoint new counsel to represent the prisoner if he makes no objection thereto, and proceed anew." McCartney v. United States, 343 F.2d 471, 472 (9th Cir. 1965).

[12] "Here the court-appointed counsel had the transcript but refused to proceed with the appeal because he found no merit in it. . . . We cannot say that there was a finding of frivolity by either of the California courts or that counsel acted in any greater capacity than merely as *amicus curiae* which was condemned in *Ellis, supra.* Hence California's procedure did not furnish petitioner with counsel acting in the role of an advocate nor did it provide that full consideration and resolution of the matter as is obtained when counsel is acting in that capacity. . . .

"The constitutional requirement of substantial equality and fair process can only be attained where counsel acts in the role of an active advocate in behalf of his client, as opposed to that of *amicus curiae*. The no-merit letter and the procedure it triggers do not reach that dignity. Counsel should, and can with honor and without conflict, be of more assistance to his client and to the court. His role as advocate requires that he support his client's appeal to the best of his ability. Of course, if counsel finds his case to be wholly frivolous, after a conscientious examination of it, he should so advise the court and request permission to withdraw. That request must, however, be accompanied by a brief referring to anything in the record that might arguably support the appeal. A copy of counsel's brief should be furnished the indigent and time allowed him to raise any points that he chooses; the court—not counsel—then proceeds, after a full examination of all the proceedings, to decide whether the case is wholly frivolous. If it so finds it may grant counsel's request to withdraw and dismiss the appeal insofar as federal requirements are concerned, or proceed to a decision on the merits, if state law so requires. On the other hand, if it finds any of the legal points arguable on their merits (and therefore not frivolous) it must, prior to decision, afford the indigent the assistance of counsel to argue the appeal." Anders v. California, 386 U.S. 738, 744, 18 L.Ed.

EC 7-5 A lawyer as adviser furthers the interest of his client by giving his professional opinion as to what he believes would likely be the ultimate decision of the courts on the matter at hand and by informing his client of the practical effect of such decision.[13] He may continue in the representation of his client even though his client has elected to pursue a course of conduct contrary to the advice of the lawyer so long as he does not thereby knowingly assist the client to engage in illegal conduct or to take a frivolous legal position. A lawyer should never encourage or aid his client to commit criminal acts or counsel his client on how to violate the law and avoid punishment therefor.[14]

EC 7-6 Whether the proposed action of a lawyer is within the bounds of the law may be a perplexing question when his client is contemplating a course of conduct having legal consequence that vary according to the client's intent, motive, or desires at the time of the action. Often a lawyer is asked to assist his client in developing evidence relevant to the state of mind of the client at a particular time. He may properly assist his client in the development and preservation of evidence of existing motive, intent, or desire; obviously, he may not do anything furthering the creation or preservation of false evidence. In many cases a lawyer may not be certain as to the state of mind of his client, and in those situations he should resolve reasonable doubts in favor of his client.

EC 7-7 In certain areas of legal representation not affecting the merits of the cause or substantially prejudicing the rights of a client, a lawyer is entitled to make decisions on his own. But otherwise the authority to make decisions is exclusively that of the client and, if made within the framework of the law, such decisions are binding on his lawyer. As typical examples in civil cases, it is for the client to decide whether he will accept a settlement offer or whether he will waive his right to plead an affirmative defense. A defense lawyer in a criminal case has the duty to advise his client fully on whether a particular plea to a charge appears to be desirable and as to the pros-

---

2d 493, 498, 87 S.Ct. 1396, 1399–1400 (1967), *rehearing denied*, 388 U.S. 924, 18 L.Ed.2d 1377, 87 S.Ct. 2094 (1967).

See Paul, *The Lawyer As a Tax Adviser*, 25 Rocky Mt. L.Rev. 412, 432 (1953).

[13] *See* ABA Canon 32.

[14] "For a lawyer to represent a syndicate notoriously engaged in the violation of the law for the purpose of advising the members how to break the law and at the same time escape it, is manifestly improper. While a lawyer may see to it that anyone accused of crime, no matter how serious and flagrant, has a fair trial, and present all available defenses, he may not co-operate in planning violations of the law. There is a sharp distinction, of course, between advising what can lawfully be done and advising how unlawful acts can be done in a way to avoid conviction. Where a lawyer accepts a retainer from an organization, known to be unlawful, and agrees in advance to defend its members when from time to time they are accused of crime arising out of its unlawful activities, this is equally improper."

"See also *Opinion 155*." *ABA Opinion* 281 (1952).

CODE OF PROFESSIONAL RESPONSIBILITY

pects of success on appeal, but it is for the client to decide what plea should be entered and whether an appeal should be taken.[15]

EC 7-8 A lawyer should exert his best efforts to insure that decisions of his client are made only after the client has been informed of relevant considerations. A lawyer ought to initiate this decision-making process if the client does not do so. Advice of a lawyer to his client need not be confined to purely legal considerations.[16] A lawyer should advise his client of the possible effect of each legal alternative.[17] A lawyer should bring to bear upon this decision-making process the fullness of his experience as well as his objective viewpoint.[18] In assisting his client to reach a proper decision, it is often desirable for a lawyer to point out those factors which may lead to a decision that is morally just as well as legally permissible.[19] He may emphasize the possibility of harsh consequences that might result from assertion of legally permissible positions. In the final analysis, however, the lawyer should always remember that the decision whether to forego legally available objectives or methods because of non-legal factors is ultimately for the client and not for himself, In the event that the client in a non-adjudicatory matter insists upon a course of conduct that is contrary to the judgment and advice of the lawyer but not prohibited by Disciplinary Rules, the lawyer may withdraw from the employment.[20]

EC 7-9 In the exercise of his professional judgment on those decisions which are for his determination in the handling of a legal matter,[21] a lawyer should always act in a manner consistent with the best interests of his client.[22] However, when an action in the best interest of his client seems to him to be unjust, he may ask his client for permission to forego such action.[23]

EC 7-10 The duty of a lawyer to represent his client with zeal does not militate against his concurrent obligation to treat with consideration all persons involved in the legal process and to avoid the infliction of needless harm.

EC 7-11 The responsibilities of a lawyer may vary according to the intelligence, experience, mental condition or age of a client, the obligation of a public officer, or the nature of a particular proceeding. Examples include the representation of an illiterate or an incompetent, service as a public prosecutor or other government lawyer, and appearances before administrative and legislative bodies.

EC 7-12 Any mental or physical condition of a client that renders him incapable of making a considered judgment on his own behalf casts additional responsibilities upon his lawyer. Where an incompetent is acting through a guardian or other legal representative, a lawyer must look to such representative for those decisions which are normally the prerogative of the client to make. If a client under disability has no legal representative, his lawyer may be compelled in court proceedings to make decisions on behalf of the client. If the client is capable of understanding the matter in question or of contributing to the advancement of his interests, regardless of whether he is legally disqualified from performing certain acts, the lawyer should obtain from him all possible aid. If the disability of a client and the lack of a legal representative compel the lawyer to make decisions for his client, the lawyer should consider all

---

[15] See ABA Special Committee on Minimum Standards for the Administration of Criminal Justice, *Standards Relating to Pleas of Guilty* pp. 69-70 (1968).

[16] "First of all, a truly great lawyer is a wise counselor to all manner of men in the varied crises of their lives when they most need disinterested advice. Effective counseling necessarily involves a thoroughgoing knowledge of the principles of the law not merely as they appear in the books but as they actually operate in action." Vanderbilt, *The Five Functions of the Lawyer: Service to Clients and the Public*, 40 A.B.A.J. 31 (1954).

[17] "A lawyer should endeavor to obtain full knowledge of his client's cause before advising thereon. . . ." ABA Canon 8.

[18] "[I]n devising charters of collaborative effort the lawyer often acts where all of the affected parties are present as participants. But the lawyer also performs a similar function in situations where this is not so, as, for example, in planning estates and drafting wills. Here the instrument defining the terms of collaboration may affect persons not present and often not born. Yet here, too, the good lawyer does not serve merely as a legal conduit for his client's desires, but as a wise counselor, experienced in the art of devising arrangements that will put in workable order the entangled affairs and interests of human beings." *Professional Responsibility: Report of the Joint Conference*, 44 A.B.A.J. 1159, 1162 (1958).

[19] See ABA Canon 8.

"Vital as is the lawyer's role in adjudication, it should not be thought that it is only as an advocate pleading in open court that he contributes to the administration of the law. The most effective realization of the law's aims often takes place in the attorney's office, where litigation is forestalled by anticipating its outcome, where the lawyer's quiet counsel takes the place of public force. Contrary to popular belief, the compliance with the law thus brought about is not generally lip-serving and narrow, for by reminding him of its long-run costs the lawyer often deters his client from a course of conduct technically permissible under existing law, though inconsistent with its underlying spirit and purpose." *Professional Responsibility: Report of the Joint Conference*, 44 A.B.A.J. 1159, 1161 (1958).

[20] "My summation of Judge Sharswood's view of the advocate's duty to the client is that he owes to the client the duty to use all legal means in support of the client's case. However, at the same time Judge Sharswood recognized that many advocates would find this obligation unbearable if applicable without exception. Therefore, the individual lawyer is given the choice of representing his client fully within the bounds set by the law *or of telling his client that he cannot do so*, so that the client may obtain another attorney if he wishes." Thode, *The Ethical Standard for the Advocate*, 39 Texas L.Rev. 575, 582 (1961).
Cf. Code of Professional Responsibility, DR 2-110 (C).

[21] See ABA Canon 24.

[22] Thode, *The Ethical Standard for the Advocate*, 39 Texas L.Rev. 575, 592 (1961).

[23] Cf. ABA Opinions 253 (1946) and 178 (1938).

circumstances then prevailing and act with care to safeguard and advance the interests of his client. But obviously a lawyer cannot perform any act or make any decision which the law requires his client to perform or make, either acting for himself if competent, or by a duly constituted representative if legally incompetent.

EC 7-13 The responsibility of a public prosecutor differs from that of the usual advocate; his duty is to seek justice, not merely to convict.[24] This special duty exists because: (1) the prosecutor represents the sovereign and therefore should use restraint in the discretionary exercise of governmental powers, such as in the selection of cases to prosecute; (2) during trial the prosecutor is not only an advocate but he also may make decisions normally made by an individual client, and those affecting the public interest should be fair to all; and (3) in our system of criminal justice the accused is to be given the benefit of all reasonable doubts. With respect to evidence and witnesses, the prosecutor has responsibilities different from those of a lawyer in private practice: the prosecutor should make timely disclosure to the defense of available evidence, known to him, that tends to negate the guilt of the accused, mitigate the degree of the offense, or reduce the punishment. Further, a prosecutor should not intentionally avoid pursuit of evidence merely because he believes it will damage the prosecution's case or aid the accused.

EC 7-14 A government lawyer who has discretionary power relative to litigation should refrain from instituting or continuing litigation that is obviously unfair. A government lawyer not having such discretionary power who believes there is lack of merit in a controversy submitted to him should so advise his superiors and recommend the avoidance of unfair litigation. A government lawyer in a civil action or administrative proceeding has the responsibility to seek justice and to develop a full and fair record, and he should not use his position or the economic power of the government to harass parties or to bring about unjust settlements or results.

EC 7-15 The nature and purpose of proceedings before administrative agencies vary widely. The proceedings may be legislative or quasi-judicial, or a combination of both. They may be *ex parte* in character, in which event they may originate either at the instance of the agency or upon motion of an interested party. The scope of an inquiry may be purely investigative or it may be truly adversary looking toward the adjudication of specific rights of a party or of classes of parties. The foregoing are but examples of some of the types of proceedings conducted by administrative agencies. A lawyer appearing before an administrative agency,[25] regardless of the nature of the proceeding it is conducting, has the continuing duty to advance the cause of his client within the bounds of the law.[26] Where the applicable rules of the agency impose specific obligations upon a lawyer, it is his duty to comply therewith, unless the lawyer has a legitimate basis for challenging the validity thereof. In all appearances before administrative agencies, a lawyer should identify himself, his client if identity of his client is not privileged,[27] and the representative nature of his appearance. It is not improper, however, for a lawyer to seek from an agency information available to the public without identifying his client.

EC 7-16 The primary business of a legislative body is to enact laws rather than to adjudicate controversies, although on occasion the activities of a legislative body may take on the characteristics of an adversary proceeding, particularly in investigative and impeachment matters. The role of a lawyer supporting or opposing proposed legislation normally is quite different from his role in representing a person under investigation or on trial by a legislative body. When a lawyer appears in connection with proposed legislation, he seeks to affect the lawmaking process, but when he appears on behalf of a client in investigatory or impeachment proceedings, he is concerned with the protection of the rights of his client. In either event, he should identify himself and his client, if identity of his client is not privileged, and should comply with applicable laws and legislative rules.[28]

EC 7-17 The obligation of loyalty to his client applies only to a lawyer in the discharge of his professional duties and implies no obligation to adopt a personal viewpoint favorable to the in-

---

[24] *See* ABA Canon 5 and Berger v. United States, 295 U.S. 78, 79 L.Ed. 1314, 55 S.Ct. 629 (1935).

"The public prosecutor cannot take as a guide for the conduct of his office the standards of an attorney appearing on behalf of an individual client. The freedom elsewhere wisely granted to a partisan advocate must be severely curtailed if the prosecutor's duties are to be properly discharged. The public prosecutor must recall that he occupies a dual role, being obligated, on the one hand, to furnish that adversary element essential to the informed decision of any controversy, but being possessed, on the other, of important governmental powers that are pledged to the accomplishment of one objective only, that of impartial justice. Where the prosecutor is recreant to the trust implicit in his office, he undermines confidence, not only in his profession, but in government and the very ideal of justice itself." *Professional Responsibility: Report of the Joint Conference*, 44 A.B.A.J. 1159, 1218 (1958).

"The prosecuting attorney is the attorney for the state, and it is his primary duty not to convict but to see that justice is done." *ABA Opinion* 150 (1936).

---

[25] As to appearances before a department of government, Canon 26 provides: "A lawyer openly . . . may render professional services . . . in advocacy of claims before departments of government, upon the same principles of ethics which justify his appearance before the Courts . . . ."

[26] "But as an advocate before a service which itself represents the adversary point of view, where his client's case is fairly arguable, a lawyer is under no duty to disclose its weaknesses, any more than he would be to make such a disclosure to a brother lawyer. The limitations within which he must operate are best expressed in Canon 22 . . . ." *ABA Opinion* 314 (1965).

[27] *See* Baird v. Koerner, 279 F.2d 623 (9th Cir. 1960).

[28] *See* ABA Canon 26.

terests or desires of his client.[29] While a lawyer must act always with circumspection in order that his conduct will not adversely affect the rights of a client in a matter he is then handling, he may take positions on public issues and espouse legal reforms he favors without regard to the individual views of any client.

EC 7-18 The legal system in its broadest sense functions best when persons in need of legal advice or assistance are represented by their own counsel. For this reason a lawyer should not communicate on the subject matter of the representation of his client with a person he knows to be represented in the matter by a lawyer, unless pursuant to law or rule of court or unless he has the consent of the lawyer for that person.[30] If one is not represented by counsel, a lawyer representing another may have to deal directly with the unrepresented person; in such an instance, a lawyer should not undertake to give advice to the person who is attempting to represent himself,[31] except that he may advise him to obtain a lawyer.

Duty of the Lawyer to the Adversary System of Justice

EC 7-19 Our legal system provides for the adjudication of disputes governed by the rules of substantive, evidentiary, and procedural law. An adversary presentation counters the natural human tendency to judge too swiftly in terms of the familiar that which is not yet fully known;[32] the advocate, by his zealous preparation and presentation of facts and law, enables the tribunal to come to the hearing with an open and neutral mind and to render impartial judgments.[33] The duty of a lawyer to his client and his duty to the legal system are the same: to represent his client zealously within the bounds of the law.[34]

EC 7-20 In order to function properly, our adjudicative process requires an informed, impartial tribunal capable of administering justice promptly and efficiently [35] according to procedures that command public confidence and respect.[36] Not only must there be competent, adverse presentation of evidence and issues, but a tribunal must be aided by rules appropriate to an effective and dignified process. The procedures under which tribunals operate in our adversary system have been prescribed largely by legislative enactments, court rules and decisions, and administrative rules. Through the years certain concepts of proper professional conduct have become rules of law applicable to the adversary adjudicative process. Many of these concepts are the bases for standards of professional conduct set forth in the Disciplinary Rules.

EC 7-21 The civil adjudicative process is primarily designed for the settlement of disputes between parties, while the criminal process is designed for the protection of society as a whole. Threatening to use, or using, the criminal process to coerce adjustment of private civil claims or controversies is a subversion of that process;[37] further, the person against whom the criminal process is so misused may be deterred from asserting his legal rights and thus the usefulness of the civil process in settling private disputes is impaired. As in all cases of abuse of judicial process, the improper use of criminal process tends to diminish public confidence in our legal system.

EC 7-22 Respect for judicial rulings is essential to the proper administration of justice; however, a litigant or his lawyer may, in good faith and

---

[29] "Law should be so practiced that the lawyer remains free to make up his own mind how he will vote, what causes he will support, what economic and political philosophy he will espouse. It is one of the glories of the profession that it admits of this freedom. Distinguished examples can be cited of lawyers whose views were at variance from those of their clients, lawyers whose skill and wisdom make them valued advisers to those who had little sympathy with their views as citizens." *Professional Responsibility: Report of the Joint Conference*, 44 A.B.A.J. 1159, 1217 (1958).

"No doubt some tax lawyers feel constrained to abstain from activities on behalf of a better tax system because they think that their clients may object. Clients have no right to object if the tax adviser handles their affairs competently and faithfully and independently of his private views as to tax policy. They buy his expert services, not his private opinions or his silence on issues that gravely affect the public interest." Paul, *The Lawyer as a Tax Adviser*, 25 Rocky Mt. L. Rev. 412, 434 (1953).

[30] *See* ABA Canon 9.

[31] *Id.*

[32] *See Professional Responsibility: Report of the Joint Conference*, 44 A.B.A.J. 1159, 1160 (1958).

[33] "Without the participation of someone who can act responsibly for each of the parties, this essential narrowing of the issues [by exchange of written pleadings or stipulations of counsel] becomes impossible. But here again the true significance of partisan advocacy lies deeper, touching once more the integrity of the adjudicative process itself. It is only through the advocate's participation that the hearing may remain in fact what it purports to be in theory: a public trial of the facts and issues. Each advocate comes to the hearing prepared to present his proofs and arguments, knowing at the same time that his arguments may fail to persuade and that his proof may be rejected as inadequate. . . . The deciding tribunal, on the other hand, comes to the hearing uncommitted. It has not represented to the public that any fact can be proved, that any argument is sound, or that any particular way of stating a litigant's case is the most effective expression of its merits." *Professional Responsibility: Report of the Joint Conference*, 44 A.B.A.J. 1159, 1160-61 (1958).

[34] *Cf.* ABA Canons 15 and 32.

[35] *Cf.* ABA Canon 21.

[36] *See Professional Responsibility: Report of the Joint Conference*, 44 A.B.A.J. 1159, 1216 (1958).

[37] "We are of the opinion that the letter in question was improper, and that in writing and sending it respondent was guilty of unprofessional conduct. This court has heretofore expressed its disapproval of using threats of criminal prosecution as a means of forcing settlement of civil claims. . . .

"Respondent has been guilty of a violation of a principle which condemns any confusion of threats of criminal prosecution with the enforcement of civil claims. For this misconduct he should be severely censured." *Matter of Gelman*, 230 App. Div. 524, 527, 245 N.Y.S. 416, 419 (1930).

CODE OF PROFESSIONAL RESPONSIBILITY

within the framework of the law, take steps to test the correctness of a ruling of a tribunal.[38]

EC 7-23 The complexity of law often makes it difficult for a tribunal to be fully informed unless the pertinent law is presented by the lawyers in the cause. A tribunal that is fully informed on the applicable law is better able to make a fair and accurate determination of the matter before it. The adversary system contemplates that each lawyer will present and argue the existing law in the light most favorable to his client.[39] Where a lawyer knows of legal authority in the controlling jurisdiction directly adverse to the position of his client, he should inform the tribunal of its existence unless his adversary has done so; but, having made such disclosure, he may challenge its soundness in whole or in part.[40]

EC 7-24 In order to bring about just and informed decisions, evidentiary and procedural rules have been established by tribunals to permit the inclusion of relevant evidence and argument and the exclusion of all other considerations. The expression by a lawyer of his personal opinion as to the justness of a cause, as to the credibility of a witness, as to the culpability of a civil litigant, or as to the guilt or innocence of an accused is not a proper subject for argument to the trier of fact.[41] It is improper as to factual matters because admissible evidence possessed by a lawyer should be presented only as sworn testimony. It is improper as to all other matters because, were the rules otherwise, the silence of a lawyer on a given occasion could be construed unfavorably to his client. However, a lawyer may argue, on his analysis of the evidence, for any position or conclusion with respect to any of the foregoing matters.

EC 7-25 Rules of evidence and procedure are designed to lead to just decisions and are part of the framework of the law. Thus while a lawyer may take steps in good faith and within the framework of the law to test the validity of rules, he is not justified in consciously violating such rules and he should be diligent in his efforts to guard against his unintentional violation of them.[42] As examples, a lawyer should subscribe to or verify only those pleadings that he believes are in compliance with applicable law and rules; a lawyer should not make any prefatory statement before a tribunal in regard to the purported facts of the case on trial unless he believes that his statement will be supported by admissible evidence; a lawyer should not ask a witness a question solely for the purpose of harassing or embarrassing him; and a lawyer should not by subterfuge put before a jury matters which it cannot properly consider.

EC 7-26 The law and Disciplinary Rules prohibit the use of fraudulent, false, or perjured testimony or evidence.[43] A lawyer who knowingly[44] participates in introduction of such testimony or evidence is subject to discipline. A lawyer should, however, present any admissible evidence his client desires to have presented unless he knows, or from facts within his knowledge should know, that such testimony or evidence is false, fraudulent, or perjured.[45]

EC 7-27 Because it interferes with the proper administration of justice, a lawyer should not suppress evidence that he or his client has a legal obligation to reveal or produce. In like manner, a lawyer should not advise or cause a person to secrete himself or to leave the jurisdiction of a tribunal for the purpose of making him unavailable as a witness therein.[46]

EC 7-28 Witnesses should always testify truthfully[47] and should be free from any financial inducements that might tempt them to do other-

---

[38] "An attorney has the duty to protect the interests of his client. He has a right to press legitimate argument and to protest an erroneous ruling." Gallagher v. Municipal Court, 31 Cal.2d 784, 796, 192 P.2d 905, 913 (1948).

"There must be protection, however, in the far more frequent case of the attorney who stands on his rights and combats the order in good faith and without disrespect believing with good cause that it is void, for it is here that the independence of the bar becomes valuable." Note, 39 Colum.L.Rev. 433, 438 (1939).

[39] "Too many do not understand that accomplishment of the layman's abstract ideas of justice is the function of the judge and jury, and that it is the lawyer's sworn duty to portray his client's case in its most favorable light." Rochelle and Payne, *The Struggle for Public Understanding*, 25 Texas B.J. 109, 159 (1962).

[40] "We are of the opinion that this Canon requires the lawyer to disclose such decisions [that are adverse to his client's contentions] to the court. He may, of course, after doing so, challenge the soundness of the decisions or present reasons which he believes would warrant the court in not following them in the pending case." *ABA Opinion* 146 (1935).

Cf. ABA Opinion 280 (1949) and Thode, *The Ethical Standard for the Advocate*, 39 Texas L.Rev. 575, 585–86 (1961).

[41] See ABA Canon 15.
"The traditional duty of an advocate is that he honorably uphold the contentions of his client. He should not voluntarily undermine them." Harders v. State of California, 373 F.2d 839, 842 (9th Cir. 1967).

[42] See ABA Canon 22.

[43] *Id. Cf.* ABA Canon 41.

[44] See generally *ABA Opinion* 287 (1953) as to a lawyer's duty when he unknowingly participates in introducing perjured testimony.

[45] "Under any standard of proper ethical conduct an attorney should not sit by silently and permit his client to commit what may have been perjury, and which certainly would mislead the court and the opposing party on a matter vital to the issue under consideration. . . .
. . . .
"Respondent next urges that it was his duty to observe the utmost good faith toward his client, and therefore he could not divulge any confidential information. This duty to the client of course does not extend to the point of authorizing collaboration with him in the commission of fraud." In re Carroll, 244 S.W.2d 474, 474–75 (Ky. 1951).

[46] See ABA Canon 5; *cf. ABA Opinion* 131 (1935).

[47] *Cf.* ABA Canon 39.

wise.[48] A lawyer should not pay or agree to pay a non-expert witness an amount in excess of reimbursement for expenses and financial loss incident to his being a witness; however, a lawyer may pay or agree to pay an expert witness a reasonable fee for his services as an expert. But in no event should a lawyer pay or agree to pay a contingent fee to any witness. A lawyer should exercise reasonable diligence to see that his client and lay associates conform to these standards.[49]

EC 7-29 To safeguard the impartiality that is essential to the judicial process, veniremen and jurors should be protected against extraneous influences.[50] When impartiality is present, public confidence in the judicial system is enhanced. There should be no extrajudicial communication with veniremen prior to trial or with jurors during trial by or on behalf of a lawyer connected with the case. Furthermore, a lawyer who is not connected with the case should not communicate with or cause another to communicate with a venireman or a juror about the case. After the trial, communication by a lawyer with jurors is permitted so long as he refrains from asking questions or making comments that tend to harass or embarrass the juror [51] or to influence actions of the juror in future cases. Were a lawyer to be prohibited from communicating after trial with a juror, he could not ascertain if the verdict might be subject to legal challenge, in which event the invalidity of a verdict might go undetected.[52] When an extrajudicial communication by a lawyer with a juror is permitted by law, it should be made considerately and with deference to the personal feelings of the juror.

EC 7-30 Vexatious or harassing investigations of veniremen or jurors seriously impair the effectiveness of our jury system. For this reason, a lawyer or anyone on his behalf who conducts an investigation of veniremen or jurors should act with circumspection and restraint.

EC 7-31 Communications with or investigations of members of families of veniremen or jurors by a lawyer or by anyone on his behalf are subject to the restrictions imposed upon the lawyer with respect to his communications with or investigations of veniremen and jurors.

EC 7-32 Because of his duty to aid in preserving the integrity of the jury system, a lawyer who learns of improper conduct by or towards a venireman, a juror, or a member of the family of either should make a prompt report to the court regarding such conduct.

EC 7-33 A goal of our legal system is that each party shall have his case, criminal or civil, adjudicated by an impartial tribunal. The attainment of this goal may be defeated by dissemination of news or comments which tend to influence judge or jury.[53] Such news or comments may

---

[48] "The prevalence of perjury is a serious menace to the administration of justice, to prevent which no means have as yet been satisfactorily devised. But there certainly can be no greater incentive to perjury than to allow a party to make payments to its opponents witnesses under any guise or on any excuse, and at least attorneys who are officers of the court to aid it in the administration of justice, must keep themselves clear of any connection which in the slightest degree tends to induce witnesses to testify in favor of their clients." In re Robinson, 151 App.Div. 589, 600, 136 N.Y.S. 548, 556–57 (1912), aff'd, 209 N.Y. 354, 103 N.E. 160 (1913).

[49] "It will not do for an attorney who seeks to justify himself against charges of this kind to show that he has escaped criminal responsibility under the Penal Law, nor can he blindly shut his eyes to a system which tends to produce perjured testimony, and to suppress the truth. He has an active affirmative duty to protect the administration of justice from perjury and fraud, and that duty is not performed by allowing his subordinates and assistants to attempt to subvert justice and procure results for his clients based upon false testimony and perjured witnesses." Id., 151 App.Div. at 592, 136 N.Y.S. at 551.

[50] See ABA Canon 23.

[51] "[I]t is unfair to jurors to permit a disappointed litigant to pick over their private associations in search of something to discredit them and their verdict. And it would be unfair to the public too if jurors should understand that they cannot convict a man of means without risking an inquiry of that kind by paid investigators, with, to boot, the distortions an inquiry of that kind can produce." State v. LaFera, 42 N.J. 97, 107, 199 A.2d 630, 636 (1964).

[52] ABA Opinion 319 (1968) points out that "[m]any courts today, and the trend is in this direction, allow the testimony of jurors as to all irregularities in and out of the courtroom except those irregularities whose existence can be determined only by exploring the consciousness of a single particular juror, New Jersey v. Kociolek, 20 N.J. 92, 118 A.2d 812 (1955). Model Code of Evidence Rule 301. Certainly as to states in which the testimony and affidavits of jurors may be received in support of or against a motion for new trial, a lawyer, in his obligation to protect his client, must have the tools for ascertaining whether or not grounds for a new trial exist and it is not unethical for him to talk to and question jurors."

[53] Generally see ABA Advisory Committee on Fair Trial and Free Press, Standards Relating to Fair Trial and Free Press (1966).

"[T]he trial court might well have proscribed extrajudicial statements by any lawyer, party, witness, or court official which divulged prejudicial matters . . . . See State v. Van Dwyne, 43 N.J. 369, 389, 204 A.2d 841, 852 (1964), in which the court interpreted Canon 20 of the American Bar Association's Canons of Professional Ethics to prohibit such statements. Being advised of the great public interest in the case, the mass coverage of the press, and the potential prejudicial impact of publicity, the court could also have requested the appropriate city and county officials to promulgate a regulation with respect to dissemination of information about the case by their employees. In addition, reporters who wrote or broadcast prejudicial stories, could have been warned as to the impropriety of publishing material not introduced in the proceedings. . . . In this manner, Sheppard's right to a trial free from outside interference would have been given added protection without corresponding curtailment of the news media. Had the judge, the other officers of the court, and the police placed the interest of justice first, the news media would have soon learned to be content with the task of reporting the case as it unfolded in the courtroom—not pieced together from extrajudicial statements." Sheppard v. Maxwell, 384 U.S. 333, 361–62, 16 L. E.2d 600, 619–20, 86 S.Ct. 1507, 1521–22 (1966).

CODE OF PROFESSIONAL RESPONSIBILITY

prevent prospective jurors from being impartial at the outset of the trial [54] and may also interfere with the obligation of jurors to base their verdict solely upon the evidence admitted in the trial.[55]

"Court proceedings are held for the solemn purpose of endeavoring to ascertain the truth which is the *sine qua non* of a fair trial. Over the centuries Anglo-American courts have devised careful safeguards by rule and otherwise to protect and facilitate the performance of this high function. As a result, at this time those safeguards do not permit the televising and photographing of a criminal trial, save in two States and there only under restrictions. The federal courts prohibit it by specific rule. This is weighty evidence that our concepts of a fair trial do not tolerate such an indulgence. We have always held that the atmosphere essential to the preservation of a fair trial—the most fundamental of all freedoms—must be maintained at all costs." Estes v. State of Texas, 381 U.S. 532, 540, 14 L.Ed.2d 543, 549, 85 S.Ct. 1628, 1631–32 (1965), *rehearing denied*, 382 U.S. 875, 15 L.Ed.2d 118, 86 S.Ct. 18 (1965).

[54] "Pretrial can create a major problem for the defendant in a criminal case. Indeed, it may be more harmful than publicity during the trial for it may well set the community opinion as to guilt or innocence. . . . The trial witnesses present at the hearing, as well as the original jury panel, were undoubtedly made aware of the peculiar public importance of the case by the press and television coverage being provided, and by the fact that they themselves were televised live and their pictures rebroadcast on the evening show." *Id.*, 381 U.S. at 536–37, 14 L.Ed.2d at 546–47, 85 S.Ct. at 1629–30.

[55] "The undeviating rule of this Court was expressed by Mr. Justice Holmes over half a century ago in Patterson v. Colorado, 205 U.S. 454, 462 (1907):

The theory of our system is that the conclusions to be reached in a case will be induced only by evidence and argument in open court, and not by any outside influence, whether of private talk or public print."

Sheppard v. Maxwell, 384 U.S. 333, 351, 16 L.Ed.2d 600, 614, 86 S.Ct. 1507, 1516 (1966).

"The trial judge has a large discretion in ruling on the issue of prejudice resulting from the reading by jurors of news articles concerning the trial. . . . Generalizations beyond that statement are not profitable, because each case must turn on its special facts. We have here the exposure of jurors to information of a character which the trial judge ruled was so prejudicial it could not be directly offered as evidence. The prejudice to the defendant is almost certain to be as great when that evidence reaches the jury through news accounts as when it is a part of the prosecution's evidence. . . . It may indeed be greater for it is then not tempered by protective procedures." Marshall v. United States, 360 U.S. 310, 312–13, 3 L.Ed.2d 1250, 1252, 79 S.Ct. 1171, 1173 (1959).

"The experienced trial lawyer knows that an adverse public opinion is a tremendous disadvantage to the defense of his client. Although grand jurors conduct their deliberations in secret, they are selected from the body of the public. They are likely to know what the general public knows and to reflect the public attitude. Trials are open to the public, and aroused public opinion respecting the merits of a legal controversy creates a court room atmosphere which, without any vocal expression in the presence of the petit jury, makes itself felt and has its effect upon the action of the petit jury. Our fundamental concepts of justice and our American sense of fair play require that the petit jury shall be composed of persons with fair and impartial minds and without preconceived views as to the merits of the controversy, and that it shall determine the issues presented to it solely upon the evidence adduced at the trial and according to the law given in the instructions of the trial judge.

The release by a lawyer of out-of-court statements regarding an anticipated or pending trial may improperly affect the impartiality of the tribunal.[56] For these reasons, standards for permissible and prohibited conduct of a lawyer with respect to trial publicity have been established.

EC 7-34 The impartiality of a public servant in our legal system may be impaired by the receipt of gifts or loans. A lawyer,[57] therefore, is never justified in making a gift or a loan to a judge, a hearing officer, or an official or employee of a tribunal.[58]

EC 7-35 All litigants and lawyers should have access to tribunals on an equal basis. Generally, in adversary proceedings a lawyer should not communicate with a judge relative to a matter pending before, or which is to be brought before, a tribunal over which he presides in circumstances which might have the effect or give the appearance of granting undue advantage to one party.[59] For example, a lawyer should not communicate with a tribunal by a writing unless a copy thereof is promptly delivered to opposing counsel or to the adverse party if he is not represented by a lawyer. Ordinarily an oral communication by a lawyer with a judge or hearing officer should be made only upon adequate notice to opposing counsel, or, if there is none, to the opposing party. A lawyer should not condone or lend himself to private importunities by another with a judge or hearing officer on behalf of himself or his client.

EC 7-36 Judicial hearings ought to be conducted through dignified and orderly procedures designed to protect the rights of all parties. Although a lawyer has the duty to represent his client zealous-

---

"While we may doubt that the effect of public opinion would sway or bias the judgment of the trial judge in an equity proceeding, the defendant should not be called upon to run that risk and the trial court should not have his work made more difficult by any dissemination of statements to the public that would be calculated to create a public demand for a particular judgment in a prospective or pending case." *ABA Opinion* 199 (1940).

Cf. Estes v. State of Texas, 381 U.S. 532, 544–45, 14 L. Ed.2d 543, 551, 85 S.Ct. 1628, 1634 (1965), *rehearing denied*, 381 U.S. 875, 15 L.Ed.2d 118, 86 S.Ct. 18 (1965).

[56] *See* ABA Canon 20.

[57] Canon 3 observes that a lawyer "deserves rebuke and denunciation for any device or attempt to gain from a Judge special personal consideration or favor."
See ABA Canon 32.

[58] "*Judicial Canon 32* provides:

"'A judge should not accept any presents or favors from litigants, or from lawyers practicing before him or from others whose interests are likely to be submitted to him for judgment.'

"The language of this Canon is perhaps broad enough to prohibit campaign contributions by lawyers, practicing before the court upon which the candidate hopes to sit. However, we do not think it was intended to prohibit such contributions when the candidate is obligated, by force of circumstances over which he has no control, to conduct a campaign, the expense of which exceeds that which he should reasonably be expected to personally bear!" *ABA Opinion* 226 (1941).

[59] *See* ABA Canons 3 and 32.

CODE OF PROFESSIONAL RESPONSIBILITY

ly, he should not engage in any conduct that offends the dignity and decorum of proceedings.[60] While maintaining his independence, a lawyer should be respectful, courteous, and above-board in his relations with a judge or hearing officer before whom he appears.[61] He should avoid undue solicitude for the comfort or convenience of judge or jury and should avoid any other conduct calculated to gain special consideration.

EC 7-37 In adversary proceedings, clients are litigants and though ill feeling may exist between clients, such ill feeling should not influence a lawyer in his conduct, attitude, and demeanor towards opposing lawyers.[62] A lawyer should not make unfair or derogatory personal reference to opposing counsel. Haranguing and offensive tactics by lawyers interfere with the orderly administration of justice and have no proper place in our legal system.

EC 7-38 A lawyer should be courteous to opposing counsel and should accede to reasonable requests regarding court proceedings, settings, continuances, waiver of procedural formalities, and similar matters which do not prejudice the rights of his client.[63] He should follow local customs of courtesy or practice, unless he gives timely notice to opposing counsel of his intention not to do so.[64] A lawyer should be punctual in fulfilling all professional commitments.[65]

EC 7-39 In the final analysis, proper functioning of the adversary system depends upon cooperation between lawyers and tribunals in utilizing procedures which will preserve the impartiality of tribunals and make their decisional processes prompt and just, without impinging upon the obligation of lawyers to represent their clients zealously within the framework of the law.

DISCIPLINARY RULES

DR 7-101 Representing a Client Zealously.

(A) A lawyer shall not intentionally:[66]

(1) Fail to seek the lawful objectives of his client through reasonably available means[67] permitted by law and the Disciplinary Rules, except as provided by DR 7-101(B). A lawyer does not violate this Disciplinary Rule, however, by acceding to reasonable requests of opposing counsel which do not prejudice the rights of his client, by being punctual in fulfilling all professional commitments, by avoiding offensive tactics, or by treating with courtesy and consideration all persons involved in the legal process.

(2) Fail to carry out a contract of employment entered into with a client for professional services, but he may withdraw as permitted under DR 2-110, DR 5-102, and DR 5-105.

(3) Prejudice or damage his client during the course of the professional relationship[68] except as required under DR 7-102(B).

(B) In his representation of a client, a lawyer may:

(1) Where permissible, exercise his professional judgment to waive or fail to assert a right or position of his client.

(2) Refuse to aid or participate in conduct that he believes to be unlawful, even though there is some support for an argument that the conduct is legal.

DR 7-102 Representing a Client Within the Bounds of the Law.

(A) In his representation of a client, a lawyer shall not:

(1) File a suit, assert a position, conduct a defense, delay a trial, or take other action on behalf of his client when he knows or when it is obvious that such action would serve merely to harass or maliciously injure another.[69]

(2) Knowingly advance a claim or defense that is unwarranted under existing law, except that he may advance such claim or defense if it can be supported by good faith argument for an extension, modification, or reversal of existing law.

(3) Conceal or knowingly fail to disclose that which he is required by law to reveal.

(4) Knowingly use perjured testimony or false evidence.[70]

(5) Knowingly make a false statement of law or fact.

(6) Participate in the creation or preservation of evidence when he knows or it is obvious that the evidence is false.

(7) Counsel or assist his client in conduct that the lawyer knows to be illegal or fraudulent.

(8) Knowingly engage in other illegal conduct or conduct contrary to a Disciplinary Rule.

(B) A lawyer who receives information clearly establishing that:

(1) His client has, in the course of the representation, perpetrated a fraud upon a person or tribunal shall promptly call

---

[60] Cf. ABA Canon 18.

[61] See ABA Canons 1 and 3.

[62] See ABA Canon 17.

[63] See ABA Canon 24.

[64] See ABA Canon 25.

[65] See ABA Canon 21.

[66] See ABA Canon 15.

[67] See ABA Canons 5 and 15; cf. ABA Canons 4 and 32.

[68] Cf. ABA Canon 24.

[69] See ABA Canon 30.

[70] Cf. ABA Canons 22 and 29.

CODE OF PROFESSIONAL RESPONSIBILITY

upon his client to rectify the same, and if his client refuses or is unable to do so, he shall reveal the fraud to the affected person or tribunal.[71]

(2) A person other than his client has perpetrated a fraud upon a tribunal shall promptly reveal the fraud to the tribunal.[72]

DR 7-103 Performing the Duty of Public Prosecutor or Other Government Lawyer.[73]

(A) A public prosecutor or other government lawyer shall not institute or cause to be instituted criminal charges when he knows or it is obvious that the charges are not supported by probable cause.

(B) A public prosecutor or other government lawyer in criminal litigation shall make timely disclosure to counsel for the defendant, or to the defendant if he has no counsel, of the existence of evidence, known to the prosecutor or other government lawyer, that tends to negate the guilt of the accused, mitigate the degree of the offense, or reduce the punishment.

DR 7-104 Communicating With One of Adverse Interest.[74]

(A) During the course of his representation of a client a lawyer shall not:

(1) Communicate or cause another to communicate on the subject of the representation with a party he knows to be represented by a lawyer in that matter unless he has the prior consent of the lawyer representing such other party [75] or is authorized by law to do so.

(2) Give advice to a person who is not represented by a lawyer, other than the advice to secure counsel,[76] if the interests of such person are or have a reasonable possibility of being in conflict with the interests of his client.[77]

DR 7-105 Threatening Criminal Prosecution.

(A) A lawyer shall not present, participate in presenting, or theaten to present criminal charges solely to obtain an advantage in a civil matter.

DR 7-106 Trial Conduct.

(A) A lawyer shall not disregard or advise his client to disregard a standing rule of a tribunal or a ruling of a tribunal made in the course of a proceeding, but he may take appropriate steps in good faith to test the validity of such rule or ruling.

(B) In presenting a matter to a tribunal, a lawyer shall disclose: [78]

(1) Legal authority in the controlling jurisdiction known to him to be directly adverse to the position of his client and which is not disclosed by opposing counsel.[79]

(2) Unless privileged or irrelevant, the identities of the clients he represents and of the persons who employed him.[80]

---

[71] See ABA Canon 41; cf. Hinds v. State Bar, 19 Cal.2d 87, 92-93, 119 P.2d 134, 137 (1941); but see ABA Opinion 287 (1953) and Texas Canon 38. Also see Code of Professional Responsibility, DR 4-101(C)(2).

[72] See Precision Inst. Mfg. Co. v. Automotive M. M. Co., 324 U.S. 806, 89 L.Ed. 1381, 65 S.Ct. 993 (1945).

[73] Cf. ABA Canon 5.

[74] "Rule 12. . . . A member of the State Bar shall not communicate with a party represented by counsel upon a subject of controversy, in the absence and without the consent of such counsel. This rule shall not apply to communications with a public officer, board, committee or body." Cal.Business and Professions Code § 6076 (West 1962).

[75] See ABA Canon 9; cf. ABA Opinions 124 (1934), 108 (1934), 95 (1933), and 75 (1932); also see In re Schwabe, 242 Or. 169, 174-75, 408 P.2d 922, 924 (1965).

"It is clear from the earlier opinions of this committee that Canon 9 is to be construed literally and does not allow a communication with an opposing party, without the consent of his counsel, though the purpose merely be to investigate the facts. Opinions 117, 95, 66," ABA Opinion 187 (1938).

[76] Cf. ABA Opinion 102 (1933).

[77] Cf. ABA Canon 9 and ABA Opinion 58 (1931).

[78] Cf. Note, 38 Texas L.Rev. 107, 108-09 (1959).

[79] "In the brief summary in the 1947 edition of the Committee's decisions (p. 17), Opinion 146 was thus summarized: Opinion 146—A lawyer should disclose to the court a decision directly adverse to his client's case that is unknown to his adversary.

. . . .

"We would not confine the Opinion to 'controlling authorities'—i.e., those decisive of the pending case—but, in accordance with the tests hereafter suggested, would apply it to a decision directly adverse to any proposition of law on which the lawyer expressly relies, which would reasonably be considered important by the judge sitting on the case.

". . . The test in every case should be: Is the decision which opposing counsel has overlooked one which the court should clearly consider in deciding the case? Would a reasonable judge properly feel that a lawyer who advanced, as the law, a proposition adverse to the undisclosed decision, was lacking in candor and fairness to him? Might the judge consider himself misled by an implied representation that the lawyer knew of no adverse authority?" ABA Opinion 280 (1949).

[80] "The authorities are substantially uniform against any privilege as applied to the fact of retainer or identity of the client. The privilege is limited to confidential communications, and a retainer is not a confidential communication, although it cannot come into existence without some communication between the attorney and the—at that stage prospective—client." United States v. Pape, 144 F.2d 778, 782 (2d Cir. 1944), cert. denied, 323 U.S. 752, 89 L.Ed.2d 602, 65 S.Ct. 86 (1944).

"To be sure, there may be circumstances under which the identification of a client may amount to the prejudicial disclosure of a confidential communication, as where the

CODE OF PROFESSIONAL RESPONSIBILITY

(C) In appearing in his professional capacity before a tribunal, a lawyer shall not:

(1) State or allude to any matter that he has no reasonable basis to believe is relevant to the case or that will not be supported by admissible evidence.[81]

(2) Ask any question that he has no reasonable basis to believe is relevant to the case and that is intended to degrade a witness or other person.[82]

(3) Assert his personal knowledge of the facts in issue, except when testifying as a witness.

(4) Assert his personal opinion as to the justness of a cause, as to the credibility of a witness, as to the culpability of a civil litigant, or as to the guilt or innocence of an accused;[83] but he may argue, on his analysis of the evidence, for any position or conclusion with respect to the matters stated herein.

(5) Fail to comply with known local customs of courtesy or practice of the bar or a particular tribunal without giving to opposing counsel timely notice of his intent not to comply.[84]

(6) Engage in undignified or discourteous conduct which is degrading to a tribunal.

(7) Intentionally or habitually violate any established rule of procedure or of evidence.

DR 7-107 Trial Publicity.[85]

(A) A lawyer participating in or associated with the investigation of a criminal matter shall not make or participate in making an extrajudicial statement that a reasonable person would expect to be disseminated by means of public communication and that does more than state without elaboration:

(1) Information contained in a public record.

(2) That the investigation is in progress.

(3) The general scope of the investigation including a description of the offense and, if permitted by law, the identity of the victim.

(4) A request for assistance in apprehending a suspect or assistance in other matters and the information necessary thereto.

(5) A warning to the public of any dangers.

(B) A lawyer or law firm associated with the prosecution or defense of a criminal matter shall not, from the time of the filing of a complaint, information, or indictment, the issuance of an arrest warrant, or arrest until the commencement of the trial or disposition

---

substance of a disclosure has already been revealed but not its source." Colton v. United States, 306 F.2d 633, 637 (2d Cir. 1962).

[81] See ABA Canon 22; cf. ABA Canon 17.

"The rule allowing counsel when addressing the jury the widest latitude in discussing the evidence and presenting the client's theories falls far short of authorizing the statement by counsel of matter not in evidence, or indulging in argument founded on no proof, or demanding verdicts for purposes other than the just settlement of the matters at issue between the litigants, or appealing to prejudice or passion. The rule confining counsel to legitimate argument is not based on etiquette, but on justice. Its violation is not merely an overstepping of the bounds of propriety, but a violation of a party's rights. The jurors must determine the issues upon the evidence. Counsel's address should help them do this, not tend to lead them astray." Cherry Creek Nat. Bank v. Fidelity & Cas. Co., 207 App.Div. 787, 790-91, 202 N.Y.S. 611, 614 (1924).

[82] Cf. ABA Canon 18.

"§ 6068. . . . It is the duty of an attorney:
. . . .
"(f) To abstain from all offensive personality, and to advance no fact prejudicial to the honor or reputation of a party or witness, unless required by the justice of the cause with which he is charged." Cal.Business and Professions Code § 6068 (West 1962).

[83] "The record in the case at bar was silent concerning the qualities and character of the deceased. It is especially improper, in addressing the jury in a murder case, for the prosecuting attorney to make reference to his knowledge of the good qualities of the deceased where there is no evidence in the record bearing upon his character. . . . A prosecutor should never inject into his argument evidence not introduced at the trial." People v. Dukes, 12 Ill.2d 334, 341, 146 N.E.2d 14, 17-18 (1957).

[84] "A lawyer should not ignore known customs or practice of the Bar or of a particular Court, even when the law permits, without giving timely notice to the opposing counsel." ABA Canon 25.

[85] The provisions of Sections (A), (B), (C), and (D) of this Disciplinary Rule incorporate the fair trial-free press standards which apply to lawyers as adopted by the ABA House of Delegates, Feb. 19, 1968, upon the recommendation of the Fair Trial and Free Press Advisory Committee of the ABA Special Committee on Minimum Standards for the Administration of Criminal Justice.

Cf. ABA Canon 20; see generally ABA Advisory Committee on Fair Trial and Free Press, Standards Relating to Fair Trial and Free Press (1966).

"From the cases coming here we note that unfair and prejudicial news comment on pending trials has become increasingly prevalent. Due process requires that the accused receive a trial by an impartial jury free from outside influences. Given the pervasiveness of modern communications and the difficulty of effacing prejudicial publicity from the minds of the jurors, the trial courts must take strong measures to ensure that the balance is never weighed against the accused. And appellate tribunals have the duty to make an independent evaluation of the circumstances. Of course, there is nothing that prescribes the press from reporting events that transpire in the courtroom. But where there is a reasonable likelihood that prejudicial news prior to trial will prevent a fair trial, the judge should continue the case until the threat abates, or transfer it to another county not so permeated with publicity. . . . The courts must take such steps by rule and regulation that will protect their processes from prejudicial outside interferences. Neither prosecutors, counsel for defense, the accused, witnesses, court staff nor enforcement officers coming under the jurisdiction of the court should be permitted to frustrate its function. Collaboration between counsel and the press as to information affecting the fairness of a criminal trial is not only subject to regulation, but is highly censurable and worthy of disciplinary measures." Sheppard v. Maxwell, 384 U.S. 333, 362-63, 16 L.Ed.2d 600, 620, 86 S.Ct. 1507, 1522 (1966).

CODE OF PROFESSIONAL RESPONSIBILITY

without trial, make or participate in making an extrajudicial statement that a reasonable person would expect to be disseminated by means of public communication and that relates to:

(1) The character, reputation, or prior criminal record (including arrests, indictments, or other charges of crime) of the accused.

(2) The possibility of a plea of guilty to the offense charged or to a lesser offense.

(3) The existence or contents of any confession, admission, or statement given by the accused or his refusal or failure to make a statement.

(4) The performance or results of any examinations or tests or the refusal or failure of the accused to submit to examinations or tests.

(5) The identity, testimony, or credibility of a prospective witness.

(6) Any opinion as to the guilt or innocence of the accused, the evidence, or the merits of the case.

(C) DR 7-107(B) does not preclude a lawyer during such period from announcing:

(1) The name, age, residence, occupation, and family status of the accused.

(2) If the accused has not been apprehended, any information necessary to aid in his apprehension or to warn the public of any dangers he may present.

(3) A request for assistance in obtaining evidence.

(4) The identity of the victim of the crime.

(5) The fact, time, and place of arrest, resistance, pursuit, and use of weapons.

(6) The identity of investigating and arresting officers or agencies and the length of the investigation.

(7) At the time of seizure, a description of the physical evidence seized, other than a confession, admission, or statement.

(8) The nature, substance, or text of the charge.

(9) Quotations from or references to public records of the court in the case.

(10) The scheduling or result of any step in the judicial proceedings.

(11) That the accused denies the charges made against him.

(D) During the selection of a jury or the trial of a criminal matter, a lawyer or law firm associated with the prosecution or defense of a criminal matter shall not make or participate in making an extrajudicial statement that a reasonable person would expect to be disseminated by means of public communication and that relates to the trial, parties, or issues in the trial or other matters that are reasonably likely to interfere with a fair trial, except that he may quote from or refer without comment to public records of the court in the case.

(E) After the completion of a trial or disposition without trial of a criminal matter and prior to the imposition of sentence, a lawyer or law firm associated with the prosecution or defense shall not make or participate in making an extrajudicial statement that a reasonable person would expect to be disseminated by public communication and that is reasonably likely to affect the imposition of sentence.

(F) The foregoing provisions of DR 7-107 also apply to professional disciplinary proceedings and juvenile disciplinary proceedings when pertinent and consistent with other law applicable to such proceedings.

(G) A lawyer or law firm associated with a civil action shall not during its investigation or litigation make or participate in making an extrajudicial statement, other than a quotation from or reference to public records, that a reasonable person would expect to be disseminated by means of public communication and that relates to:

(1) Evidence regarding the occurrence or transaction involved.

(2) The character, credibility, or criminal record of a party, witness, or prospective witness.

(3) The performance or results of any examinations or tests or the refusal or failure of a party to submit to such.

(4) His opinion as to the merits of the claims or defenses of a party, except as required by law or administrative rule.

(5) Any other matter reasonably likely to interfere with a fair trial of the action.

(H) During the pendency of an administrative proceeding, a lawyer or law firm associated therewith shall not make or participate in making a statement, other than a quotation from or reference to public records, that a reasonable person would expect to be disseminated by means of public communication if it is made outside the official course of the proceeding and relates to:

(1) Evidence regarding the occurrence or transaction involved.

(2) The character, credibility, or criminal record of a party, witness, or prospective witness.

(3) Physical evidence or the performance or results of any examinations or tests or the refusal or failure of a party to submit to such.

(4) His opinion as to the merits of the claims, defenses, or positions of an interested person.

(5) Any other matter reasonably likely to interfere with a fair hearing.

CODE OF PROFESSIONAL RESPONSIBILITY

(I) The foregoing provisions of DR 7-107 do not preclude a lawyer from replying to charges of misconduct publicly made against him or from participating in the proceedings of legislative, administrative, or other investigative bodies.

(J) A lawyer shall exercise reasonable care to prevent his employees and associates from making an extrajudicial statement that he would be prohibited from making under DR 7-107.

DR 7-108 Communication with or Investigation of Jurors.

(A) Before the trial of a case a lawyer connected therewith shall not communicate with or cause another to communicate with anyone he knows to be a member of the venire from which the jury will be selected for the trial of the case.

(B) During the trial of a case:

(1) A lawyer connected therewith shall not communicate with or cause another to communicate with any member of the jury.[86]

(2) A lawyer who is not connected therewith shall not communicate with or cause another to communicate with a juror concerning the case.

(C) DR 7-108(A) and (B) do not prohibit a lawyer from communicating with veniremen or jurors in the course of official proceedings.

(D) After discharge of the jury from further consideration of a case with which the lawyer was connected, the lawyer shall not ask questions of or make comments to a member of that jury that are calculated merely to harass or embarrass the juror or to influence his actions in future jury service.[87]

(E) A lawyer shall not conduct or cause, by financial support or otherwise, another to conduct a vexatious or harassing investigation of either a venireman or a juror.

(F) All restrictions imposed by DR 7-108 upon a lawyer also apply to communications with or investigations of members of a family of a venireman or a juror.

(G) A lawyer shall reveal promptly to the court improper conduct by a venireman or a juror, or by another toward a venireman or a juror or a member of his family, of which the lawyer has knowledge.

DR 7-109 Contact with Witnesses.

(A) A lawyer shall not suppress any evidence that he or his client has a legal obligation to reveal or produce.[88]

(B) A lawyer shall not advise or cause a person to secrete himself or to leave the jurisdiction of a tribunal for the purpose of making him unavailable as a witness therein.[89]

(C) A lawyer shall not pay, offer to pay, or acquiesce in the payment of compensation to a witness contingent upon the content of his testimony or the outcome of the case.[90] But a lawyer may advance, guarantee, or acquiesce in the payment of:

(1) Expenses reasonably incurred by a witness in attending or testifying.

(2) Reasonable compensation to a witness for his loss of time in attending or testifying.

(3) A reasonable fee for the professional services of an expert witness.

DR 7-110 Contact with Officials.[91]

(A) A lawyer shall not give or lend any thing of value to a judge, official, or employee of a tribunal.

(B) In an adversary proceeding, a lawyer shall not communicate, or cause another to communicate, as to the merits of the cause with a judge or an official before whom the proceeding is pending, except:

(1) In the course of official proceedings in the cause.

(2) In writing if he promptly delivers a copy of the writing to opposing counsel or to the adverse party if he is not represented by a lawyer.

(3) Orally upon adequate notice to opposing counsel or to the adverse party if he is not represented by a lawyer.

(4) As otherwise authorized by law.[92]

---

[89] *Cf.* ABA Canon 5.
"*Rule 15.* . . . A member of the State Bar shall not advise a person, whose testimony could establish or tend to establish a material fact, to avoid service of process, or secrete himself, or otherwise to make his testimony unavailable." Cal.Business and Professions Code § 6076 (West 1962).

[90] *See* In re O'Keefe, 49 Mont. 369, 142 P. 638 (1914).

[91] *Cf.* ABA Canon 3.

[92] "*Rule 16.* . . . A member of the State Bar shall not, in the absence of opposing counsel, communicate with or argue to a judge or judicial officer except in open court upon the merits of a contested matter pending before such judge or judicial officer; nor shall he, without furnishing opposing counsel with a copy thereof, address a written communication to a judge or judicial officer concerning the merits of a contested matter pending before such judge or judicial officer. This rule shall not apply to ex parte matters." Cal.Business and Professions Code § 6076 (West 1962).

---

[86] *See* ABA Canon 23.

[87] "[I]t would be unethical for a lawyer to harass, entice, induce or exert influence on a juror to obtain his testimony." *ABA Opinion* 319 (1968).

[88] *See* ABA Canon 5.

CODE OF PROFESSIONAL RESPONSIBILITY

CANON 8

A Lawyer Should Assist in Improving the Legal System

ETHICAL CONSIDERATIONS

EC 8-1 Changes in human affairs and imperfections in human institutions make necessary constant efforts to maintain and improve our legal system.[1] This system should function in a manner that commands public respect and fosters the use of legal remedies to achieve redress of grievances. By reason of education and experience, lawyers are especially qualified to recognize deficiencies in the legal system and to initiate corrective measures therein. Thus they should participate in proposing and supporting legislation and programs to improve the system,[2] without regard to the general interests or desires of clients or former clients.[3]

EC 8-2 Rules of law are deficient if they are not just, understandable, and responsive to the needs of society. If a lawyer believes that the existence or absence of a rule of law, substantive or procedural, causes or contributes to an unjust result, he should endeavor by lawful means to obtain appropriate changes in the law. He should encourage the simplification of laws and the repeal or amendment of laws that are outmoded.[4] Likewise, legal procedures should be improved whenever experience indicates a change is needed.

EC 8-3 The fair administration of justice requires the availability of competent lawyers. Members of the public should be educated to recognize the existence of legal problems and the resultant need for legal services, and should be provided methods for intelligent selection of counsel. Those persons unable to pay for legal services should be provided needed services. Clients and lawyers should not be penalized by undue geographical restraints upon representation in legal matters, and the bar should address itself to improvements in licensing, reciprocity, and admission procedures consistent with the needs of modern commerce.

EC 8-4 Whenever a lawyer seeks legislative or administrative changes, he should identify the capacity in which he appears, whether on behalf of himself, a client, or the public.[5] A lawyer may advocate such changes on behalf of a client even though he does not agree with them. But when a lawyer purports to act on behalf of the public, he should espouse only those changes which he conscientiously believes to be in the public interest.

EC 8-5 Fraudulent, deceptive, or otherwise illegal conduct by a participant in a proceeding before a tribunal or legislative body is inconsistent with fair administration of justice, and it should never be participated in or condoned by lawyers. Unless constrained by his obligation to preserve the confidences and secrets of his client, a lawyer should reveal to appropriate authorities any knowledge he may have of such improper conduct.

EC 8-6 Judges and administrative officials having adjudicatory powers ought to be persons of integrity, competence, and suitable temperament. Generally, lawyers are qualified, by personal observation or investigation, to evaluate the qualifications of persons seeking or being considered for such public offices, and for this reason they have a special responsibility to aid in the selection of only those who are qualified.[6] It is the duty of

---

[1] ". . . [Another] task of the great lawyer is to do his part individually and as a member of the organized bar to improve his profession, the courts, and the law. As President Theodore Roosevelt aptly put it, 'Every man owes some of his time to the upbuilding of the profession to which he belongs.' Indeed, this obligation is one of the great things which distinguishes a profession from a business. The soundness and the necessity of President Roosevelt's admonition insofar as it relates to the legal profession cannot be doubted. The advances in natural science and technology are so startling and the velocity of change in business and in social life is so great that the law along with the other social sciences, and even human life itself, is in grave danger of being extinguished by new gods of its own invention if it does not awake from its lethargy. Vanderbilt, *The Five Functions of the Lawyer: Service to Clients and the Public*, 40 A.B.A.J. 31, 31–32 (1954).

[2] See ABA Canon 29; Cf. Cheatham, *The Lawyer's Role and Surroundings*, 25 Rocky Mt.L.Rev. 405, 406–07 (1953).
"The lawyer tempted by repose should recall the heavy costs paid by his profession when needed legal reform has to be accomplished through the initiative of public-spirited laymen. Where change must be thrust from without upon an unwilling Bar, the public's least flattering picture of the lawyer seems confirmed. The lawyer concerned for the standing of his profession will, therefore, interest himself actively in the improvement of the law. In doing so he will not only help to maintain confidence in the Bar, but will have the satisfaction of meeting a responsibility inhering in the nature of his calling." *Professional Responsibility: Report of the Joint Conference*, 44 A.B.A.J. 1159, 1217 (1958).

[3] See Stayton, *Cum Honore Officium*, 19 Tex.B.J. 765, 766 (1956); *Professional Responsibility: Report of the Joint Conference*, 44 A.B.A.J. 1159, 1162 (1958); and Paul, *The Lawyer as a Tax Adviser*, 25 Rocky Mt.L.Rev. 412, 433–34 (1953).

[4] "There are few great figures in the history of the Bar who have not concerned themselves with the reform and improvement of the law. The special obligation of the profession with respect to legal reform rests on considerations too obvious to require enumeration. Certainly it is the lawyer who has both the best chance to know when the law is working badly and the special competence to put it in order." *Professional Responsibility: Report of the Joint Conference*, 44 A.B.A.J. 1159, 1217 (1958).

[5] "Rule 14. . . . A member of the State Bar shall not communicate with, or appear before, a public officer, board, committee or body, in his professional capacity, without first disclosing that he is an attorney representing interests that may be affected by action of such officer, board, committee or body." Cal.Business and Professions Code § 6076 (West 1962).

[6] See ABA Canon 2.
"Lawyers are better able than laymen to appraise accurately the qualifications of candidates for judicial office. It is proper that they should make that appraisal known to the voters in a proper and dignified manner. A lawyer may with propriety endorse a candidate for judicial office and seek like endorsement from other lawyers. But

CODE OF PROFESSIONAL RESPONSIBILITY

lawyers to endeavor to prevent political considerations from outweighing judicial fitness in the selection of judges. Lawyers should protest earnestly against the appointment or election of those who are unsuited for the bench and should strive to have elected [7] or appointed thereto only those who are willing to forego pursuits, whether of a business, political, or other nature, that may interfere with the free and fair consideration of questions presented for adjudication. Adjudicatory officials, not being wholly free to defend themselves, are entitled to receive the support of the bar against unjust criticism.[8] While a lawyer as a citizen has a right to criticize such officials publicly,[9] he should be certain of the merit of his complaint, use appropriate language, and avoid petty criticisms, for unrestrained and intemperate statements tend to lessen public confidence in our legal system.[10] Criticisms motivated by reasons other than a desire to improve the legal system are not justified.

EC 8-7 Since lawyers are a vital part of the legal system, they should be persons of integrity, of professional skill, and of dedication to the improvement of the system. Thus a lawyer should aid in establishing, as well as enforcing, standards of conduct adequate to protect the public by insuring that those who practice law are qualified to do so.

EC 8-8 Lawyers often serve as legislators or as holders of other public offices. This is highly desirable, as lawyers are uniquely qualified to make significant contributions to the improvement of the legal system. A lawyer who is a public officer, whether full or part-time, should not engage in activities in which his personal or professional interests are or foreseeably may be in conflict with his official duties.[11]

EC 8-9 The advancement of our legal system is of vital importance in maintaining the rule of law and in facilitating orderly changes; therefore, lawyers should encourage, and should aid in making, needed changes and improvements.

DISCIPLINARY RULES

DR 8-101 Action as a Public Official.

(A) A lawyer who holds public office shall not:

(1) Use his public position to obtain, or attempt to obtain, a special advantage in legislative matters for himself or for a client under circumstances where he knows or it is obvious that such action is not in the public interest.

(2) Use his public position to influence, or attempt to influence, a tribunal to act in favor of himself or of a client.

---

the lawyer who endorses a judicial candidate or seeks that endorsement from other lawyers should be actuated by a sincere belief in the superior qualifications of the candidate for judicial service and not by personal or selfish motives; and a lawyer should not use or attempt to use the power or prestige of the judicial office to secure such endorsement. On the other hand, the lawyer whose endorsement is sought, if he believes the candidate lacks the essential qualifications for the office or believes the opposing candidate is better qualified, should have the courage and moral stamina to refuse the request for endorsement." *ABA Opinion* 189 (1938).

[7] "[W]e are of the opinion that, whenever a candidate for judicial office merits the endorsement and support of lawyers, the lawyers may make financial contributions toward the campaign if its cost, when reasonably conducted, exceeds that which the candidate would be expected to bear personally." *ABA Opinion* 226 (1941).

[8] See ABA Canon 1.

[9] "Citizens have a right under our constitutional system to criticize governmental officials and agencies. Courts are not, and should not be, immune to such criticism." Konigsberg v. State Bar of California, 353 U.S. 252, 269 (1957).

[10] "[E]very lawyer, worthy of respect, realizes that public confidence in our courts is the cornerstone of our governmental structure, and will refrain from unjustified attack on the character of the judges, while recognizing the duty to denounce and expose a corrupt or dishonest judge." Kentucky State Bar Ass'n v. Lewis, 282 S.W.2d 321, 326 (Ky. 1955).

"We should be the last to deny that Mr. Meeker has the right to uphold the honor of the profession and to expose without fear or favor corrupt or dishonest conduct in the profession, whether the conduct be that of a judge or not. . . . However, this Canon [29] does not permit one to make charges which are false and untrue and unfounded in fact. When one's fancy leads him to make false charges, attacking the character and integrity of others, he does so at his peril. He should not do so without adequate proof of his charges and he is certainly not authorized to make careless, untruthful and vile charges against his professional brethren." In re Meeker, 76 N.M. 354, 364–65, 414 P.2d 862, 869 (1966), *appeal dismissed*, 385 U.S. 449, 17 L.Ed.2d 510, 87 S.Ct. 613 (1967).

[11] "*Opinions 16, 30, 34, 77, 118* and *134* relate to Canon 6, and pass on questions concerning the propriety of the conduct of an attorney who is a public officer, in representing private interests adverse to those of the public body which he represents. The principle applied in those opinions is that an attorney holding public office should avoid all conduct which might lead the layman to conclude that the attorney is utilizing his public position to further his professional success or personal interests." *ABA Opinion* 192 (1939).

"The next question is whether a lawyer-member of a legislative body may appear as counsel or co-counsel at hearings before a zoning board of appeals, or similar tribunal, created by the legislative group of which he is a member. We are of the opinion that he may practice before fact-finding officers, hearing bodies and commissioners, since under our views he may appear as counsel in the courts where his municipality is a party. Decisions made at such hearings are usually subject to administrative review by the courts upon the record there made. It would be inconsistent to say that a lawyer-member of a legislative body could not participate in a hearing at which the record is made, but could appear thereafter when the cause is heard by the courts on administrative review. This is subject to an important exception. He should not appear as counsel where the matter is subject to review by the legislative body of which he is a member. . . . We are of the opinion that where a lawyer does so appear there would be conflict of interests between his duty as an advocate for his client on the one hand and the obligation to his governmental unit on the other." In re Becker, 16 Ill.2d 488, 494–95, 158 N.E.2d 753, 756–57 (1959).

Cf. *ABA Opinions* 186 (1938), 136 (1935), 118 (1934), and 77 (1932).

CODE OF PROFESSIONAL RESPONSIBILITY

(3) Accept any thing of value from any person when the lawyer knows or it is obvious that the offer is for the purpose of influencing his action as a public official.

DR 8-102 Statements Concerning Judges and Other Adjudicatory Officers.[12]

(A) A lawyer shall not knowingly make false statements of fact concerning the qualifications of a candidate for election or appointment to a judicial office.

(B) A lawyer shall not knowingly make false accusations against a judge or other adjudicatory officer.

CANON 9

A Lawyer Should Avoid Even the Appearance of Professional Impropriety

ETHICAL CONSIDERATIONS

EC 9-1 Continuation of the American concept that we are to be governed by rules of law requires that the people have faith that justice can be obtained through our legal system.[1] A lawyer should promote public confidence in our system and in the legal profession.[2]

EC 9-2 Public confidence in law and lawyers may be eroded by irresponsible or improper conduct of a lawyer. On occasion, ethical conduct of a lawyer may appear to laymen to be unethical. In order to avoid misunderstandings and hence to maintain confidence, a lawyer should fully and promptly inform his client of material developments in the matters being handled for the client. While a lawyer should guard against otherwise proper conduct that has a tendency to diminish public confidence in the legal system or in the legal profession, his duty to clients or to the public should never be subordinate merely because the full discharge of his obligation may be misunderstood or may tend to subject him or the legal profession to criticism. When explicit ethical guidance does not exist, a lawyer should determine his conduct by acting in a manner that promotes public confidence in the integrity and efficiency of the legal system and the legal profession.[3]

EC 9-3 After a lawyer leaves judicial office or other public employment, he should not accept employment in connection with any matter in which he had substantial responsibility prior to his leaving, since to accept employment would give the appearance of impropriety even if none exists.[4]

EC 9-4 Because the very essence of the legal system is to provide procedures by which matters can be presented in an impartial manner so that they may be decided solely upon the merits, any statement or suggestion by a lawyer that he can or would attempt to circumvent those procedures is detrimental to the legal system and tends to undermine public confidence in it.

EC 9-5 Separation of the funds of a client from those of his lawyer not only serves to protect the client but also avoids even the appearance of impropriety, and therefore commingling of such funds should be avoided.

EC 9-6 Every lawyer owes a solemn duty to uphold the integrity and honor of his profession; to encourage respect of the law and for the courts and the judges thereof; to observe the Code of Professional Responsibility; to act as a member of a learned profession, one dedicated to public service; to cooperate with his brother lawyers in supporting the organized bar through the devoting of his time, efforts, and financial support as his professional standing and ability reasonably permit; to conduct himself so as to reflect credit on the legal profession and to inspire the confidence, respect, and trust of his clients and of the public; and to strive to avoid not only professional impropriety but also the appearance of impropriety.[5]

---

[12] Cf. ABA Canons 1 and 2.

[1] "Integrity is the very breath of justice. Confidence in our law, our courts, and in the administration of justice is our supreme interest. No practice must be permitted to prevail which invites towards the administration of justice a doubt or distrust of its integrity." Erwin M. Jennings Co. v. DiGenova, 107 Conn. 491, 499, 141 A. 866, 868 (1928).

[2] "A lawyer should never be reluctant or too proud to answer unjustified criticism of his profession, of himself, or of his brother lawyer. He should guard the reputation of his profession and of his brothers as zealously as he guards his own." Rochelle and Payne, The Struggle for Public Understanding, 25 Texas B.J. 109, 162 (1962).

[3] See ABA Canon 29.

[4] See ABA Canon 36.

[5] "As said in Opinion 49 of the Committee on Professional Ethics and Grievances of the American Bar Association, page 134: 'An attorney should not only avoid impropriety but should avoid the appearance of impropriety.'" State ex rel, Nebraska State Bar Ass'n v. Richards, 165 Neb. 80, 93, 84 N.W.2d 136, 145 (1957).

"It would also be preferable that such contribution [to the campaign of a candidate for judicial office] be made to a campaign committee rather than to the candidate personally. In so doing, possible appearances of impropriety would be reduced to a minimum." ABA Opinion 226 (1941).

"The lawyer assumes high duties, and has imposed upon him grave responsibilities. He may be the means of much good or much mischief. Interests of vast magnitude are entrusted to him; confidence is reposed in him; life, liberty, character and property should be protected by him. He should guard, with jealous watchfulness, his own reputation, as well as that of his profession." People ex rel. Cutler v. Ford, 54 Ill. 520, 522 (1870), and also quoted in State Board of Law Examiners v. Sheldon, 43 Wyo. 522, 526, 7 P.2d 226, 227 (1932).

See ABA Opinion 150 (1936).

CODE OF PROFESSIONAL RESPONSIBILITY

DISCIPLINARY RULES

DR 9-101 Avoiding Even the Appearance of Impropriety.[6]

(A) A lawyer shall not accept private employment in a matter upon the merits of which he has acted in a judicial capacity.[7]

(B) A lawyer shall not accept private employment in a matter in which he had substantial responsibility while he was a public employee.[8]

(C) A lawyer shall not state or imply that he is able to influence improperly or upon irrelevant grounds any tribunal, legislative body,[9] or public official.

---

[6] *Cf.* Code of Professional Responsibility, EC 5-6.

[7] *See ABA* Canon 36.

"It is the duty of the judge to rule on questions of law and evidence in misdemeanor cases and examinations in felony cases. That duty calls for impartial and uninfluenced judgment, regardless of the effect on those immediately involved or others who may, directly or indirectly, be affected. Discharge of that duty might be greatly interfered with if the judge, in another capacity, were permitted to hold himself out to employment by those who are to be, or who may be, brought to trial in felony cases, even though he did not conduct the examination. His private interests as a lawyer in building up his clientele, his duty as such zealously to espouse the cause of his private clients and to defend against charges of crime brought by law-enforcement agencies of which he is a part, might prevent, or even destroy, that unbiased judicial judgment which is so essential in the administration of justice.

"In our opinion, acceptance of a judgeship with the duties of conducting misdemeanor trials, and examinations in felony cases to determine whether those accused should be bound over for trial in a higher court, ethically bars the judge from acting as attorney for the defendants upon such trial, whether they were examined by him or by some other judge. Such a practice would not only diminish public confidence in the administration of justice in both courts, but would produce serious conflict between the private interests of the judge as a lawyer, and of his clients, and his duties as a judge in adjudicating important phases of criminal processes in other cases. The public and private duties would be incompatible. The prestige of the judicial office would be diverted to private benefit, and the judicial office would be demeaned thereby." *ABA Opinion* 242 (1942).

"A lawyer, who has previously occupied a judicial position or acted in a judicial capacity, should refrain from accepting employment in any matter involving the same facts as were involved in any specific question which he acted upon in a judicial capacity and, for the same reasons, should also refrain from accepting any employment which might reasonably appear to involve the same facts." *ABA Opinion* 49 (1931).

See *ABA Opinion* 110 (1934).

[8] *See ABA Opinions* 135 (1935) and 134 (1935); *cf.* ABA Canon 36 and *ABA Opinions* 39 (1931) and 26 (1930). *But see ABA Opinion* 37 (1931).

[9] "[A statement by a governmental department or agency with regard to a lawyer resigning from its staff that includes a laudation of his legal ability] carries implications, probably not founded in fact, that the lawyer's acquaintance and previous relations with the personnel of the administrative agencies of the government place him in an advantageous position in practicing before such agencies. So to imply would not only represent what prob-

DR 9-102 Preserving Identity of Funds and Property of a Client.[10]

(A) All funds of clients paid to a lawyer or law firm, other than advances for costs and expenses, shall be deposited in one or more identifiable bank accounts maintained in the state in which the law office is situated and no funds belonging to the lawyer or law firm shall be deposited therein except as follows:

(1) Funds reasonably sufficient to pay bank charges may be deposited therein.

(2) Funds belonging in part to a client and in part presently or potentially to the lawyer or law firm must be deposited therein, but the portion belonging to the lawyer or law firm may be withdrawn when due unless the right of the lawyer or law firm to receive it is disputed by the client, in which event the disputed portion shall not be withdrawn until the dispute is finally resolved.

(B) A lawyer shall:

(1) Promptly notify a client of the receipt of his funds, securities, or other properties.

(2) Identify and label securities and properties of a client promptly upon receipt and place them in a safe deposit box or other place of safekeeping as soon as practicable.

(3) Maintain complete records of all funds, securities, and other properties of a client coming into the possession of the

---

ably is untrue, but would be highly reprehensible." *ABA Opinion* 184 (1938).

[10] *See ABA* Canon 11.

"Rule 9. . . . A member of the State Bar shall not commingle the money or other property of a client with his own; and he shall promptly report to the client the receipt by him of all money and other property belonging to such client. Unless the client otherwise directs in writing, he shall promptly deposit his client's funds in a bank or trust company . . . in a bank account separate from his own account and clearly designated as 'Clients' Funds Account' or 'Trust Funds Account' or words of similar import. Unless the client otherwise directs in writing, securities of a client in bearer form shall be kept by the attorney in a safe deposit box at a bank or trust company, . . . which safe deposit box shall be clearly designated as 'Clients' Account' or 'Trust Account' or words of similar import, and be separate from the attorney's own safe deposit box." Cal.Business and Professions Code § 6076 (West 1962).

"[C]ommingling is committed when a client's money is intermingled with that of his attorney and its separate identity lost so that it may be used for the attorney's personal expenses or subjected to claims of his creditors. . . . The rule against commingling was adopted to provide against the probability in some cases, the possibility in many cases, and the danger in all cases that such commingling will result in the loss of clients' money." Black v. State Bar, 57 Cal.2d 219, 225–26, 368 P.2d 118, 122, 18 Cal.Rptr. 518, 522 (1962).

CODE OF PROFESSIONAL RESPONSIBILITY

lawyer and render appropriate accounts to his client regarding them.

(4) Promptly pay or deliver to the client as requested by a client the funds, securities, or other properties in the possession of the lawyer which the client is entitled to receive.

DEFINITIONS*

As used in the Disciplinary Rules of the Code of Professional Responsibility:

(1) "Differing interests" include every interest that will adversely affect either the judgment or the loyalty of a lawyer to a client, whether it be a conflicting, inconsistent, diverse, or other interest.

---

* "Confidence" and "secret" are defined in DR 4-101(A).

(2) "Law firm" includes a professional legal corporation.

(3) "Person" includes a corporation, an association, a trust, a partnership, and any other organization or legal entity.

(4) "Professional legal corporation" means a corporation, or an association treated as a corporation, authorized by law to practice law for profit.

(5) "State" includes the District of Columbia, Puerto Rico, and other federal territories and possessions.

(6) "Tribunal" includes all courts and all other adjudicatory bodies.

(7) "A bar association representative of the general bar" includes a bar association of specialists as referred to in DR 2-105(A)(1) or (4).

INDEX TO CODE OF PROFESSIONAL RESPONSIBILITY

References are to Pages

A

Acceptance of Employment.
See Employment, acceptance of.
Acquiring interest in litigation.
See Adverse effect on professional judgment, interests of lawyer.
Address change, notification of, 552.
Administrative agencies and tribunals,
    former employee, rejection of employment by, 587, 588.
    improper influences on, 579, 584.
    representation of client before, generally, 575–584, 585.
Admiralty practitioner, 547, 555
Admission to practice,
    duty of lawyers as to applicants, 541, 542.
    requirements for, 541, 542.
Advancing funds to clients, 564, 568.
    court costs, 564, 568.
    investigation expenses, 564, 568.
    litigation expenses, 564, 568.
    medical examination, 564, 568.
    personal expenses, 569.
Adversary system, duty of lawyer to, 576, 584.
Adverse effect on professional judgment of lawyer, 563–569.
    desires of third persons, 567, 568, 569.
    interests of lawyer, 563–565, 568.
    interests of other clients, 565–567, 569.
Adverse legal authority, duty to reveal, 577, 581.
Advertising, 545, 551.
See also Name, use of.
    announcement of change of association, 552.
    announcement of change of firm name, 552.
    announcement of change of office address, 552.

Advertising—Cont'd
    announcement of establishment of law office, 552.
    announcement of office opening, 552.
    announcement of organization of which lawyer is officer or director, inclusion of name and profession of lawyer in, 551.
    availability as associate, 556.
    availability as consultant, 556.
    bar association, by, 543–544.
    books written by lawyer, 551.
    building directory, 546, 552.
    cards,
        announcement, professional, 552.
        professional, 546, 552.
    city directory, 551–552.
    commercial publicity, 551.
    compensation for, 551.
    directories,
        building, 546, 552.
        city, 551–552.
        legal, 552–553.
        telephone, 552–553.
    display, 551.
    jurisdictional limitations of members of firm, required notice of, 554.
    law lists, 552, 553.
    law office, identification of, 552.
    law office establishment, 552.
    legal directories, 552, 553.
    legal documents, 551.
    legal journals, 556.
    legal notices, 551.
    letterheads,
        of clients, 552.
        of law firm, 552.
        of lawyer, 552, 553, 554, 555.
    limited practice, 555–556.
    magazine, 551.
    name, 551.

592   CODE OF PROFESSIONAL RESPONSIBILITY
References are to Pages

Advertising—Cont'd
See Name, use of.
  newspaper, 551.
  news story, 551.
  office, identification of, 552.
  office address change, 552.
  office building directory, 546, 552.
  office sign, 552.
  political, 551.
  public notices, 551.
  radio, 551.
  reasons for regulating, 545, 546.
  sign, 552.
  specialization, 547, 555, 556.
  telephone directory, 551–553.
  television, 551.
  textbook, 551.
  treatises, 551.
Advice by lawyer to secure legal services, 544, 545, 555.
  client, former or regular, 545, 555.
  close friend, 545, 555.
  employment resulting from, 545, 555.
  motivation, effect of, 544, 545.
  other laymen parties to class action, 555.
  relative, 545, 555.
  volunteered, 544, 545, 555.
  within permissible legal service programs, 555.
Advocacy, professional, 571–584.
Aiding unauthorized practice of law, 559, 560.
Ambulance chasing.
See Recommendation of professional employment.
Announcement card.
See Advertising, cards, announcement.
Appearance of impropriety, avoiding, 564, 587–588.
Appearance of lawyer.
See Administrative agencies, representation of client before; Courts, representation of client before; Legislature, representation of client before; Witness, lawyer acting as.
Applicant for bar admission.
See Admission to practice.
Arbitrator, lawyer acting as, 567.
Argument,
  before jury, 577, 580, 582.
  before legislature, 575.
  before tribunal, 577, 580.
Associates of lawyer, duty to control, 539, 558, 561, 562, 578.

Association of counsel.
See also Co-counsel; Division of legal fees.
  client's suggestion of, 565.
  lawyer's suggestion of, 565.
Assumed name.
See Name, use of, assumed name.
Attempts to exert personal influence on tribunal, 578, 579, 584.
Attorney-client privilege, 558, 561.
See also Confidences of client; Secrets of client.
Attorney's lien.
See Fee for legal services, collection of.
Availability of counsel, 543, 547, 549, 550.

B

Bank accounts for clients' funds, 588.
Bar applicant.
See Admission to practice.
Bar associations,
  advertising by, 544.
    bar examiners, assisting, 541.
      disciplinary authority, assisting, 541, 542.
    legal service programs, 554, 555.
  minimum fee schedule.
See Fee for legal services, determination of minimum fee schedule.
Bank charges on clients' accounts, 588.
Barratry.
See Advice by lawyer to secure legal services; Recommendation of professional employment.
Bequest by client to lawyer, 564.
Best efforts.
See Zeal.
Bounds of law,
  difficulty of ascertaining, 572.
  duty to observe, 572, 573.
  generally, 571–584.
Bribes.
See Gifts to tribunal officer or employee by lawyer.
Building directory.
See Advertising, building directory.
Business card.
See Advertising, cards, professional.

C

Calling card.
See Advertising, cards, professional.

Candidate.
See Political activity.
Canons, purpose and function of, 540.
Card.
See Advertising, cards.
Change of office address.
See Advertising, announcement of change of office address.
Change of association.
See Advertising, announcement of change of association.
Change of firm name.
See Advertising, announcement of change of firm name.
Character requirements, 541, 542.
Class action.
See Advice by lawyer to secure legal services, parties to legal action.
Clients.
See also Employment; Adverse effect on professional judgment of lawyer; Fee for legal services; Indigent parties, representation of; Unpopular party, representation of.
   appearance as witness for, 564, 565, 568.
   attorney-client privilege, 558, 561.
   commingling of funds of, 588.
   confidence of, 560-562.
   counselling, 573, 574, 580.
   property, protection of, 588.
   restraint of, 578.
   secrets of, 560-562.
Co-counsel.
See also Association of counsel.
   division of fee with, 556-557.
   inability to work with, 558.
Commercial publicity.
See Advertising, commercial publicity.
Commingling of funds, 588.
Communications with one of adverse interests, 581.
   judicial officers, 579, 584.
   jurors, 578-580, 584.
   opposing party, 576, 581.
   veniremen, 578, 584.
   witnesses, 577, 578, 584.
Compensation for recommendation of employment, prohibition against, 554.
Competence, Mental.
See Instability, mental or emotional; Mental competence of client, effect on representation.
Competence, professional, 550, 570, 571.

Confidences of client, 560-562.
Conflicting interests.
See Adverse effect on professional judgment of lawyer.
Consent of client, requirement of acceptance of employment though interests conflict, 563, 568, 569.
   acceptance of value from third person, 548, 569.
   advice requested from another lawyer, 561.
   aggregate settlement of claims, 569.
   association of lawyer, 548, 556.
   foregoing legal action, 574.
   multiple representation, 566, 569.
   revelation of client's confidences and secrets, 561, 562.
   use of client's confidences and secrets, 561, 562.
   withdrawal from employment, 558.
Consent of tribunal to lawyer's withdrawal, requirement of, 557.
Consultant.
See Advertising, availability as consultant.
Contingent fee, propriety of,
   in civil actions, 548, 564, 568.
   in criminal actions, 548, 556.
   in domestic relation cases, 558.
Continuing legal education programs, 570.
Contract of employment,
   fee provisions, desirability of writing, 548.
   restrictive covenant in, 557.
Controversy over fee, avoiding, 548.
Copyright practitioner, 547, 555.
Corporation, lawyer employed by, 567, 569.
Corporation, professional legal.
See Professional legal corporation.
Counsel, designation as,
   "General Counsel" designation, 552.
   "Of Counsel" designation, 552.
Counseling.
See Client, counseling.
Courts.
See also Consent of tribunal to lawyer's withdrawal, requirement of; Evidence, conduct regarding; Trial tactics.
   appointment of lawyer as counsel, 549, 550.
   courtesy, known customs of, 580, 582.

CODE OF PROFESSIONAL RESPONSIBILITY
References are to Pages

Courts—Cont'd
   personal influence, prohibitions against exerting, 579, 584.
   representation of client before, 576–582.

Criminal conduct,
   as basis for discipline of lawyer, 542.
   duty to reveal information as to, 542, 562.
   providing counsel for those accused of, 549, 550.

Criticism of judges and administrative officials, 585, 586, 587.

Cross-examination of witness.
   See Witnesses, communications with.

D

Deceased lawyer,
   payment to estate of, 559, 560.
   use of name by law firm, 546, 553.

De facto specialization, 547.

Defender, public.
   See Public defender office, working with.

Defense against accusation by client,
   privilege to disclose confidences and secrets, 562.

Defense of those accused of crime, 549, 550.

Delegation by lawyer of tasks, 558.

Desires of third parties, duty to avoid influence of, 567, 569.

Differing interests, 565, 589.
   See also Adverse effect on professional judgment of lawyer.

Directory listing.
   See Advertising, directories.

Disciplinary procedures, 540.

Disciplinary rules,
   application of, 540.
   purpose and function of, 540.

Disciplinary sanction, 540.

Discipline of lawyer, grounds for,
   advancement of funds to client improper, 568–569.
   advertising, improper, 551, 554.
   associates, failure to exercise reasonable care toward, 562.
   bribery of legal officials, 584.
   circumvention of disciplinary rule, 542.
   clients' funds, mismanagement of, 588.
   communication with adverse party, improper, 581.
   communication with jurors, improper, 584.

Discipline of lawyer, grounds for—C't'd
   confidential information, disclosure of, 562.
   conflicting interests, representation of, 568–570.
   crime of moral turpitude, 542.
   criminal conduct, 542, 581.
   differing interests, improper representation of, 568, 570.
   disregard of tribunal ruling, 581.
   division of fee, improper, 556, 560.
   employees, failure to exercise reasonable care toward, 562.
   evidence, false or misleading, use of, 580.
   extra judicial statement, improper, 582–584.
   failure to act competently, 571.
   failure to act zealously, 580.
   failure to disclose information concerning another lawyer or judge, 543.
   failure to disclose information to tribunal, 581.
   fair trial, requirement of, 540.
   false accusations, 587.
   false statement in bar application, 542.
   fees,
      charging contingent fee in criminal case, 556.
      charging illegal or clearly excessive, 556.
      failure to return unearned, 557.
   further application of unqualified bar applicant, 542.
   guaranty of financial assistance, 568–569.
   holding out as a specialist, 555, 556.
   holding out as having limited practice, 555, 556.
   illegal conduct, 542, 581.
   improper argument before tribunal, 581, 582.
   institution of criminal charges, 581.
   investigation of jurors, 584.
   malpractice, 571.
   moral turpitude, crime of, 542.
   penalties imposed, 540.
   public office, improper use of, 586, 587.
   publicity, improper, 551.
   recommendation of professional employment, prohibited, 554, 555.
   restrictive covenant, entering prohibited, 557.

CODE OF PROFESSIONAL RESPONSIBILITY
References are to Pages

Discipline of lawyer, grounds for—C't'd
  secrets, disclosure of, 561, 562.
  solicitation of business, 555.
  specialization, notice of, 555, 556.
  suggestion of need of legal services, prohibited, 554, 555.
  unauthorized practice of law, 560.
    aiding laymen in, 560.
  violation of disciplinary rule, 542.
  withdrawal, improper, 557–558.
Disclosure of improper conduct,
  of another lawyer, 543.
  of bar applicant, 542.
  of judge, 543.
  toward juror or veniremen, 578, 584.
Discretion of government lawyer, exercise of, 581.
Discussion of pending litigation with news media.
  See Trial publicity.
Diverse interests.
  See Adverse effect on professional judgment of lawyer.
Division of legal fees,
  consent of client, when required for, 548, 556, 557.
  reasonableness of total fee, requirement of, 548, 556.
  with associated lawyer, 548, 556.
  with estate of deceased lawyer, 560.
  with laymen, 560.
Dual practice, holding out as being engaged in prohibited, 554.

E

Education,
  continuing legal education programs, 570.
  of laymen to recognize legal problems, 545, 585.
  of laymen to select lawyers, 545, 585.
  requirement of bar for applicant, 541.
Elections.
  See Political activity.
Emotional instability.
  See Instability, mental or emotional.
Employees of lawyer,
  delegation of tasks, 558.
  duty of lawyer to control, 539, 558, 561, 562, 578.
Employment.
  See also Advice by lawyer to secure legal services; Recommendation of professional employment.

Employment—Cont'd
  acceptance of,
    generally, 550.
    indigent client, on behalf of, 549, 550.
    instances when improper, 545, 550, 555, 557, 561, 563, 564–570, 587, 588.
    unpopular cause, on behalf of, 550.
    when unable to render competent service, 550, 570.
  contract of,
    desirability of, 548.
    restrictive covenant in, 557.
  public, retirement from, 587, 588.
  rejection of, 550, 555, 557, 561, 563, 564–570, 587, 588.
  when arbitrator or mediator, 567.
  withdrawal from,
    generally, 551, 557–558, 564–565, 565–566, 567, 568, 569, 574.
    harm to client, avoidance of, 551, 557, 565, 566.
    mandatory withdrawal, 557, 568, 569.
    permissive withdrawal, 557, 558, 568, 574.
    refund of unearned fee paid in advance, requirement of, 551, 557.
    tribunal, consent to, 549, 557.
Estate of deceased lawyer.
  See Division of legal fees, with estate of deceased lawyer.
Ethical considerations, purpose and function of, 540.
Evidence, conduct regarding, 577, 580, 582.
Excessive fee.
  See, Fee for legal services, amount of, excessive.
Expenses of client, advancing or guaranteeing payment of, 564, 568, 569.

F

Fee for legal services,
  adequate fee, need for, 547.
  agreement as to, 548, 556.
  amount of,
    excessive, clearly, 556.
    reasonableness, desirability of, 547.
  collection of,
    avoiding litigation with client, 548.
    client's secrets, use of in collecting or establishing, 562.
    liens, use of, 564, 568.
  contingent fee, 548, 556, 564, 568.

596 CODE OF PROFESSIONAL RESPONSIBILITY

Fee for legal services—Cont'd
  contract as to, desirability of written, 548.
  controversy over, avoiding, 548.
  determination of, factors to consider,
    ability of lawyer, 547, 548, 556.
    amount involved, 556.
    customary, 556.
    effort required, 556.
    employment, likelihood of preclusion of other, 556.
    experience of lawyer, 548, 556.
    fee customarily charged in locality, 556.
    fee schedule, 548.
    interests of client and lawyer, 547.
    labor required, 556.
    minimum fee schedule, 556.
    nature of employment, 548, 556.
    question involved, difficulty and novelty of, 556.
    relationship with client, professional, 556.
    reputation of lawyer, 548, 556.
    responsibility assumed by lawyer, 548.
    results obtained, 548, 556.
    skill requisite to services, 556.
    time required, 548, 556.
    type of fee, fixed or contingent, 556.
  division of, 548, 556, 560.
  establishment of fee, use of client's confidences and secrets, 562.
  excessive fee, 547, 556.
  explanation of, 548.
  illegal fee, prohibition against, 556.
  persons able to pay reasonable fee, 547, 548.
  persons only able to pay a partial fee, 546, 548.
  persons without means to pay a fee, 547–549.
  reasonable fee, rationale against over charging, 547.
  rebate, propriety of accepting, 548, 569.
  refund of unearned portion to client, 557.
Fee of lawyer referral service, propriety of paying, 554.
Felony.
See Discipline of lawyer, grounds for, Illegal conduct.
Firm name.
See Name, use of, firm name.

Framework of law.
See Bounds of law.
Frivolous position avoiding, 573, 580.
Funds of client, protection of, 588, 589.
Future conduct of client, counseling as to.
See Clients, counseling.

G

"General counsel" designation, 552.
Gift to lawyer by client, 564.
Gifts to tribunal officer or employee by lawyer, 579, 584.
Government legal agencies, working with, 554, 555.
Grievance committee.
See Bar associations, disciplinary authority, assisting.
Guaranteeing payment of client's costs and expenses, 564, 568–569.

H

Harassment, duty to avoid litigation involving, 550, 557.
Holding out,
  as being engaged in both law and another field, 554.
  as limiting practice, 547, 555.
  as partnership, 547, 553.
  as specialist, 547, 555, 556.

I

Identity of client, duty to reveal, 575, 581, 585.
Illegal conduct, as cause for discipline, 542, 580.
Impartiality of tribunal, aiding in the, 576, 577–579, 581–584.
Improper influences,
  gift or loan to judicial officer, 579, 584.
  on judgment of lawyer.
See Adverse effect on professional judgment of lawyer.
Improvement of legal system, 585–587.
Incompetence, mental.
See Instability, mental or emotional; Mental competence of client.
Incompetence, professional.
See Competence, professional.
Independent professional judgment, duty to preserve, 563–570.

CODE OF PROFESSIONAL RESPONSIBILITY

References are to Pages

Indigent parties,
  provision of legal services to, 547, 549.
  representation of, 547, 549, 550.
Instability, mental or emotional,
  of bar applicant, 542.
  of lawyer, 542, 558
  recognition of rehabilitation, 542.
Integrity of legal profession, maintaining, 539, 540, 541, 542, 586.
Intent of client, as factor in giving advice, 573.
Interests of lawyer.
  See Adverse effect on professional judgment of lawyer, interests of lawyer.
Interests of other client.
  See Adverse effect on professional judgment of lawyer, interests of other clients.
Interests of third person.
  See Adverse effect on professional judgment of lawyer, desires of third persons.
Intermediary, prohibition against use of, 567, 568, 569.
Interview,
  with opposing party, 576, 581.
  with news media, 578–579, 582–584.
  with witness, 577–578, 584.
Investigation expenses, advancing or guaranteeing payment, 564, 568–569.

J

Judges,
  false statements concerning, 587.
  improper influences on,
    gifts to, 579, 584.
    private communication with, 579, 584.
  misconduct toward,
    criticisms of, 586.
    disobedience of orders, 576–577, 581.
    false statement regarding, 587.
  name in partnership name, use of, 547, 553.
  retirement from bench, 587, 588.
  selection of, 585–586.
Judgment of lawyer.
  See Adverse effect on professional judgment of lawyer.
Jury,
  arguments before, 577, 580, 582.
  investigation of members, 578, 584.
  misconduct of, duty to reveal, 578, 584.
  questioning members of after their dismissal, 578, 584.

K

Knowledge of intended crime, revealing, 562.

L

Law firm.
  See Partnership.
Law lists.
  See Advertising, law lists.
Law office.
  See Partnership.
Law school, working with legal aid office or public defender office sponsored by, 554, 555.
Lawyer-client privilege.
  See Attorney-client privilege.
Lawyer referral services,
  fee for listing, propriety of paying, 554.
  listing of type referrals accepted, propriety of, 556.
  request for referrals, propriety of, 554.
  working with, 547, 554.
Laymen.
  See also Unauthorized practice of law.
  need of legal services, 543, 585.
  recognition of legal problems, need to improve, 543, 585.
  selection of lawyer, need to facilitate, 545, 547, 585.
Legal aid offices, working with, 549, 554, 555.
Legal corporation.
  See Professional legal corporation.
Legal directory.
  See Advertising, legal directories.
Legal documents of clients, duty to safeguard, 561, 562.
Legal education programs.
  See Continuing legal education programs.
Legal problems, recognition of by laymen, 543–544, 585.
Legal system, duty to improve, 585–587.
Legislature,
  improper influence upon, 588.
  representation of client before, 575, 585.
  serving as member of, 586.
Letterhead.
  See Advertising, letterheads.
Liability to client, 540, 571.
Licensing of lawyers,
  control of, 559.
  modernization of, 559, 585.

Liens, attorneys', 564, 568.
Limited practice, holding out as having, 547, 555, 556.
Litigation,
  acquiring an interest in, 564, 568.
  expenses of, advancing or guaranteeing payment of, 564, 568–569.
  pending, media discussion of, 578–579, 582–584.
  responsibility for conduct of, 573–574, 580.
  to harass another, duty to avoid, 550, 557.
  to maliciously harm another, duty to avoid, 550, 557.
Living expenses of client, advances to client of, 564, 568–569.
Loan to judicial officer, 579, 584.
Loyalty to client.
See Zeal.
Lump-sum settlements, 569.

M

Mandatory withdrawal.
See Employment, withdrawal from, mandatory.
Mediator, lawyer serving as, 567.
Medical expenses, 564, 568–569.
Mental competence of client, effect on representation, 574.
Mental competence of lawyer.
See Instability, mental or emotional.
Military legal service officers, working with, 554–555.
Minimum fee schedule.
See Fee for legal services, determination of, factors to consider, minimum fee schedule.
Misappropriation,
  confidences of client, 561, 562.
  property of client, 588, 589.
  secrets of client, 561, 562.
Misconduct.
See also Discipline of lawyer.
  of client, 548, 557–558, 562, 578.
  of juror, 578, 584.
  of lawyer, duty to reveal to proper officials, 543.
Misleading advertisement or professional notice, prohibition of, 545–546, 553.
Moral character, requirement of, 541, 542.

Moral factors considered in counseling, 574.
Moral turpitude, crime of as ground for discipline, 542.
Multiple clients, representation of, 561, 565–567, 569.

N

Name, use of,
  assumed name, 546, 553.
  deceased partner's, 546, 553.
  firm name, 546, 553.
  misleading name, 546, 553.
  partners who hold public office, 547, 553.
  predecessor firms, 546, 553.
  proper for law firm, 546, 553.
  proper for lawyer in private practice, 546, 547, 553.
  retired partner, 546, 553.
  trade name, 546, 553.
  withdrawn partner's, 546–547, 553.
Need for legal services, suggestion of.
See Advice by lawyer to secure legal services.
Negligence of lawyer, 571.
Negotiations with opposite party, 576, 581.
Neighborhood law offices, working with, 549, 554, 555.
Newspapers,
  advertising in, 551.
  news releases in, during or pending trial, 578–579, 582–584.
  news stories in, 551.
Non-meritorious position, duty to avoid, 576, 580.
Non-profit organization, legal aid services of, 554–555.
Notices.
See Advertising.

O

Objectives of client, duty to seek, 571–573, 580.
"Of Counsel" designation, 552.
Offensive tactics by lawyer, 580.
Office building directory.
See Advertising, building directory.
Office sign, 552.
Opposing counsel, 564, 576, 580, 581, 582.
Opposing party, communications with, 576, 581.

P

Partnership,
  advertising.
  See Advertising.
  conflicts of interest, 569.
  deceased member,
    payments to estate of, 560.
    use of name, 546, 553.
  dissolved, use of name of, 546, 553.
  holding out as, falsely, 546, 554.
  members licensed in different jurisdictions, 554.
  name, 546, 553.
  nonexistent, holding out falsely, 546, 554.
  non-lawyer, with, 559, 560.
Patent practitioner, 547, 558.
Payment to obtain recommendation or employment, prohibition against, 545, 554.
Pending litigation, discussion of in media, 578–579, 582–584.
Perjury, 573, 577, 580.
Personal interests of lawyer.
See Adverse effect on professional judgment of lawyer, interests of lawyer.
Personal opinion of client's cause, 550.
Phone directory, listing in.
See Advertising, telephone directory.
Political activity, 551, 585, 586.
Political considerations in selection of judges, 585, 586.
Potentially differing interests.
See Adverse effect on professional judgment of lawyer.
Practice of law, unauthorized, 558–560.
Prejudice to right of client, duty to avoid, 551, 557, 576.
Preservation of confidences of client, 560–562.
Preservation of secrets of client, 560–562.
Pressure on lawyer by third person.
See Adverse effect on professional judgment of lawyer.
Privilege, attorney-client.
See Attorney-client privilege.
Procedures, duty to help improve, 585.
Professional card of lawyer.
See Advertising, cards, professional.
Professional impropriety, avoiding appearance of, 564, 587–589.
Professional judgment, duty to protect independence of, 563–570.
Professional legal corporation, 567, 569, 589.
Professional notices.
See Advertising.
Professional status, responsibility not to mislead concerning, 547, 553.
Profit-sharing with lay employees, authorization of, 560.
Property of client, handling, 588–589.
Prosecuting attorney, duty of, 575, 581.
Public defender office, working with, 554, 555.
Public employment, retirement from, 587, 588.
Public office, duty of holder, 585, 586, 587.
Public opinion, irrelevant to acceptance of employment, 550.
Public prosecutor.
See Prosecuting attorney, duty of.
Publication of articles for lay press, 543–544, 545.
Publicity, commercial.
See Advertising, commercial publicity.
Publicity, trial.
See Trial publicity.

Q

Quasi-judicial proceedings, 575.

R

Radio broadcasting.
See Advertising, radio.
Reasonable fee.
See Fee for legal services, amount of.
Rebate, propriety of accepting, 549, 569.
Recognition of legal problems, aiding laymen in, 543–545.
Recommendation of bar applicant, duty of lawyer to satisfy himself that applicant is qualified, 541, 542.
Recommendation of professional employment, 545, 554, 555.
Records of funds, securities, and properties of clients, 588.
Referral service.
See Lawyer referral services.
Refund of unearned fee when withdrawing, duty to give to client, 557.
Regulation of legal profession, 559, 585.
Rehabilitation of bar applicant or lawyer, recognition of, 542.
Representation of multiple clients.
See Adverse effect on professional judgment of lawyer, interest of other clients.

Reputation of lawyer, 545.
Requests for recommendation for employment, 554.
Requirements for bar admission, 541, 542.
Respect for law, 541.
Restricted covenants, propriety of, 557.
Restrictive covenant, 557.
Retention of employment.
See Employment.
Retirement.
See also, Name, use of, retired partner.
 from judicial office, 587, 588.
 from public employment, 587, 588.
 plan for laymen employees', 559, 560.
Revealing of confidences, 560–562.
Revealing of secrets, 560–562.
Revealing to tribunal,
 jury misconduct, 578, 584.
 representative capacity in which appearing, 575.
Runner, prohibition against use of, 554.

S

Sanction for violating disciplinary rules, 540.
Secrets of client, 560–562.
Selection of judges, duty of lawyers, 585, 586.
Selection of lawyer, 545–547, 551–554.
Self-interest of lawyer.
See Adverse effect on professional judgment of lawyer, interests of lawyer.
Self-representation, privilege of, 559.
Settlement agreement, 569.
Solicitation of business, 554, 555.
See also Advertising; Recommendation of professional employment.
Specialist, holding out as, 547, 555, 556.
Specialization,
 admiralty, 547, 555.
 holding out as having, 547, 555, 556.
 patents, 547, 555.
 trademark, 547, 555.
Speeches to lay groups, 544.
State of mind of client, effect of in advising him, 573.
State's attorney.
See Prosecuting attorney.
"Stirring up litigation."
See Advertising; Advice by lawyer to secure legal services; Recommendation of professional employment.
Stockholders of corporation, corporate counsel's allegiance to, 566.

Suit to harass another, duty to avoid, 550, 557.
Suit to maliciously harm another, duty to avoid, 550, 557.
Suggested fee schedule.
See Fees for legal services, determination of minimum fee schedule.
Suggestion of need for legal services.
See Advice by lawyer to secure legal services.
Suppression of evidence, 577, 584.

T

Technical and professional licenses.
See Advertising, law lists.
Telephone directory.
See Advertising, telephone directory.
Television and radio programs.
See Advertising, radio; Advertising, television.
Termination of employment.
See Confidences of client; Employment, withdrawal from.
Third persons, desires of.
See Adverse effect on professional judgment of lawyer, desires of third persons.
Threatening criminal process, 576, 581.
Trademark practitioner, 547, 555.
Tradename.
See Name, use of, trade name.
Trial publicity, 578–579, 582–584.
Trial tactics, 576–584.
Tribunal, representation of client before, 572, 573, 575–582, 584.
Trustee, client naming lawyer as, 564.

U

Unauthorized practice of law.
See also Division of legal fees; Partnership, non-lawyer, with.
 aiding a layman in the prohibited, 558–560.
 distinguished from delegation of tasks to sub-professionals, 558.
 functional meaning of, 558.
 self-representation by layman not included in, 559.
Undignified conduct, duty to avoid, 579, 580.
Unlawful conduct, aiding client in, 573, 580.
Unpopular party, representation of, 550.

Unreasonable fees.
See Fee for legal services, amount of.
Unsolicited advice.
See Advice by lawyer to obtain legal services.

V

Varying interests of clients.
See Adverse effect on professional judgment of a lawyer, interests of other clients.
Veniremen.
See Jury.
Violation of disciplinary rule as cause for discipline, 542.
Violation of law as cause for discipline, 542, 580.
Voluntary gifts by client to lawyer, 564.
Volunteered advice to secure legal services.
See Advice by lawyer to secure legal services.

W

Waiver of position of client, 580.
Will of client gift to lawyer in, 564.
Withdrawal.
See Employment, withdrawal from.
Witness,
   communications with, 577, 578, 584.
   false testimony by, 577.
   lawyer acting as, 564, 565, 568.
   member of lawyer's firm acting as, 568.
   payment to, 578, 584.
Writing for lay publication, avoiding appearance of giving general solution, 545.

Z

Zeal,
   general duty of, 571–574, 580.
   limitations upon, 571, 572, 576–584.

INDEX

References are to Pages

See also Code of Professional Responsibility, 539–589

ACCIDENTS, 98–99.

ACCOUNTANTS, 135–137, 139–140.

ADAMS, JOHN, 93.

ADJUDICATION, 18–22, 331.

ADMINISTRATION OF JUSTICE, 146.

ADMINISTRATION OF LAW, 11, 23, 406–407.
Adversary system in, 37.
Judges' functions, 528–530.
Lawyers' role, 24, 240–241.
Public responsibility, 403–409.

ADMINISTRATIVE AGENCIES
See Government Lawyer.

ADMISSION TO PRACTICE, 17, 149, 487–493.
Bar examinations, 15–17.
Civil disobedience and, 490–493.
Communist and, 498–500.
Due process, 500.
Internship, 474–475.
Moral character, 489–493.
Public responsibility, 404.
Requirements, 191.

ADVERSARY SYSTEM, 6, 11, 28, 36–37, 173, 237, 387, 399.
See also Advocate.
Alternatives, 329–333.
Excessive zeal, 169.
Law administration, 37.
Political trials, 96.
Right to counsel, 40.

ADVERTISING
See also Solicitation of Business.
Permissible, 123, 125.
Prohibited, 67–68.

ADVICE
Disobey law, 244–245.
Dummy to avoid liability, 245.
Office lawyers', 244–249.

ADVOCATE, 20, 154, 243, 289, 508.
See also Adversary System.
Adjudication, 18.
Art of, 278–279.
Candor, 8, 169, 259, 297–316.
Character, 14.
Client relationship, 280.
Collective bargaining, 332–333.
Decision making, 29.
Divorce cases, 308–312.
Duty of, 298.
Efficiency of, 8.
Emotion, appeal to, 289–292, 368.
Identity of client, 300–301.
Judge and, 279.
Lawyer as, 13.
Office lawyer and, 243.
Persuasive subtleties, 293–294.
Preparation, 288–289.
Professional responsibility, 280.
Prosecutor as, 364.
Testimony of, 317–319.
Trial, nature of, 272–279.
Witnesses, 308, 317–328.
Work of, 272–333.
Zeal of, 280–297.

ALLARD, ROBERT E., 520.

AMBULANCE CHASING
See Solicitation of Business.

AMICUS CURIAE, development, 344.

ANDERSON, DILLON, 21–22.

APPELLATE COURTS, 472.
Judges, 512–513.
Trial courts and, 507–508.

ARBITRATION, 331–332.

ASSOCIATION OF AMERICAN LAW SCHOOLS, 27–29.

ATTORNEY-CLIENT RELATIONSHIP
See Client-lawyer Relationship.

Thurman et al., Cs. Legal Prof. UCB

INDEX
References are to Pages

BAKER, NEWTON D., 26.

BAMBERGER, JULIAN, 81.

BAR ASSOCIATIONS, 150, 165.
    American Bar Association,
        House of Delegates, 90–99, 163, 165.
        Professional ethics, 163–164.
        Section of Individual Rights and Responsibilities, 399–400.
    American Bar Foundation, 164, 359–361.
    American Judicature Society, 164, 339, 520.
    American Law Institute, 164, 338–339.
    American Trial Lawyers Association, 114.
    Continuing education, 474–476.
    Disciplinary proceedings, 493.
    Fee schedules, 445, 447, 449.
    General Council of the Bar, 200.
    Integrated bar, 157–161.
    Law Society, The, 198–199.
    Leadership, 399–403.
    Legislative changes, 339.
    Local, 61.
    National Bar Association, 164.
    National Conference of Bar Examiners, 487.
    National Conference of Commissioners on Uniform State Laws, 339.
    National Lawyers Guild, 91, 164.
    Security funds, 460.
    Self-governing bar, 149, 160, 165.
    Specialization, 462.

BAR EXAMINATIONS, ASSUMPTIONS, 15–17.

BAR EXAMINERS, NATIONAL CONFERENCE OF, 487.

BARGAINING
    See also Negiotiation and Settlement.
    Plea, 252, 363–365.

BARRATRY, 56, 121–122.

BARRETT, EDWARD L., 508.

BARRISTERS, 196–199.
    Fee schedule, 444.
    Legal power over, 148.
    Obliged to accept case, 411–412.
    Standards of, 91–92.

BARRY, DONALD D., 9, 380.

BEALE, JOSEPH H., JR., 211.

BEAR, JOSEPH, 34.

BELLI, MELVIN, 112, 114.

BENTLEY, ERIC, 278.

BERMAN, HAROLD J., 9, 380.

BIRKENHEAD, LORD, 481.

BLAUSTEIN, ALBERT, 379–380.

BRADY, FRANK W., 253–254.

BRANDEIS, LOUIS D., 343–344.

BREACH OF PROMISE, 293–294.

BREITEL, CHARLES D., 362.

BRENNAN, WILLIAM J., JR.
    Government lawyers, 373.
    Individual ideals, 182.
    Judicial administration, 530.
    Public leadership, 393–394.

BROUGHAM, LORD, 280–281.

BROWN, ESTHER LUCILLE, 371–372.

BROWN, ROME G., 224–225.

BROWNELL, EMERY A.
    Lawyers, attitude toward, 172.
    Legal aid organizations, 81.

BUCHAN, JOHN, 279.

BUCKNER, EMORY, R.
    Advocate's preparation, 288–289.
    Deceitful client, 323.

BURGER, WARREN E.
    Legal education, 471–473.
    Legal service available, 57.

BUSINESS COUNSELOR, 227–229, 257.

BYRNE, LAURENCE A., 509.

CANDOR
    Advocate's, 8, 169, 259, 297–316.
    Controversy and, 304–305.
    Evidence, 301–304.
    Facts and law, 306–308.
    Negotiations and, 259.
    Negotiator's, 267.

CANONS OF PROFESSIONAL ETHICS, 166.
    See also Code of Professional Responsibility, 539–589.

CARD, PROFESSIONAL, 123–125.

INDEX

CARDOZA, BENJAMIN N.
Appellate judge's function, 512–513.
Fiduciary's duties, 171.
Legal education, 470.
Memorial on Milburn, 20–21.
Trust in lawyer, 142.

CARE AND COMPETENCE, 456–464.

CARLIN, JEROME E.
Fee division, 450–451.
Individual ethics, 183–184.

CARR, ROBERT K., 351–352.

CASE
Control over, 435–439.
Facts in, 36.
Method of education, 471–472, 477–480, 483–484.
Offered, 188, 411–414.
Preparation of, 288–289, 337, 356.
Refused, 180.

CAVANAUGH, J. J.
Non-lawyer role, 30–31.
Public leadership, 397–398.

CAVERS, DAVID F., 239.

CENSURE, 151, 264.

CHAMPERTY, 56, 121–122.

CHANDLER, HENRY P., 530–531.

CHANIN, ROBERT H., 98–99.

CHARACTER REQUIREMENTS FOR LAWYERS, 489–493.

CHEATHAM, ELLIOTT E.
Client's whole problem, 227.
Lawyer's roles, 10–12, 24–25.
Lay experts, 128–129.
Political trials, 95–97.
Work setting, 35–37.

CHOATE, JOSEPH HODGES, 293–294.

CHOATE, RUFUS, 203–204.

CHRISTENSEN, BARLOW F., 68–69.

CHURCHILL, SIR WINSTON, 481.

CIVIL CASES, RIGHT TO COUNSEL, 51–54.

CIVIL DISOBEDIENCE, 490–493.

CIVIL PROCEDURE, FEDERAL RULES OF, 299.

CIVIL RIGHTS ACT OF 1964, 85.

CLARK, HERBERT W., 324.

CLARK, THOMAS C., 503.

CLERKSHIP, 475–476.

CLIENT-LAWYER RELATIONSHIP, 224, 411–468.
Advertising and, 118–119.
Advocate's, 280.
Commencement of, 428–430.
Confidence and, 69–71.
Confidential communications, 232, 321, 323, 351, 418, 428, 430, 454–456.
Conflicting interests, 414, 415, 417–418, 419–423.
Consequences of, 435–468.
Contract and, 442.
Decision making, 28.
Established, 411–434.
Fees, 443–454.
Fiduciary character, 128, 443, 454.
Financial, 439–454.
Gifts and, 439–441.
Injuries to third parties, 464–468.
Liability for advice, 246–249.
Loyalty, 414–428.
Negotiation of, 258, 265–267.
Privileged, 320.
Tax counselor, 231.
Termination of, 430–434.

CLIENTS
Case offered, 188, 411–414.
Deceitful, 321–324.
Diversity of, 55–56, 60.
Duty to, 308–316.
Identity of, 300–301.
Loyalty to, 146.
Negotiation and, 258, 265–267.
Personal injury and death claims, 100.
Settlement and, 437.

COCKBURN, LORD, 281.

CODE OF PROFESSIONAL RESPONSIBILITY
See also Appendix, 539–589.
Advocate's candor, 298.
Authoritative sources, 192.
Confidential communications, 454–455.
Control of trial, 438.
Fees, 444–445.
Law administration, 406–407.
Lay experts, 128.
Lobbyist standards, 339.
Professional sanctions, 166.
Publicity and solicitation, 118–119.

606 INDEX

References are to Pages

COHEN, JULIUS, 336–338.

COLLECTIVE BARGAINING, 332–333.

COMLEY, JOHN M., 29.

COMPETENCE, 48–49, 456–464, 466–468.

COMPROMISE, 250–271.

CONARD, ALFRED F., 115–116.

CONCILIATION, 29, 264–265.

CONFIDENTIAL COMMUNICATIONS, 232, 321, 323, 454–456.
  Commencement of, 430.
  Conflicting interests, 417–418, 428.
  Disclosures, 300–301.
  Legislative investigating committee, 351.

CONFLICTING INTERESTS
  See also Loyalty.
  Amicus curiae and, 344.
  Confidential communication, 417–418, 428.
  Corporation lawyer, 227.
  Defense counsel, 43, 411–414.
  Disqualification for, 420–421.
  Extension of knowledge, 409–410.
  Family counselor, 237.
  For and against same client, 416.
  Future negotiations, 266.
  Government lawyers, 47, 374–375.
  Lawyers in politics, 385.
  Liability insurance, 425–428.
  Liquidation and reorganization, 423–425.
  Municipal attorney's, 373, 374.
  Mutual consent, 419–423.
  Opposing former client in related matters, 417–418.
  Reorganization, 423–425.
  Representing both parties, 415.
  Settlements, 426–427.
  Solicitation and, 73–74.
  Tax counselor, 267.
  Title company lawyer, 130.

CONNER, LESLIE L., 509.

CONTEMPT OF COURT, 69–70, 135–137.

CONTINGENT FEES, 105, 120–121, 349.
  Commencement of relationship, 428–430.
  Continuance of case, 437.
  Criminal cases, 445.

CONTINGENT FEES—Cont'd
  Interference with, 431–433.
  Legal aid organizations, 81.
  Lobbying and, 347–348.
  Personal injury claims, 111–113.
  Settlements and, 266, 431.
  Supplemented, 444.

CONTINUING LEGAL EDUCATION, 474–475.

CONTRACTS
  Client-lawyer, 439–442.
  Described, 19.
  Illegal, 347–349.
  Lobbying, 347–349.

CONTROL OVER CASE, 435–439.

CORPORATION LAWYERS, 25, 62–64.
  Conflicting interests, 227.

CORPORATION PRACTICING LAW, 69–80.

COSTIGAN, GEORGE P., JR., 281.

COUNCIL ON LEGAL EDUCATION FOR PROFESSIONAL RESPONBILITY, INC., 389.

COUNSEL
  Civil cases, 51–54.
  Competence, 48–49, 460–461.
  Corporation, 360, 422–423.
  Defense, 39–51, 309–310, 411–414.
  Investigating committee, 353.
  Middle class and, 76–78, 84.
  People's, 88–89.
  Policy-makers, 372.
  Poor persons, 83–85.
  Post-trial, 44–45.
  Pre-trial, 43–44.
  Provided, 91.
  Reimbursement of, 49–50.
  Trial court, 39–42.
  Witnesses and, 150.

COUNSEL, RIGHT TO, 27, 39, 40, 41, 80, 84, 90, 210, 330.
  Choice of, 414–415.
  Civil disorders, 47.
  Committee witnesses, 351.
  Conflicting interests, 414–415.
  Constitutional, 42–51.
  Criminal cases, 87, 460–461.
  Federal courts, 42.
  Juvenile, 47–48.
  Mentally ill, 52.
  Misdemeanors, 45–47.

INDEX

References are to Pages

COUNSEL, RIGHT TO—Cont'd
  Personal injury claims, 103–104, 113–114.
  Poor persons, 43, 44, 45, 80–88.
  State courts, 43.

COUNSELING, 13, 18, 20, 68, 154.
  Business, 227–229, 257.
  Characteristics of, 14–15.
  Corporate, 205.
  Labor union, 235–236, 251–252, 259, 295–297.
  Precedents, 14–15.
  Shift in emphasis to, 206.
  Tax, 229–234, 251, 259, 267.

COUNTY ATTORNEY
  See Prosecutor.

COURTS
  See also Judge.
  Control of legal profession, 148–155.
  Federal standards, 193.
  Function of, 214, 275–276.
  Information, 274.
  Legislative investigation, 354.
  Organization and administration, 526–532.
  Protect attorneys, 154–155.
  Sanctions on clients, 147.
  Supports and sanctions, 148–155.
  Television in, 178–180.

CRAVATH, PAUL D., 33.

CREIGHTON, JOSEPH R., 63–64.

CRIMINAL CASES
  Contingent fees, 445.
  Counsel, 87, 460–461.

CRIMINAL JUSTICE ACT OF 1964, 43, 54, 85–86.

CRIMINAL PROCEDURE, FEDERAL RULES OF, 365.

CULLINAN, EUSTACE, 324.

CURTIS, CHARLES P., 288.

DARRELL, NORRIS, 229–234.

DARROW, CLARENCE, 295–297.

DAVIS, JAMES C., 401.

DAVIS, KENNETH CULP, 362.

DAWSON, JOHN P., 331.

DEFAMATION, 464–468.

DEFENSE COUNSEL, 39–51.
  Advocate's candor, 309–310.
  Conflicting interests, 43, 411–414.
  Reimbursement, 49–50.

DISBARMENT, 301–304, 325–327, 496.
  Moral character, 489–490.
  Moral turpitude, 497–498.
  Not criminal punishment, 151.
  Professional misconduct, 284–286.
  Purpose of, 285–286.
  Right of silence, 500–501.
  Solicitation of business, 94–95.

DISCIPLINARY PROCEEDINGS, 149, 287, 306–307, 466, 493–501.
  Advertising, 120.
  Civil disobedience and, 490–493.
  Court power, 150–152.
  Disqualification, 417–418, 420–421.
  Due process, 501.
  Failure to prosecute, 363.
  Grievance committee, 493–495.
  Personal injury claims, 263–264.
  Professional misconduct, 496.
  Public responsibility, 404.

DISTRICT ATTORNEY
  See Prosecutor.

DIVISION OF FEES, 449–452.

DIVORCE, COOPERATION IN, 308–316.

DODD, E. MERRICK, JR., 156.

DOUGLAS, PAUL H.
  Conflict of interest, 385.
  Ethics, 162–163.
  Lobbyist, 342–343.
  Loyalty conflicts, 145.
  Standards, 171.

DRINKER, HENRY S.
  Candor, 299, 308–315.
  Competence, 457.

DUE PROCESS
  Bar admission, 500.
  Disciplinary proceedings, 501.
  Lawyer and, 405–406.

ECONOMIC OPPORTUNITY ACT OF 1964, 54, 85–86.

ECONOMICS OF THE PROFESSION
  See Fees.

EDGERTON, HENRY W., 194–195.

EDUCATION, LEGAL
See Legal Education.

ELECTION OF JUDGES, 520.

ELSON, ALEX, 57.

EMOTION, APPEAL TO, 289–292, 368.

EMPLOYEES, LEGAL SERVICES TO, 69–80.

ENGLAND
Barristers, 91–92, 148, 196–199, 411–412, 444.
Change of tone in courts, 149–150.
Compared with U. S., 199–201.
Fee system, 444.
History of profession, 196–199.
Inns of Court, 196–198.
Judicial appointment, 517.
Law Society, 198–199.
Legal Aid organizations, 82, 199.
Legal profession, 196–201.
Legal services for the hated, 91–92.
Periodical office accounting, 173.
Pre-trial publicity, 174.
Publicity and solicitation, 121.
Solicitors, 123, 196–198, 412.
Union counsel, 75.

ERSKINE, LORD THOMAS, 92, 411–412.

ETHICS
See Professional Ethics.

EULAU, HEINZ, 378–379.

EVASION, 244–249.

EVIDENCE
Candor about, 301–304.
Rules of, 18, 41.

EVIDENTIARY MATERIALS, 336.

EVIDENTIARY RULE, 455–456.

FACTS
Adjudication and, 18.
Candor about, 306–308.
Case, 36.
Dealing with, 472.

FAIR TRIAL, PUBLICITY AND, 173–178.

FAIR TRIAL AND FREE PRESS, ADVISORY COMMITTEE ON, 177.

FALSE IMPRISONMENT, 464–468.

FAMILY COUNSELOR, 236–238.

FEDERAL CONFLICT OF INTEREST ACT OF 1962, 374–375.
Disqualification limits, 421.

FEDERAL CRIMINAL JUSTICE ACT OF 1964, 43, 85–86.

FEDERAL INCOME TAX, LOBBYING REGULATION, 346.

FEDERAL JUDICIARY, COMMITTEE ON, 518.

FEDERAL REGULATION OF LOBBYING ACT, 345.

FEDERAL RULES OF CIVIL PROCEDURE, 299.

FEDERAL RULES OF CRIMINAL PROCEDURE, 363.

FEDERAL SYSTEM, 189–195.

FEES
Attorney's claim for, 452–454.
Barristers' schedule, 444.
Choate's, 203–204.
Client-lawyer relationship, 443–454.
Contracts, 443.
Cutting, 449.
Division of, 449–452.
Excessive, 102, 445–446.
Finance plans for, 72.
Lawyers', 80–81, 93.
Legal advice, 66–68.
Negotiator's, 265–266.
Problems, 232–233.
Referral, 450–451.
Retained by group employer, 69.
Schedules, 445, 447, 449.
Settlements and, 446.
Splitting with specialist, 462.

FEINSINGER, NATHAN P., 331–332.

FIDUCIARY
Duties, 171.
Functions, 224–225.
Obligations, 385–386, 444.

FINANCIAL RELATIONS
Fees, 443–454.
Gifts and contracts, 439–443.

FORSYTHE, WILLIAM, 280.

FRANCE
Judicial selection, 516–517.
Procedural system, 215–217.

LAWYERS—Cont'd
  Public attitude toward, 172–173.
  Public leadership, 7, 22–27, 38.
  Qualities of, 32–34, 481–482, 487–488.
  Referral, 66–69, 127.
  Roles, 5–31.
  Setting of work, 35–37, 144.
  Specialization, 59–60.

LAY EXPERTS, 35–36, 45.
  See also, Unauthorized Practice.
  Control of litigation, 73.
  Legal services available, 128–141.

LEGAL AID, 81–87, 387, 390.
  Contingent fees, 81.
  English, 82, 199.
  Public responsibility, 394.
  Publicity for, 127.
  Standards of, 459.

LEGAL EDUCATION, 1–2, 5–6, 380–381, 469–487.
  Apprenticeship period, 474–475.
  Assumptions of, 15–17.
  Case method, 471–472, 477–480, 483–484.
  Clerkship, 475–476.
  Clinical, 389.
  Continuing, 474–476.
  Curriculum, 390–391.
  English, 201.
  Future, 476–487.
  Judges', 532.
  Professional responsibility, 473–474.
  Specialization, 462.

LEGAL ETHICS,
  See Professional Ethics.

LEGAL PROFESSION, 24.
  Adaptability, 30.
  Court control of, 148–155.
  English, 196–201.
  Forces which shape, 209–213.

LEGAL SERVICES, 13, 55–141, 387, 403, 411.
  For employees, 69–80.
  For the poor, 81–82, 85.
  Group, 69–80.
  Office of Economic Opportunity program, 85–88.

LEGAL SYSTEMS
  Other countries', 213–219.
  United States, 201–213.

LEGISLATION, 18–22.

LEGISLATIVE FUNCTION OF LAWYER, 24–25.

LEGISLATIVE INVESTIGATING COMMITTEES, 351–354.
  Confidential communication, 351.
  Court and, 354.
  Lawyer and, 335–336.
  Precedents, 336.

LEGISLATOR
  Lawyer as, 238–240.
  Prosecutor as, 365.
  Quality of, 350.

LEGISLATURE, 334–354.

LePAULLE, PIERRE, 215–217.

LIABILITY INSURANCE COMPANIES, 99–100, 104.
  Conflict of interest, 425–428.
  Prompt, limited payments, 116.

LIENS, 433, 452–454.

LIQUIDATION AND REORGANIZATION, 423–425.

LITIGATION, 15–16.
  Control of, 72.
  Defined, 29.
  Ends of, 276.

LOBBYISTS, LAWYERS AS, 336–350.

LOYALTY, 33, 144–147, 156.
  See also Conflicting interests.
  Judges', 144.
  Lawyers', 146–147.
  Reconciliation of, 144–146.
  To client, 146, 414–428.

LUMMUS, HENRY T., 199–200.

LUND, THOMAS G., 196–199.

McCOOK, PHILIP J., 288.

MacDONNELL, SIR JOHN, 275–276.

McDOUGAL, MYRES S., 20.

MacKINNON, F. B.
  Contingent fees, 112–113.
  Publicity and solicitation, 121.

MADDOCK, CHARLES S., 63.

MAINTENANCE, 56, 109–110, 121–122.

MALICIOUS PROSECUTION, 464–468.

MARDEN, ORISON S., 64.

MARK, IRVING, 98–99.

MATHEWS, ROBERT E., 399–400.

MAYER, MARTIN, 223–224.

MAZOR, LESTER J., 298.

MEDIATION, 331–332.

MEDINA, HAROLD R.
Administration of justice, 526–528.
Qualities of judges, 503.

MICHAEL, JEROME, 289–290.

MIDDLE CLASS
Counsel and, 76–78, 84.
Legal services available, 66–80.
Need for lawyer, 51.

MILBURN, JOHN G., 20–21.

MILLER, JOHN S., 457.

MINIMUM FEE SCHEDULES, 445, 447, 449.

MISDEMEANORS, 45–47.

MISSOURI PLAN, 520–521.

MORE, SIR THOMAS, 183.

MORELAND, ALLEN B., 353–354.

MORGAN, CHARLES, 93.

MORGAN, EDMUND M., 274–275.

MOULTON, LORD, 184–185.

MUNICIPAL ATTORNEYS, 373–374.

NADER, RALPH, 390–393.

NAHSTOLL, RICHARD W., 15–17.

NEGOTIATION AND SETTLEMENT, 16, 18, 19, 28, 75.
Candor in, 259, 267.
Client and, 258, 265–267.
Compromise and, 250–271.
Concessions and, 260.
Conciliation, 264–265.
Conflicting interests for future, 266.
Criticized, 257.
Fees, 265–266.
Impediments to, 268–269.
Importance, 253–257.

NEGOTIATION AND SETTLEMENT— Cont'd
Personal injury claims, 251, 254, 256, 267.
Pretrial, 252, 255–257.
Skills, 258–265.
Threats, 263–264.

NEIGHBORHOOD LEGAL SERVICES, 391–392, 394.

NELLES, WALTER, 292.

NEVINS, ALLAN, 145.

NEW YORK COUNTY LAWYERS' ASSOCIATION, 167.

NEWSPAPERS, 173–178.

NILES, RUSSELL D.
Judicial elections, 519.
Specialization and competence, 463.

NON-PROFIT CORPORATION PRACTICING LAW, 70.

ODGERS, W. BLAKE, 149–150.

OFFICE OF ECONOMIC OPPORTUNITY
Legal Services Program, 85–88.
Neighborhood Legal Services, 391–392, 394.
People's counsel, 89.

OFFICER OF THE COURT, 142, 153–154, 156, 171, 174, 267, 285, 320, 336, 443.

ORGANIZED PROFESSION,
See Bar Associations

O'TOOLE, THOMAS J., 475–476.

PAINE, THOMAS, 411.

PARTISANSHIP, 6, 11, 36, 221, 329.
Judge's, 510–512.
Limits of, 272, 280, 380.
Paradox of, 36–37.
Prosecutor and, 366.
Public service, 404.

PARTNERSHIPS, 58–59.

PAULSEN, MONRAD G., 275.

PERSONAL INJURY AND DEATH CLAIMS, 98–117, 290–292, 321.
See also Contingent Fees.
Solicitation of Business.

INDEX

References are to Pages

PERSONAL INJURY AND DEATH CLAIMS—Cont'd
Changes proposed, 113–117.
Development of, 205.
Disciplinary proceedings, 101–105, 263–264.

PERSUASION AND ADVOCACY, 293–294.

PIKE, JAMES A., 226–227.

PLEA-BARGAINING, 252, 363–365.

POLITICAL LEADERSHIP, 378–386.

POLITICAL TRIALS, 95–97, 275–276.

POOR PERSONS
Counsel, 83–85.
Defense of, 49–50.
Law school and, 486.
Legal services available to, 80–89.
Need for lawyer, 27, 40, 52–54, 56.
Right to counsel, 43, 44, 45, 80–89.

PORTER, CHARLES, 379–380.

POST-CONVICTION RELIEF, 138.

POUND, ROSCOE
Advocate system, 277.
Judicial process, 215.
Lawyers' history, 7–9.
Lawyer's public responsibility, 377.
Profession defined, 155.
Trials and advocates, 276.

POVERTY
See Poor Persons.

POWELL, LEWIS F., JR., 403.

PRACTICAL LAWYER, THE, 410.

PRACTICE OF LAW, WHAT IS, 128–141.

PRIVILEGED COMMUNICATION,
See Confidential Communications.

PROFESSION, DEFINED, 155, 376, 410.

PROFESSIONAL ANNOUNCEMENT, 123–125.

PROFESSIONAL CARD, 123–125.

PROFESSIONAL ETHICS, 150–152, 168.
American Bar Association, 163–164.
And Grievances, Committee on, 167.
Functions of, 162–165.

PROFESSIONAL ETHICS—Cont'd
Prosecutor's, 370–371.
Standards and, 183–184.

PROFESSIONAL RESPONSIBILITY, 1–2, 13, 210.
See also Report of the Joint Conference on Professional Responsibility.
Advocate's, 280.
Education for, 473–474.

PROFESSIONAL SPIRIT, 8.

PROFESSIONAL STANDARDS
Individual, 188–189.
Lobbyists', 339–344.
Support for, 155–170.

PROSECUTOR, 46, 362–371.
As advocate, 364.
As judge, 364–365.
As legislator, 365.
County attorney, 356–359.
Decisions of, 362–366.
District attorney, 369.
Essential, 40.
Ethics, 370–371.
Private practice and, 370–371.
Public, 355, 356–361.
Qualities of, 363.

PUBLIC AFFAIRS, 386–403.

PUBLIC DEFENDER, 83, 394.

PUBLIC RESPONSIBILITY, 228–229.
Government lawyers, 394.
Law administration, 403–409.
Lawyer and, 376–410.
Tithing for, 388–389.

RANDALL, FRANK H., 265.

REED, STANLEY F., 14–15.

REFERRAL, 66–69, 127.

REORGANIZATION, CONFLICTS, 423–425.

REPORT OF THE JOINT CONFERENCE ON PROFESSIONAL RESPONSIBILITY
Administration of law, 404–405.
Background, 12n.
Counselor-at-law role, 221–222.
Individual understanding, 182–183.
Legislative role, 238–239.

INDEX

References are to Pages

REPORT OF THE JOINT CONFERENCE ON PROFESSIONAL RESPONSIBILITY—Cont'd
Prosecution, 366.
Public leadership, 395–397.
Roles, 12–14.
Trial judge's function, 508–509.
Trials, 272–273.

RETAINER, ACCEPTANCE OF, 344.

RIESMAN, DAVID, 182.

RIGHT TO COUNSEL,
See Counsel, Right to

ROOT, ELIHU, 61.

ROSENBERG, MAURICE, 503, 504–506.

ROSTOW, EUGENE V.
Professional ethics, 162.
Public leadership, 400.

RUTLEDGE, WILEY, 32.

SACCO–VANZETTI CASE, 92–93.

SANCTIONS, PROFESSIONAL, 167.

SCHACHTER, OSCAR, 486–487.

SEGAL, ROBERT M., 235–236.

SELF-GOVERNING BAR, 149, 160, 165.

SETTLEMENTS, 300, 331.
See Negotiations and Settlement.

SEYMOUR, WHITNEY NORTH
Business counselor, 228–229.
Large city firm, 59–62.
Legislative investigations, 352.
Public leadership, 395.

SHAWCROSS, SIR HARTLEY, 91–92.

SHULER, ALBERT W., 363–365.

SIDGWICK, HENRY, 2.

SKILL, 456–464.

SLANDER, 464–468.

SMITH, JOHN W., 350.

SMITH, REGINALD HEBER
Complaints against lawyers, 9–10.
Law administrator, 240.
Legal services for the poor, 80–81.
Partnerships, 58.

SOLICITATION OF BUSINESS, 122, 150–152, 168, 349.
Announcements, 124.
Conflicting interests, 73–74.
Disbarment, 94–95.
Group legal services, 69–71.
Hated, the, 93–94.
Legal services made available, 117–127.
Personal injury and death claims, 101–111.
Protected, 72–75.
Public causes, 72, 94, 127.

SOLICITORS, 196–198, 412.
Periodic accounting, 198.
Purchase of practice, 123.

SOLO PRACTITIONER
Legal services made available, 57–58.
Specialization, 462.

SOPER, MORRIS AMES, 97.

SPECIALIZATION
Competence, 461–464.
Development of, 204–205.
Publicity for, 125–126.

SPRAGUE, JOHN D., 378–379.

STACY, W. P., 172.

STANDARDS
Authoritative sources of, 189–195.
Diversity, 167–170.
Factors and, 143.
Fundamental sources of, 209–213.
Interrelation, 171–172.
Legal profession, 142–147.

STASON, E. BLYTHE
Career judiciary, 516.
Judicial appointment, 517.
Judicial elections, 520.
Legal education, 475.

STEWART, POTTER, 515.

STIRRING UP LITIGATION,
See Solicitation of Business.

STOLZ, PREBLE, 79.

STONE, HARLAN F., 23.

STUDENTS,
See Legal Education.

SUIT, COLLUSIVE, 273.

SUNDERLAND, EDSON R., 145–146.

INDEX

References are to Pages

SUPPORTS AND SANCTIONS, 147–189.

SUPREME COURT,
See United States Supreme Court.

SUSPENSION, 151, 327.

SWAINE, ROBERT T.
Cravath on loyalty, 419.
Lawyer's leadership role, 23–24.

TAFT, WILLIAM HOWARD, 530.

TAX
Conflicting interests, 267.
Counselor, 229–234, 251, 259, 267.
Fraud, 413.
Negotiation and, 257.
Unauthorized practice, 135–137.

TELEVISION, 178–180.

TERMINATION OF RELATIONSHIP, 432–433.

TESTIMONY OF LAWYER, 317–319.

THIRD PERSONS, INJURIES TO, 464–468.

THREATS OF CRIMINAL PROCEEDINGS
Negotiations, 263–264.
Plea-bargaining, 365.
Tort cases, 263.

THURMAN, SAMUEL D., 473–474.

TITLE COMPANIES, 129–131.

TRAYNOR, ROGER J., 531.

TREVELYAN, GEORGE M.
Forces of change, 212.
Legal services for the hated, 92.

TRIAL
Judge, 502–512.
Nature of, 272–279.

TWEED, HARRISON
Counsel for poor, 83.
Large city law firm, 62.
Public leadership, 395.

TYDINGS, JOSEPH D., 529.

UNAUTHORIZED PRACTICE, 6, 69–72, 128–141, 149, 150.
See also Lay Experts.
Accountants, 135–137, 139–140.
Committee on, 72.

UNAUTHORIZED PRACTICE—Cont'd
Inefficiency of, 8.
Settlements, 266.
Title companies, 129–131.

UNION OF SOVIET SOCIALIST REPUBLICS
Judicial elections, 520.
Lawyer's influence, 380.
Legal profession, 9.

UNIONS,
See Labor Unions.

UNITED STATES
Compared with England, 199–201.
Legal system, 201–213.

UNITED STATES SUPREME COURT
Criticism of, 407–409.
Justices' activities, 25–26.

UNLAWFUL PRACTICE,
See Unauthorized Practice.

UNPOPULAR CLIENT
Case offered, 412.
Legal services available to, 89–97.
Need for lawyer, 27.
Solicitation of business, 93–94.

VAN ALSTYNE, ARVO, 255–257.

VAN VOORHIS, JOHN, 111–112.

VANDERBILT, ARTHUR T.
Candor about facts and law, 306–307.
Judge's extrajudicial functions, 513–514.
Lawyers and politics, 382–383.
Lawyer's roles, 13–14.
Lay experts, 132.

VOORHEES, THEODORE
Group legal service, 79.
Negotiation skills, 258–261.

WALD, PATRICIA M., 52–53.

WARNER, JOSEPH B., 273.

WARREN, EARL
Advocate's candor, 299–300.
Contentiousness, 214–215.
Law administration, 408–409.

WASHINGTON LAWYER, 340–343.

WATSON, ANDREW S.
  Counselor-at-law, 223.
  Panel appointment of judges, 521.

WECHSLER, HERBERT, 513.

WEINSTEIN, JACK B., 356–359.

WESTWOOD, HOWARD C., 87–88.

WHITEHEAD, ALFRED NORTH
  Forces of change, 212.
  Organization, 480.

WIGMORE, JOHN H.
  Chinese legal system, 217–218.
  Evidentiary rule, 455.

WILLISTON, SAMUEL
  Candor, 307–308.
  Contracts, 443.

WINTERS, GLENN R.
  Judicial elections, 520.
  Judicial tenure, 526.

WIRTZ, WILLARD W., 332–333.

WITHDRAWAL,
  See Client-lawyer Relationship.

WITNESSES
  Adverse, 327–328.
  Advocate and, 317–328.
  Compensation of, 325–327.
  Counsel and, 150.
  For lawyer, 324.
  Lawyer as, 317–321.
  Treatment of, 8.

WORKMEN'S COMPENSATION, 99, 117.

WYZANSKI, CHARLES E., JR., 510.

END OF VOLUME